A HISTORY OF THE ANCIENT CHAPEL OF BIR
JOHN BOOKER

Publisher's Note

The book descriptions we ask booksellers to display prominently warn that this is an historic book with numerous typos, missing text or index and is not illustrated.

We scanned this book using character recognition software that includes an automated spell check. Our software is 99 percent accurate if the book is in good condition. However, we do understand that even one percent can be a very annoying number of typos! And sometimes all or part of a page is missing from our copy of a book. Or the paper may be so discolored from age that you can no longer read the type. Please accept our sincere apologies.

After we re-typeset and design a book, the page numbers change so the old index and table of contents no longer work. Therefore, we usually remove them.

Our books sell so few copies that you would have to pay hundreds of dollars to cover the cost of proof reading and fixing the typos, missing text and index. Therefore, whenever possible, we let our customers download a free copy of the original typo-free scanned book. Simply enter the barcode number from the back cover of the paperback in the Free Book form at www.general-books.net. You may also qualify for a free trial membership in our book club to download up to four books for free. Simply enter the barcode number from the back cover onto the membership form on the same page. The book club entitles you to select from more than a million books at no additional charge. Simply enter the title or subject onto the search form to find the books.

If you have any questions, could you please be so kind as to consult our Frequently Asked Questions page at www.general-books.net/faqs.cfm? You are also welcome to contact us there.

General Books LLC™, Memphis, USA, 2012. ISBN: 9781459011236.

❊ ❊ ❊ ❊ ❊ ❊ ❊ ❊

Higins, my sister Elizabeth's three children, x a piece, in holl xxx. 16. To three other her childringe, for learninge also, William, Thomas and Robert Beech, xxx, that is x a piece. 17. To William Browhill my sister Agnes' sonne, x. 18. To Robert Birche, my eldest brother's childe, for learninge, as to the other seaven before of my nephes, x. 19. To his eldest sonne, my nephew, also a student in the lawes, vj and Titus Livius. 20. To William, my brother George's sonne, towards learninge, x. 21. To his other children amonge them vj. 22. To George, my brother, Fabiani Chronicle, and vj sylver spoones of myne, that he haithe in kepinge. 23. To the rest of my sister Ans children x amonge them equallie. 24. To the other children of my brother Thomas viij equallye, and Raufe to have James Pilkingtons, the Busshop of Durham, thre books, all in one bunden booke, that nowe I have. 25. To my brother Thomas, to be an heir lowme, my Geneva Bible, there printed in Englishe, and the sylver bear pott, parcel gilte, covered, that cost iiij. Also Munsters Cosmographie, in Latten, for George, his sonne. 26. To the doughters of my sister Elizabeth x, that is to his sic eldest, Elizabeth, iiij, and to the other two iiij a peice. 27. To my ant Mosse, or yf she be not, to John and Anne Mosse xx. 28. To my ant Becke, Nicholas, Thomas Becke, Cicily Holande, my cosings, x for a token in gold; the holl xK 29. To my neighbours at Birche, 4 as greave, ij vj a peice. To Raufe Barche ij vj, or his childe. 30. To the poorest in Risshum amongst them v. 31. To the poorest in Wythinton v. To the poorest in Didisbury v. 32. To Robert Bewicke of Durham ij vj. 33. To my trustie servant John Johnson, at Sedgefeilde, iiij and my best Lattyn Testament, with Beza's notes. To the other John Johnson, of Stanhop, iiij x. To Richard Rawlinge, minister, who with Johnsons,

ister, my Greike and Lattyn Testament with Erasmus's Annotations; Aristotells Moral Philosophic of Argiroples Translation, with an epitome before it; Metamorphosis of Ovid, with a Commentary, and Ovidius de Fastis, with a lardge Comment. 34. To John Peirson and his wyfe, my wyves servants, vj vi-ij. To Richard Pursglove iiij. To Ewen Halliwell ij". 35. The rest of my Englishe books to be geven to men and children of Stanhop parishe and Durham, that can reid, except that if my brother desireth A Replye to Mr. D Whitgifte, by Thomas Cartewrighte, is Raufe Wedowes booke, delyver with yt to hym Roderike Mors and Al. Nowell against Dorman. My books of the Lawes of this Realme I leave to Thomas my brother, for his children as he thinketh, or to George his sonne, for hym and brethren. 36. The seaven newe volomes of Civill Lawe I geve to Anthony Higgins, with the Annotations of Budseus upon the Pandects. The Canon Lawe books to G. Higgins. 37. All Greeke and Hebrewe books or halfe Greke and Hebrewe, to William and Tho. Beech. Plato, in Lattyn, to go with Greeke Plato; and Latten parts of Aristotle to go with the Greeke. 38. To William Browell the books of Erasmus, with Melanctbon's Logiko and Rhet., Cicero's Works to Edward Higgins, Logike, Arithmetike, Cosmographie and books of Astronomy in Latten, and the poets. 39. To Robert Birche all books of profane and ecclesiasticall histories, as the Fyve Centuries, in three volumes, Sledane, Eusebius. My Latten Gramer books to be geven to three poore Latten schollers at any grammar scholls. 40. All my Lattyn Divinitie books to be geven to those of my nephews that first be teachers in the Ecclesiasticall Ministerey. Seneca and Budteus de Contemptu rerum fortuitarum to Richard Dalton. The fyrst gyft of some books before sheweth that I meane not of them in lardger wordes after. 41. If dowtes in thes legaces, I geve to my executors aucthoritie to do as by godlie discretion they shall thinke good, and dare answere before that Judge that seith our mynde, before which Jesus Christ all must appeare; and thoughe over the funeralls, debts and legaces paid, all goods be the executors, yet my will I do declaire to be, that yf the part remayning be greit, they shall of the remayning parte help poore neighbours, partlye by guifts and partlye by lending freelye to the needye, especialye the godlye, for they ar but stuerds, under God, the true Owner, and I was and am. The disposers, bestowers and executors of this my last will and testament I maike and appointe my brother Thomas or his sonne George for hym, yf he be not leyvingo or not very willinge to execut; and with the one of them my other brother, George Birche; or, yf George be not lcyvinge, I appoint Anthony Higgins executor, prayinge my executors to agree and let not my goods trewlie gotten to helpe, be an occasion to hurte them or others. Subscriptio confirmat hoc esse Testamentum.

Gulielmus Birch. Testis Richardus Rawlinge. Probat. xxx mensis Novembris anno Domini 1575.

On the death of Thomas Birch Gent. in 1595, he was succeeded, as already intimated, by his eldest son George Birch.

George Birch added to the original extent of the family estate by his marriage with Anne, daughter and heiress of John Bamford Gent., and the consequent annexation of the Holt demesne in Withington, as well as other lands.

At the time of their marriage they stood to each other in the relation of step-brother and sister, the mother of the latter having recently become the second wife of Thomas Birch, the father of George Birch.

He died, as appears from his inventory, in 1601, and was buried at the Collegiate Church, February 15, leaving issue George Birch his eldest son, William, Thomas, John, Edmund and James.

His inventory, "taken and praised" the 24th day of February 1601, shows the value of his goods and chattels to have been £191 5s. lOd.; among the items which occur are the following: — In apparell for his bodie vj; item in bookes xl; item in pewter lxxij poundes at vj a pound xxxvj; item a bakspitte, a fleshooke, ij tostinge irons and ij fringepans; item a pair of bellies xvj; item ij chers and iiij stols wrought with neeld work xxxiijs viij; item a case of trenchers ij'.

Shortly after her husband's death the widow executed a deed bearing date February 12, 1602, settling all the lands she inherited from her late father John Bamford upon her eldest son George Birch and his heirs, subject however to a life interest in a house and Surtecs Society's Publications, Voi. xxii, pp. cxcxir.

certain lands called the Forty Acres to the use of her son William Birch; and also a life interest in a tenement in the parish of Middleton, in the tenure of John Kay, and one close in Spotland called Smythie Scholfeild, to the use of her son Thomas Birch; and also of a life interest in a tenement in the parish of Rochdale, in the tenure of Robert Chadwick, to the use of her son John Birch; and as to the remainder of her lands the same to be to herself for her life; and all these several uses ended, the whole of her inheritance to go to the use of her eldest son George Birch and his heirs for ever. She married secondly Francis Dukinfield.

On the death of George Birch in 1601, he was succeeded by his eldest son George, who had not attained his full age. In his minority he was committed to the guardianship of one of the Mosleys. He married shortly afterwards, in 1606, Anne, daughter of Ellis Hey of Monkshall in the parish of Eccles, Gent. The marriage settlement is dated September 30, 1606, and speaks of the marriage as having then already taken place. The contracting parties are George Birch of Birch Hall in Withington Gent. on the one part, and Ellis Hey of the Monkes Hall in Eccles Gent. and Adam Smith of Manchester, mercer, on the other part. The deed witnesses that George Birch does covenant and grant to and with the said Ellis Heye and Adam Smith for and in consideration of a marriage already had and solemnized between the said George Birch and Anne his now wife, daughter of the said Ellis Hey, and for and in consideration of the sum of i?300 already paid and to be paid by the said Ellis Hey to the said George Birch, and in consideration of the better maintenance and stay of living of the said Anne, wife of the said George Birch, and for the assuring and conveying of a competent and sufficient jointure to the use of the said Anne, that he the said George Birch shall and will before the Feast of Easter next convey and assure unto the said Ellis Hey and Adam Smith all that part and portion of the capital messuage or tenement called Birch Hall in Withington, and all and every the fields, closes, clausures and parcels of land hereafter named, that is to say the Barn Field, the Two Oaks, the Seven Acres, the Five Acres, the Long Small Meadow, the Three Acres, the Old Marled Earth, the Wood Field, the Wheat Croft, the Fall, the Pighowt and the Calf Croft, to the use and behoof of the said George Birch and his assigns for and during the term of his natural life; and after the death of the said George Birch, then to the use and behoof of the said Anne, wife of the said George Birch, for the term of her life, in lieu and in full satisfaction of all and every her dower and jointure during the minority of any heir male that may issue, and so long as she keep herself unmarried; but if any heir male should attain the age of twenty-one years in the life-time of the said Anne Birch, or if the said Anne Birch marry again then the estate to be forfeited and to be charged with an annual payment of i?30 for her use.

By this marriage George Birch had issue an only son, Thomas Birch, his successor, and a daughter Anne, married in 1629 to John, son and heir of John Kinsey of Blackden in the county of Chester Gent. Her marriage-portion " was £300, being in lewe and full recdmpence and satisfaction of her childes pte and filiall porcon of the goodes and chattells" of her deceased father.

George Birch died in 1611, having scarcely reached the age of thirty years. His will is dated July 28, 1611. He describes himself as of Hindley Birche in the county of Lancaster gentleman, " sicke in bodye but of good and p'fect remembrance, thankes be given to God." First and principally he commends his soul into the hands of Almighty God, trusting to be saved by the blood-shedding and passion of Jesus Christ; and his body he commits to the earth to be buried in Jesus Chapel in Manchester Church. He gives and bequeaths towards the repairing of the said Jesus Chapel ten shillings. To Elizabeth Parsivall he gives ten shillings; and to the poor of Manchester parish ten shillings. To Ellis Chadwick of the parish of Bochdale he bequeaths forty shillings. And touching the rest and residue of all his goods, debts and chattels, his will and mind is that they shall be equally divided into three parts, whereof he reserves one part to himself, the second he bequeaths to Anne Birch his wife, and the third he gives to Anne Birch his daughter. He charges his own third part with the payment of his legacies and funeral expenses; and the rest and residue of this his third part he bequeaths in equal portions to his wife and child. His will and mind is that " my brother James Birche shall have all that belongeth unto him uppon accompt paid unto him win the space of one yeare after my decease." He gives to his brother William Birch his best cloak, and to Thomas Birch his brother his cloak best but one; all the rest and residue of his apparel to be divided amongst his brothers. He gives to Mr. Deane of Ripone one gowne and cloth to cover the pulpit wall. And of this his last will and testament he makes, constitutes and ordains Mr. Anthonie Higgens, Dean of Ripon, Ellis Hey his father-in-law, and Anne Birch his wife his true and lawful executors. The will was proved at Chester October 16, 1611. The inventory of his goods and chattels was under i?200.

The inquisition post mortem of George Birch, the testator, was taken at Manchester on Thursday September 9, of the age of five years and four months; and that the said messuages, lands and tenements in Birch and Rusholme within the aforesaid George, and is at the time of the taking of this inquisition of the age of August, 9 James I. (1611), and that Thomas Birch is son and heir of premises, died at Eccles on the 22nd Birch already given, and then proceeds to say that the said George Birch, being seised of all and every the aforesaid recites the marriage covenant of George chester aforesaid. The inquisition next three gardens and three tofts in Manchester, and in a moiety of three messuages, with a certain messuage called The Holt, in Withington aforesaid; and of demesne as of fee of and in eight acres of wood in Withington, lately occupied the said George Birch was seised in his said George Birch deceased. And that of Anne Dokenfield, wife of Francis Dokenfield Gent, mother of the aforesaid Rusholme as aforesaid, after the death third part of the aforesaid messuages, cottages, gardens, &c. in Birch and and also of and in the reversion of a Withington in the county of Lancaster; sixty acres of pasture and ten acres of wood, in Birch and Rusholme within acres of land, twenty acres of meadow, tages, three gardens, two orchards, forty messuages called Birch Hall, two cotas of fee, of and in two parts of two orge Birch he was seised in his demesne the day before the death of the said Gejurors; who say upon their oaths that on Thomas Bradshawe of Salford Gent, Henry Bamford of Shore Gent, and Joseph Scholes of Chadderton Gent, orge Buckley of Whitefield Gent, Richard Lenny of Rochdale Gent, Geley of Ashton-under-Line Gent, Ashton of Herod Gent, Robert BardesChadwick of Wolstenholme Gent, John , Richard Bury of Gooden Gent, John Edmund Whitehead of Birchen... Gent. Butterworth of Woldhouse (?) Gent, James Hall of Droylsden Gent, Ralph stenholme of Wolstenholme Gent, worth of Haworth Gent, Francis WolAshton of Shepley Gent, Edmund Hato him directed, on the oaths of Robert Eschaetor, by virtue of a writ of the king 1613, before Edward Rigbie Esquire,

the manor of Withington are held, and at the time of the decease of the said George Birch were held of Rowland Mosley Esquire as of his manor of Withington, in free socage, by fealty and a rent of three shillings and twopence; and that the premises named in the aforesaid indenture are worth yearly in all outgoings clear of deductions twenty shillings; and that the rest of the premises in Withington are worth yearly in all outgoings, &c., forty shillings; and that the aforesaid lands and tenements in Withington, lately occupied with the aforesaid messuage called The Holt, is held of the said Rowland Mosley Esquire as of his manor of Withington, by knight's service, namely, by the fiftieth part of a knight's fee and a rent of twopence, and is worth yearly in all outgoings, &c., six shillings and eightpence; and that the aforesaid messuages and lands in Manchester are held of the said Rowland Mosley Esquire as of his manor of Manchester, by knight's service, namely by the fiftieth part of a knight's fee and a yearly rent of twelve pence; and at the time of the death of the said George were held of Sir Nicholas Mosley, now deceased, as of his manor of Manchester a like payment, and are worth yearly in all outgoings, &c., ten shillings. And the aforesaid jurors further say that the said Anne Birch widow, late wife of the said George Birch, is now surviving and in full life at Manchester; and that the said Anne, wife of the aforesaid Francis Dokenfield, is surviving and in full life at Manchester; and that the aforesaid Ellis Hey have received the outgoings and profits of the lands, tenements and premises from the time of the death of the aforesaid George up to the day of the taking of this inquisition. And the jurors further say that the aforesaid George Birch had no other or more manors, messages, lands, tenements or hereditaments, on the day of his death so far as they could ascertain.

Thomas Birch, on succeeding to the estates of the family at the death of his father, had but attained the age of three years. He was born in 1608, and baptised at Eccles on the 5th of June in that year. He lived in the eventful days of Charles I, and in the civil dissensions of that unsettled period espoused the popular side. At the commencement of the war he offered His active services to the Parliament, and on the 13th of June 1642 received from Lord Wharton his commission as captain in a regiment of foot. On the 15th of January following, a circumstance occurred which brought him in collision with one of the royalist leaders Lord Strange, afterwards Earl of Derby, and laid the foundation of a personal hostility to that nobleman, which was never afterwards extinguished. On the occasion of a banquet given in Manchester to Lord Strange, a number of adherents to the royalist cause accompanied him thither, — the high sheriff, Lord Molineux, Sir Alexander Radcliffe, Sir Gilbert Hoghton, Mr. Holt of Stubley, Mr. Farrington, Mr. Prestwich, Mr. Tildesley, &c. It is probable that this assemblage had some political significance, and was an expression of sympathy towards Lord Strange, whose recent appointment by the king to the lieutenancy of the county had been annulled by the parliament in favour of their own partisan Lord Wharton. Be this as it may, they were met by an armed band, headed by Captain Birch, who disputed their passage, and gave orders to his men to fire upon them. This, the rain (which was falling heavily at the time) prevented, putting out their matches, and the royalists taking courage repelled the attack, and forced their assailants to disperse, Captain Birch hiding himself under a cart which happened to be standing in the street. This event gained for him the sobriquet of "Lord Derby's carter," and is the cause assigned by Seacombe for Birch's malice towards Lord Derby, which, whenever an opportunity occurred, was too apparent to pass unnoticed. On the 14th of December in that year he received from Lord Wharton his commission as major in the regiment of Colonel Ralph Assheton. His first distinction was his success before Preston on the 13th of February 1643, which town he

and his companions in arms, Major-General Sir John Seaton, Colonel Holland, Major Sparrow and Captain Booth was from Manchester on the 10th instant, and their forces consisted of three companies of foot, to which about double that number of troops was added from Bolton and Blackburn. The assault lasted for two hours, and was attended with considerable loss on both sides. Amongst the killed were Adam Morte, a circumstance occurred which brought mayor of Preston, and his son; Captain Hoghton (brother of Sir Gilbert Hoghton), Major Purvey, &c. The prisoners numbered two hundred, including Captain Farrington, Captain Preston, Mr. George Talbot (son of Sir John Talbot), Mr. Richard Fleetwood, Mr. Blundell, Mr. Thomas Hoghton and Captain Hoghton (nephews of Sir Gilbert Hoghton), Lady Hoghton and Lady Girlington. From Preston Major Birch proceeded to Lancaster, which surrendered to him almost without resistance.

On the 10th of March following he was appointed colonel of a foot regiment by Ferdinando Lord Fairfax, and in April he was named as one of the committee of sequestrations for Lancashire, "for sequestering the estates of notorious delinquents." In June 1644 the town of Liverpool, stormed by Prince Rupert, was retaken after the lapse of a few days by the parliamentary forces, and Colonel Birch was appointed governor.

For the next five years his name does not occur in any of the enterprises undertaken. His connection with Liverpool continued unbroken, and in October 1649 he was elected to represent that constituency in parliament in place of Sir Richard Wynn deceased.

About this time his duties as sequestrator brought him into contact with Humphrey Chetham, the founder, and that in relation to *Souse of Stanley*, p. 133.

his then contemplated foundation. Having matured his plans, Mr. Chetham was desirous of purchasing certain lands in Manchester called the College, late the property of the Earl of Derby, but then under sequestration; and to this end he

applied to the committee for sequestrations, to whom a petition was addressed, and the following answer prepared:—

Whereas there is a howse and outhowseing with th' appurtenances in Manchester, called the Colledge, which was sequestred as parte of the inheritance of the Earle of Derbie, the which have yeilded noe proffit to the publicke duringe the tyme the same hath bin sequestred nor is likelie to doe unles the same bee repaired which will require a great sume of money, the same beinge very ruinous and in greate decay as wee are informed; and whereas Humfrey Chetham Esquire hath desired the same to bee employed for a pious use, viz for an habitacon for some poore children or aged and infirme ould folkes, which hee intends to manteine and provide for at his owne costes and charges, and will make the same or some partes thereof habitable and fitte for that purpose; — Wee whose names are subscribed of the committee of sequestracons for the countie of Lancaster, beinge willinge to further soe good a worke, doe give way and leave soe farre as in us lyes to the said Mr. Chetham to have and use the said colledge howse with th' appurtenances to and for the use and purpose aforesaid; wherevnto wee doc the rather consent for that wee are thereunto solicited by some of the cheife inhabitantes of the townes of Manchester aforesaid and Salford in the said countie of Lancaster. In witnes whereof wee have hereunto set our handes the tenthe daie of September anno Dni 1649.

This document was signed by Peter Egerton, John Starkie, Thomas Fell and Edward Butterworth. On its being submitted to Colonel Birch for his signature, he refused to append it unless Mr. Chetham would pledge himself to apply the premises named to the purpose indicated; he therefore returned the paper, having first inscribed on the margin the following memorandum: — September 20th 1649. I, Humphrey Chethem Esquire, do undertake to maintaine twentie poore people at the colledge, viz. aged persons w blank ev'ie one p ann. and younge boyes to learningo w allowance of blank p ann. ffor w purpose I will settle a durable and constant estate of this value out of lands for ever as assurance to that purpose may be thought fitt and drawne up by councell learned in the lawes. In pnce and witnes of blank.

This insolent dictation led to a temporary abandonment of Mr. Chetham's design, that worthy individual justly regarding Colonel Birch's refusal as a suspicion that his motives were corrupt. The original document is still preserved in the Chetham library. Beneath Colonel Birch's proposal, which has been cut out but afterwards restored, are two explanatory memoranda: — Mem. That the forementioned termes and conditions were pposcd by Mr. Tho. Birch of Birch Chappell to Mr. Chetham when James Lightbowne &c. were sent to the said Tho. Birch for his hand and consent (hee being then a comittee man for sequestration) w said pposalls when Mr. Chetham saw them was much offended that Mr. Birch should bee soe lordly to comand ov soe charitable an intention, and therefore did refuse to buy the colledge.

Mem. When Majo Radcliff one of y ffeofees saw the aboves sawcie pposell of the said Tho. Birtch, hee cut it forth as may app, w is still p'served that if this in after ages bee taken notice of it may and will appeare that always the greatest pretenders for reformation doe not prove reformers.

The whole is endorsed, — "The Order ffor the Colledg from the Comittee hindred by Mr. Birtch. Let this be kept for a lasting monument."

On the 5th of November 1649 Colonel Birch again rendered himself conspicuous as a sequestrator by a forcible attempt to seize upon the revenues of the Church of Manchester. Warden Heyrick having refused to give up peaceable possession, Colonel Birch placed himself at the head of a company of soldiers, and having broken open the door of the chapter house, compelled the surrender of the charter chest, the contents of which, says Walker, "were sent up to London, where they perished in the fire, to the great detriment of the college." *Suffering! of the Clergy*, p. 88.

See also *Foundation in Manchester*, vol. i. pp. 293-1.

Colonel Birch's name next appears in the month of February following when he submitted to the House of Commons a proposition for raising the necessary funds for strengthening the garrison of Liverpool. The sum of £600 had been already voted for that purpose, and Colonel Birch's recommendation to parliament was " that power may be given to the said Thomas Birch, Captain William Duckenfield, Peter Ambrose and Giles Meadowcroft, Gentlemen, or any two of them, to grant and renew so many leases for three lives, according to former rates, unto such of the Earl of Derby's tenants in Lancashire who have faithfully adhered to the parliament in the late wars, as may forthwith raise and extend to the sum of i?600, by the said Colonel Birch to be employed for the use aforesaid."

In December 1650, by a vote of the House, arrears of pay to the amount of £805 13s. 8d. were awarded to Colonel Birch, being after the rate of fifteen shillings a day as captain, twenty-four shillings as major, and forty-five shillings as colonel. It does not, however, appear that this sum, though awarded, was actually paid; for in January 1651-2 reference is again made to it as still owing, and as being about to be allowed to him "as so much doubled monies in the purchase of any lands of delinquents."

The year 1651 was memorable to Colonel Birch as affording him the long sought for opportunity of retaliating on Lord Strange (now Earl of Derby) for the discomfiture he had already suffered at his hands. After the disastrous battle of Worcester, the earl retracing his steps towards Lancashire, on his way thither encountered a troop of the enemies' horse, by whom ho was taken prisoner. "The terms on which he surrendered were that he should have quarter given him for life, and condition for honourable usage; but being now in his enemies' hands, Bradshaw, Rigby and Birch design him to be a victim to their inveterate malice Birch, because his lordship had trailed him under a haycart at Manchester, by which he got even among his own party the deserved epithet of the Earl of Derby's carter. These three, assisted by Sir Richard Houghton, Commons' Journals, vol. vi. pp. 356-7.

representing to Cromwell how unsafe it would be not only to that country but to the whole nation to suffer that man to live, got a commission to try him by a pretended court-martial, the result of which was that he was beheaded at Bolton," October 15, 1651.

In the mouth of November 1651, within a few days of the Earl of Derby's execution, Colonels Birch and Dukinfield were despatched to the Isle of Man to summon the countess, who had escaped thither for refuge, to surrender the island for the use of the parliament. On the 2nd of November they stormed the Castle of Ilushin and Peter Castle, and by the treachery of an officer named Christian, to whom the deceased earl had committed the keeping of his wife and children, the island was surrendered, and the countess and her children were given up to the invaders, who refused her request that she might be permitted to retire to Peel Castle, and with her family thence to embark to France or Holland. They were conveyed in the first instance to the castle of Liverpool, where Colonel Birch was their gaoler, but were afterwards sent to Chester Castle as a place of greater security.

In 1653 Colonel Thomas Birch was again returned by the constituency of Liverpool, in Cromwell's second parliament, which met on the 4th of July. Their deliberations were but short, the session being abruptly terminated by its dissolution on the 12th of the following December. In the succeeding parliament the name of Colonel Thomas Birch appears, and again as the representative for Liverpool. This was the parliament which conferred on Cromwell the title of Lord Protector; its sitting terminated January 22, 1656. In September 1656 he was again returned for Liverpool, but was not permitted to take his seat, the Lord Protector having exercised an assumed right of rejecting such of the members elected as were not wholly favourable to his views, Colonel Birch being of the number. In common with the other secluded members (upwards of a hundred) he signed the remonstrance to the Protector. His name appears in the parliament summoned by Richard Cromwell, which met in 1659; and on the 4th of July in that year, after the reading Seacombe's *House of Stanley,* pp. 114-115. Ibid, pp. 143-144. of a long report about the demolition of the castle of Liverpool, wherein Colonel Walton reports from the Council of State that it will be for the service of the State that the said castle be demolished and made untenable, together with the walls and towers; it was resolved that this house doth agree with the Council of State that the castle of Liverpool and the walls thereof be demolished and the towers made untenable, and that £S5 mentioned in the report as the estimated value of the lead and materials thereof be forthwith paid unto Walter Frost, Esquire, for the use of the Commonwealth, and that the dwelling-house therein with the site and materials of the said castle be conveyed unto Colonel Thomas Birch and his heirs in consideration of the demolishing thereof and for recompence of his charges therein. On the 11th of August he received permission from the House to go into the country, and on the 22nd of that month a letter from him was read before the House, written from Northwich in Cheshire, announcing the defeat of Sir George Booth, in which affair it is presumed Colonel Birch was engaged. He is found also on several committees about this time, for reviving the jurisdiction of the counties palatine of Chester and Lancaster, and for settling the militia of London, on which latter committee Colonel John Birch his kinsman was one of his associates. It does not appear that he had a seat in parliament after the Restoration; his name only occurs in relation to a past transaction, involving the privileges of parliament: — On the 30th of June 1660 Sir Ralph Assheton acquainted the House that a person who sat in the last parliament took a bond of «P 100 for the doing of some particular service in the House; upon which it was resolved that Sir Ralph Assheton be required to name the person; whereupon Sir Ralph Assheton named Thomas Birch of Liverpool. Commons' Journals, vol. vii. p. 704. The muster-rolls of this date contain an order on Colonel Birch for one light horse. The summons addressed to him is as follows: —

By vertuo of a warr' under ye hand and seale of y" Eight honorable Charles Earle of Derby, dated 9 Octobris instant, to us directed and a list thereunto annexed whereby yo are charged with one light horse, yo are hereby required to furnish and send out ". said light horse oompleatly armed and in all poyntes fitt for service, to y«

Thus closed the public career of Colonel Thomas Birch as far as can now be gathered. He lived for some years after his retirement, and died in 1678, in the seventy-first year of his age. His inventory is dated August 14.', 1678. It estimates the "value of his goods and chattels" at i?184 13s. lid., but contains nothing entitling it to a more extended notice. We may form, however, some idea of the size of Birch Hall, the residence of the family, in Colonel Birch's time, from an enumeration of the apartments which the inventory supplies: — The hall, the garden parlour, the little parlour, the white chamber, the middlemost room, the painted chamber, the dining room, the red chamber, Mrs. Birch's chamber, old Mrs. Birch's chamber, the yellow chamber, the old wench's chamber. rendevous at Bury on Thursday the 18 of this instant October by one of the clocke in yc after noone, there to receive further orders from Thomas Greenehaulgh EsqTM who is appoynted their captaine, and yo are further required to send with your sayd horse 30 dayes pay after 2" p' diem; hereof faile not at your perill. — Given under our handes this 11lh day of October 1660.

Your lov. friends
Tno. Blown j S Constables.
To Collonell Birch, theise p'sent.

The will of Colonel Birch is not to be found either in the Diocesan Registry of Chester or at Doctor's Commons; nor is any copy of it known to exist. ' Birch Hall as it now is, if not altogether modern, has yet been so modernised as to present no features of attraction to the antiquarian investigator. Portions of the original structure yet remaining show it to have been one of the black and white half-timbered houses so common in Lancashire.

From a MS. in the autograph of Colonel Birch it appears that the distance between Birch Chapel and the Collegiate Church of Manchester was about four miles. This was in 1640, when the route lay over Ardwick Green. Marche 9th 1640. A true and p'feete note of the distance betwene Birche Chappell and the Churche of Manchester after 5 yeardes and an halfe to tho pole and 320 poles to a mile, beinge measured the day and yeare above written, the ordinarie lane way thorough Birchall flbuld, and so to Ardwick Greene; — it is in all just 4 miles and 52 poles, viz.

ftlrst to the yate gowing out of the medowe into the lane by the horsepoole from the Chappell is 80 poles, w is a q't of a mile.

Thence to the yate gowinge out of Anne Edges ffould is another q.

Thence to the Brouke short of Rusholme is halfe a mile — all w make one mile.

Thence to the midle of the greene is at Ed. Baguleyes house is 1 q't'.
o

He married in October 1623 Alice, eldest daughter of Thomas Brooke of Norton in the county of Chester Esq. , and by her had issue Thomas Birch his eldest son, George, Matthew, Andrew, and Peter the twin brother of Andrew, of whom more hereafter; and five daughters, Anne wife of Alexander Rigby of Burgh Esq., Alice wife of John Robinson of Bruckshaw Esq., Ellena wife of Thomas Holcroft of Hurst Esq., Mary and Deborah.

His wife survived him, dying in 1697. Her will is dated September 23, 1696, and is as follows: — In the name of God amen. I, Alice Birch, widdow of Thomas Birch Esquire of Birch in Lancashire, being in perfect memory and understanding but decaied in strength, doe upon the twenty-third day of September 1696, make this my last will and testament, revoking all others whatsoever. First I humbly commend my soul to God who gave it, in sure and certain hopes of his mercifull I acceptance through the mediation of Jesus Christ our only mediator and advocate. And as for my body £ desire it may be decently interred by my late beloved husband at the discretion of my executor. Item I do hereby constitute, appoint and declare my son George Birch, now living with me, to be my true and lawfull executor to all intents and purposes, to demand and receive all rights, profits and emoluments w shall be due unto me, and to discharge all due debts and claims to which I am subject at my death. Item I give and bequeath to my well beloved children now surviving or that shall survive at my decease, to each a gold ring of twenty shillings value, to be kept in memory of me their

Thence to Tho: Shelmerdine his Breckline is another 1 q t.

Thence to the little Plat finge beyond John Davies house is 1 qt·.

Thence to the furthest tree in Raphe Hudsons furthest feild upon the right hand *is* 1 qt, w makes another mile — viz. 2 miles, ffrom thence to Edward Richardson alias Wolworke his house as we come to Ard wieke Greene is 3 q'tr̃m of a mile and 48 poles. From Edward Wolworkes house to Manchester Churche is one mile one quarter and 4 poles.

So that the Totall is ut supradict' 4 miles and 52 poles.

From the House of Birche to Manchear' Churche is as neere as possibly bo 4 miles of this measure and this way.

By nice Tho: Birche.

mother. Item I give to my servant Ann Wilkinson, for her good and faithful services, one year's wages over and above her just arrears at my death. Witnesses: Pet. Birch, William Birch, Sarah Righway. Proved at Chester August 31, 1697.

Colonel Birch was succeeded by his eldest son Thomas, who was baptised at the Collegiate Church October 15, 1704.

George Birch, eldest son and heir of George Birch of Birch Esquire her sole executor. Proved at Chester June 23, 1704.

Thomas Birch the younger, on succeeding to the estates, mortgaged in 1701 Birch Hall and the demesne to his uncle Dr. Peter Birch, the sum borrowed on security of the lands being ?1,000; and in October 1702 he charged his lands with a further mortgage of £250. On the 25th of February 1703 he re-settled his estates, limiting them to the use of himself for his life, and to such further uses as he should by his will appoint, with remainder to his brothers Thomas Birch and William Birch in succession, with further remainder to the Rev. Peter Birch D.D. He died, as already stated, without issue and intestate; and upon the death of his brothers Thomas and William, also without issue, the estates reverted to the Rev. Peter Birch D.D., their father's younger brother. To this member of the family Anthony Wood refers. He was son of Thomas Birch of the ancient and genteel family of the Birches of Birch in Lancashire. He was born in that county; educated in Presbyterian principles, and afterwards retiring with Andrew his brother to Oxford in 1670, they lived as sojourners in the house of John Foulks, an apothecary, in St. Mary's parish, became students in the public library, and had a tutor to instruct them in philosophical learning, but yet did not wear gowns. At length Peter, leaving Oxford for a time, did afterwards return with a mind to conform and wear a gown. Whereupon Dr. John Fell, taking cognizance of the matter, he procured certain letters from the Chancellor of the University in his behalf, which being read in a Convocation held May 6, 1673, you shall have the contents of them as they follow: — Peter Birch, whom these letters concern, did lately live among you, not so regularly either in relation to the church or the government of the University as he ought, yet withall, as I have understood, that before he went from among you, he declared his conformity to the church by receiving the sacrament publicly. Immediately after he was called away by his father, with *Alietue Oxoniensef*, vol. iv. p. 659.

whom he hath with great importunity prevailed to permit him to return to the

1629, and was consequently in his fiftieth year. He married in December 1658 Beatrix, daughter of William Cotton of Bellaport in the county of Salop Esquire. He was much addicted to antiquarian studies. Many of his MSS. were in the possession of Gregson, some of them being printed by that author in his *Fragments Relating to Lancashire*. The date of his death is unknown, but he was dead in 1 700. He had issue three sons. — George, eldest son and heir, died unmarried and intestate in 1704, being at the time high sheriff of the county of Lancaster; his inventory is dated June 19, 1704, it estimates the total value of his "goods and chattels" at i?136 7s. 6d. ; Thomas, a captain in the Earl of Orrery's regiment, who succeeded to the estates on the death of his brother, but who also died unmarried; and William, to whom the estates descended on the death of his brother; living in 1723, but died also unmarried. Ho had issue also eight daughters, of whom Elizabeth was the wife of the Rev. John Tetlow, minister of Birch Chapel, Joyce Birch, her sister, makes her will April 28, 1704. She describes herself as of Birch in the county of Lancaster, spinster. She commits her soul to God and her body to Christian burial in such decent manner as shall seem meet to her executor. And for her worldly estate she orders, gives and disposes of the same in manner and form following: — First it is her will and mind that her funeral expenses be paid out of her whole estate. Also it is her will that all and every the sum and sums of money left and given unto her by William Cotton of Bellowport in the county of Salop Esquire, deceased, and now remaining in his executors hands (viz. William Oldfelt Esquire and Philip Cotton Esquire) shall be disposed of as follows: She gives and bequeaths all and every the said sum and sums of money to her two affectionate brothers George and Thomas Birch, to be equally divided betwixt them. She appoints her said loving and affectionate brother

University (though he was pressed to go to Cambridge, where he was sometime since matriculated), choosing to testify his change of mind and receive his education there, where he had formerly lived a dissenter. "Iis my desire that he may be bachelor of arts after he has performed his exercises, and to compute his time from his matriculation in Cambridge, &c. The Chancellor then told the venerable Convocation in his said letters, — That when so many run away from the church you would think fit to encourage one who addresseth himself a free and thorough convert, &c. After the said letters were read there was some clamour in the house against the passing of them; and Ralph Rawson of Brazennose College, concerning himself more than the rest in the matter (for he said openly that fanatics are now encouraged and loyalists set aside, &c.), he got the ill-will of Dr. John Fell, who always showed himself forward in gaining proselytes, Dr. R. Bathurst and others of that mind. On the 12th day of the said month of May 1673, Peter Birch was matriculated as a member of Christ Church, he being then about twenty-one years of age, and being soon after admitted bachelor of arts he was made one of the chaplains or petty canons of that house by the said Dr. Fell. Afterwards he proceeded in arts, preached several times in and near Oxford, was curate of St. Thomas's parish, afterwards rector of St. Ebbe's Church for a time, and a lecturer at Carfax; and being recommended to the service of James Duke of Ormond, he was by him made one of his chaplains. Afterwards he became minister of St. James's Church within the liberty of Westminster, chaplain to the House of Commons in 1689, and prebend of Westminster in the place of Dr. Simon Patrick, promoted to the see of Chichester, in which dignity he was installed the 18th of October the same year. He graduated B.A. 1673, M.A. 1674, B.D. 1683, and D.D. 1688. Dr. Birch published several sermons: — 1. Sermon before the House of Commons on John xxvi. 3, printed at the Savoy, 1689; 2. Sermon before the House of Commons January 30, 1693, on 2 Sam.

i. 21, London 1694, in the 20th page of which were several expressions which caused some of the said house, as was then reported, to cry out " Ad Igncm." On the 20th of February following was published an answer to the latter sermon, entitled "A Birchen Hod for Dr. Birch, or some animadversions upon his sermon preached before the Honourable House of Commons at St. Margaret's, Westminster, January 30, 1693," &c.

He married Sybil, youngest daughter and coheir of Humphrey Wyrley of Hampstead in the county of Stafford Esquire, by whom he had issue two sons, Humphrey Birch and John Wyrley Birch.

He died in 1710. His will is dated June 27, 1710, and is as follows: —

In the name of God amen. I, Peter Birch, Doctor of Divinity and Prebendary of St. Peter's Church, Westminster, being sick and weak in body but of sound and perfect understanding (praised be Almighty God for the same) do make this my last will in manner following. First I give and bequeath to my eldest son Humphrey all my real estate, manors, messuages, cottages, lands, tenements, hereditaments and appurtenances whatsoever or wheresoever within the counties of Stafford and Warwick, and to his heirs for ever, paying yearly out of the same to my youngest son John.£200 at two even payments; to wit at Michaelmas and Lady Day; the first payment to be made at which of the said days shall first happen next after my decease, my said eldest son subjecting himself to the settlement made before my marriage with his mother, who was the youngest daughter of Humphrey Wyrley of Hamstead in the parish of Handsworth and said county of Stafford Esquire, now deceased. Item I give all my real estate, mortgages, leases, manors, messuages, cottages, lands, tenements, hereditaments and appurtenances whatsoever in the county of Lancaster or elsewhere in the kingdom of Great Britain, and not before devised, to my eldest son; and also all my goods, cattells and chattells of what kind soever the same be, to my said youngest son John and his heirs and assigns for ever.

And I hereby revoke all former wills by me made; and I do hereby make and appoint my dear sister Deborah Birch sole executrix of this my last will, and guardian to both my said sons until they shall severally attain to the age of one and twenty years, and I beg sho will take care of the education of them, and forthwith take them into her care and custody for that purpose. And my mind and will is that she shall receive and gather all the rents of all my estate by herself and agents, and out of the same for her trouble and care thereabouts she shall receive and take to her own use during her natural life, without rendering any account for the same, one hundred pounds yearly at Michaelmas and Lady Day by even portions, the first at which of the said feasts shall first happen next after my decease. And my mind and will is further that in case she shall depart this life before my said sons shall attain to the age of one and twenty years, that then my friend Nicholas Geast of the parish of Handsworth in the said county of Stafford shall be guardian, and have the guardianship of both my said sons until they shall attain to the several ages of twenty-one years; and I desire he will take care of the education of them and forthwith take them into his care and custody for that purpose; and my mind and will is then that he shall by himself or agents receive and take all my rents of all my said estate, and manage the same to the best advantage of my said sons, taking thereout only i?100 per annum for his care and trouble thereabouts until they and both of them shall attain to the said age of twenty-one years, without rendering any account thereof. And my mind and will is further, that all the charges and expenses whatsoever that either my said sister or the said Nicholas Geast shall be put to or expend in and about the managing my said estate or education or maintenance of my said children or anyways relating to either, shall be paid and allowed to them or both or either of them out of my said estate. And my mind and will is that neither my mother-in-law, Mrs. Wyrley, nor any of the family of the Wroths shall have anything whatsoever to do with the guardianship of my said children or the management of my said estate or any part thereof. And I desire my said friend Nicholas Geast will assist my said sister. In witness whereof, &c. Proved in the Prerogative Court of Canterbury January 15, 1710-11.

On the death of Dr. Peter Birch he was succeeded in his estates » by his son Humphrey, who took the name of Wyrley. In 1743 he executed a deed barring the entail of the estates, and the following year, for the consideration of the payment of £6,000, conveyed Birch Hall and one hundred and sixty-eight acres of land to George Croxton of Manchester, merchant. From Mr. Croxton it passed in 1745 to Mr. John Dickenson of Manchester, merchant, in whose representative, Sir John William Hamilton Anson Bart., it is now vested. The arms of Birch of Birch are described by Dugdale as azure 3 fleurs-de-lis with a serpent entwined proper. Baines, in his pedigree of the family (History of Lancashire, vol. ii. p. 537) has incorrectly substituted the arms of Birch of Birch or Bruch near Warrington.

The town residence of the Dickensons, successors of the old local family at Birch, was situated in Market-street Lane. Here Mr. John Dickenson, the purchaser of the Birch Hall estate, lodged and entertained the Pretender on the occasion of his visit to Manchester in 1745. It is stated that the bed on which he lay was removed to Birch Villa, where it was sold a few years ago on the death of Miss Dickenson. The house itself in Market-street, from the circumstance, received the name of the Palace. It was afterwards converted into an inn, when it was known as the " Palace Inn. " It has more recently been rebuilt as a warehouse, and now bears the designation of the " Palace Buildings."

A branch of the Birch family settled in Ardwick within Manchester parish and entered a pedigree at the visitation of Sir William Dugdale in 166"1. The precise point from which they spring is not ascertained, but their claim of descent was admitted, and the same arms were accorded to them as those borne by the Birches of Birch, differenced by a trefoil on the crest and a canton or in the arms. Samuel Birch of Ardwick Gent. resided there about the time of the Restoration. He married Mary Smith of Dob in tho parish of Manchester, at whose death in 166() the Rev. Henry Newcome preached her funeral sermon, and from the published diary of this celebrated divine we learn that on March 22, 1662, he had a "precious day" with Mr. Samuel Birch, who had then recently purchased the Ordsal estate, and removed thither.

Mr. Birch died in 1668-9, and was buried at the Collegiate Church. His will is dated July 8, 1667, and is as follows: — In the name of God amen. I, Samuell Birche, of Ardwicke in the county of Lancaster Gentleman, beinge weake in body but of perfect myud and memorie, thankes bee to Almighty God for the same, and knowinge tho uncertainty of this transitory life, and that all flesh must yeild unto death when it shall please God to call, doe constitute, ordayne, make and appoint this my last will and testament in-manner and forme following: And I doe hereby revoke and disannull all will and wills, testament and testaments heretofore by mee made and declared either by word or wrytinge, and this is onely to bee taken for my last will and testament, and none other, ffirst and principally I committ my soule into the hands of Almighty God, trustinge through the meritts of Jesus Christ to bee eternally saved; and my body to tho earth, cxpcctingc a joyfull resurrection, to bee buryed in such decent and Christian manner as to my executor hereafter herein nominated shall bee thought meete and convenient. And for the estate which it hath pleased God to bestowe upon mee my mynd and will is and I give and dispose of the same in manner followinge, that is to say, ffirst I give and bequeath unto the poore the summe of tenn pounds to bee distributed amongst them at the tyme of my interrment at the discretion of my executor out of my whole personall estate, and in his absence att the discretion of my sonnes Samuell Birch, John Bent, Edward Ratclifte and Peeter Antrobus Gentlemen. Item I give and bequeath unto my sonne John Birch of Whittebourne in the county of Hereford EsqTM all my lands, tenements, leases, and all. deeds, evidences, wrytings and rescripts touching and concerninge the same. Item I give unto my said sonne John Birch all the standinge bedds, all the wainscottes and all the tables win my house, and all the stone troughs, hewen stone, the ladders and all the screw presses in and about the house. And for all the rest and residue of my personall estate, goods, cattells, moneys and plate, my mynd and will is the same to bee devided into ffoure equall parts; and I give and bequeath the same to bee equally devided and distributed amongst my four children; that is to say, Shusanna Bent, Elizabeth Antrobus, Sarah Ratclifte and Thomas Birch, clarke. And lastly, I doe hereby constitute, ordayne, nominate and appoint my dearest sonne John Birch of Whittbourne in the county of Hereford EsqTM to bee the sole executor of this my last will and testament, hopinge hee will duely execute the same. In witnes whereof I the said Samuell Birch have hereunto sett my hand and seale the day and yeare first above written. Alsoe I give and bequeath unto my dearest sonne John Birch the clocke and bell with all thinges belonginge unto the same, before the sealinge and delivery hereof. And whereas I have since my declaracon of this my will, and before this day, given to my daughters Elisabeth and Sarah either twentie poundes, with an intent that they should in consideracon thereof give full discharges for any demand of any part of my personall estate at my decease, which discharge being not yet given to my content, my mind and will now is that my two daughters aforesaid shall have no part of my personall estate other then what shall amount unto above twentie pounds a peice for my sonne Thomas Birche and my daughter Susanna Bente to equall them with theire other sisters, and then the overplus, whatever it may be, to bee devided in four equall parts, as I have said before, and to my four children paid or delivered, my debts, legacies and funerall charges first paid out by my executor herein named.

Witnesses, Edmund Pesivall, Edward Hartley, John Halle.

The sum total of the inventory is but £93 13s. 0£d.

The eldest surviving son of the testator, designated by the will as John Birch of Whitbourne, was the celebrated Colonel John Birch, an officer in the Parliamentary Forces, who took an active part in the occurrences of the eventful period in which he lived. He was born in 1616 (not 1626 as erroneously stated in Burke), and was baptised at the Collegiate Church, Manchester, on the 7th of April in that year. It is reported of him that in his youth, being of great stature, he enlisted in the army, and that on the circumstance being made known to his kinsman, the afterwards celebrated Colonel Thomas Birch of Birch Hall, he was received with favour, and his promotion was rapid. Be this, however, as it may, in 1643 he had risen to the rank of major, and on the 14th of October 1644, a petition from Colonel John Birch was presented to the House of Commons, praying to have as satisfaction for the sum of *£1,500* lent in the service of the state, such property of one Henry Hudson, a delinquent, as is not already discovered. In May 1645 he was in command of the Kentish regiment at Plymouth, and became later in the year, by a vote of the house, governor of Bridgewater, subject to the approval of Sir Thomas Fairfax and the concurrence of the House of Lords. About this time too he entered parliament as member for Weobley, under which date and in which capacity he is alluded to by Oldmixon (vol. i. p. 299), who asserts the general moderation of his political opinions; that he sometimes voted with the Presbyterians and sometimes with the Independents; and generally went with those who voted for satisfaction and security till it was known that Oliver and his party meant the death of the king by it. On the 1st of September 1645, with Colonel Pride for his associate, he was at the siege of Bristol; and in the month of December he and Colonel Morgan, uniting their forces, took the city of Hereford by stratagem, sending into the city at night six men disguised as labourers. These surprised the sentinels, and being seconded, by a sudden assault, in which Colonel Birch led on the foot and Colonel Morgan the cavalry (in all two thousand men), they were in a short time masters of the city. They captured eleven pieces of ordnance, forty lords, knights and gentlemen of consideration, whom they sent prisoners to Gloucester. Colonel Birch was instated as governor of the city by a vote of the House of Commons, and a public thanksgiving was decreed in recognition of this seasonable success. A story is related of Colonel Birch at this stage of his career which strongly illustrates the insecurity of the times in which he lived. Soon after the taking of Hereford, Dr. Herbert Croft, afterwards Bishop of that see, preaching at the Cathedral, inveighed boldly and sharply against sacrilege, at which some of the officers then present began to mutter amongst themselves, and a guard of musqueteers in the church were preparing their pieces, and asked whether they should fire at him, but Colonel Birch the governor prevented them. On the 23rd of March following two letters from Colonel Birch were read before the house, relating to the capture of Sir Jacob Astley and a victory over the forces under his command at Stow on the Wold in Gloucestershire, and again a public thanksgiving was decreed. In March 1646, Colonel Birch, Colonel Morgan and Sir William Brereton, with their joint forces, marched to Worcester, and summoned the city to surrender to the Parliament, assuring them that the king had no forces to relieve them; to which summons the inhabitants answering that had such been the case they should have known the king's pleasure, the besiegers replied that they would give them a short respite in order that they might the better inquire and prevent their own ruin. They consequently withdrew from Worcester, and falling upon the town of Bridgewater, carried it by storm. In the following May Ludlow Castle surrendered to Colonel Birch, and at his request a supply of ammunition was forwarded to him for operations against Goodrich Castle and Ragland Castle. At the close of the year he took the solemn league and covenant. On the 1st of March 1646-7, it having been determined that the city of Hereford should be disgarrisoned, and that the Castle of Hereford should be kept a garrison with one hundred and three score foot in it, he ceased to occupy the post of governor, which was conferred on Whitelock's *Memorials,* p. 190. *Athetue Oxonienses,* vol. iv. p. 311, note.

' Whitelock's *Memorials,* pp. 205-206.

Colonel Samuel Moore. After resigning the governorship of Hereford, ho actively employed himself in collecting troops for service in Ireland, with the intention of accompanying them thither. Circumstances, however, occurred which rendered his presence and influence needful at home, to appease the discontent of the army, which from the pay of the soldiers having been too long withheld, began to manifest symptoms of insubordination. On the 11th of June 1647, ho was requested, together with three other members, to prepare a letter, which they were authorised to send to General Fairfax, desiring that the army might remain stationary, and not advance within forty miles of London, his name being at the same time added to a committee which charged itself with the duty of putting London in a posture of defence. The delay in acting upon his original intention of crossing to Ireland seems to have led to an abandonment of his design, and whatever was the destination of the troops their colonel remained in England. Early in the ensuing year he was placed on a committee to consider in what manner such churches, houses, towns, &c. as have been burnt, demolished and spoiled since these wars may be repaired, and on the 25th of January he was chosen one of a commission to proceed on an important state mission from the parliament of England to that of Scotland, his brother commissioners being the Earls of Nottingham and Stamford, Bryan Stapleton, Wil-

ucational bequest has been lost to the school, as will appear from the following extract taken from the Digest of Ect-ums on Education for 1818: — A school in Ardwick endowed by the family of the Birches with £8 per annum, which was regularly paid to the clerk of the chapel, but about nine years ago he absconded, after having collected the pew-rents, which, with the £8, he appropriated to his own use; since which time the trustees have been in entire ignorance of the manner in which the £8 was raised, and the school has been at a very low ebb." the two largest silver candlesticks and the waiter, which he hereby gives to his said nephew Samuel Birch. To his sister-in-law Margaret Lilly he gives the usual furniture of and belonging to such of his bed-rooms as she shall make choice of; and afterwards the like furniture of or belonging to any two other of his bed-rooms or chambers to his said brother George Birch as he shall think proper.

By a second codicil, dated April 24, 1753, he revokes the grant made in the first codicil of the lands in Higher Ardwick, therefore in the several tenures of himself and John Chapman, and which by that codicil were bequeathed to his nephew Thomas Birch and his heirs for ever, and by this codicil gives such part of them as yet belongs to him to his (testator's) sister-in-law Margaret Lilly for her life, and after her death to his nephew Thomas Birch, his heirs and assigns. His household furniture he gives to the said Margaret Lilly, and also his pew or seat in Ardwick Chapel gives the same to his said nephew, his heirs and assigns. In lieu of the interest of £300 bequeathed by his will to his nephew John Walker, he directs that £100 and no more shall be put out at interest for his said nephew's use, and after his death the principal to be distributed as in the will. the £300 was directed to be divided. The legacy of £700 bequeathed by the will to the child or children of his late niece Elizabeth, wife of Thomas Gardner, which legacy by the first codicil was reduced to £400, is now by this present codicil further reduced

and Maria (died 1813).

leaving issue Thomas (died in 1796). George, of Ardwick, who died in 1794; and died in January 1811; goons, war as Colonel of Preston's Light Dragoons the army, who served in the American 8, 1781 s.p.; Samuel, a major-general in son, of the Inner Temple, who died June beth Hill, Thomas, his eldest surviving 1757, leaving issue by his wife Elizabeth He died at Ardwick December 18, terwards to go to the curate. him until he be reimbursed, the rents afrents of such gallery being secured to to erect a west gallery in the chapel, the source we learn that he pledges himself sion, the manor-house. From the same successors, owners of his capital mansion Chapel, Ardwick, and by the consecration deed a vault at the east end of the chapel is reserved to himself and to his he presented the site for St. Thomas's 1747 high sheriff of the county. In 1740 of the peace for Lancashire, and was in born in 1690. He was in the commission resided at Lower Ardwick, and was Samuel Birch, another brother, Holy Communion. lowing year a silver flagon for use at the chapel at Gorton, presenting in the following year self in promoting the rebuilding of the and in 1753 he actively employed himself ers for the consecration of the chapel; Chapel, Ardwick, as one of the petitioners consecration deed of St. Thomas's of the testator, occurs in 1740, in the The name of George Birch, a brother

James Hall. sociates her in the trust with the said that of his brother George Birch, and associates of his sister-in-law Margaret Lilly for Thomas Birch. He substitutes the name bequeaths such residue to his nephew he there names as his executors, and he partner in trade James Hall, whom also for George Birch, and to his brother al estate made in his will to his brother the bequest of the residue of his personal to the £5 given by his will. He revokes chester, joiner, he gives £55 in addition her £100 only. To Mary Wood, of Manchester, garet Lilly, and instead thereof he gives en in his will to his sister-in-law Margaret Lilly. He revokes the bequest of £200 given

to £100, to be paid as already directed.

On the 9th of March 1795, pursuant to a decree in chancery in a cause Watson v. Birch, several freehold estates in the township of Ardwick and a moiety of a lime-stone quarry, late the property of Thomas Birch Esq. deceased, were offered for sale; a purchaser was found, but disputes having arisen as to the validity of the sale, the estates were directed to be resold, and they finally passed into other hands on the 1st of February 1796.

On the east side of the township, near to its junction with Newton and Gorton, is an estate called Slade, or more anciently, Milkwallslade. The name Slade signifies in the Anglo-Saxon a plain or open tract of land, a term sufficiently descriptive of its true character; but the meaning of its earlier designation Milkwallslade it is more difficult to conjecture.

Michewall Diche is given in 1484 as one of the boundaries of certain lands in Birch, conveyed by William Birch to his son Robert; and its proximity of the Nico or Nicker Ditci which forms the southern boundary of the Slado Hall estate suggests that these may both be modifications of the same word; its etymology, however, has not yet been decided.

The first proprietors of whom we know anything were the family of Manchester, whose association with the township we have already seen. By a deed undated but executed about the year 1270, Thomas, son of Geoffrey, son of Luke de Manchester, confirmed to his brother Jordan certain lands in Didisford and Milkewallslade, being the same lands which Geoffrey his father had given him, together with one acre of meadow in Banereris, and all the land his father held in Akedone. This deed was witnessed by Geoffrey, Dean of Manchester; Ad or W de Hulton, Matthew de Birch, William le Norreis, Robert son of Symon de Manchester, Richard de Honeford, William de Didisb'y and John the Clerk.

In the 23 Edward III (1349) the estate is found vested in Robert de Milkewallslade, who being in all probability a member of the family of Manchester, had taken the name of Milkewallslade from the place of his abode, as was customary in those early times. Ho may possibly have been a son or grandson of Jordan de Manchester, the last recorded proprietor. He married Ellen or Elena, daughter of Robert del Platt of Platt within Rusholme, and had issue Robert his heir and a younger son named John.

In 1349 Robert de Milkwallslade tho elder settled his estates, limiting them to himself for his life, and after his decease to his elder son Robert and his lawful heirs, with remainder in case of

R failing issue to John his younger son, with further remainder in a like contingency to the right heirs of himself and Elena his wife.

In the reign of Elizabeth the name of the estate was abbreviated into Slade, and the names of the owners also suffered a similar abridgment. Slade Hall, though still in possession of the family, had ceased to be their residence, a lease of the premises having been made to Richard Siddall of Manchester, yeoman, which was afterwards renewed to Edward Siddall his son. Meanwhile the Slades had retired to an estate in Staffordshire. An indenture made the 20th of April in the 19 Elizabeth (1577) between Rauffe Slade of Breerehurst in the county of Stafford Gent. on the one part, and Roger Greene alderman of Congleton in the county of Chester on the other part, witnesseth that these parties in consideration of a marriage hereafter to be had between Thomas Slade, son and heir apparent of the said Ralph, and Marie Bellotte, daughter of Robert Bellotte late of Moreton in the county of Chester Gent. deceased, agree that Rauffe Slade doth covenant and grant with Roger Greene, &c., by these presents that the said Thomas Slade shall, by God's permission and sufferance, before the feast of Holy Pentecost next, marry the said Marie Bellotte if she will be ready, consent and agree. and the laws of holy church on her part will it permit and suffer, &c. a like covenant here following by Roger Greene for Marie Bellotte. Ralph Slade then proceeds to covenant that before such marriage he will convey to John Lawton of Lawton in the county of Chester Esq., Philippe Bellotte of Moreton Gent., and Richard Podmore and Richard Whelocke of the parish of Wolstanton in the county of Stafford, yeomen, one certain messuage, &c., called Milkwalleslade, and all lands, &c., thereto belonging, with the yearly rent of 26s. 8d. situate and being in Withington in the county of Lancaster, and now or late in the tenure and occupation of Edward Syddall, to the following uses: — To the use of the said Ralph Slade for his life, afterwards to that of the said Thomas Slade and the lawful heirs of him and the said Marie Bellotte; in default of such issue to the lawful issue of Thomas Slade; in default of such to the right heirs of Ralph Slade for ever, free from all former grants, jointures, dowers, &c. ; the lawful dower of Jone Norst, wife of the said Ralph, and one lease of tho said messuage, lands, &c., to the said Edward Syddall for the term of forty-two years (of which thirty are unexpired), and whereon is reserved the yearly rent of 26s. 8d. payable to the said Ralph, &c., always excepted. Ralph Slade further covenants that before the next court to be holden at Thurstfield within the manor of Tunstall in the county of Stafford, he will surrender, according to the custom of the manor, one capital messuage, &c., at Brerehurst, wherein the said Ralph doth now dwell, and twenty-seven acres of land, &c., into the hands of Geoffrey Rowley of Wedgewood and the said Richard Podmore, two customary tenants of the said manor, to the end that they should present the same at the said court after the solemnization of the said marriage, before the steward, &c., to the use of the said Thomas Slade and his heirs male by the said Marie Bellotte &c. &c. as before on condition that Thomas Slade at the said court, after his marriage and immediately after the surrendering of the premises aforesaid to his use, make a petit estate or surreuder, according to the custom of the manor, to the said Ralph and Jone his wife, of two parts of the said messuage and of two parts of all buildings thereto belonging, and of eighteen acres of the said twenty-seven acres to the use of the said Ralph and Jone his wife, during their lives, they yielding and paying two parts of all rents, &c., due and payable for the said two parts during their occupation. Upon condition also that the said Thomas, at the said court, after solemnization of the marriage, make a good and lawful estate by surrender or otherwise, according to the custom of the manor, to the said Marie Bellotte, of the third part of the said messuage and buildings and of nine acres of the customary lands, residue of the said twenty-seven acres, to Marie Bellotte for her life, with remainder to the said Thomas Slade and his heirs male. Provided the said Thomas and Marie shall inhabit and dwell together with the said Ralph and Jone at the said capital messuage, and do the work and labour of the said Ralph and Jone, so long as they can agree together, Ralph and Jone finding to Thomas and Marie and their children meat, drink, clothing and all other things necessary, meet and convenient for living; and if they cannot agree together then Thomas and Marie to have the said nine acres of customary lands with the third part of the said capital messuage, &c., during the life of Ralph and Jone, with remainder to Thomas and Marie as aforesaid. In consideration of which covenants, &c., the said Roger Greene doth covenant to pay Ralph Slade at or before the solemnization of the marriage *£40* as the proper goods, filial portion or child's part of goods of the said Marie. Ralph Slade consents to be bounden in his " escripte obligatory" bearing date with these presents, to the said Roger Greene in the sum of *£200*. In witness whereof, &c.

The date of the first association of the family of Siddall with the Slade Hall estate was antecedent to the year 1565, which time accords with the above recited indenture. Edward, son of Richard Siddall of V ithington yeoman, obtained a lease of the premises for a term of forty-two years. There had been an earlier lease of the premises to Richard Siddall, the father, who resided at Slade Hall in 1558, as his will testifies: —

Will Of Richard Siddall.

In the name of God amen. The 22

Field; and also all the part, purpartie and porcon of the said George Siddall of and in that comon or moore in Kersal aforesaid, commonly known by the name of Kersal moore or Kersal wood; and all that rent of three shillings and four pence issuing out of that messuage in Awdwynshawe in the county of Lancaster, now or late in the tenure of Raphe Hobson Gent.

In addition to this transfer of the Kersal estate George Siddall, who must be regarded as the spendthrift of the family, alienated in 1627 to John Beswick of Manchester chapman and his heirs for ever, two closes of land in Grindlow Marsh within Gorton, in extent five acres, and known by the respective names of the Two Acres and the Cullenfield. The purchase money paid was £10.

On the 25th August 1629 he grants a seven years' lease of his " capital messuage called Milkwall Slade or Slade" to John Kinsey, of Blackden in Goosetree in the county of Chester Gent., in consideration of the payment by John Kinsey of the sum of £160; the lease included also all lands belonging to the said George Siddall in Witbington, Gorton and Grindlowe, &c., and at the termination of the seven years specified the lease was renewed for the further period of forty years, to commence from the death of Katharine, wife of George Siddall. Mr. Kinsey had married, the month preceding the date of the first lease, Anne, daughter of George Birch of Birch Gent., and sister of the afterwards celebrated Colonel Thomas Birch M.P.

In 1664 Mr. Siddall was summoned to appear before Sir William Dugdale, Norroy King of Arms, when holding his Visitation of the county of Lancaster, to register his descent and justify his title of gentleman or esquire, and his right to bear such coat of arms and crest as he usually bears. Mr. Siddall was at this time residing in Birchall houses in Rusholme, his own estate being under lease to Mr. Kinsey. It does not appear that the family of Siddall was heraldic. Ho died at an advanced age, and probably outlived his son Thomas, John, eldest son of Thomas Siddall, being declared executor under the will of his grandfather.

There is nothing in the later descent of the family to call for special notice; the line of succession has continued unbroken to the present time. It is now vested in John Siddall Gent., who has ceased to reside at the hall, and is living abroad. He is married, and has male issue.

Slade Hall is situated a few yards to tho west of the London and North Western line of railway. Though some parts of the house have been modernised, and considerable alterations have from timo to time been made in the internal arrangements, it still retains sufficient traces of its former self to render it deserving the notice of the antiquary. It appears to have been erected about the middle of the sixteenth century, a supposition which is borne out by the date 1585 and the letters E. S. and G. S. corresponding with the initials of Edward Siddall, the purchaser of the estate, and George Siddall, his son and successor, which appear over the principal doorway, and exhibits the general features and characteristics common to the timber houses of that period. The structure is in the form of a parallelogram, with two gables of unequal size projecting from the north or principal front. The building is constructed almest entirely of wood, a stone foundation supportiug the massive oak timbers which form the framework, the latter connected by horizontal wallpieces of the same material, carried along tho face of the building, these being firmly bolted to the upright posts, and receiving additional strength from diagonal bracing ribs, the intervening spaces being filled with a plaster of clay and rushes, and whitened on the surface. The windows are square, exhibiting a number of lights divided by substantial timber mullions, and crossed by a transom of the same material. The house is of two stories, the upper story projecting a little beyond the lower, and the roof overhanging this again, a peculiarity frequently met with in buildings of this class; the several gables have bargeboards, simple in character, and terminated by hip-knobs, slightly ornamented.

The interior presents little to call for attention, if we except somo of the upper rooms, where some ornamental plaster-work of very fair execution still remains in a tolerable state of preservation. In a room on the north side of the house the ceiling is embellished in stucco-work, and on one of the walls are three heraldic shields. The centre one, encircled by a garter, and surmounted by the letters

E. R., bears the arms of Queen Elizabeth, in whose reign the hall was built: Quarterly 1st and 4th, az. three fleurs-de-lis or for France; 2nd and 3rd, gules three lions passant, guardant or for England. Supporters: Dexter, a lion rampant, guardant and crowned or. Sinister: A dragon gules. To the left of this shield is another, divided into eleven quarterings, containing the arms of the Stanley family and their alliances, the first five quarters of which are 1st, arg. on a bend az. three bucks heads, caboshed or, for Stanley; 2nd, or on a chief indented az. three plates, for Lathom; 3rd, gu. three legs conjoined in the fesse point, in armour ppr. garnished and spurred or, for Isle of Man; 4th, chequy or and az. for. Warren; 5th, gu. two lions passant arg. for Strange. Supporters: Dexter, a griffin. Sinister: a buck, both or and ducally collared and chained az. This shield is surrounded by a garter, and over it arc the letters E. D., the initials of Edward Earl of Derby, who died in 1572, so celebrated by Camden for his magnificenco and liberality. To the right of the centre coat of arms is another shield of eleven quarterings, which cannot be identified, a coronet and supporters denoting it to be that of a peer. Above the shield are the. letters E. S. On another wall is depicted a hunting scene with stag and dogs in plaster-work, somewhat rude in execution; and near it an eagle with wings endorsed, preying upon an infant in its cradle, the crest of the Stanley family.

Birch Chapel, dedicated to St. James, was erected by the Birch family, and consecrated in the reign of Elizabeth. Dr. Hibbert Ware conjectures that it was

T

Chronicles of Manchester, p. 83.

built sometime between the years 1558 and 1573, but we have it on Bishop Gastrell's authority that it was consecrated by his predecessor Dr. Chaderton, whose episcopate commenced in 1579 and terminated in 1595; and in confirmation of this wo find that in 1573, when injunctions were given by the Archbishop of York to the Warden of Manchester, exhorting him and the Fellows to diligent and constant preaching every Sunday in the Church of Manchester or in one of the chapels of ease connected with it, Birch Chapel is not included, whilst the chapels of Stretford, Chorlton, Didsbury, Gorton, Denton, Newton and Blackley are all named. Like most of the other chapels in the parish of Manchester its early use was doubtless limited to the family on whose estate it was erected, and their immediate dependents, afterwards extending its influence as the surrounding population increased and possessing a more public character. At first it was wholly unendowed; the income of the officiating minister arising exclusively from the voluntary contributions of the inhabitants of Rusholme and its neighbourhood, and these being at all times precarious, the chapel was frequently left without ministerial superintendence. Such was the case in 1598, as we learn from the Visitation returns of that year, — " Bircho chapel in Rusholme latelie erected and now voyd of a curate. " In 1636 Mr. Bentley's income from the chapel-wage, as this contribution was termed, amounted to £17 2s. 7d. It was in 1640 that a subscription was first commenced for the purchase of land, " to bee laid to the Birch chapell," and intended as a permanent endowment-fund. The number of contributors was sixty-seven, and the amount raised was ¡740 8s. 8d. Amongst the donors' names we find " ould M Birche £5 ; Raphe Worsley £4; Thomas Shelmerdine £2: Mr. Siddall of Slade £1 6s. 8d.but as the interest of the sum thus collected was too small to supersede the necessity for the customary annual subscription, " moneyes" were also Hollingworth's

gathered for the charges of procuringe meanes for the ministry at Birch Chapell," Mr. Raphe Worsley heading the list with 8s., followed by old Mrs. Birch 5s. 3d, Mr. Birch 5s. Mr. Siddall 3s. 4d. and Anne Edge 2s. 6d. The special fund for the endowment of the chapel was expended the same year in the purchase of a small estate, two acres in extent, of the inheritance of Mr. Thomas Siddall of Slade, situated at Longsight, and known by the name of the Great Pendleton, to which Colonel Birch added as a gift about an acre of land from his own estate at Grindlow Marsh in Gorton, which adjoined the two acres already purchased, and caused the whole to be conveyed to himself, promising to reconvey both estates to such trustees as the inhabitants should appoint. The unsettled period of the Commonwealth succeeding, no reconveyance was immediately made, but in 1658 Colonel Birch, unknown to the inhabitants of Rusholme, settled the lands upon his eldest son Thomas Birch and his heirs to the following uses: " to the use and behoofe of one orthodox preaching minister of the gospell, to be constantly resident, to performe divine service att the chappell att Birche in the parish of Manchester and county of Lancaster, and to the use and behoofe of such his successors as shall be orthodox preaching ministers, and constantly resident att the said chappell for ever." On its being made known to the inhabitants that Colonel Birch had constituted his son sole trustee they expressed their dissatisfaction, and requested of him that he would reconvey the estate to a body of trustees elected by the inhabitants; and accordingly by a deed dated December 20, 1672. Colonel Birch and his son Thomas made a new conveyance of the land to George Birch Gent. (son and heir of Thomas Birch the younger, and grandson of the colonel), Raphe Worsley of Platt Gent, John Siddall of Slade Gent, Oliver Edge of Birchall Fold Gent, Robert Birch of Grindlow Gent, George Worsley of Blakestake Gent, Thomas Hartley of Moss Side yeoman, Ralph Cowper of Cringlebrook yeoman, Raphe Nicholson of Cringlebrook yeo-

man, Isaac Hall of Levenshulme yeoman, and John Bradshaw of Fallowfield yeoman. n this latter conveyance, however, the terms of the former trust were changed, and no doubt with a view of detaching the benefits of the endowment from the episcopal and conferring them on the Presbyterian form of worship, which had in the interim become more popular. Instead of the rents, issues and profits being limited specifically to Birch Chapel as in the former deed, they are directed " ever hereafter, to the pleasure of Almighty God, to bee yearly from time to time, justly, truely, carefully, faithfully and wholly disposed of, distributed and imployed for the good and benefit of the inhabitants in or neere Birche for the time beinge, in such manner and sorte as all or the greater parte of the trustees aforesaid shall order and appoint." Such a perversion of the intentions of the original contributors to the fund naturally gave offence to all who remained staunch to the old form of church government, and a threatened misapplication of the rent of the estate on the part of George Birch Gent., one of the trustees, was met by a strong remonstrance, and laid the foundation for disputes, which were not settled until the year 1743. In that year a case was prepared for counsel, and submitted to Mr. Edward Chetham, who decided that the second deed executed by Colonel Birch was valid in so far as it transferred the trust from the exclusive control of his own family into the hands of a body of trustees appointed by the inhabitants, but that the application of the funds must be regulated by the deed first executed, which limits to Birch Chapel the lands in question and their yearly profits. The duties of the trustees of the chapel lands were not only to collect the rents as they became due, but also to superintend the collecting and disbursing of all other sums of money raised for church purposes. The custom appears to have been to have a weekly collection from the congregation. From this fund, to which was afterwards added the rent of the chapel lands, Mr. Finch received by agreement ten shillings for each Sunday, and all

liam Ashurst and Robert Goodwin, Esqrs. In February 1647-8, we find him in Edinburgh, accomplishing his mission, and on the 15th of that month honourable mention was made in the House of Commons of his diligence and zeal. He seems to have returned home in August 1648, when a more formal expression of the thanks of the House awaited him, and the following month he was deputed by parliament to proceed into Lancashire and the other counties where Scotch prisoners were, to inquire which of those prisoners were forced men, and to discharge all such on condition of their not serving again. This occurred shortly after the defeat and capture of the Duke of Hamilton near Preston. On the 22nd of November 1648, he was appointed high steward of the borough of Leominster, an office at the disposal of parliament, and now void by reason of the delinquency of Sir Walter Pye; and was the following day added to a commission whose duty it was to consider of the castles, garrisons, &c. that are to be razed and made untenable. In the last parliamentary struggle between the Presbyterians and Independents, which precipitated the catastrophe of the king's death, and which is known in history as "Pride's purge," unable to quell the storm which he had assisted to raise, Colonel Birch was in the number of those leading Presbyterians who were secluded and thrown into prison for counselling further overtures to the king against the impatient desires of the Independents, backed by the army, for a total subversion of the monarchy. With the king's death the parliamentary career of Colonel John Birch met with a temporary interruption, for although re-elected for Weobley after the dissolution of the Long Parliament in 1653, he had lost all sympathy with the usurper whose ambitious designs were now no longer concealed, and but few opportunities occurred for resisting them. He had discovered when it was too late that Cromwell's aims were after a power even more arbitrary than had been claimed by the deposed and murdered king. From a letter addressed by the Governor of Hereford to the Lord Protector, dated Hereford, March 17, 1654, we ascertain that at this time he was in active opposition to the constituted authorities: — " Colonel Birch," he says, " coming hither now in the middle of the assizes (the city being very full of all sorts of people) gave out before the judges, as they themselves told me, that the present insurrections (Salisbury and the rest) did not consist of cavaliers, but a company of silly quakers, with some other disaffected persons. He also told me the same, and added further that the greatest matter was our own jealousies and fears. Considering this, and what we know of his carriage when the Scots were in Worcester, and his behaviour of late, I feared such speeches were coals cast abroad to kindle divisions among the good people here, and to hinder their uniting against the common enemy. I thought it my duty for the safety and peace of these parts, and agreeable to your former orders, to secure him, which I have done; and as his sword was taking from him he (refusing to deliver it) said, Though my sword is short now it may be long enough within a while (the sword hanging by his side being a little short sword), and very angrily asked me whether I had orders to secure him. I answered, If I have not you will question me? He replied, Yes, that I will. I said again, I believe it. So we parted, and he is in custody. I have sent a party to possess his moated house (which I find is very strong with drawbridges; it is also well provided) lest at this time it might be surprised and manned against your highness, and be a great scourge to this country. I beseech your highness speedy order concerning this person and his house, whether I shall continue a guard there or make it untenable."

In November 1655, he is found yet a prisoner by Major-General Berry, Cromwell's new vice-gerent of the county, who, writing to the government, says: " I met with (as a prisoner here) Colonel Birch, who hath applied himself to me as to a little king that could redress every grievance. I confess upon examination of the business, though

there were some grounds of jealousy, yet I cannot see any great reason he should now be kept in restraint. It is true the man is popular in these parts, and he loves to be so. He is taken for a great wit, and guilty of some honesty, and upon that account able to do hurt if he have a mind to it; but he professeth desire of peace and settlement, and saith he is for the same things that we are, but could have been glad to have them in another way; but seeing the time is not yet for it, nor we fit for it, he thinks we had better have it as it is than make disturbance. And truly I think it were an easy matter to gain him if he be worth getting. But, not to trouble you with my thoughts, I shall tell you my actions: I have desired the governor (whose prisoner he is) to give him liberty to be at his own house upon his promise to appear when he shall be called for."

In 1656 he is named (Oldmixon, vol. ii. p. 429) as one of the northern conspirators in league with Captain Penruddocke, whose unsuccessful efforts to check the growing ambition of Cromwell cost him his life. He was returned again for Weobley in the Protector's Thurloe's State Papers, vol. iii. p. 261. Ibid. Vol. iv. p. 237.

third parliament, which assembled in September 1656, but was secluded, not being allowed to take his seat because he refused the engagement, a fate shared by nearly a quarter of the representatives returned by the country. The death of Cromwell in 1658 having opened a way for the restoration of the monarchy, a council of state of thirty-one members being appointed, the name of Colonel John Birch is of the number, and on the 26th of April he is found with his parliamentary associates negociating for the king's return. The month of May 1660 was occupied in preparing instructions for those charged with the delivery of a letter inviting the king; in preparing for his majesty's reception; in drawing up the bill of general pardon, indemnity and oblivion; and for confirming to the people the privileges of parliament, Magna Charta and other rights; in all which arrangements Colonel John Birch was conspicuous.

Immediately after the Restoration he was appointed one of six commissioners for disbanding the army and navy, and with this event the more distinguished portion of Colonel Birch's career may be said to have closed, though not less active or useful in the succeeding years of his public life. His name occurs in September 1666, on a committee of the House inquiring into the cause of the great fire in London, and on the 1 9th of January following he was deputed by the House to bring in a bill for the rebuilding of the city. He continued to represent Weobley until his death in 1691. Colonel Birch was twice married, his first wife being Alice, daughter of Thomas Deane, citizen of Bristol. She died September 10, 1676, leaving issue John Birch of Ordsal in the county of Lancaster Esquire, his eldest son, who died without male issue; Samuel Birch of Whitbourne in the county of Hereford Esquire, who married twice, but died s.p.; Thomas and George both died unmarried; and also three daughters, Mary, Elizabeth and Sarah, to the last of whom Colonel Birch bequeathed his estates on condition that she should marry her cousin John, second son of her uncle the Rev. Thomas Birch. This marriage took place, but dying without issue John Birch Esq. was succeeded by his brother Samuel, who dying in 1752, also without issue, devised his estates to his nephew (the son of his sister Eliza

Q beth) John Peploe, who in consequence assumed the additional name of Birch, and now represents that branch of the family. By his second marriage with Winifred, daughter of Matthew Norris of Weobley Esq., Colonel Birch had no issue.,

He was buried in the chancel of Weobley Church, where there is a monument to his memory — a full-length figure in armour standing beneath a canopy. The monument bears the following inscription: " In hope of resurrection to eternal life. Here is deposited the body "of Colonel John Birch, descended of a worthy family in Lancashire. As the dignities he arrived at in the Field, and the esteem universally yielded him in the Senate House exceeded the attainments of most, so they were but the moderate and just rewards of his courage, conduct, wisdom and fidelity. None who knew him denied him y character of asserting and vindicating y laws and liberties of his country in war and of promoting its welfare and prosperity in peace. He was borne y 7th of September 1626, and died a member of the honourable House of Commons, being burgess for Weobley, May y 10th, 1691."

The second son of Samuel Birch Gent. (the aforesaid testator) and younger brother of Colonel John Birch, was named after his father Samuel, and was baptised at the Collegiate Church, Manchester, in 1620-1. From the circumstance that he is named in his father's will without any bequest being assigned to him it is inferred that provision had been already made to him during his father's lifetime. He was commonly known as Major Birch, and appears to have adopted the profession of arms without reaping many laurels, his name and deeds being eclipsed by the reputation of his elder brother. His estates lay in Ardwick and Gorton, and at this latter place he The error before alluded to respecting the date of Colonel John Birch's birth is perpetuated by his monument. In Wood's *Athena Oxonienses,* vol. i. p. 118, the correct date of his birth (or rather baptism) is given, viz. April 7, 1616. We have Wood's authority for stating that in May 1694 the inscription on Colonel Birch's monument became a subject for episcopal interference. The bishop, with his attendants, went to Weobley, and defaced the inscription, " the minister and churchwardens thinking some words thereon were not right for the church institution. " The colonel's nephew, he adds, designs to bring an action against the bishop for defacing it.

was interred in the year 1693. He died, leaving John Birch his son and successor, who was baptised at Gorton Chapel in 1652. By his will made in 172-John Birch, who describes himself as of Manchester Gentleman, bequeaths his soul to God and his body to be buried in such decent sort as his executors Bhall determine. And as touching the disposition of his temporal estate, he gives and bequeaths all that his messuage and tenement with appurtenances situate and being in Over otherwise Upper and Lower Ardwick in the county of Lancaster, containing by common estimation seventeen acres and a half, late in the possession of James Goddard, and now or late in that of Daniel Woosencroft, and all those two closes of land in Upper and Lower Ardwick aforesaid, containing by estimation three acres of land, and commonly called by the names of the two Rough Fields, and also that other close also situated in Ardwick, commonly called the Hollow Meadow, containing two acres of land, to his beloved wife Elizabeth for her life, and after her decease to his son Thomas Birch and his heirs, subject nevertheless to the charge hereafter specified and declared, namely the sum of =P200, to be paid therefrom to his (testator's) son George Birch, to be paid within twelve months after the decease of Elizabeth, testator's wife. He proceeds to recite an indenture of settlement bearing date June 4, 1712, whereby with the concurrence of his son Samuel he charges certain of his estates with an annuity of £25 *to* his wife Elizabeth from and after his (testator's) decease. He died in 1728, and was buried September 21st at Gorton Chapel, his funeral sermon being preached by his kinsman Samuel Peploe Lord Bishop of Chester. Thomas Birch, who is styled of Higher Ardwick, merchant, succeeded his father, sharing, however, the Ardwick estate with his younger brother Samuel, who also is styled of Lower Ardwick. In 1730 he rebuilt the manor-house at Ardwick, but died s.p. May 5, 1753. His will is dated January 13, 1746. He therein directs that his debts and funeral expenses, &c., be paid, and that his body be interred in a decent and Christian manner at the discretion of his executors. To his brother Samuel Birch and Elizabeth his wife he gives J£25 apiece to buy them mourning with. To his nephew Thomas Birch i?600. To his nephews Samuel and George (sons of the said brother Samuel Birch) *£i00* aforesaid, to be paid as they shall severally reach the age of twenty-one years. To his brother George Birch he gives all that and those his messuages, dwelling-houses, gardens, &c., in Higher Ardwick, now in the several tenures of himself and John Chapman, and which were devised to him by his late father John Birch, for and during the term of his natural life; and after his death he devises the same to his esteemed friend and partner in trade James Hall and nephew-in-law Thomas Gardner of Manchester aforesaid, chapman, in trust for the heirs of the body of his said brother George Birch lawfully issuing; and in default of such issue he gives the said premises, &c., to his (testator's) said nephew Thomas Birch and his heirs; and in default of such issue to his said nephew George Birch; and in default of such issue to his said brother George Birch; and in default of such issue to his said nephew Samuel Birch and his heirs; and in default, &c., to his said nephew George Birch; and in default, &c., to his said nephew Thomas Birch and his heirs; and in default, &c., to his (testator's) right heirs for ever. His lands in Droylsden, now in the occupation of John Redfern, he leaves to his brother George Birch and his heirs and assigns for ever; to whom also he gives all his messuage or dwelling-house, warehouses, stables, &c., in Manchester aforesaid, in or near a certain street there called Deansgate, and now in testator's own possession, and which he holds by lease from the Warden and Fellows of Manchester. All that his messuage, &c., in Deansgate, now in the holding of Robert Tyrer, he gives to his said nephew George Birch and his heirs; and in default of such issue in succession Thomas Birch and Samuel Birch and their heirs for ever. He wills that the sum of £300 be put out at interest, the proceeds thereof to be paid to his nephew John Walker, son of James Walker of Man-chester, merchant, for his life, and after his death the principal sum to be paid to such child or children as he may leave, in equal portions, to be paid on their severally reaching the age of twenty-one years; but in case his said nephew John Walker should die without children which shall attain such age, then he bequeaths the said sum of £300 unto such child or children of his (Walker's) late sister Elizabeth Gardner, late wife of the said Thomas Gardner, as shall be then living, equally to be divided; but in case there should be no such children then the said sum of £300 to be distributed amongst his (testator's) next of kin in manner as intestate's personal estate. Also to such child or children of his said niece Elizabeth Gardner as shall be living at his decease, the sum of £700, equally to be divided, the share of any child dying to be divided amongst the survivors; and if all die before attaining the age of twenty one then the £700 to be distributed amongst his next of kin in manner aforesaid. To his brother George Birch he gives the sum of £200 in money, and all his silver plate. To his nephew Robert Jackson £300, to be paid two years after testator's decease. To the aforesaid James Hall £100. To his sister-in-law Margaret Lilly i?200. All his messuages, &c., which he holds in fee-simple on the south-side of a certain street in Chester called Northgate, he bequeaths to his sister-in-law Margaret Lilly and her heirs and assigns for ever. All his messuages, &c., in the said street which he holds by lease from the Dean and Chapter of Chester, he gives to the said Margaret Lilly for and during his right and title to the same. He wills that within two years after his death the sum of £200 be put out at interest by and in the names of his said brothers Samuel and George Birch, the interest to be for ever continued and applied to the instruction and learning of poor children belonging to Higher and Lower Ardwick," to be taught to read perfectly by some sober and discreet master and mistress, who shall for the time being reside and dwell within Higher or Lower Ardwick aforesaid; and for the better preservation and continuing my said intended charity I do expressly will and declare that the owner and proprietor for the time being of the capital messuage or mansion-house in Lower Ardwick aforesaid, now in the possession of my said brother Samuel Birch, as also of my messuage or dwelling-house in Higher Ardwick herein before mentioned to be in the possession of myself and John Chapman, shall at all times for ever hereafter be the trustees and managers thereof; and that the said df200 shall in their names only from time to time be put out at interest upon personal security only for the uses and purposes herein before mentioned." To each of his servants who shall be in his service at the time of his death he gives £5 for mourning. To Mary, daughter of James Wood of Manchester, joiner, £5. All the rest, residue and remainder of his goods, chattels, &c., he gives to his said brother George Birch and the said James Hall, equally to be divided, whom he also names as his executors.

Witnesses, Thomas Clowes, Joseph Allen, Peter Heywood.

By a codicil to his will, dated March 6, 1748, he revokes the several devises of his messuages, &c., named in his will, and he hereby gives and devises his said first-mentioned messuages, &c., therein mentioned as in the possession of himself and John Chapman, to his said nephew Thomas Birch, his heirs and assigns for ever. And as for and concerning the said other messuages, &c., therein mentioned as purchased from Worral Millington, he gives and devises the same to his said brother George Birch and his assigns for the term of his natural life, and from and after his decease he gives the same to his said nephew Samuel Birch, his heirs and assigns for ever. He revokes the legacy of £700 bequeathed in his will to the child or children of his late niece Elizabeth, wife of Thomas Gardner, and in lieu thereof he gives to such child or children i?400 only. Also he gives to his nephew Robert Jackson df?300 over and above the df300 given to him in the will. The silver plate bequeathed in the will to his brother George Birch, to be confirmed to him, except This ed-

daye of May in the yere of o lord God a Mccccclviijth. I Ric Sedull of VVithington in the countie of Lancas? yoman, beyng at this p'sent somthinge deceasid but thankes unto God of sounde and pYect memorie, and cosidering y' death to every man is most c'teine and the bower and tyme to all men most unc'teine; willing therefore by the help of God to make all thinkes in pYect redines in such man! and sorte as shalbe to *y* glory of God and cofart of my wife and children, do ordeine and make this my testamet wherein is conteined the effecte of my last will, in maS and forme following: Y' is to saye ffirste and principally I offer, geve and bequeth my soule to Almightie God my maker and redem, trusting y by the merits of Christes passion and bloode sheding to be one of that number that shalbe elect and chosen into elastinge glorie; and my bodie to be buryed in the p'ishe church of Machester or where it shall please God to appoynt. Also coVnyng y dispocicon of all and singuler my lands, tacke and tenemcts it is my will and mynd y the same shalbe and remene thereaft named and mecioned, y is to saie it is my will and mynd and also I do assigne and geve all and evy my p'te and porcion of all and singuler y lands and tenemets w y app'tenances now lying and beyng in Keyrsall w latly I bought and p'rchasid, as by writings thoreof made more at larg may appere, to Edward Sidall my eldiste sonne and to his heres male of his bodie lawfully begotten, and for default of such issue y same to come and remene unto Thom's Sidall my sone and to his heirs male of his bodie lawfully begotten; and for default of such issue y same to com and remene and be to my right heires for evr. Also 1 doe assigne and geve y shope w I have in the M'keth strete w th' app'teiices w I latly purchasid, to Edward Sidall my sone aforesaid and to his heires male of his bodie lawfully begotten; and for default of suche issue y same to remene and come to Thom's Sidall my yongest sone aforesaid and to his heres male of his bodie lawfully begotten; and for default

come to my right heres for evV; forseying alwayes, and it is my will and mynd y Ellysabeth now my wife shall have, hold, enioye and occupio y same shope duryng her naturall life if she kepe her sole and unmaried; and if she do m'reye then this my legacie of y said shoppe to be voyd unto her, any thinke before metioned to ye cotrarie made in any wise notwstandinge. Also it is my will and mynde and also I do assigne and appoynte ye house meas'e or tent w I now dwell in w th app'rtenances (called y Mylkewall Slade) to Edward my sone, duryng suche terme as I have in aft ye decease of Elizbeth my wife forsaid unto whom I assigne y same meas'e and tent duryng the lif naturall of y said Elisabeth, toward the brynging upp of my children, if she kepe her sole and unmaried, or els not. Also I do assigne and geve unto my yongest sone Thom's Sidall above said, all and evy my lands and tenem'ts v I latly purchasid in Most on w th' app'tences and to his heres male of his bodie lawfully begotten; and for default of such issue to co and remene to Edward Sidall my sone and his heres male of his bodie lawfully begotten; and for default of such issue y remander vof to come to my right heres for evr. Also I do assigne and bequeth by y cosent and assent of Edward my sofie all and singuler y my meas'e and tenem lyeing and beyng at Diddisbury w th apptefices and evy p'te and p'cell yof ymediately aft y decease of Elisab3 my wife whoe it is my mynd and will y she have the same duryng her life if she kepe her soule and unmaried, and if she m'rye then y saide Thom's Sidall to have y same ymediately aft she doth m"rye if my lease and terme in the same so long continewe. Also it is my will and mynd and I do assigne, name and appoynto y Elisabeth, now my wife, shall have, occupie and enioye one close or p'cell of ground caled y M'led Yearth lyeing and beyng in the Houghe durynge her life, if she kepe her sole and unmaryed, if my lease or graunt yof so long continewe, the rev'cion whereof shall come and remene ymediatly aft my her deceass or mariag unto Edward Sidall my said sofie duryng my terme

and... in y same to his heres or assignes. Also it is my will and mynd y Edward Sidall my sofie according to his former p'myse shall and will wout coneng, craft or gile make or cause to be made a sure and lawfull surrend and assuranc in the lawe, such as shall or may be lawfull devised or advised by his counsell of in or apon one mease or tefit in Diddisbury aforesaid, to have and to hould y said mease or tefit to y said Elizabeth duryng her life or untill she do m'ry and aft her life or m'ryage to Thom's my sofie and his assignes duryng all such tyme and terme as he the said Edward bath in the same or thereaft may have by reason or occasion of any form graunt or lease before made when it shall or maye be hereaft lawfully demanded or required by the said Thom's or his assignes. And if the said Edward Sidall my sofie do refuse, or desire thus to do, then these my legacies and the benefitts before written and evy of them to be utterly voyd and of none effect to the said Edward, eny thing before written and mencioned to y cotrarie made in any wise notvstanding. And cocernyng y dispocicon of all and singuler goods and catteles it is my will and mynd y the same aft my fourth bryngiug and funerall expenciys discharged shalbe devidid in to thre ptes, y is to saie one pte unto my self, an oth pto unto my pore children and ye thrid and and last pte unto my wife, accordingc to y lawe. Of w my pte of goods it is my will and mynd y' Edward my sone have vj' xi ijs iiij; also I do geve and bequeth unto Anne my dought ov and beside hir child pte and porcion of goodes due unto her xl8. Also I geve and bequeth to my sone Edward my best Jacked, my chamlet dublet, my bat, and my heng; also I geve and dispose y rest of myne app'rell not bequethed, to Thom's my sone v my second henger and my Also I geve and bequeth to.... v. Also it is my will and mynd y' the rest of my pte of goods and cattcles not bequethed and disposid shalbe devided betwixt my wife and children hereaft named equally, y is to saye Edward, Alis, Elizabeth, Genet, Anne and Ellin. Also it is my will and mynd y' if it happen, as God defend y', any of my said children, eth my wife or any of them, do denye or refuse to stand to this my true and last will in man and forme aforesaid, then he or she and they or any of them so denyeing or refuseing shall have no benefite, gayne nor advantag' of any legacie so before to him or hir and theme geven so denying or refusing, and the p'te of them so denying to be equally devided amongest the rest of those w are content and pleasid, any thing menchnd or wryten to the contrarie notwithstandinge. Also I order, constitute and make Elisabeth my wife, Edward Sidall and Thom's Sidall my sonnes, my true and lawfull execut' to execute, p'forme, accomplishe and fulfill this my testamet and last will in man and forme aforesaid according to the true intent, menyng, p\port and effecte yof. And also I most hartely require my most trustie and loving frendes Thom's Birch Gent, Witīm Sidall and John P'cevall yomen, to be y sup'visors of this my last will and testamet, to see the same accomplishd and fulfilld in man and forme aforesaide, these beyng witenesses and p'sent, Thomas Birch Gent, Banduli Kenyon and John Glover y writer hereof, with others.

Proved at Chester.

His inventory amounted to £249 5s. 3d.

The third part of the lands of Kersal referred to in his will were purchased by testator in the year 1548 from Ralph Kenyon of Gorton, to whom a conveyance had been made of the entire manor by Ralph Sacheverell and Philippa his wife under the authority of letters patent dated July 20, 2 Edward vi. They had until recently formed part of the possessions of the Priory of Lenton iu the county of Nottingham, but had been confiscated to the crown on the suppression of monasteries in the reign of Henry VIII.

In 1565 a renewal of the lease of Slade Hall was granted to Edward Siddall, and before the time specified therein had expired the first step was taken by the lessee for the absolute purchase of the estate. The several parties possessing an interest in the lands of Slade were, as we have already seen, Ralph Slade, to whom they were secured for his life, and Thomas Slade his son, to whom the reversion and remainder had been conveyed. By indenture dated the 7th of June 22 Elizabeth (1580) Edward Siddall agreed to purchase the reversion from Thomas Slade, and on the 9th of June 26 Elizabeth (1584) the estate was absolutely conveyed to Edward Siddall by Ralph Slade and Joane his wife. The following is an abstract of the deed of conveyance: —

This indenture dated the 9th of June 26 Elizabeth (1584) between Raphe Slade of Brerehurst in the county of Stafford Gent, and Joane his now wife upon the one part, and Edward Siddall of Withington in the county of Lancaster upon the other part, witnesseth that the said Raphe and Joane for the consideration of £10 to them paid before sealing, by the said Edward Syddall, have given, granted to the said Edward Syddall, &c., all their right, estate, title, &c, which they or either of them now have of in or to that messuage with the appurtenances called Milkewalleslade in Withington, and the buildings, orchards, gardens, &c., thereto belonging, and of and in the reversion of the said premises, &c., to have and to hold the said messuage, &c., to the sole and proper uso of the said Edward Syddall, &c., for ever.

Edward Syddall, after completing the purchase, rebuilt the house the following year in its present form, and dying February 18, 1588, was succeeded by his son George, who was then twenty-five years of age.

The inquisition post mortem of Edward Siddall was taken at Bolton the 23rd of September 30 Elizabeth (1588). It is as follows: —

Indented inquisition taken at Bolton 23rd of September 30 Elizabeth, before Thomas Hesketh Esquire, escheator of our Lady the Queen in the said county by virtue of a writ of the Queen " de diem clausit extremum" to him directed, after the death of Edward Syddall late of Slade in the said county, in the said writ named, on the oaths of Peter Heywood Gent., Alexander Leyver Gent, Richard Leighe Gent, Richard Sococroft Gent.

Ralph Greene Gent, Richard Wood Gent, Ralph Haughton Gent, Henry Hardy Gent, Robert Hardy Gent, Ralph Bridge Gent, George Allonson Gent, George Kenyon Gent, Thomas Kaye Gent, Robert Ravalde Gent, Henry Chetham Gent, William Bamford Gent, and Robert Butterworth Gent, who say on their oaths that on the day before the death of the said Edward Syddall, &c., the said Edward Syddall was seised in his demense as of fee, of and in one capital messuage or tenement called the Milkewall Slade with the appurtenances, and of and in certain closes of land containing by estimation twenty-four acres situate, &c., in Rusholme and Withington, &c.; also of and in certain other closes and meadows with their appurtenances containing by estimation twenty acres of land, in Gorton, &c.; also of and in one burgage or tenement and one shop with appurtenances situate, &c., in Manchester; and also of and in the third part of the manor of Kerksawe otherwise called Kerksall with the appurtenances; and of and in one burgage or tenement, two cottages, the third part of a water-mill, the third part of one other cottage and three acres of land; and of and in the third part of one other cottage and one garden; and of and in forty acres of land, ten acres of meadow, thirty acres of pasture, four acres of wood, and the third part of a certain waste whether called by the name of Kersall Wood or Kersall Moor situate, &c., in Kersawe alias Kersall aforesaid; and of a certain free rent of twelve pence yearly, payable out of certain lands and tenements called Lees in the parish of Oldham, &c, and parcel of the said manor of Kersall; and of a certain other free rent of three shillings and four pence yearly, payable by a s certain Robert Hobson as parcel of the said manor of Keksall; and of a certain other freehold rent of five pence yearly, payable by Agnes Lees, a parcel of the said manor of Kerksall. And the said Edward Syddall of the said manors, messages, lands, &c., by a certain indented writing of his, gave and granted all and singular the said manors, &c, and premises in the said indented deed named, to the use of the said Edward Syddall for the term of his life, and after his decease to the use of Elizabeth Syddall the then wife of the said Edward, and to George Syddall their son, and heir apparent of the said Edward Syddall in the said writ named, and the lawful heirs of the said George; and failing all issue, then to the use and benefit of Thomas Syddall, younger son of the same Edward Syddall in the said writ named, and his heirs male, &c.; and in default thereof to the right heirs of Edward Syddall in the said writ named, for ever. In virtue whereof and in pursuance of a certain act in the parliament of our Lord Henry VIII., late King of England, and in the twentyseventh year of his reign, " For transferring of uses in possession" made and provided, the same Elizabeth and George, after the death of the said Edward, were seised of all and singular the said manors, messuages, lands, &c., namely the said Elizabeth in her demesne as of fee tenement for the term of her life, and the said George in his demesne as of like fee. And the said jurors further say on their oaths that the said Edward Syddall, &c., then so seised of all and singular the said manors, messuages, lands, &c., in all and singular the premises, died seised of such estate at Milkwallslade aforesaid, the 18th of February in the thirtieth year of the reign of our Lady the Queen; and that the said George Syddall is son and next heir of the same Edward, and is aged at the time of the taking of this inquisition twenty-five years and more. And further the jurors, &c., say that the said messuage or tenement called Milk wall Slade and the rest of the premises in Riseholme and Withington aforesaid are worth yearly in all outgoings clear of deductions twenty-six shillings and eightpence; and that the said lands and tenements in Gorton aforesaid are worth yearly in all outgoings clear of deductions sixteen shillings; and that the said burgage and shop in Manchester aforesaid is worth yearly in all sixpence; and that the said third part of the manor of Kirkshawe or Kerksall aforesaid is worth yearly in all outgoings clear of deductions £4. And further the jurors, &c., say that the said messuage or tenement called Milkwall Slade of the said lands or tenements in Riseholme and Withington aforesaid, are held and at the time of the death of the said Edward Syddall, &c., were held of Nicholas Langford Esquire by fealty, and paid two shillings and sixpence yearly for all services and demands whatsoever; and that the said lands and tenements in Gorton aforesaid and the said burgage and shop in Manchester aforesaid are held at the time of the death of the said Edward Syddall were held of John Lacy Esquire, lord of Manchester, by fealty as well as by all services, &c.; and that the said third part of the manor of Kerksawo otherwise Kerksall, and the rest of the premises in Kerksawe aforesaid are held at the time of the death of Edward Syddall, &c., were held of the said lady the Queen that now is, in capite, namely by the twelfth part of one knight's fee. And further the said jurors, &c, say that the said Edward Syddall had no other or more manors, lands or tenements on the day of his death, had or held in demesne or by service, as far as the said jurors in any way could ascertain. In testimony whereof to one part of this inquisition the said escheator as well as the said jurors have set their seals, and to the other part of the said inquisition which remains in the custody of the said jurors the said escheator has set his seal the day and year first above written.

George Siddall succeeded to the Slade Hall estate, as already intimated, on the death of his father in 1588, being at that time twenty-five years of age. He married Frances Kay, who if not herself a native of Yorkshire, was connected by ties of affinity with Richard Kay, of Dodworth, in that county. He appears to have conveyed his lands in Kersal to his son George Siddall. He died November 14, 1616. His inquisition p.m. taken at Bolton December 20 in that year, makes no reference to his Kersal property, which had already been transferred to his son. He died seised of Slade Hall and twenty-four acres of land, of twenty acres of land in Gorton, and of a burgage, tenement or shop in Manchester.

George Siddall, his son and heir, was in his twenty-ninth year when he succeeded his father in the family inheritance in 1616. By a deed executed in his father's life time, dated March 22, 1613, he conveyed a part of his lands in Kersal to George Kenyon Gent., for the consideration of £150. They aro described as two closes in Kersal called the Round Meadow and the Little Bed Stone, and four acres of Kersal moore or Kersal wood, " to bee taken out of the parte belonging and which of right ought to belong to me George Siddall, in commune or upon dyvision, partition, improvement or inclosure of y said moore. The greater portion, however, of the estate was transferred by the said George and Katharine his wife immediately after his father's death. By indenture dated November 2, 1616, George Siddall and Katharine his wife, in consideration of the sum of i?365, grant, bargain, sell and confirm to William Leaver, of Darcy Leaver, all and singular the messuages, lands, &c, as follows, namely, all that messuage and tenement situate in Kersal, now or late in the tenure or occupation of John Aston, and all that other messuage in Kersal, in the occupation of Abraham Seddon; also one full third part of the messuage in Kersal, in the occupation of William Digle, and also one third part of the water corn mill in Kersal, commonly called Kersal Mylne, now in the tenure of Bichard Holland Esq.; also all that and those the barn, stable and shippon in Kersal aforesaid, now or late in the tenure or occupation of the said George Siddall and of Adam Gartside, of Prestwich, yeoman; together with a bay of building in 'Kersal aforesaid at the end of the shippon, now or late in the tenure of George Kenyon Gent.; also all those closes, &c., in Kersal, namely, the Oakes, now or late in the tenure of George Siddall and George Kenyon; the Barn Field, now in the tenure of George Kenyon; the two Thistle Fields, the Horse Hey, the Warthe, the Bottoms Wood Field, and the Bottoms Wood, now or late in the tenure of the said Adam Gartside; together with a third part of the close lying in Kersal aforesaid, commonly known as the Meane

A history of the ancient chapel of Birch • John Booker

expenses incurred in keeping the chapel in repair were hence defrayed. In 1679, after the payment to Mr. Finch of the stipulated sum, there remained of the total amount collected in the chapel a surplus of £1 15s. 2d, "out of w surlTie Mr. ffinch had ten shillinges of a gratuity because he had beene sicke, soe there remained £1 5s. 2d., out of v was paid seven shillinges and six. pence for repaire of the Chappell and eight shillinges six pence more was lost in bad and broken money; soe then there remained nine shillings two pence w was paid in pte of a greater suiire ffor the continuation of the liberty att the Chappell."

In 1651 this estate produced to Mr. John Wigan, then minister of the chapel, the sum of £3 10s., to which until recently had been added a certain annual grant from sequestrations, now withdrawn. This was declared to be its annual value at the commencement of the last century, when a return was made of its value to Bishop Gastrell. The voluntary contributions of the inhabitants in aid of the endowment amounted at the latter period to about £9. The estate remained in possession of the chapel until very recently, and formed in part the site of the old parsonage-house. In 1850 it was thought desirable to sell the house, which was much dilapidated, and also a plot of land, in extent 7,197 square yards, being part of the field lying on the north-east side of the turnpike road at Longsight in Gorton. This was done under the authority of a commission issued by the Bishop of the Diocese. The house realised £75, and the land £199 10s., being at the rate of two pence per square yard at twenty years purchase. The proceeds of the sale were applied in 1851 to the erection of a new parsonage-house nearer to Birch Chapel. The remainder of the estate is let on chief, and produces an income of £30 per annum.

In 1708 Warden Wroe returns the value of Birch Chapel at £3 10s., which was of course exclusive of the voluntary contributions of the inhabitants; and in 1720 the Rev. Thomas Wright, who held the chapels of Didsbury and Birch together, estimates the "contribution" of the Birch congregation at =£16 per annum, whikt that of Didsbury, owing to certain dissensions which prevailed, had dwindled to £5 4s. "My friends in Manchester," he says, " advise mo to preach three Sundays at Birch and one at Didsbury."

In 1747 John Dickenson Esq, who by his then recent purchase of the Birch estate, had become patron of the chapel, contributed i?200 towards its endowment. This was met by a grant from the Governors of Queen Anne's Bounty, and an estate called Schoolshill, situated upon Gilbert Moss in Cheadle Mosley in the parish of Cheadle and in the county of Chester, was purchased in 1763 for the sum of i?630, Mr. Dickenson at the time of its purchase adding i?30 to the amount of his previous contribution. It consisted of a farm house, cottage, and thirty-two acres of land, and was exchanged in 1798 for a farm house, outbuildings and 19a. 2r. 22p. Cheshire measure, also in Cheadle, producing in 1849 an annual rent of £65. The London and North Western Railway intersects this estate, and has paid i?600 for the land required, which sum has been invested in the funds. In 1780 Miss Mary Dickenson gave, with a like object, the sum of i?200, which was met by a grant from Queen Anne's Bounty of a corresponding amount, and in 1782 this sum of £400 was expended in the purchase of an estate called Moorside in Castleton near Rochdale, consisting of a house, outbuildings and eight acres of land. This produced in 1849 an annual rent of 1735.

On the 16th of June 1650 an inquisition was taken at Manchester before Richard Standish, James Ashton, Alexander Barlow, Thomas Birch, Robert Mawdesley, John Hartley and Peter Holt Esquires, Commissioners under the Great Seal of England, with a view to effecting a more equitable adjustment of ecclesiastical districts. The commissioners report that " in the township of Wythington are the four chapels of Didesbury, Birch, Chorleton and Denton, which chapels are fit to be made a district parish." Their report is correct as to Withington *manor* though not of the *township.* They add, moreover, that "Chorleton on Medlock hath neither church nor chapel nor benefice, and the inhabitants resort to Birch and Manchester: part of the township near Birch should be annexed to it, and the other part continued to Manchester." These suggestions were not carried out.

In March 1850 Birch was returned as a district chapelry under 59 George III. cap. 134, its annual value being estimated at i?180. It was constituted a rectory under the provisions of the Manchester Rectory Division Act, by an order in council dated June 8, 1854.

The registers of the chapel are all of a recent date, commencing in the year 1752, the earlier volumes having been lost.

A ground-plan of Birch Chapel, undated, but which may be referred to the year 1640 or thereabouts, is still in existence: the family from the Hall is not included in the enumeration of seatowners, and it is difficult to account for the omission.

The Chapel-Book, which bears date 1636, is more comprehensive, giving at once the adjacent hamlets connecting themselves with the chapel at that period, and also a list of the families then resident in the several localities, and the amount paid by each in support of the ministrations at Birch Chapel.

Birche and Birch hall houses.

M Anne Birche, 25
Mr. Thomas Birche, 20
Oliver Edge, 258
Thomas Greaves, 4
John Ridinges, 2
Tho. Birch, blacksmith, 2
Henry Hughes, 4
Edmund Whiticar, 2

Slade and Rushford.

Mr. Kinsey, 6 8
Mr. Sidall, 138 4
Joseph Ken ion, 6
Abram Kenion, 48
M Adkinson, 48

Grinlow and Chorlton.

Thomas, Wolwerke, 8
John Bradshaw, 4
George Pomfret, 2

Thomas Persivall, 43
John Hunt, 2
Edmund Knowles, 2
Widow Williamson, 3 4
James Boden, 2
Robert Radcliffe, 2'
Adam Hulme
William Streete
William Jobson
Jacob Taylor, 48
Levenshulme.
Widow Percival, 5
John and Robert Dickonson, 4
Allexander Birch, 2 6
Isack Halle, 3 4
Richard Johnson, 5
John Shelmerdine, 48
Robert Broome
Thomas Timperley, 3
William Mellor
William Nicholson, 6
Nicholas Baylie, 2
Widow Taylor, 28
Robert Taylor, I
Raphe Glossop, 4
Richard Smith
Themas Hobson, 38
Edward Gorton, 2
John Hobson, jun.
Widow Bouker, I
John Birch, 23
James Bouker, 2
John Percivall, 48
Richard Percivall, 2
Nicholas Wimbell, 4«
Rodger Bewsicke, 2» 8
   Raphe Marlor
Joseph Stoppard, 3
Thomy Smith, 18
Rushulme.
Raphe Worsley, 288
Thomas Shelmerdine, 13 4
Charles Worsley, 4
William Shelmerdine, 8
Thamas Travis, 10
John Davie of Manchester, 4
Thomas Shelmerdine, sen., 3 4
Marie Davie, 18 4
Adam Sidall, 2 4
John Wilkinson, whelewrit, 4
Robert Bouker, 3 4
Richard Travisse, 6 8
Renould Parkinson, 3
Margret Dickonson, 18 4
Thomas Janney, 48

John Davie, 2 8
Edward Baguley, 38 4
William Birch, *18* 4
Thomas Bamford, 2
Edward Worsley, 2
Thomas Hartley, Moss-side, 4
   Matthew Barlow, Heaton
Edmund Smith, 48
ffallowfeild, Ladie Barne, §c.
Robert Bamford, 4
Thomas ffletcher, 4
Widow Bordman, 38
Richard Bordman, 2
George Sidall, 6
James Redich, 4
Robert Bradshaw, 6
Elizabeth Blomiley, 2
John Barlow, 48
George Blomiley, 2
John Smith alias England, I 4
Withington and housend.
Robert Brook, 2
Nicholas Langford, I 4
Alice Baguley, 2s 8
William Langford, 3"
John Wood, 28
ffrancis Wood, I 4
Randle Sedon, I 4
William Blomiley, 2
Dcaffe Margret, 2

The subordination of Birch Chapel to Manchester Church is shown in the payment of tithes to the Warden and Fellows of Manchester as rectors of the entire parish. In 1701 the tithes of Rusholme proper, in which township Birch Chapel is situated, were leased by the Warden and Fellows to Mr. Worsley for J65. The tithes chargeable on the Birch demesne were farmed by Mr. Birch for £3 15s., and on Birchall £ 14s. , and Mr. Siddall was lessee of the tithes of his own estate of Slade, and paid five shillings and sixpence; making a total of *£10* 14s. 6d. In 1848 the rent-charge, payable to the Dean and Chapter of Manchester in lieu of tithes over the whole township of Rusholme was £84. No district was ever assigned to Birch Chapel, that apparently given to it in the ChapelBook of 1636 being merely conventional, suggested by convenience, and not recognised or sanctioned by any authority.

The earliest known allusion to Birch Chapel represents it as deprived of ministerial superintendence; this would be within a few years of the date of its erection; the Visitation returns of 1598 thus referring to it: " Birche Chapel in Rusholme latelie erected and now voyd of a curate.

The first minister whose name has been recorded is one Richard Lingard, curate of the chapel in 1622. Of him nothing more than his name is known. At the time indicated he was within a year of the termination of his incumbency. In 1623 the Rev. Thomas Norman was found discharging the duties of the office, having relinquished the chapel at Gorton, where his name occurs in 161821. It is uncertain how long he remained at Birch, but from the recurrence of his name in the Gorton register in 1641 and later in 1650, it is conjectured that after a brief stay at Birch he returned to his former charge at Gorton. He was still resident in Rusholme in the capacity of Curate of Birch Chapel in October 1632, at which time he buried a daughter (Elizabeth) at the Collegiate Church, and even as late as April 3, 1633, when his daughter Sarah was also buried. In 1635 a Mr. Bentley officiated at Birch, and is described in the registers of Didsbury Chapel of that year, at which time and place he christened one of his children, as preacher at Birch Chapel, being followed by a Mr. Hall, who was resident there in a like capacity in 1641.

In 1646 the Rev. John Wigan, leaving Gorton, fixed his residence at Birch, " where he set up congregationalism," this being about tho-time when the Independents or Congregationalists first prominently opposed the Presbyterian form of church government. Adam Martindale *(Life,* p. 61) speaks of these new opinions as " tugging hard at Gorton to get in there in the days of Mr. Wigan, my prede u cessor, who spent his afternoons' sermons constantly to promote it, and meeting with remoras too weighty to be removed, he was then using all endeavours to get it up at Birch, which in time he effected." The difference in his views on church matters led to his seclusion from his Presbyterian brethren, who made an effort, though an unsuccessful one, to secure his adhesion, the result of which is stated in the proceedings of that body under the date June 9, 1647. — " The members of y last classis appointed to deal with Mr. Wigan returned answer that the said Mr. Wigan was not desirous to meet them as members of a class but as fellow-brethren; promised to return his scruples to you in writing; not yet done." Mr. Wigan afterwards left Birch, and indeed ceased from the ministry. Having entered the army he became first a captain and afterwards a major. Martindale makes another allusion to him (*Life*, p. 75) when speaking of the revolutions in church and state which succeeded the death of Charles I.: — "Diverse of the ministers of the classis hurried about and imprisoned at Liverpool and Ormskirke till it came even to peaceable Mr. Angier; those of Manchester, viz. Mr. Heyrick and Mr. Hollinworth put to pensions (if they got them), the colledge lands being sold and the colledge itself to Mr. Wigan, who now being turned Antipædobaptist and I know not what more, made a barne there into a chappell, where he and many of his perswasion preached doctrine diametrically opposite to the ministers perswasion under their very nose." From the Parliamentary Commissioners' Report of 1650 it appears that Mr. John Wigan was still at Birch. He is therein described as "a painfull godly preaching minister," and as having " received some maintenance out of the sequestrations, but all orders expiring about midsummer 1650 he then depended on the contributions of the people." His resignation followed shortly after. Of his children, Elizabeth was married February 19, 1656, to Mr. Daniel Dunbaven of Warrington, and Lydia June 10, 1658, to the Rev. William Morris of Manchester.

Proceedings of the First Manchester Classis, a MS. in the Chetham Library, *Lansdowne MSS.*, 459, fo. 5.

On the 13th of July 1659, the Rev. Robert Birch, minister of Birch Chapel, was present at a meeting of ministers convened in Manchester, for the purpose of settling amicably the differences of opinion prevailing amongst them in religious matters. At this meeting it was agreed to " lay to heart all unnecessary distances and unbrotherly carriages one towards another and engage in this accommodation in all unfeigned love and steadfast resolution, to pray one with and for another, and to lay aside to their utmost all words and carriages that may violate or prejudice this Christian communion." Mr. Birch was probably a member of the family possessing the patronage of the chapel. Refusing to conform he was silenced on the passing of the Act of Uniformity in 1662, and afterwards altogether abandoning the ministeral function, practised as a physician and surgeon. He died in 1693. His will, which is dated June 24, 16.92, was proved at Chester October 4, 1693, and is as follows: —

I, Robert Birch, of Grindalowe within the township of Chorltonn alias Chorlton roe in the county of Lancaster, clerk, being weak in body but of sound and perfect memory, thanks be to Almighty God, do make, constitute, ordain and declare this my last will and testament, in manner and form following, revoking by these presents all former wills and wills heretofore by me declared either by word or writing. And first, I give and commit my soul into the hands of Almighty God, assuredly believing through the merits of Jesus Christ to be eternally saved; and my body to the earth to be buried in such decent manner as to my executrix hereafter herein named shall be thought meet. And now for the settling of my temporal estate and such lands, goods, chattels and debts as it hath pleased God to bestow upon me, I do order, give, devise and bequeath the same in manner and form following: And first, I will that my debts, if any such be, my funeral expenses and the probate of this my last will and testament, be paid out of my whole personal estate by my executrix hereafter herein named. Item I give, devise and bequeath unto Mary, my loving wife, all that my messuage and lands situate, lying and being in Chorlton roe aforesaid, containing by estimation sixteen acres of land or thereabouts, to have and to hold to her and her assigns for her natural life. And as touching and concerning my personal estate, I do give, devise, dispose and bequeath the same in manner and form following, that is, first I give and bequeath unto all such of my grandchildren as shall be living at the time of my decease ten shillings apiece to be paid out of my said personal estate; and afterwards it is my will and mind that my personal estate be divided into three equal parts, the first part whereof I give and bequeath to Mary, my loving wife; and as for and concerning the other two parts, it is my will and mind and I give and bequeath the same to be equally divided amongst my three daughters, Margaret, Mary and Martha, share and share alike. And lastly, I do hereby constitute, ordain, nominate and appoint Mary, my loving wife, to be the sole and whole executrix of this my last will and testament, trusting she will duly execute the same. In witness whereof I the said Robert Birch unto this my last will and testament have set my hand and seal, &c.

Witnesses, Eliezer Birch, Jane Manifould, John Hall.

The inventory of his "goods and chattels" amounted to £111 10s. 11d.

Of his successor nothing is known, and it is not until after the lapse of ten years that the blank is filled up in the chain of succession. During that interval, in 1670-1, Adam Martindale, himself ejected from Rostheme in 1662, states (*Life*, p. 193) that he "preached publickly in two neighbour chapells, Gorton and Birchbut this, it is probable, he did with no regularity, and when permitted to do so, then only perhaps by the connivance of Colonel Birch, the laws against nonconformity being pressed with the utmost rigour. At this time the nonconformists of the neighbourhood assembled at Birch Hall for the occasional celebration of divine service. Even this they were compelled to do by stealth, the Conventicle Act (as it was called) adjudging that "every person above sixteen years of age present at any meeting under pretence of any exercise of religion in other manner than is the practice of the Church of England, where there are five persons more than the household, shall for the first offence be sent to gaol three months or pay £5; for the second offence double; and for the third transportation for seven years, or a fine of £100." On Sunday November 18, 1666, Colonel Birch, in contravention of this law, permitted two wandering ministers from Germany to preach at Birch Hall. They were engaged from nine to three speaking very fluently, denouncing all manner of woe to England, in exhorting the people to fly and take refuge in Germany. They sang two German hymns with well-tuned voices, the purport of one of which, when sung at the house of an old commonwealth officer, beginning "Hark, how the trumpet sounds!" might well excite some alarm in the minds of the neighbouring royalists. The magistrates took the opportunity of putting the Conventicle Act in force against Colonel Birch and several persons who were present at this meeting, amongst whom was the wife of Ralph Worsley, a gentleman of Rusholme, ancestor of the Worsleys of Platt, friends of the Nonconformists.

In 1672 tho Rev. Henry Finch was appointed to the chapel. Mr. Finch was born in the parish of Standish in the county of Lancaster, and baptised September 8, 1633. He was educated at Wigan and Standish schools, and afterwards proceeded to the university. His earlier ministrations were in the Fylde country, until in 1656 he obtained the vicarage of Walton. From this living he was ejected in 1662 on the passing of the Act of Uniformity, and returned to Warrington, where his wife's friends resided. " By the Corporation Act in 1665 he was forced to remove again, and the kind providence of God brought him to Manchester, though he was a stranger to the place and the people. Thither he fled several other ministers (it not Hunter's *Life of Oliver Metwood*, p. 188.

This act, moro generally known as the " Fire Mile" Act," prohibited Nonconformist ministers from approaching within fire miles of any parish, town or place wherein they had acted as ministers, or within five miles of any city, town corporate or borough, upon forfeiture, for every such offence, of the sum of £40. The' only means by which the rigour of this act could be avoided was by taking an oath denying the lawfulness under any pretence whatsoever of taking arms against the king, and any alteration of the government either in church or state. being a corporation) who lived in great harmony and usefulness to the town and adjacent country. Here, also, he ordinarily joined in public worship with the Established Church till the liberty in 1672, when he renewed his beloved work of preaching publickly, at Birch Chapel, with great diligence and cheerfulness. His great prudence and wise management kept him employed when his brethren were silenced by the recalling of their licenses." On the passing of the Act of Toleration Mr. Finch certified his Majesty's Justices assembled in court at Manchester July 26, 1689, that he intends his own house in Manchester, as also the place called Birch Chapel within the parish of Manchester,.for his preaching to their Majesties Protestant subjects dissenting from the Church of England, assembling there for their religious worship; at which court upon the said Mr. Finch his notifying the said chapel for that purpose, Dr. Wroe, Warden of the Collegiate Church in Manchester, came into the said court and excepted against his the said Mr. Finch preaching in the said Chapel of Birch, shewing that the same is one of the consecrated chapels appertaining to the Warden and Fellows of the said Collegiate Parish Church of Manchester, and did absolutely deny his consent to the said Mr. Finch his admittance to officiate there. All which is certified by

Rogkr Kenyon,
Clerk of the Peace, com. Lane. Once during the term of Mr. Finch's ministrations at Birch, "they thrust a conformist

into his place, but for want of maintenance that project dropped, and Mr. Finch continued with his flock in that place till the chief proprietor died, whose heir took the chapel from him." This event occurred in 1697. On his retirement from Birch Chapel, Mr. Finch, assisted by his friends and some of the more influential members of his late congregation, erected a nonconformist chapel at Platt in Rusholme, of which he became the first minister. He died November 13, 1704, in the 6eventy-second year of his age. " He was," says Calamy, " a great blessing and help to the younger ministers, who loved and honoured Calamy's *Abridgment*, vol. ii. pp. 404-407. Ibid.

him as a father, and his behaviour to them was full of condescension and tenderness. He greatly resented anything that broke in upon order or tended to-the reproach of the ministry; in particular the bold intruding of forward and rash young men without examination and trial. As he was of sound and healing principles in religion, so his thoughts about civil government were according to the English constitution. He absolutely refused the Engagement, and was desirous of King Charles's return. After the defeat of Sir George Booth, the sequestrators seized all of Mr. Finch's estate they could meet with, which he had certainly lost for his love to the king if the speedy turn of affairs had not prevented. He rejoiced at the revolution of 1688, and entirely fell in with it; and yet he had a greater tenderness for those who refused the oaths, and lost their places for conscience sake; to some of them he was a charitable contributor while he lived. His preaching was clear and methodical, and was adapted to convince the mind and to move the passions. He lived, according to his profession, a peaceable life in all godliness and honesty." After the dismissal of Mr. Finch, there occurs an interval of two years, in which no settled curate seems to have been appointed, or if any such there was his name is now unknown.

On the 17th September 1699, George Birch Esq. nominated the Rev. Samuel

Taylor M.A. of Emmanuel College, Cambridge, "to serve at my domestick chappell of Birch, and I do allow him what belongs to it, which, with the contribution which the congregation will make, will probably amount to 620 a year and upwards, if your lordship shall please to admit him into Holy Orders." Mr.

The following extracts from the registers of the Collegiate Church relate to the family of Mr. Finch: — 1665, Dec. 14, Bapt. Nathan, son of Mr. Henry Finch of Manchester, clerk. 1667, July 24, Bapt. Hannah, daughter of Mr. Henry Finch of Manchester, clerk. 1669-70, March 14, Bapt. Elizabeth, daughter of Mr. Henry Finch of Manchester, clerk. 1671-2, Jan. 3, Bapt. James, son of Mr. Henry Finch of Manchester, clerk. 1680, May 1, Bur. Nicholas, son of Mr. Henry Finch, cleric. 1704, Nov. 16, Bur. Mr. Henry Finch of Salford.

Taylor was a native of Gorton, being baptized there December 26, 1675. The duration of his residence at Birch is uncertain, but it is conjectured that he vacated some time before 1707, since in that year Warden Wroe writes thus: " Chorleton and Stretford have no settled curates, for want of endowment; Birch is in the same condition, having only £3 10s. belonging to it." In 1717 the Rev. Joseph Dale was discharging the duties of curate, but with no prospect of permanency. He held the Chapel of Chorlton also in conjunction with that of Birch. On the 11th of July 1720, the Rev. Thomas Wright B.A. was nominated by William Birch Esq. "to my chapel at Birch." He received a nomination to Chorlton Chapel the same day from the Warden and Fellows of Manchester. Mr. Wright was educated at the Manchester Grammar School, and afterwards at Brazenose College, Oxford. He was appointed to a Hulmian Exhibition March 12, 1714. He resigned both chapels January 10, 1721-2, after a short incumbency of eighteen months. On the resignation of Mr. Wright, the Rev. John Tetlow B.A. was nominated as his successor by William Birch of Birch Esq. The patron in this and the preceding nomination was the younger brother of George Birch Esq., who died in 1704. Mr. Tetlow married Elizabeth Birch, a sister of the patron, and daughter of Thomas Birch Esq. and his wife Beatrix Cotton. He continued in the enjoyment of the living until his death in 1742. He was succeeded by the Rev. John Leech B.A. of Katharine Hall, Cambridge, whose nomination is dated June 22, 1742, and is signed by Humphrey Wyrley of Hampstead in the county of Stafford Esq., "the true and undoubted patron of the Chappell of Birch." Mr. Leech was a native of Audenshaw in the parish of Ashton-under-Lyne, and was ordained to the incumbency. His stay was but short, and the vacancy caused by his resignation was filled by the Rev. Robert Twyford B.A. of Brazenose College, Oxford, curate of Didsbury, who continued to hold the two chapels until his death in 1746; he was buried at Didsbury. Mr. Twyford was succeeded at Birch by his son, the Rev. William Twyford B.A. of St. John's College, Cambridge, whose nomination bears date March 17, 1746, and is signed by John Dickenson Esq. as patron. He received also a nomination to Didsbury Chapel in succession to his father on the 15th of May following, under the hand of Sir John Bland Bart. Finding himself unable to supply both chapels he tendered his resignation of Birch to the Bishop of Chester April 27, 1752, and two days after we have recorded the nomination of the Rev. Thomas Aynscough M.A. of St. John's College, Cambridge; patron John Dickenson of Manchester Gent. Mr. Aynscough was a son of the Rev. Radley Aynscough, formerly Fellow of the Collegiate Church, Manchester, and was ordained to the incumbency of Birch. He was himself elected a Fellow of the Collegiate Church November 12, 1761, and resigned Birch Chapel the following year. He died senior Fellow November 8, 1793, and was buried within the Collegiate Church. On the 16th of March 1762, the Rev. Miles Lonsdale M.A., Fellow of Brazenose College, Oxford, was nominated to the chapel by Mr. John Dickenson on the resignation of the Rev. Thomas Aynscough. Mr. Lonsdale was educated at the Manchester Grammar School, and was an exhibitioner at Brazenose College on the Hulme foundation. He held the chapel for about seven years, and resigning October 16. 1769, was succeeded by the Rev. Henry Ainsworth. Mr. Ainsworth was, it is presumed, a native of Gorton, being baptised there September 24, 1737. For three years previous to his appointment to Birch he was curate of Rostherne in Cheshire. He married Elizabeth, daughter of Mr. Philip Rothwell of Longsight, and dying May 16, 1795, was buried at Birch. On the death of Mr. Ainsworth the Rev. Rowland Blayney B.A. was nominated by Mr. John Dickenson to " the augmented curacy of Birch." Mr. Blayney was the son of the Rev. — Blayney, Curate of Whitchurch, Shropshire, and Master of the Grammar School there. The term of his incumbency was protracted; he died May 30, 1838, having held the chapel forty-three years, and was succeeded by the Rev. Francis Philips Hulme B.A., whose nomination, signed by John Dickenson Esq., is dated October 13, 1838. Mr. Hulme died within a few months of his appointment, June 1, 1839, and was buried at Birch. On the 14th of June 1839, the Rev. George Gardner Harter M.A. was nominated to the vacant chapel by John Dickenson Esq., to hold the same in commendam, under promise of resignation in favour of either of the patron's grandsons, George Henry Greville Anson or Archibald Edward Harbord Anson. Mr. Harter resigned February 26, 1840. On Mr. Harter's resignation the Rev. Oliver Ormerod M.A. was nominated by Mr. Dickenson on like condition of resignation. He resigned in 1841, and was succeeded by the Rev. George Dugard M.A. of St. John's College, Cambridge, whose nomination, subject to the conditions binding on his predecessors, was dated March 29, 1841, and signed by Mr. Dickenson. Mr. Dugard was ordained in 1828 to the Curacy of St. Am's, Manchester. In 1830 he became Curate of Prestwich. In 1831 he was appointed to the Incumbency of St. Andrew's, Manchester, which he resigned in 1841, being also from 1834 to 1837 Librarian at the Chetham Hospital. In 1846, in accordance with the terms of his nomination, he vacated Birch Chapel, which he had held for about five years. In 1847 he was nominated to the Incumbency of Barnard Castle, and in 1849 to the Mastership of St. John's Hospital, Barnard Castle. In 1850 he became Honorary Canon of Durham on the nomination of the Bishop.

On the 27th of June 1846, the Rev. George Henry Greville Anson M.A. was nominated to the chapel, on the resignation of Mr. Dugard, by his brother, John William Hamilton Anson of Devonshire Place in the county of Middlesex Esq. Mr. Anson had previously held the Curacy of the parish church of Leeds. He is the present Incumbent of the chapel.

The following is a list of the Curates of Birch Chapel as far as their names can now be traced: — 1598 No Curate.
1622 Richard Lingard. 1623 Thomas Norman.
1635.1636 — Bentley.
1641 — Hall.
1646.1650 John Wigan.
1659.1662 Robert Birch.
1672-1697 Henry Finch.
1699-Samuel Taylor.
1707 No Curate.
1717 Joseph Dale. 1720-1721 Thomas Wright. 1721-1742 John Tetlow.
1742-John Leech.
-1746 Robert Twyford.
1746-1752 William Twyford.
1752-1762 Thomas Aynscough.
1762-1769 Miles Lonsdale.
1769-1795 Henry Ainsworth.
1795-1838 Rowland Blayney.
1838-1839 Francis Philips Hulme.
1839-1840 George Gardner Harter.
1840-1841 Oliver Ormerod. 1841-1846 George Dugard. 1846-George Henry Greville Anson.

Birch Chapel (the earlier structure) was erected, as already intimated, in the reign of Elizabeth. It was of brick, covered with grey slates, and consisted of a nave, 8the roof of which at its eastern extremity bore a plain cross, and at the west a small octagonal turret or bell-cot; there was no chancel. A small cottage-like erection, with a separate entrance on the south, was known as the Dickenson Chapel. The entrance to the main structure itself was in the western gable. Internally it was filled with oaken pews, supplying accommodation for about three hundred and fifty persons, none of the sittings being free. The pulpit, also of oak, was situated in the centre of the nave near to the east end. On the 4th of May 1753, a faculty was granted to John Dickenson of Manchester, merchant, owner and proprietor of divers messuages or tenements and lands in the township and chapelry, empowering him at his own cost to raise the roof of the chapel seven feet, and to enlarge the chapel by taking down the wall at the east end and rebuilding it twelve feet beyond, extending at the same time the north and south walls. In 1803, the chapel being out of repair, substantial alterations were effected by the curate, the Rev. Rowland Blayney, at a cost of about i?200; and in 1811 it was further decorated and an organ added, towards the expense of which Mr. Dickenson the patron contributed i?20. The rapid increase which has taken place in the population of Rusholme since the beginning of the present century having rendered increased church accommodation necessary, in 1845 the foundation-stone of a new church, designed to supersede the older structure, was laid.

The present church is situated about twenty yards to the east of the site of the old chapel. It is an exceedingly beautiful specimen of ecclesiastical architecture, built from designs furnished by Mr. James Macduff Derick of Oxford. The style adopted is that known as lancet or early English, which prevailed during the earlier part of the thirteenth century; and in the various details and internal fittings this style has been carefully adhered to. The church is built entirely of stone, in random courses, and is remarkable for simplicity, exhibiting externally an almost entire absence of ornament, at the same time showing the elegant effect that may be obtained by a proper attention to proportion in the arrangement and distribution of the several parts. The plan aomprises a nave, chancel and side aisles, with a square tower, surmounted by an octagonal spire flanking the western end of the south aisle. The tower is of three heights or stories, separated by string-courses, and supported by twostage buttresses with plain set-offs, placed rectangular-wise; the basement story of the tower forms a porch, the entrance being by an elegant arched doorway on the south side; the belfry windows are of two lights, trefoiled, the space between the heads pierced with a quatrefoil, and surmounted by a moulded dripstone; above these a plain corbel-table gives support to the cornice. An octagonal broach spire rises from the outer face of the tower, without any intervening parapet; the four sides which face the cardinal points slope down to the eaves, each diagonal face of the spire being connected at the base with an angle of the tower by a semi-pyramidal projection, rising from the angle, and terminating in the oblique face of the spire. There are three tiers of spire lights with acute pedimental heads, placed alternately on the four cardinal and four oblique sides. The height from the basement to the apex of the spire is 128 feet. The nave is divided into six bays by buttresses of two stages with moulded set-offs, carried up to and terminating in the corbel-table, the area of the tower circumscribing the length of the south side to the extent of one bay. The windows, set upon a string-course, are of two lights, lancet-headed, and surrounded by dripstones with plain corbels. The clerestory windows are of three lights each, with lancet heads, alternating with flat pilaster-like buttresses. The length of the nave is 80 feet, the width 48 feet, and the height from the ground floor to the ridge 50 feet, the elevation of the clerestory being about 12 or 13 feet. The chancel, 33 feet by 16 feet, is lighted on either side by three single light windows, with moulded weatherings, separated by buttresses of two stages, and at the eastern end by a triplet, above

The interior of this beautiful church is very effective in appearance, the whole of the details being in keeping with the exterior, evincing great accuracy of taste and a nice appreciation of the characteristics and peculiarities of the style. The nave is separated from the side aisles by five cylindrical shafts with richly carved capitals, supporting six pointed arches, surrounded by mouldings terminating in ornamental corbels, and above which rises the clerestory. The roof of the nave and chancel is of timber-work, plain and simple in construction, acutely pointed and open to the ridge without tie-beams, the walls being connected by curved bracing-ribs springing from wall-pieces resting upon corbel-heads, at an angle of 60, formed by the sides of equilateral triangles, and so disposed as to form equilateral arches. On the north side of the chancel is a chapel having an opening into the north aisle, built to contain the organ. The pulpit is of Caen stone, situated on the south side near the junction of the chancel with the nave, the reading-desk occupying a corresponding position on the north side; in addition to these, there is an ornamental lectern. The chancel is lighted by a large triplet with detached shafts, filled with exquisitely stained glass; the centre light containing representations of St. John the Baptist, the Saviour, surrounded by emblems of the four evangelists — the lion, the eagle, the angel and the ox, St. James (the patron saint of the church), and the Alpha and Omega at the top. The north side light represents the Nativity, St. Peter, and the Crucifixion, with the emblem of the Crucifixion — a pelican feeding her young. In the south side light are representations of the Baptism of our Saviour, St. Paul, and the Resurrection, surmounted by the phoenix the emblem of the Resurrection. The tympanum above is filled with a large wheel window, divided into twelve compartments, and decorated with various devices in coloured glass, the *Agnus Dei* being in the centre. The western end of the nave is lighted by a large stained glass window of two lights, surmounted by a quatrefoil, similar in design to one in Stone Church, Kent. The side windows of the nave and chancel are filled with glass of Mosaic pattern, burnt in. The seats are of pitch-pine, varnished, and entirely open. There are no galleries, with the exception of a small one over the western entrance, access to which is gained by a staircase in the tower. An octagonal stone font is appropriately placed near the south entrance to the church. The floor of the nave and chancel is paved with beautiful encaustic tiles.

It will be seen by the foregoing description that there are two principal entrances to the church — one through the western gable and the other on the south side of the tower; in addition to these, there is a priest's entrance on the south side of the chancel. The church will afford accommodation for 750 persons, 400 of the sittings being free. The cost of its erection was about £4,300, the principal contributors towards the object being John William Hamilton Anson Esq. the patron, and his brother, the Rev. G. H. Anson, incumbent of the church. The Manchester and Eccles Church Building Society subscribed £500, and a liberal subscription was entered into by the inhabitants of the township.

It was consecrated July 1, 1846, the consecration sermon being preached by the Bishop of Chester from 2 Cor. x. 3-5.

Adjacent to the church are large and commodious schools, built of brick of different colours, arranged in diaper-like patterns in the style prevalent during the reigns of Henry VIII. and Elizabeth. Over the entrance is a label with the inscription, "Birch School, 1841."

The same year witnessed the erection of two other churches in Rusholme. — Trinity Church situated on the Platt estate, and erected at the sole expense of Thomas Carill Worsley of Platt Hall Esq. at a cost of about £3,600, is wholly built of terra-cotta which gives it a novel and rather pleasing effect and consists of a nave 75 feet by 20 feet, a chancel 24 feet by 20 feet, and two side aisles each 15 feet in width, the latter being separated from the nave on either side by five arches. There is no gallery; the pews, or rather seats, are all open, and the building is calculated to accommodate 700 persons. The tower is placed at the south-west angle and thrown open to the church. Together with the spire, which is octagonal and 150 feet in height, it is a striking feature in the edifice. The architecture of the two entrance doors is rich and pleasing. The interior framework of the lofty roof is composed of oak and left exposed, thus adding greatly to the general effect. High over the elevated arch, separating the chancel from the nave, is placed the decalogue. The foliated capitals of the pillars from which the arches in the side aisles spring are very rich, as are also the corbels and string-course running along the interior of the nave. The floor, both of the nave and chancel, is laid with indented tiles, the chancel floor being elevated two steps above the body of the church. The church was consecrated June 26, 1846, by the Bishop of Chester, who preached on the occasion. The remaining church, dedicated to St. John, and situated locally in Rusholme, is placed on the confines of that township at its point of junction with Gorton. It was designed specially for the inhabitants of the hamlet of Longsight, and its description will therefore fall more appropriately under the head of Gorton Chapel. The foundation-stone was laid March 28, 1845, by Miss Marshall of Ardwick House, one of the chief contributors to its erection, who subscribed £1,000 towards the endowment and £300 towards the structure itself. The cost of the tower and spire was mainly defrayed by Mrs. Marshall (mother of the foundress), who gave £1700 with that object. The site was given by John William Hamilton Anson Esq. The church was consecrated June 26, 1846, (the day on which Trinity Church also received consecration), the sermon being preached by the Bishop of Chester from 1 Pet. iii. 18.

The founder of the dissenting interest in Rusholme was the Rev. Henry Finch,

a friend of the Rev. Henry Newcome, in whose autobiography his name frequently occurs. Though avowedly dissenting from the Established Church he was appointed, as we have seen, to Birch Chapel by Colonel Thomas Birch the patron, and continued with more or less interruption to officiate there during the life of Colonel Birch and of his son and successor until, on the death of the latter in or about the year 1697, he was displaced by Mr. George Birch the next heir, who, having no sympathy with Mr. Finch in his Presbyterian opinions, took advantage of his open violation of the law in officiating as a dissenter in an episcopal chapel, and thus obtained his dismissal. On his retirement from Birch Chapel Mr. Finch began to preach in private houses. This was in October 1697, at which time several houses in the township were licensed for the purpose, amongst others those of Mr. Ralph Worsley of Platt and Mr. Oliver Edge of Birch Hall Fold. The form observed in these licenses is as follows: — Com Lane. These are to certifye that att a Generall Q Sessions of the peace held att Manchester the 14th day of October anno Dni 1697, the Dwelling House of Mr. Raph Worslcy of Platt within Rusholme is recorded for a meeting place ffor an assembly of Protestantes dissenting from the Church" of England ffor ye exercise of theire religious worshipp in, according to an Act of Parliament intituled an Act for exempting their Ma Protestant subjects dissenting from the said Church of England from the pennaltyes of certaine Lawes according to the letter and purport of the said A ct. — Given under my hand the day and yeare above written.
Roger Kenyon,
   Clicus pacis ibm.

The amount of "wage" collected for Mr. Finch's maintenance whilst thus exercising his office was i?16 perannum, and the contributors to the fund numbered fifty individuals, including Mr. George Birch, whose name, however, does not occur as countenancing dissent in the efforts which were afterwards made to establish it in the township. On the 30th of May 1699, a meeting was convened of those inhabitants who were desirous of securing a continuance of Mr. Finch's ministrations, when the following resolutions were adopted: — 1. Wee whose names are hereunto subscribed doe declare our earnest and hearty desire that there may be a Building erected for the Worshipp of God ffor the benefit and convenience of that congregation w now attends upon the ministry of Mr. ffinche. 2. Wee doe promise and declare that wee will duely attend the worshipp of God in such place when erected. 3. ffurther wee doe promise to contribute to the maintenance of such Dissenting Minister or Ministers as shall be unanimously elected to officiate in the said place.

This document is signed by twenty-four individuals, including Mr. Raphe Worsley and Mr. Ebenezer Edge.

The next step was to raise the requisite funds for giving effect to their wishes. A site, the south-east corner of a close called the Blake Flatt, in extent about twenty roods, was given by Mr. Raphe Worsley, who contributed in addition the sum of £10; Mr. Finch gave £20; and with the following smaller donations the promoters were soon enabled to begin the work: — £ a. d.

Mr. Edge of Warrington 6 0 0
Richard Whittaker 5 0 0
Mr. Thomas Butterworth 1 10 0
Mr. Alexander Boardman 1 10 0
Mr. Birche, minister 1 0 0
Adam Barlow 1
ObadiahHulme 1 y
Mr. Charles Worsley 1 0 0
Mrs. Okell 1 0 0
Francis Wood 1 0 0
Mr. Siddall 1 0 0
Mad. Gill 1 0 0
Mrs. Loyd 0 10 0

The structure was of brick, and it is on record that 39,008 bricks were required to complete it. The chief items of disbursement were: — £ s. d.
ffor Brickes 19 10 0 ffor 56 Loads of Lime at 18 per load 4 4 0
Peter Ryland, Bricksetter 4 2 6
   Randle Thorneley &c. ffor Slate 4 15 6 ffor Timber 10 0 0
Jeremiah Kirsley for Slateinge and Mosse... 2 13 8
ffor Boardes for Doores and Weatheringe and
for 50 yards of sparrs at 3 per yard 2 8 2
Three Loades of fflaggs and carriage 17 6 ffor meate, drinke, ale, Pipes and Tobaccer att y Rearinge, being y sixth day of October.. 0 19 0 ffor Glass six score and foure foote at 4£ y foot 2 6 6
The Smith for Bandes for Doores w Barres and Bolts and window rods 1 12 10 ffor Recordinge our Chappell 0 16 ffor the Pulpitt Quishion 1 3 3
John Odcroft's Bill for yᵉ Pulpitt, Sounder, seates, wainscott &c 18 7 11

The total amount expended on the chapel was about df?95. It was not completed until the close of the year 1700. At its inauguration Mr. Grimshaw officiated, and received five shillings for his services.

In 1706 a formal conveyance of the chapel was made to certain trustees by Mr. Raphe Worsley. By Indentures of Lease and Release, dated respectively October 25 and 26, 1706, Raph Worsley conveys to Charles Worsley, his heir apparent, John Finch the elder, Ebenezer Edge, Richard Whittaker, John Siddall, Eleazer Birch, Francis Wood the elder, Robert Walker, Robert Bradshaw the elder, Obadiah Hulme and Thomas Shelnierdine, their heirs and assigns, the said edifice, chapel, oratory and meeting-place and the said parcel of land wherein the same now stands, to hold unto the said grantees their heirs and assigns for ever; upon trust that the said grantor and grantees and their heirs shall permit the said edifice, chapel and oratory from time to time and at all times thereafter so long as the law of this realm will permit, connive at, tolerate, allow or indulge the same to be used as a meeting-place and assembly of a particular church or congregation of Protestants dissenting from the Church of England for the free exercise of their divine and religious worship therein, on such days and times by such minister and ministers as in the said indenture of release are mentioned, and shall be qualified according to the true intent and meaning of an act of parliament made in the first year of the reign of

King William and Queen Mary, entitled "an act.for exempting their majesties' Protestant subjects dissenting from the Church of England from the penalties of certain laws," or according to some other act of parliament thereafter to be made in favour of such dissenting Protestants; and that the said small parcel of land shall be used at all times for the convenience and better enjoyment of the said chapel; and that no person shall be interred within the said chapel or parcel of ground without the consent of the major part of the said trustees in writing made under their hands (except the said trustees and their families); and that if the law of this realm will not permit the performance of the said trusts or such public and religious worship as aforesaid, that then the said trustees and their heirs shall and may convert and dispose of the said edifice and small parcel of ground to such pious and charitable uses as the said trustees or the major part of them shall think most fit; and that for the better continuance of the said trust and supply of new trustees when nine or fewer of the said trustees shall be dead, then the survivors of them shall elect nine or more or fewer other able, sufficient, sober, honest and religious persons most likely to favour and promote the said uses and trusts to be trustees with them or him so surviving; and in like manner elections of trustees to be made from time to time for ever when there shall be but three or fewer trustees living; and that after such election and elections the surviving trustees shall with all convenient speed by good conveyances convey and assure the said edifice and small parcel of ground to such persons and their heirs as shall be so elected, to the use as well of the person or persons so conveying and of their or his heirs as of the persons so newly elected and their heirs under and upon the trusts in the reciting indenture directed and none other.

The trust-deed of the chapel requires " the minister or ministers or teachers of the said congregation to be a Protestant able minister or ministers of the gospel, who is of the Presbyterian judgment and practice as to church discipline and government, and not of any other persuasion, and to pray and preach God's word, administer the sacraments of the New Testament, and perform all offices and duties belonging to that sacred function there, so as every such minister or ministers shall be orthodox and sound in the faith of our Lord Jesus Christ, and such as hold and profess the doctrinal articles of the Church of England, required to be subscribed by the pastor or teacher of such congregations, and as are qualified by an act," &c., the Toleration Act.

The following platform or ground-plan, with the allotment of seats, dates from the time of the erection of the chapel: —

Platt Chapel has received from time to time various donations and bequests towards the formation of an endowment-fund for the support of a resident minister. The following, though probably an incomplete list, includes most of the contributions towards that object: — 1. Extract from the will of Raphe Worsley, dated June 11, 1725: — "I give and bequeath one hundred pounds sterling to my son Mr. Charles Worsley and Mr. Peter Worsley my grandson, in trust that the lawful interest thereof shall be yearly paid and given to such orthodox, gospel, dissenting, preaching minister as shall be constantly resident at Platt Chapel or meeting-place for public worship; and if liberty in or at any time to come shall be restrained, it is then my will and mind that the interest and produce of the said one hundred pounds be given and bestowed for the benefit and relief of the most religious poor people, whether housekeepers or others, within Rusholme, Fallowfield and Birchall Houses, at the discretion of my executors and their successors for the time being." 2. Abstract of the will of John Dickenson of Levenshulme, dated September 11, 1750:—Proved at Chester August 22, 1763. He gives and devises all his messuage and tenement, &C, in Levenshulme to his brother-in-law Thomas Whitelegg and his heirs, on trust that the said Thomas Whitelegg shall within twelve months next after testator's decease pay unto the several persons hereinafter named the several sums of money hereinafter mentioned; i.e. to his wife Alice, his brother Robert Dickenson, his sister Mary Dickenson, his brother-in-law Thomas Fletcher and Elizabeth his wife, testator's cousins John Worthington and Robert Worthington, his brother Robert Oldham, James Thorp and Thomas Richardson, the sum of £20 each; unto his brother-in-law James Whitelegg i?10; to John Pearson and Thomas Pearson (sons of his brother-in-law John Pearson), his cousins Thomas Worthington, Alice Oldham (mother of the said Robert Oldham), his brothers-in-law Richard Vost and Thomas Vost, his cousins John Worthington, Daniel Hampson, William son of testator's brother-in-law Thomas Nicholson, the Rev. Mr. John Whitaker and Richard Whitaker his son £5 each. To his executors (Thomas Whitelegg, Richard Whitaker and Robert Worthington) he gives the sum of i?60 in trust that they " distribute and divide the same amongst such industrious and necessitous persons residing within the township of Levenshulme aforesaid not receiving public alms or relief, in such shares and proportions as they my said executors or the survivors of them shall in their discretion think meet. And unto Charles Worsley of Platt Esq., Peter Worsley of the same Esq., John Siddall of Slade within Withington Gent., the said Richard Whittaker, Thomas Irlam of Withington Gent., and Thomas Fletcher of Levenshulme aforesaid Gent., Thomas Siddall of Burnage Gent., Thomas Fletcher of Withington aforesaid Gent., and George Hobson of Levenshulme aforesaid yeoman, the sum of.£100 upon trust, and to the intent and purpose that the said Charles Worsley, &c., do and shall from time to time and at all times hereafter put the same sum of £100 out at interest, and the interest and produce thereof yearly pay and apply to and for the use and benefit and for the better support and maintenance of such Protestant minister of the gospel, dissenting from the Church of England, as for the time being shall preach or officiate at or in the chapel or place of meeting of Protestant dissenters for the public exercise of religious worship in Rusholme in the said county of Lancaster, commonly called or known by the name of Platt Chapel. And for the better and more effectual management and continuance of the same trust I do hereby order and direct that when the same trustees shall (by death) be reduced to the number of three survivors, then such survivors or the survivors or survivor of them shall with all convenient speed after such reduction elect and choose so many honest, sober and religious persons to be trustees concerning the same premises as will with the then surviving old trustees complete and make up the number of nine trustees, and such surviving trustees shall assign the securities that shall be had and taken for the said last-mentioned sum of £100, so that the legal interest of and in the said securities shall and may be vested in such old and new trustees upon the trust aforesaid, and that the like method and course shall be had and practised from time to time and at all times hereafter when and as often as the trustees for the time being shall be reduced to the number of three." 3. J3y her will (date unknown) Mrs. Margaret Johnson bequeathed the sum of £100 towards the endowment of the chapel, the interest to be applied yearly for that purpose. Her executor was Mr; John Carill Worsley.

4. By her will (date unknown) Mrs. Fletcher of Levenshulme bequeathed the sum of £20 with a like object. 5. By his will (date unknown, but supposed to be about 1799) Bobert Hyde of Burnage gives and bequeaths " unto the minister for the time being of the dissenting chapel at Platt in the said parish of Manchester for ever, in case that chapel shall continue what is generally called a dissenting chapel, the sum of £5 yearly and every year to be paid to the minister for the time being by my executors on every the 25th day of December."

In 1810 the trust-money of the chapel, amounting to the sum of i?566 2s. 8d. was expended in the purchase of chief rents in Stockport, which produce £35 7s. 8d. per annum.

In 1790-1 the chapel was taken down and rebuilt in its present form on the old site; it was re-opened for public worship May 11, 1791.

The first minister of Platt Chapel was, as already stated, the Rev. Henry Finch. He did not long survive the erection of the chapel, dying in 1704 in the seventy-second year of his age. His successor was the Rev. Robert Hesketh, one of Franklands pupils, whose academy at Rathmel in Yorkshire he entered in 1692. After completing his course of study he appeared as a candidate at the provincial meeting of Lancashire ministers at Bolton on the 14th of April 1696, and again in Manchester on the 4th of August in the same year. He began his ministry as pastor of a congregation of nonconformists at Carnforth near Lancaster, where he also married. On the death of the Rev. Henry Finch in 1 704 he removed to Platt. During his residence here, which continued till 1712, he contracted a second marriage April 6, 1708, with Miss Hannah Sykes of Leeds. Little is known of his subsequent life.

The Eev. John Whitaker was next in succession to Mr. Hesketh. He was ordained at Knutsford August 3, 1714, and for his thesis advocated the affirmative of the question " An infantes fidelium sint baptizandi!" At the time of Mr. Whitakers settlement at Platt Chapel his congregation numbered two hundred and fifty persons. His ministrations there terminated with his death in 1752. The next minister was the Rev. Robert Andrews. He was a native of Bolton, and a member of an eminent nonconformist family which had been seated for nearly two centuries at Little Lever and Rivington. He received his theological education under Dr. Caleb Rotheram at Kendal, and having completed the usual course of study entered upon the duties of his profession at Platt Chapel. The precise period of Mr. Andrew's stay is uncertain, but it did not exceed three years. He afterwards presided over a Presbyterian congregation at Bridgenorth, where he remained until mental derangement compelled him to withdraw from the pulpit. He was a man of considerable scholarship and taste. In 1757 he published a volume of poems entitled " Eidyllia," to which he prefixed a violent attack upon rhyme. Some time previously he had sent to the press " Animadversions on Dr. Brown's Essays on the Characteristics," and a Criticism on the Sermons of his friend the Rev. John Holland. His latest work was a " Translation of Virgil in blank verse," which is not destitute of merit, though it has the strange peculiarity of conveying the sense of his author line for line. This handsome volume in Baskerville's type now finds a place among the curiosities of literature. Mr. Andrews married Miss Hannah Hazlewood, and died about the year 1766. The pulpit of Platt Chapel was next filled by the Rev. John Houghton, a native of Liverpool, born in 1730, whose studies for the ministry were pursued partly at Northampton under Dr. Doddridge, and partly at the University of Glasgow. This was his first settlement. In 1755 he married Mary Pendlebury, a connexion of the Worsleys of Platt, the marriage-settlement being dated June 21st in that year; and in 1758 he removed to Hyde in Cheshire, and subsequently to Nantwich, Elland and Wem. About the year 1788 he again removed to Norwich, where his son, the Rev. Pendlebury Houghton, was settled as one of the ministers of the Octagon Chapel, and where he opened a classical school. Here he died in April 1800, aged seventy. The next minister in succession was the Rev. Richard Meanley, one of Dr. Caleb Rotheram's pupils, who removed to Platt from Nantwich in the year 1758, and continued there till his death in 1794. The chapel was now supplied by students for the next three years. In 1797 the Rev. George Checkley, who had received his education at Daventry under Dr. Caleb Ashworth, and been settled in the ministry for upwards of thirty years at Hyde and Ormskirk, was invited to Platt, and spent there the last ten years of his life. He died February 6, 1807, in the sixty-third year of his age, and was twice married, his second wife being a sister of the late Mr. Touchet of Manchester. Mr. Checkley had an estate at Ashley near Altringham, to which he had retired previously to his last settlement with the intention of passing there the remainder of his days, but the proximity and society of Mr. Worsley and a numerous circle of personal, literary and religious friends in Manchester drew bim from his retirement, and probably rendered this last the happiest period of his life. For three years after the death of Mr. Checkley the chapel was temporarily supplied by the Rev. Joseph Lawton Siddall till the year 1810, when the present minister, the Rev. William Whitelegge, removed from Full wood near Bristol, where he had resided a year or two, to take charge of the congregation at Platt.

The earliest return of the population of Rusholme is in the year 1714, at which time it contained but 40 families, representing probably an aggregate of 200 persons. Of these families five were dissenters. In 1774 the number of families had increased to 67, consisting of 351 individuals, and residing in 63 houses. Of its then inhabitants one hundred and fifty were under the age of 15 years; forty-three above 50; nine above 60; eight above 70; and three above 80. In 1801 the population had reached 726; in 1811 it amounted to 796; in 1821 to 913; in 1831 to 1,078; in 1841 to 1,868; and in 1851 to 3,679, being an increase on the past ten years of 97 per cent.

In 1655 the township contained 14 ratepayers, but no separate return is made of the amount of rate collected, it being included in the total of Withington. Amongst the names of the Rusholme ratepayers at this period are Mr. Worsley, Mr. Worsley of Heild heuse, Lieutenant-Colonel Worsley and George Worsley. In.Birchall houses, Thomas Birch Esq., Mr. Siddall of Slade, Captain Edge and Thomas Birch. In 1854 the ratepayers numbered 1,027, and the rate collected was.£981 lis. 7d.; the gross value of property in the township rated for the poor being i?32,287 0s. 3d.

In 1692 the annual value of real property in Rusholme, as assessed to the land-lax, was i?146 13s. 4d. In 1815 its value, as assessed to the county-rate, was £3,608; in 1829, £5,748; in 1841, £15,281; and in 1853, £27,903.

In 1854 there were in Rusholme 69 county voters. The number of public-houses was two, and of beer-houses sixteen. The London and North Western Railway passes through the township. There is no river or canal, neither is there a mill or manufactory of any kind. The Wesleyans, Independents, Baptists and Unitarians have each a place of worship.

The superficial area of Rusholme, as given by Messrs. Johnson in their survey, is 960 acres; the Ordnance Survey returned it at 973a. 3r. 15p.; Mr. Hickman's Computation in the Census Returns of 1831 is 1,040 acres, which corresponds with the return of the Tithe Commissioners. In the year 1 844 the lands of the township were divided amongst one hundred and twenty owners, of whom the following are the principal: —

A. R. p.

Anson, Sir John William Hamilton Bart. (Birch Hall,&c.) 220 2 21

Worsley, Thomas Carill Esq. (Platt estate, &c.).. 153 1 22

Egerton, Wilbraham Esq 99 3 6

Rushton, Edward, Executor of 53 0 38

Holford, John Esq 50 3 19

Denison, Joseph Esq 39 1 29

Siddall, John Esq. (Slade Hall) 24 0 9

Cobden, Richard Esq 21 2 39

Assuming the area to be 1,040 acres it was divided as follows: — Arable land, 20 acres; meadow and pasture, 960 acres; site of buildings, 60 acres. Victoria Park lies towards the north of the township. It consists of about 200 acres of land, laid out in gardens, ornamental grounds, roads, &c., for villa residences. The Victoria Park Tontine was projected in 1836, with a capital of,£750,000, in 7,500 shares of £100 each. In 1850 sixty-five houses had been already erected in the park, the inmates numbering about 390 persons.

Rusholme has no 'charity exclusively its own; it participates, however, in several endowments which extend their operations over the entire parish of Manchester.

The hamlet of Longsight, though in part within Rusholme, is situated chiefly within the township of Grorton. Its description and history will fall, therefore, more legitimately under the head of the latter township.

A Roman road intersects the township, and according to Whitaker, "appears advancing towards Manchester from the south-east, traversing the whole breadth of the parish on the south, and still carrying a considerable ridge in several parts of it. It is particularly conspicuous at Birch, and is popularly represented as a breast-work thrown up against the Danes, and denominated Nico (or Devil's) Ditch.' This description by Whitaker is not, however, quite correct, the historian having confounded the name of a neighbouring Saxon dyke or embankment with the old Roman road which is separate and distinct from it.

Recent investigations show the Roman road to be an ancient Whitaker's *History of Manchester,* vol. i. pp. 235-6, second edition. Communicated by Mr. John Higson, of Droylsden, author of the *Gorton Historical Recorder.* vicinal way. By the inhabitants of the locality it is designated as the "Pink Pank Lane/' and it is generally known as the old London Road. The old people state it was currently believed in their younger days that one branch went from Rochdale and another from Manchester (uniting in the hamlet of Kirkmanshulme in the township of Newton Heath) to Macclesfield, and from thence to London. After leaving Levenshulme, near the junction of that township, Reddish and Gorton, it crosses the Nico Ditch and enters the township of Gorton shortly afterwards, taking a turn and proceeding along a portion of the margin of the Gorton race-course (where it is laid to the field); directly after leaving the course at the south-west angle, it exists in something like its primitive state until it enters Kirkmanshulme, where it presently afterwards divides into two heads, one passing Knutsford Vale Printworks, and winding backwards up Ked Lane, re-enters the township of Gorton. It next diverges where the lane is crossed by the Hyde road, and after a few more turns crosses the Gorton or Corn Brook, and enters the township of Openshaw. This portion is known as "Th' Owd Green ione." After passing over the old and new Ashton roads it proceeds through Philips' Park, and thence to Rochdale. Returning to Crow Croft, Kirkmanshulme, the other branch passes on to the Stockport road, and for a short distance blends or identifies itself with that ancient Roman road, crossing the Rush-brook with it at Rushford, but shortly afterwards diverging to the left, where it is modernised for a considerable distance, but still retains the name of Birch Lane. Near Birch School (at the back of St. John's, Longsight), it takes a sndden turn, where doubtless Whitaker saw it; it proceeds through Birch Hall fold, and thence probably winds round to old Mancunium.

Another striking feature in the geography of Rusholme township, and which may be placed side by side with the preceding, the better to mark the distinction which Whitaker has failed to recognise, is the Nico or Nicker Ditch, a rivulet or stream, and a rampart of earth raised, according to tradition, by the Saxons as a defence against their invaders the Danes, who towards the close of the ninth century seized upon Manchester, and ravaged the surrounding country. Its formation was apparently anterior to the general cultivation of the land through which it passes, if not to the colonization of the district; else why is it that it acts as a boundary to so many townships? Its source or commencement is found to be in the Audenshaw division of the parish of Ashtonunder-Lyne, on the site of Ashton Moss; it seems here to be a natural stream, and acts as a drain to a portion of that morass. Crossing the Ashton New Road a little to the south-east of Droylsden Church, and running under the canal it begins its functions at Ashuett Lane by dividing Droylsden from Audenshaw. Winding obliquely round the hamlet of Fairfield it renounces Droylsden and embraces Openshaw; passing under the Old Ashton Road near Se'nthorns Wells (Seven Thorns Wells, from a tradition that seven thorns anciently grew there) and crossing the Manchester, Sheffield and Lincolnshire Railway, it begins to form the Waterworks Reservoir. It now changes Openshaw for Gorton, after receiving a tributary brook from Dane Wood, Audenshaw. The united stream (Gore Brook) now forsakes the ancient embankment, and proceeds through Gorton, Kirkmanshulme, Rushohne, &c. (at Birch Church it again falls into the embankment line); at Longsight it is named the Rush, and gives name to a hamlet Rushford, at the place where the old Roman road and vicinal way conjointly passed over it, and also to the township of Rusholme. Returning once more to the line of division, it runs nearly in the centre of the higher reservoir, faithfully embracing Gorton, from hence to the Midway, Stockport road. On the opposite side, near "Deb-dale Lane," the ditch may be traced leaving Audenshaw for Denton, crossing the Hyde road, the old Denton road, the Stockport Canal, &c., leaving Denton for Reddish, and shortly after (near Winning Hill) leaving Reddish for Levenshulme; then crossing the vicinal way (Pink Pank Lane) it proceeds straight forwards to the Midway, Stockport road, where Gorton gives place to Rusholme (it here forms the ring fence of the Slade Hall estate); it flows on in rather an oblique direction until it regains the Gore or Rush Brook near Birch Church, Rusholme (which brook is said to be the site of the embankment), until it arrives near Ouse Moss. It is a singular fact that the hedge is on the Gorton or Manchester side all along, which seems to imply that when the land was first divided into fields, the remains of the old breast-work were used as a cop or backing, the thorns being simply planted upon it.

APPENDIX.

Goildhouses.—Family Op Trafford. *(pp. 2-5.J* 1. — Sciant p'sentes et futuri q ego Math fit Matb.1 de Hav'sege dedi &c. Ric' de Trafford viginti acras t're p pticam viginti duo pedm ppinquiore de Tollache, incipiendo ad magna mussam et ascendendo Gosselache usq, ad divisas de Plat et sic a divisis de Plat i transverso versus Grenclow-lache ac com pastur' in villa de Wyddine; Tend et Hend de me &c. sibi et hedib3 suis exceptis viris religiosis et judeis. Redd inde annu m et hedib3 meis una calcaria ferri vt tres denarios argenti p omi seculari servicio ad Annunc' be Marie salva mihi et meis una via debita et usitata versus Mamcestr. Hiis testib3 Dno Ada de Biri, fre yvone canonico de Bello capic' Brother Ivo, canon of Bello Campo, *i.e.* Beauchief Abbey in Derbyshire, WiHo de Didesbur', Ric de Most', Rob Redig' et aliis. — s. d. — *Trafford Evidences, Lane. MSS.*

Indorsed: " Fossa Rici trafford jux" Goselache." — Seal: Green wax imperf. bearing arms of Hathersage De Haverseche. 2. — Sciant &c. Ego Nicholaus de Longeford dnus de Wythinton dedi &c. Henrico de Trafford militi quamdam placeam vasti mei in villa de Wythinton infra has divisas incipiendo ad Goslache ad le Hontlon del Plat sequendo viam regale versus borial usq, in Grenlowlache et sic descend Grenlow lache usq, occidental usq, in Kemlache et sic de Kemlache ex transverso versus australem p puteos et fossata facta usq, in Le Yhildhouse digth et sic ascendendo usq, in Goslache et sic ascendendo Goslache usq, in p'dcm Hontlone del Plat q est p'ma divisa. Hend et Tend de me p'dco Henr' et hedib3 de corpe suo legit' pcreat, Redd septemdecim solid argenti ad duos ann' term' viz. medietat' ad festu Annunci b Marie et aliam medietate ad festu sci Mich p oib3 serviciis secularib3. Et si contingat pdct Henr' obiere sine herede de corpe suo legit' pcreat'; rem mihi et hedib3 mei. Hiis testib3 Dom Rico de Byronu milite, Mag Ricardo de Trafford rectore ecclie de Chedle, Ricardo de Hulton, Johe de Asshton Johe de hulton, Roblło de Asshton et aliis. Datu ap Wythinton die Veneris in fest' sci Mathie apostoli A Edwardi filii Edwardi undecimo.

Indorsed: "Yeeldhouse redd xvy8 11 Edw. 2." Seal: White paste, bearing shield with arms of Longford. Legend: Sigillvm Nich De Lonoford. — *Trafford Evidences, Lane. M.SS.* 3. — Oib3 xpi fid &c. Symon de Gousil salfm &c. — Noverit' me concess' remiss' &c. Henrico de Trafford &c. homag' ct servic trium soliditar quidam annu redd' et omnia alia exactio' et demand' in quib3 mihi tenebatur de quadam tenemeto q de me tenuit in Withinton q vocatur le Gyldehousys p concessione &c. qm Roger' de Penilbury michi fecit p cartam suam q quid homag' et servic p'fat Henr' et an'cessores sui face solebant p'fato Rogero et antecessorib3 suis p p'dco tenem' q de me an'cessorib3 meis tenuit; Redd' duob3 solid' annuat'. Hiis testib3 Diio Galfrido de Bracebrigge, Galfrido de Chadirton, Rico de Radeclive, Thom de Heton, Robfo de Shorsworth, Ric6 de Moston et aliis. — s. d. — *Trafford Evidences, Lane.* MSS. 4. — Oib3 &c. Rog' de Penilbury salfm in dno semp'. Noverit' me concessisse assignasse remisisse &c. Henrico de Trafford atornato et assignato Symonis de Gousul militis homagiu et serviciu trium soliditar cujusdam annu redditus et omnimodas alias exaccoes et demandas quas ab eodem Henric' v'l hedib3 suis exig'e pot'o de quadam tenemeto que vocatur Gyldehousis in Wytbinton que quide tenemen' ego des Rog' de p'fato Symone capitali diio meo tenui in eadem villa. Hiis testib3 Dno Galfrido de Bracebrigg, Galfro de Chadirton, Rico de Radeclive, Thoma de Heton, Robto de Shorisworthe, Rico de Moston et aliis. — s. d. — *Trafford Evidences, Lane.* MSS. 5. — Sciant p'sentes et futuri q ego Helias filius Robft ? Rogi de Peuelburie dedi &c. Henrico filio Roberti filii Radulphi de Trafford pro homagio et servicio suo totam terram de Gildehusestide cu p'tin inter has divisas scilicet de Goselache usq, ad pullum ubi Matheus filius Willelmi levavit fossatum ad vertendam aquam ad molendinum suum, et per pullum descendeudo usq, ad fossatum quod ego feci, et ita per illud fossatum usq, ad mussam, et de mussa usq ad Goselache — cum communione omnium libertatum quas liberi homines predicti Mathei domiui mei habent sicut carta testatur quam habeo de predicto Matheo de prefata terra. Reddendo inde annuatim mihi quatuor solidos pro omni servicio et consuetud,

et duos solidos prenominat' Math fil Willi et hed qui habebunt unam viam per Alsedum prefate terre p'scpti Henrici ad cariauda fena sua. Hiis testib3 Ricardo filio Henrici, Robto de Burunn, Ricardo de Perepont, Witto de Radeclive, Alexandra filio Gilberti de Harewode, Henrico filio Galfridi de Mamecestr, Petro de Burnhill, Alexandro de Pilkinton, Matheo de Rcdich, Hugone de Stretford, Ada de Ormeston, Robto filio Hugonis de Mascy, Ricardo clico de Mamecestr. — *Trafford Evidences, Lane.* MSS. 6. —Sciant &c. q ego Nichus de Longeforde dSus de Wythinton concessi et reddidi Henr' de Trafford militi et hedib3 suis et oib eor' tenentib3 in Wythinton die cocessionis huj indent ut jus commune sue coniuna turbarie in coniun turbarie die Yliildhous mosse ad turbas fodendas sctand et capiend p voluntate eor' ad tenementa sua in Wythinton. Ita scilicet q liceat pdico Henr' et hedib3 suis ac oib3 eor" tenentib3 in Wythinton cartare turbas sine molest ct absq, impediin. Hiis testib3 Dno Ricardo Byron milite, mag Rico de Trafford rectore ecclie de Chedle, Ricardo de Hulton, Johe de Asshton, Johe de Hulton, Robto de Asshton et aliis. Dat ap Wythington die Ven'is in festo S Mathie apostoli anno regni regis Edwardi filii regis Edwardi undecimo 1317. — *Trafford Evidences, Lane.* MSS. — Seal: White paste, " Sigillvm Nich. de Longford," with shield of arms.
7. — Sciant &c. Ego Math Cissor' de Mamecestr' dedi &c. Nicho fil Henr' de Trafford militis oes terras meas et tenementa in Rysshum in vitt de Wythinton sine alkmo retenemeto et tenend' dcto Nicho et hedib3 de corpe suo legit' pcreat cu oib3 libtatib3 in boscis planis s'viciis. Et si contingat q p'dcus Nichol' obiere sine hered' de corpore suo legit' pcreat &c.; rem Galfrido fr! ejusdem Nichi, rem Thome fri ei, rem' Robto fri ejusdem Thome, rem Rico fri Robt', rem' Henrico fri ejusdem Rici. Hiis testib3 Henr' de Trafford milite Rico de Trafford fre ei Matheo de Haydock, Rico de Moston, Johe fit Thome de Ashton, Willo de R clico et aliis. Datu ap Rysshum die Ascension dni anno Edwardi fil regis Edwardi nono. — *Traf-*

ford Evidences, Lane. MSS. Indorsed:' " Carta de terr' in Risholme. " Seal: White paste. Legend: Siqil Math De c.... rest imperfect.
Family Of Rusholme.
Cpp. 5, 6.J
1. — Sciant ofiis psntes & futi q ego Hnr de Russu dedi & cessi & Lac psenti carta mea firmavi GalP fil Luc de Mammecestr' p homagio & servico suo qndam pte t're mee infra divisas de Russu videl3 unu mesuagiu ad capd pti mei in pte aqloii juX Huttelone & longitudiue qndeci pcatas & latitudine qtuor pcatas & unam ac m t're cu? unu capd extendit se ad illam t'ram & alid capd v'sus pomeriu meu & unam ac'm pti in pto de Russu & unam acm t're cui? unu capd extend ad illu ptu & alid capd i lemenegate v'sus occidente & unam dimid ac'm t're cui capd unu extendit se v'sus pdcam ac'm & alid capd I goselache & una selione q vocat' le qwikehaggedelonde cui unu capd extend se i goselache & alid cap i lemenegate & unam dimid ae"m t're cui unu extend se i le huttelone & alid cap i goselache & sex ac"s t're q jacent jux t'ra Hug de Asselu q"r unu cap extendit se i goselache & alid cap i vet' foveii. Hend & Tcnda de me & hedib3 meis s' & hedib3 suis libe quete & pacifice cu comi pasta & cu oib3 libtatib3 & aysiamtis ville de Russu ptinlib3 Reddendo inde annuati m & hedib3 meis de se & hedib3 suis unu par albar' cyrothecar' ad natale dfii p omi servico exaccoe & demanda ego v & hedes mei tota pdcam tra cu ptinenciis pdeo Galfr' & hedib3 suis ta oiiis holes & femias warentizabim9 imppetuu. Et ut h mea donaco rata sit & stabil huic psnti scpto sigillu meu apposui, hiis testib3 Dno WiH de Heeton, Rob. de Redich, Rob. de Aston, Symon fil Luc, Jord fil eid & Ad fre suo, Henr' fil Huhelet & aliis. — *Birch Evidences,* penes Sir John "William Hamilton Anson, Bart.
The seal, which is pendant and oval in shape, is of green wax and in remarkably good preservation, bears in the centre a device, a lozenge divided into four parts by two cross-crosslets which intersect each other. The legend: Sigil Henri De Rvsvm. 2. — Sci omib3 psens

sept visu vel audit' q ego Hricus de RusschQ mera & spontanea volutate mea remisi & qet clamavi p me & hredib3 meis dno meo dno Matheo de Hatirseg' & hredib3 suis homagiu & servisscїu Galfridi filii Luc de Mamecest'a & hredu suo & totius terre q idem Galfridus tenuit in villa Ruschu scil unu par cirothecar albar annuati ad pentecosten. Ita scil q no liceat m' n hredib3 meis vel alicui noie meo vel hredu meo aliq ius vel clamiu in homagio & servisscio dti Galfridi filii Luc vel hredu suo vel terre q id G. de me tenuit in villa de Ruschum in possum vendicare vel optinere. Et in hui rei testimoniu huic psenti scpto sigillum meu apposui, hiis testib3 Dno GahV de Chetham, Robto de Biru, WiHo le Noreis, Ric de TrFord, Symone fil Luc de Mamecestr', Johe de Leya clerico & aliis.—*Birch Evidences,* penes Sir John William Hamilton Anson, Bart.

3. — Sciant omes psentes & futi q ego H5r' de RussG penit' qeteclamavi Galf. filio Luc de Mamecestr' & hedib3 suis vl assignatis suis totu ius q heo vl hfe poto in viginti acris tre qs tenet de Rob' de Hulton i villa de Russu. Ita qdem q nec ego n aliqi hedum meo aliq ius vl clameum i p'dcis viginti acris t're cu ptinenciis de ceto exig'e pot'im imppetuu. Et q'a volo q h mea q'eteclamacio rata & stabilis p manet huic psnti scpto sigillu meu apposui, hiis tcstib3 Galf' de Chetha, Rob. de Buru, WiH de Heeton, Rob. de Redich, Ric. de Moston, Symofi fit Luc, Ric. fil Rant, Ad. de Farneworke, Henr' fil Huheloth & aliis. — *Birch Evidences,* penes Sir John William Hamilton Anson, Bart.

Seal pendant: A fleur-de-lis. Legend: Henricus Bussum. 4. — Sciant omS tam psentes q"m futi q ego Henric' de Russum dedi cessi & hac psenti carta mea firmavi Hugoni de Haselum & heredib3 suis vel suis assignatis p homagio & servicio totam t'ram mea que est int' altam stratam de Russeford & t'ram d'ei Hugois & dimidia bovata t're in villa de Russum ele Holt cu oib3 ptinenciis Teneudas & Habendas sine ullo retenemto de me & hedib3 meis sibi & hedib3 suis vel suis assignatis in feodo & heditate libe & qete pacifice & integre cu oib3 libtatib3 comunis & aisiaintis infra villa de RussQ & ext pdce terre ptinetib3, Reddedo inde annuatim m' & hedib3 meis de se & hedib3 suis vel suis assignatis vj den' ad duos terminos statute8 scil ad nativitate Sci Johis Bapt. iij den' & ad festu Sci Michael iij denar' p oib3 serviciis reb3 & ilemandis. Et ego Henric' & hedes mei p'noiatas t'ras & ele Holt cu ptinentiis p'noiato Hugoi & hedib3 suis vel suis assignatis tra 5s hoies & femias imppetuu warantizabim. Ut igit' h donatio cessio & firmacio robur ppetue firmitatis obtuleat psenti carta sigilli mei imp'ssione corroboram, hiis testib3 Dno G. de Cheta, Robto de Hulton, Ric. de T'ford, Jordan de Rabi, Galfrido fit Luce, Rob. fit Leysig, Symoe fil Luc, Rogo fit Rand', Ric. fre ei Randulpho clico & aliis.—*Birch Evidences,* penes Sir John William Hamilton Anson, Bart.

Family Of Manchester.
(pp. 6, 7.J

1. — Sciant psentes & futuri q ego Witts fil Henr fil Houlot of Mamecestr dedi concessi & hac psenti carta mea confirmavi Jordano fil Witti de ffawfeld & heredib3 suis q"mdam ptem t're mee in villa de Russum, videlicet tres acras terre cu ptinentiis jacentes int' ter' Henr' de Trafford ex ut"q, pte que se extendunt in longitudine de t'ra Matild del Holt usq, in altam viam v'sus Stokeport, Habend & Tenend eidem Jordano & hedibus suis de dno capitali feodi libe quete bfie & in pace cu oinib3 libtatib3 & aysiamentis pdicf t're ptinentibus. Reddendo inde annuatim dco drio capitali tres denar' argent ad duos anni t'minos videlic. ad natat drii unii denar' & obolu & ad festum Sancti Johis Bapt'e unu denar' ct obolu

B B de quatuor denar' iu quibus pdcus Witts tenetur annuatim solnt pdco dno capitali. Et ego v pdcs Witts & heredes mei pdcam t'ram cii ptinenf suis sicut pdcm est pdco Jordano & heredib3 suis cont'omes gentes imppetuu warantizabim et defendem. In cui rei testimoniu huic scpto sigillu meu apposui, hiis testibus Alexo del Byrches, Galfrid de Strongwas, Witto de Honeford, Thom de Chorlton, Stepho de Redich & aliis. Dat ap Mamecestf die dnica px post festm Sci Mftin anno regni reg Edwardi vicesimo nono. — *Birch Evidences,* penes Sir John William Hamilton Anson, Bart.

2. — Sciant psentes & fluti q ego Johes de Annacotes fill Robti de Mammecesstf dedi concessi & hac psenti carta mea confirmavi Jordano fil Witti de ffalwefeld & hered' suis q"mdam ptem terre mee in t'ritorio de Russum scilicet totam pte meam de una cultura que vocat' Grenclowe field jacet int' t'ram Henrici de Traflbrd ex una pte & t'ram Witti fil Henrici de Mamecestr ex alta cu? unii capnd extendit se usq, ad regiam viam que se ad Ynce (?) ducit & aliud capnd extendit se usq, ad unam cult'am que vocat' le Somer Werkeddeffeld; et una dimid' acr' pti jacente in le Brodemedwe int' t'ram Henrici de Traflbrd ex ufq, pte et unu capnd se extendit usq, ad ripam que est subtus le Birchenewode & aliud capnd extendit se usq, ad Clayffeld. Hnd & tenenti pro me & hered meis de capitali dno dci tenemt sibi & hered' suis & assign' suis libe quete bene et in pace jure hereditar' integre & honorifice cu libera introitu & exitu & cu omib3 aliis aysiamtis & libfatib3 dce t're ubiq, spctantib3 5 Po bac aute donacoe dedit m' dcs Jordan qdam sumam pecunie p manib3. Et ego dcs Robfs & hered mei & assign mei totam pdcam t'ram & ptm cu suis ptinenc' ut pdcm est dco Jordano & hered & assign suis cont omes hoies & feminas p pdea suma pecne imppetuu warantizabim aquietabim et defendem. Et ut hec mea donaco & psentis carte mee conffirmaco rata & stabit pmaneat sigilli mea eam imp'ssione roboravi, hiis testib3 Rogo de Barlowe, Rico de Redich, Alex de Birches, Galfrido de Strongwas, Witto de Honford, Rogo de Denton, Thom de Cholrton & multis aliis. — *Birch Evidences,* penes Sir John William Hamilton Anson, Bart.

Seal: A lion rampant. Legend: s Iohi Db Ibernie.

Families Op Mosedon, Honford And Bexwick. *(PP. 7, S.J* 1. — Sciant psentes & ffuturi quod ego Henricus Mosedon dedi concessi & hac psenti carta mea confirmavi Matheo de Byrches &

heredibus suis totam ptem meam totius aque de Gorebroc sili3 de Halegateforde usq, Russeforde cum attachiacone stagni sui ubiq, usq, ad t'ram meam ubicumq, ei commodius fint infra pdcas divisas salva destruccone prati mei infra dcas divisas. Habend & Tenend de me & heredib3 meis sibi & heredibus suis libere quiete integre & in pace cu omib3 libtatib3 & omnimodis aysiamentis pdce aque, spectantib3 sine aliquo retenemento mei vel heredum meor', Reddendo inde annuatim m' & heredib3 meis de se & heredib3 suis una sagittam barbatam ferri die nativitatis Beati Johis Bapt. p omnib3 s'viciis s'claribu3 exaccoib3 & demandis predce aque cum stagno infra pdcas divisas ptinentib3. Et ego v pdcus Henricus & heredes mei totam ptem meam totius aque predce cum attachiacone eiusdem ubiq, infra pdcas divisas pdto Matho & heredib3 suis cont omes hoies & feminas imppetuu warantizabimus & defeudemus. In cuius rei testimonium huic psenti scpto sigillum meum apposui, hiis testib3 Rogo de Midilton, Alex de Pilkinton, Rico de Workedeley, Rico de Moston, Johe de Ayneswerthe, Tho. fil Galfr. fil Luc de Mamecest', Tho. Bexwic, Henr. de Byrches clico & aliis.— *Birch Evidences,* penes Sir John William Hamilton Anson, Bart.

2. — Ego Agnes ux Henr. de Honford dedi Rico f. meo ter' in Ruschun &c. q Matilda de Holt ten in noie dotis &c. ; rem. Galfr. fri ejusd Rici; rem. pdce Agneti &c. Test. Rico de Hulton, W de Radeclive, Rogo de Midleton, Rico de Redish, Jo de Hulton &c. — *Harl.* MSS. 2112, fo. 143. 3. — Sciant psentes et futuri q ego Rogerus Bexwik dedi concessi et hac psenti carta mea confirmavi Miloni Bexwik filio meo omia illa terras & tenta reddit' rev'coes et s'vicia cum suis ptinen jacent' in Grenelawe et Risshum in com Lancastr que nup pquesivi de Willo Heyld. Habend & tenend pdict' terras & tenta reddit' rev'coes et s'vicia cum omib3 et singlis suis ptin pfat Miloni Bexwik hered' et assignat' suis imppetmi de capit' dnis feod' illius p s'vicia indc debit' et de jure consuet'. Et ego v pfat Rogerus Bexwik et hered' mei omia pdict' terras et tenta reddit' rev'coes & s'vicia cum omib3 et singlis suis ptin pfat Miloni Bexwik filio meo hered' et assignat' suis contra omes gentes warrautizabim et imppetuu defendem p psentes. Ac insup sciant me pfat Rogerum Bexwik attornasse deputasse et in loco meo posuisse dilect' michi in Xpo Johem Bamford gen'osum et Jacobum Sbalcros meos veros & legittimos attornat' conjunctim & divisim ad intrand omia pdict' terras & tenta cu ptin et post talem ingressum inde p me et noie meo plenam et pacificam possessionem et seisinam pfat Miloni Bexwik ad deliband scdm vim formam et effectum hui prsentis carte mee inde ei confect' rat' & graf bent et hitur' totum et quicquid diet' attornat' mei noie meo fecrnt seu eor' alter fecit in pmissis. In cui rei testimoniu huic psenti carte mee sigillum meum apposui. Dat vicesimo octavo die Junii anno regni regis Henrici octavi post conquestum Anglie vicesimo secundo. — *Birch Evidences,* penes Sir John William Hamilton Anson, Bart.

Family Op Platt. *pp.* 12-24J *Platt Evidences penes Charles Carill Worthy Esq.* 1. — Notu sit 001103 tam p'sentib3 q"m futuris q ego Matheus filius Willi dedi et concessi et hac p'senti carta mea confirmavi t'ram de Plat hospitali de Jerlm in puram et ppetua elemosiuam cu pastara que ad Wytintonam p'tinet. Ego et her' mei p'dcam t'ram p'dco hospitali cont hoies univ'sos warantizabo, scilicet de magna fossa usq, ad finem inferiorem pne fosse usq, crux incidit in arbore et de pna fossa usq, iu goselache et p goselache usq, ad semita eite (?) que iacet int' Plat et Russhum et p semita eite (?) usq, in gorebroc et p gorebroc usq, ad maram Willi de Honford et sic usq, in magnam fossam. Test' Jordano de Diddesb, Hamel fil Onti et filii Rog. de Barlowe et Ric. Breton et Rob Diacon' et Hug. de Plat et Ric. et tota curia de Wydenton.

2. — Notu sit omib3 tam p'sentib3 futuris q ego Garii de Neopol prior frift hospital Jerlomit' in Anglia de coi assensu et voluntate frfn capitli nro concessi et hac p'senti carta confirmavi Rico de la More et her' suis t'ram de Bikerstath qua hem ex dono Ade til RadI et t'ram de Perr quam hem ex dono Willi Dolfini et t'ram de Grewinton halfsnede et duas bovatas t're de Ranchorior et passagiii de Ranchior et t'ram de Halctoii et t'ram de Plette qua hem ex dono Mathei filii WiHi et t'ram de Acton quam hem ex donacone Gilberti filii Radi et omcs t'ras quas hem de adquesitu ipius et quas ipe vel her' cius pot'unt pquirer' domui nre usq, ad Valencia dim marc' Tenendas et hendas de domo nra jur' hereditario liber' quiete et honorifice. Reddendo in singlis annis domui nre in thalamo nro apud London quatuor solidos esterlingor ad capitlm mm p festu Sci Michis p omib3 s'viciis et placitis et exaccoib3 ad nos indc p'tinentib3. Ita q fres nfi de Standee nullam sup ipm vel heredes suos heant potestate causandi eos vel auferendi pecuniam eor' nec alicui respondeant nisi nobis vel locu nrm tenentib3 apud London. Prefatus v Riciis et her' sui manntenebunt et regent una navem sup aqua de Merse apud Ranchorier in caritate quam J ones constabilar' Cestrie dederat aii Rico et her' suis ad istam elemosinam tenendam, ut omes qui Dei amore fnsitu p'fate aque petierint passagiu heant. In obitu v suo et heredu suor' similit' t'cia ps omiu catallor' suor' p salute aie sue domui nfe remanebit. Hiis testib3 fratre Alano, fre Wittmo capellano, fre Gilberto de Ver, fre Robto fit Rici, fre Gilberto de Wilton, fre Henr. de Dalby, fre Nicho de Cardinel, fre Wirlmo de yp", fre Gilberto, fre Ysaac, fre Samsone, Walto clico. Anno Incarnacois Millio centesimo nonagesimo. 3. — Sciant p'sentes et futuri q ego Wittus fil Rici de More dedi concessi et hac p'senti carta mea confirmavi Henr. fil Gilbti cum Cesilia fil mea et her' suis ab eadm pcreatis in libm maritagiu totam medietate t're mee de Plette et messuagia sua et una acram t're ad dictam messuagiam spectante sine ullo r'tenemeto cu omib3 p'tin, Habend sibi et her' suis pcreatis de me et her' meis libe quiete integr" et honorifice in bosco in plano in pcis in pasturis cu omib3 lib'tatib3 et asiamentis ad p'fata t'ram p'tinentib3. Ita q p'dcus Henr. et Cesilia et her' pcreati

sui tenebunt p'dcam t'ra de me et her' meis tam libe qua ego illam teneo de frib3 hospitalis Jerlm p't sex denar' quos p'dcus Henr' et her' sui reddunt annuatim michi et her' meis ad festu Sci Bartholomeu p omib3 s'vic's et consuctudine et exaccone. Ego siquidem Willmus et her' mei warantizabim p'dcam t'ram sicut illam quam dedi in libni mari This and the preceding deed are on the same parchment, which is headed " Copia carte original'." The first deed is endorsed " Hec carta p'dca apud Yeveley jux» Longeford in com' Derb'," and the latter " et hec carta p'x p'dca in manu Rob'ti Taliol de p'ochia de Wrenbury jux8 Abbathiam de Cumbremer' in com' Cestrie." tagiu cum Henr. et Cesilia fil mea et her' suis pcreatis cont» oes hoTes et feias warantizabunt et dependent imppetuu, Hiis testib3 Wittmo de Norton fre, Wittmo de Norros, Rogo de Middulton, Alexandr' de Pilkinton, Adm de Pennilbury, Jordano Norreis, Witto de Diddesbury, Matho clico et aliis.

Inscribed on the back of this deed is the following genealogical note: 4. — Univ'sis xpi fidelib3 ad quos ltte p'seutes p'ven'int fir Helias de Smethetun hmlis pr'or ffrm hosp' Jrtm in Anglia salm in dno. Nov'it univ'sitas v'ra nos de communi consilio et assensu totius capituli n'ri dedisse et concessisse et hac p'senti carta n'ra confirmasse Ric fil Ade de ffarnewurthe et heredib3 suis omem me dietatem t're n're de la Platte quam medietatem Adam clicus de nobis quondam tenuit. Habend et tenendam d'cam medietatem t're de la Platte de nobis sibi et hedib3 suis in hereditate libere et quiete bene et in pace cu omib3 commun et aessiamentis in pascuis in viis in semitis in aquis et in omib3 locis ubi cummuns vel aessiamentum dco tenemento pertinet vel p'tinere potuit; Reddendo inde aunuatim ipe et heredes sui domui nfe quatuor solidos argent' ad festum Sci Math p omib3 s'viciis et exacconib3 et con8uetudinib3 ad nos p'tinentib3 et in obitu suo et hcdum suor' t'ciam partem catallor' suor' mobilium et immobilium ubicunq, fuint inventa. Nos v d'cam medietatem t're de la Platte cu omib3 communis et aessiamentis sicut p'notatum est dco Ric fit Adc de ffarnewurthe et heredib3 suis cont omes homines et fferninas imppetuu warantizabimus quam diu donator illius domui n're illa pot'it warantizar'. Et ut hec n'ra donaco rata et stabilis pmaneat p'sentem cartam sigiH capituli n're roboramus, Hiis testibus Dno Ada de Bury, Diio Galfrid de Chetham, Dno Galfrid capttan, Ric de Trafford, Ric de Bondini', Rjc de Mostun, Heur. de la Platte et multis aliis.

5. — Sciant p'sentes et fut'i q ego RogS del Plat dedi concessi et hac p'senti carta mea confirmavi Elene filie Heur. del Plat duas acras terre jacentes in hameH del Plat in viH de Wythinton, videl't illas acrs qs Cecilia mat' mea recup'avit coram justiciar' dm' Reg' in banco p quoddm Bre q vocat' Cui vita que quidm d'ce acr' extendunt del Thornidiche usq, ad le Goselache, Hend et tenend eidm Elene et hedib3 suis et assignatis de capital driis feodi illius p s'vicia inde debita et consueta libe quiete et in pace cu oib3 juril3 lib'tatib3 et asiamentis p'dcc terr p'tinentib3. Et ego vero p'dcus Rog'us et hedes mei p'dcas duas acras t're cu p'tin in olb3 ut p'dcm est p'dcis Elene et hedib3 suis et assignatis contra omes gentes warantizabim et impp'm defendem. In cuj rei testimoniu huic p'senti carte sigillu meu apposui hiis testib3 Johe Cissor' de Mameestr, Thoma le Marchal, Robfo del Plat, Johe Bibby, Nicho clico et aliis. Dat' ap le Plat die Sabti px post fm Sci Andree ap'li anno regni reg' Edwardi decimo septimo. 6. — Omib3 xpi fidelib3 hoc septum visur' vel auditur', WiHs fil Hugois de Laghokf saltm in Dno. Novitis me remisisse relaxasse et oino p me et hedib3 meis imppet'm quietu clamasse'Robto fit Rici de farneworthe et hedib3 vel suis assignatis totu jus meu et clameu q hui vel aliquo modo here potui in medietate totius hamelli del Plat in viH de Wythinton que quid' medietas idem Rob's huit p successionem heditariam post mortem Rici de ffarneworthe p'ris sui, Ita scit3 q n ego p'dcus WiHs n hedes mei n aliq's alius noie nro aliq'd jur' vel clamei in p'dca medietate seu in pte ejusdem illi' hamelli de cet'o exig'e vel vindicare potim9 s'c't penit p hoc s'cm meu exclusi sim imppctuu. Et pr'tra ego p'des WiHs et hedes mei p'dcam medietate toti hamelli del Plat in 01D3 ut p'dcm est p'dco Robto et hedib3 vel suis assignatis cont' omes holes warantizabim. In cui rei testimoniu huic scpto sigillu meu apposui, Hiis testib3 Dnis Henr. de Trafforde, Rogo de Pilkynton militib3, Rico de Hulton, Johe de Hulton, Robto de Asshton, Robto de Grottoii, Nicho de Wyrkesworthe clico et aliis. Dat' ap le Plat die Jovis in crstino Sci Swythen epi anno regni reg' Edward fit reg' Edwardi octavo. 7. — Die Lune px ante festu Sci Andree ap'l i anno Dni Millesimo t'centes vicesimo qrto f'ca vent' int' Rogeru del Platte ex una p'te et Robertu fil Rici del Platt f ex alt'a pte sub hac forma q pastura que se extendit ab hostio dci Rogi usq, ad le Geldebrockf dividit int' dcos Rogti et Robtm, et fossatm q se extendit a vico usq, ad le Gelde broke p'dict' est totu sup pcelam dci Robti. Pret'a dcus RogS quiet clamavit p se et hede Robto et heredib3 suis totum jus suii et clamiu q habuit seu aliquo modo habere poterit in toto tenemeto a d'co fossato usq, ad Gelde hrocke int' vicu et le Herneflatte. Pret'a d'c's Rogg concessit Robto et heredib3 suis t'ciam pte suam in le name undecipherable una cu quadam butea jacente in Gosecroft in escambio p t'ra d'ci Robti jacente in le fal d'ci Rogi. In cui rei testimoniu huic p'senti sc'pto sigillu meu apposui, hiis testib3 Rogo dno de Barrlowe, Johe de Worthinton, Thoma le Marchal de Mameestr, Johe fre eius, Johe Bibby de Mamcestr et aliis. Dat' ap Lancastr die et anno supdcis. c c 8. — Sciant p'sentes et futuri q ego Elena fil Henr. del Platf dedi concessi et hac p'senti carta mea confirmavi Rico fil Robti del Platf un m acram t're cum p'tin jacentem in hamello del Platf in villa de Wythinton quam hui ex dono et feoffamento RogI del Plat que quidem acra t're jacet in quodam campo vocato le Bruches cujus unu capnd se extendit del Thomidiche usq, ad le Goselache, HenSam et tenendam p'dcam t'ram cu ptin pdco Rico et hedib3 de corpe suo pcreat' de capit' dnis feodi illius p

s'vicia inde debita et de jure consueta libe quiete bene et in pace cu omib3 lib-tatib3 et aysiamentis dce t're p'tinentib3 imppetuu. Et si contingat q idem Ricus obierit sine hede de corpe suo pcreato trie post decessum ipius Rici p'dca t'ra cu ptin integre remanebit Johi fratri ejusdem Rici et hedib3 de corpe suo pcreat', Tenend de capit' dnis feodi illius p s'vicia inde debita et de jure consueta imppetuu. Et si contingat q idem Jobnes obierit sine hede de corpe suo pcreato tiic post decessum ipius Jobis p'dca t'ra cu ptin integre remanebit Robto del Plat patri p'dicor' Rici et Johis hedib3 et assignatis suis Tenend de capit' dnis feodi illius p s'vicia inde debita et de jure consueta imppetuu. Et ego vero p'dca Elena et hedes mei p'dcam t'ram cu ptin p'dco Rico et hedib3 suis p'dcis et p'dco Job! et hedib3 suis p'dcis si idem Ricus obierit sine hede de corpe suo pcreato, et p'dco Robto et hedib3 suis si idem Johes obierit sine hede de corpe suo pcreato warantizabim conta omes hoies imp-petuu. In cuj rei testimoniu huic p'senti carte sigillu meu apposui, hiis testib3 Rogo de Barlowe, Henr. de Trafford, Johe le Taillour de Mamcestf, Rico fil Thome de Mamcestr, Thoma fil Rici de Bosedon, Robfo de Milkewalleslade, Thoma fil Alani de Aynesworthe et ali-is. Dat' apud le Plat die Jovis px post festu Sci lichis Archangli anno regni Edwardi reg' Angi t'eii a conquestu decimo septimo et regni sui t&ancie quarto. 9. — Sciant p'sentea et fut'i q ego Elena fil Henr' del Plat dedi concessi et hac p'senti carta mea confirmavi Johi fil Robti del Plat una acram t're cum ptin in villa de Withinton quam hui ex dono et feoffamento Rogi del Plat que quidem acra t're jacet juxta le Yeldehousdiche in hamello del Plat in quodam campo quod vocat' le Bruches cuj unu capnd se extendit del Thorni-diche usq, ad le Goselache. Hend et tenend p'dcam t'ram cu ptin p'dco Johi et heredib3 de corpore suo legitie pcreat' de capit' dnis foodi illins p s'vicia inde dehita et de jure consueta libe quiete bene et in pace cu omib3 lib'tatib3 et aysiamentis dce t're ptinentib3 imp-petuu. Et si contingat q idem Johes obierit sine herede de corpore suo legi-tie pcreat' tunc post decessum ipius Jo-his p'dca t'ra cu ptin integre remanebit Rico fratri ejusdem Johis et heredib3 de corpore suo legitie pcreat', Tenend de capit' dnis feodi illius p s'vicia inde debita et de jure consueta imppetuu. Et si contingat q idem Ricus obierit sine herede de corpore suo legitie procreato tunc post decessu ipius Rici p'dca t'ra cum ptin integre remanebit Robto del Plat patri p'dcor' Johis et Rici heredib3 et assignatis suis, Tenend de capit' dnis feodi illius p s'vicia inde debita et de ju-re consueta imppetuu. Et ego vero p'dca Elena et heredes mei p'dcam t'ram cu ptin p'dcis Johi Rico et RoMo et hered-ib3 suis warantizabim et defendem cont omes holes imppetuu in forma supdca. In cuj rei testimoniu huic psenti carte in-dentate sigillu meu apposui, hiis testib3 Henr' de Trafford, Rogo de Barlowe, Thoma fil Alani de Aynesworthe, Johe le Taillo de Mamcestr, Rico fil Thome le Mareschal de Mameestr, Thoma fil Rici de Bosedoii, Robto de Milke-walleslade et aliis. Dat' apud le Plat die Jovis px post festu Sci Michis Archangti anno regni reg' Edwardi t'eii post conquestum Angl decimo septimo et ffranc quarto. 10. — Ceste endanture faite en-tre Eleyne la fille Henry del Platf la puisnesse d'une pte et Robt del Platf d'autre pte testmoigne que come le dit Robf ad graunte a dite Eleyne p sa chartre endente une maea et dis3 acres de sa fre en Platf en la ville de Wythyng-ton a avoir et tenir a meisme cesty Eleyne a t'me de sa vie del avaunt dit Robt et de ses heris rendaunt dou3e den-ers p an sicome en la chartre endentee entre eux de ces faites plus pleinement est contenu. Lavaunt dite Eleyne voetf et graunte p lui q si ele soit en eyde a William fit3 Alisaundre del Bothe en ascune maSe ou p doner de ses lieus ou chateux ou p pole ou demplendre les tenement3 quels meisme cesty Eleyne re-couveri vers lavaunt dit William a Lan-castr' p assise de nouvele disseisine de-vaunt Mons. William Basset et ses com-paignouns Justices a assises pndre en le countie de Lancastr' assignes. Et de quels tenement3 meisme cesty Eleyne ad enfeffe lavaunt dit Robt et ses heris et ses assignes sicome p la chartre p lavaunt dite Eleyne a lavaunt dit Robert de ceo faite plus pleinemeut est contenu q a dong's bien lise al dit Robert et a ses heris et a ses assignes entrer les avaunt dit3 mees et t're et les retenir sann3 countre dit del avaunt dite Eleyne et ensement q la chartre endente de ceo faite ne soit de valu. Ensement sramcol? lavaunt dite Eleyne q a quel houre q ele liesse les avaunt dit3 tenement3 a ascun fors q al avaunt dit Robt ou a ses heris q a dong's bien lise al avaunt dit Robt et a ses heris dentrer les avaunt dit3 ten-ement3 et les retenir sann3 countredit del avaunt dite Eleyne et q ele soit os-hte de. chescun mani'e daccionn a de-maundre les tenement3 avauut dit3. Par quele graunte lavaunt dit Robt graunte p lui et p ses heris q si lavaunt dite Eleyne ne soit de pouver detenir les tenemen-t3 avant dit3 en sa meyne dcmeigne le dit Robt graunte po lui et p ses heris a prendre la Pre en sa meyn demeigne ou en la meyn des heris et rendronnt al dite Eleyne p tote sa vie dis south sous p an a deux t'mes del an cest a savoir la moitee a la feste de Seynt Michel larchangel et lautre moitee a la feste de Seynte Joh"n le Baptistre p oueles egales porciouns. A quele chose faire a loyalment p fourn-er lea avant dit3 Eleyne et Robt en-trechaungablement onnt mys leur seals. Ceux sonnt les tesmoignes Johan de Aynesworth, Adam de Hoppewode, Roger de Chaditron, Roger de Shotellesworth le puisne, et Thomas le fil3, Aleyn de Aynesworthe et autres. Done a Bury le dismeigne pchayn ap's la feste de Seynt Bartholomeu l'apostol, L'an du regne Edward roi d'Angle?re tierc3 puis le conquest dis et octoisme et de son regne de Fraunce quinte. . 11. — Sciant p'sentes et fut'i q ego Elena fil-ia Henrici del Plates junior dedi conces-si et hac p'senti carta mea confirmavi Robto del Plates hedib3 et assignatis su-is duo messuagia viginti et quatuor acras t're et una acram pti cu p'tin in Wythyngton que quidem ten d'ca Elena recupavi v'sus Wittm fil Alexi del Bothe p assiam nove disseie coram WiHo Basset et sociis suis Justic' ad as-sias nove disseie in com Lancastr' as-sign' capiend, Hend et Tenend oia p'dca ten cu suis p'tin p'fato Robto hedib3 et assignatis suis de capit' dnis feodi illius p s'vicia inde debita et de jure consueta libe quiete bene et in pace cu libo introitu et exitu et cu coia pasture et cu omib3 aliis p'tin dco teii p'tinentib3 in eade villa. Et ego vero p'dca Elena et hedes mei oia p'dca ten cu suis p'tin in omib3 sicut p'dcm est p'fato Robto hedib3 et assignatis suis cont omes holes warantizabim et imppetuu defendem. In cuj rei testimoniu huic p'senti carte sigillu meii apposui, hiis testib3 Nicho de Longeford milite, Henr. de Trafford, Robto fit Henr.? de Trafford militis, Jordano de Claydefi, Robto de Chorleton, Thoma de Holt, Robfo de Mylkwalslade et aliis. Dat' apud le Plates die Lune px post festu Sci Cuthbti epi anno regni Edwardi reg' Angt t'cii a conquestu decimo octavo et regni sui ffrancie quinto. 12. — Hec carta indentata testat' q Robtus del Plat dedit concessit et hac psenti carta sua indentata confirmavit Rico filio suo et heredi omia t'ras et ten sua cu edificiis que huit die confecconis psentiu in villa de Wythynton, Hend et Tenend omia p'dca t'ras et ten cu edificiis et cu ptin p'dco Rico et hered de corpore suo legitie pcreatis libe quiete bene et in pace cu omib3 libfatib3 et aysiamentis pdcis t'ris et ten cu edificiis in villa de Wythinton ptin' de capit' dnis feodi illius p s'vicia que ad p'dca t'ras et ten cu edificiis ptinent imppetuu. Et si contingat q p'dcus Ricus obierit sine herede de corpore suo legitie pcreaf tunc post decessum ipius Rici omia p'dca terre et ten cu edificiis et cu ptiu integre remaneant Johi fri ejusd Rici et hered de corpe suo legitie pcreatis Hend et Tenend omia p'dca t'ras et ten cu edificiis et cu ptin p'dco Johi de capit' dnis feodi illius p s'vicia que ad p'dca t'ras et ten cu edificiis ptin imppetuu. Et si contingat q p'dcus Johes obierit sine herede de corpe suo legitie pcreaf tunc post decessum ipius Johis omia p'dca terre et ten cu edificiis et cu ptiu' integf remaneant Robto fil Robti de Milkewalleslade juniori et hered masclis de corpe suo legitie pcreatis Hend et Tenend omia pdca t'ras et ten cii edificiis et cu ptin p'dco Robto fil Robti de capit' dnis feodi illius p s'vicia que ad p'dca t'ras et ten cu edificiis ptinent' imppetuu. Et si contingat q p'dcus RoWus fil Robti obierit sine herede tnascio de corpe suo legitie pcreat' tunc post decessum ipius Robti fil Robti omia p'dca t're et ten cu edificiis et cu ptin' integre remaneant Johi fil Robu de Milkwaleslade fri p'dco Robto fil Robu et hered masclis de corpe suo legitie pcreat' Hend et Tenend omia p'dca t'ras et ten cii edificiis et cu ptin p'dco Johi fit Robti de capi dnis feodi illi p s'vicia que ad p'dca t'ras et ten cu edificiis ptinent imppetuu. Et si contingat q p'dcus Johes fil Robti obierit sine herede masclo de corpe suo legitie pcreat ' tunc post decessum ipius Johis fil Robti omia p'dca t ' re et ten cu edificiis et cu p'tin integ' remaneant Robto fil A&e de ffernilegh de Sadulwrthffryth et hered masctis de corpe suo legitie pcreat' Hend et Tenend omia p'dca t'ras et ten cu edificiis et cu ptin p'dco Robto fil Ade de capit' dnis feodi illi p s'vicia que ad p'dca t'ras et ten cu edificiis ptinent imppetuu. Et si contingat q p'dcus Robtus fil Ade obierit sine hered mascto de corpe sno legitie pcreat' tunc post decessum ipius Robu fil Ade omia p'dca t're et ten cu edificiis et cu ptin integr' remaneant Wilto fil Edward Heth de Sadulworthfryth et hered masctis de corpe suo legitie pcreat' Hend et Tenend omia p'dca t'ras et ten cu edificiis et cu ptin p'dco Witto de capit' dnis feodi illius p s'vicia que ad p'dca t'ras et ten cu edificiis ptinent imppetuu. Et si contingat q p'dcus Wiltus obierit sine hered masctis de corpe suo legitie pcreat' tunc post decessum ipius With omia p'dca t're et ten cu edificiis et cu ptin integr' remaneant Margarete fit Robti del Plat et heredib3 masctis de corpe suo legitie pcreat' Hend et Tenend omia p'dca t'ras et ten cu edificiis et cu ptin p'dce Margarete de capit' dnis feodi ill? p s'vicia que ad pdca t'ras et ten cu edificiis ptinent imppetuu. Et si contingat q p'dca Margareta obierit sine hered mascto de corpe suo legitie pcreat' tunc post decessum ipius Margarete omia p'dca t're et ten cu edificiis et cu ptin rectis heredib3 ipius Robti del Plat integr' remaneant Hend et Tenend omia p'dca t'ras et ten cu edificiis et cu ptin p'dcis rectis hed ipius Robti del Plat de capit' dnis feodi illius p s'vicia que ad p'dca t'ras et ten cu edificiis ptinent imppetuu. Et p'dcus vero Robtus del Plat et hered sui omia p'dca t'ras et ten cu edificiis et cu ptin p'dco Rico et heredib3 de corpe suo legitie pcreat' ut p'dcm est, et ecia p'dco Johi fri ejusdm Rici et heredib3 de corpe suo legitie pcreat' ut p'dcm est, et ecia p'dco Robfo fit Robti et heredib3 masctis de corpe suo legitie pcreat' ut p'dcm est, et ecia p'dco Johi fit Robn et hered masctis de corpe suo legitie pcreat' ut p'dcm est, et ecia p'dco Robto fil Ade et hered masctis de corpe suo legitie pcreat' ut p'dcm est, et ecia p'dco WiHo et heredib3 masctis de corpe suo legitie pcreat' ut p'dcm est, et ecia p'dce Margarete et heredib3 masctis de corpe suo legitie pcreat' ut p'dcm est, et ecia rectis heredib3 ipius Robti del Plat cont oes gentes warantizabim et imppetuu defendem. In cuj rei testimoniu hviic p'senti carte indentate sigillu suum apposuit, hiis testib3 Nicho de Longeford chivaler, Tboma de Trafford, Rogo de Barlow, Thoma del Holt, Robto de Cborlton, Henr. fit Robt del Birches et aliis. Dat' ap Wythinton die Sabti px ante fm See Margarete virgis anno regni regis Edwardi t'eii a conquestu vicesimo t'cio regni vero firancie decimo. 13. — Pateat univ'sis p p'sentes me Robtm del Plat dedisse et vendidisse Rico fit meo et heredi omia bona mea mobilia et immobilia quecuq, bui die confecconis psentiu in villa de Wythynton. Ita vero q nec ego dcus Robfus nec executores mei nec aliquis alius noie nro seu jure nro aliquid juris vel clameu in pdcis bonis here exig'e vel vendicare pofm9 infitm? ac ab omni accone sim exclusi imppetuu. In cuj rei testimoniu p'sentib3 sigillu meu apposui. Dat' apud Wythynton die Sabf i px ante fni See Margarete virginis anno regni regis Edwardi fen a conquestu vicesimo t'cio regno vero firancie decimo. 14. — In noie Dei amen. Anno dni Mccc sexageso die Veneris in fasto Sci Mauri Abbat' Ego Robart de Platte do testamct meu iu hnc mod. Impprimis lego aiam mea Deo et be Marie et oib3 scis et corp' meu ad sepcliend in simiterio Macest', et meli auer' coram corpe meo in noie mortuar' ad fidelit' ministrandfh. Istos constituo executores meos scilicet Johm filiu meu et Loretam uxor" meam ut ministrat oia bona mea sicut meli aie mee viderit. In cui rei testimoniu huic testameto sigiH meu apposui.

Endorsed: Ut hoc testamet pbatii fact' cora decano Macest? & administr' honor' dat' fuit ex'b3. In cu rei test' sigillu offii' i nfi psentib3 apposuim. Dat' Macestf in vigilia Sci Mathie ap'li anno Dni Mccc sexageio.

15. — Sciant p'sentes & futuri q ego Johnes del Plat dedi concessi et hac p'senti carta mea confirmavi Johi le fiytheler, Wittmo le fiytheler, Johi de Poynton, Wittmo Davie, Rico Braybon capltis, Nicho & Ade fil meis & Johi & Rico fit Rici del Plat omia t'ras & ten, pta, redditus & s'vicia cu edificiis & cQ omib3 suis p'tin que hui die confecconis p'senciii in hamello del Plat in villa de Withyngton, Hend & Tend omia p'dca t'ras & ten, pta, redditus & s'vicia cu edificiis & cu omib3 suis p'tin p'fatis Johi le fiytheler, Wittmo le fiytheler, Johi de Poynton, Wittmo Davie, Rico Braybon capltis, Nicho & Ade fit meis & Johi & Rico fit Rici del Plat her & assignatis suis libe quiete integre bene & in pace de capitalib3 dnis feodi illi p s'vicia inde debita et de jure consueta imppetuu. Et ego v p'dcus Johes del Plat et her mei omia p'dca t'ras et ten, prta, redditus & s'vicia cu edificiis et cu omib3 suis p'tin p'fatis Johi de fiytheler, Wittmo le fiytheler, Johi de Poynton, Wittmo Davie, Rico Braybon capltis, Nicho et Ade fit meis et Johi et Rico fit Rici del Plat her' et assignatis suis cont omes gentes warantizabim et imppetuu defendem. In cuf rei testimoniu huic p'senti carte sigillu meu apposui hiis testib3 Johne de Radeclif de Chadurton, Robfo de Chorlton, Ad de Barlawe, Johiie de Neuton & Henrico le Marshal de Mamcestf et aliis. Dat' apud le Plat die Sal&i pxia post festu Sci Andree ap'li anno regni regis Edwardi t'cii a conquestu Anglie quadgesimo octavo. 16. — Sciant p'sentes et futuri q ego Johes del Plate dedi concessi et hac p'senti carta mea confirmavi Galfro filio Johis Edmundson le clerke &

Alonie filie mee totam t'ciam ptem omi t'rar' et tenemetor' meor' cu ptin suis que hui seu aliquo modo here pofo infra comitatu Lancastr Hnd et Tend totam p'dcam p'tem

D D omi pdcor t'rar' et ten cu omib3 ptin suis pfatis Galfro et Alonie et hedib3 int' eosd de corpib3 eordm Galfri et Alonie lie legitime pcreatis de me ad totam vitam mei p'dci Johis sine omi s'vicio sclari exaccone et demand. Ego vero p'dcus Johes del Plat et hedes mei totam p'dcam t'ciam ptem omi p'dcor' terrar' et ten cu omib3 ptin suis p'fatis Galfro et Alonie et hedib3 int' eosdm Galfrm et Alonia lie legitime pcreatis ad totam vitam meam cont omS gentes warantizabim. In cu'? rei testfn huic p'senti carte sigillu meu apposui hiis testib3 Badpho de Badcliff, Johiie de Badcliff de Chadurton, Johfie de Badcliff de Ordessatt, Henr' de CromptoS, WiHo del Crosse et multis aliis. Dat' apud le Plat die Martis in festo translacois Sci Thome martiris anno regni regis Bici sedi post conquestu septio.

17. — Pateat univ'sis p psentcs me Nichm filiu Johis del Plat dedisse concessisse Bobto Colayn capellano omia bona niea et catalla in le Plat in villa de Wythington. Ita v nee ego p'des Nichus nec her' mei nee aliquis alius noie nro aliqua accon in p'dcis bonis seu catatt de ceto exig'e vel vendicare pot'irn ac ab om'i accoe sim exclusi imppetuu. In cui rei testimoniu psentib3 sigillu meu apposui. Dat' apud le Plat in villa de Wythington die dnica px post festu Sci Cedde epl anno regni reg' Bici sedi post conquestu Anglie q"rto decio. 18. — Sciant psentes et futuri q ego Nichus filius Johis del Plat dedi concessi et hac psenti carta mea confirmavi Bobfo Colayn capellano oia t'ras et ten mea cu ptin in le Plat in villa de Wythington, Hend et Tenend omia p'dca t'ras et ten cu ptin p'dco Bobio her' et assign suis libere quiete integre bene et in pace de capital dnis feodi illius p s'vicia inde debita et de jure consueta imppetuu. Et ego v p'des Nichus et heredes mei omia p'dca t'ras et ten cu ptin p'dco Bobto her' et assiguatis suis cont» omes gentes warantizabim9 imppetuu. In cur rei testimoniu huic p'senti carte mee sigillu

meu apposui hiis testib3 Rado de Prestewyche, Rado de Barlawe, Wittmo Bolder, Johne de Strangeways et Rico Bybby et aliis. Dat ' apud le Plat die dnica px post festu Sci Cedde epi anno regni regis Rici scdi post conquestii Anglie quarto decio.

Seal: Green wax; Device — a shield vair placed obliquely, its sinister chief surmounted by a helmet from which spring two standards. Legend: " Philipe de Premieres." 19. — Sciant psentes et futuri q ego Robtus Colayn capellanus dedi concessi et hac psenti carta mea indentata confirmavi Nicho filio Johis del Plat omia t'ras et ten mea cu ptin que hui ex dono et feoffamento p'dci Nichi in le Plat i villa de Wythington, Hend et Tenend omia p'dca t'ras et ten cu ptin suis p'dco Nicho et her' de corpe suo legitie pcreaf libere quiete beue et in pace de capitalib3 dnis feodi illius p s'vicia inde debita et de jure consueta imppetuu. Et si contingat q p'dcs Nichus obierit sine her' de corpe suo legitie pcreat ' volo q omia p'dca t'r et ten cu p'tin suis remaneat Alone sorori p'dci Nichi et her' ipius Alone de corpe suo legitie pcreat ' Hend et Teneud omia p'dca t'ras et ten cu ptin p'dce Alone et her' de corpe suo legitie pcreat ' libere quiete bene et in pace de capitalib3 dnis feodi illius p s'vicia inde debita et de jure consueta imppetuu. Et si contingat q p'dca Alona obierit sine her' de corpe suo legitime pcreat ' volo q omia p'dca t'r et ten cu ptin remaneant Emmote ux'i Jolns del Slade et her' ipius Emmote de corpe suo legitime pcreat ' Hend et Tenend omia p'dca f ras et ten cu ptin p'dce Emmote et her' de corpe suo legitime pcreat ' libe quiete bene et in pace de capital dnis feodi illius p s'vicia inde debita et de jur' consueta imppetuu. Et si contingat q p'dca Emmota obierit sine her' de corpe suo legitime pcreat ' volo q omia p'dca t'r et ten cu ptin remaneant Johi del Plat juniori dco filio Rici del Plat filii Robu del Plat et her' ipius Johis de corpe suo legitime pcreat' Hend et Tenend omia p'dca t'ras et ten cu ptin p'dco Johi del Plat juniori et her" de corpe suo legitie pcreat' libere quiete bene et in pace de capitalib3 dnis feodi illius p s'vicia inde debita et de jur' consueta imppetuG. Et si contingat q p'dcs Johes del Plat junior obierit sine her' de corpe suo legitie pcreat' volo q omia p'dca t'r et ten cu ptin rectis her' p'dci Nichi integre rem'eant Hend et Tenend omia p'dca t'ras et ten cu ptin pdcis rectis her' libe quiete bene et in pace de capitalib3 dnis feodi illius p s'vicia inde debita et de jur' consueta imppetuii. Et ego v p'dcs Robtus Colayn et her' mei oia p'dca t'ras et ten cu 01D3 ptin suis p'dco Nicho et her' de corpe suo legitie pcreat' ut p'dcm est, et ecia p'dce Alone et her' de corpe suo legitie pcreat' ut p'dcm est, et ecia p'dce Emmote et her' de corpe suo legitie pcreat' ut p'dcm est, et ecia p'dco Johi del Plat juniori et her de corpe suo legitim pcreat' ut p'dcm est, et eciam p'dcis rectis her' ipius Nichi ut p'dcm est cont omes gentes warantizabim imppetuii. In cui rei testimoniu huic psenti carte indentate sigillu meu apposui hiis testib3 Radulpho de Radecliff milite, Henrico de Trafford, Radulpho de Prestewyche, Johne de Barlowe et Radulpho de Barlowe et aliis. Dat' apud le Plat in villa de Wythingtoii die Ven'is px post festu Sci Gregorii pape anno regni reg' Rici scdi post conquestii Anglie quarto decimo.

20. — Sciant psentes et futuri q ego Nichiis del Platte dedi concessi et hac psenti carta mea indentata confirmavi Rado de Radeclif militi et Rado fil ejus omia mesuagia t'ras et ten mea cu ptin in le Platte in villa de Wythyngtori except' uno mes' et duab3 acris t're vocat' Goscrofthous et una pcella fre vocat' le Medhap, Hend et Tenend omia p'dca mes' t'ras et ten cu ptin pMcis Rado et Rado at t'mnm vite p'dci Radi de Radeclif milit' salvo Wilhno del Byrches et hered suis unam via ulta p'dcam t'ram cii curro suo et oib3 aliis car'agiis suis a domq dci Witti usq, ad coem viam in Risshum. Redendo inde annuati michi hered et assign' meis p p'mos octo annos post dat' p'sent' viginti solidos argenti ad festu nativit' Sci Johis baptist' et natal dni p equales porcoes et faciend capitalib3 dnis feodi illius s'vicia inde debita et de jure consuet' et redendo inde annuati michi et hered meis p quolifo anno quo p'dci Radi et Radi teneant et habeant p'dca mes' fras et ten cu p'tin ulta p'dcos octo annos decem marcas argenti ad festa p'dca p equales porcoes et faciendo capital dnis feodi illius s'vicia inde debita et de jure cons'. Et si contingat p'dcm annuale viginti solidi ad alique t'mnm quo solvi debent a retro esse in pte vel in toto seu p'dcm annuale redditu decem marcar' ad alique t'mnm quo solvi debent aret' esse in pte vel in toto et p viginti dies px sequ alique t'mnm p'dcm q tnc bene liceat michi p'fato Nicho hered et assign meis in p'dcis mes' t'ris et ten cu ptin inre et ea in statu meo p'stino retinere et pacifice possidere sine concencoe p'dci Radi et Radi seu alicui alt'ius et p'dci Radus et Radiis sustentabunt omes domos supd'cas t'ras et ten edificat' et eas in adeo bono statu seu meliori quo eas receperunt ad finem t'mni sui dimittent. Et ego v p'dcus Nichiis et hered mei omia p'dca mes' t'ras et ten cu ptin p'dcis Rado et Rado ad t'mnm vite p'dci Radi de Radeclif milit' in forma p'missa cont omes gentes warantizabim et defendem. In cui rei testimoniu huj carte mee indentate sigillu meu apposui. Dat' apud Wythyngton die dnica px post ffn Ascencois dni anno regni reg' Ric' scdi sexto decimo. 21. — Sciant p'sentes et futuri q ego Nichiis del Platte dedi concessi et hac psenti carta mea confirmavi Thome de Hultoii rectori ecclie de Bury omia t'ras et ten mea cu omib3 suis ptin in hamella de Russhu in villa de Wythyngton, Hend et Tenend omia p'dca terras et ten cu omIb3 suis ptin p'fato Thome her' et assignat' suis libe quiete bene et in pace de capital dnis feodi illi p s'vicia inde debita et de jure consuet'. Et ego v p'dict Nichus et her' mei omia p'dct terr' et ten. cu oib3 suis ptin p'fato Tbome her' et assignat' suis cont omes gentes warantizabim et imppetuu defendem. In cui9 rei testimcn huic psenti carte mee sigillu meu apposui, testily Rado de Stanelay milit', Johe de Ashton milit', Johe de Hulton, Edmudo de Workesley, Johe de Baumfort et aliis. Dat' apud Ruschu die dnica px post fin Sci Cedde epi anno regni reg' Henr' qnti post conquestni Anglie p'mo. 22. — Sciant p'sentes et futuri q ego Thomas de Hulton rector ecclie de Bury dedi concessi et hac p'senti carta mea confirmavi Rico filio Nichi del Plat et Ka?ine uxi ejusd et heredib3 int' eosd lie legitime pcreatis dimidia p'tem uni campi qui vocat' le Plat fold cu oib3 suis ptin que hui ex dono et feoffameuto p'dict' Nichi del Plat in le Plat in villa de Wythyngtoii cuj unu capfit extendit se ad domii Edi de Workesley et aliud in le Rissbu Broke, Hend et Tend p'dca dimidia p'tem p'dcti campi cu oib3 suis p'tin p'fat' Rico et Ka?ine uxi ejusd et heredib3 int' eosd lie pcreatis libe quietc bene et in pace de capital dnis feodi illi p s'vicia inde debita et de jure consueta imppetuu. Et ego v p'dict Thomas de Hulton rector ecclie de Bury et heredes mei p'dicta dimidia p'tem p'dcti campi p'dict Rico et Ka?ine et heredib3 int' eosd lie legitime pcreatis ut p'dictu est contra omes gentes warantizabim et imppetuu defendem. In cui rei testimoniu huic p'senti carte mee sigillu meu apposui hiis testib3 Ed mo de Trafford, Johe de Hulton de ffarneworth, Johe de Trafford sen' et multis aliis. Dat' apud le Plat in villa de Wythyngton die M'curii px ante festu Sci Nichi epi a regni regis Henrici quinti post conquestu Anglie tercio. 23. — In x sibi... Johannis Platt & Constancie cosortf? sue ftY Jacob frm mino P'ston Gardian & s'rv servus salt'm & p 25. — In noie Dni amen. Ego Ricardus Plat Anglicus scutifer lego seu contribuo aiam mea Deo oipotenti & beate Marie virgini & omib3 scis & reliuquo corpus meu seu cadaver vermib3 atq, sepeliri in pro sci s samtini foro men Dioc' Malden. cupimus q de bonis michi a Deo collate p salute aie mee pvide. P'mo facio seu ordino test' seu ultiam volu'tem in modum qui sequitur. Primo volo & cupio q malefacta mea atq, debita si po possibile sit restaurentur ac eciam emendentur. Deinde ea que debeo & legata mea infra scripta, volens et ordinans q si aliquid residm inventu fuit ultra ea que distribuo in fine dier' meor' q p manm executoris nri Johnis Plat filii mei disponatur et ordinat meliori modo q ei p salute mea q vidit' exped'i. Primo do & lego eccie p'd' in qua corpus meu p mic' jacet seu requiescit unu nobile auri p sepultura mea. Post meo fessori vero

Johani Richebery seu aie mee medico tria nobilia auri. Itf Gaufrido filio meo quadra nobilia cedo, & residm volo & ordino q p manus executoris Johns Plat filii mei disponat & ordinef & ipm stituo Johnm Plat executore meu, dans & cedcns ei executori meo plenam p'tatem & madatum spale omia & singla p'missa exeque'di augendi c'di ac eciam defalcandi & in melius disponedi si ncce fuit put executor meus legitime stitutus pot'it & debuerit p salute aie mee face. Volo & ordino q istud test'm seu ultima voluntas duret usq, ad imppetuum. In cui9 rei testimoniu sui acta eit' hec cora Johe Richebery pbro et in domo habitacionis dicti testatoris p'ntib3 Johe Gauwen & Roberto Boston, Johe Nuehyc cu plib3 aliis testib3 fide dignis ad p'missa vocatf piterq. rogatf. Act' anno Dni Mccccxxxix die quarta meg Septebris. J. Ruschebery.

Seal, pendant, of greenish wax, vesica-shaped, bearing in a three-gabled niche a Priest or Bishop in vestments or robes, perhaps mitred, holding in his left hand a palm branch, or rather an aspergam or sprinkler. Legend in Lombardic capitals: Sigillcm CURIE ECCLIE SCI PETRI SOI8TAMECO.

26. — Sciant p'sentes et futuri qi ego Johes del Plat concessi tradidi et ad firma dimisi Katarine nup ux'i Rici del Plat unm mesuag vocat' Goscrofthous cum quodTM orreo et duab3 acris t're et uno gardino p'dcti mesuag' p'tinent in le Plat in hamella de Risshum, Hend et Tend eidm Ka?ine ad t'minm vite sue, Reddendo inde annuati p'dco Johi hered et assignat' suis quatuor solid' legal monete ad festu Nat. Sci Johis Bapt' p omib3 s'viciis. Et si contingat p'dict reddit' a retro esse in pte vel in toto ad festu p'dcm q tiic bene liceat p'fat' Johi hered et assign suis in p'dco mesuag' distring'e et districoes sic capt' asportarc et penes se retinere quousq, de p'dco reddif omes arreras ejusd fu'unt eidm Job! hered seu assignat' suis plenar' fuit satisflon. In cui rei testimoniu huic p'senti scr'pto meo sigillu meu apposui hiis testib3 Rado Birches, Robto Byrches, Witto Hunt et multis aliis. Da apud le Plat xxvj die Augusti anno regni reg' Henr' sexti post conquestu vicesimo octavo. 27. — Frater RicuS minist' dom Sci Robfi juxta Knaresburgh Ordis see t'nitatis et Redempcois captiof qui snt icarcati incarcerati p fide Jhu x a paganis Johni Plat et Constancie ux' sue saltfii et sincam in dno caritatem. Cum i p'vilegiis aplicis p sacsanctum sedfn apHcam nob et ordini nri p'dicto ab antiq's tempib3 indultis et p eandem eodm de novo canoice cSfirmatis que cet'a qdm spaba tineant indulta tiuere sbsequentf Dinib3 v'e peccantib3 & cofess qui adsu fee n tacie3 dci ordis man vorrexint' adint'ees sex anos & octoginta dies de i mota peia relaxim. Eciam cocedim q oes cofratres et cosorores dci ordis qui dedint c'tam p ? porcionem honor' suor" et annuati frat'b3 v'l nu ars eiusdem ordis bnficia q sol'int possint S elig'e annuati frat'b3 v'l nnors eiusdem ordis bnficia p sol'it possint S elig'e annuati ydoneu p'sb'um cu cofessore qui eor' cofcssionib3 dil'get auditis eis p comiss peia i pendc valeat salutare n taha sint pp que sedes aptica E E sat iuxta cosut de se q'lib3 cosuet habit se'psum Richo frat' nuatis & eidm sepult'am ecia facit n5 neque co q'cuq, morte moriat' n noiata sint excoit. Si quis bnfactor infra ann moriat' de oib3 pccatis suis ve' cotcis & cofess' est de nfa gra spali absolut ca de abusionib3 no obstante. Nos vfe devocois qua frat' nctati dicti ordis hmtic postulat' macipari s'viciu cosid'antes afft'm vos in cbfratre & cdsorore n'ri ordis te nove p'sonam aute nob indulta admHam & cois dun ve' dictis & aliis p'vilegiis nfi ordis cofratib3 emseru indultis scdm forma & essenc eordm libe p finam vrox max ad saltm. Adiam isup vob bnficiu dco gra spati p cu in nfo cSventuali ca rey obitum vfum p'sonem fca f'int exhibico trar eadm p vob net comendaco que p fratfy nfis defunctis ibm fieri cosvent. In cui rei testimon sigillu nrm p'sentib3 e appensu. Dat' domo nro p'dicto anno dni Millmo cccc l vj.

Endorsed: Aucte dei pfis oipotetf & beor Sci Pet'i & Pauli aptor ei de aucto toti mat'is ecclie & papal indulgecie m» in hac pte missa ego absolvo te ab o'ib3 pecat' tuis oblit' de quib3 velles fiteri si tue occurrerent memorie & semel in vita de oib3 casib3 sedi aptice quomodolibt' reservatf & de quib3 sedes ipa cet' inc'to sulenda. Aucte dni pape pii sccudi absolvo te eciam articto mortf plena remissione omiu pecor' tuor' in *qntu* claves ecclie se extedt aucte istar' trar' aplicar' tibi do & cedo in noie p'ris &c.

28. — Sciant presentes & futuri q nos Cnstancia nup uxor Johis Platte & Ricus Platte filius & heres p'dict Johis & Cnstancie dedim concessim9 & hac presenti carta nfa indentat' confirmavim Wittmo Addeshede de Mamcestr' unm burgagiu nfm jacens in le Milnegate infra villam de Mamcestre inf tenement' Johis Bradford ex una pte & tenement' p'dict Rid modo in tenura uxis Nichi Shelm'dyn ex alt'a parte & continens in longitudine ab alta via usq, ad aquam de Irke quod quid'm burgagiu modo est in tenura p'dicti Wilh Addeshed. Hcnd & Tenend p'dict' burgagiu cu omIb3 comoditatib3 libtatib3 & aliis suis p'tin p'fat "Wittmo heredib3 & assignat' suis imppetuu. Reddendo inde annuati nobis p'fat' Cnstanc & Rico heredib3 & assignat' nris septem solidos legalis monete Anglie ad ffesta Natalis Dni & Nat' Sancti Johis Bapt' p equales porciones, et capit' Dnis feodi iH annuati duodecim denar' ad ffest' diet ville de Mamcestr' visitat' & consuet'. Et si contingat diet' reddit' septem solidor' a ret esse in pte vel in toto ad aliquod ffest' quo solvi debeat & p viginti dies extunc px sequent' tunc bene liceat nobis p'fat Cnstan2 & Rico heredib3 & assignat' nfis in diet' burgagio distringe & districciones sic capt' abducc asportare effugare impcare & penes nos retinere quousq, de p'dict, reddit' cum arreragiis eiusd'm sique fuint plenar' fu'imus satisffact'. Et si contingat diet' reddit' septem solidor' a ret esse in pte vel in toto ad aliquod ffest' quo solvi debeat & p quadraginta dies extunc px sequent' et sufficiens districcio in diet' burgag inveniri non pot'it tunc bene liceat nobis p'dict' Cnstancie & Rico heredibus & assignat' nris in diet' burgagiu cum ptin reintrTe rehabere & in pristino statu retiner' hac carta & seisin a inde hit in aliquo non obstant'. Et nos vero p'dict' Cnstanc & Ricus & heredes nostri p'dict ' burgagiu cum omnibus libtatib3

fraunchesiis & aliis eius ptin p'fat Wittmo heredibus & assignat' suis in forma p'dict' contra omes gentes warrantizabimus acquietabim & imppetuum defendmus. Et ult'ius nov'itis nos p'fat' Cnstancia & Ricum attornasse & in loco nfo posuisse dilectfn nobis in xpo Thoma Bradford capellanii ac vicariu collegii de Mameestre & Henricum Leylond fideles attornat' nros con' & di ad deliband pro nobis & noib3 nris p'fat' Willmo plenam & pacificam possessions & seisinam de & in p'dict' burgagiu cu ptin s'cdm vim forma & effcm p'sent' carte nre indentat' rat' & grat' hent & hitur' quicquid iidm attornat' nri noie nro fecint seu co alt' fecit in p'missis. In cui rei testimoniu huic p'senti carte nre indentat' sigilla nfa apposuim9 hiis testibus Thoma Olgrevc, Johii Rudde, Johe Bradford, Radulpho Prowdeluffe, laurencio Hulmc & aliis. Dat' duodecimo die Augusti anno regni regis Henrici septimi post conquestum Anglie quinto. 29. — This endentnre made betwene Robt Mascy son & heire of Edward Mascy gentilman Cnstance late the wiff of John Platte and Ric' Platte his son opoii that one ptie, and Laurence Kyrkhalgh of Manchestr' opon that oy ptie, — Wittenessith that the said Laurence grauntes by thes p'sentes to wedde and take to wiff Cnstance Mascy sust of the said Robt afor the ffest of Saynt Bartholomew next to come aft the date herof if the said Cnstance Mascy will then aggree, ffor the which the said Robt Mascy guntes to pay or cause to be paied to the said Laurence or his assignes xiiij mrcs of leale money of Euglond in man' & forme folowyng, that is to witte yerely xiij iiij at the ffestes of the nativite of Saynt John the Baptist & the birthe of oure Lord by even porcions duryng x yeres unto such tyme as the said x mrcs be fully content & paied. And the saides Cnstance late the wiff of John Platte & Ric' Platte graunte by thes p'sentes that the said Laurence shall have & yerely recyve xxvj viij of such tenntes as yai have assigned hym within the towne of Mamchestr' duryng the t'me of v yeres next suying the date herof, that is to witte unto the tyme the said Laurence have receyved of the said teniftes x mrcs, and ov'r this the said Robt Mascy grauntes by thes p'sentes that he shall make or cause to be made a sure and a lawfull astate of all the londes and tencmentes, rentes, rev'sions & s'vices w yaire appurtennce that the said Robt now has or stondes seased of or may have or stonde seased of within the counties of Lancastr' & Chestr' or oy places within the realmes of England or Irland to iij certen psons by the said Robt Mascy & Laurence to be named, To have and to holde to the said certen pscns yaire heires & yaire assignes to th'entente that the saides feoffees shall make or cause to be made a sufficiant & a lawfull astate to the said Robt Mascy & to the heires of his bodic lawfully begetten of all the saides londes & tenementes, rentes, rev'sions & s'vices w yaire appurteiince. And if it happen the said Robt Mascy wtoute heires of his bodie lawfully begetten to discesse that then all the said londes & tentes, rentes, rev'sions & s'vice imediatly aft the discesse of the said Robf shall descende, rev'te, remayii or come to the said Ciistance Mascy sust of the said Robt & to the heires of hir bodie lawfully begetten, dower or dowers of wiff or wiffes of the said Robt alwayes except; and for defaute of heires of the said Ciistance, that then all the said londes, tenementes, rentes, rev'sions & s'vices, except before excepted, to remayn to the right heires of the said Rob't for ev'; and thes astates to be made afor the ffest of the nativite of Saynt John the Baptist next to come aftr' the date herof. Also the said Robt grauntes that he & ij sufficiant p'sons wt hym shall be bounden to the said Laurence by yaire obligacion of C mrc, which obligacon shall have such condicon that if the said Robt opon his ptie well & truly holde, kepe & pforme all man' of grauntes & coviintes comprised in thes endentures, that then that obligacion be voide & elles to stonde in strength & effect. In witenesse wherof to thes p'sent endentures the pties aforsaid enfchaungeably have sett yaire scales, thes wittenesse Ric' Bexwik th'elder, Henr' Leylond, Rog' Sondeforth & oy. Yeven the xxiiij day of July the yere of the regne of Kyng Henr' the vij' aft' the conquest of Englond the ix. 80. — Sciant presentes et futuri q ego Johes Platt de Rysshulme in com Lane. gen'os' dedi concessi et hac pnti carta mea indentat' confirmavi Jahamie Lawrance relict' Jacobi Lawrance nup de Mamcest' defunct' duo messuag' sive teiit nuc in sepalib3 tenuris sive occupatiob3 Margaret' relict' Edmundi Duncuthley et Radulphi Duncuthley in Risshulm in coin Lancast' predict' et duas clausuras sive p'cellas terr' vocat' Hallefelde et Brucfelde nuc in tenura sive occupacoe mei predict' Johis Platt Habend et tenend omia et singla predict' messuag' t'ras ct tenta ac alta premiss' cu oib3 et singtis suis ptinen prcfatc Jahane Lawrance et assiguat' suis p t'mno vite ipius Jahane in noie totius dotis et junctur' eidm Jahane contingent. Et ego vero p'dict Johes Platt et bered' mei omia predict messuag sive tenta cu duabus clausur' sive pcellis terre predict' ac cet'a premissa cu suis ptin' prefat' Jahanne Lawrence durant' tota vita naturali ipius Jahanne in forma predict' cont oes gentes warantizabim9 et imppetm defendem p presentes. Ac insup sciatis me prefat' Johem Platt attornassc deputasse et in loco meo posuisse dilectos michi in Chro Thoma Jackeson ct Radulpbu Birche de Ma'cest' meos veros et lcgittimos attornat conTM et di an intrand p me et in noie meo in oia et singla predict' messuag terr' et tent ac cet'a premiss' cu 0105 et singtis suis ptin. Et post talem ingress' inde p me et in noie meo plena et pacific! possessions et seisina prefat' Jahanne Lawrance ad deliberand' s vim forma et effectu hujus p'ntis carte mee indentat' ei confect Rat et grat' hent et habitur' totu et quicquid ent' attornat' mei noie meo fecint seu eoru alt' fecit in premissis. In cujus rei testTM huic present' carte mee indentat' sigillu mcu apposui. Dat' tercio die Junij anno regni Edwardi Sexti Dei gra Anglie ffrauncie et Hib'nie regis fidei defensoris ac in t'ris sub xpo ecclie Anglica et Hibernie an'dict' capitis supremi primo. 31. — Sciant psentes et futuri q ego Johes Plate de Ryssholme in com Lane' gen'osus p cert' causis me moventib3, dedi concessi et hac p'senti carta mea indentat' confirmavi Wittmo Plate filio meo juniori quandam messuag' sive pcella terre jacent' sive existent' in Rysholme p'dict' in com p'dict' que extendit unu acru et dimidiu terre vocat' the Crofte sup Ryssholme Grene et nuc in tenur' et occupacoe mei p'dct Job! Plate, Hend et Tend p'dict messuagiu sive pcella terre cu omib3 et singtis suis ptin p'fat Wittmo et assignat' suis durante vita ipius Wittmi. Reddendo inde annuatim michi p'dict Job! hered et assignat' meis unu granu pepi ad festu natalis dni si petit p omib3 reditt et s'vic pviso semp q p'dict Willm Platte fecit s'viciu suu ad p'dict' Johem Plate et hered suos tamdiu p'fat' Willm Platte & assignat' snis habuerit sive occupaverit p'dict mesuag' sive pcella terre, et si p'fat Willm9 negat facer' s'viciu suu ad p'dict Johem et hered suis q tunc bene licebit michi p'dict' Johi Platte hered et assignat' meis in p'dict' messuagiu sive pcella terre cu ptin rehere p rehabere et in p'stino statu nro ea retinere hanc psenti carta indentat' et seisina inde delibat' ulla modo non obstant'. Et ego vero p'fat Johes Plate & hered mei omia p'dict' messuag' sive pcella terre cu omib3 et singtis suis ptin p'fat Wittmo Platte et assignat' suis cont omes gentes warrantizabim et defendem imppetuu p p'sentes. Ac insup sciant me pfat' Johem Platt attonasse deputasse et in loco me posuisse dilect' michi in xpo Richardu Platte seniore et Johe P'cevatt meos veros et legittimos attornat' conjunctim et divisim ad intrandu p me et in noie meo in p'dict' messuagia sive pcella terre cu ptin. Et post talem ingressu inde p me et in noie meo plena et pacific! possessions et seisina p'fat' Wittmo Platte ad deliband scdm vim forma et effect' hnj psentis carte mce indentate inde ei confect' rat' et grat' hent et hitur totu et quicquid diet' attonat' me noie meo fecnt seu eor' alt' fecit ' in pmissis. In cui rei testimoniu huic psenti carte mee indentat' sigillu meu apposui. Dat' decimo tercio die Augusti anno regni regis Edwardi sexti Dei gra' Anglie ffrancie et Hibernie regis fidei defensoris et in terr' ecclie Anglicane et Hibernie sup'mi capitis secudo. 32. —

This indentur made the viij daye of Marche in the sext yer' of the reigne of our Sav/aign lorde Edward the sext by the grace of God Kyng of England ffranncc & Ireland defendo of the faithe and of the Churche of England and also of Ireland in erthe the supme hede — betwen Rauff Hunt of Chorleton in the pyisshe of Manchestr' in the countye of Lane' husbandman apon the one ptye, and Rychard Platte son & heyr apparinte of Jhon Platte of Ryssholme in the seid pisshe & countye gent' apon the other ptye — wittenessithe that the scid Rauff Hunt for a certen some of good & lawfull money of England to hym fully payd before the date of thes psentes by the forseid Rychard Platte haithe by the lycence consent & agrement by the Ryght Wourshipfull Jhon Bothe of Barton in the countye aforseid esquier & landlord to the seid Rauff Hunt haith dymysed grnnted sette betaken & to ferme letten & by thes psentes dothe dymyse griinte sette betake & to ferme lette to the seid Rychard Platte one close called lyttle Shote conteynyng three acres & a halfe lyeng in Chorleton afforseid pcell of the tenement whyche one Margaret Hunt wydowe late wyffe of Jhon Hunte disceased & the seid Rauffe Hunt have & hold of the seid Jhon Bothe as tenntes at wylle to the same Jhon, To have & to hold the seid close w th'appteiinces to the seid Rychard Platte & hys assignes from the daye of the dysceasse of the seid Margaret Hunt wydowe duryng the t'me & space of sex yeres next aftr immedyatly folloyng the same daye of the discease of the seid Margaret & fully to be complete fynysshed & endet wtoute lette or impedymcnt of the seid Rauff Hunt hys wyffe chyldren executors admynystrators or assignes or of any of them duryng the seid t'me yeildyng & paying therfore yerely aft' the dyscease of the seid Margaret Hunt to the seid Rauffe Hunt hys executors or assignes one pepercorne at the feaste of Penthecoste if it be lawfully asked and demaunded for all rentes s'vyces & demaundes to the seid close belongyng duryng the t'me aforseid. In wittenes wherof the ptyes afforseid to thies psentes inden-

tures interchnngeablye have sette ther seailles the daye & yer' fyrste above wrytten. 33. — This indenture made the ffourthe daie of Marche in the ffirste yere of the reigne of our Sovereigne ladie Mary by the grace of God of Englannde ffrannce and Irelande quene deffender of the ffaythe and in earthe next under God the supreame heade of the churche of Englannde and also of Irelannde — betwene Johane Platt wydowe late wiffe of John Platt in the countie of Lane' gent. deceased upon th'on partie, and Ric' Platte sonne and heir of the said John Platt aforsaid gent. upon th'other partie — wittenessith that the said Johane ffor dyvers and soundrye good reasonable causes & consideracons in the daie of the date hereof her speciallye moving have demysed graunted sett betaken and to ferme letten and by these presentes indenture dothe demyse, graunte, sett, betake and to ferme lett unto the said Richard Platt too messuages or tenementes now or late in the severall tenures or occupacons of Margarete late wiffe of Edmound Duncuthley and Rauffe Duncuthley in Rysshulme aforsaid and also too closes or parcels of ground called Hall ffelde and Brucke ffelde now or late in the tenure or occupacon of John Platt aforsaid deceassed, To have and to holde all and singuler comodities easementes liberties proffettes and advantages to the same appertaynyng or in any wyse belonginge to the said Richard Plat his heirs executours or assignes ymmediatlye next after the daie of the date hereof unto th'ende and terme and during all the tyme and t'me of the liffe naturall of the said Johane Plat widow and during all suche terme title and interest as she hathe in too or upon the same or in to and upon every part or parcell thereof, yelding and paying therfor yerelie unto the said Johane Platt widow or her assignes the some of ffoure markes thre shillinges ffoure pense of good and lawfull money of Englannd at too feastes or termes in the yere, that is to saie at in or upon the ffeaste daye of Sainct John Bap xxviij iiij, and at in or upon the feaste daye of the birthe of o Lord Jesu Christe other xxviij8 iiij by even porcons, fforseing alwayes and it is of both the said parties covnted and agreed that the firste payment shall coniense & beginn at the ffeaste of Sainct John Bap next eusuyng the daie of the date hereof. And if it happen the said yerelie rent of iiij merkes iij iiij or any part or parcell thereof to be behinde unpaid in part or in all by the space of ffourtie dayes at any or anther of the said ffeastes at w yt ought to be paid at, then yt shalbe lawfull to aud for the said Johane Platt widow or her assigues to entre in, have agayne and repossede the said too messuages or terites and the said too percels of ground and all other the premysses with th'appurtennces, and in her former or ffirst estate to stande, any thing or thinges herein conteyned or specyfied to the contrary made in any wise notwithstanding. In wytnesse whereof to these present indentures the parties aforsaid enterchangeable have setto thair scales the daye and ycre ffirste above wryten. 34. — Devotis & in xpo sibi dilectf Bychero Plate & Annes frat' Matheus Evys pror covent frm ordinis P'dicato Cestr' licet indignus saltni & augmentu cotinuu celestiii grap exigente v're devocois affectu que ad nrm hetf ordinem & coventu vobis offii missajp oronu p'dicacom jeiunio abstinecia vigilia labor' cetof bonor que p fres nri covent Diis fieri dederit univ'sos pticipacone cocedo tenore p'sencih spale in vita pit pariter ct in morte. Volo insup et ordino vt post decess v'ros aie v're frm tociu covent oronib3 recomendenf in nro conventuali capitulo si v'ri ibidm obit fuerint nuciati & immigant p ipis misse et orones sic' p frib3 nfis & amycis deffunctf fieri cosuevyt. In cui cocessiois testimoniu sigiltm officii mei psentib3 ef appensu. Dat' Cestrie in festo purifficacio beate Marie anno Dni Mccccc qu!gentesimo v.

Seal: Red wax, vesica-shaped, bearing two priestly figures, much defaced. Legend, also defaced: Sigillum Prioris Pre...ica Predicatorum.

35. — To all trew Christen people to whome thes prentes shall come. John Hunte of the parrishe of Mamch in the countye of Lancastre comonly called John Hunte of the ffieldes or Make stake, husbandman, sendethe gretinge. Whereas I have and holde one mease or tenemeute withe th'appurtenanncS commonly called Huntes of the ffielde or Blake Stake, set, standinge, lyenge and beinge in the parrishe of Manch in the countye of Lancastre now in the holdinge of me the said John Hunte and myne assignes for and duringe the tyme and terme of xxi yeres of the demyse and graunte of the worshipfull John Boothe of Barton in the countye of Lancastre esquier as by a writinge or dede indented thereof made beringe date the xvij daye of Auguste in the thrid yere of the raingne of the Queues mooste excellent maiestie that nowe ys more at large yt may appeare: Know ye me the said John Iluntc for dyvers and sundre good reasonable causes and consideracons me in this behalff esspecially movinge, to have geveu, graunted, surrendred, assigne and sett overr unto Margaret Platte doughtcr of Richarde Platte of Rissheholme in the countye of Lancastre gent. all my right, tytle, estate, use, possession, clame and demaunde what so ever whiche I have in and to the saide mease or tenemente withe th'appurtnnces or in or to any parte or pcell thereof, or hereafter shall and maye have or of right owe to have in and to the same, To have and to holde enioy and occupie all and singuler as well the saide mease or tenemente withe th'appurtennces and every parte & parcell thereof and all my right, tytle, estate, use, possession, clame and demaunde what so ever w I have or hereafter shall and maye have or of right owe to have in and to the same or in or to any parte or pcell therof, as also the said lease or writtinge indented to the said Margaret Platt and her assignes duringe the tyme and terme of so many yeres as are yet to come unexpired mencyoned in the said lease or writinge indented, without let, varyance, sute, troble, striffe, debate, disturbance, ympedyment or agaynesainge of me the said John Hunte my executours, admynystratours or assigncs or any of us or any other pson or psons for us or in our names by our willes, consent or abetement in eny maner. In witnes whereof I the said John Hunte have caused this to be made, and hare putto my sealc and signed the same withe my hande the xix daye of Aprill in the twelthe yere of the raingne of our soveraingne Ladie Elizabethe by the grace of God of England ffraunce and Irelande Quene, deffendo1 of the faythe &c. 36. — Sciant p'sent' et futur quod nos Ricus Platt de Platt in coin Lancastr' gen. et Johes Platt Alius et heres apparens p'd Rici pro et in consideracone cujusdam maritag' in posterrh habend et celebrand inter me p'd Johem Platt ex una p'te et Elizabetham Birche filiam Thome Birche de Hindley Birche in com p'd gen. ex altera p'te. Dedimus, concessimus et hac p'senti charta nfa indentata confirmavimus p'd Elizabethe Birche omia illa messuagia terras tents reddit' s'vic et hereditamets cu p'tin in Withington vulgariter vocat' et nuncupat' le Haull fielde continent' in se p estimacoem quinq, acras et dimid' acr' terre duas clausur' terre et pasture vocat' Brocke fielde continent' in se p estimacoem sex acras ct dimid' acr' terre, pratu sive clausur' terre et pasture vocat' le Middope cu p'tin continent' in se p estimacoem una roda terre et tent cu suis p'tiuen' modo in tenura et occupacoe Wittmi Platt fratris p'dci Rici et assignator' suor' existen' parcet t hereditament' p'd Rici neenon rev'coem ct rev'coes omniu ct singtor pmissor' cu primo et proxime accidere et evenire contiger'. Habend et Tenend oia et singta p'd messuagia terras, tent, reddit', s'vic' et hereditamet ac cetera quecuq, p'missa cu suis ptin et rev'coem ac rev'coes eorndem cu acciderint p'fat Elizabethe Birche et assignatis suis pro terino vite sue et durante toto termino vite naturalis p'd Elizabethe Birche absq, impetuoe alicujus vasti pro et in noie totius jucture sue. Et nos vero p'd RicBs et Johes Platt et heredes nri omia et singta p'd messuagia, terras, tent, reddit', s'vic et hereditament' ae cetera quecuq, p'missa cu suis p'tin ac rev'coem et rev'coes eorndem p'fat Elizabethe Birche et assignatis suis pro termio vite sue et durante toto termio

vite naturalis p'd Elizabethe Birche pro et in noie totius juncture sue contra omes hoies warrantizabimus et imppetuu defendemus p psentes. In cuius rei testimoniii ptes supradict' sigilla sua alternatim psentibus apposuerunt. Data xv die Decembris anno regni dne nre Elizabethe Dei gra' Anglie ffrauncie et Hibernie regine fidei defensor' &c. decimonono. 37.— Lane. Inquisico indentata apud Wiggan in com Lane. Decimo die Septembris anno regni dne nre Elizabeth dei gra Anglie ffrauncie et Hibnie regine fidei defensor' &c. tricessimo quinto coram Thoma Hesketh ar' escaetor dne regine coin sui pallantini Lane, RoMo Pilkington aro feodar' dce dne regine com pred' Jacobo Woorthington et Rado Haghtone gener' virtute comissionis dee dne regine in natura Bris Brevis de diem clit clausit extremu pred' comissionar' et aliis direct' et huic inquisicol annexat' ad inquirend' post mortem Richi Platt gen. defunct' p sacrni Thome Lane an, Robti Hindley gener., Rogeri Bradshawe gen., Johis Dewhurste gen., Thome Markland gen. , WiHi Ascrofte gen., Milonis Gerrard gen. et Thome Tarlton gen. Qui dicunt sup sacr'm suu q Richardus Platt in dicta comissione noiat die ante obitu suu fuit seifus in dnico suo ut de feodo de et in uno mess' viginti octo acr' terr' duobus acr' prati decem acr' pastur' cu ptin Rysheholme in Wythington in dco *com* Lane', ac de et in uno burgagio et uno gardino cu p'tin in Manchester in coin pred. Et sic inde seit existens pred Richus Platt die ante obitu suu p chartam sua indentata geren' dat decimo quinto die Decembris anno regni dee dne regine decimo nono, dedit et concessit cuidam Elizabethe Platt vidue nup uxor' Johis Platt defunct' p nomen Elizabethe Birche cem acr' terr' prati et pastur' cu ptin in Rysheholme pred' pceft premissor' Heud et Tend pred' Elizabethe p terminu vite sue que quidem Elizabetha adhuc superstes est et in plena vita existit vi3 apud Risheholme pred in com pred. Et ulterius jurator' pred dicunt q pred Richus Platt sic de p'dict' mess' terr' et tentis seit existen' quarto die Augusti anno Dni 1590 condidit et constituit ultima voluntate sua inscript'

et sigillo ipius Rici sigillat' et p eandem voluntatem dedit et concessit Issabell Platt uxor' pred' Rich! Platt unii cotagiu et quatuor decem acr' terr' prati et pastur et unii croft contin' p estimacoem dimid acr' cu ptin in Rysheholme ali' pcerl premissor', Hend et Tencud pred Elizabeth sic p termin' vite sue put p pred voluntate jurator' pdict' sup capcoem hujus iuquisicois in evidenc osten' plenius liquet et apparet, que quidem Issabella adhuc superstes est et in plena vita existit vi3 apud Rysheholme pred in com pd. Et juratores ulterius dicunt q pred messuag terr" et tenta cu suis p'tin in Rysheholme pred tenent et tempore mortis pred Richi tenebant de dha regina ut de nup hospitali Sci Johis Jretem in Anglia p annual reddit' quatuor solid et reddendo ad mortem cujuscunq, tenentis ejusdem terraru p'tem catellor' mobiliii ejusdem tenentis p omib3 servic', et valent p ann in oib3 exitib3 ultra reprisas vigint' sex solid et octo denar'. Et quod pdict mess' burgag' et gardin' cu suis p'tin in Manchester pred in com pred tenentur et tempore mortis p'd Richardi tenebant de dno de Manchester in socagio p reddit' de duodece denar' p omib3 servic' et valent p ann in oib3 exitibus ultra reprisas ij. Et q pred Richus Platt in dca comissione noiat obiit de tali statu ut p'fertur seifus scdo die Junii ultiin preterit'. Et q Edmundus Platt est filius et heres pred Richardi et est etatis die capcois hujus inquisicois octo annor' octo mensiu et viginti septem dier Et ulterius juratores dicunt q pred Richus Platt dca comissione noiat nulla alia sive plura messuag' terra tenta aut hereditamenta huit seu tenuit de dca dna regina nec de aliquibus aliis p'sonis in emfo revercoe nec in servico dicto die quo obiit in dco com Lane' aliter q'm ut sup'dict' est. In cujus rei testimoniu uni p'ti hujus inquisicois tam pfat comissionar' q'm jurator' pred sigilla sua apposuerunt alter' vero p'ti hujus inquisicois penes p'fat jurator' remanen' p'fat comiss' sigilla sua apposuerunt. Datu die anno et loco primo suprad.

Family Of Birch.
(pp. V0-104J

1. — Sciant psentes et futuri quod ego Matheus filius Mathei de Hav'sage cou-

cessi et confirmavi Matheo filio Mathei de Byrchis et heredib3 suis tota t'ram dc Hyndley Byrchis pro homag' et s'vicio suo; videlicet infra has devisas Incipiendo ad magna fossam, deinde ex transverso usque ad devisas del Plat, et deinde aput Aquilonem usque in Gorbroke; assendendo fluvium aque de Gorbroke usque ad vadu de Kusseford et deinde sequendo le Matregate usque ad magna fossam, et sequendo magna fossam usque ad divisas del Plat. Et sciend' est q p'dictus Matheus quietus erit de pannageo in nemore meo de Wythyngton de omnibus porcis suis et molet bladum suum hopurfre ad omnes molend' meos sine multura infra feodu de Wythyngton. Tenend et Habend sibi et heredib3 suis de me et heredib3 meis in feodo et in hereditate libe quiete pacifice iutegre in boscis in planis in pasturis in moris in aquis in exitibus in introitibus et in oib3 aliis aysiamentis et libel-tatib3 ad villam de Wythyngton ptinent'. Reddendo inde annuatim michi et heiedib3 meis tres solidos argenti de se et heredib3 suis pro omnib3 serviciis exacconib3 consuetudinib3 videlicet xviij denar' ad Annunciationem Beate Marie et xviij denar' ad festii Beati Michaelis. Et ego pfat' Matheus et heredes mei istam confirmacoem dicto Matheo et heredibus suis contra omnes homines et feminas imppetuum warrantizabimus et defendemus. Et ut hec mea concessio et cofirmaco rata et stabilis impptuum p'maneat huic psenti scripto sigillu meum apposui hiis testib3 Domino Galfrido de Chetham, Ad'de Buri, Wittmo Doly militib3, Roberto de Buru, Rychardo de Trafford, Rob' de Redyche, WiHmo de Heyton, Rycho de Chorleton, Witto de Dudusbury, Thoma de Barlowe et aliis. — *Birch Evidences,* penes Sir J. W. H. Anson, Bart.

2. — O103 xpi fidelib3 &c. Robfus fit Alexi del Birchis saltm in dno. Noverit' me remisisse &c. Robto fil Henr' de Trafford et hedb3 suis totum jus et clamiu que unquam hui in molendino del Birches q idem Robtus fil p'dcti Henr' huit ex dimissione Alexi del Birches pris mei simul cii una domo una acre t're juxta p'dcm erat cu stagnis attachmentis stagnor' piscar' sectis

molendini cu sufficient' cursu aque p pipas et fossata ad d'ctum molendinu cu refullo aque infra divisas del Birches in longitudine et latitudine ad voluntatem p'dco Robto fil Henr' cu sufficient' place t're ad ventiland commoda blad' dco molendino cu suffic' via infra divisas del Birches ad cariand' blad' ad dct molend' cu equis vel qualitercunq, venientes et ad recariand' sine impedimento alicuj hiis testib3 Rico de Byron, Henr' de Trafford militib3, Rico de Hulton, Johe de Asshtoii, Johe de Hulton, Wittmo de Moston, Galfrido de Hulm, Nicho de Wirkesworthe clico et aliis. Dat' ap Trafford die Sci Oswaldi reg' anno regni regis Edwardi til regis Edwardi sexto decimo. — *Trafford Evidences, Lane.* MSS. 3. — Sciant psentes et futuri q ego Robtus fil Alexand' del Birchis dedi concessi et hac psenti carta mea confirmavi Johi de Hulton heredib3 et assignatis suis omes terras meas et ten mea in le Birchis in villa de Withinton cu edificiis et cu omib3 boscis et p'tis et cu rev'coe omniu tYar et ten bSci et p'ti que qdm Johanna dam ux Alexand' del Birchis tenet in dotem cu acciderit. Hend et Tend p'dco Johi heredib3 et assignatis suis de dHo capitali feod' illi p s'vicia inde debita et consueta libe et quiete cu om!b3 lib'tatib3 et ptin p'dcis t'ris et ten ubiq, ptin. Et ego v p'dcs Itobts et heredes mei omes p'dcas t'ras et ten cu edificiis boscis et p"tis et cu rev'coe p'dce dotis in omib3 sicut p'dcm &c. p'dco Johi heredib3 et assignatis suis ta omes gentes waranti3abim et imppetuu deffendem'. In cuj rei testimoniu huic p'seuti carte sigillu meu apposui hiis testib3 MathS de Haydoc sen de Salford, Rico de Holond, Henr' de Par, Henr' de Bruches, Galfrid de Strangwas, Henr' de Wytfeld, Witto clico et aliis. Dat' ap le Birchis die Jovis px an fm nat Johis Baptis' anno regni regis Edwardi fil regis Edwardi duodecimo. — *Birch Evidences,* penes Sir J. W. H. Alison, Bart. 4. — Hec indentura testat q Johes de Hulton dedit concessit et hac psenti carta sua confirmavit Robto del Birchis omes t'ras et ten que p'dcs Johes huit de dono et feofamento p'dci Robti del Birchis in villa de Wythyngton cu oib3 suis ptin sn aliquo retenemento videl3 cu edificiis et cu oib3 gardinis boscis et p"is et unu molendinu aqticu et cu rev'coe omn t'rar' et ten bosci et p"ti que Joha dam ux Alexand del Birchis tenet in dotem cu acciderit, Hend et Tenend p'dco Robto ad tota vita sua de capitalib3 dnis feodi illius p s'vicia q ad p'dca Ten ptineut ad tota vita ipi RoHi et post decessum ipi Robti oia p'dca ten cu ptin integre remaneat Henric' filio p'dict' Robti de Birchis, Tend et Hend p'dco Henr' et heredib3 de corpore suo pcreat' de capitalib3 dnis feodi illi p s'vicia que ad p'dca ten ptinert imppetuum. Et si p'dcs Henr' obierit sn hered de corpe suo pcreat' tunc post decessum ipr Henr' omia p'dca ten cu ptin integ remaneant heredib3 int' p'dcm de Strangwas, Henr' de Wytfeld, WiHo clico et aliis. Dat' apud le Birchis die Sabat px post fm Ap'lor Petri et Pauli anno regni regis Edwardi M regis Edward' duodecimo. — *Birch Evidences,* penes Sir J. W. H. Anson, Bart. 5. — Nov'int univ'si p psentes me Wittm del Birches del Birches attornasse et in loco meo posuisse dilectos michi in xpo Johem de Bamford et Wittm del Plat de Risshum coniuncti et divisi ad liband' p me et noie meo Rico Whiteacres et Johi le Wright capellanis plena et pacifica seisina in omib3 messuag' t'ris et ten reddtis et s'viciis meis cu ptin in villa de Wythyngton sedm vrm forma et effectu cuiusdam carte mee eisdm Rico et Johi le Wright hedib3 et assign' suis inde confect' put in eadm continet' rat' et conrat' bent et hetur' quidquid Johes de Bamford et Witts del Plat noie meo fecint vel alt' eor' noie meo fecit in p'miss'. In cuius rei testimoniu p'sentib3 sigillu meu apposui. Dat' die Martis px ante festum See Marie Magdalene anno regni regis Henrici Sexti post conquestu Angl septimo. — *Birch Evidences,* penes Sir J. W. H. Anson, Bart. 6. — Sciant psentes et futuri q ego Witts del Birches del Birches dedi concessi et hac psenti carta mea confirmavi Rico de Whitacres et Johi de Wright capellanis hedib3 et assign' suis omia messuag' t'ras et ten redditus et servicia mea cu ptin in villa de Wythyngton, Hend et Tend omia p'dict' messuag t'r et ten redditus et servicia cu ptin Rico et Johi hedib3 et assign' suis imppetuu de capitalib3 dnis feodi illius p servicia inde debita et de iure consnet'. Et ego vero p'dict' Witts et hedes mei omia p'dict' mesuag' t'ras et ten redditus et s'vicia cu ptin p'dcis Rico et Johi hedib3 et assign suis contra omes gentes waranti3abim et imppetuu defendem. In cui rei testimoniu huic p'senti carte mee sigillu meu apposui hiis testib3 Johe de Barlawe, Jacobo de Prestwicli, Johe de Chetam, Johe del Slade, Hug' del Slade et aliis. Dat' apud le Birches die Martis px ante festu See Marie Magdalene anno regni regis Henrici Sexti post conquestum Anglie septimo.

Sciant psentes et futuri q nos Ricus de Whitacres et Johes le Wright capellani dedim9 concessim9 et hac psenti carta nra indentat' confirmavim9 Witto del Birches del Birches et Margaret' uxi eius omia illa mesuag' t'ras et ten reddit' et s'vicia cu ptin in villa de Wythyngton que nup huim9 ex dono et concessione p'dci WiHi, Hend et Tend omia p'dca mesuag' t'ras et ten reddit' et s'vicia cu ptin p'dcis Witto et Margarete ad t'minm vite eor', ita q post decessum p'dcor' Witti et Margarete volum concedim9 q omia p'dict' mesuag' t'ras et ten reddit' et s'vicia cu ptin integre remaneaut Radulpho fil p'dicor' Witti et Margaret' et hedib3 masculis de corpore suo legitime pcreat, Hend et Tend omia p'dict' mesuag t'ras et ten reddit' et s'vicia cu ptin p'dict' Radulpho et hedib3 mascul' de corpore suo legitime pcreat', tend de capit' dnis feodi illius p s'vicia inde debit' et de iure consuet'. Et si contingat p'dict' Radulphum sine hede mascul' de corpore suo legitime pcreat' obire tunc volum et concedim q omia p'dict' mesuag' t'ras et ten redditus s'vic' cu ptin integre remaneant Robto fratri p'dcti Radi et hedib3 masculis de corpore suo legitime pcreat'. Et si contingat p'dict' Robtum sine hede mascul' de corpore suo legitime pcreat' obire tunc volum et concedim q omia p'dict' mesuag' t'ras et ten reddit' et s'vicia cu ptin integre remaneant Edmudo fratri p'dci Robti et hedib3 masculis de corpore suo legitime pcreat'. Et si contingat p'dict' Edmudu sine hede mascul' de corpore suo legitime pcreat' obire tunc volum et concedim q omla p'dict' mesuag' t'ras et ten reddit' et s'vicia cu ptin integre remaneant Thome fratri pdcti Edmudi et hedib3 masculis de corpore suo legitime pcreat' obire tunc volum et concedim q omia p'dict' mesuag' t'ras et ten reddit' et's'vicia cu ptin integre remaneant et rev'tant rectis hedib3 p'dcti Witti imppetuu. Et nos vero p'fat' Ricus et Johes et hedes nri omia p'dict' mesuag t'ras et ten reddit' et s'vic cu ptin p'dctis Witto et Margarete ad terminu vite eor', ac ecia p'dict' Radulpho, Roberto, Edmudo et Thome ac ecia rectis hedib3 p'dcti cu accidcret ut p'dcm est contra omes gentes waranti3abim et imppetuu defendemus. In cui9 rei testimoniu huic p'senti carte nre indcntate sigilla nra apposuim9 hiis testib3 Johe dc Barlawc, Jacobo de Prestwich, Witto del Plat, Johe del Slade, Hug' del Slade et aliis. Dat' apud le Birches die Mercurij ps post festum Sci Jacobi Apti anno regni regis Henrici Scxti post conquestum Anglie septimo. — *Birch Evidences*, penes Sir J. W. H. Anson, Bart.

7.— Sciant p'sentes et futuri q ego Radus Byrches dedi cocessi et hac psenti carta mea confirmavi Joh'i fferro capellano omia mesuagia t'ras tenta reddit et servicia mea cu ptin in Wythyngton et alibi in com Lancastr', Hcnd et Tend omia p'dca mesuagia t'ras tenta reddit' et servicia cu ptin p'fat' Johi heredib3 et assign' suis de dno capitali p servic' iude debit' et cousuet' imppetuu. Et ego p'dict' Radus et hercdes mei ola p'dict' mesuag' t'ras tenta reddit' et servic' cu ptin p'fat' Johi heredib3 et assignat' suis contra omes gentes waranti3abim. In cui rei testimoniu huic psenti carte mee sigillu mee apposui hiis tcstib3 RobertoWorkesley armig'o, Thurstano Tildcsley, Wittmo Hilton et aliis. Dat' vicesimo die Juuij anno regni regis Henrici Sexti post conquestu Anglie vicesimo septimo.

Sciant psentes et futuri q ego Johes fferro capellanus dimisi, tradidi et hac p'senti carta mea indctata delibavi Rado Byrche3 oia mesuagia fras et tent cu ptin que fuerut p'dicti Radi in villa de Wythyngton et alibi in com Lancastr' que quidm mesuagia t'ras et tenta nup habui michi heredib3 et assignatis meis p cartam diet' Radi, Hend et Tend omia p'dict' mesuagia terras et tenta cu ptin pfat' Rado et heredib3 de corpe suo legitie pcreatis remanere eodm t'nc diet' Rado et rectis heredib3 suis. In cui rei testimon huic carte mee iudentat sigillu meu apposui hiis testib3 Robto Workesley armig'o, Thurstano Tildesley,.Wilhno Hilton et aliis. Dat' vicesimo p'mo die Junij anno regni regis Henrici Sexti post conquestu Anglie vicesimo septimo. — *Birch Evidences*, penes Sir J. W. H. Anson, Bart.

8.— Sciant psentes et ffuturi q ego Wittms Byrches deByrches dedi concessi et hac psenti carta mea confirmavi Robto Byrches filio meo duas p'cellas terr' iacent' in le Byrches p'dict' continent' duodecim acras terr' int' Michcwall Diche ex pte australi et unu mesuag' vocat' VVynnerhey ex pte boreali put includentur p sepes et limites et modo in tenura p'dict' Wittm, Habend et Tenend p'dict' p'cell terr' cu omib3 suis ptin p'fat' RoWo ad terminu vite sue Ita q post decessum p'fat Robf i p'dict p'ceH terr continent' duodecim acras terr cu omib3 suis ptin integre remaneant rectis hereo mascul' mei p'dict Wittmi imppetuu de capit' dnis feod' illi p s'vic' inde debit' et de iure consuet'. Et ego vero p'fat' Wiftmus et hered mei p'dict' duodecim acras terr' cu ptin p'fat Robfo durante vita sua cont' omes gentes warranti3abim et defendemus p p'sentes. Et ult'ius nov'itis me p'fat Wiltm attornasse et in loco meo posuisse dilect' michi in xpo Thoma AValker de Diddisburie meu veru legitimu attornat' ad dcliband p me et in noie meo p'fat Robfo plenam et pacifica possessione et seisina de et in p'dict' pcetl terr' continent duodecim acras terr' et cu omib3 suis ptin sedm vera forma et effectu p'sentis carte mee rat' et conrat' hent et hetur' et quicquid idm attornat' meus noie meo fecerit in p'miss. In cui rei testimoniu sigillu meu apposui hiis testib3 Henric Longford armig', Wilhno Bradford capello, Rico Bomford, Georgio Rediche, Thoma ffletcher et multis aliis. Dat' p'mo die mensis Marcii anno regni regis Ricardi t'cii post conquest' Anglie secudo. — *Birch Evidences*, penes Sir J. W. H. Anson, Bart. '

Families Of Slade Of Slade And Siddall Of Slade.

(pp. 121-136.;

1. —Notu sit omnib3 scriptam visuris vel audituris q ego Thom. fil Galf. fil Luc de Mamecestr' concessi et hac presenti carta mea confirm avi Jordano fri meo et hedib3 suis p homagio et s'vicio suo totam t'ram q Galf. pater meus sibi dedit in Didisford et Milkewallslade, et unam acram prati in Banereris et totam t'ram q pr meus tenuit in Akedone, Tenend et Habend de me et hedib3 meis sibi et hedib3 suis libe et quiete in feodo et hereditate cu omib3 libtatib3 et cleam'tis d'tis t'ris ptin. Reddendo et faciendo servicium tam dnis capitalib3 q m' in omib3 et p omia sic tinet' in carta q idem Jord" *h't* de p'dicto Galf. patre meo. In cuj rei testimoniu huic scpto sigillu meii apposui, hiis testib3 Diio Galf. tuc Dec. Mam, Ad. or W de Hulton, Matho de Birch, Witto le Norreis, Robto filio Sym. Mamecestr', Ric' de Honeford, Witto de Didisb'y, Johe clico at aliis.

2. — Sciant presentes et futuri q ego Noel de Loggeford dedi et cessi et hac presenti carta mea confirmavi de me et hedib3 meis Jordano filio Galfridi filio Luco de Mamecestr' et hedib3 suis tota t'ram mea q Ric Ridehorn tenebat de me ad t'em in territorio de Didisbury, Tendam et Habenda in feodo et heditate libe et q'ete et integre cu omib3 munib3 aisiamentis et libertatib3 infra divisas ville de Withingtuu et Didisbury ptinentib3 cu exitib3 ct serviciis, Reddo annuatim mihi et hedib3 meis de se et hedib3 suis q'ndm quindecim den arg ad duas anni t'ios scil septe den ob ad festu Sci Michael et septem den arg ob ad Annuncionis See Marie p oib3 serviciis suetudinib3 t demand nob pertinentib3. Et ego diet' Noel et heredes mei ista dcta t'ra cu libtatib3 et aisiam'tis d'to Jord et hedib3 suis sic' p'dcm est tra oes hoies et feminas ippetum warenti3abim. In cuj testim' ut douaco mea rata et stabilis p'maneat huic scpto sigill meu apposui hiis testib3 Dno Galfrido de Schetha, Witto de Hea, Ric' de Most',

Matbeo de Birch, Ric' de Honeford, Thom de Barf, Henr' de T'fford, Jord de Stokep' clico et aliis. 3.—Sciant presentes et futuri q ego Robtus de Milkewalleslade dedi concessi et hac presenti carta mea confirmavi Heur' fil Thom' de Aynesworth unu messuagiu et omia t'ras et ten mea que bui die confeccionis p'sent' in Withynton, Hend et Tend p'dto Henr' hedib3 et assignat' suis libe quiete bn et in pace cu libo introitu et exitu ad eadem et cu omi pastur' omib3 averiis suis in omib3 locis ville p'dte et cu omib3 aliis libertatib3 et asiament' pdtis ten ubiq, ptinentib3 de capitalib3 dnis feod illo ten p s'vic que ad pdta ten ptinent imppetii. Et ego vero p'dict' Robtus et hefes mei pdtu messuag' et pdta fras et ten cu suis ptinent' et p'dtam coem pastur' p'dti Henr' hedib3 et assignatis suis contra omes gentes warantiabim et imppetii defendem. In cuj testimon' huic p'senti carte mee sigillu meii apposui, Hiis testib3 Nicho de Longford chivaler, Henr' de T'fford chivaler, Robto de Trafford, Thom de Trafford, Thom del Holt, Robto del Plat et Henr' fil Robti del Byrches. Dat' apud Withynton die Jovis px post fm t'nslacois Sfi Thom Archiepi anno regni regis Edwardi t'cii post conquestum vicesimo t'cio. 4.— Hec carta indentata testatur q Henr' fit Thome de Aynesworth dedit concessit et hac presenti carta sua confinnavit Robto de Milkewalleslade unum messuagium et omia t'ras et ten cu ptin que habuit de dono et feoffamento p'dti Robti in villa de Withynton sine aliquo retenemento, Hend et Tend omia p'dta t'ras et ten cu ptin p'dto Robto ad totam vita suam de capitalib3 dnis feodi illius p servicia que ad p'dta t'ras et ten ptineut ad totam vitam ipius Robti; et post decessum ipius Robti omia p'dta t're et ten cum ptin integre remaneant Robto fil Robti de Milkewalleslade juniori, Hend et Tend omia p'dta t'ras et ten cu ptin pdto Robto fil Robti et hedib3 de corpore suo legitime procreatis de capitalib3 diiis feodi illius per servic' que ad p'dta t'ras et ten ptinent impetuum. Et si pdtus Robtus fil Robti obierit sine herede de corpore suo legitime procreato tunc post decessum ipius Robti fit Robti omia p'dta t're &c. integre remaneant Johi fil Robti de Milkewalleslade fri p'dti Robti fil Robti, Hend et Tend omia pdta t'ras &c. pdto Johi et hered de corpore suo legitie procreatis de capitalib3 dnis feodi illius p servicia que ad pdta t'ras &c. imppetuum. Et si pdtus Johes obierit sine herede &c. tunc post decessum ipius Johis omia pdta terre &c. integre remaneant heredib3 int' pdtm Robtm de Milkewalleslade et Elena ux'em sua fil Robti del Plattes legitie procreatis, Hend et Tend omia p'dta t'ras &c. sibi et hedib3 suis de corporib3 suis legitie procreatis de capitalib3 dnis feodi illius p servicia que ad p'dta t'ras &c. ptinent imppetum. Et si ipi heredes obierint sine hered &c. tunc post decessum pdcor hered omia pdte t're &c. integre remaneant rectis H H hered ipius RobTi de Milkewalleslade Habend et Tenend de capitalib3 dnis feodi illius p servic' que ad pdta t'ras &c. ptinent imppetuum. Et pdti Henr' ct heredes sui pdtm messuagium &c. pdto RoMo de Milkewalleslade ad totam vitam suam ut pdtm est and in turn all the other contingent or reversionary grantees are warranted against all men for ever contra omes holes waranti3abimus imppetuum. In cuf rei testimoninm ptib3 huf indent' ptes alternatm sigilla sua apposuerunt, Hiis testib3 Nicho de Longford chivaler, Henr' de Trafford chivaler, Robto de Trafford, Thoma de Trafford, Thoma del Holte, Robto del Platt et Henr' fit Robti del Burches. Dat' apud Withynton die Ven'is px post f'm Sci Jacobi Apti anno regni regis EdwardH'cii post conquestm vicesimo t'cio regni vero sui ffrancie decimo.

5. — Lane. Inquisitio indentata capt. apud Bolton in com. p'dict. vicesimo tercio die Septembris anno regni dne nre Eliz Sec. tricessimo. Coram Thoma Heskcthe aro escaetor dfie Regine in com p'dcto virtute Bris diet dne regine de diem clausit extrem' eidem escaetor' direct et huic? inquisitionem consuet. p. m. Edwardi Syddall nup de Slade in com p'dct in dicto brevi noiat p sacrum Petri Heywood gen., Alex Leyver gen. , Richi Leighe gen., Richi Scocroft gen. , Radi Greene gen., Richi Wood gen., Radi Haughton gen., Henrici Hardi gen. , Robti Hardi gen., Radi Bridge gen., Georgii Allonson gen., Georgii Kenyon gen., Thome Kaye gen., Robti Ravalde gen., Henrici Cheetam gen., W Bamforde gen., et Robti Butterworthe gen. Qui dicunt sup sacrum suu q dfn ante obitum p'd Edwdi Syddall in B'vi p'dict noiat idem Edwdus &c. fuit seitus in dominico suo vel de feodo de et in uno capitalli messuagio sive tento vocat le Mylkwall Slade cu ptin & de et in quibusdam clausur' terr' continent' p estimacionem vigint quatuor acr, scituat' jacen' et existen' in Risholme et Withington in com p'dto; ac de et in quibusdam aliis clausuV terr' et prati cum p'tin continen' p estimacoem vigint acr terr scituat &c. in Gorton &c., necnon de et in uno burgagio sive tefito et una shopa cu ptin scituat &c. in Manch; ac etiam de et in tertia pte manerii de Kerksawe alias diet Kerssall cu ptin in com p'dct; ac de et in uno burgagio sire tent, duobus cottagiis tertia p'te unius molendini aquatici, tertia pte unius alii cottagii et trium acrarum terr; ac de et in tertia pte unius alii cottagii et unius gardini, et de et in quadraginta acr terr decem acf prati trigint acr pastur, quatuor acris bosci ac de tertia pte cujusdem vasti sive noie vocat' Kersall Woodde ats Kersall more, scituat &c. in Kersawe ats Kersall p'dct; ac de quodfii libo reddt' duodecim denariorum annuat soulubil de quibusdam terris et tentis vocat Lees in pochia de Oldham in com p'dt, ut pcell p'dt manerii de Kerksall; ac de quodam alio libo reddit' iij iiij annuat solubil p quendam Robt. Hobson ut p'cell ejusdem manerii de Keksall; ac de quodam alio libo redd' quinque denariorum annuat solubil p Agnetem Lees ut pcell ejusdem manerii de Kerksall. Et idem Edwdus Syddall de p'dt manerib3 messuagiis, terris &c. p quoddam scrii suu indentat dedit et concessit oia et singula p'dt maneria &c. premissis quibusdam ffeofatis in p'dt facto indentato noiat ad usii p'dct Edwdi Sydall pro termino vite et post ejus decessum ad usu E Syddall ad tunc uxor' p'dt Edwardi, et Georgii Syddall ad tunc filii et here' apparen d'ti Edwdi Syddall in brevi p'dto noiat et hered masculorum

de corpe pdti Georgii letime procreand, et pro desitu t'lis exitus tunc ad opus et usu Thome Syddall filii junior' ejusdem Edwdi Syddall, in brevi p'dto noiat et hered masculorum &c. et pro dessitu &c. rectorum hered p"d Edwdi Syddall, in bri &c. impptium, virtute cujus ac vigore cujusdam act' in p'liamento dni Henrici nup Regis Anglie anno regni sui viccsimo septimo de usibus in possessionem transferend nupcr edit et pvisus, iidem E et Georgius post mortem p'dti Edwdi fuerunt seif de *dib)* et singulis pdt maner mess'giis terris &c., vi3 p'dt E in domco suo ut de libo tento p term vite sue, et p'dt Georgius in domco suo ut de feod taliat. Et jurator' p'dt ulterius sup sacr' suii dicunt q p'dtus Edwdus in br'i &c. sic inde seit de oib3 et singulis p'dt mafl mess'giis terris &c. obiit de tali statu inde seitus apud Milkwall Slade p'dict, decimo octavo die Februarii anno regni die dne regine tricesimo; ac q p'dtus Georgius Syddall est filius et prop' heres ejusdem Edwdi in bri &c. et est etatis tcmpe capconis hujus inquisit' viginti quinquc annorum et amplius. Et ulterius jurat' &c. dicunt q p'dt mess'gii sive tent vocat' Milkwall Slade ac cetera p'miss in Risheolme et Witbington p'dct valent p annu in *dib* exitib3 ultra reprisis viginti sex solid' octo denarior'; Et q p'dt terr' et tent in Gorton p'dt valent p annum in oib3 &c. sexdecim solid'; ac q p'dt burgag' et shoppa in Manchester p'dt valet p annum in oib3 &c. sex denarios, et q p'dt tertia pars de manerio de Kerksawe alias Kerksall p'dct valet p ann. in oib3 &c. quatuor libras. Et ulterius juratores &c. dicunt q p'dt messuag' sive tent vocat' le Milkwall Slade et p'dt terr et tent in Risheholme et Withington p'dt, tenent' et tempore mortis ejusdem Edwdi Syddall in bri &c. tenebantur de Nicho Langford aro p fidelitatem et reddit' duorum solid' et sex denariorum p annum pro oib3 serviciis et demandis quibuscunque; et q p'dt terr et tent in Gorton p'dt et p'dt burgagium et shoppa in Manchester p'dt tenentur et tempe mortis &c. tenebantur de Johe Lacy aro dno de Manchester pro fidelitate tantum pro oib3 serviciis &c.; et q p'dt tertia pars manerii de Kerksawe als Kerksall ac ceter' premiss' in Kerksall p'di tenentur et tenebantur de dcta dna regina nunc in capite, vi3 p duodecima p'te unius feod militis. Et ulterius p'dt jurat' &c. dicunt q p'dtus Edwdus Syddall in bri &c. nulla alia sive plura man' terr sive tent die obitus sue huit seu ten' in dnico vel in servicio pro ut jurator' p'd aliquo modo constare poterrim. In cujus rei testim uni p'ti hujus inquisicionis tum p'd escaetor quum p'dt jurator' sigilla sua apposuerunt, alteri vero pti hujus inquisicionis penes p'fat jurat' remanent' p'd escaetor sigillum suum apposuit die et anno primo suprad'.

Tho. Hesketh, Escaet.

Endorsed: Delibert infra nolat Petro Hewood gen. qui primus jurat fuit in inquisitione p'dt vicesimo septimo die Septembris anno regni dee dne regine tricesimo secund' forma statu in hujusmodi casu provisus p me Thoma Hesketh, escaetor coin p'dt.

Tho. Hesketh, Escaet.

INDEX.
Abraham, John, 55.
, Robert, 55.
Addeshede, William, 210, 211.
Adkinson, M, 143.
Adshead, William, 20.
Ainsworth, Elizabeth, 153.
, Henry, clerk, curate of Birch, 153, 155.
Alcocke, Joseph, 165.
Alexander, John, 30.
Allen, Joseph, 118.
, Mary, 55.
, Thomas, 54.
Allonson, George, gent., 129, 234.
Ambrose, Peter, gent., 94.
Andrews, Key. Robert, 169.
Angler, Mr. John, of Benton, 60, 146.
Annacotes, John de, 7, 186.
Anson, Archibald Edward Harbord, 154.
, George Henry Greville, clerk, 154, 155, 158. , John William Hamilton, Esq. , 154, 158, 160. , Sir John William Hamilton, Bart., 104, 171, 183-188. Antrobus, Elizabeth, 107. , Peter, gent., 107.
Arderne, John, 64.
Ardwick School endowed, 117.
Arstindall, James, sen., 165.
, James, jun., 165.
Ascrofl, William, gent., 21, 221.
Ashton, James, Esq., 141.
, John, gent., 88.
, John, 182. , Sir John de, 206. , Robert, gent., 88. , Thomas, 182. , William, clerk, rector of Prestwich, 70.
Ashurst, William, Esq., 110.
Ashworth, Br. Caleb, 170.
ABsheton, Sir Ralph, 96.
Asshton, John de, 180, 182, 224.
, Robert de, 180, 182, 193.
Aspinwall, George, 142.
, Hezekiah, 165.
Asselum, Hugh de, 183.
Astloy, Sir Jacob, 109.
Aston, John, 132.
, Robert de, 183.
Aynesworthe, Alan de, 194, 195, 197.
, Henry de, 232, 233, 234. , John de, 187, 197. , Thomas de, 194, 195, 197, 232, 233.
Aynscough, Radley, clerk, fellow of Coll.
church, Manchester, 153, 155., Thomas, clerk, curate of Birch, 153.
Baguley, Alice, 144.
, Edward, 97, 142, 144.
Bainbrige, Ann, 54. —, Sherwood, 54.
, Thomas, clerk, 54.
Bainbrig, Nicholas, 55.
, Sarah, 55. , Thomas, 55.
Baley, Nicholas, 142, 143.
Bamford, Anne, 8, 77, 85.
, Barton de, 7.
, George, gent., 74. , Henry, gent., 88. , John de, 227. , John, Esq., 7, 77. , John, gent., 18, 74, 85, 188. , Robert, 142, 144. , Thomas, 142, 144. , Thomas, jun. , 142. , William, gent., 129, 234.
Barch, Raufe, 83.
Bardesley, Robert, gent., 88.
Bardsley, Robert, 36.
Barlawe, Adam do, 201.
, John de, 228, 229.
, Radulphus, 203.
Barlow, Adam, 161, 165.
, Alexander, Esq., 141.
, John, 41, 142, 144, 165.
, Matthew, 144, 165.
, Thomas de, 71, 224, 232.
Barlowe, John de, 204.
, Badulphua do, 204.
, Roger de, 187, 189, 193, 195, 200.
Barton, Nicholas, 37.
Basset, Mr. William, 196, 197.

Bathurst, Dr. R, 101.
Baumfort, John de, 206.
Baylcy, Hannah, 11.
——, John, 165.
——, Richard, 11.
   Bcake, Peter, 54, 55.
Bealey, James, 165.
Beck, Marion, 72.
——, Thomas, gent., 72, 74.
   Becke, Nicholas, 83.
——, Robert, 73.
——, Thomas, 83.
   Beech, Robert, 83.
——, Thomas, 83, 84.
——, William, 83, 84.
   Bckke, Maryon, 72, 73.
——, Thomas, 72, 73.
   Bellottc, Marie, 122-124.
——, Philippe, of Moreton, gent., 122.
   Bent, John, gent., 107., Susanna, 107.
   Bentley, Mr., clerk, curate of Birch, 137, 145, 154.
Berry, Colonel, 43.
——, Major-General, 112.
   Beswick, John, 133.
——, Miles, 8.
——, Roger, 8.
   Bewicke, Robert, 83.
Bewsicke, Roger, 143.
Bexwie, Thomas, 187.
Bexwik, Miles, 188.
——, Richard, 213.
——, Roger, 188.
   Bibby, John, 192, 193.
Birch, Alexander, 142, 143.
——, Alice, 77,79,80; will of, 98,99,113.
——, Andrew, 98.
——, Anne, will of, 77, 86-89, 98, 133.
——, of Ardwick, family of, 106-120.
——, Beatrix, 99.
   Birch, of Birch, family of, 70-104. O
——, Deborah, 98, 102.
——, Edmund, 85.
——, Eliezer, 148, 163.
——, Elizabeth, 21, 22, 77, 78, 83, 99, 113, 115, 120, 152., Ellena, 98.
——, George, Esq., 8, 100, 151, 152.
——, George, gent., 20, 86; will of, 87; inquisition of, 88-90, 133, 138, 139, 160, 161.
Hall, description of, 97.
——, Humphrey, 102, 104.
——, James, 72, 85, 88.
——, Colonel John, M.P., 96, 107; memoir of, 108-114; joins the parliamentary army, 108; appointed to the command of the Kentish regiment, *ibid.;* governor of Bridgewater, *ibid.;* elected M.P. for Weobley, *ibid.;* lays siege to Bristol, *ibid.;* surprises and takes the city of Hereford, *ibid.;* of which city he is appointed governor, 109; protects Dr. Herbert Croft from violence in the cathedral of Hereford, *ibid.;* defeats a detachment of the royalists at Stow-on-the-Wold and takes prisoner Sir Jacob Astlcy, *ibid.;* summons Worcester to surrender to the parliament, *ibid.;* carries Bridgewater by storm, *ibid.;* storms Ludlow castle, Goodrich castle and Ragland castle, *ibid.;* takes the solemn league and covenant, *ibid.;* resigns the governorship of Hereford, *ibid.;* collects troops for service in Ireland with the intention of accompanying them thither, 110, but is detained in England by symptoms of insubordination in the army, *ibid.;* receives authority to prohibit the approach towards London of General Fairfax and the army, and charged with the duty of putting the city in a posture of defence, *ibid.;* proceeds on an important state mission to the parliament of Scotland, and receives the thanks of the commons of England for his services, *ibid.;* appointed high-steward of Leominster, *ibid.;* re-elected for Weobley, but secluded for his equivocal support of the Lord Protector, *ibid.;* thrown into prison by order of the governor of Hereford as an enemy to the public peace, *ibid.;* but liberated after an incarceration of several months, 112; negociates for the king's return, 113; re-elected for Weobley after the restoration, *ibid.;* commissioned to superintend the disbanding of the army and nary, *ibid.;* chosen a member of the committee to enquire into the cause of the great fire in London, and deputed to bring in a bill for the rebuilding of the city, *Hid.;* his death, *ibid.;* family connexions, *ibid.;* monument in Weobley church, 114.
   Birch, John, of Ordsal, Esq., 113.
——, John, of Manchester, gent., will of 115.
——, John, of Whitbourne, Esq., 108.
——, John, 85, 86, 142, 143.
——, John Pcploe, Esq., 114.
——, John Wyrley, Esq., 102.
——, Joyce, will of, 99.
——, Major, 114.
——, Margaret, 148.
——, Martha, 148.
——, Marv, 98, 106, 113, 147, 148.
——, Matthew, 98, 232.
——, Matthew do, 70, 121, 231.
——, Peter, 98, 99.
——, Peter, D.D., memoir of, 100-102; will of, 102., Raufe, 83.
——, Robert, 66, 72, 83, 84, 121.
——, Robert, clerk, fellow of Coll. church, Manchester, 77-79, 81.
——, Robert, of Qrindlow, gent., 138.
——, Robert, clerk, curate of Birch, will of, 147, 154.
——, Samuel, gent., 106; will of, *ibid,lli.*
——, Samuel, 107, 115-120.
——, Samuel, of Whitbourne, Esq., 113.
——, Major-General Samuel, 120.
——, Sarah, 113.
——, Sybil, 102.
——, Thomas, Esq., 120, 171.
——, Thomas, of Higher Ardwick, will of, 115-119.
——, Thomas, 9, 75, 83-86, 88, 98-100, 113, 115, 116, 118-120, 138, 142, 143, 171.
——, Thomas, clerk, 72, 107, 113.
——, Mr. Thomas, gent., 11,22,76; marriage-covenant, 77; will of, 78-81, 85, 152.
——, Colonel Thomas, M.P., 87, 89; memoir of, 90-98; enters the parliamentary army, 90; collision with Lord Strange, *ibid.;* success beforo Preston, 91; seizes upon Lancaster, *ibid.;* named as one of the committee of sequestration for Lancashire, *ibid.;* appointed governor of Liverpool, *ibid.;* elected to represent Liverpool in parliament, *ibid.;* frustrates for a timo tho benevolent intentions of Humphrey Chetham the founder, 91-93; forcibly attempts to seize upon the revenues of the church of Manchester, 93; submits to parliament a proposition for strengthening the garrison of Liverpool, 94; compasses the death of Lord Strange, *ibid.;* storms the castle of Rushin and

Peter castle, and summons the Countess of Derby (Lady Strange) to surrender the Isle of Man to the use of parliament, 95; the island given up to Col. Birch, and the countess and her children conveyed asprisoncrs to Liverpool, *ibid.;* re-elected for Liverpool, but not permitted to take his seat by the Lord Protector, *ibid.;*
again elected in the parliament summoned by Richard Cromwell,*ibid.;* entrusted by parliament with the dismantling of the castle of Liverpool, 96; defeats
Sir Greorge Booth near Northwich, *ibid.;*
his death, 97; family connexions, 98, 108, 133, 138, 139, 141, 149, 160.
   Birche, William, 30,72, 77-80, 83, 85, 86,
88, 99, 100, 121, 142, 144, 152, 165.
, William, clerk, warden of Manchester, 73-75; his ordination by Bishop Ridley, 81; nominated chaplain to King Edward VI., *ibid.;* appointed warden of the Coll. church, Manchester, *ibid.;* resigns tho wardenship, and retires to the rectory of Stanhope, *ibid.;* his will, 81-85.
, M' Anne, 143.
, Elizabeth, 220-222.
, George, 9, 72, 77-83, 85-87, 98, 99, 113, 115-120.
, Maryon, 75, 76.
, Mr., minister, 161.
, Radulphus, 214.
, Sir Thomas, priest, 74.
, Thomas, 220.
   Birches, Alexander del, 71, 187.
, Edmund del, 72, 228, 229.
, Henry del, 71, 200
, Margaret del, 72, 228, 229.
. Matthew del, 71.
, Ralph del, 72, 209, 228, 229.
, Robert del, 71, 72, 200, 228, 229.
   Birches, Thomas del, 72, 228, 229.
, William del, 71, 227, 228, 229.
   Birchis, Alexander del, 224-226.
, Henry del, 225.
, Johanna del, 225, 226.
, Robert del, 224-226.
   Biri, Adam de, 179.
   Birum, Robert de, 184.
   Bland, Sir John, Bart., 153.
   Blayney, Rowland, clerk, curate of Birch,
153, 155,156.
Blomiley, Arnold, 80.
, Elizabeth, 144.
, George, 144.
, Widow, 142.
, William, 144.
   Blundell, Mr., 91.
   Boardman, Mr. Alexander, 161, 165.
, Robert, gent., 41.
   Boden, James, 143.
   Bold, Peter, Esq., 41, 42.
   Bolder, William, 203.
   Bolton, Alice, 25.
market, value of toll in 1653, 50.
, Thomas, 25.
   Bomford, Richard, 231.
Bondini, Richard de, 192.
Booker, Peter, 51.
Booth, Captain, 91.
, Elizabeth, 27.
, Sir George, 96.
, John, 27, 37, 49.
, Martha, 27.
, Mary, 27, 49, 61.
, Sarah, 27.
   Bordman, Richard, 144.
, Widow, 142, 144, 165.
   Bosedon, Richard de, 194,195.
, Thomas de, 194, 195.
   Boston, Robert, 208.
   Bothe, Alexander del, 16, 191, 196, 197.
, Ellen del, 16.
, Right Worshipful John, Esq., of Barton, 216, 219.
, William del, 16,196, 197.
   Bouker, Dorothy, 66.
, James, 143.
, Jane, 65.
, Robert, 144.
, Widow, 143.
   Boulton, Alice, 26.
, Thomas, 25, 26.
   Bowker, Robert, 142.
Bracebriggc, Golfridus de, 180, 181.
   Bradford, John, 20, 210, 212.
, John, the martyr, 20.
, Thomas, vicar of the college of Manchester, 20, 211.
, William, capellanus, 231.
   Bradshaw, Anne, 26.
, John, 138, 143.
, Miles, 66.
, Richard, 36.
, Robert, 142, 144.
, Robert, the elder, 163.
, Roger, gent., 21, 221.
   Bradshaw, Thomas, gent., 88.
, Widow, 142, 165.
, William, 142.
   Braybon, Richard, 201.
Breckhill, Thomas, 165.
Brereton, Sir William, 109.
Breton, Richard, 189.
Briddock, Ralph, gent., 41.
Bridge, Ralph, gent., 129, 234.
Briset, Jordan, Knt., 13.
Briskoe, Mr., 38.
Brook, Robert, 144.
Brooke, Alice, 98.
, Thomas, Esq., 98.
   Broome, Henry, 142.
, Robert, 143.
, Thomas, 29.
   Browhill, William, 83, 84.
Browne, Thomas, 97.
Brownehill, William, 80.
Brownsword, Cieeley, 25, 35.
, JohD, 25, 52, 57.
   Broxupp, John, gent, 41.
Bruchcs, Henry de, 225, 226.
Buckley, Arthur, gent., 41.
, George, gent., 88.
   Burches, Henry del, 234.
, Robert del, 234.
   Buri, Sir Adam de, 224.
Burdsell, John, 37.
Burnhill, Peter de, 181.
Burtche, Thomas, 73.
, William, 73.
   Burton, Daniel, 165.
Burunn, Henry de, 181.
, Richard de, 181.
, Robert de, 181, 184, 224.
   Bury, Adam de, 71, 192.
, Richard, gent., 88.
   Butler, Major, 43.
Buterworth, Captain, 36.
Butterworth, Edward, 92.
   Butterworth, Ralph, gent., 88.
, Robert, gent., 129, 234. , Mr. Thomas, 161.
   Buxton, Michael, 41.
Bybby, Richard, 203.
Byrche, Aunes, 73, 75.
, Elizabeth, 73, 75.
, George, marriage-covenant of, 72, 73; will of, 74-76. , James, 76, 77. , Jennet, 73, 75, 77, 79, 80. , Margaret, 73, 75. ,

Thomas, 73, 78. , Thomas, gent., 8, 9, 73, 127. , William, 72, 73.
   By relics, Alexander del, 186.
, Henry de, clericus, 187. , Henry del, 233. , Matthew de, 7, 187, 223. , Radulphus de, 229, 230. , Robert, 209, 230, 233. , William del, 204, 205, 230.
   Byrom, Edward, gent., 41.
Byron, Lord, 45.
, Sir Richard de, 180, 182, 224.
, Robert de, 71.
   Cardinel, Nicholas de, 190.
CariR, Hannah, 67.
, John, Esq., 67.
   Chadirton, Galfridus de, 180, 181.
, Roger de, 197.
   Chadwick, Ellis, 87.
, John, gent., 88. , Robert, 86.
   Chapman, John, 116, 118, 119.
Checkley, Rev. George, 170.
Chester, John, constable of, 190.
, Bishop of (Dr. Chadderton), 137.
, Bishop of (Dr. Gastrell), 137. , Bishop of (Dr. Peploe), 115. , Bishop of (Dr. Sumner), 159, 160.
   Chetham, Mr. Edward, 139.
, Elizabeth, 77. , Sir Geoffrey de, 71, 224. , Geoffrey de, 184,185, 192. , Henry, gent., 129. , Humphrey, Esq., thefounder,91-93. , Mr. James, 80. , John de, 228. , John of Nuthuret, Esq., 77.
   Cholrton, Thomas de, 187.
Chorleton, Robert de, 197, 200, 201., Thomas, 74.
   Chorlton, John, clerk, 11.
, Richard de, 71. , Thomas de, 186.
   Cissor, John de, of Manchester, 5, 192.
, Matthew de, of Manchester, 5, 182.
   Clarke, Alice, 25.
, George, the founder, 25, 27.
   Claxton, Elizabeth, 54, 55.
, Hamond, gent., 54, 55. , Paulina, 55. , Susan, 55.
   Clayden, Jordan de, 197.
   Cleyburne, William, B.D., prebendary of Eipon, 73.
Cliffe, Deborah, 61.'
Clowes, Thomas, 118.
Cobden, Richard, Esq., 172.
Colayn, Robert, capeUanus, 202-204.
Colliar, Thomas, 165.
Constable, Sir William, 47.
Constantine, Mr., clerk, 64.
Conventicle act enforced at Birch, 148.

Coppocke, John, 165.
Corporation act, 149.
Cotton, Beatrix, 99,152.
, Philip, Esq., 99.
, William, Esq., 99.
   Couper, Lieutenant, 49.
Cowper, Ralph, 138.
Croft, Dr. Herbert, 109.
Crompton, Henry de, 202.
Crosse, William del, 202.
Croxton, George, 104.
Culcheth, Mr. Thomas, 62.
Cundall, Maister, of Ripon, 73.
   Dalby, Henry de, 190.
Dale, Joseph, clerk, curate of Birch, 152, 155.
Dalton, Richard, 82, 84.
Davenport, Sir Humphrey, 11.
, Katharine, 9.
, Robert, gent., 9.
   Davie, John, 144.
, Mary, 142, 144. , William, 201.
   Davies, John, 98.
   Dawson, John, 27.
, Widow, 165.
   Deacon, Robert, 189.
Deane, Alice, 113.
, Esther, 63.
, Mr., 56, 58. , Thomas, 113.
   Delves, Mr., 52.
Denison, Joseph, Esq., 172.
Denton, Roger de, 187.
Derick, Mr. James Macduff, 156.
Derby, Countess of (Charlotte de la Tre mouille) 95., Earl of (Charles Stanley, 8th earl of), 96.
, Earl of (Ferrars), 2. , Earl of (James Stanley, 7th earl of), 94, 95.
Desborough, General, 43.
Dewhurst, John, gent., 21, 221.
Diccouson, John, 9.,
Dickanson, John, 165.
Dickenson, Alice, 166.
, Henry, gent., 41. , Mr. John, 104, 140, 141, 153-156. , John, of Levenshulme, abstract of will, 166-168. , Miss Mary, 141. , Mary, 166. , Miss, 104. , Robert, 165. , Thomas, gent., 41.
Dickonson, Margaret, 144.
, Robert, 143. , Widow, 142.
   Diddesb' Jordan de, 189.
Diddesbury, William de, 191.
Didesbur', William de, 179.
Didisb'y, William de, 231.

Didsbury, William de, 71, 121.
Digle, William, 132.
Dikonson, John, 142, 143.
Doddridge, Dr., 169.
Dolfinus, William, 189.
Doly, Sir William, 71, 224.
Duckenficld, Captain William, 94.
Dudusbury, William de, 224.
Dugard, George, clerk, curate of Birch, 154, 155.
Dukinfield, Anne, 88, 89.
, Colonel, 95.
, Francis, gent., 86, 88, 89.
   Dunbaven, Mr. Daniel,of Warrington, 146.
, Elizabeth, 146.
   Duncuthley, Edmund, 21, 213, 217.
, Margaret, 21, 213, 217. , Ralph, 213, 217.
   Dyconson, J4hn, 9., Richard, 9.
Eaton, Mr., 38.
Edge, Anne, 11, 97, 138.
, Captain, 10, 171. , Ebenezer, 11, 161, 163. , Hannah, 11. , John, 11. -, Katharine, 11. , Mary, 11. , Mr., 161, 165. , Oliver, 10; will of, 11,138,143,160. , Captain Oliver, will of, 11. , Thomas, 11.
   Edmundson, Alonia, 17.
, Geoffrey, 17, 201, 202. , John, 17, 201.
   Egerton, Peter, 92.
, Wilbraham, Esq., 171.
   Elcocke, Thomas, 165.
England, John, 144.
Entwisscll, Alexander, Esq., 10.
Evys, Matthew, prior of Chester, 218.
Fairfax, Ferdinando Lord, 91.
, Sir Thomas, 108, 110.
   Fallowfield, Jordan de, 6, 7.
, William de, 6,7. ffalwcfeld, Jordan de, 186. , William de, 186.
   Farneworke, Adam de, 184, 191, 192.
Farncworth, Adam de, 15, 191, 192. —
—, Richard de, 15, 192, 193.
, Robert de, 15, 192, 193.
   Farrington, Captain, 91.
, Mr., 90.
   Faulkner, John, 41. ffawfeld, Jordan de, 185. ffawfeld, William de, 185, Fell, Dr. John, 100, 101.
, Thomas, 92.
   Ferneley, Adam de, 17.
, Robert de, 17. '
   Fernilegh, Adam do, 198, 199.
, Robert de, 198, 199.

Ferror, John, capellanus, 229, 230.
Finch, Elizabeth, 151.
——, Hannah, 151.
, Henry, clerk, curate of Birch, 11, 139, 149-151, 155, 160, 161, 165, 168.
, James, 151. , John, the elder, 163. , Mr. , 64. , Nathan, 151. , Nicholas, 151.
Fleetcroft, Robert, gent., 41.
Fleetwood, Mr. Richard, 91.
Fletcher, Elizabeth, 166.
, George, 165. , John, 165. , Martini, 64.
, Mrs., of Levenshulme, 168. , Raph, 32.
, Richard, 165. , Thomas, 231.
Ford, Alexander, gent., 26.
, Isabel, 26. , William, gent., 26.
Foulks, John, 100.
Frost, Walter, Esq., 96.
Fytbeler, John le, 201., William le, 201.
Galfridus, dean of Manchester, 231.
Gardner, Elizabeth, 117-119.
, Thomas, 116-119.
Gamett, John, 165.
Garside, Joane, 38.
Gartside, Adam, 132.
Gauvven, John, 208.
Gaythorne, Anne, 11.
, John, 11.
, Thomas, 11.
Geaat, Nicholas, 103.
Gee, Elizabeth, 25.
, George, clerk, 25, 26.
, Jonathan, 41. , Raph, 25.
Gerrard, Miles, gent., 21, 221.
Gill, Madam, 162.
Gilliam, John, gent., 41.
Gillibrand, Mary, 165.
Girlington, Lady, 91.
Glossop, Raphe, 143.
Glover, John, 127.
Goate, Mary, 55.
Goddard, James, 115.
Goffe, Colonel, 43.
Goodwin, Robert, Esq., 110.
Gorton, Edward, 143.
Gousil, Symon de, 180.
Gousul, Sir Simon de, 3, 181.
, Simon de, 2.
Gratrieke, Henry, 165.
Greatres, Thomas, 81.
Greaves, Thomas, 143.
Green, Alexander, gent., 41.
, Isaae, gent.. 14.
Greene, Mr. Alexander, 66.
, Ralph, gent., 129, 21. , Roger, of Congleton, 122, 124.

Greenebaulgh, Thomas, Esq., 97.
Grelle, Robert, 2.
Grotton, Robert de, 193.
Grimshaw, Mr., 162.
Guildhouses, the, 3-5,179-182.
Gylsford, Miles, 73.
Gymer, Katharine, 55.
Haghtone, Radulphus, gent., 221.
Hale, Adam, 80.
Hall, Isaae, 138, 142, 143.
, Mr., clerk, curate of Birch, 145,154, ,
James, gent., 88. , James, 116-119.
Halle, John, 107, 142, 148.
Halliwell, Ewen, 84.
, Richard, gent., 41.
Hampson, Daniel, 166.
Hardey, Elizabeth, 80.
Hardman, John, 36, 165.
Hardy, Henry, gent., 129, 234.
, Robert, gent., 129, 234.
Harewode, Alexander de, 181.
, Gilbert de, 181.
Harison, John, clerk, 60, 64.
Harmcr, Samuel, gent., 41.
Harrison, James, 165.
Harter, George Gardner, clerk, curate of
Birch, 153-155. Hartley, Edward, 107.
, John, Esq., 41. , John, gent., 41. , John, 10. , Thomas, 49, 138, 142, 144.
Haselum, Hugh de, 6, 184, 185.
Hathersage, Matthew de, 2, 4-6, 70.
Hatirseg', Matthew de, 184.
Haughton, John, 78.
, Ralph, gent, 21, 129, 234.
Hav'sege, Matthew, 179, 223.
Haward, Alice, will of, 70.
, Samuel, 70.
Haworth, Edmund, gent., 88.
Haydock, Matthew de, seneschal of Salford, 182, 225, 226.
Hazlewood, Miss Hannah, 169.
Hea, William de, 232.
Healdhouscs, vide Guildhouses.
Heeton, William de, 183,184.
Heginbothom, Beulah, 64.
, Cassandra, 64.
——, Henry, 64.
—, Joane, 63, 64., William, 63, 64.
Heginbothom, William, the younger, 63;
will of, 64.
Hesketh, Rev. Robert, 168, 169.
, Thomas, Esq., 21,129,221,234,237.

Heth, Edward, 17, 199.
, William, 17, 199.
Heton, Thomas de, 180, 181.
Hey, Anne, 86.
, Ellis, gent., 86, 88, 89.
Heylde, William, 8, 188.
Heyrick, Richard, warden of Manchester,
4, 93, 146.
Heyton, William de, 224.
Heywood, Peter, gent., 129, 234, 237.
, Peter, 118.
Higgen, Elizaboth, 73.
, Mr. Thomas, 73.
Eiginbotom, Martha, 39.
, William, 39.
Higson, Mr. John, 172.
Hill, Elizabeth, 120.
Hilton, William, 229, 230.
Hindley, Robert, gent., 21, 221.
Hobson, George, 167.
, John, 142, 165.
, John, jun., 143.
, Raphe, gent., 133.
, Robert, 130, 235.
, Thomas, 143.
Hoghton, Captain, 91.
, Sir Gilbert, 90, 91.
, Lady, 91.
, Mr. Thomas, 91.
Holand, Cecily, 83.
, James, 79.
Holcroft, Ellena, 98.
——, Thomas, Esq., 98.
Holford, John, Esq., 172.
, Thomas, Esq., 5.
Holland, Colonel, 91.
, Rev. John, 169.
, Richard, Esq., 132.
Hollinworth, Mr., of Manchester, 146.
, Richard, clerk, 60.
Holond, Richard de, 225, 226.
Holt, Matilda del, 6, 7, 185, 188.
, Mr., of Stubley, 90.
, Thomas de, 197, 200, 233, 234.
Honeford, Richard de, 121,188, 231, 232.
, William de, 186.
Honford, Agnes de, 7, 188.
, Geoffrey de, 7, 188.
, Henry de, 7, 188.
, William de, 7,14, 187, 188.
Hoppewode, Adam de, 197.
Houghton, Rev. John, 169.

, Rev. Pendlebury, 170.
, Raphe, 80.
, Sir Richard, 94.
  Houlme, George, 80.
Hoult, John, 142.
Hudson, Beulah, 64.
, Henry, 108.
, Raphe, 98.
  Hughes, Henry, 142, 143.
, Thomas, 165.
  Hull, Cecilia del, 191.
Hulm, Galfridus de, 224.
Hulme, Adam, 143.
, Charles, 63.
, David, 63.
, Edward, 165.
, Francis Philips, 'clerk, curate of Birch, 153, 155.
, George, 81.
, John, 165.
, Laurence, 212.
, Obadiab, 161, 163.
, Mr. Robert, of Reddish, 80.
, Thomas, 165.
, William, 165.
  Hulton, Adam de, 121, 231., Elizabeth, 78.
, John de, 180, 182, 188, 193, 206, 224-226.
, John de, of Farnworth, 206.
, Richard de, 180, 182, 188, 193, 224.
, Thomas de, rector of Bury, 205, 206.
, Robert de, 6, 184, 185.
, William de, 121, 231.
, William, 78.
  Hunt, John, 142, 143, 216, 219, 220.
, Margaret, 216.
, Rauff, 216.
, William, 209.
  Hyde, Mr., clerk, 39., Robert, 168.
  Hygen, Anthony, clerk, dean of Ripon,
will of, 73, 82, 84, 85, 88.
, Edward, 73, 82.
, Elizabeth, 73.
, George, 73, 82, 84.
, John, 73.
, Robert, 73.
, Thomas, will of, 73.
  Hyndsone, Jenet, 80.
  Ivo, Brother, canon of Beauchief abbey.
  Jackson, Thomas, 214.
Jackson, Richard, 83.
, Robert, 117, 118.

, William, 32, 41.
  Jankens, Richard, 80.
Janney, Thomas, 142, 144.
Jepson, Alice, 77, 78.
, Mr., 57.
  Jepsonne, John, 77.
  Jerusalem, Knights Hospitallers of, 12-15, 189-191, 222. Jerzey, Peter, 59.
Jobson, William, 143. Johnson, John, 83.
, Mrs. Margaret, 168. , Johnson, Richard, 142, 143. , Robert, 31.
  Jolley, Mr., 38.
  Jones, Edmund, clerk, 60.
  Kay, Frances, 131.
, Jchn, 86. , Richard, 131.
  Kaye, Thomas, gent., 129, 234.
Kelsey, Colonel, 43.
Kenion, Abram, 143.
, M Dorathie, 38, 49.
, Joseph, 142, 143.
  Kenyon, Dorothy, 67.
, Edward, B.D., rector of Prestwich, 60.
, George, gent., 129,132, 234. , Ralph, of Gorton, 127. , Randull, 127. , Mr. Roger, M.P., 49. , Roger, of Parkhead, gent., 49. , Roger, clerk of the peace, 150, 160.
  Key, Corporal, 36.
Kinsey, Anne, 87.
, Jchn, gent., 87, 133, 143.
  Kirsley, Jeremiah, 162.
Knot, Elizabeth, 11.
Knowles, Edmund, 142, 143.
Kyrkhalgh, Laurence, 212, 213.
  Lacy, John, Esq., 131, 236.
Laghokes, Hugh de, 192.
, William de, 192, 193.
  Lagoe, Dorothy, 50, 65.
, Waldive, Esq., 50.
  Lambert, Lord, 43.
Lancashire, James, 41.
Lane, Thomas, Esq., 21.
Langford, Edward, 165.
  Langford, Nicholas, 144.
, Nicholas, Esq., 131, 236. , William, 144.
  Lawranee, James, 21, 213.
, Jane, 21, 213, 214.
  Lawton, John, of Lawton, Esq., 122.
Leaver, William, of Darcy Leaver, 132.
Leech, John, clerk, curate of Birch, 153, 155.
  Lees, Agnes, 130, 235.
Lees, Mr. John, 67.

Leeze, James, 38.
Leighe, Richard, gent., 129, 234.
Lenny, Richard, gent., 88.
Leya, John le, 184.
Leylond, Henry, 211, 213.
Leyver, Alexander, gent., 129, 234.
Lightbowne, James, 93.
LiUy, Margaret, 117, 119.
Lingard, Richard, clerk, curate of Birch, 145, 154. Livesey, Raph, 32. Lomax, Mr., 56.
Longeford, Nichobma de, 179, 180, 182. Longford, Henry, arm., 231.
, Nicholas de, 2, 3, 4. , Sir Nicholas de, 72, 197, 200, 232, 234. , Nigel de, 2. , Noel de, 231, 232.
  Lonsdale, Miles, clerk, curate of Birch, 153,155. Loyd, Mrs., 162. Lyne, Roger, 165.
  Make, W., 165.
Mamecestr', Galfridus de, 181, 183, 184, 187, 231, 232.
, Henry de, 181, 185, 186. , Houlot de, 185. , Jordan de, 186, 231, 232. , Luke de, 183, 184, 231, 232. , Richard de, 194. , Robert de, 186, 231. , Symon de, 184, 231. , Thomas de, 187, 194, 231.
  Manchester, Geoffrey de, 5, 6,121.
, Geoffrey, dean of, 121. , Henry de, 6, 7. , Houlot de, 6. , Jordan de, 121. , Luke de, 5, 6. , Robert de, 7. , Robert, son of Symon de, 121.
  Manchester, Thomas, son of Geoffrey, son of Luke de, 121.
, William de, 6, 7, 185, 186.
  Manifould, Jane, 148.
Marchal, Henry de, 201.
, Richard le, 195.
, Thomas le, 192, 193, 195.
  Markland, Thomas, gent., 21, 221.
Marler, Robert, gent., 41.
Marlor, Raphe, 144.
Marshall, Miss, 159.
, Mrs., 160.
  Martindale, Adam, clerk, 148.
Mascy, Constance, 212, 213.
, Edward, 212.
, Hugh de, 181. , Robert de, 181, 212, 213.
  Massey, Anne, 26.
, Edward, gent., 26. , Hamnct, 26. , Henry, 63. , Isabel, 26, 39. , Joel, 26. , Katharine, 26. , Margaret, 26. , Randle, 26.
  Massie, Edward, gent., 27.

Meadowcroft, Giles, gent., 94.
Meanley, Rev. Richard, 170.
Meeke, William, clerk, 60.
Mellor, William, 143.
Middulton, Roger de, 191.
Midilton, Roger de, 187, 188.
Milkewalleslade, Ellen de, 16,17,121,122, 233.
——, John de, 17, 121, 122, 198, 233.
——, Robert de, 16, 17, 121, 194, 195, 198, 232-234. ——, Robert de, the younger, 17, 121, 198, 233.
Millington, Worral, 116, 118.
Minshall, Mr. Thomas, 66.
Molineux, Lord, 90.
Moore, Colonel Samuel, 110.
More, Cecilia de la, 15.
——, Richard de la, 14, 189, 190. , William de la, 15, 190.
Morgan, Colonol, lOf 109.
Morris, Lydia, 146.
——, William, clerk, 146.
Morte, Adam, mayor of Preston, 91.
Mosedon, Henry de, 7, 187.
JUosley, Sir Edward, 11., Rowland, Esq. , 89.
Mosley, Sir Nicholas, 89.
——, Oswald, gent., 25.
Mossc, Anne, 83.
——, John, 83. , Robert, 74. , William, 165.
Moston, Richard de, 179-182, 184, 187, 192, 232.
——, William de, 224.
Moulins, Roger de, 14.
Mylkwalslade, Robert de, 197.
Naplouse, Gamier de, 14, 189.
Neuton, John de, 201.
Newcome, Mr., clerk, 64, 106, 160.
Nicholson, Isaac, 165.
——, Ralph, 138.
——, William, 142, 143, 166.
Nield, Henry, gent., 41.
Noreis, William le, 184.
Norman, Elizabeth, 67, 145.
——, James, Esq., 67.
——, Sarah, 145. , Thomas, clerk, curate of Birch, 145, 154.
Norreis, Jordan, 191.
——, William le, 121, 231.
Norris, Matthew, Esq., 114.
——, Winifred, 114.
Norros, William de, 191.
Norst, Jone, 123.
Norton, William de, 191.

Nuehye, John, 208.
Oderoft, John, 162.
Offerton, Robert, 165.
Okell, Mrs., 162.
Oldfelt, William, Esq., 99.
Oldham, Alice, 166.
——, Robert, 166.
Olgreve, Thomas, 211.
Ormerod, Oliver, clerk, curate of Birch, 154, 155.
Ormestou, Adam de, 181.
Ormond, James, Duke of, 101.
Orrell Elizabeth, 64., ranees, 64.
Ottiwell, Elizabeth, 27, 29, 31, 38, 39, 65.
——, James, gent., 41. , Joseph, clerk, 27, 38, 39.
Ottywell, Elizabeth, 55.
——, John, 55.
Ouldam, George, 26.
Ouldham, John, 41.
Oweo, Robert, gent., 41.
Palgrave, Mary, 54.
——, Nathaniel, clerk, 54.
Par, Henry de, 225, 226.
Parkinson, Renolds, 66, 142, 144.
Parte, John, 165.
Patrick, Dr. Simon, bishop of Chichester, 101.
P'ceral, John, 127, 215.
Pearson, John, 166.
——, Thomas, 166.
Pedigrees: —
Biroh of Ardwick, 120.
of Birch, 102.
Dickenson of Birch, 105.
Edge of Ruaholme, 12.
Platt of Platt, 24.
Siddall of Blade, 136.
Worsley of Crompton, 68.
of Putt, 66.
Peirson, John, 83.
Pendlebury, Mary, 169.
Penilbury, Elias de, 4, 181.
——, Robert de, 181.
——, Roger de, 3, 180, 181.
Pennilbury, Adam de, 191.
Penruddocke, Captain, 112.
Peploe, Elizabeth, 114.
——, John, 114.
Percival, Widow, 143.
Peropont, Richard de, 181.
Perscvall, Elizabeth, 80, 87.
PersiTall, George, 80, 81.
——, John, 142, 143.

——, Richard, 142,148., Thomas, 142, 143.
——, Edmund, 107.
Pilkington, Robert, Esq., 21, 221.
Pilkinton, Alexander de, 181, 187, 191.
Pilkynton, Sir Roger de, 193.
Plat, Hugh de, 189.
——, Roger de, of Holyngreye, 191.
——, William del, 227,229.
Piatt, Adam del, 201.
——, Alonia del, 17, 201-204. , Amabilia del, 16, 191. , Annes, 21, 218. , Cecilia del, 15, 16,191, 192. , Constance, 18-20, 206, 209, 211, 212 , Edmund, 22, 23, 78, 80, 222. , Elizabeth, 21, 22, 77, 222.
Piatt, Ellen del, 15,16,121,192,194,195, 197, 233.
——, Ellen del, the younger, 16,195,196. , family of, 12-24. , Geoffrey del, 16, 191. , Geoffrey, 18, 208. , Henry del, 15,16, 191,194, 195. , Henry del, the younger, 16, 197. , Isabella, 21, 22, 222. , Jane, 20. , Joane, 22, 217, 218. , John, 18; indulgence granted to, by Pope Pius II., 19: letters of affiliation addressed to, ibid., 20, 21, 22, 206, 208, 209, 212-217, 220-222. , John del, 16, 17, 194, 195, 198, 200-203, 209. , John del, the younger, 17, 203, 204. , John, gent., 77. , Katharine del, 17,18,206,207, 209. , Loreta del, 16, 200. , Margaret del, 16, 17,199, 200, 219. , Nicholas del, 17, 201-206. , Ralph, gent., 78. , Richard, 20; letters of affiliation granted to, 21; inquisition p.m. of, ibid., 22, 207. , Richard del, 15-17; will of, 18, 193-198, 199, 200, 201, 206, 209. , Robert del, 15; will of, 16,17,121, 192-195, 233, 234. , Roger del, 15, 16, 192-195. , William, 20, 214, 215, 220.
Platte, Henry de la, 192.
——, John, 74. , Richard, 210-212, 216-222.
——, Richard, sen., 215.
Playford, George, 54, 55, , Henry, of Northrepps, 51.
——, John, 54, 55. , Mary, 51. , Nicholas, 54, 55. , Richard, 54.
Podmore, Richard, 122, 123.
Pomfret, George, 142, 143.
Poole, Raphe, 66.
Pope, William, 54, 55.
Poynton, John de,.,?1.
Prescot, George, 11"2.
Prestewyche, Radulphus de, 203, 204.
Preston, Captain, 91.

Prestwich, Edmund, Esq., 10.
, James de, 228, 229. , Mr., 90.
Prestwiche, Radulphus, 207.
Pride, Colonel, 108.
Prowdeluffe, Radulphus, 212.
Pursglove, Richard, 84.
Purvey, Major, 91.
Pye, Sir Walter, 111.
Rabi, Jordan de, 185.
Radcliff, Major, 93.
, John de, of Ordsal, 202.
, Radulphus de, 202, 204.
Radcliffe, Sir Alexander, 90.
, Robert, 143. , Sir "William, 78.
Radeclif, John de, of Chadderton, 201, 202.
, Radulphus de, 204, 205. , Sir Ralph, 204, 205.
Radeclive, Richard de, 180, 181.
, William de, 181, 188.
Ratcliffe, Edward, gent., 107.
, Sarah, 107.
Rathband, Nathaniel, clerk, 60.
Rawlinge, Richard, minister, 83, 85.
Rawson, Ralph, 101.
Reade, Henry, 142.
Redfern, John, 116.
Reddish, Robert de, 71.
Redich, James, 142, 144.
, Matthew de, 181. , Richard de, 187, 188. , Robert de, 183, 184. , Stephen de, 186.
Rediche, George, 231.
Redig', Robert, 179.
Rediot, Edward, 73.
Redyohe, Robert de, 224.
Renshaw, Jonathan, 165.
Richardson, Edward, 98.
, George, 41.
, Thomas, 166.
Richebery, John, clerk, 18, 208.
Ridehorn, Richard, 232.
Ridge, Jane, 64.
Ridinges, Abednego, 142.
———, John, 143.
Ridings, John, 41.
Rigbie, Edward, Esq., 88.
Rigby, Alexander, Esq., 98.
, Anne, 98.
, Cicely, 25. , Nicholas, 25.
Righway, Sarah, 99.
Robinson, Alice, 98.
Robinson, John, Esq., 98.
Rogers, Thomas, 55.
Rotheram, Dr. Cale, 169,170.

Rothwell, Mr. Philip, 153.
Rowbotham, Edward, 165.
Rowley, Geoffrey, 123.
Rudd, John, 212.
Rupert, Prince, 91.
Ruschebery, J., 208.
Rusholme, township of; derivation of name, 1; the several hamlets of which it consists, *ibid.;* its early proprietors, 2—24; its more recent possessors, 25136; erection and endowment of Birch chapel, 137-141; ground-plan of chapel, 142; hamlets connecting themselves with the chapel, 143; its ecclesiastical relations, 144; curates of chapel, 145-155; description of chapel, 155; chapel rebuilt, 156-159; erection of Trinity church and St. John's, Longsight, 159; origin of dissent in the township, 160; erection of Piatt chapel, 161-164; ground-plan of Piatt chapel, 165; endowment provided, 166-168; list of ministers, 168-170; population returns of township, 170; valuation of township, 171; its area, *ibid.;* Roman road, 172; Nicker ditch, 172-175.
Rusholme, Henry de, 5, 6.
Rushton, Edward, 171.
Russchun, Henry de, 184.
Russum, Henry de, 183-185.
Ryland, Peter, 162.
Sacheverell, Philippa, 128.
, Ralph, 128.
Schetham, Galfridus de, 232.
Scholar, Ruth, 67.
Scocroft, Richard, gent., 129, 234.
Schofield, Anthony, 11.
Scholes, Joseph, gent., 88.
, Master, clerk, 64.
Scoles, Hugh, capollanus, 207.
Seaton, Major-General Sir John, 91.
Seddon, Abraham, 132.
Sedon, Randle, 144.
Sergeant, Cassandra, 64.
, Clemence, 67.
, Hannah, 67. , Peter, gent., 64. , Thomas, gent., 67.
Shalcross, James, 188.
Shclm'dyn, Nicholas, 210.
Shelmerdine, Edmund, 37.
, Elijah, 165.
, John, 142,143. 165. , Mary, 37. , Nicholas, 20. , Peter, 63. , Thomas, 23, 98,137, 142, 144, 163, 165. , Thomas, sen., 144. , William, 142, 144.

Sholcrosse, Steven, 142.
Shotellesworth, Roger de, the younger, 197.
Sidal, Adam, 144.
Siddall, Alice, 127., Anne, 127.
, Edward, 10, 122-127; inquisition of, 128-131, 134.
, Elizabeth, 125-127, 130. , Ellen, 127.
, Genet, 127. , George, 128, 130-134, 142, 144. , George, gent., 27. , John, 133, 163. , John, geut., 133, 138, 165, 167, 172. , Rev. Joseph Lawton, 170. , Katharine, 132, 133. , Martha, 27. , Mr., of Slade, 137, 138, 142-144, 162,171. n, of Slade, family of, 121-136. , Thomas, 125-127, 130,133, 138. , Thomas, of Burnage, gent., 167. , Richard, 10, 122; will of, 124-127. , William, 127.
Skippon, Major-General, 43.
Slade, Emmota del, 17, 203, 204.
Hall, description of, 134.
, Hugh de, 228, 229. , John del, 17, 203, 228, 229. , Jone, 123, 124, 128. , Rauffe, gent., 122-124,128. , Thomas, marriage-covenant of, 122 124, 128.
Smethton, Elias de, prior of the Knights
Hospitallers in England, 15, 191.
Smith, Adam, 86.
, Edmund, 142,144. , John, 144,165. , Mary, 106. , Richard, 143. , Thomas, 144.
Sondeforth, Roger, 213.
Sparrow, Major, 91.
Stampe, M, 66.
, Philip, gent., 41.
Standish, Richard, Esq., 142.
Stanelay, Sir Ralph de, 206.
Stapleton, Bryan, Esq., 110.
Starkie, John, 92.
Stokcport, Jordan de, clerk, 232.
Stonehewer, John, 27, 37, 38.
, Martha, 27, 37.
, Mary, 37.
Stoppard, Joseph, 144.
Strangeways, John de, 203.
Strangwayes, Katharine, 8.
, Philip, Esq., 8.
, Thomas, 8. , William, gent., 8, 9.
Strangwaies, John, 9.
Strangweis, Philip, Esq., 9.
, Thomas, 9.
Streete, William, 143.
Stretford, Hugh de, 181.
Strongwas, Galfridus de, 186, 187, 225,

227.

Syddall, Edward, of Slade, 234-236. , Elizabeth, 235, 236. , George, 235, 236. , Thomas, 235.

Sykes, Miss Hannah, of Leeds, 168.

Taillour, John le, of Manchester, 194,195. Talbot, Mr. George, 91.

, Sir John, 91.

Talior, Robert, 142,143.

Tarlton, Thomas, gent., 21, 221.

Taylor, Jacob, 143.

, Samuel, clerk, curate of Birch, 151, 152, 155.

, Widow, 143.

Tele, Agnes, 191.

, John, 191.

Teliare, Edward, 80.

Tetlow, Elizabeth, 99.

, John, clerk, curate of Birch, 99,152, 155.

Thomeley, Handle, 162.

Thorp, James, 166.

Thropp, Anne, 11.

——, William, 11.

Tildeeley, Edward, Esq., 10.

, Mr., 90.

, Thurstan, 229, 230.

Timperlev, Thomas, 142, 143.

Touchet, Mr., of Manchester, 170.

Trafford, Edmund, 207.

, Edmund de, 206.

, Sir Edmund, 4. , Geoffrey de, 5, 182. , Henry de, 8-7, 71, 179-182, 185, 186, 194, 195, 197, 204, 224, 232., Sir Henry de, 2, 4, 5, 179, 182,193, 224, 232, 234. , Trafford, John de, 206. , Nicholas de, 5, 182. , Ralph de, 181. , Richard de, 2, 5, 71, 182, 184, 185, 192, 224. , Richard de, rector of Cheadle, 180, 182. , Robert de, 5, 71,181,182,197, 224, 232, 234., Thomas, 207. , Thomas de, 5, 182, 200, 233, 234.

Travis, George, 23.

, Widow, 165.

Traviss, Richard, 142, 144.

, Thomas, 142, 144.

Twyford, Robert, clerk, curate of Birch, 152, 155.

, William, clerk, curate of Birch, 152, 155.

Tyrer, Robert, 116.

Ver, Gilbert de, 190.

Vost, Richard, 166., Thomas, 166.

Walker, Elizabeth, 27.

, George, 27. , James, 116. , John, 116,

117, 119. , Robert, 163, 165. , Thomas, 30, 230.

WaltoD, Colonel, 96.

West, Thomas, Lord De la Warre, 7.

Whalley, Commissary-General, 43.

Wharton, Lord, 90, 91.

Whelocke, Richard, 122.

Whelwrighte, John, 80.

Whitaker, Mr., 63.

, Rev. Mr. John, 166, 169.

, Richard, 166, 167.

Whiteacrcs, Richard, capellanus, 227-229. Whitehead, Edmund, geut., 88. Whitelegg, James, 166.

, Thomas, 166, 167.

Whitelegge, Rev. William, 170.

Whiticar, Edmund, 142, 143.

Whittaker, Richard, 161, 163, 165.

, Widow, 165.

Whitworth, John, gent., 41.

Wigan, Elizabeth, 146.

, John, clerk, curate of Birch, 140, 145, 146, 154.

, Lydia, 146.

Wilde, Mr., of Rochdale, 56, 57.

Wildman, Major, 44.

Wilkcnsone, Henry, 80.

Wilkinson, Anne, 99.

, John, 142, 144.

, John, jun., 142. , Richard, 165. , Thomas, 66.

Williamson, Widow, 142, 143.

Willinson, Ellen, 65.

Wilson, Peter, 55.

Wilsone, Margaret, 80.

Wilton, Gilbert de, 190.

Wimbcll, Nicholas, 143.

Wolstenholme, Francis, gent., 88.

Wolwerke, Thomas, 142,143.

, Edward, 98.

Wood, Francis, 144, 162, 165.

, Francis, the elder, 163. , James, 118. , John, 144. , Mary, 118, 119. , Richard, gent., 129, 234. , William, 165.

Woorthington, James, gent., 221.

Woosencroft, Daniel, 115.

Woosencrofte, Martha, 165.

Workedeley, Richard de, 187.

Workesley, Edmund de, 206.

, Elias de, 25.

, Robert, ar., 229, 230.

Worsley, Alice, 70.

, Charles, 25-27, 80, 31, 35-37, 50, 52, 58, 61, 64-67, 70, 142, 144,162. , Charles, gent., 14. , Mr. Charles, 29,

80, 38, 62, 63,162, 166. , Lieut-Col. Charles, 87, 38. , Major-General Charles, M.P., 38, 39; memoir of, 39-51; obtains a commission in the parliamentary army, 39; raises a regiment, *ibid.;* appointed to the command of Cromwell's own regiment of foot, 40; is present at the dissolution of the long parliament, *ibid.;* takes possession of the speaker's mace, *ibid.;* elected M.P. for Manchester, 41; appointed to the command of the army in the counties of Lancaster, Chester and Stafford, 42; proceeds to eject scandalous ministers and schoolmasters, 44; disarms papists and malignants, *ibid.;* carries into execution the laws against drunkenness, swearing and profanity, 45; prohibits horse-racing in Cheshire, *ibid.;* proposes to the Protector to extend the taxation of delinquents' estates to incomes of £50 per annum, 46; sequestrates the estates of delinquents, *ibid.;* much troubled by the sect of Quakers, *ibid.;* suppresses alehouses, *ibid.;* summoned to London by the Protector, 47; where, on his arrival, he dies and is buried in Westminster abbey, *ibid.;* his character, as drawn by his contemporaries, 48; provision made for his widow and children by the Protector and his council, *ibid.;* alleged indignity offered to his remains, 49; his family connexions, *ibid.;* his portrait, sword and fac-simile of autograph, 50, 61, 63, 66, 67,171.

Worsley, Charles, Esq., 167.

, Charles, clerk, will of, 54.

, Charles Carill, Esq., 67, 189.

, Cieeley, 25.

, Clemence, 67.

, Clementia, 62, 63, 67.

, Deborah, 62, 63, 67.

, Dorothie, 38, 50, 66, 70.

, Edward, 25, 26, 39,142, 144.

, Edward, clerk, 27, 29, 31, 39, 51-55, 58, 65.

, Elizabeth, 25, 27, 38, 65.

, Elizabeth Carill, 67.

O, family of, 25-70.

, George, 27, 29, 30, 31, 37, 39, 58, 59,65, 66,138, 171.

, Isabel, 26, 39.

i John Carill, Esq., 67, 168.

Worsley, John Carill, clerk, 67.

, Martha, 27-29, 30, 35, 39, 49, 63, 65, 66.
, Mary, 27, 36, 37, 49,52,54, 55, 65.
, Mr., 165,170, 171.
, Mr., of Heild House, 171.
, Nicholas, 25.
Otes 25.
1 Peter, 62, 63, 67, 166, 167.
, Ralph, gent., 4, 11, 14, 23, 25-27 i will of, 28-32 *(vide* also 61-63), 35, 37-39, 49, 51-53, 55, 57-59, 61, 64-66, 70, 138, 144,149, 160-163, 166.
, Raphe, 137, 142.
, Raphe, clerk, 27, 29, 31, 57-60, 65.
, Roger, 38, 50, 66, 70.
, Sarah, 39, 49, 62, 63; will of, 64-66, 70.
, Thomas, 37.
, Thomas Carill, Esq., 67, 159, 171.
Worthington, Esther, 63.
, James, gent., 21.
, John de, 193.
, John, 166.
, Robert, 166,167.
Wosencroft, James, 142.
Wright, John le, capellanus, 227-229.
, Thomas, clerk, curate of Birch, 140, 152, 155.
Wrigley, Henry, 97., Samuel, 165.
Wroe, Richard, D.D., warden of Manchester, 150,152.
Wynn, Sir Richard, 91.
Wyrkesworthe, Nicholas de, clerk, 193, 224.
Wyrley. Humphrey, Esq., 102, 104,152.
, Mrs., 103.
, Sybil, 102.
Wytfeld, Alice de, 71, 226. , Henry de, 71, 225-227.
Yieldhouscs, *vide* G-uildhouses.

INDEX TO PLACES IN THE HISTORY OP BIRCH CHAPEL.
VOL. XLVII.
Akedone, 121, 231.
Altham, 38.
Altrincham, 170.
Ardwick, 10,106,114-120; Green, 97-8;
House, 160. Ascalon, 14. Ashley, 170.
Ashton-under-Lyne, 27, 64, 88,152, 173 4; Moss, 174. Aston, 27.
Audenshaw (Awdwynshawe), 133,

152, 174. Aylsham, 54.
Bamford, 7, 18.
Banereris, 121.
Banke, The, 25.
Barnard Castle, 154.
Barnelanton, 25.
Barn Field, 86, 132.
Barwicke, 37.
Beauchief Abbey, 179.
Bellaport, 99.
Birch (Birche, Byrcne), 1, 8, 20, 22, 70, 72, 75-6, 82-3, 98, 104, 106, 121, 133, 141, 143, 145-6, 148, 152, 172.
Chapel, 35, 38-9, 63, 93, 99, 137, 139-40, 142-5, 147-50, 153-5, 160.
Church, 174-5.
Hall, 86, 88, 97, 100, 104, 108, 148-9.
Hall (Birchal) Fold, 97, 138, 160, 173.
(Birchall) Houses, 10-11, 62, 133, 143, 166, 171. Lane, 104,173; Mill, 71,76; School, 159. Birchen, 88.
Birchenewode, 7, 186.
Birchis (Byrches), 224, 280.
Birch (Byrch) Wood, 76.
Blackburn, 46, 91.
Blackden, 87, 133.
Black (Blako) Flatt, 23, 161.
Blackley, 23, 27, 137.
Blakestake, 27, 39, 138, 219.
Bolton, 36, 50, 91, 95, 129, 131, 168-9, 234.
Bottom Wood, 132; Field, 132.
Breadic Buttes and Lands, 25.
Brcerehurst (Brerehurst), 122-3, 128.
Bretherton, 61.
Bridgewater, 108-9.
Bristol, 108, 113, 170.
Broad Croft, 23.
Broad (Brode) Meadowe, 7, 76, 79, 186.
Bruch (Warrington), 104.
Bruches, 195.
Brucke (Bruc-) Field, 21, 214, 217.
Bruckshaw, 98.
Burgh, 98.
Burnage, 1, 167-8.
Bury, 47, 97.
Calfe Crofte, 76, 87.
Canterbury, 103.
Carfax, 101.
Camforth, 168.
Castleton, 141.
Chadderton, 88.

Cheadle, 141.
Mosley, 141.
Cheetam Hill, 37.
Cholford, 60.
Chester, 11,14,21-2,32,44, 47, 63-1, 66, 78, 88, 97-100,115,117, 127,147,166. 2 INDEX TO THE HISTORY OF BIRCH CHAPEL.
Ohorlton, 1,10,137,141,143,147,152,216.
Clayffeld, 7, 186.
Clerkenwell, 13.
Clithero, 49.
Coley, 11.
Congleton, 122.
Corley, 36.
Corn Brook, 173.
Cringlebrook, 138.
Croft, 25.
Croston, 61.
Crow Croft, 173.
Cullenfield, 133.
Dane Wood, 174.
Daventry, 170.
Deansgate, 116.
Denton, 137, 141, 174.
Didsbury (Didisbury, 4c.), 30,89,83,126, 137,140-1, 152, 232.
Chapel, 49,145, 153.
Didisford, 121, 231.
Dighton, 73.
Dob, 106.
Dodworth, 131.
Dole, 26.
Droylsden, 88, 116, 174.
Durham, 37, 82, 84. Gaile, 82.
Eccles, 37, 86, 89, 90.
Egmanton (Egmenton), 27, 29.
Elland, 170.
Ellesmere (Elsmere), 27, 55.
Entwissell, 10.
Fairfield, 174.
Fall, The, 87.
Fallowfield, 62, 138, 144, 166.
Five Acres, 86.
Forty Acres, 86.
Fullwood, 170.
Gatisheade, 82.
Geldebrook, 15, 193.
Gloucester, 109.
Gooden, 88.
Goodrich Castle, 109.
Goosecroft (Gosecroft), 15, 193.
Goosecroft House, 18.

Goosetree, 133.
Gore Brook, 7, 14, 71, 174-5, 187.
Gorse Crofts, 4.
Gorton, 1,10,114,120-1,127,130-1,1378,140,145,152,159,172-3,175,235-6.
Gorton Chapel, 115, 159.
Goscrofthous, 209.
Goslache (Goselache), 2-6, 14-15, 179, 181, 192, 195.
Gravel Hole, 26.
Great Brook Field, 23.
Great Ditch, 14.
Moss, 2.
Pendleton, 138.
Greenackers, 38.
Grindlow (Grenlow, Grenclow, 4c.), 8,30, 143,147,186,188; Field, 7; Lache, 2, 3, 179-80; Marsh, 133, 138.
Guildhouse, *see* Healdhouse.
Halegateford, 7, 187.
Half-acre, The, 25.
Hall Cliff, 26; Croft, 23.
Field (Hallefelde),21,23,214,217.
Hamilton, battle of, 38.
Hampstead, 102,152.
Handford, 7.
Handsworth, 102-3.
Hanging Ditch, 36.
Meadow, 26.
Harrock, 25.
Haworth, 88.
Healdhouses (Heald-house, Guild, Yeeld), 3-5,29,171,179-82; Ditch.3,195; Moor,4.
Hereford, 109, 111 Castle, 109.
Herneflatte, 15, 193.
Hindley (Hyndley) Birch, 78,87,220,223. Hobearthe, The, 25.
Holt, 85, 89,185; Hall, 7; Market, 64-5.
Horse Hey, 132.
Houghend (Housend), 144.
Houghton, 82.
Houlgate Meadow, 25.
Hulme, 10.
Hurst, 98.
Hyde, 169-70; Boad, 173.
Ince, 7.
Irke, River, 210.
Isle of Man, 95.
Jerusalem, Pilgrimage, 12.
Eed Lane, 173.
Kemlache, 3, 180.

Kenerdey (Kenerden), 37 *bit*.
Kersal (Kersawe, Kerksawe, Kerksall.
Keksal, Key-sail, Kirkshaw), 10, 125, 127, 129-83, 235-6. Wood, 129.
Kiln Croft, 23.
Kirk Deighton, 73.
Kirkmanshulme, 173-4.
Knutsford, 48, 16a. Vale, 173.
Lady Barn, 144.
Lancaster, 168.
Lawton, 122.
Leeds, 168.
Lees, 129.
Leigh, 25.
Lenton Priory, 128.
Leominster, 110.
Letheringsett, 29, 51, 54-5.
Levenshulnie, 1, 29, 138, 143, 166, 168, 173-4. Little Brook Field, 23.
Lever, 169.
Bed Stone, 132.
Liverpool, 14, 91-5,146,169; Castle, 46. London, 38, 47, 56-7, 96, 101, 110, 173, 190; Fire, 113. Long Eyes, 23.
Longsight, 1, 138, 140, 153, 159,172-4.
Long Small Meadow, 86.
Ludlow Castle, 109.
Macclesfield, 27,173.
Man, Isle of, 135.
Manchester, 1, 4-5, 8, 10-11, 16, 20-3, 25-8, 30-1, 35, 37, 39, 41, 45, 49-50, 52-3, 58-fiO, 67, 70, 72-3, 77, 79, 82, 86-91, 97, 104,106, 108,114, 116,11819, 121-2, 124, 129, 131, 133, 137-8, 140-1, 144, 146,149-55,168,170, 1725, 221.
Meane Field, 132.
Menegate, Le, 5.
Mersey, River, 14.
Michewall Diche, 72, 121.
Middleton, 86.
Middlewich, 45.
Middope, 23.
Midway Rirer, 174-5.
Milgate (Milngate), 27, 37.
Milkwallslade, 121,125,128, 130-1, 133, 231, 234, 236.
Milne Knolle, 76.
Monk shall, 86.
Moorside, 141.
Moreton, 122.
Moss-Side, 1, 3, 138.
Moston, 27, 62,125.

Much Woolton, 14.
Nantwich, 11, 169-70.
Newcastle, 37, 82.
Newham Green, 25, 37.
New Intack, 26; Pale, 9.
Newton, 1,27,36,121,137; Heath, 173.
Nico (Nicker) Dith, 121, 172-8.
Northampton, 169.
Northerden, 37.
North Repps, 54-5.
Northwich, 96.
Norton, 98.
Norwich, 54-5, 170.
Nuthurst, 77.
Nuum Green, 37.
Oakes, 132.
Oldham, 129.
Old Marled Earth, 75, 87.
Openshaw, 173-4.
Ordsal, 106, 113.
Ormskirk, 146, 170.
Ouldearthe, The, 25.
Ouse Moss, 175.
Owd Green Lone, 173.
Oxford, 38, 55-7, 60, 101.
Palace Buildings, 104; Inn, 104.
Park Head (near Whalley), 38, 49, 66-7.
Peel Castle, 95.
Philips' Park, 173.
Pighowt, 87.
Pighell, 75.
Pike End, 23.
Pilkington, 67.
Pingot, The, 23.
Pink Pank Lane, 173, 175.
Piatt, 1-5, 7, 12-16, 18, 23, 26-8, 30, 35, 37-8, 41, 48-50, 57-9, 61, 63-7, 70-1, 77,121,138,149-50,160,167-70,192, 195-6, 201, 204, 206, 220.
Chapel, 62, 166-9; Hall, 159.
Plattinge, 98.
Plymouth, 108.
Preston, 36, 43-4, 91, 110.
Prestwich, 50, 67, 70, 132, 154.
Qwikehaggedlonde, Le, 5.
Ragland Castle, 109.
Bathmel, 168.
Reddish, 80,173-4.
Rhodes, 25.
Ripon, 74.
Rivington, 169.
Rochdale, 56, 86-8, 141, 173.
Rostherne, 148, 153.

Rough Fields, 115.
Round Meadow, 132.
Runcorn, 14.
Runton, 27, 51-2, 65.
Rush, 174.
   Rush-brook, 173, 175.
   Rushford (Russeford), 6, 7, 71, 143, 173 4, 184, 187. Rushin Castle, 95.
   Rusholme (Rushulme, Riseholme, Ruschun, &c.), 1-3, 5-10, 12, 15-16, 18, 21, 22-3, 25, 27-8, 35-7, 52-3, 57-9, 62, 64, 77-8, 83, 88, 97, 121, 129-30, 133, 137,144, 145,149-50,156,159-60, 166-7, 170-5, 182, 184-6, 188, 215-17, 202, 205, 213, 219, 221-2, 234, 236.
   Green, 20; Meadow, 5, 25.
   Saddleworth-frith, 17.
Salisbury, 111.
   Salford (Sawford), 25-6, 39, 63-1, 70, 82, 88, 151. Salthouse, 55. SchoolshiU, 140. Scaven Falls, 25. Seven Acres, 86.
   Thorns Wells, 174.
   Shepley, 88.
Shore, 88.
Short Eyes, 23.
Skipton, 37.
   Slade, 121-2, 129, 133, 138, 143-4, 167, 171, 231.
   Slade Hall, 10, 121-2, 124, 128,131,134, 172, 195.
Small Meadow, 76.
Smithy door, 31.
   Somer Werkeddeffeld, 7, 186.
Standish, 149; Moor, 36.
Stall.in!. 44.
Stanhope, 81-4.
   Stockport (Stopperd),6,82,185; Road, 173.
   Stone Church, 158.
   Stony Lands, 23.
   Stow on the Wold, 109.
   Strangeways, 8-9.
   Street ffould, 62.
   Stretford, 137, 152.
   Swyudley Woodhouscs, 26.
   Taylor's Tenement, 62.
Thistle Fields, 132.
   Thornditch (Thornidiche), 15, 195.
Three Acres, 87.
Tiberias, Battle of, 14.
Tildesley, 10.
Tollache, 2.
Tunstall, 123.
Two Acres, 133. Oaks, 86.
   Uttoxeter, 36.

Victoria Park, 172.
Warrington, 36, 47, 146.
Warthe, 132.
Weardale, 81.
Wedgewood, 123.
Wem, 170.
Weobley, 108, 111-14.
Westminster, 66, 101-2; Abbey, 47.
Wetherby, 73.
WhaUcy, 38, 50.
Wheat-(Wheyte) croft, 26, 76, 87.
Wheatficld (Whitefield), 25, 88.
Whitbourne (Whittebourne), 107-8,113.
Whitchurch, 153.
Wigan, 10, 26, 36, 149, 221.
Winning Hill, 174.
Winstor, 67.
Withens, The, 25.
Withington (Withinton, Wythington, Ac.), 1-4, 7-10, 14, 16, 21, 23, 25, 28, 70,83,85-6,88-9,122,124,128-9,133, 141,144, 167,171, 179-82, 189, 192-4, 198, 200, 202-6, 220-1, 223-5, 227, 229-30, 232-3, 235-6.
Wode-ende, 75.
Wodesloy, 75.
Woldhouso, 88.
Wolstauton, 122.
Wolstenholme, 88.
Wood Field, 87.
Knowle. 79.
Worcester, 10, 40, 94, 109, 111.
Worral Millington, 116, 118.
Worslcy, 25, 50.
Wrenbury, 39.
Wyddine, 2.
Wydenton, 189.
Wynnerhey, 72, 230.
Yarmouth, 52.
Yieldhouse, *see* Healdhouse.
Charles Simms & Co., Plinters, 53, King St1eet, Mancheste1 ERRATA.
Page 7, line 24, *for* William the Honford *read* William de Honford.
„ 44, line 24, *for* ef *read* of.
„ 49, last line (note), *for* of Piatt *read* at Piatt.
„ 66, Worsley pedigree, *for* dau. of Hudson *read* dau. of. Hudson.
„ 72, line 16, *for* 16th of April *read* 12th of April.
„ 89, line 80, *for* a like payment *read* by a like payment.
DIRECTIONS TO BINDER.
Pedigree of Worsley of Piatt *to face*

page 67
„ Birch of Birch „ 102
„ Birch of Ardwick „ 120 REMAINS HISTORICAL & LITERARY CONNECTED WITH THE PALATINE COUNTIES OF LAN-CASTEE AND CHESTEE, PUBLISHED BY THE jpETHAM SOCIETY.
VOL. XLVIII. COUNCIL For 1858-59. JAMES CROSSLEY, Esq,, F.S.A., President. REV. F. R. RAINES, M.A., F.8.A., Hon. Canon Of Manchester,
Vice-president. WILLIAM BEAMONT.
THE VERY REV. GEORGE HULL BOWERS, D.D., Dean Of Manchester REV. JOHN BOOKER, M.A., F.8.A. REV. THOMAS CORSER, M.A., F.S.A. MATTHEW DAWES, F.S.A., F.G.S. JOHN HARLAND, F.S.A. EDWARD HAWKINS, F.R.S., F.S.A., F.L.S. THOMAS HEYWOOD, F.S.A. W. A. HULTON.
REV. JOHN HOWARD MARSDEN, B.D., Canon Of Manchester, Disney Professor Of Classical Antiquities, Cahbridoe. ARTHUR H. HEYWOOD, Treasurer.
WILLIAM LANGTON, Hon. Secretary.
OF THB COLLECTION OF TEACTS FOR AND
AGAINST POPERY
(published In Ok About The EEIGN OF JAMES II.) IN THE MANCHESTER LIBRARY FOUNDED
BY HUMPHREY CHETHAM,
IN WHICH IS INCORPORATED, WITH LARGE ADDITIONS AND
BIBLIOGRAPHICAL NOTES, THE WHOLE OF
_PECK'S LIST OP THE. TRACTS IN THAT CONTROVERSY, WITH HIS REFERENCES. TO WHICH ARE ADDED
A TABULAR INDEX TO THE TRACTS IN BOTH EDITIONS OF GIBSON'S PRESERVATIVE, AND A REPRINT OF DODD'S CERTAMEN UTRIUSQUE ECCLESLE.
EDITED BY THOMAS JONES, B. A., LIBRARIAN OF THE CHETHAM LIBRARY. PART I. PRINTED FOR THE CHETHAM SOCIETY.
M.DCCC.LIX.
PEEFACE
The Library founded by Humphrey Chetham, as part of his noble Educational Charity, contains a more than ordinarily complete Collection of the Tracts published on both sides in the Roman Catholic Controversy which

was waged with so much learning, ability, and argumentative skill in the latter part of the reign of Charles the Second, and throughout the whole of that of his successor.

As it appeared desirable that a specimen of the contents of this Library should be afforded by a detailed account of some portion of it, which might be easily separable from the remainder, in the series of publications which bear the honoured name of its founder, it was conceived that a Catalogue of these Tracts, taking Peck's elaborate and valuable "A complete Catalogue of all the Discourses written, both for *and* against *Popery,* in the Time of King *James* II. Containing in the Whole, An Account of Four hundred and Fifty seven Books and Pamphlets, a great Number of them not mentioned in the three former Catalogues. With References after each Title, for the more speedy finding of a further Account of the said Discourses, and of their Authors, in sundry Writers: And An Alphabetical List of the Writers on each Side. A Tract very necessary for these Times, and for all those who are desirous to complete their Sets of those Pieces, or would sort them to the best Advantage. Drawn up in a new Method, By *Francis Peck,* M.A. Hector of *Godeby,* near *Melton* in *Leicestershire. Aid Avcrtyfiias Kal Evfrjfiias.* 2 Cor. vi. 8. London: Printed and Sold at St. *John's* Gate; by A. Dodd, without List as its groundwork, and giving therefore a complete bibliographical view of the Controversy, would not be unacceptable to the Members of the Chetham Society, more especially as the List referred to has never been reprinted, and has now become exceedingly scarce. That a reprint of it was not subjoined to the late republication of Bishop Gibson's *Preservative* by the Reformation Society appears an unaccountable omission.

The plan adopted in the present work has been to give the Tract of Peck entire, incorporating with it whatever additions, which it will be seen at once are not slight or inconsiderable, the Editor was able to collect from the sources which have been open to him, and relieving the dryness of a mere catalogue of books by historical and bibliographical notes and references. It will be observed that all the Tracts and Books not numbered are additions to Peck's original List. The marginal letters (£ indicate the Chetham Library, *B. M.* the British Museum, *B. L.* the Bodleian Library, *T. C. D.* Trinity College, Dublin, *M. L.* Archbishop Marsh's, Dublin, and *S. C.* Sion College Library, as the depositories in which the books thus marked are respectively to be found.

It is rather remarkable that scarce as Peck's Tract undoubtedly is, the Chetham Library possesses three copies of it, in which extensive MS. additions have been made, *Temple Bar*; J. Stag and J. Fox, in *Westminster-Hall*; E. Nutt and Mrs. Cook, at the *Royal Exchange.* 1735. Price 23." 4to pp. 62; title, preface and contents, pp. 8. For an account of Francis Peck and his writings, see Nichols's *Literary Anecdotes,* Voi. i. p. 507, et seqq. partly by the Rev. John Clayton, M.A., Fellow of the Collegiate Church, Manchester, and partly by another annotator less known, who subscribes himself E. Syddal (vid. p. 11), and was probably the Edward Syddal or Siddal of Fallowfield, who appears in the Pedigree of the Siddal family as of Slade Hall in the Parish of Manchester. These MS. additions encouraged the Editor in his endeavours to make the List of Controversial Tracts as nearly complete as possible. Similar additions have been supplied from an interleaved copy of Peck, kindly placed at his service by the Rev. John Taylor Allen, M.A., Ex-Librarian of the Chetham Library, which formerly belonged to Bishop White Kennett, and furnishes fresh proofs of the patient and laborious industry of that indefatigable writer.

But the most useful assistance which the Editor has derived from any source, and to which the present work must owe its principal value and main recommendation, is from the liberality and learned and careful research of the eminent theological scholar, James Henthorn Todd, D.D., of Trinity College, Dublin. Dr. Todd had made large collections for a second edition of Peck with a view to their being printed at the Clarendon Press, Oxford, and had proceeded as far as chap, xviii. No. 220, when, on learning that a similar publication was in progress in the Chetham Series, he most kindly placed his MS. materials in the hands of the present Editor, in order to be made available for the For an account of this able and learned man see *Byrom's Remains,* Toi, i. part ii. p. 509. See Booker's *Chapehy of Birch,* Chetham Series, p. 136. work now in the reader's hands. Those who refer to the notes and additions to which the initials *J. H. T.* are subjoined will have no difficulty in estimating the extent of the obligation under which Dr. Todd has placed the Members of the Chetham Society and all who take an interest in the publication to which he has afforded so rich a contribution.

The Editor has much pleasure in availing himself of this opportunity of acknowledging also his obligations to the Rev. John I. Dredge; to Robert Travers, Esq., M.A., M.B. of Trinity College, Dublin, who on this as on other occasions has been his faithful guide and counsellor; and especially to James Crossley, Esq., F.S.A., President of the Chetham Society, by whose valuable counsels and suggestions the volume has been greatly benefited. He has to lament that to one zealous co-operator all expression of gratitude is now vain; the effective aid of the Rev. Robert Ryland Mendham, B.A., of Sutton Coldfield, having been lost to him by death shortly after this volume was commenced.

In such a multitudinous series of titles it is almost impossible to avoid occasional inaccuracies, and any corrections therefore which the Editor may receive he will gladly insert and most thankfully acknowledge in the concluding part of this Catalogue.

T. J.

As a proof of the rarity of Peck's *Catalogue,* it may be mentioned that this gentleman (who possesses a large collection of the Tracts) has for years sought in vain for a copy of Peck. PREFACE TO PECK'S CATALOGUE.

There being *three* Catalogues of this sort by three very eminent persons already printed, the reader will be perhaps surprised at my here offering him a *fourth*.

But 1. The *two first* Catalogues were printed while the controversy was yet on foot. This appears from their very titles. *The present state of the controversy.* And, *A continuation of the present state of the controversy.* And, for this reason, neither of those two could be complete.

2. The *third* Catalogue (tho' it came not out 'till 1689) mentions only the writers *against* popery; and not *all* those neither by a great many. For which reason, and as it is in a manner perfectly silent as to the writers *for* popery, it may be said to be, tho' not so defective as the two former Catalogues in the *one* respect, yet much more so in the *other*. 3. The titles of the several discourses written by the *Romanists* are (so many of them as are mentioned in the *two first* Catalogues) so contracted and abridged, that Viz. The Present State of the Controversie between the Church of England and the Church of Rome; Or, An Account of the Books written on both sides. In a Letter to a Friend. By William Claget, D.D. Imprimatur Guil. Needham. May 7, 1686. pp. 36, 4to Lond. 1687.

A Continuation of the Present Controversy between the Church of England and the Church of Rome. Being a full Account of the Books that have been of late written on both sides. By William Wake. pp. 76, Epistle, Dedic., &c, pp. 12, 4to Lond. 1688.

The Catalogue of all the Discourses published against Popery during the Reign of King James II. By the Members of the Church of England, and by the Non-conformists. With the names of the Authors of them. By Edward Gee, M.A. pp. 34, 4to Lond. 1689.

None of these Tracts are reprinted in Gibson's *Preservative.—Ed.* (whatever any other person may do) I must frankly own, I often could not so well understand their account of the discourses written *against* popery, for want of a better account of the discourses written *for* popery.

And, for all these reasons, I could not forbear frequently wishing for a more complete account of the several writers and discourses *on both sides;* and, as no abler hand appeared to go about it, have at length attempted to do it myself. And this I have done, 1. By giving *the title* of each book *pro* and *con* (when I had it by me) *at large*. Or (where I had it not) as full as I could gather it from the former Catalogues or any other books which my little study afforded.

2. By inserting proper *references* after the title of each tract, which will carry the reader (if he pleases) to the places where he will meet with many curious remarks in the former Catalogues and in some other books, relating to these discourses and their several authors: Particularly to all those in the second edition of Mr. *Wood's Athena Oxonienses.* Which volumes (coming not out 'till 1721) I have diligently read over, almost with this one view. And, 3. By exhibiting, in the close, an alphabetical *List of the Writers on both sides;* with farther references after each name: Whereby may be presently seen what discourses of this sort each person there mentioned hath wrote.

The collecting of all these additions, the reader may well think, have cost me a great deal of pains. But they have also afforded me a great deal of knowledge and pleasure. And, if they are of the same advantage to others who have occasion to look into these matters (as I think they will) I shall have still the more satisfaction.

CONTENTS OP PART I.

Chap. I. Of certain discourses published before the end of
the reign of K. Charles II 1
Coles, *page* 1; Shaw, 2; Lloyd, 3; Williams, 9; Claget, 10;
Stanley, 11; Cave, 11; Owen, 11.
Chap. II. Of the Royal Papers (viz. two of K. Charles II.
and one of the Duchess of York's) and of the discourses
written about them 13
Hudleston, 13; Duchess of York, 14; Stillingfleet, 15, 16;
Dryden, 16; Parker, 17; Morley, 18; Charles II., 13, 18;

Burnet, 19; Grascome, 19; Jenkins, 20.
Chap. III. Of the discourses written upon the design of
abrogating the penal laws and test 21
Parker, 21; Goodwin, 21; Wake, 21; Burnet, 24, 65, 66;
Care, 25, 68; Phillips, 29; Walsingham, 42; Penn, 64, 67,
68; Clarendon (Hyde), 66; Lloyd, 66; James, 66, Johnson,
66; L'Estrange, 68; Milton, 68; Denton, 68; Cawley, 69;
Whitby, 6!); Ayres, 71; Blackerby, 72; Locke, 72.
Chap. IV. Of the discourses written on occasion of the
King's most gracious letters of indulgence 74
Halifax (Savile), 74, 85; Care, 76; L'Estrange, 76; Darell,
77; Burnet, 80, 81, 82, 92; Clifford, 82; Ferguson, 82; Fagel,
83, 84; Stewart, 84; Herbert, 87; Johnston, 87; Atkyns, 88;
Bp. of Rochester (Sprat), 89, 97; Nye, 89; Langhorn, 90;
Wilson, 90; Anglesea (Annesley), 90; Payne, 92; Nicholets,
92; Sherlock, 95; Ayres, 96; Stillingfleet, 97; Bp. of Hereford (Croft), 97; Manby, 99.
Chap. V. Of the discourses written in the representing
controversy 102
Gother, 102; Stillingfleet, 104; Sherlock, 104, 106; Seller,
b
PIOI
105; Claget, 106, 110; Williams, 107, 110; Patrick, 108;
Taylor, 108, 109, 111; Stratford, 110.
Chap. VI. Of the discourses written in the expounding
controversy 112
Bossuet, 112, 114, 115; Johnston, 112, 115, 116; Wake,
113, 115, 117; John Gilbert, 114; Claget, 116; Walker, 117;
Buckley, 118; Dodwell, 118; Jurieu, 119; Claudius Gilbert,
119; De Brueys, 120; Burnet, 120; Camus, 120; Claude,
123; Le Jay, 123; Gautier, 123; Benoit, 124; Freschot, 124;

Bray, 124; Jones, 124; Laval, 125.

Chap. VII. Of the discourses written on occasion of Mr.

Thomas Godden's conference with Dr. Edward Stillingfleet, Dean of S. Paul's 126

Stillingfleet, 126, 128, 129, 131, 133, 134; Sargeant, 127,

129, 130, 134; Ellis, 127, 128; Williams, 132; Dillingham,

135.

Chap. VIII. Of the discourses written on occasion of the

conference between Father Andrew Pulton and Dr.

Thomas Tennison 136

Pulton, 136, 137, 138, 140; Tenison, 137, 138; Meredith,

137; Cressener, 137; Harrington, 140.

Chap. IX. The sequel of the conference between father Andrew Pulton and Dr. Thomas Tennison; or, an account

of the *Speculum ecclesiasticum,* and of the discourses

written thereupon 141

Ward, 141, 145; La Placette, 141, 142; Tenison, 141,144;

Wharton, 142, 143.

Chap. X. Of the discourses written in the dispute between

Dr. William Sherlock and Father Lewis Sabran, about

the doctor's *Preservative against popery* 146

Sherlock, 146, 147; Sabran, 146, 147; Giles, 146.

Chax. XI. Of the discourses written about the conversions

of several persons to the church of Rome, with their

motives; and the churchmen's replies 148

Tillotson, 148; Bassett, 148; Bambridge or Bainbrigg, 149;

Manby, 150; King, 151; Sclater, 152; Gee, 153; Gother, 154

Boyse, 155; Salgado, 155; Burnet, 156, 158; Patrick, 156

Musgrave, 156; Carolan, 156; Briber, 157; Creasy, 157

Bacon, 159.

Chap. XII. Of the discourses written by the country parson and the Romish missionary 160

Ashton, 160, 161, 162; Comber, 163, 164.

Chap. XIII. Of the popish discourses written by way of advice to the protestant pulpits; with the churchmen's replies 165

Gother or Leybourn, 165, 166; Williams, 165, 166; Sherlock, 166.

Chap. XIV. Of the Romanist's charge of schism and heresy upon the church of England; with the churchmen's replies 168 Altham, 168; Williams, 168; Sherlock, 169; Hickes, 169;

Saywell, 171; Steward, 172; Burnet, 174; Sergeant, 176;

Sall, 176.

Chap. XV. Of the Romanist's charge of an agreement of the church of England with the church of Rome. With

the churchmen's replies 179

Sherlock, 180; Williams, 180; Lloyd, 181; Du Moulin, 181.

Chap. XVI. Of the discourses written by the Romanists reflecting upon the reformation of the church of England. With the churchmen's replies 182

Heylin, 182; Claget, 183, 192, 200; Woodhead, 187, 196; Hutchinson, 192; Smalridge, 193; Atterbury, 190; Deane, 198; Burnet, 199; Ward, 200; Schelstrate, 201; Stillingflcet, 202; Stratford, 203, 204; Hascard, 204; Davis and Coke, 205; Twysden, 205; Fulwood, 205; Tillotson, 205; Sanderson, 205.

Chat. XVII. Of the discourses written by the Romanists reflecting upon the validity of the orders of the church of England. With the churchmen's replies 206

Burnet, 207; Browne, 207; Milburne, 208; Seller, 208;

Whitfield, 209; Prideaux, 211; Mareden, 211; Champ or

Champney, 212; Talbot, 212; Lewgar, 213; Fuller, 214;

Ward, 214; Constable, 215; Earbery, 216; Williams, 216;

Brown, 217.

Chap. XVIII. Of the discourses written of the unity, authority, and infallibility of the church 218 Woodhead, 218-221, 234; Tenison, 224; Hooper, 224;

Sherlock, 225, 240; Patrick, 226, 236; Williams, 226; Free-

ADVERTISEMENT.

The word *State,* refers to the present *State* of the controversy. By William Claget, D.D. See No. 71.

The word *Contin.,* refers to a *continuation* of the *present state,* of the controversy. By William Wake, D.D. See No. 438.

The word *Cat.* refers to the *catalogue* of all the discourses, published against Popery in the reign of K. James II. By Edward Gee, M.A. See No. 438.

The words *Ath.* and *Fasti* refer to the pages of the I. and II. volumes of the *Athenm* and *Fasti Oxonienses,* 2d edition. This mark 4i is set before all the popish pieces.

This mark is set against all such of the pieces *pro* and *con.,* as I have by me, in my private collection.—F. P. This mark has not been retained, as no opportunity of access now remains to Peck's Collection.

The references to Dr. Todd's notes to Gibson's *Preservative* are to the folio edition in three volumes, and in the Editor's notes *vol.* designates the reprint in quarto, and *folio* the original edition. — Ed.

A CATALOGUE OF THE DISCOURSES, WRITTEN

For *and* Against *Popery, in the time of* K. James II.

CHAP. I. *Of certain Discourses published before the End of the Reign of K. Charles II.* HEOPHILUS and Philodoxus, or several conferences between two friends, the one a true son of the Church of England, the other fallen off to the Church of Rome. Concerning, 1. Prayer in an unknown Tongue. 2. Half Communion. 3. Worship of Images. 4. Invocation of Saints. By Gilbert Coles, D.D. Fellow of Winchester Coll. Oxon. pp. 221, 4to Lond. 1674 See Wood's *Alh. Ox.* vol. ii. col. 560. (Edit. Bliss, vol. iii. col. £ 1067.) Republished, 4to, 1679, under the title of "A Dialogue between a Protestant and a Papist concerning," &c. , with the former as a second title-page. Coles died in 1676. "Wood saith, that he became Fellow of the College near Winchester, but soon after was ejected by the Visitors appointed by the Parliament; which I know

B not what to make of: because I do

not apprehend how the Visitors power reach'd that College: and I have been informed that none of the Fellows there were turned out.... However that be, 'tis certain this Mr. Coles was depriv'd of a Fellowship either in this College New College or that near Winchester for some time; and so was in part a Sufferer: but he was so much belov'd by the Society that they reelected him."— Walker's *Account of the Numbers and Sufferings of the Clergy,* part ii. p. 129.

C 5n 2. Origo Protestantium; or an answer to a Popish MS. of *N. N.* that which answer would fain make the Protestant catholick religion bear date at the very time when the Roman popish commenced in the world. Wherein Protestancy is demonstrated to he elder than Popery. To which is added a Jesuit's Letter; with the Answer. By John Shaw, Rector of Whalton in Northumberland, and preacher at St. John's in Newcastle. pp. 133, 4to Lond. 1677 *Ath. Ox.* vol. ii. col. 832. *Edit.* Bliss, vol. iv. col. 256.) *N. N.* introduces the subject of the Nag's Head Ordination. Amongst the principal works on the validity of the English Ordinations, are Mason, De Ministerio Angl., fol. 1625, the same work translated by John Lyndsay, fol. 1728; the works of Bramhall, fol. Dubl. 1677, Oxf. 1842-45, arid Burnet on English Ordinations, 1677; and especially M. Courayer's Dissertation sur la Validite des Ordin. Angl.; Defence de la Dissertation, and Supplement, Brux. 1723, translated by Dan. Williams, 1727-28, and of which there is an analysis in *The Present State of the Republic of Letters,* 1728; Bp. Ellington's Validity of English Ordinations, 1809. Browne's Concio ad Clerum, 4to, Cantab. 1628, contains from the original MS. in Corpus Christi College, Cambridge, the Instrument,— " Rituum atq. ceremoniarum ordo in consecrando Reverendissimo in Christo patre Mattheo Parker Cantuarensi Archicpo in Sacello suo, apud Maneriu suum de Lambeth, die Dnico 17 viz. die mensis Decembris Anno Doni 1559, habit." This, with other documents, is also given by Bramhall from the Registry of the See of Canterbury. See Collier's Ecclesiastical History of Great Britain, vol. ii. p. 4G0. In reference to the Reformed Churches may be mentioned the following treatises: — Certain Briefe Treatises written by diverse Learned Men, concerning the ancient and moderne government of the Church. (By Richard Hooker, Lancelot Andrewes, Martin Bucer, John Rainoldes, James Archhishop of Armagh, and Edward Brerewood.)

Wherein, hoth the Primitive Institution of Episcopacie is maintained, and the Lawfulnesse of the Ordination of the Protestant Ministers beyond the Seas likewise defended. By John Duree and Francis

Mason. 4to Lond. 1641. See also chap. xvii.

, 3. A calm answer to a violent discourse of N. N. a seminary priest for the invocation of saints, with a reflection upon the covetousness and imposture of the popish clergy. 4to 1677

The same? N. N. Translated out of French " The Proceedings of J,, the General Assembly of the Clergie of France Assembled in the year

1682 at Paris, and in the year 1685 at S. Germains in Laye, concerning Religion. Lille, 1686." Among the articles of the Doctrine of the

Church here defended is that of the Invocation of Saints, of Relicks,

and of Images. This writer exemplifies the remark made by Macaulay that the style of the Roman Catholic divines of the period was disfigured with foreign idioms, " The edict of the King which defends prohibits the Ministers of all others of the Pretended Reformed Religion to Preach or compose books," &c.

4. Considerations touching the true way to suppress Popery in %, this Kingdom, by making a distinction between men of loyal and disloyal principles in that communion. On occasion whereof is inserted an historical account of the Reformation in England. By William Lloyd. pp. 164, 4to Lond. 1677

The publishing of this book made a great noise. — *Peck. Ath. Ox.* vol. ii. col. 1090. *Edit.* Bliss, vol. iv. cols. 714, 889.) Bishop Lloyd, born in 1627, died 1717. See also Biographia Britannica,

Williams's Biographical Dictionary of Eminent Welshmen.

No chapter having been apportioned to Allegiance, I shall here give a list of such Tracts, published at this period, as are not found in

Watt's Bibliotheca Britannica, s. v. Allegiance and Oath of Allegiance,

that legal tie by which subjects are bound to their Sovereign.

The Protestant Religion is a sure Foundation and Principle of a true 5.,

Christian, and a good Subject, a great Friend to Humane Society; and a grand Promoter of all Virtues, both Christian and Moral. By diaries Stanley, Earl of Derby. The second edition. 4to Lond. 1671.

" This piece contains a dedication ' To all Supremo Powers, by what titles soever dignified or distinguished, *i.e.* to Emperors, Kings, Sovereign Princes, Republics, &c.:' on Epistle to the Reader; another longer in the second edition; and the Work itself, which is a Dialogue between Orthodox, a royalist, and Ciccodsemou, one popishly affected. His lordship is warm against the church of Rome, their casuists and the Jesuits, and seems well read in the fathers and in polemic divinity, from both of which his style has adopted much acrimony. He died in 1672. His father was the brave James, Earl of Derby; his mother, the heroine who defended Latham House, grand-daughter of the great Prince of Orango; — a compound of Protestant heroism that evaporated in controversy." — Walpole's *Royal and Noble Authors,* vol. iii

The Great Loyalty of the Papists to Charles I. 4to Lond. 1673

Popery absolutely destructive to Monarchy. 18mo Lond. 1673

The Papal Tyranny as it was exercised over England for some ages represented by Peter Du Moulin. 4to Lond. 1674 The Controversial Letters, or the Grand Controversio concerning the Pope's Temporal Authority between two English Gentlemen; the ono of the Church of England, the other of Rome. By Peter Walsh.

4to Lond. 1673-75

A Letter to the Catholics of England, &c. &o. &c. By Father Peter Walsh. 8vo Lond. 1674

History and Vindication of the Irish Remonstrance, &c. By Peter Walsh. 1661. Reprinted, fbl. Lond. 1674 England's Independency upon the Papal Power historically and judicially stated, out of the Reports of Sir John Davis and Sir Edw. Coke. By Sir John Pettus. 4 to Lond. 1674

Some Considerations of Present Concernment; how far Romanists may be trusted by Princes of another Persuasion. By Henry Dodwell. 8vo Lond. 1675

A Reply to a Person of Honour, his pretended Answer to the Vindication of the Protestant Religion in the point of Obedience to Sovereigns, and to the Book of Papal Tyranny. By Peter Du Moulin. 4to Lond. 1675 A Seasonable Question, and an Useful Answer; contained in an Exchange of a Letter between a Parliament Man in Cornwall and a Bencher of the Temple, London. By Andrew Marvell. Lond. 1676

The Jesuits' Loyalty, in Three Tracts, written by them against the Oath of Allegiance, with the Seasons of Penal Laws. 4to Lond. 1677

Answer to Three Treatises published under the title of "The Jesuits' Loyalty." By Peter Walsh. 4to Lond. 1678

"Peter Walsh was the honestest and learnedest man I ever knew among them. He was of Irish extraction, and of the Franciscan'order: and was indeed in all points of controversy almost wholly protestant: but he had senses of his own, by which he excused his adhering to the church of Rome: and he maintained, that with these ho could continue in the communion of that church without sin: and he said that he was sure he did some good staying still on that side, but that he could do none at all if ho should come over. He thought, no man ought to forsake that religion in which he was born and bred, unless he was clearly convinced that he must certainly be damned if he continued in it. He was an honest and able man, much practised in intrigues, and knew well the methods of tho Jesuits, and other missionaries." —Burnet's *Oion Times*, vol. i. p. 195. An account of his life is given by Sir James Ware; and from him, by Chalmers, in his General Biographical Dictionary, and by Charles Butler, in his Historical Memoirs respecting the English, Irish and Scottish Catholics, 1819, vol. ii. p. 491.

The Catholic Cause, or the horrid Practice of Murdering Kings justified and commendod by the Pope in a Speech to hie Cardinals upon the barbarous Assassination of Henry III. of France, who was stabbed by Jaques Clement, a Dominican Fryar. 4to Lond. 1678

Reprinted in the seventh volume of the Harleian Miscellany. See Foulis's History of Popish Treasons and Usurpations, pp. 546-61.

The Grand Design of tho Papists in the reign of our late Sovereign Charles I., and now carried on against his Present Majesty, his Government, and the Protestant Religion. 4to Lond. 1678

Reprinted in the eighth volume of the Harleian Miscellany.

Popery and Tyranny lording it over the Consciences, Lives, Liberties and Estates both of King and People. By Sir Roger L'Estrange.1 4to Lond. 1678

The Common Interest of King and People; shewing the original antiquity and excellency of Monarchy compared with Aristocracy and Democracy, and particularly of our English Monarchy; and »hat absolute Papal and Presbyterian Popular Supremacy are utterly inconsistent with Prerogative, Property and Liberty. By John Nalson. 8vo Lond. 1678

A Vindication of the Sincerity of the Protestant Religion in the point of Obedience to Sovereigns. Opposed to the doctrine of Rebellion authorised and practised by the Pope and tho Jesuits. In answer to a Jesuitical Libel, entitled, Philonax Anglicus. By Peter Du Moulin. The Fourth Edition, in which moro light is given about the Horrible Popish Plot, whereby our late Sacred Sovereign Charles I. was murdered. 4to Lond. 1679

A Letter from a Jesuit in Paris to his Correspondent in London. Shewing the most effectual way to ruin the Government and Protestant Religion. 4to Lond. 1679

Truth and Honesty in Plain English. Or a Brief Survey of those Libels and Pamphlets printed and published since the Dissolution of tho last Parliament. Together with a Letter to the Reverend and Worthy Pastors of the Separate Congregations. By a True Lover of Monarchy and the Anglican Church. 4to Lond. 1679

An Appeal from the Country to the City for the Preservation of his Majesties Person, Liberty, Property, and the Protestant Religion. 4to Lond. 1679

An Exact Account of Romish Doctrine in the case of Conspiracy and Rebellion, by pregnant Observations collected out of the express Dogmatical Principles of Popish Priests and Jesuites. 4to Loud. 1679

An Account of the Growth of Popery, and Arbitrary Government in England; J£ J., more particularly from the long Prorogation of Parliament of Nov. 1675, ending the 15th Feb. 1676, till the last Meeting of Parliament, the 16th of July, 1077. By Audrew Marvell. Fol. Lond. 1678

Reprinted in " State Tracts" in 1689. Second Part of the Growth of Popery unto 1682. By Andrew Marvell. 4to Cologne 1682

Tins second part is not generally known.

Popery, or the Principles aud Positions approved by the Church of Rome « (when really believed and practised), arc very dangerous to all, and ' to Protestant Kings and Supreme Powers more especially pernicious and inconsistent with that Loyalty which (by the Law of Nature and Scripture) is indispensably duo to Supremo Powers. By Thomas Barlow, Bishop of Lincoln. 4to Lond. 1679

Brutum Fulmen, or the Bull of Pius V. against Q. Elizabeth, with Observations and Animadversions. By the Same. 4to Lond. 1681

The King-Killing Doctrine nf the Jesuits, translated from the French. By Peter Bellon. ito Lond. 1679

The Jesuits' Catechism according to St. Ignatius Loyola for the Instructing and Strengthening of all those which are weake in that Faith. Wherein the Impiety of their Principles, Pernitiousness of their Doctrines, and Iniquity of their Practises are declared. 4to Lond. 1679

The Jesuits Unmasked; or Politick Observations upon the Ambitious Pretensions and Subtle Intreagues of that Cunning Society. Presented to all High Powers as a Seasonable Discourse at this Time.
4to Lond. 1679

Christian Loyalty; or a Discourse, wherein is asserted that just Royal Authority and Eminency, which in this Church and Realm of England, is yielded to the King. Especially concerning Supremacy in Causes Ecclesiastical. Together with the Disclaiming all Foreign Jurisdiction; and the Unlawfulness of Subjects Taking Armes against the King. By William Falkncr. 8vo Lond. 1679

An Exact Discovery of the Mystery of Iniquity as it is now in practice among the Jesuits and other their Emissaries. With a particular Account of their Anti-christian and Devillish Policy. 4to 1679

The Case put concerning tho Succession of the D. of York. With some Observations upon the Political Catechism, the Appeal, &c., and Three or Four other Libels. 2nd edit. enlarged. By Sir Roger L'Estrange.J
Lond. 1679

Seasonable Advice to all true Protestants in England in this present Posture of Affairs. Discerning the present Designs of the Papists, with other remarkable Things, tending to tho Peace of the Church, and the Security of the Protestant Religion. By a Sincere Lover of his King and Country. Ito Lond. 1679

A Seasonable Memorial in some Historical Notes upon the Liberties of the Press and Pulpit, with the Effects of Popular Petitions, Tumults, Associations, Impostures, and disaffected Common Councils. To all good Subjects and true Protestants. By Sir Roger L'Estrange, partly in favour of the succession of the Duke of York. 4to Lond. 1680

Roman Catholic Principles in reference to God and the King. 1680? Reprinted in 1684 and 1686 This tract will bo found in Butler's Lives of the Catholics, 1819, vol. ii. p. 313, and in the ninth volume of the Somers Tracts, p. 59. A new edition, by the Rev. John Kirk, was published in 1815, 8vo. Prefixed is an elaborate inquiry respecting the previous editions and the author.

Three Great Questions concerning the Succession, and tho Danger of Popery. Fully examined in a Letter to a Member of the Present Parliament.
4to 1680

Tho Truo Protestant Subject, or the Nature and Rights of Sovereignty discussed and stated. Addressed to the Good People of England.
Ito Lond. 1680

A Seasonable Address to both Houses of Parliament concerning the Succession, the Fears of Popery, and Arbitrary Government. By George Savile, Marq. of Halifax. 4to 1681
In the Somers Tracts.

A Conference about the next Succession to the Crown of England. By R. Doleman. Reprinted, 1681

The Case of Protestants in England under a Popish Prince, if any shall happen to wear the Imperial Crown. 4to 1631

Loyalty asserted, in Vindication of tho Oath of Allegiance. 8vo 1681

Jus Csesaris ot Ecclcsin? vere dictsc (Anglicc). By William Douton. Folio, Lond. 1681
To which he added, an Apology for the Liberty of the Press.

A Dialogue between the Pope and a Phanatie concerning Affairs in England. By a Hearty Lover of his Prince and Ccuntry. 4to Lond. 1681

Ursa Major et Minor, shewing that there is no such Fear as is factiously pretended of Popery and Arbitrary Power. Lond. 1681

No Protestant Plot, or the present pretended Conspiracy of Protestants against the King and Government discovered to be a Conspiracy of the Papists against the King and his Protestant Subjects. (By Antony Ashley Cooper, Earl of Shaftesbury.) 4to Lond. 1681

A Letter to a Friend containing certain Observations upon some Passages which have been published in a late Libel, intituled, The Third Part of
No Protestant Plot; and which do relato to the Kingdom of Ireland.
4to Lond. 1682

Last Efforts of Afflicted Innocence; being an Account of the Persecution of the Protestants of France, and a Vindication of the Reformed Religion from the Aspersions of Disloyalty and Rebellion charged on it by the Papists, translated from the French by W. Vaughan. 1682

The Loyalty of Popish Principles examined in answer to a late Book entitled " Stafford's Memoirs." By Robert Hancock. 4to Loud. 1682

The Power Communicated by God to the Prince, and the obedience required of the Subject, &c. By the most Reverend Father in God, James, late Lord Archbishop of Armagh and Primato of all Ireland. Faithfully published out of the original copy, by Robert Saunderson, L. Bishop of Lincoln, with his Lordship's Preface thereunto. 8vo Lond. 1683

The Judgment of an Anonymous Writer concerning these following particulars: 1. A Law for Disabling a Papist to Inherit the Crown, &c. &c. The second edition. 4to Lond. 1681

This was first published in 1674 under a different title: see *Biographia Britannica,* Suppl., p. 95, ». D. Dr. Geo. Hickes was the writer.

The Royal Apology, or Answer to the Rebel's Plea, wherein the anti-dp « monarchical Tenents, first published by Doleman the Jesuit, to promote ' a Bill of Exclusion against King James. Secondly, practised by Bradshaw and the Regicides in the actual Murder of King Charles the 1st. Thirdly, republished by Sidney and the Associators to Depose and Murder his Present Majesty, are distinctly considered. With a Parallel between Doleman, Bradshaw, Sidney, and other of the True Protestant Party.

4to Lond. 1684

Watt ascribes this work to Sir R. L'Estrange as well as to Assheton.

Jus Regium: or, The just and solid Foundations of Monarchy in general: and more especially of the Monarchy of Scotland: maintain'd against Buchannan, Naphtali, Dolman, Milton, &c. By Sir George Mackenzie.
12mo Lond. 1684

In the same volume, That the Lawful Successor can not be debarr'd from Succeeding to the Crown, &c.

The Case of Resistance of the Supreme Powers Btated and resolved according to the doctrine of the Holy Scriptures. By William Sherlock. 8vo Lond. 1684

Religion and Loyalty; or a demonstration of the power of the Christian Church within itself, the supremacy jf sovereign power over it, the duty of passive obedience or non-resistance to it, exemplified out of the Records of the Church and the Empire, from the beginning of Christianity to the end of the reign of Julian. By Sam. Parker, D.D., Bishop of Oxford. " 8vo Lond. 1684

Religion and Loyalty, the second part; or the history of the concurrence of the imperial and ecclesiastical jurisdiction in the government of the Church, from the beginning of the reign of Jovian to the end of the reign of Justinian. 8vo Lond. 1685

The Apostate Protestant. A Letter to a Friend, occasioned by the late reprinting of a Jesuit's Book about Succession to the Crown of England, pretended to have been written by B. Doleman. By Edw. Pelling.
4to Lond. 1685

The first edition was published in 1682. Ascribed by Watt to Sir B. L'Estrange also. On B. Doleman's, i.e. B. Parson's Conference about the next Succession to the Crown of England, see Brady's Introduction to the Old English History (fol. Lond. 1684), pp. 339-412.

Bemarks upon the reflections of the Author of Popery misrepresented, &o. on his Answerer; particularly as to the deposing Doctrine, &c. 4c. By Mr. Abednego Seller. ' 4to Lond. 1686 The same writer published The History of Passive Obedience since the
Reformation. 4to Amsterdam 1689.

Popery anatomized; or tho Papists cleared from the false Imputations of Idolatry and Bebellion. 4to 1686

An Answer of a Minister of the Church of England to a Seasonable and Important Question proposed to him by a loyal and religious Member of the present House of Commons, viz., What Bespect ought the true
Sons of the Church of England in point of Conscience and Christian
Prudence to bear to the Beligion of that Church, whereof the King is a Member. 4to Lond. 1687

How the Members of the Church of England ought to behave themselves under a Boman Catholic King, with reference to the Test and Penal
Laws. By a Member of tho same Church. 12mo Lond. 1687

f, 5L, The Catholic Balance; or a Discourse determining the Controversies con cerning I. The Tradition of Catholic Doctrines; II. The Primacy of St. Peter and tho Bishop of Bome; III. The Subjection and Authority of the Church in a Christian State; according to the suffrages of the primest antiquity, pp. 136. 4to Lond. 1687

The True Test of the Jesuits, or the Spirit of that Society disloyal to God, their King, and Neighbour. 4to Amsterdam, 1688

The Jesuits' Beasons Unreasonable. Or Doubts proposed to the Jesuits upon their Paper presented to Seven Persons of Honour for NonException from the common favour voted to Catholics. 4to 1688 The True Spirit of Popery, or the treachery and cruelty of the Papists exercised against Protestants in all ages and countries when Popery hath the upper hand. 4to 1688 An Impartial Query for Protestants, viz. Can Good come out of Galilee, or can a Popish Buler propagate the Beformed Beligion. 4to 1688 The Obligation resulting from tho Oath of Supremacy to assist and defend the Prerogative of the Dispensative Power belonging to the King.
Fol. 1688

An Enquiry into the Measures of Submission to the Supreme Authority; and of tho Grounds upon which it may be lawful or necessary for Subjects to defend their Beligion, Lives and Liberties. 1688 Allen's (Will.) alias Col. Titus Killing no Murder, proving it lawful to kill a Tyrant. 4to 1689

Beprinted in the fourth volume of the Harleian Miscellany: first published in 1659. A Col. Sexby is said to have been the real author of this work, but this is denied in the Clarendon Papers, vol. Hi. p. 343.

Ascham's (Anthony) Seasonable Discourse of what is lawful during the Confusions and Revolutions of Government. First published in 1649.
4to 1689

Brutus (Junius) Vindicise contra Tyrannos; or, a Defence of Liberty against Tyrants, or of the Prince over the People, and of the People over the Prince, translated. 4to 1689
This translation was first published in 1618. The original is by some ascribed to Ilubert Languet, by others to Theodore Jieza. See Placcii Theatrum Anonymorum, and The General Biographical Dictionary, x. 305, folio. It was translated by Walker, the presumed executioner of Charles L

Sidney Redivivus, or the Opinion of the late Colonel Sidney as to Civil Government. 4to 1689

A Treatise of Monarchy, containing two Parts: I. Concerning Monarchy in General; II. Concerning this Particular Monarchy. Wherein all the main questions, occurrent in both, are stated, disputed, and determined.
4to Lond. 1689
Reprinted in the sixth volume of the Harleian Miscellany.

Brief H istorical View of the Behaviour of the Jesuits and their Faction for the first 25 years of Q. Elizabeth's Reign. 4to Lond. 1689

The Jesuit's Memorial, for the intended Reformation of England, under *Qt*
their first Popish Prince. Published from the Copy that was presented to the late King James II. With an Introduction, and some
Animadversions. By Edward Gee. 8vo

Lond. 1690

It would occupy too much spaco to enumerate the Tracts relative to the Revolution. See " A Collection of State Tracts, publish'd on occasion of the Late Revolution in 1688. And during the Reign of King William III," 3 vols, fol. Lond. 1705.

5. Christianity abused by the Church of Rome, and Popery shewed *B. L.* to be a corruption of it, being an answer to a late printed paper given out by Papists, in a Letter to a Gent. By John Williams, M. A. 4to Lond. 1679 *Note.* The printed paper is printed with it. — *Peck. Ath. Ox.* vol. ii. col. 1120. *Edit.* Bliss, vol. iv. col. 769.) Bishop of Chichester, horn in 1634, died 1709. Among his works are Boyle Lecture Sermons, and History of the Gunpowder Treason. On the abuses of Christianity introduced by ecclesiastical and papal tyranny and corruptions the following works may be consulted: — Gratii Fasciculus rerum expetendarum et fugiendarum etc. 2 voll. fol. 1690; Hus et Hieronymi Monumenta; Illyrici Catalogus Testium Veritatis, 1618 fol.; Wolfii Lectiones Memorabiles, 2 voll. fol. 1600; Onus Ecclesise a Joanne Episcopo Saltsburg. 1531 fol.; Mornayi Mysterium Iniquitatis seu Histoiia Papatus. Quibus gradibus ad id fastigii enisus sit quamque acriter omni tempore ubique a piis contra intercessum, 1611 fol. See also Hallam's Literature of Europe, vol. i. 132, &c.; Mendham's Literary Policy of the Ch. of Bome, 15, 16. Among modern controversial writers it will be sufficient to mention Penrose's Bampton Lectures, 1808; "An Attempt to prove the Truth of Chris

C tianity from the Wisdom displayed in its original Establishment, and from the History of false and corrupted Systems of Religion."

C 1L 6. A persuasive to an ingenuous tryal of opinions in religion. By Nicholas Claget, M.A. *(Gibson,* vol. xvi. folio 3) pp. 57, 4to

Lond. 1685

Cat. No. 3. Contin. p. 2. *(Edit.* Bliss, vol. iii. col. 640.) "A plain practical useful discourse." — *Chetham* MS. Archdeacon Clagett was born 1654, died 1727. By Bliss and Gibson this is ascribed to Wm. Clagett. Wrongly, for I learn from Mr. J. R. Smith he has a copy in which is written by J. Kettlewell that it was presented to him by the author Nicholas Claget.

£. 2,, 7. The difference of the case between the separation of the Protestants from the Church of Rome, and the separation of Dissenters from the Church of England. By Will. Claget, D.D. preacher to the society of Gray's Inn. (G. xiv. fol. 3).

pp. 71, 4to Lond. 1683 Cat. No. 9. Contin. p. 2. *(Edit.* Bliss, vol. iii. col. 640.) Born in 1646, died 1688. " The Case of Indifferent Things used in God's Worship, stated on behalf of Dissenters," here referred to, was written in reply to a Discourse on the same subject by Dr. Williams, Bishop of Chichester, which with a Vindication appears in the London Cases. See also Bishop Sanderson's admirable Sermon, " Puritan Prejudices and Censures against the Regular Episcopal Clergy, considered and answered," (in the fourth vol. of Wordsworth's Christian Institutes); Bancroft's Survey of the pretended holy discipline, 4to, Lond. 1593; and Dangerous positions and proceedings, etc., 8vo, Lond. 1595; Thorndike's Just Weights and Measures, 4to, Lond. 1680. Much information concerning the principles and practices of the Nonconformists may also be found in Walton's Life of Hooker, in Hooker's Preface to his Ecclesiastical Polity, especially the first four sections, in the Preface to " Cosins's Conspiracy for pretended Information," and in Edwards's Gangrsena. 4to Lond. 1646. On the causes of schism and nonconformity, see Spry's (Bampton Lecture) Sermons, " Christian Unity doctrinally and historically considered," Oxf. 1817.

C 8. A discourse concerning the devotions of the Church of Rome, especially as compared with those of the Church of England;

in which is shewn, that, whatever the Romanists pretend, there is not so true devotion among them, nor such rational provision for it, nor encouragement to it, as is in the Church established by law amongst us. By William Stanley, D.D. (G. viii.

folio 2.) pp. 67, 4to Lond. 1685

Cat. No. 10. Contin. p. 5. Dean of St. Asaph, born 1647, died

1731. "A useful and judicious discourse if we except the Author's erroneous opposition to the doctrine of Praying for the Saints departed." *Chetham* MS. See Reflections on the Devotions of the Roman Church, by John Patrick, 8vo Lond. 1686.

9. A discourse of the unity of the catholick Church maintained d, in the Church of England. By William Cave, D.D.?

pp. 57, 4to Lond. 1684 Cat. No. 13. Contin. p. 4. — *Peck.* " By Dr. Thorp, as he told me himself." E. Sydall. — *Chetham* MS. See chap, xxxvi of the Discourses written of the Notes of the Church. 10. The proselyte of Rome called back to the communion of the £. 5,,

Church of England. By L. W. pp. 27, 4to Lond. 1679

The Creed of Pope Pius IV. is here cited. See also Altham's

Comments, &c., 4to, Lond. 1687; Gardiner's Brief Examination of the present Roman Catholic Faith, &c, fol., Lond. 1689; the Tridentine Gospel, or Papal Creed, &c, with Notes by W. Ramsay, Lond. 1672. Protestant Journal, 1831, pp. 18-29.

11. A true and lively representation of Popery, shewing that Popery £, jk, is only new modelled Paganism, and perfectly destructive of the great ends and purposes of God in the Gospel. By Thankful Owen. pp. 82, 4to Lond. 1679 Mr. Thankful Owen designed a book for the press, which he entitled Imago Imaginis; the design of which was to shew, that Rome

Papal is an Image of Rome Pagan. See *Fasti Oxon.* vol. ii. col. 52.

Edit. Bliss, vol. iv. col. 91.) But whether it was ever completed and printed, I find not. — *Peck.* A Dissenter, born in 1619, died 1681. The resemblance between Paganism and Popery has

been often adverted to by writers on the Romish controversy, but the chief works devoted expressly to the illustration of it are the following: — Du Pre's Conformity of Ancient and Modern Ceremonies, translated from the French, 1745; Stopford's PaganoPapismus, or an Exact Parallel between Rome-Pagan and RomeChristian, in their Doctrines and Ceremonies, published in 1675; *Eikwv Tov Brjpiov,* or the Image of the Beast, by Delaune, the well-known Nonconformist, 1684; Middleton's Letter from Rome, showing an exact Conformity between Popery and Paganism, or the Religion of the present Romans derived from that of their Heathen Ancestors; Popery the Religion of Heathenism, by Ignotus J. Poynder, published in 1818, which contains along with a summary of the conformity of Popery to Ancient Paganism, a full proof of its similarity to Modern Hinduism; Poynder's Alliance between Popery and Paganism. The Abbe de la Berthier, the author of the following treatise, was a prisoner in the Bastile, and being asked why he troubled himself to write against the Constitution Unigenitus, made answer that he took Priest's Orders with no other view than to preach and defend the Truth which is wounded by that Constitution;.... that if his enemies pleased they might put him to death, which he was resolved to suffer rather than retract one tittle of what he had written. " A Parallel of the Doctrine of the Pagans, with the Doctrine of the Jesuits; and that of the Constitution Unigenitus issued by Pope Clement XI. Divided into several chapters and sections, shewing the contrary Sentiments of the Pagans and Jesuits. Translated (by Stephen Whatley) from the Original printed in France. To which are added, Copies of the said Constitution, and of the 101 Propositions of Father Quesnel thereby condemned." 8vo Dubl. 1726 It is here proved that the Jesuit authors have advanced infamous principles in regard to almost every department of duty, which had been denounced even by Heathen writers. See also The Jesuits Morals by Anthony Arnauld translated from the French, fol. Lond. 1670. To the list given above may be added Francis De Croy's Harmony of the Romish Church with Gentilism, Judaism, and ancient Heresies. Translated from the French by Hart, 4to Lond. 1620. — "Sicut Christus ex Judteis et Gentibus unum facit, ita Antichristus Judseorum et Gentium abominationes in unum coacervat." Christianismi Restitutio a Serveto 1553. Reprinted 1790.

CHAP. II. *Of the royal papers (viz. two of K.* Charles II. *and one of the Duchess of* York's,) *and of the discourses written about them.* 12. P A Short and plain way to the faith and church, composed Ct. iL. many years since by that eminent divine Mr. Richard Hudleston, of the English congregation of S. Benedict, and now published for the common good by his nephew Mr. John Hudleston of the same congregation. To which are annexed his late Majesty's K. Charles II. papers found iu his closet after his decease. As also a brief account of what occurred on his death-bed in matters of religion. pp. 38, 4to Loud. 1688 See Contin. p. 27 and 57. The Publisher to the Reader. " The Malignity of the times, and the Disasters ensuing thereupon for above these Forty years, have been too pernicious to be soon forgot. There are none so ignorant who have not heard of the Defeat of his Late Majesties Army by the Rebels at Worcester on the 3d of September 1651. And of the then Preservation of His Sacred Life and Person by the care and fidelity of his Catholic Subjects, of whom I acknowledg myself the most unworthy. In this sad Conjuncture it was that the desolate King after having been harassed to and fro, night and day in continual fatigues and perils, from Wednesday the Day of the Battel till Sunday following (the particulars of which are out of the sphere of my present design to enlarge upon) at last found an Asylum and Refuge at Mr. Whitgrave's House at Moseley in Staffordshire, whither Divine Providence not long before brought me, and where I had first the Honor of Attending upon him. During this Retreat, whilst Mr. Whitgrave, his Lady, and Mother, (who alone of all the Houshold were Privy to the Secret) were often busied in watching and other discharges of their Duty towards his Accommodation and Safeguard, His Majesty was pleased to entertain himself for the most part with me in my chamber, by perusing several of my Books, amongst others he took up this present Treatise then a Manuscript, lying on the table of a Closet adjacent to my Chamber. He read it; He seriously considered it, and after mature deliberation pronounced this Sentence upon it (viz.) I have not seen nny thing more Plain and clear upon this subject: the Arguments here drawn from Succession, are so conclusive, I do not conceive how they can be denied," &c. &c. Richard Hudleston was the youngest son of Andrew Hudleston of Farrington Hall in Lancashire. John Hudleston was a younger brother of the renowned family of the house of Hutton-John, in the county of Cumberland. Among " the Boscobel Tracts relating to the Escape of Charles II. after the Battle of Worcester," &c. &c., is Whitgreave's Narrative. For a relation of the reconciliation of Charles II. to the Church of Rome, see also Lingard, vol. x. p. 109; Macaulay, vol. i. pp. 434-436, who adds, "I have seen in the British Museum, and also in the Library of the Royal Institution, a curious broadside containing an account of the death of Charles. It will be found in the Somers Collection. The author was evidently a zealou3 Roman Catholie, and must have had access to good sources of information. I strongly suspect that he had been in communication, directly or indirectly, with James himself. No name is given at length, but the initials are perfectly intelligible, except in one place. It is said that the D. of Y. was reminded of the duty which he owed to his brother by P.M. A.C.F. I must own myself quite unable to decipher the last five letters. It is some consolation that Sir Walter Scott was equally unsuccessful. Since the first edition of this work was published, several very ingenious conjectures touching these mysterious letters have been communicated to me; but I am convinced that the true solution has not yet been suggested. "—Ibid. pp. 437-438. The true solution has doubtless been supplied in Notes and Queries (2nd series, vol. i. pp. 110, 247), from Memoirs of the Rev. John

Huddleston, reprinted in 1816.— "Pere Mfansuete A Capuchin Friar, Confessor to the Duke." A copy of this contemporary broadside will be found, No. 1120, in the collection of Proclamations, Broadsides, Ballads, and Poems, presented to the Chetham Library, Manchester, by James O. Halliwell Esq., F.R.S. 13. "i Reasons of her leaving the communion of the church of England, and making herself a member of the Roman catholick church. Written by her grace the Duchess of York, for the satisfaction of her friends. pp. 6. Prefixed are Charles the Second's Papers, pp.8. "James now (1686) took a step which greatly disconcerted the whole Anglican party. Two papers, in which were set forth very concisely the arguments ordinarily used by Roman Catholics in controversy with Protestants, had been found in Charles's strong box, and appeared to be in his handwriting. These papers James showed triumphantly to several Protestants, and declared that, to his knowledge, his brother had lived and died a Roman Catholic. One of the persons to whom the manuscripts were exhibited was Archbishop Sancroft. He read them with much' emotion, and remained silent. Such silence was only the natural effect of a struggle between respect and veneration. But James supposed that the Primate was struck dumb by the irresistible force of reason, and eagerly challenged his Grace to produce, with the help of the whole episcopal bench, a satisfactory reply. ' Let me have a solid answer, and in a gentlemanly style; and it may have the effect which you so much desire of bringing me over to your Church.' The Archbishop mildly said, that in his opinion, such an answer might, without much difficulty, be written, but declined the controversy on the plea of reverence for the memory of his deceased master. This plea the King considered as the subterfuge of a vanquished disputant.

He ordered these tracts to be printed with the utmost pomp of typography, and appended to them a declaration attested by his sign manual, and certifying that the originals were in his brother's own hand. James himself distributed the whole edition among his courtiers and among the people of humbler rank who crowded round his coach. He gave one copy to a young woman of mean condition whom he supposed to be of his own religious persuasion, and assured her that she would be greatly edified and comforted by the perusal.

In requital of his kindness she delivered to him, a few days later, an epistle adjuring him to come out of the mystical Babylon, and to dash from his lips the cup of fornications." Macaulay, vol. ii., pp. 44-5.

14. An answer to some papers lately printed, concerning the £. authority of the catholic church in matters of faith, and the reformation of the church of England. By Edward Stillingfleet, D.D. pp. 72, 4to Lond. 1686

Cat. No. 31. Contin. p. 28. Bishop of Worcester, born in 1635, died 1699. Stillingfleet, who was renowned as a consummate master of all the weapons of controversy, gave James deep offence by publishing an answer to the papers which had been found in the strong box of Charles the Second. He is generally acknowledged to have occupied the very first place among those illustrious men who, in that important crisis of our history, brought great talents and prodigious learning to bear upon the exposure of Popery. — Macaulay, vol. ii. p. 149. "A clear and solid answer to the Papers undertaken herein to be examined." — *Chatham MS.*

C %, 15. A defence of the papers written by the late King of blessed memory and Duchess of York, against the answer made to them. By John Dryden. pp. 126, 4to Lond. 1686

Contin. p. 28. Born in 1631, died 1700. " The help of Dryden was welcome to those Roman Catholic divines who were painfully sustaining a conflict against all that was illustrious in the Established Church...... It seemed that it was no light thing to have secured the cooperation of the greatest living master of the English language. The first service which he was required to perform in return for his pension was to defend his Church in prose against Stillingfleet. But the art of saying things well is useless to a man who has nothing to say; and this was Dryden's case. He soon found himself unequally paired with an antagonist whose whole life had been one long training for controversy. The veteran gladiator disarmed the novice, inflicted a few contemptuous scratches, and turned away to encounter more formidable combatants." — Macaulay, vol. ii. p. 198.

£. 1L. 16. *Jf* A reply to the answer made upon the three royal papers.

Contin. p. 28. The author of this pamphlet is honoured by Stillingfleet, in his Vindication, with a very respectful rejoinder.

CIL. 17. A vindication of the answer to some late papers concerning the unity and authority of the catholick church, and the reformation of the church of England. By Edward Stilling

Cat. No. 32. Contin. p. 28. See 14.

18. An answer to father Huddleston's short and plain way, &c. as above. No. 12.

Contin. p. 57. "To this there is an Answer almost fniished by a very Learned Person, who will demonstrate to the World, how little that Book had in it to convince." 19. A discourse sent to the late K. James, to persuade him to embrace the protestant religiou; with a letter to the same purpose. By Samuel Parker, Lord Bishop of Oxon.

pp. 46, 4to Lond. 1690 *Ath. Ox.* vol. ii. col. 280. *(Edit.* Bliss, vol. iv. col. 225.) Republished, 8vo, 1714, under the title of "A Letter sent by Sir Leolyn Jenkins," &c. See 20. In the " Life of Sir Leoline Jenkins, Judge of the High Court of Admiralty, and Prerogative Court of Canterbury, &c. Ambassador and Plenipotentiary for the General Peace at Cologne and Ninicguen, and Secretary of State to K. Charles II." &c. &c. , by William Wynne, 2 vols. fol. Lond. 1724, there are two Letters addressed by him to the Duke of York, respecting which his Biographer remarks, in defence of his Protestantism: " To this (his bounty to the French Protestants in the year 1681) may be justly added the many affectionate and pressing Instances he had made to his Royal Highness to persuade him to return to the Communion of the Church of England both by Letter and Conversation. Dr. Parker's Letter to Sir Leoline Jenkins (?) is already in print, and the Lord Clarendon's Letters on the same subject, which I have some reason to think were published by Sir Leoline's mean3, in order to promote and encourage others in the like Addresses. There is likewise a Letter in the following Collection to his Highness when he was retired to Scotland, (vol. ii. p. 690,) wrote just after the Debates in the House of Commons, upon the Bill of Exclusion, full of affectionate expressions and pathetick arguments to induce him to forsake the Roman Catholick Religion, but was no more than, as he there says, what he had often presumed to urge in his private and occasional Conferences with him. ' I will presume,' says Sir Leoline, ' humbly to say that besides what you owe to the Injunctions of your Martyr Father, and the rest of the Protestant World, you are bound in Justice 1. To the Church of England. 2. In submission to the King your Royal Brother. 3. In natural Affection to your Children. 4. In charity to these Three unhappy Nations, to use all the Means possible to inform yourself, whether you can with a safe Conscience return again to this Communion.'" The Injunctions of Charles I. will be found in a Broad *n* side, No. 1144, in the Collection of Proclamations, &c, presented to the Chetham Library, Manchester, by James 0. Halliwell Esq., F.R.S., viz.: " Not Popery but the Protestant Religion the Support of the Crown Confirmed out of the Mouth of the Blessed Martyr K. Charles I. of Pious Memory. With other of his Sayings and Instructions concerning both Religion and Government, worthy to be seriously considered by all Protestants."

C 5. Letter to Ann, Duchess of York, a few months before her death.

By Geo. Morley, Bishop of Winchester. 1670 "Of this letter of Morley, dated Jan. 1670, there is a copy indorsed by the hand of Lord Clarendon himself. There is, besides, a most able and pathetic letter written by that illustrious exile himself to his daughter, and another full of respectful but manly remonstrance to the Duke, on occasion of the rumours which had reached him concerning the change in her Royal Highness's religious faith. These are dated in 1668. The last paper in the series is a letter by Lord Cornbury to the Duke of York on the same subject, dated December 26, 1670. They are so full of interest, that I had purposed to print them here entire; but the great space, which they would occupy, forbids me. I trust however that the public will soon obtain them by some other channel." — Phillpotts' Letters to Charles Butler, Esq., p. 330. The first is in the collection of " Several Treatises written upon seve-ral Occasions by the Right Reverend Father in God George Lord Bishop of Wiuton," 4to Loud. 1683; the second and third in the third volume of the Harleian Miscellany; the second and fourth in the Supplement to the Clarendon State Papers, pp. 38-41.

C iL. A true relation of the late King's death. One folio half sheet.

See 12 supra. No. 1120 of the Collection of Proclamations, Broadsides, Ballads, and Poems, presented to the Chetham Library by James 0. Halliwell Esq., F.R.S. Also in State Tracts, 1660-89.

4T«fL Copies of two papers written by the late King Charles II. of blessed memory; as also a copy of a paper written by the late Duchess of York, *ut supra* 13.

Folio and 4to. pp. 14, 4to Loud. 1686 Reprinted in the fifth volume of the Harleian Miscellany.

Remarks on the two Papers, writ by his late Majesty King Charles ft IT. concerning Religion. By Gilbert Burnet, D. D.

4to Hague, 1687

This was the third answer to King Charles's Tracts published in the reign of James. Of these answers Dr. Lingard appears to have heen ignorant. In vol. x. p. 215, he writes thus: "A question respecting their King Charles's Tracts authenticity was soon raised by persons who, with Evelyn and Burnet, maintained that both papers displayed a much greater proficiency in controversial learning than the laughter-loving Monarch had ever possessed. On the other side competent judges, acquainted with the handwriting of Charles, pronounced them genuine, and, from the erasures and corrections and interlineations with which they abounded, drew the conclusion that they were not mere copies of documents presented to that Prince, but compositions of his own, which he had revised and improved on different occasions. It was speedily known that numerous conversions to the Roman Catholic creed had occurred among the nobility and the dependants on the Court: the example of the higher was gradually imitated by the lower classes; and the more zealous of the Catholic body were careful to reprint editions of the two tracts, which they triumphantly dispersed among their neighbours. But the most unaccountable thing was the torpor with respect to them of the Protestant press. During the whole reign of James nothing was published in the shape of refutation; *not a writer came forward to enter the lists against the royal theologian*. This was a circumstance to which James has alluded with evident marks of satisfaction."—James's Memoirs, vol. ii. p. 9. In the same page is added, "There was something of an answer published by an unknown hand; but the drift of it was rather to prove that the papers were not the late King's, than any reply to the arguments in it." Reprinted in State Tracts, 1660-89.

An Answer to a book, entituled, A short and plain way to the ft Faith and Church. By Samuel Grascome, a Priest of the Church of England. pp. 210, 8vo Lond. 1703

" It may perhaps be objected, that I have said nothing to the Two Papers of King Charles the Second, nor to the Account which the younger Huddleston gives of his Death, printed at the end of that small Treatise I have good reason to call in question

Mr. Huddleston's Sincerity and fair dealing in that relation. For I have been told by a person of no mean Quality and Known Integrity, who attended his

Majesty from the time presently after his fall in that fatal Distemper to the last minute of his Life, excepting the space of about one half hour, when he and others were desired to withdraw, to make room for some other company, whereof Mr. Huddleston was one, that the King at that time was not able to speak three words together without great difficulty, and those so brokenly and unintelligibly that they were forced to guess at his meaning. Now let any man well consider all the Formalities and parts which Mr. Huddleston tells us he then acted, and you will scarce allow it to be done with any decency in less than an hour and a half (although nothing should have passed at that time between the King and Queen to hinder or interrupt his proceedings) and that is three times as long as he was there. But the strangest thing of all is that he puts long speeches in the King's Mouth, and makes him speak them Readily and Chearfully; whereas that Honourable Person tells me, that when he and the others went in again to the King, they observed his speech to fail more, and so it continued to his death. Now how came he to speak so well and readily then, who could do it neither before nor after *f.— Pref.*

A Letter to the King, when Duke of York, persuading him to return to the protestant Religion, wherein the chief errors of the Papists are exposed. By an old Cavalier and faithful son of the church of England as established by law.

A single sheet. 4to 1688 Probably the same as the Letter addressed by Sir Leoline Jenkins to the Duke of York in Scotland in 1680 above referred to.

CHAP. III. *Of the discourses written upon the design of abrogating the penal Laivs and Test.* 20. Reasons for abrogating the test imposed upon all members of ©, %, parliament. First written for the author's own satisfaction,

and now published for the benefit of all others whom it may concern. By Samuel Parker, L. Bp. of Oxon.

pp. 131, 4to Lond. 1688

See Contin. p. 50. *Ath. Ox.* vol. ii. col. 820. *(Edil.* Bliss, vol. iv.

col. 820.) Born in 1640, died in 1687. A defence of the Declaration of Indulgence, or rather a defence of the doctrine of transubstantiation. This piece called forth many answers, particularly one from

Burnet, written with extraordinary vigour and acrimony. See Enquiry into the Reasons for abrogating the Test, &c. , *infra.*

21. Transubstantiation a peculiar article of the Roman catholick £. fL. faith, which was never owned by the antient church or any of the reformed. In answer to a late discourse called, Reasons for abrogating the test. By Goodwin, a dissenting teacher in London. pp. 48, 4to Lond. 1688

See Cat. p. 33. Contin. p. 50. I can find no notice of this writer although not a theologian *Kara (TV/J,f3e/3r)KO;.* " How unsuccessfully he (Bp. Parker) has managed this design of expounding transubstantiation has been shewn in a late Discourse proving transubstantiation to be the peculiar doctrine of the Church of Rome, and in the Preface to the Examination of the New Articles of the Roman Creed by Catholic Tradition. "— Wake.

22. A discourse concerning the nature of idolatry, in which a late C H, author Samuel L. Bp. of Oxon'sJ true and only notion of

Idolatry in his reasons for abrogating the test, as above, No.

20. is considered and confuted. By William Wake, M.A.

Pref. pp. xvi., 96, 4to Lond. 1688

See Cat. No. 160. Contin. p. 50. Born in 1657, died in 1737. " Archbishop Wake was early and long engaged in controversy with the papists; and of all the great Divines who stood forward in defence of the Church of England in that protracted and memorable contest he, after Stillingfleet, was at once the most profoundly skilled in the learning, the most acute, solid and judicious in the argument of his cause. His gentle spirit led him to be moderate; but to convince you how he really thought and wrote of the Church of Rome, I will beg leave to add one or two quotations from his works in return for yours. The charge of idolatry is repeatedly enforced by him, and that not incidentally and by the way, but directly and argumentatively. The title of one of his chapters is as follows. That the Church of Rome thus worshipping of images is truly and properly guilty of idolatry.... Of the Adoration of the Host he says, the Church of England, consequently to her principles of the Bread and Wine remaining in their natural substances, professes that she thinks it to be Idolatry, and to be abhorred of all faithful Christians. Of the Sacrifice of the Mass, that it both makes up the chiefest part of the Popish worship, and is justly esteemed one of the greatest and most dangerous errors that offend us. See Exposition of the Doctrines of the Church of England. "— Letter to Charles Butler, Esq. By the Rev. Henry Phillpotts, D.D. The question so laboriously dilated upon in Moncwii Aaron Purgatus sive de Vitulo Aureo simul Cheruborum Mosis, Vitulorum Jeroboami, Theraphorum Mich a formam et historiam Explicantes, Atrebati, 1606, (of which there is an analysis in Poole's Synopsis ad Exod. xxxii.) viz. Whether the Golden Calf was set up in honour of Apis, the Egyptian god, or symbolically in honour of Jehovah, was involved in the controversy between Godden and Stillingfleet, and again in the revival of that controversy between Parker and Wake. " I shall not discuss the question of Moncaius," who believed Aaron and the Levites to have offered relative worship only, whilst the rest of the congregation were guilty of apostasy — says the Rev. Dr. Townsend in *Scriptural Communion with God,* or *the. Pentateuch and the Book of Job,* vol. ii. p. 287 — "neither shall I enquire into the accuracy of the opinion of Pfeiffer and of the majority of commentators, that it was set up in honour of Apis. I believe that it was framed in honour of the God of the patriarchs, the God of Israel, Jehovah." Our learned author has evidently misrepresented the opinion of Pfeiffer, as will appear from the following extract from his *DifficiUorum S. S. Locorum Centurim,* Ultrajecti 1704, p. 131. Eum vitulum Israelite non habebant pro Deo sed verum

Dcum *representative et symbolice* colere volebant illo. Nec enim vitulum eduxisse se ex iEgypto (cujus materiam potius ipsi secum ex Egypto asportarant) nec Aaron tani emote mentis erat.... Nihilominus tamen idololatriam Israelite comniittebant, quia Deum aliter colere intendebant quam coli volebat. Confer B.D. Chemnitius P. 4. Exam. C. T, p. m. 22. seq. D. Gerhardus de Lege Mor. § 92. D. D. Caloyius Bibl. Illustr. h. 1. pag. 454. B. D. Dannhawerus Coll. Decal. p. 95. D. Klotzius de Angelol. p. 11. seq. D. Keslerus im Pabsthum p. 446. 476. Mich. Haveman Theogn. Proleg. § 8. Hackspanius Not. Bibl. P. 1. pag. 390. Vossius de Theol. Gent. 1. p. 10. Seeing then the theory of MoncEcius supported by so many consentient authorities, we cannot but be surprised that it has so severely been condemned by the learned Lutheran Divine, Jo. Henr. Mains, in his Historia Animalium Scripture Sacra; viz. " Ac juste denique ille purgatus impuri hominia a Paulo V. et Alexandre VII. Pontificibus indici librorum prohibitorum insertus, purgatorioque igni subjectus est." That from the use of animals as symbols of the divine nature, animal worship originated, is shown by Jamblicus de Myster. Egypt. s. ii. c. 1. &c. &c. See Jurieu's Critical History of the Doctrine and Worship of the Church, vol. ii. p. 178; Kircher's Obeliscus Fampbilius, c. 1 ; Vossius de Idolatria; Cudworth's Intellectual System; Faber's Origin of Pagan Idolatry. In a curious work on " Ancient Alphabets and Hieroglyphics," written in Arabic by Ibn Wahshih, and translated by M. Joseph Hammer, London, 1806, 4to, there is a singularly formed hieroglyphic symbol, called by Kircher, Anima Mundi. See GSdipus iEgyptiacus, vol. ii. p. 415, vol. iii. p. 405, and Prodromus Coptus, cap. ix. Of this symbol the author says, " This figure is expressive of the most sublime secret, called originally, Bahumed and Kharuf, (or calf,) viz., The Secret of the Nature of the World, or The Secret of Secrets, or The Beginning and Return of every thing." On which M. Hammer remarks: " It is superfluous to recall here to the memory of the reader the great antiquity and mysterious sense of the idolatrous veneration in which the calf has been continually held," &c. Pref. p. xiii, and pp. 22, 23. On Symbol-Idolatry see also Brocklesby's Explication of the Gospel-Theism and the Divinity of the Christian Religion, fol. Lond. 1706, Book i. c. 7.

The first Apologists indeed exulted in a religion more dogmatical and spiritual than that of the subjects of the ceremonial law, and zealously and severely condemned the frequent defections of the Jews, which were no other than the joining foreign worship to the worship of the God of Israel; and in this they acted with much good judgment, inasmuch as Christianity could not have been established but upon the abandonment by the Pagans of their inveterate prejudices concerning intercommunity of worship. So great was the influence of this principle that in the same time and country the Jews of Jerusalem added the Pagan idolatries to their religion, while the Pagans of Samaria added the Jewish religion to their idolatries. For instances of Jewish intercommunity, see Apthorpe's Letters on the Prevalence of Christianity. The truth of Christianity was acknowledged by the Pagans; they only wanted the compliment to be returned. As this could not be done, there was a necessity for the Christians to assign the reasons for their refusal. And this gave birth to so many confutations of idolatrous worship. See Warburton's Div. Leg. B. ii. s. 6. Severe laws of the Church were established against such as mingled the Jewish religion and the Christian together, and who are specified and condemned in the laws of Honorius in the Theodosian code. Lib. xvi. tit. viii. On the evils infused into the Church, both Jewish and Christian, by Pagan Philosophy, see Gale's Court of the Gentiles, Part iii. B. 2, c. i., 4to Lond. 1677.

C, IL. 23. A discourse concerning transubstantiation and idolatry; being an answer to the L. Bishop of Oxford's plea to those two points. By Gilbert Burnet, D.D. pp. 36, 4to Lond. 1688

" The wisdom of our Legislators is demonstrated in singling out this to be the sole point of the Tests for Imployments; since it is perhaps the only point in Controversy in which the whole Church of Rome holds the Affirmative, and the whole Reformed hold the Negative." This treatise is in the ninth volume of the Somers Tracts, p. 151, and is thus described: "Samuel Parker, D.D. Bishop of Oxford, a man of some talents and activity, disgraced himself during this busy period by his implicit compliance with the arbitrary commands of James II. This involved him in a dispute with Dr. Burnet, who treated him as unmercifully as Andrew Marvel had done upon a former occasion. Indeed Parker had exalted the king's supremacy in terms which amounted to direct blasphemy. Burnet's account of the controversy is as follows: — 'He wrote a book against the tests full of petulant scurrility, of which I shall only give one instance. He had reflected much on the popish plot, and on Oates's evidence; and upon that he called the test the sacrament of Oatesian villainy. He treated the parliament that enacted the tests with a scorn that no popish writer had yet ventured on; and he said much to excuse transubstantiation and to free the church of Rome from the charge of idolatry. This raised such a disgust of him, even in those that had been formerly hut too much influenced by him, that, when he could not help seeing that,

he sunk under it. I was desired to answer his book with the severity that he deserved; and I did it with an acrimony of style that nothing but such a time and such a man could in any sort excuse. It was said the king sent him my papers, hearing that nobody else durst put them into his hands, hoping it would raise his indignation and engage him to answer them.'" — Burnet's *History of His Own Time,* vol. iii. p.

1265. (Edit 1724, vol. i. p. 740.)

24. Draconica, or, an abstract of all the penal laws touching matters £, L.

of religion and the several oaths and tests thereby enjoined;

with brief observations thereupon. The third edition, with considerable additions. By Henry Care.

pp. 40, 4to Lond. 1688

In reply to this tract and the same au-

thor's Animadversions (41 infra) was published, A Seasonable Discourse showing the necessity of Union among Protestants, &c., *ut infra.*
25. A discourse for taking off the test and penal laws about reli-£, L, gion. Pref. pp. vi, 40, 4to Lond. 1687
Dr. More's discourse on the Real Presence is here quoted, in which " he can not escape a falling in with Transubstantiation any other way than by closing with a Notion manifestly false and Platonic." 26. The judgment and doctrine of the clergy of the church of Eng-£. 1L.
land concerning the King's prerogative in dispensing with penal laws. Asserted by the Lords Archbishops Bancroft, Laud and Usher. The Lords Bishops Sanderson and Cartwright. The Reverend Doctors Sir Thomas Ridley LL.D.
,
Dr. Heylin, Dr. Barrow, Dr. Sherlock, Master of the Temple,
Dr. Hicks, Dr. Nalson and Dr. Puller. And by the Anonymous Author of the Harmony of Divinity and Law. Together
E with the concurring Resolutions of our Reverend Judges, as most consonant and agreeable thereunto
Imperfect, pp.. 4to Lond. 1687.
ft i. 27. An Answer to a late pamphlet, entitled, The judgment and doctrine of the clergy, &c. as above, No. 26, shewing that this is not asserted by the Archbishops Bancroft, Laud, and Usher; Bp. Sanderson; the Doctors Heylin, Barrow, Sherlock, Hickes, Nalson, Puller; so far as appears from their words cited in this pamphlet. In a letter to a friend. pp. 39, 4to Lond. 1687 This tract shows that even those writers who advocated non-resistance and passive obedience did not consequentially include the dispensing power among the rights and privileges of sovereignty. " The Laws of England are the King's Laws, but when they are made Laws by the King King's authority they become the Laws of the Land, the Rule of his own Government, and his Subjects' obedience." " He concludes this pamphlet with some few Authorities for Liberty of Conscience. I shall not now examine how pertinent they are, for I will give no other Answer but this; when he has answered all the Presbyterian arguments against Toleration, but especially that Book call'd Toleration Discuss'd and the arguments of Dr. Parker, now the Right Reverend Bishop of Oxford, in his Ecclesiastical Policy; when he can prove that Liberty of Conscience is the doctrine and practise of the Church of Rome, and the Standing Rule of the Inquisition, then I will consider further on this Argument."

The works from which testimonies to this "judgment" (Tracts 26, 27) are derived are as follow:

Jovian; or, An Answer to (Samuel Johnson, Author of) Julian, the Apostate. By George Hickes, D.D. 8vo Lond. 1683

A Vindication of the Monarchy and Government long established in the Church and Kingdome of England against the pernicious assertions &c. of the Inuorators during the last Parliament in the Eeign of Charles I. By Sir Robert Poyntz. 4to Lond. 1661

The Church, her doctrines and the opposing heresies; a Sermon preached at St. Paul's Cross. By Richard Bancroft, Archbishop of Canterbury.

Lond. 1588.

Q£ Reprinted in Hickes's Bibliotheca Scriptorum Ecclesise Angl. 1709, and in Tracts of the Anglican Fathers, vol. i. The substance of this Sermon will be found in Collier's Eccl. History, vol. ii. p. 609.

View of the Civil and Ecclesiastical Law; wherein the practice of them is streitned and may be relieved within this land. By Sir Thomas Ridley, one of the Masters in Chancery. Oxford 1607, 4to. 2nd edit. Oxf. 1634, 4to. 3rd edit. Oxf. 1661. 4th edit., Oxf. 1676, 8vo. All these editions, except the first, contain Notes by John Gregory, A.M., of Christ College.

Conference between Bishop Laud and Fisher the Jesuit, with an answer to the exceptions of A. C. Fisher. The first edition was printed along with White's Replie to Jesuit Fisher's answere to certaine questions propounded by King James, fol. Lond. 1624. The second edition was published separately, much enlarged, 1639, fol.; the third in 1673, with important alterations; the fourth in 1686, with trifling variations from the third; the fifth, 1849, in Lib. of Anglo-Cath. Theol., Oxon. In this edition the whole of Fisher's Account of the Conference, with his notes, to which Laud's Relation is a reply, and of which some portions only were given in the former editions, is incorporated from the only copy known to exist, and the numerous quotations from the Fathers and Schoolmen are printed with their context. — " He quotes a saying of his Laud's out of his book against Fisher, but never directs us where to find it," &c. It will be found in page 211 of the third edition. Of the nine questions proposed to Fisher the last is — " Deposing Kings and transferring their Dominions by Papal Authority either directly or indirectly."

The Power communicated by God to the Prince and the Obedience required of the Subject, &c. By James Ussher, Archbishop of Armagh. Published by his grandson, James Tyrrcl, after the Restoration, with a Preface by Bishop Saunderson. 8vo Lond 1661

In the eleventh volume of Archbishop Usshor's Works, Dublin, 1847—" The reverend Author without meddling with these Punctilios of the Law undertaketh no more but to declare and assert the Power of Sovereign Princes, as the godly Fathers and Councils of the ancient Catholick Church from the evidence of Holy Scripture, and the most judicious Heathen Writers by discourse of Reason from the light of Nature, have constantly taught and acknowledged tho some." Pref. D. 3.

Cases of Conscience. By Robert Sanderson, D.D. Translated by Robert Codrington. 12mo Lond. 1660

Compare his "De Obligatione Conscientise Prselectiones Decem." 12mo Lond. 1676. Republished in 1851, with a translation by Professor Whewell. See also Wordsworth's Christian Institutes, vol. iii. This eminent Divine published also, " Judgment concerning Submission to Usurpers, 1678."

A Sermon preached upon the Anniversary Solemnity of the happy Inauguration of our dread Sovereign James 2. 6th February 1685-6. By Thomas Cartwright, Bishop of Chester. The Jacobite devotion of this " still viler sycophant than Parker" may be gathered from the following extract from his Diary printed for the Camden Society. " May 29, 1687. I was at the first sermou, and after at the King's levee, who ordered me to deliver my address at 10 after the rising of the cabinet council, which was graciously accepted and answered with a speech of his Majesty's to this effect — My Lord, I could expect no less than such a loyal address as this from a prelate of such approved loyalty as you have been, and am fully convinced that, where my bishops are loyal, the clergy of the Church of England will easily be ruled by them in any thing relating to my service; and I do assure you and them that whilst they continue their duty, they shall never find me unmindful of my engagements to them, but ready to make good all that I have promised them, and to stand by them as long as I live; but when the bishops are wanting in doing their duties, I can not but expect their clergy shall be unmindful of theirs."

The extract given from Dr. Heylin respecting " the King's *sometimes* passing by a Statute with a Non-obstante" is not to be found by any reference given Sere or in the Answer. It occurs in " The Stumbling Block of Disobedience and Rebellion: cunningly laid by Calvin in the Subjects way, discovered, censured and removed." (Iu his Historical and Miscellaneous Tracts, foI. Lond. 1681.)

Treatise on the Pope's Supremacy. By Isaac Barrow, D.D. Master of Trinity College, Cambridgo. 4to Lond. 1688. Fol. Lond. 1683, vol. i. The places where to find them are given in the Answer viz. pp. 311-318, 400, 4to. This excellent and elaborate treatise is given in the first volume of the Supplement to Gibson's Preservative from Popery, 8vo Lond. 1849; and "The Nature and Extent of the Papal Claims to Supremacy, whether in Things Temporal or Spiritual," from the same Treatise will be found in Wordsworth s Christian Institutes, vol. iv. " Of the life of this luminary of mathematical science and ornament of the English church, it is hardly necessary to say a word, as a biography of him will bo met with in every Cyclopaedia and Collection of Lives;" Worthington's Diary and Correspondence, vol. i. p. 66. A few passages, however, from Abraham Hill's Account of his Life, prefixed to his works, are too interesting to be omitted. " Besides the particular assistence he gave to many in their studie, he concerned himself in every thing. that was for the interest of his College; upontho single affair of building their Library, he writ out quires of Paper, chiefly to those who had been of the College, first to ingnge them and then to give them thanks, which he never omitted: these Letters he esteemed not enough to keep copies of, but by the generous returns he brought in, they appeared to be of no small value; and those Gentlemen that please to send back their Letters will deserve to be accounted further Beiielactours to their Library In this place seated to his ease and satisfaction he yielded the day to his public business, and took from his Morning sleep many hours to increase his stock of Sermons and write his Treatise of the Pope's Supremacy. He understood Popery both at home and abroad, he had narrowly observed it, militant in England, triumphant in Italy, disguised in France, and had earlier apprehensions than most others of the approaching danger, and would have appeared with the forwardest in a needful time; for his ingagement in that Cause, and his place in your Friendship Dr. Tillotson's I would (with the leave of the most worthy Dean of St. Paul's, his highly respected Friend) call him another Dr. Stillingfleet." Sec also Ward's Lives of the Professors of Gresham College, fol. Lond. 1740. How delightful it is to see such men as Dr. Barrow and his successor in the Mathematical Chair, Sir Isaac Newton, thus "yielding the day to public business." " I do not love to be printed on every occasion, much less to be dunned and teased by foreigners about mathematical things, or to be thought by our own people to be trilling away my time about them when I am about the King' business." (Newton to Flamsteed.) The "particular Branches of Sovereignty," as set down by Dr. Barrow, will be found in pp. 274, 287, 297, 318, 319, 323, 311, 357, 365, 382, 388, 396, 398, 400, and arc collected in Toi Cleri pro Rege, ut infra. The Case of Resistance of the Supreme Powers stated and resolved, according to the doctrine of the Holy Scriptures. By William Sherlock, D.D. Master of the Temple, and Dean of St. Paul's. Lond. 1684

" A pension was bestowed on him by Charles: but that pension James soon took away; for Sherlock, t hough he held himself bound to pay passive obedience to the civil power, held himself equally bound to combat religions errors, and was the keenest and most laborious of that host of controversialists who, in the clay of peril, manfully defended the Protestant faith. In little more than two years he published sixteen treatises, some of thom large books, against the high pretensions of Rome. Not content with the easy victories which he gained over Bueh feeble antagonists as those who were quartered at

Clerkenwcll and the Savoy, he had the courage to measure his strength with no less a champion than Bossuct, and came out of the conflict without discredit. Nevertheless Sherlock still continued to maintain that no oppression could justify Christians in resisting the kingly authority." (Maeauhy, vol. iii. pp. 457-8.) In vol. iv. of the same work is fully told the story of his conversion from Jacobitism by a passagoin the eighth chapter of Bishop Overall's Convocation Book, 1606, concerning the Government of God's Catholick Church and the Kingdoms of the Whole World. 4to Loud. 1690. In justification of his conduct he published a pamphlet entitled The Case of Allegiance to Sovereign Powers stated, 4to Lond. 1691.

The Common Interest of King and People; shewing the original antiquity and excellency of Monarchy, compared with Aristocracy and Democracy, and particularly of our English Monarchy; and that Absolute,

Papal and Presbyterian Popular Supremacy are utterly inconsistent with Prerogative, Property and Liberty. By John Nalson. 8vo

Lond. 1678

The Moderation of the Church of England considered. By Timothy Puller, f

D.D. 8vo Lond. 1679. A new Edition, with an Introductory Preface,

by the Rev. Robert Eden. Lond. 1818

The Harmony of Divinity and Law, in a Discourse about not Resisting of Sovereign Princes, on Prov. xxx. 31. By George Hickes, D.D. 4to

Lond. 1684. Anon.

This learned divine and philologist advocated passive obedience and the theory of divine right in several other works, *e.g.* The Judgment of an Anonymous Writer, &c., already enumerated in page 7, Jovian, &c.—A Letter to the Author of a late Paper, entitled, a Vindication of the Divines of the Church of England, &c., in Defence of the History of Passive Obedience, (the Author of the Vindication, Dr. Fowler, Bishop of Gloucester) 1689.— A Discourse of the Soveraign Power, in a Sermon preached Nov. 28, 1682, before the Artillery Company, 1713. Ho here says (Collection of Sermons, vol. i. p. 315): "God hath reserved wicked Princes and Tyrants for his punishment, and hath allowed their Subjects no Arms against them, but the Arms of the Catholick and Apostolical Church, even the primitive Artillery of Prayers and Tears."—The celebrated story of the Theban Legion no Fable, in answer to the Objections of Dr. Gilbert Burnet's Preface to his Translation of Lactantius de Mortibua Persecutorum, with some Remarks on his Discourse of Persecution; written in 1687, though not published till 1711. His favourite argument for passive obedience drawn from the story of the Theban Legiou has been annihilated by John Dubourdieu in an Historical Dissertation upon the Thebean Legion, plainly proving it to be Fabulous, 1696.

28. Samuel Lord Bp. of Oxford, his celebrated reasons for abro-(£. ft. gating the test and notions of idolatry answered by Samuel Archdeacon of Canterbury. By John Phillips, (?) nephew to John Milton. The third edition. pp. 22, 4to Lond. 1688 See *Ath. Ox.* vol. ii. col. 850 and 1119. *(Edit.* Bliss, vol. iv. col. 820.) To understand this title-page, it is necessary that the reader be informed that, in reward of Bishop Parker's obsequiousness to King James, he had, upon being preferred to the see of Oxford, obtained permission to hold the archdeaconry of Canterbury in commendam with that preferment. The archdeaconry he had obtained by distinguishing himself in the controversy between the church of England and the dissenters; and as, in the present struggle, he assumed the appearance of compassion and affection for the latter class of protestants, his antagonists fail not to reproach him with the very different sentiments he formerly entertained respecting non-conformists. These are chiefly drawn from Parker's work, entitled " A Discourse of Ecclesiastical Polity, wherein the Authority of the Civil Magistrate over the Consciences of Subjects in Matters of external Religion is asserted." This treatise appeared about 1673-4, and greatly offended the dissenters, as appears from the intemperate titles to several answers to which it gave occasion, as, for example, " Insolence and Impudence triumphant, Envy and Fury enthroned." The vindication of the test and penal laws, which the Ecclesiastical Polity contains, is in this tract placed by Burnet in contrast with Parker's Defence of the Indulgence.— Somers Tracts, ix. 160.

The author, whether Burnet or Phillips, here adopts Horace's maxim: Ridiculum acri

Fortius ac melius magnas plerumque secat res."

Lib. ii. Sat iv. 14. " There is another reason, why His Majesty was graciously pleas'd to think Force in Matters of meer Religion directly contrary to the

Interest of Government, and that is, Spoyling of Trade. Trade!

cries the Arch-Deacon; Trade! No. Let grass grow about the Custom-House, rather than abate one Tittle of my Ecclesiastical

Polity Ho is a very silly Man, and understands nothing of the follies, passions and inclinations of Human Nature, who sees not there is no Creature so ungovernable, as a Wealthy Phanatick, (p. 51.) And therefore (p. 48) I confess I can not but smile, when I observe how some, that would he thought wonderful grave and solemn Statesmen, labour with mighty projects of setting up this and that Manufacture in their respective Towns and Corporations, and how eagerly they pursue these petty attempts beyond the great Affairs of a more Publick Concernment (meaning the dreadful and terrible execution of the Penal Laws;) and how wisely they neglect the settlement of a whole Nation, for the Benefit of a Village or Burrough! Very pleasant Ecclesiastical Polity! No Man must eat or drink, or maintain his Family: the grand relation of Human Necessities, depending one upon another, must stand still to oblige the Arch-Deacon's Ecclesias tical Polity. Here's a Quietus est for above the Third Part of the

Nation. None but those that can swallow a Surplice, and adore the

Parochial Levite, must weave Camlets at Norwich, make Bays at

Colchester, Spurrs at Rippon, Nayls at Brummigeham, or Saddles at

Burford. For why? There is not any sort of people so seditious, as the Trading Part of the Nation."

29. The reasonableness of the church of England's test and just-£. fL, ness of her reformation, asserted; in answer to the Bp. of

Oxon's fallacious reasons and precarious assertions against it.

Also the worship of images, adoration of the host, and invocation of saints proved idolatry; by the catholick doctrine of the holy scripture, the ancient fathers, and all reformed churches.

By which the writings of the doctors, Stillingfleet, Tillotson,

More, &c. are cleared from the charge of anti-catholick, antichristian, phanatical, &c. pp. *22,* 4to 1688

" That men as loyal as himself and as far from being fanatical or unlearned entertained different notions of idolatry I shall insert the following passages," &c. p. xi. The authors here quoted are Whit-

gift, Abbot and Laud. Another contemporary equally learned might have been cited, viz. Bilson in " The True Difference betweene Christian
Subjection and Unchristian Rebellion," &c. 4to Lond. 1685. The fourth part.
30. Vox cleri pro rege; or the rights of the imperial sovereignty of £. fL, the crown of England vindicated in reply to a late pamphlet
No. 27 *supra* pretending to answer a book, entitled The judgment and doctrine of the clergy of the church of England,
concerning the King's prerogative in dispensing with penal laws. In a letter to friend. pp. Pref. xv., 68, 4to 1688
There was a second edition, with an Historical Account appended of the Convocation, 1689. In 16.90 was published An Answer to
Vox Cleri, &c. Among other works here cited as concurring in this judgment is Patriarcha: or the Natural Power of Kings, Lond. 1680,
8vo, by the Learned Sir Robert Filmer Baronet, " one of the most learned and loyal Gentlemen of the last Age, who as the Author of the Epistle Dedicatory to his Grace the present Duke of Beaufort (Edm. Bohun) says of him, dared to be true to the Crown when his

Fidelity could entitle him to Nothing, but the glory of living and dying a Good Subject, with the hazard of his Life and Fortunes." His " Power of Kings and in particular of the King of England," Lond. 1648-1680, concludes thus: — " The Councel of Many wise men may be better than of One; but to resolve, determine, and to command, One will always perform it better than Many; He which hath advisedly digested all their Opinions, will soon resolve without contention: the which many cannot easily perform: it is necessary to have a Soveraign Prince, which may have Power to resolve and determine of the Opinions of his Council." He wrote several other political works, e.g. The Anarchy of a Limited and Mixed Monarchy; in answer to Phil. Hutton's Treatise on Monarchy, 8vo. Lond. 1646, 1648, 1679. Observations concerning the Original of Government against Hobbes, Milton, Grotius, Hutton, &c., 4to. Lond. 1652. The Freeholders Grand Inquest touching the King and his Parliament, written by Sir Richard Hobhouse, 8vo. Lond. 1679. Defense against the Mistakes and Misrepresentations of Algernon Sidney Esq. in a Paper delivered by him to the Sherifs upon the Scaffold in Tower Hill, on Friday December 7, 1683, before his Execution there, fol. Lond. 1684. Sidney's Paper will be found in State Tracts 1660-1689. The most celebrated of his works, the " Patriarcha," in which the author derives all power from paternal authority and from Adam, occasioned some of the best works on government not only in this country but likewise on the continent, e.g. Locke's Two Treatises of Government. In the former, the false Principles and Foundation of Sir Robert Filmer and his Followers are detected and overthrown. The latter, an Essay concerning the true Original Extent and End of Civil Government, 8vo Lond. 1690. Sir James Tyrrel's Patriarcha non Monarcha. The Patriarch Unmonarch'd: being Observations on a late Treatise and diverse other Miscellanies, published under the name of Sir R. F. Bart, In which the falseness of those Opinions that would make Monarchy Jure Divino are laid open; and the true Principles of Government and Property (especially in our Kingdom) asserted. 8vo Lond. 1681. Algernon Sidney's Discourses concerning Government, fol. Lond. 1698.

On the doctrine of an Original Contract, or Compact, the following works may also be consulted: —
Lex, Bex: The Law and the Prince. A Dispute for the just Prerogative of King and People. Containing the Reasons and Causes of the most necessary Defensive Wars of the Kingdom of Scotland, and of their Expedition for the ayd and help of their Dear Brethren of England.
In which their Innocency is asserted, aud a full answer is given to a
Seditious Pamphlet, Intituled, Sacroaaneta Regum Majestas, or The Sacred and Royal Prerogative of Christian Kings; under the name of J. A. But penned by Jo. Maxwell the Excommunicate P. Prelat.
With a Scripturall Confutation of the Ruinous Grounds of W. Barclay,
H. Grotius, H. Arnisteus, Ant. de Domi. P. Bishop of Spalato, and of other late Anti-Magistratical Royalists; as, The Author of Ossorianum,
D. Fern, E. Symmons, the Doctors of Aberdeen &c. By Samuel Rutherford. 4to Loud. 1644-1657. Anon.

Ordered to be burnt by the hands of the common hangman. See Craig's Right of Succession, Pref. 1703. In pp. 111-15 is discussed this Question, Whether or no the King be univocally, or only analogically, and by proportion a father?

The Tenure of Kings and Magistrates; proving that it is lawful, and hath been held so through all ages, for any who have tho power, to call to account a Tyrant or wicked King, and after due conviction to depose and put him to death, if the ordinary Magistrate have neglected or denied to do it. By John Milton. 4to 1650

A Sermon preached at Scoon in Scotland, Jan. 1,1651, at the Coronation of Charles the Second. By Robert Dowglas, Minister at Edinburgh, Moderator of the Commission of the General Assembly. 1660 Reprinted in the first volume of the Phenix.

De Corpore Politico, or the Elements of Law, Moral and Politick. By Thomas Hoboes. 8vo Lond. 1650. Leviathan, or the Matter, Form and Power of a Commonwealth Ecclesiastical and Civil. By the same. Fol. Lond. 1651. A Dialogue between a Philosopher and a Student of the Common Laws of England. By the same. 1681. Moral and Political Works of T. H. with his Life. Fol. Lond. 1750. Edited by Sir William Molesworth, 11 volumes 8vo. Lond. 1889

See Worthington's Diary, part i. p. 277, note.

The Art of Lawgiving, in three Books. The first, shewing the foundations and superstructure of all kinds of Government. The second, shewing the Frames of the Commonwealths of Israel and of the Jews. The third, shewing a

Model fitted to the present State or Balance of this Nation. 1659. In Toland's edition of Sir John Harrington's Works. Fol, 1700. Also in the same volume, written not by Harrington but John Hall, The Grounds and Reasons of Monarchy consider'd and exemplify'd in the Scotish Line, &c. On Hobbes' and Harrington's Models of Government see Tenison's Epistle Dedicatory to his Examination of Hobbes's Creed Examin'd. 4to Lond. 1670

A Brief History of the Succession of the Crown of England, &c., collected out of the Records of the most authentick Historians.

From a Folio, printed in the year 1688-9. In State Tracts 1660-89, fol. was answered by the intrepid advocate of an indefeasible hereditary right of the Crown, Robert Brady, in A True and Exact History of the Succession of the Crown of England, &c. Lond. 1681. The Second Edition much inlarged. Together with Reflections upon the Bill of Exclusion, and a full and satisfacfactory Answer to Mr. Hunt s Argument in his Postscript about the succession of the Children of Robert the Second, King of Scotland, by Elizabeth Mure his pretended Concubine and Eufame his Wife. One of the Three Tracts of the Author's Introduction to the Old English History. Fol. Lond. 1684. There was another Answer, entitled, The Great Point of Succession Discussed.
F

An Essay on the Original and Nature of Government. By Sir William Temple. Written in the year 1672. VoL i. of Miscellanea, pp. 55-82.
8vo 1705

Both Hohbes and his adversary Cumberland, Sanderson, Overall, and Paley, the advocates of divine right, as well as Sir W. Temple, were of opinion that civil government originated in Patriarchal power. The Tryall of Dr. Henry Sacheverell before the House of Peers for High Crimes and Misdemeanours, &c. Fol. 1710

Especially the Extracts from Divines, pp. 154-186.

On the tendency of Dr. Sacheverell's Sermons see A New Catechism with Dr. Hickes's Thirty-nine Articles, in the twelfth vol. of Somers Tracts, p. 178. Scripture Politicks; or an impartial Account of the Origin and Measures of Government, ecclesiastical and civil, taken out of the Books of the Old and New Testament. With a Postscript relating to the Report of the Committee of Convocation about the Bishop of Bangor's Preservative and Sermon before the King. To which is subjoined The Supposal, or a New Schcmo of Government. By William Winston. 8vo 1717 Lord Bohngbroke's Dissertation on Parties, in vol. ii. his Works. 4to 1764 A Treatise of the Social Compact; or the Principles of Politio Law, translated from the French of John James Rousseau-12mo Lond. 1763 An Utopian government! See Coleridge's Friend, voL i. p. 324, On the Grounds of Government as laid exclusively in the Pure Reason; or a statement and critique of the Theory of Rousseau and the French Economists. "All the different philosophical systems of political justice," says Coleridge, "all the Theories on the rightful Origin of Government are reducible in the end to three classes, correspondent to the three different points of view, in which the Human Being itself may bo contemplated." The system of Hobbes ascribes the origin and continuance of Government to fear. The second system derives it from human prudence, the invisible powers of our nature, whose immediate presence is disclosed to our inner sense. The third and last system denies all rightful origin to government except as far as it is derivable from principles contained in the Reason of Man, and judges all the relations of men in society by the laws of moral necessity, which is the common duty of all men. Coleridge declares himself an adherent of the second system, in which the human being is considered as an animal gifted with understanding, or the faculty of suiting measures to circumstances. This theory appears to be supported by Aristotle, who ascribes Government to connate principles or moral sentiments, those lifeblent characteristics of humanity by which are instinctively impelled as well to civil as to domestic society. The origin and constitution of Human Society, considered as the necessary result of the physical and moral conditions impressed on our nature by the Creator, is beautifully exhibited in the fifth, sixth and seventh chapters of Dr. Chalmers' Bridgewater Treatise; and in the sixth Lecture of Archbishop Whateley's Political Economy.

Blackstone's Commentaries on the Laws of England, first edit. 4to Oxf. 1765-69. Book i. chap. 6. " As to the terms of the original contract between king and people, these I apprehend to be now couched in the coronation oath, which by the statute 1 W. and M. st. i. c. 6 is to be administered to every king and queen, who shall succeed to the imperial crown of these realms, by one of the archbishops or bishops of the realm, in the presence of all the people; who on their parts do reciprocally take the oath of allegiance to the crown."

The Spiritual and Temporal Liberty of Subjects in England, &c. By Anthony Ellys, D.D. 4to Lond. 1765. Part ii. pp. 226-257.

Lord Hardwick's State Papers, vol. ii. p. 401, " Notes of what passed in the Convention upon the day the question was moved in the House of Commons concerning the Abdication of King James II., the 28th of Jan. 1688-9. 2 vols 4to 1778
The doctrine of Hooker, Aquinas and Suarez will be found in Hallam's Literature of Europe, part iv. chap. 4, part iii. cbap. 4.

Some of the objections which have been urged against the doctrine of the Social Contract are noticed by Whewell in the second volume of " The Elements of Morality, including Polity," Lond. 1848. See also Burke's "Appeal from the New to the Old Whigs.

In opposition to the notion of an original Contract and in favour of the Divine Right of Kings, the following works may be consulted: —

The Rebels' Catechism; composed in an easy and familiar way to let them see the heinousness of their offence, the weakness of their strongest subterfuges, and to recall them to their duties both to

God and Man. 4to 1643

In the Harleian Miscell. vol. vii. p. 434. IL. Bishop Sanderson's Preface to Usher "On the Power of the Prince," *ut supra*.

Sacrosancta Regum Majestas; or the 8acred and Royal Prerogative of Christian Kings. Wherein Sovereignty is by Holy Scriptures, reverend Antiquity and sound Reason asserted, by discussing of five Questions. And the Puritanical, Jesuitical, Anti-Monarchical Grounds are disproved, and the untruth and weakness of their new devised State-principles are discovered. 4to Oxon, 1644: 8vo Lond. 1680 An example of a royalty thus emanating directly from on high is seen in the line of David established on the throne of Judah; and a claim to a resemblance to this right is expressed or implied in the language of Oriental monarch, and of many princes of the house of Stuart (see A Defence of the Right of Kings by James I.) and of the house of Bourbon. "It is," writes Louis XIV. (see his Memoires Historiques in the second and third volumes of his works, 6 vols. 8vo 1806), "the will of Heaven who has given kings-to man that they should be revered as his vicegerents, he having reserved to himself alone the right to scrutinise their conduct." On the doctrine of the Jesuits, *the Majesty of the People,* see Baxter's *Key for Catholics,* edit. by Allport, 1839, p. 412.

Tho Serpent-Salve; or a Remedy for the Biting of an Aspe. Wherein the Observators Grounds are discussed and plainly discovered to be unsound, seditious, not warranted by the Laws of God, of Nature, or of Nations, and most repugnant to the known Laws and Customs of this Realm, &c. First printed in the year 1643. The Catching of the Leviathan; or the Great Whale. Demonstrating out of Mr. Hobbs his own Works, That no man who is thoroughly an Hobbist, can be a good Christian, or a good Commonwealths-man, or reconcile himself to himself. Because his Principles are not only destructive to all Religion, but to all Societies: extinguishing the Relation between Prince and Subject, Parent and Child, Master and Servant, Husband and Wife; and abound with palpable contradictions. 1658. Schism Guarded, and beaten back upon the Right Owners, *(cc.* Sect. v. 1658. By John Bramhall, D.D., Abp. of Armagh. Folio, Dubl. 1677. 5 voll. 8vo. ai Lib. of Anglo-Cath. Theology. Oxf. 1842-45.

Three Sermons, preached at Lancaster, and in the late Guild of Preston. j£ Wherein the nature of Subjection to the Civil Magistrate is explained, the duty proved, and the Clergy justified in pressing the same upon their Fellow-Subjects. By Thomas Gipps, Rector of Bury in Lancashire, Chaplain to the Right Honourable the Earl of Darby. 4to Lond. 1683.

A Defence of Sir Robert Filmer against the Mistakes and Representations of Algernon Sidney Esq.; in a Paper delivered by him to the Sheriffs upon the Scaffold, &c. By Edmund Bohun. 1684 Among the upholders of the patriarchal theory may be mentioned Chrysostom, Bp. Andrews and the Caroline Divines (see Hurd's sixth Dialogue), Fleury, Bossuet and their followers in France. (See Sir James Stephen's Lectures on the History of France, vol. ii., " The Absolute Monarchy of Louis XIV.")

"It was," writes Hallam in his Constitutional History of England, "at this time 16851 that the university of Oxford published their celebrated decree against pernicious books and damnable doctrines, enumerating as such above twenty propositions, which they anathematized as false, seditious and impious. The first of these is, that all civil authority is derived originally from the people; the second, that there is a compact, tacit or express, between the king and his subjects: and others follow of the same description. They do not explicitly condemn a limited monarchy, like Filmer, but evidently adopt his scheme of primogenitary right, which is incompatible with it

This decree was publicly burned by an order of the house of lords in 1709: nor does there seem to have been a single dissent in that body to a step that cast such a stigma on the university. But the disgrace of the offence was greater than that of the punishment." This decree will be found in State Tracts from tho year 1660 to 1689, part ii. p. 154; Collier's Ecclesiastical History of Great Britain, vol. ii. p. 902; Sacheverell's Tryall, p. 162; Somers Tracts, vol. viii. p. 420.

Hickes's Jovian, *ut supra*. Especially the Preface.

Vindicia) Juris Regii, or Remarks upon a Paper entitled, An Enquiry into the measures of Submission to the Supreme Authority. By Jeremy Collier. 4to 1689. Dr. Sherlock's Case of Allegiance considered, with some Remarks upon his Vindication. By the same. 4to 1691. A Persuasive to Consideration, tendered to the Royalists, particularly those of the Church of England. By the same. 4to 1693.

Sir Thomas Craig's Right of Succession to the Kingdom of England against the Sophisms of Parsons the Jesuite, &o. Fol. Lond. 1703. Especially chap, xviii.

"One of the contrivances of the Jesuits was by searching into the origin of civil power, which they brought rightly, though for this wicked purpose, from the people; for they concluded that if the original power could be shown to have no divine right, but to be of human, and even popular institution, the liberty which the pope took in deposing would be less invidious: thus the Jesuits reasoned. The argument was pushed with great vigour by Harding and his brethren in Elizabeth's reign, but afterwards with more learning and address by Bellarmine, Mariana and others. (Note. This notion was stated even so early as Henry's rejection of the supremacy. Cardinal Pole insists strongly on this origin of kingship in his book, Pro ecclesiastica e unitatis defensione, lib. i. p. 74.) To combat this dangerous position so prejudicial to the power of kings and which was meant to justify the attempts of violence on the lives of heretical princes, the Protestant divines went into the other extreme, and to save the person of their sovereign, preached up the doctrine of Divine Right. Hooker, superior to every prejudice, followed the truth. But the ze8t of our reforming and reformed divines stuck to the other opinion, which, as appears from the Homilies, the Institution of the Christian Man, and the general stream of writings in those days, became the opinion of the church, and was indeed the received Protestant doctrine." — Hurd's Moral and Political Dialogues, vol. iv. p. 61.

Hume's Essays. 4to Lond. Vol. i. part ii. Essay xii.

Paley's Principles of Moral and Political Philosophy, Book vi. chap. i. The arguments against the theory of an original contract are stated with great ability in chap. iii. But, as Coleridge observes, " the contempt lavished by him on the notion of an original contract, though sufficiently compatible with the tenets of a Hume, will seem strange to us in the writings of a Protestant clergyman, who surely owed some respect to a mode of thinking which Ood himself had authorized by his own example, in the establishment of the Jewish constitution." These arguments will also be found in Bishop Sanderson's Preface to Usher " On the Power of the Prince," § 15-18.

I shall not attempt to give the golden chain of champions of monarchy from the Heroic ages down to our own days. Some links will be found in Mackenzie's Jus Regium *(ut supra* p. *7)* and Duport's f. %.

Gnomologia Homerica ad Iliad. 2, v. 204.

Ovk ar/adov irovicoipa,vir)' ets Koipavos earm Eh /3ao-iKevs etc. There are now living two eminent monarchists, Guizot and Palgrave. The former, in his Lectures on European Civilization, ha3 accurately distinguished the varieties of regal power which have prevailed at different periods, Barbarian, Imperial or Roman, Feudal, Religious, and Constitutional. On the Divine Right see also Hayward's Life and Raigne of Henrie the iiii., pp. 101-110, 4to Lond. 1599; Wolley's Loyalty amongst Rebels; The True Royalist, or Hushay the Archite, Lond. 1662. For other authorities on both sides see Dr. Doddridge's Lectures. Hooker, Baxter, Horsley, Burke, and Paley contended that all government is in such sort of divine institution that be the form of any particular government what it may, the submission of the individual is a principal branch of that religious duty which each man owes to Ood; but the principles which they advanced ascribed no greater sanctity to monarchy than to any other form of established government. See Wordsworth's Christian Institutes, vol. iii.

I shall conclude this digression into the field of Political Philosophy with a list of Tracts on non-resistance and passive obedience. Their name is Legion, but I shall confine it to those works which, having been collected in the State Tracts referred to in p. 9 and d. 2,. similar publications, are easily accessible —

Memorial to the Prince and Princess of Orange. By Major Wildman. Vol. i. p. 36. An Enquiry into the present State of Affairs, &c. By Dr. O. Burnet, pp. 128-133. A Justification of the Prince of Orange's Descent, pp. 134-148. Some Remarks upon Government, and particularly upon the Establishment of the English Monarchy, relating to this present Juncture. In two Letters, written by and to a Member of the Groat Convention, pp. 149-62, Four Questions Debated, pp. 163-66. Important Questions of State, Law. Justice and Prudence, both civil and religious, pp. 167-74. Short Considerations relating to the Settling of the Government, pp. 175-78. The Proceedings of the Present Parliament justified by the Opinion of H. Grotius, pp. 178-84. A Defence of their Majesties K. William and Q. Mary, pp. 186-208. A Defence of the Proceedings of the Late Parliament, anno 1689, pp. 209-216. A Discourse of the Nature of the present Conventions in both Kingdoms, pp. 218-24. The Supremacy Debated, or The Authority of Parliaments (formerly owned by Romish Clergy) the Supremest Power, &c., pp. 231-36. A Letter from a French Lawyer to an English Gentleman upon the present Revolution, p. 236. Reflections upon the Great Revolution. Written by a Lay-Hand in the Country, pp. 242-65. The Advantages of the Present Settlement and Danger of a Relapse, pp. 265-80. The Nullity of King James's Title, pp. 280-84. A Dialogue between a Jacobite and a Williamite, pp. 285-300. Examination of the Scruples about the Oath of Allegiance, pp. 300-18. The Case of Allegiance consider'd. By Samuel Masters, B.D. pp. 318-33. Some Considerations touching Succession and Allegiance, pp. 334—40. The Case of the Oaths Stated, pp. 340-47. Non-resistance and Passive Obedience no way concerned in the present Controversies. By Edm. Bohun. pp. 347-67. The Doctrine of Passive Obedience and Jure Divino disprov'd, and Obedience to the present Government prov'd from Scripture, Law and Reason, pp. 368-71. The Letter which was sent to the Author of the Doctrine of Passive Obedience, &c. answered and refuted, pp. 371-86. Political Aphorisms, or the true Maxims of Government display'd. By way of Challenge to Dr. William Sherlock and Ten other new Dissenters: and recommended as proper to be read by all Protestant Jacobites. pp. 386-402. Agreement between the present and former Government, pp. 409-39. A Resolution of certain Queries concerning Submission to the Government, pp. 439-65. Reflections upon the Opinions of some Modern Divines concerning the Nature of Government in general, and that of England in particular. With an Appendix, containing, I. The Seventy-fifth Canon of the Council of Toledo; II. The original Articles in Latin, out of which the Magna Charta of King John was fram'd; III. The True Magna Charta of King John in French; by which the Magna Charta in Matth. Paris is clear'd and justify'd, and the Alterations in the Common M. C. discover'd. All three Englished. By P.eter A.llix D.D. pp. 466-541. An Historical Account of the English Government, sect. III. and sect. VI. A Discourse concerning the Unreasonableness of a new Separation on account of the Oaths. With an Answer to the History of Passive Obedience, so far as relates to them. Bv Bishop Stillingflect. pp. 598614. A Vindication of the Same. By J. Williams, D.D. pp. 615-30.

A Letter writ by a Clergyman against the New Separation, pp. 631-634.

Vol. ii. — An Answer to the late King James's Declaration to all his pretended Subjects in the Kingdom of England, pp. 61-70. Plain English: or an Inquiry concerning the Real and Pretended Friends to the English Monarchy. With an Appendix concerning the Coronation Oath administered Dr. Edward Fowler?, pp. 10-4-15. Reflections upon K. James's Letter to his Privy Counsellors, pp. 23 4—42. A Letter to a Friend concerning a French Invasion, pp. 243-52. A Second Lettor, pp. 253-65. The Earl of Warrington's Charge, pp. 342-46. A Dialogue between Whig and Tory, pp. 371-92. An Inquiry into the Nature and Obligation of Legal Rights, pp. 392—412. An Essay concerning Obedience to the Supremo Powers and the Duty of Subjects in all Revolutions, pp. 431-61. Ail Essay concerning the Laws of Nations and the Rights of Sovereigns, pp. 462-75. A Defence of the Archbishop's Sermons on the Death of the Queen, &c. &c. pp. 522-38. Argument shewing, That a Standing Army is inconsistent with a Free Government, &c. by John Trenchard1, pp. 564-613. A Letter against Restraining the Press, pp. 614-26.

Vol. iii.—The Revolution vindicated; in an Answer to the two Memorials, and the Protestation against the Peace treated at Reswick, and other vT. 3L. Papers published in the late King James's Name. In which particularly the Matter of the Abdication, or the Sense in which King James is said to have abdicated, is more fully explain'd than has yet been done, pp. 694-728.

The Declaration of his Highness, William Henry, Prince of Orange, Ac. Of the Reasons inducing him to appear in Arms in the Kingdom of England, for preserving of the Protestant Religion, and for restoring the Laws and Liberties of England, Scotland and Ireland, is given entire in the Tryall of Dr. Sacheverell, pp. 179-185. State Tracts, 1660-89. Part ii., pp. 420-26. The opinion of Orotius referred to in the first volume, *ut supra,* was that our non-resistance should be ever measured by the intention of those who first framed the society. "The Rights of War and Peace," b. i. c. iv. s. 7. See also Puffendorf "de Jure Natures et Gentium," lib. vii. o. 7, s. 7. "The maxim, Fiat Justitia ct mat Coelum, let justice be performed though the universe be destroyed, is apparently false, and by sacrificing the end to the means, shews a preposterous idea of the subordination of duties." Hume's Essays, xiii., On Passive Obedience.

The political Treatises of Samuel Johnson, Chaplain to Lord Russel, were 5L, collected in one volume, folio, 1710, *e.g.* Julian the Apostate; being an Account of his Life, and the sense of the primitive Christians about his Succession, &c. (published in 1682). Julian's Arts to undermine and extirpate Christianity; together with Answers to Constantius the Apostate, and Jovian (published in 1689 in reply to Hickes's Jovian, 1689). Remarks on Dr. Sherlock's book, entitled, The Case of Resistance of the Supreme Powers stated and resolved (published 1689). An Argument proving that the abrogation of King James was according to the Constitution of the English Government (published 1692). Of Magistracy, Of Prerogatives by Divine Right, Of Obedience, Of Laws, (published 1688, reprinted in State Tracts, pp. 1660-1689, part ii. pp. 269-72, and in the Fifth Collection of Papers relating to the present Juncture of Affairs in England, 4to 1688). The Trial and Examination of a late Libel, *ut infra.* See Biographia Britannica. His Reflections on the History of Passive Obedience (pp. 251-56), in reply to Seller's History, *ut infra.*

All these inquiries are collectively discussed in " Bibliotheca Politica; or an Inquiry into the Ancient Constitution of the English Government." In thirteen Dialogues. Lond. 1694. The first dialogue relates to the question, whether monarchy be of divine right? the second, whether hereditary succession to crowns be a divine institution: the third, whether resistance of the supreme power by a whole nation, can be justified by the law of nature, or the gospel: the fourth, whether absolute non-resistance is enjoined by the gospel, or was the doctrine of the primitive church: the fifth, whether the king be the supreme legislative authority, and whether the parliament be a fundamental part of the government, or proceeds from the favour of kings: the sixth, whether the commons of England was one of tho three estates of the kingdom, before the 49th of Henry III.: the seventh, the same question continued: the eighth, continuation of the same subject: the ninth, whether by the ancient laws and constitution of this kingdom, as well as by the statutes of the 13th and 14th of Charles II., all resistance of the king, or of those commissioned by him, is expressly forbidden upon any pretence whatsoever: the tenth, whether a king of England can ever fall from, or forfeit his royal dignity, for any breach of an original contract, or wilful violation of the fundamental laws of the kingdom; and whether King William the Conqueror did not acquire, by virtue of his conquest, an absolute and unconditioned right to the crown of these realms: the eleventh, in what sense civil power is said to be derived from God, &c.: whether the appointment of William Prince of Orange be in accordance to the constitutional maxims of the English Constitution: the twelfth and thirteenth dialogues are on matters of little public moment. C 3L. 32. A reply to the new test of the church of England's loyalty.

I find in "The Law of Christ respecting Civil Obedience, especially in the Payment of Tribute, &c, by John Brown D.D.," extracts on the Right of Resistance from numerous authorities, references to the most valuable of which I here subjoin: —

Locke on Civil Government, chap. xix. Paley's Mor. and Pol. Phil., book vi. chap. iii. Hutcheson's Elements of Ethics, book iii. M'Crie's Review of the first series of the Tales of my Landlord. Edinburgh Christian Instructor for 1817. "We can appeal to divines and dignitaries of the Church of England, who have sanctioned the principles of resistance on which our ancestors acted — to Jewel, Hooker, Bilson, Bedel, Burnet, Hoadly, and King. But this is unnecessary, as the whole convocation, the Church of England representative, in Elizabeth's reign, publicly acknowledged it 'glorious to assist subjects in their resistance to their sovereigns, and their endeavours to rid themselves of their tyranny and oppressions.' " Sir James Mackintosh's View of the Reign of James II. from his Accession to the Enterprise of the Prince of Orange, chap. x. Jus Populi; or, a Discourse wherein clear satisfaction is given as well concerning the Right of Subjects as the Right of Princes: showing how both are consistent, and where they border one upon the other; as also what there is divine and what there is humane in both; and whether is of more value and extent, pp. 63-65, 4to Lond. 1664. It has been ascribed, obviously in mistake, to Milton.

" The reader," adds Dr. Brown," who wishes to see what can be said against a principle which is so powerfully supported in these extracts, and in favour of its opposite, will do well to consult a small but most elaborate dissertation, in the form of a sermon, entitled Passive Obedience, or the Christian Doctrine of not resisting the Supreme Power, proved and vindicated upon the Principles of the Law of Nature, in a discourse preached at the College Chapel, by George Berkeley, M.A., Fellow of Trinity College, Dublin, (afterwards Bishop of Cloyne). 'Nec vero aut per senatum aut per populum solvi hac lege possumus.'— Cic. fragm. de rep. Lond. 1713. This without doubt, and beyond comparison, the ablest defence of Passive Obedience and Non-resistance on philosophical principles consistent with revelation, is a curious display of the characteristic extreme acuteness, yet unsoundness of the mind of its singularly gifted and most estimable author— 'ingeniosa et sagax hariolatio viri disertissimi.' The scriptural argument in favour of these doctrines is fully stated in Dean Sherlock's ' Case of Resistance,' &c And the argument from the doctrine and practice of the primitive Christians may be found in Archbishop Usher's tract, entitled, The Power communicated by God, &c Few questions have been more thoroughly discussed. A specimen of the advocacy of what we regard as the right side is presented to the reader, and it is but justice to say that if that side of it which we consider untenable has been disgraced by the impiety of Hobbes and the unprincipled meanness of Parker — the learning of Usher, the judgment of Sanderson, the wit of South, the subtilty and candour of Berkeley, and the sanctity of Ken, are more than enough to entitle to careful consideration any principle which they entertained, &c. Abednego Seller, in his History of Passive Obedience since the Reformation, 4to Amsterdam, 1689, maintained that the Church of England "in contradistinction both to Papists and to Dissenters has constantly asserted the principles of Obedience to Princes, as the beet ages of Christianity practised it."

Kurd's remark cited *supra*, p. 37, on the opinion of most of our reforming and reformed Divines, is illustrated also in Jovian (chap. 10), in which are produced not only Statutes and Judgments of Convocations, but numerous authorities both legal and ecclesiastical. Kcttlowell, in his Treatise on Christianity, A Doctrine of the Cross; or, Passive Obedience under any pretended Invasions of Regal Rights and Liberties (in the second volume of his Works, fol. Lond. 1719), adduces also the Statutes, and concludes, p. 181: "By all which I conceive it plainly appears, 1. that the Two Kouscs sit with the King in Parliament, and concur in making laws, not as co-ordinate Powers that are equal to him, but as subordinate under bim; not in place of Sovereigns, but of Subjects under him, thoir sole Sovereign." The theory of a co-ordinate monarchy had been adopted to justify the war which the two houses were waging against King Charles I., and is the subject of a short pamphlet, entitled, A fuller Answer to a Treatise written by Dr. Ferno, entitled, "The Resolving of Conscience," 1642, 4to., the writer of which, according to Dr. Wordsworth, in Christian Institutes, vol. iii. p. 14, was Charles Herle, rector of Winwick in Lancashire, one of the licensers of the press under the two houses, a member of the Assembly of Divines, &c. &c. The subordination of the Three Estates of Scotland, Lords temporal and spiritual, and Commons, is zealously advocated in Abercromby's Martial Achievements of the Scots Nation, folio, Edinb. 1715. See Index in vol. ii. s.v. Antimonarchical Authors Confuted, (George Ridpath, Scc.)

On the other side Sir Robert Howard, in the History of the Reigns of Edward and Richard II., Lond. 1690, quotes reformed Divines asserting and supporting a contrary doctrine, viz. Zuinglius, Calvin, Bucer, Poter Martyr, Para?us, &c. (as wo are frequently reminded by Papal writers, *e.g.* Brercley or Anderton, Parsons, Patenson); extracts the original agreement in Magna Charta, and the opinion of Bracton and Fortescue; and subjoins from Hooker's Ecclesiastical PoUty the rationale of civil governments, according to which they have only an executive government committed to them by the pco idable adversary of the Patriarchal Scheme of Fihner, vol. ii. pp. 250-86.

In the ninth vol. of the Somers Tracts, p. 1!5.

"Hitherto we have only soen the most decent part of the controversy, which at this time raged between the King and the Church of England, when they stood forth on each side in their own characters, and for that reason were obliged to observe decorum; but in the two following pieces (A New Test and Some Considerations, &c.) or in the first of them at least, we shall find that the same temper and decency were not always observed. The Church of England, it is plain, could not act up to her own professions, and tho moment she hesitated, the king forgot her servieos. In the expostulations that followed, the gall of each party overflowed; and, as on the one hand, the courtiers would not allow the churchmen to be loyal, so, on the other, the churchmen were resolved not to lose tho first opportunity that offered to make the courtiers cat their words, or, if not, to make them sensible that they had given them a sufficient provocation to be otherwise." Somers' Tracts, vol. ix. p. 195.

31. A new test of the Church of England's loyalty. pp. 8, 4to Lond. 1687
C ML 33. The new test of the church of England's loyalty examined by the old test of truth and honesty. pp. 10, 4to 1687

" But however who can endure to hear Papists crying up Moderation, and exclaiming against Sanguinary Laws? For this is for the Kettle to accuse the Pot of Blackness," p. 5. See the thirteenth chapter of Puller's Moderation of the Church of England, 8vo Lond. 1679. New edition, by the Rev. Robert Eden, M.A., F.S.A., Lond. 1843. Gray's (Bampton Lecture) Sermons on the Principles upon which the Reformation of the Church of England was established. 1796. See Serm. VII. Conf. Mendham's Pius V., pp. 62 et seq.

34. *b* An instance of the church of England's loyalty. 4to 1687
In the ninth vol. of the Somers Tracts: — " This is another arrow from the same quiver which afforded the New Test of the Church of
England's loyalty. It rips open the history of Mary Queen of Scots,
and is obviously the work of some angry catholic." p. 203.

B.M. 35. *i* A reply to the two answers of the new test of the church of
England's loyalty. 4to 1687
C 1 36. Reflections upon the new test and the reply thereto; with a letter of Sir Francis Walsingham's concerning the penal laws made in the reign of Q. Elizabeth. (Sir F. W.'s Letter to Monsieur Critoy concerning the Queen's proceedings against both Papists and Puritans.) pp. 20, 4to 1687

Respecting Queen Elizabeth's " grace towards such as in her wisdom she knew to be Papist in conscience, and not faction and singularity," dilated on in Sir F. Walsingham's Letter, and, on the other hand, "the undutiful and traiterous affection borne against her Majesty by her Roman Catholic subjects," I shall give the testimonies not only of Protestants but of those who are represented as persecuted, in *chronological order,* because the lenity of the Queen and the Government for the first ten years of her reign is acknowledged by Parsons himself, and in the works of the Seculnr Priests *ut infra;* and the institution of a seminary at Douay in 1569, followed by another at Rome ten years later, which together sent three hundred priests into the English harvest (as Rishton in his Continuation of Sanders de Schism. Angl. relates) with the deposing bull of Pius V. (dated by Sanders February 27, 1.56.9-70; by Catena in his Italian translation of it in his Life of Pius V. February 25, and 5 Kal. Martii 1570 in the Bullarium Magnum) would naturally make some difference in the views and conduct of the English Government. At the same time the books here referred to will be found to contain a " Vindication " of the English Catholics under Queen Elizabeth.

A Bull granted by the Pope to Dr. Harding and others, by reconcilement and assoyling of English Papistes, to undermine Faith and Allegiance to the Quene; with a true Declaration of the Invention and Truthes thereof, and a Warning of Perils thereby imminent not to be neglected. By Thomas Norton. The bull is dated " anno 1567, die Jouis, 14 Aug." This and several similar articles by Norton were printed by John Daye, all without dates. See Watt, s. v. Norton, and the British Librarian, p. 1042; also Archaeologia, vol. xxxvi. pp. 105-19.

A Viewe of a seditious Bul sente into Englande from Pius Quintus, Bishop of Rome, Anno 1569. By John Jewel, Bp. of Salisbury. " Bishop Jewel has left some able and eloquent strictures upon the manifesto of Pius V. in his View of *a* Seditious Bull, &c. Scarcely any portion is more remarkable for his characteristic excellences than that in which he chastised the low-minded reflexion of the pontiff upon the shelter afforded to the unhappy persons whom he persecuted out of his country, and who, he would be doubly mortified to find, had escaped his fury by finding an asylum in the dominions of the British Queen. And yet it appears from the orders for enquiry by Elizabeth and the Archbishop of Canterbury that great care was taken in this work of exemplary charity to distinguish between those who came into the country for conscience sake and those who came from improper motives." See Wilkins' Concilia, vol. iv. pp. 254-5; The Life and Pontificate of Saint Pius the Fifth, &c, by the Rev. Joseph Mendham M.A., Lond. 1832; Cf. Pantin's Observations on Dr. Arnold's Christian Duty. See also Bishop Barlow's Brutum Fulmen, or the Bull of Pope Pius V., concerning the damnation, excommunication, and deposition of Q. Elizabeth, as also the absolution of her Subjects of their Oath of Allegiance, with a peremptory injunction upon Pain of an Anathema, never to obey any of her Laws or Commands; with some Observations and Animadversions upon it. Whercunto is annex'd the Bull of Pope Paul the Third, containing the damnation &c. of King Henry the Eighth. " A work," says Mendham, " of great original research and value, and far from being superseded in the present age."

The End and Confession of John Felton, the rank Traytor, who set vp the trayterous Bull on the Bishop of London's Gate, 4to Lond.
1570. See Howell's State Trials, 1085.

Nic. Sanderi de visibili Monarchia Ecclesise, Libri viii., Lovanii, 1571, Antw. 1581, Witeburg. 1592. It appears that this work of Father Sanders gave great uneasiness to the Government of Queen Elizabeth, on account of its advocating the deposing power of the Pope, and defending the Bull of Pius V. To counteract his designs, Elizabeth framed her Six Celebrated Questions, which were proposed to all Catholic missionaries, and to which Questions she required explicit and satisfactory answers. Two of these Questions, the third and the fifth, applied to Father Sanders; and the fifth especially relates to this work. See Butler's English Catholics. " In this book Sanders doth avow the bull of Pope Pius V. against Qu. Elizabeth to have been lawful, and affirmeth that by virtue thereof one Dr. Moreton, an old fugitive and conspirator, was sent from Rome into the north parts of England, to stir up the first rebellion there, whereof Charles Nevile,

Earl of Westmoreland, was head captain."—Wood, vol. i. col. 471. It is full of scurrilous abuse of England and English affairs. He wrote likewise Pro defensione Excommunicationis a Pio V. late in Anglise reginam, lib. i. Printed, but afterwards suppressed by the author.

Barthol. Clerke, Fidelis Servi Subdito infideli Responsio, una cum Errorum et Calumniarum quarundam examine quse continentur in septimo libro dc V. M. E. a N. S. conscripta, 4to Lond. 1573. For other works, written in reply to Sanders on the Papal Supremacy, sec Walchii Bibl. Theolog. vol. ii. p. 210.

A brief Treatise of diuerse plaine and sure Wayes to find out the Truthe in this doubtful and dangerous time of Heresie. By Richard Bristow D.D. 16mo Antw. 1574. This work, generally entitled Dr. Bristow's Motives, was reprinted Antw. 1599, 8vo; translated into Latin by Dr. Worthington 1608, 4to. The "particular Declaration," mentioned *infra,* and Butler's Memoirs of the Catholics, give extracts from Bristow and from Sanders de V. M. E. " Whereby it is manifest they do miserably forget themselves, who feare not excommunications of Pius quintus of holy mcmorv, in whome Christ himselfe to have spoken and excommunicated ns in St. Paul, they might consider by the miracles that Christ by him as by St. Paul did worke." — Bristowe, in his Sixth Motive, fol. 31. Oliver Carter, a Fellow of Christ's College in Manchester, " writt a book in answer to Bristowe's Motives." — Hollingworth's History of Manchester.

A treatise of Schism showing that all Catholics ought to abstain from Heretical Conventicles. By Gregory Martin. Duaci 1578.

" Authoris porro ea mens est, eoque refert omnia, partim ut Regiae Majestati subjectos a parendi studio avocet, eosque tumultuosos ct seditiosos efficiat, partim ut ipsa Reginu tollatur c vita. " Bridgewater's Concert, p. 129. See in reply Lingard's History, vol. vi. p. 693, and Tierney's Dodd, vol. iv. Append. p. ccii. The Declaration of the Fathers of the Council of Trent concerning the Going unto Churches at such time as Hereticall Service is said, or Heresy preached. Edited, with a Preface, by Eupator the Rev. Joseph Mendham. 12mo Lond. 1850.

A Checke or Reproofe of M. Howlet's (Rob. Parsons') untimely Skreeching in her Majesty's Eares; with an Answeare to the Reasons alleaged in a Discourse thereunto annexed, why Catholikes refuse to go to church; wherein (amongst other things) the Papists traiterous and treacherous doctrine and demeanour towards our Soveraigne is some what at large upon occasion unfolded, their develish pretended conscience also examined, 4to Lond. 1581.

See The British Librarian, col. 1045.

A Declaration of the true Causes of the great troubles presupposed to be intended against the Realme of Englaude, &c. By Robert Parsons, 1581, 1592.

One of the rarest and most interesting volumes relating to English history ever published. It was looked upon to be so dangerous a piece as to receive an answer from Bacon, under the title, Certain Observations upon a libel printed this present year, 1592.

" From Persons we may prove the necessity of the penal laws enacted under Elizabeth against a priesthood which had then openly made a league with persecution, with treason and with massacre." Southey's Vindicise.

The Execution of Justice in England for maintenaunce of publique and Christian Peace against ccrteine Stirrers of Sedition and Adherents to the Traitours and Enemies of the Realme without any persecution of them for Questions of Religion, as is falsely reported and published by the Fautors and Fosterers of their Treasons &c. By William Cecil, Lord Rtirgleigh. 1581.

In the second volume of the Harleian Miscellany; Somers' Tracts, vol. i. p. 192; Gibson's Preservative, vol. xvii.; Stowe's Annals; and in a Collection of several Treatises concerning the reasons and occasions of the Penal Laws: i. The Execution, &c.; ii. Important Considerations, *ut infra;* iii. The Jesuits' Reasons, &c., *tit supra,* p. viii. Printed 1677, 1687,1688. " This is a defence of the penal laws against Catholics, instituted in the reign of Queen Elizabeth. These were chiefly occasioned by the violence of those Papists who acknowledged the bull of Pius V. excommunicating Queen Elizabeth, and absolving her subjects from their allegiance. In January 1581-2 a severe statute was passed, declaring those guilty of high treason who should dissuade English subjects from their allegiance, and from the established religion, or who should reconcile them to the church of Rome: and the same penalty of high treason was denounced against those who should be so dissuaded or reconciled. It is probable that this pamphlet, which has the air of being written by the royal command, was intended as a commentary on so severe an act.

Great, and natural, and laudable anxiety is shown in this curious treatise, to draw a distinction between the executions made in Queen Mary's time, on account of religion alone, and those examples which Elizabeth had made amongst the Catholics, not on account of their abstract religious tenets, but because they had warped with them political doctrines inconsistent with the safety of the state. Elizabeth was anxious to escape the reproach of persecution, and to show that in those priests who, acting on the bull of Pius V., endeavoured to excite her subjects against her, she punished, not the Catholie, but the traitor." Somers' Tracts, vol. i.

" For the complete vindication of this much injured princess (Q. Eliz.) from the main if not precisely every particular of her alleged offences, especially her conduct in respect of severity towards her papal subjects, it would be abundantly sufficient to refer any impartial reader to Lord Burleigh's Execution of Justice; to the generally received history of Europe at the time, particularly to the Life and Letters of Pius V.; and for a modern historian, to Sharon Turner, who by travelling even out of the country to the real sources of what was transacting in it, has produced a more rational and just account of the reign of Elizabeth than ever appeared before in our language. I refer with much satisfaction to the elaborate biography of her most eminent minister, Lord Burghley, by Dr. Nares." Mendham.

Rationes decern oblati Certaminis redditte Acndemicis Anglise. Ab Kdnmndo Oampiano Soc. Jesu. 1581. Claramontanse 1583. Rochelle 1585. Herbipol. 1589. Rorschachii 1606. Cadomi 1616. Colonise Agripinae 1625. Antverp. 1631. Translated into English 1671.

Campian's Rationes. or Reasons for embracing the Faith of Rome, addressed to the Universities of Oxford and Cambridge, occasioned numerous replies and rejoinders from Whitaker, Charke, Lawrence Humphrey, and from John Dorey or Duraeus, also a member of the Society of Jesus, and Parsons. The reply provoked from Whitaker, 1581, was translated by Richard Stoke under the title of "Answer to the Ten Reasons of E. C. Jesuite, in confidence whereof he offered disputation to the Ministers of the Church of England in the controversy of Faith," 4to Lond. 1706. (See Baines's Lancashire.) It was also translated under the title of " A seasonable Preservative against Popish Delusions. Or, an Answer," &c. To which is prefixed an Account as well of the Jesuit, as the Professor, together with some Remarks (subjoin'd to the Ten Reasons) upon a late boasted Performance, entitled, The Conversion and Reformation of the Church of England compar'd, &c. By Thomas Dawson, D.D. 8vo Lond. 1732. In his animadversions on the Preface, or the Letter sent by Campian to the two Universities, " The honour of our Schools and the angel of our Church, learned Whitaker, than whom our age saw nothing more memorable" Bishop Hall exclaims, " But who are you and what's the religion you profess, that you take upon you to upbraid us with cruelty? Hear me, dear Campian, and deny it, if you can, There have been more of *us* destroy'd at one sentence, in one day, and at one fiery stake, by your Party than all that you can reckon up together amongst yourselves that suffer'd at different times, and by different punishments, for the Popish Cause, all this happy reign of Queen Elizabeth." Dorey's " Confntationes " Paris 1582.

Ingolst. 1585 are inserted with a Rejoinder, in Whitnkeri Opp. fol. Genevse, 1610.

Concertatio Ecclesiae Catholicae in Anglia adversus Calvinopapistas et Puritanos sub Elizabetba Regina quorundam hominum doctrina et sanctitate illustrium renovatu et recognita. Quse nunc de novo centum et eo amplius Martyrum, sexcentorumque insignium virorum rebus gestis variisque certaminibus, lapsorum Palinodiis, novis persecutorum edictis, ac doctissimis Catholicorum de Anglicano seu muliebri Pontificatu, ac Romani Pontificis in Principcs Christianos auctoritate; disputationibus et defensionibus aucta, &c. A Joanne Aquapontano (John Bridgewater.) Aug. Trev. 1594. First edition 1583, second 1588, third 1594.

The first part contains, Duas Epistolas Edmundi Campiani the original, in English, of that addressed to Everard Mercurian, will he found in Fuller's Church History, and that of the Letter to the Lords of the Council in Strype's Annals, vol. iii. p. vi. eiusdemque Rationes decem &c. una cum Epistola alterius docti viri, in qua explicantur crudelissimse leges Calvinistarum in Catholicos edite. De Persecutione Anglicana Epistola Paris 1582, Roma; 1582, 8vo, which has been ascribed to Parsons. An English translation was printed at Douay 1582, 16mo. The second part, Martyria aliorum Catholicorum, consisting principally of extracts from the seventh book of Sanders de Visibili Monarchia, and the third book of the same author's De Origine ac Progressu Schismatis Anglicani, lib. iii. etc. Col. Agrip. 1585, Rom. 1586, Ingolst. 1588, Col. Agrip. 1590, 1610, 1628. The latter of these is the work in which were first published the "calumnies" relative to the birth and parentage of Queen Anne Boleyn. Campian's Narratio Divorcii Henrici VIII. ab uxore Catharina, published in his Opuscula, Ingolst. 1602, Mediol. 1625, Antwerp 1631, is inserted at the end of Harpsfield's Hist. Eccl. Angl. "A Diary kept by the Rev. Mr. Rishton, a prisoner in the Tower, in which he gives a description of the various modes of torture in-

flicted on the Catholic prisoners from 1580 to 1585, was first published in Latin at the end of Sanderus de Schismate." Butler's Nook of the R. C. Church. Lingard supplies some extracts from it in the Appendix. In the last edition, 1628, Rishton, or Rushton, added a third part and a fourth by way of Appendix, together with "Summarium de Morte Mariae Stuarfee." It has been translated under the title of "The Rise and Progress of the English Reformation," &c, Dublin, 1827, 8vo. At the end of the first volume of Burnet's History of the Reformation is an Appendix concerning some of the Errors and Falshoods in Sanders' Book of the English Schism. To Dr. Cowell is generally attributed Anti-Sanderus, duos continens Dialogos, in quibus varise N. S. aliorumque Romanensium Calumnies in haec Anglorum ab Excuso Pontifice Tempora confictae refelluntur, Cantab. 1593, 4to. A Life of Sanders will be found in Wood's Ath. Oxon. — To return to the Concertatio. The second part contains also " Certamina quatuor nobilium Puerorum, Thomae, Roberti, Ricardi ac Joannis Worthingtoniorum Item Georgii Hather salli nobilis, Gulielmi Crunielhulmii, Humfredi Maxfeldii laicorum, Thomse Worthingtonii et Thomse Browni Sacerdotnm." This narra-tivc gives considerable information relative to the Romanists in Lancashire. Cf. Hollingworth's Chronicle, p. 94. "Certamen Dominse Alanse, vidute fratris Illustrissimi Cardinalis Gulielmi Alani." " Palinodia Antonii Tyrelli." There is an English original of his Recantation, 1588. — The third part, " Apologia Martyrum, qua ipsorum innocentia variis rationibus demonstratur; eosque solius religionis Catholicte causa, quam susceperant propagandam et propugnandam, crudelissime enecatos fuisse." " Literae et Confessio Publica Joannis

Nicolai," etc. See Lingard's History, vol. vi. p. 343

" Apologia doctissimi viri D. Gul. Alani pro sacerdotibus societatis Jesu, cum duobus Edictis Elizabethse Reginse Anglite." Printed

Aug. Trev. 1583. Additur eiusdem

"piissinia Admonitio et

Consolatio vere Christiana ad afflictos Catholicos Anglise." Ibid. 1583. The original of the former was " Apologie, and true declaration, of the institution and endeavours, of the two English Colleges;" the one in Rome, the other now resident in Rhemes, &c. Printed at Mounts in Henault 1581, against "certaine sinistre Informations given up against the same." With the latter compare Saunders's Address to the Irish Nobility in Ellis's Second Series of Letters, vol. iii. p. 92. " Ad Persecutores Anglos pro Catholicis domi forisque persecutionem sufferentibus contra falsum, seditiosum et contumeliosum Libellum, inscriptum, Justitia Britannica *ut supra* Responsio." Ingolst. 1584, 8vo. This is Cardinal Allen's work translated, " A true and modest Defence of the English Catholicks that suffered for their faith at home and abroad, against a Libel entituled " The Execution of Justice in England." Or, Justitia Britannica; per quam liquet perspicue aliquot in Anglia perditos ciues, propter turpes proditiones, morte mulctatos esse; propter Religionem vero aut ceremonias Romanas neminem, 1584. Annexed to this celebrated volume is " De summa eorum dementia, qui habendis qurestionibus prtefuerant contra proditores quosdam, deque tormentis qute in eosdem ob Proditionem, non ob Religionem, exprompta sunt." An account of it will be found in Lingard, Append. Note 0, and in Strvpe's Annals, vol. iii., Append, p. 121. "Statutum Calvinianum in Catholicos Anglos," 1585. " Brevis descriptio reram a Cathol. Angl. gestarum." " Nomina eorum qui doctissimis in lucem editis Libris (idem et vitam Catholicam contra htereticos Anglos propugnarunt sub Elizabetha," viz. , Gul. Alanus, N. Sanderus, T. Hardingus, T. Stapletonus, T. Heskinus, T. Dornierus i. q. Dorman, R. Pointz, Jo. Marschallus, A. Langdal, H. Joliffus,

H

Jo. Rastellus, A. Copus, Jo. Yongus i. e. Harpsfeldius, R. Bristous, Greg. Martinus, G. Reinoldus, E. Campianus, R. Personius, R. Hop kineus, L. Vauxaeus. " Index Personarum quae propter fidem Catholicam passae sunt aliquando in Anglia vinculo, bonorum direptionem, exilium aut mortem sub Eliz. Regina." Foeminae quae in Anglia passse sunt pro fide Catbolica mortem etc. Cf. Lingard, cb. v. p. 344.

A briefe Historie of the Martyrdom of 12 reuerend Priests, executed within these twelve Monthes for Confession and Defence of Catholike Faith, but under false Pretence of Treason, a Note of sundrie Things that befel them in their Life and Imprisonment, and a Preface declaring their Innocence. Printed An. 1582, 8vo.

Cf. Apologia Martyrum in the Concertatio.

A particular Declaration or Testimony of the undutifull and traiterous affection borne against her Maiestic, by Edmund Campian, Jesuite, and other condemned Priestes, witnessed by their own confessions; in reproofe of those slanderous bookes and libels delivered out to the contrary by such as are maliciously affected towards her Maiestic and the State. Imprinted at London by Christopher Barker, An. Dom. 1582, 4to.

" Of so much importance and at the same time rarity (never having to my knowledge been reprinted) as to justify a particular and extensive reference," &c. See Mendham's Notes to Watson, *ut infra*, p. 76.

There is a copy in the British Museum. See Butler's Historical Memoirs of the English Catholics, in which will be found copious extracts from this important document.

Declaration of the favourable dealing of her Majesty's Commissioners appointed for the examination of certaine Traitours (Campian and others) and of tortures unjustly reported to be done upon them for matters of religion. By Lord Burghley, 1.583.

Inserted in Holingshed's Chronicle, p. 1357. Reprinted in Somers' Tracts, vol. i.

A Discovery of John Nichols, misrepresented a Jesuit; with a full Answer to his Recantation. By Robert Parsons, 8vo.

His recantation is in Bridgewater's Concertatio.

A true and plain declaration of the horrible treasons practised by William Parry the traitor against the Queenes Maiestie. The maner of his arraignment, conviction and execution, together with the copies of sundry letters of his and others, tending to divers purposes, for the proofes of Lis Treasons. Also an addition not impertinent thereunto, containing a short collection of his birth, education and course of life. Moreover, a few observations gathered of his owne wordes and writings, for the farther manifestation of his most disloyal, devilish and desperate purposes. 4to Lond. 1584.

Sec Hargrave's State Trials, vol. i. Foulis's Popish Treasons, B. vii. c. 4. The Art of Assassinating Kings, taught Lewis XIV. and James II. by the Jesuites. Wherein is discovered, the secret of the last conspiracy, form'd at Versailles in Sep. 1695, against the life of William III. king of Great Britain. And discover'd at White-Hall, Feb. 1695-6 Done out of the French. London 1691.

A Watchwoord to England to beware of Traitours and Tretcherous Practises, which have beene the ouerthrowe of many famous Kingdomes and Common Weales. Including the Myraculous preservation of Lady Elizabeth, now our most dread and gratious Queene, from extreme ealamitie and daunger of life, in the time of Q. Marie, her sister. Written by a faithfull affected Friend to his Country, who desireth God long to blesse it from Traytours and their secret Conspiracyes. Anthony Munday. 4to Lond. 1584.

A discouerie of the Treasons practised and attempted against the Queene's Maiestie and the Realme, by Francis Throckmorton, who was, for the same arraigned and condemned in Guyld Hall, in the citie of London, the 21 day of May last past. 4to Lond. 1584.

A Declaration of the Causes mooving the Queene of Englande to give aide to the defence of the people afflicted and oppressed in the Low Countries. Imprinted by Christopher Barker, 1585.

In the first volume of Somers' Tracts.

This Declaration was answered by Stapleton under the title of Apologia pro Rege Catholico Philippo II. Not in his works. Constantiae, 1592.

The True Difference betweene Christian Subjection and Unchristian Rebellion. Wherein the Princes lawfull power to commaund for trueth and indeprivable right to beare the sword are defended against the Popes censures and the Jesuits sopbismes, uttered in their Apologie and Defence of English Catholikes, against a Libel intituled, The Execution of Justice. With a demonstration that the thinges reformed in the Church of England by the Lawes of this Realme arc truely Catholike, notwithstanding the vaine shew made to the contrary in their Hhemish Testament. By T1ki. Kilson, Bp. of Winchester. Ito Oxford 1585.

In the third Part, pp. 313-545, this most accomplished scholar replies to Cardinal Allen's books here referred to. . In his booke on Purgatory, Antwerp 1565, Allen inculcates the belief in the Pope's supremacy, which subsequently he maintained so strenuously. It was probably on this account that Fitzherbert called this book an answer to Jewel. See Allen's Defence of Stanley, p. lxxii.

Epistola de Daventrise Redditione, 1586-7. Cracovite 1588. Reprinted under the title of Cardinal Allen's Defence of Sir William Stanley's Surrender of Deventer. Edited, with an Historical Introduction, by Thomas Heywood, Esq.. F.S.A., for the Chetham Society, Manchester, 1851.

A briefe Discoverie of Dr. Allen's Seditious Drifts contriued in a Pamplet written by him cone, the yeelding up of the Towne of Dcucnter, in Oueroissel, vnto the King of Spain by Sir Wm. Stanley. 4to Lond. 1588.

Cf. Important Considerations, *ut infra*.

Crudelitatis Calviniante exempla duo recentissima ex Anglia, quorum primum continet barbarum Edictum contra Catholicos, alteram exhibet indigniss. mortem illustr. viri Comitis Northumbria? occisi mense Julio hujus anni. Anno 1585.

A contemporary account of the death of the Earl of Northumberland. It was given out that the Earl had committed suicide, but the author of the above volume endeavours to prove that he was murdered, at which conclusion Dr. Lingard also arrived. See A True and Summarie Reporte of the Declaration of some Parte of the Earle of N's Treason, 8vo 1585.

A Dutiful Invective against the moste haynous Treasons of Ballard and Babington, with other their adherents, latclie executed. Together with the horrible attempts and Actions of the Queen of Scottes; and the sentence pronounced against her at Fodderingay. Newlie compiled and set foorth, in English verse, for a New-Ycares gifte to nll loyall English subjects. By William Kemp. 4to Lond. 1587.

The Censure of a loyal subject upon certaine noted speeches and behauiour of those 14 notable Traitors, (Ballard, Babington, &c.) at the place of their execution, (Lincoln's Inn Fields,) the xi. (20) and 12 (21) of September last past; etc. 4to Lond. 1587.

A Defence of the honorable sentence and execution of the Queenc of Scots: exempled with analogies and diuerse presidents of Emperors, Kings and Popes: with the opinions of learned men in the point and diuerse reasons gathered foorth out of both Lawcs Ciuil and Canon, &c. By Maurice Kyffin. 1587.

The Holy Bull and Crusado of Rome, first published by Pope Gregory XIII., and afterwards by Pope Sixtus V., for all those who desire full pardon and indulgence of their sinnes; with Declaration found in the Armada of Spain. 1588.

Admonition to the Nobility and People of England and Ireland, concerning the present warres made for the execution of his holines sentence, by the highe and mightic kinge Catholike of Spaine. By the Cardinal of England. Antvcrpise 1588.

Reprinted with a Preface by Eupator the Rev. Joseph Mendham, 12mo Lond. 1842.

The first part of this tract was intitled, A Declaration of the Sentence of Sixtus V. See Strype's Annals, vol. iii. bk. ii. ch. 18; Dodd, by Tierney, vol. iii. App. p. xliv.; and Lingard's History. The history of this work is given in Placcii Theatr. Anonvmor. f. 523, and in Schelhornii Amoenitat. T. ii. p. 385. There can be but one opinion on this precious document; and it is well expressed by one of the most candid writers that ever honoured the church of Rome, Tierney, (Dodd, vol. iii. pp. 28,29.) See also Watson's Important Considerations for a comprehensive analysis of the book; Mendham's ed. p. 57 et seq.; and for a systematic digest, see Lingard, vol. viii. p. 446, note 2.

The Hunting of Antichrist. With a caueat to the contentious. By Leonard Wright.

Of Seditious Schismatikes sprung up in our time, &c. 4to Lond. 1589.

Elizabethan Anglise Reginse Haeresim Calvinianam Propugnantis, saevissimum in catholicos sui Regni edictum, quod in alios quoq. Reipub. Christiante Principes contumelias continet indignissimas: Promulgatum Londini 29. Nouemb. 1591. Cum Responsione ad singula capita: qua non tantum sreuitia, et impietas tarn iniqui cdicti, sed mendacia quoque, et fraudes ac impostime deteguntur, et confutantur. Per D. Andream Philopatrum presbyterum ac Theologum Romanum, ex Anglis olim oriundum. Robert Parsons. Augustte 1592.

" There was much to reprehend in the scurrilous language of this instrument; and several passages in it appear to call for an answer from the leaders of the Spanish party among the exiles. Two were soon published: one by Persons under the title of Responsio ad edictum, for an accurate account of which I shall refer the reader to Mr. Butler's Memoirs, vol. iii. p. 236; and another by F. Creswell, intituled Exemplar literarum missarum e Germania ad D. Gulielmum Cecilium, consiliarium regium. Impressum Anno Domini Mdxcij."

" It is difficult to speak of these tracts with the severity which they deserve. They might please the king of Spain, and might uphold his hope of effecting the conquest of England; but they were calculated to irritate Elizabeth, to throw suspicion on the loyalty of the Catholics, and to increase the pressure of persecution. The real motive of the authors may perhaps be discovered from the conclusion of each tract. They seem to have believed that the queen wa3 alarmed, and they hoped, by adding to that alarm, to extort her assent to the following proposals: that she should make peace with Philip, should tolerate the exercise of the Catholic worship, and should allow all men, without distinction of religion, to partake of the favours and protection of government. See Responsio, p. 247; Exemplar literarum p. 170; Lingard's History, vol. vi. pp. 712, 713.

Theatrum Crudelitatum Htereticorum nostri temporis per Verstegan. Antv. 1592, 1604; Gall. 1607, 4to.

See Dodd, vol. ii. p. 428. Watt ascribes this work to Hadrian Hubert.

A Defence of the Catholick Cause: containing a Treatise of sundry Untruths and Slanders, publish'd by the Hereticks, in infamous libels as well against all English Catholicks in general, as against some in particular, &c. , by T. F. with an Apology in defence of his Innocence in a feign'd Conspiracy against her Majesty's Person, &c. By Thomas Fitzherbcrt. 1598, 1602, 8vo. See Dodd, vol. ii. p. 413.

A Watch-word to all Religious and True-hearted Englishmen, by Francis Hastings. 8vo Lond. 1598.

The Temperate Wardword against the Seditious Watchword of Sir Francis Hastings, in Behalf of the Popish Cause, by N. D. i.e. Robert Parsons the Jesuit. 1598, 4to.

The Warn word to Sir F. Hastings' Wasteword. By N. D.; 4to 1599, 1602. (The First Encounter about Blessinges and Cursinges brought in by change of Catbolike Religion in England. Cap. vi.)

An Apologie or Defence of the Watch-word against the Ward-word, publ. by an English-Spaniard, lurking under the title of N. D., deuided into eight Resistances, by Sir Francis Hastings. 4to Lond. 1600.

The Wormwood of Sir Francis Hastings' Watchword, by Robert Parsons. 8vo 1602.

A New Challenge made to N. 1). wherein O. E. offcrcth to justify that popish religion is not catholike or apostolike; secondly that it is compounded of divers novelties and heresies; thirdly that the church of Rome is not the true church of Christ Jesus. Lastly that such as have died in the popes quarrels were rather false traitors, then Christian martyrs. By Matthew SutclifTe. 4to Lond. 1600.

A Challenge concerning the Romish Church, her doctrine and practices, against Parsons, Garnet, and Blackwel. By Matthew Sutcliffe. 4to Lond. 1602.

Watson (William) Important Considerations, or a Vindication of Queen Elizabeth from the charge of Unjust Severity towards her Roman Catholic Subjects, by Roman Catholics themselves: being Important Considerations in the name of certain Secular Priests, printed in 1601. Edited, with a Preface and Notes, by the Rev. Joseph Mendham, M.A. 12mo Lond. 1831.

The Treasons here confest will be found, as stated by the Secular Priests, in Blackerby's Historical Account of Making the Penal Laws, &c. Lond. 1689.'

Decachordon of Ten Quodliberticall Questions concerning Religion and State; wherein the Author solves a hundred cross interrogatory doubts about the general contentions betwixt the Seminary Priests and the Jesuits. By William Watson. 4lo 1G02.

These two works are noticed by Mendham in his Literary Policy of the Church of Rome, p. 355.

Brief Historical Account of the Behaviour of the Jesuites &c. for the first twenty-five years of Queen Elizabeth's Reign. With an Epistle of W. Watson, a Secular Priest, shewing how they were thought of by the other Romanists of that time.

' This discourse was composed by a priest of the Church of Rome, with the consent and in the name of many more, and was then a preface to a treatise, &c. (Important Considerations, ut supra.) The Epistle is the same as that in the same treatise." In Gibson's Preservative, fol. vol. iii. p. xvii. 8vo. " For further decisive, and it should appear, sincere acknowledgments of clemency by Romanists themselves, I refer to certificates by twenty-one individuals in 1584, (Gibson, ibid.), and of thirty-two more in 1585, (Stow's Chron. p. 710); the Protestation of thirteen Secular Priests in 1602, (given at length in Dodd's History, vol. ii. pp. 2.02-3, and Butler's Historical Memoirs, vol. i. p. 261); the relation of the faction at Wisbich, (Gibson, ibid.); and the admissions of Warmingham, Barclay, Widdrington, and Peter Walsh, with others adduced in the Brief Historical account of the Jesuits," ibid, at the end. Mendham's Notes as above. To her (Elizabeth's) eternal honour she ordered seventy popish priests, either under sentence of death or awaiting it, to be released from prison, the rack and the scaffold. (Camden's Annals; Mackintosh's Hist. of England, vol. iii. p. 287; Gibson, as above, p. 22.) It was in 1580 the Jesuits first came into England, and therefore they had no right to complain of penal inflictions, since the Act against Papal Bulls was adopted in 1572. They voluntarily incurred the evil they braved and suffered from; and it was the peculiar character of these laws that they were defensive, not attacking measures. See Mackintosh, ibid. p. 161, and Sharon Turner's History of Edw. VI., Mary and Elizabeth, Book ii. ch. 32.

The following works, containing reflections on the preceding reign, were published after James's accession and at a subsequent period.

The Catholikes Supplication unto the King's Majesty; for Toleration of Catholike Religion in England: with short Notes or Animadversions in the margine. Whereunto is annexed Parallel-wise, a Supplicatorie Counterpoyse of the Protestants, unto the same most excellent Majesty. Together with the reasons of both sides, for and against toleration of diuers religions. By Gabriel Powell, pp. 39, 4to Lond. 1603.

The " Counterpoyse" is nothing more than a parody of the Supplicacation. See

Tierney's Dodd, vol. iv. Appendix p. lxxiv.

In 1604 there was also published by Gabriel Powell, A Consideration of the Papists Reasons of State and Religion, for toleration of Poperie in England, intimated in their Supplication, &c. 4to Oxford, 1604.

An exact Discoverie of Romish Doctrine in the case of Conspiracie and Rebellion, by pregnant observations: collected (not without direction from our Superiours) out of the expresse dogmaticall principles of Popish Priests and Doctors, pp. 54, 4to Lond. 1605.

The principal authors of this rebellious doctrine are here enumerated, viz. Tollet, Bellarmine, Allen, Molina, Gregorie of Valentia, Stapleton, DomiDicus Banncs. " We have also allenged The Resolution of the Jesuites Colledge of the Universitie of Salamancha in Spaine, anno 1602, as likewise Creswels Philopater, printed at Rome, Licentia Superiorum, signifying the Jesuites. What shall I neede to mention Reynolds (in his Rosseus) a Doctor of Divinity, and chiefest man in the English Seminarie at Rhemes? Father Parsons (in his Dolman) a principal Rector of the Seminarie at Rome?" There were seminaries also at Valladolid, Saville, St. Omer's and Douay.

Those who desire information respecting the contest between the Seculars and the Jesuits in these Seminaries will find their curiosity amply fed in Dodd's " History of the English College at Doway from its first Foundation in 1568 to the present year, 1713;" and "The Secret Policy of the English Society of Jesus, discover'd in a series of Attempts ngainst the Clergy, &c. &c. 1715." Cardinal Alan, or Allen, the founder of this College and of others, especially the Roman College, is eulogized in the following terms in the Preface to the Golathseus, sive de Moribus Liber Italicus, of Joannes Casa (the Italian Chesterfield), Romse, 1595: "Cardinalis Alanus (Deus bone, qualis et quantus vir) familiaribus multam stepe prudentis disputationis materiem subjecit; fecitque dubitando disceptandoque, ut et aula ejus videretur schola, et mensa cathedra pietatis et prudentise. "

We have now arrived at the year of the Gunpowder Plot, and it will not perhaps be impertinent to our subject to introduce an anecdote locally connected with Manchester, and politically with the causes of one of the most remarkable occurrences in English history. It appears that at the assizes at Manchester, in the summer of 1604, several Jesuits or seminary priests were tried, condemned and executed, under the statute 27th Elizabeth, for high treason for remaining within the realm after the time prescribed by the royal proclamation. Mr. Pound, an aged Roman Catholic gentleman residing in Lancashire, who had been imprisoned in Queen Elizabeth's time on account of his religion, presented a petition to the King complaining generally of the persecution of the Roman Catholics, and in particular of the rigorous proceedings and alarming doctrines of the Judges at Manchester. He was prosecuted by the Attorney-General in the Star Chamber for a contempt, and no pains were spared to render this judicial proceeding against an inoffensive old man as imposing as possible. Sir Edward Coke inveighed violently against the doctrines and practices of the Romanists; the Lords of the Council and Judges followed in the same strain; and in the end Mr. Pound was sentenced by the Court to be imprisoned in the Fleet during the King's pleasure; to stand in the pillory both at Lancaster and Westminster; and to pay a fine of one thousand pounds. Many members of the Court proposed to add to this severe sentence that the old man should be nailed to the pillory and have both his ears cut off. This barbarous proposition was negatived by one or two voices only. (Rushton Papers, MSS.

l of Sir Thomas Tresham, discovered at Rushton, in Northamptonshire, qnoted hy Jardine; see Winwood's Memorials, vol. ii. p. 36, where this sentence is somewhat differently stated.)

An Answere to the Fifth Part of Reportes lately set forth by Sir Edward Cooke, Knight, the Kinges Attorney generall. Concerning the ancient and modeme Municipall lawes of England, which do apperteyne to Spirituall Power and Jurisdiction, etc. By a Catholike Deuyne Robert Parsons. 4to 1606. See chap. xv.

An Epistle of Comfort to the Reverend Priestes, and to the Honorable, Worshipful and other of the Laye sort restrayned in Durance for the Catholicke Fayth. 16mo Paris 1605.

This work is presumed to be by the Martyr Southwell, and the same as that assigned to him by Dodd by the title of a Consolation for Catholics imprisoned on account of Religion. See Turnbull's edition of Southwell's Poems, Memoir, p. xxxv. *Notet and Querie,* second series, vol. iii. pp. 376, 475.

Brereley (John) Priest. James Anderton, of Lostock in Lancashire. The Protestants Apologie for the Roman Church. Divided into three several Tractes. The first concerneth the antiquity and continuance of the Roman Church and Religion, ever since the Apostles times. The second l. that the Protestants Religion was not so much as in being, at or before Luther's first appearing. 2. That the Marks of the true Church are appertcyning to the Roman, and wholly wanting to the several Churches, begun by Luther and Calvin. The third that Catholics are no less loyall and dutifull to their Soueraigue than Protestants. All which is undertaken and proved by testimonies of the learned Protestants themselves. With a conclusion to the Reuerend Judges, and other the grave and learned Sages of the law. 4to 1608.

The first edition 1604; the second 1608; the third 1615. Translated into Latin by Rayner. 4to Paris 1615. The Preface is an examination of the chargeable demeanour of the Protestants towards their Soueraignes. " There was a Printing-house suppress about three years since (1621) in Lancashire, where all Brerely his workes, with many other popish pamphlets, were printed." The Foot out of the Snare, by John Gee, 4to Lond. 1624, p. 97. Reprinted in Sir Walter Scott's edition of the Somers Tracts, vol. iii. p. 4!).

An Apologie for the Oath of Allegiance. Against the Two Breves of Pope Paulus Quintus, and the late Letter of Cardinall Bellarmine to G. Blackwell the Arch-priest. Premonition to all Most Mightie Monarches, Kings, Free Princes and States of Christendome. King James's Works, fol. Lond. 1616. In page 250 of the former and page 336 of the latter, James sacrifices to the Manes of his late Predecessor (to the propriety of these words Parsons objects in his Replie to Barlow, pp. 166-68, which, however, are defended by the latter in his Answer, *ut infra*, p. 70, *el teqq.*) by declaring his conviction that " the punishment of the Papists was ever extorted out of her hands against her will by their own misbehaviour," &c. Cf. Nowell's Confutation of Dorman, p. 258, 4to Lond. 1567. It is a curious circumstance that an answer to Sir Henry Saville's translation of King James's Apology for the Oath of Allegiance, which was made by command of the Conclave by Francisco Suarez, and entitled Defensio Fidei Catholics, was interlined by the Inquisition at Rome with the doctrine of deposing and killing Princes; though detested by the writer of the Answer. See Dr. King's Letter to Walton, prefixed to Hooker's Ecclesiastical Polity. An imperfect list of the books published on occasion of the Apology will be found in the Appendix to Harris's Life of James I. See also Lowndes's British Librarian.

An Answer to a Catholike English-Man (so by himselfe entituled), who, without a name, passed his Censure upon the Apology, for the Oath of Allegiance; which Censure is heere examined and refuted. By the Bishop of Lincoln (Willam Barlow), 4to Lond. 1609. See pp. 64-102. 'But to conclude this complaint of Queene Elizabeth's crueltie, an Italian, no Protestant shall speake; (Bizar. Histor. Genuens, p. 568.)

" So great and so apparent was the moderation of her minde, and her inbred elemencie, that (not vndeseruedly) it may bo said of her, which the ancient Histories haue left to posteritic of Alexander Seuerus, borne of his Mother Mammrea, nempe" antematon, hoc est, Citra Snngvinem; namely, that she hath gouerncd her Kingdome without bloodshed, cum svapte natvra semper a csedibus et crvdelitate abhorreat; for even her natvre doth abhorre the thovght of slavghter or ervcltie: and so he goeth on in a large discourse; in this her praise; and when he wrote thus, she had reigued twenty yeeres." p. 92.

A Discussion of the Answere of M. William Barlow D. of Divinity to the Booke intituled The Judgment of a Catholike Englishman living in banishment for his Religion &c. Concerning the Apology of the new Oath of Allegiance. Written by the R. Father, F. Robert Persons of the Society of Jesus. Whereunto since the said Father's death, is annexed a Generall Preface, &c. Permissu Superiorum. 1612. "This excellent work, (The Judgment, &c.) equally distinguished by strength of argument and eloquence, is now extremely scarce." Butler, iii. 180.

The Second Part about the Breves of Paulus Quintus. Concerning M. Barlowe his exorbitant flattery in exaggerating Queene Elizabeth's vertues and sanctity, pp. 159-228. After the Pope forbade the people to swear allegiance to the King a long controversy began among the Romanists on the extent of the deposing power; but the result was that the foreign Pontiff was obeyed. Obedience to the temporal sovereign was decided to be inconsistent with religious duty. " Widdrington, a Benedictine Monk, published a masterpiece in defence of the Oath. The Jesuits to a man refused it. The generality of the Clergy were for it. The Pope is advised with. He puts forth several Bulls to prohibit it; but they were neglected by many, in the same manner as those had lately been which absolved the English from their allegiance to Queen Elizabeth If the Jesuits could find a means to evade the Bull, which absolved all subjects from their obedience to Queen Elizabeth, under penalty of excommunication; why could not such as took the Oath of Allegiance make use of the same pretence, to excuse themselves from submitting to those Bulls, which forbid the Oath of Allegiance? " Dodd's Secret Policy of the English Society of Jesus. Lond. 1715, p. 195. Cf. The Difference between the Church and Court of Rome considered in some Reflections on a Dialogue entitled, A Conference between two Protestants and a Papist. 4to Lond. 1674. — Pseudo-Martyr; shewing that Roman Catholics in this kingdom may and ought to take the Oath of Allegiance. By John Donne, D. D. 4to Lond. 1610. — A Pattern of Christian Loyalty: whereby any prudent man may clearly perceive in what manner the new oath of allegiance, and every clause thereof, may in a true and catholikc sense, without danger of perjurie, be taken by the ronian catholikes Collected out of authors who have handled the whole matter more largely. By William Howard, an English catholike, 4to Lond. 1634 — Butler's Historical Memoirs, vol. iii. ch. 48.

The Jesuits Downefall, threatened against them by the Secular Priests for their wicked lives, accursed manners, hereticall doctrine, and more than Machiavillian police. Together with the Life of Father Parsons an English Jesuite. By Thomas James. 4to Oxf. 1612. See Richard James's Iter Lancastrense. Edited, with Notes and an Introductory Memoir, by the Rev. Thomas Corser, M.A.

Antilogia adversus Apologiam Andres e Eudsemon-Joannis Jesuits e pro Henrico Garneto Jesuita Proditore. Qua mendacissimi Monachi adversus Ecclesiam et Remp. Anglicanam violate religionis et justitise nomine calumniss refutantur; et Jesuitarum, Garneti vero maxime, proditoria consilia et conjurationes exploratissima veritate referuntur. Authore Rob. Abboto. 4to Londini 1613. Vide cap. iv. An account of this rare work will be found in Jardine's Narrative of the Gunpowder Plot. Lond. 1857. The real name of the author of the several works published under the title of Eudaemon-Joannes was L'Heureux. He was a native of Candia and a Jesuit of high reputation for learning, who taught theology at the University of Padua, and was appointed by Pope Urban VIII. Rector of the Greek College at Rome. See the Act of Parliament 3

Jacobi cap. 4, 5, where we are told by the Parliament of the hellish conspiracies of the Jesuits and Seminary Priests. For a particular narrative of the horrid Powder Plot consult Williams's History of the Gunpowder Treason, Lond. 1678, and those authors out of which he collected it, in the last page of that tract. Cf. Townsend's Accusations of History against the Church of Rome. Lond. 1826.

A thankful remembrance of God's Mercy. In an Historicall Collection of the great and mercifull Deliverance of the Church and State of England, since the Gospel beganne here to flourish, from the beginning of Queen Elizabeth. By George Carleton. Lond. 1614, 1627, 1630. The historical part is chiefly extracted from Camden's Annals of Queen Elizabeth.

Cesar's Dialogue; or a Familiar Communication, containing the first Institution of a Subject in Allegiance to his Soueraigne. By E. N. 12mo Lond. 1601. Reprinted in 1615, and entitled, God and the King; or a Dialogue shewing that our Soveraign Lord King James being immediate under God within his Dominions, doth rightfully claim whatsoever is required by the Oath of Allegiance. 12mo Lond. 1615. Another edition, imprinted by his Majesty's special Priviledge and Command. 4to Lond. 1663. With the portrait of the Merry Monarch. Another edition, published in 1727, does not advocate the divine right of the Stuarts, but that of their successful adversaries, the Hanoverians. The first impression, in which there is a fine full length portrait of Queen Elizabeth, in regal costume, in a chair of state, surrounded by her Divine Charters in the shape of texts from the Old and New Testaments, is in the possession of the Rev. T. Corser, M.A. See *Notes and Queries,* second series, vol iv. p. 141.

An Answere to a Treatise written hy Dr. Carrier, by way of Letter to his Maiestie; wheren he layeth downe sondry politike considerations; by which he pretendeth himselfe was moued, and endeureth to moue others to be reconciled to the Church of Rome, and embrace that Religion, which he calleth Catholike. By George Hakewil, Doctour of Divinity, and Chapleine to the Prince his Highnesse. 4to Lond. 1616. See p. 104 *et seqq.*

The Image of Bothe Churches, Hierusalem and Babel, Unitie and Confusion, Obedience and Sedition, (being a treatise historically discussing whether Catholicks or Protestants are the better Subjects. By Father Matthew Patenson, or Patison. Tornay 1623. An account of this curious book is given in *Notes and Queries,* first series, vol. iii. p. 469. It was dedicated to Charles I. when Prince of Wales, by his physician.

Reflections upon the Oath of Supremacy and Allegiance. By a Catholic Gentleman, an obedient Son of the Church, and loyal Subject to his Majesty £John Sergeant 1661, 12mo. "He understands by the former oath, that prescribed by queen Elizabeth; by the latter the oath prescribed by James: he shows, with great clearness, that the oath of supremacy can not be conscientiously taken by the roman catholics, and that the oath of allegiance, though in other respects defensible, was substantially objectionable, from its declaring the deposing doctrine to be heretical." Butler's Historical Memoirs, vol. iii. p. 430.

Horae Subsecivae, or a treatise shewing the original, grounds, reasons and provocations, necessitating our sanguinary Laws against Papists, made in the days of queen Elizabeth. By William Denton. Lond. 1664. 4to.

Denton's Jus Csesaris et Ecclesise has been referred to, *supra* p. 6; for his other works, Jus Regiminis, etc. see Wood, ed. Bliss, vol. iv. p. 307, col. 863.

The Late Apology in behalf of the Papists re-printed and answered, in behalf of the Royalists. 4to Lond. 1667. See pp. 22-28.

The History of Romish Treasons and Usurpations: together with a particular Account of many gross Corruptions and Impostures in the Church of Rome, highly dishonourable and injurious to Christian Religion. To which is prefixt a large Preface to the Romanists Carefully collected out of a great number of their approved Authors, by Henry Foulis. Fol. Lond. 1671, 1078, 1081. (Lib. viii. chap. ii. A Vindication of Queen Elizabeth.)

Foxes and Firebrands: or a specimen of the Danger and Harmony of Popery and Separation. Wherein is proved from undeniable matter of fact and reason, that Separation from the Church of England is in the judgment of Papists, and by sad experience, found the most compendious way to introduce Popery, and to ruine the Protestant religion. By Robert Ware. 12mo Dubl. 1680; Lond. 1682, 1689. See pp. 13-47. Cf. The Discovery of the Jesuits' College at Clerkenwell, in March 1627-8: and a Letter found in their House, (as asserted) directed to the Father Rector at Bruxelles. Edited by John Gough Nichols, F.S.A. In the Camden Miscellany, vol. ii. 1852.

The Jesuits Memorial, for the intended Reformation of England, under their first Popish Prince. Published from the copy that was presented to the late King James II. With an Introduction, and some Animadversions by Edward Gee. Lond. 1690. The original title is as follows: A Memorial of the Reformation of England: containing certain Notes and Advertisements which seem might be proposed in the first Parliament and National Council of our Country after God, of his mercy, shall restore it to the Catholick Faith, for the better Establishment and Preservation of the said Religion. Gathered and set down by R.obert P.arsons, 1500. "A book which never saw the light till of late years; it had slept in Flanders from 1588, being first adapted (as tis supposed) for that Invasion." Dodd, The Secret Policy, &c., p. 128.

The English Spanish Pilgrime. Or a new Discoverie of Spanish Popery, and Iesuiticall Stratagems. With the estate of the English PeDtioners and Fugitives under the Kiifg of Spaines Dominions, and elsewhere at this present. Also laying open the new Order of the Iesuitrices and preaching Nunnes. Composed by James Wadsworth gentleman, newly converted into his true mothers bosom, the Church of England, with the motives why he left the Sea of Rome; a late Pentioner to his Maiesty of Spaine and nominated his Captaine in Flanders: sonne to Mr. James Wadsworth Bachelor of Divinity, sometime of Emanuell Colledge in the University of Cambridge, who was perverted in the yeere 1604, and late Tutor to Donia Maria Infanta of Spaine. Published by Authority. Printed at London by T. C. for Michael Sparke, dwelling at the blue Bible in Greene-Arbor, 1630. In small 4to, pp. 95. It has belonged to " Wh. Kennett." It is a very curious piece of biography, abounding with adventures and anecdotes of English refugees.

P. 69 is a notice of Sir William Stanley, who " cozened in his old age, turned Carthusian at Austend, and gave the Carthusians there his plate, and that little money which he had, where I have heard him often complaiue of the Jesuites, and say he was heartily sorry to find them such knaves, and that if his Majesty of great Britaine would grant him pardon, and leave to live the rest of his daies in Lancashire with beefe and bagge-pudding, hee should deeme himselfe one of the happiest in the world; but this could never bee obtained of his aforesaid Majesty hee having been so great and notorious a traytour."

This rare tract is in the possession of the Rev. James Raine jun. M.A., Secretary of the Surtees Society, by whom the above description was kindly communicated.

C %, 37. Good advice to the Church of England, Roman Catholick and Protestant Dissenter. In which it is endeavoured to be made appear that it is their duty, principle and interest to abolish the penal laws and tests. Beati Pacifici. By William Penn the Quaker. pp. 61, 4to Loud. 1687

See *Ath. Oxon.* vol. ii. col. 1054. (Edit Bliss, vol. iv. col. 650.) William Penn, born in 1644, died 1718. See also Biographia Britannica. The second part of this tract contains extracts from Divines of the Church of England in favour of toleration, as Sanderson, Taylor, Lloyd, Stillingfleet, Tillotson, Burnet, Sir Robert Poyntz, Charles I. Cf. Penn's Address to Protestants upon the present conjuncture, 1679, ad calc. " William Penn, a man of such virtue as to make his testimony weighty, even when borne to the sufferings of his party, publicly affirmed at the time in page 57 of this tract that since the restoration more than five thousand persons had died in bonds for matters of mere conscience to God."—Mackintosh's History of the Revolution, p. 160.

38. The great and popular objection against the repeal of the penal C1L. laws and test briefly stated and considered, and which may serve for answer to several late pamphlets upon that subject. By a Friend to Liberty for Liberties sake. William Penn. pp. 23, 4to Lond. 1688

See *Ath. Own.* vol. ii. col. 1054.

An Enquiry into the Reasons for abrogating the test imposed on C 3L all Members of Parliament, offered by Sa. Oxon.

pp. 8, 4to 1688

Without title-page. In the ninth volume of the Somers Tracts, p. 151, where it is ascribed to Bishop Burnet. See note to No. 20 *supra.*

" His Majesty commanded the stationers not to print any answer to Bishop Parker's book. This was very surprising from a Bishop of the Church of England, and the more so when it was found that he had treated the chief Divines of it with an insolence superior to any of its open enemies. Therefore, notwithstanding the King's commands, several sharp answers came out against it; but none made greater noise than that written by Dr. Burnet; out of which we may take notice of two or three passages. He unluckily turns these words in the titlepage, Written for the Author's own satisfaction, and now publish'd for the Benefit of all others whom it may concern. But says he the words are certainly wrong plac'd, for the truth of the matter is that it was written for the Author's own Benefit, and now publish'd for the Satisfaction of all others whom it may concern... With what sensible regret must those who were edify'd with the gravity, the piety, the generosity and charity of the late Bishop of Oxford, look on, when they see such a Harlequin in his room.' Having charg'd Dr. Burnet with writing Lampoons upon the present Princes of Christendom, the Doctor retorts it upon him with this satyrical period: ' It is Lampoon enough upon the Age, that he is a Bishop, but it is a downright Reproach that he is made the Champion of a Cause, which if it is bad of itself, must suffer extremely by being in such hands.'" (Echard's history of England, vol. iii. pp. 838, 839.) Somers Tracts, pp. 153, 156, 159.

K (£. 1L. Concerning the Act imposing the test, 1678; in answer to the Bishop of Oxford (Dr. Samuel Parker's) Reasons for abrogating the test. By the E.arl of C.larendon. In Gutch's Collectanea Curiosa, vol. i. p. 313-25.

G, 1L. Answer to the Bishop of Oxford's Reasons for abrogating the test impos'd on all Members of Parliament Anno 1678, Octob. 30. In these words, " I A. B. do solemnly and sincerely, in the Presence of God, profess testifie and declare, that I do believe that in the Sacrament of the Lord's Supper there is not any Transubstantiation of the Elements of Bread and "Wine into the Body and Blood of Christ at, or after, the consecration thereof by any person whatsoever; and that the Invocation, or Adoration of the Virgin Mary, or any other Saint, and the Sacrifice of the Mass, as they are now used in the Church of Rome, are Superstitious and Idolatrous." By a Person of Quality William Lloyd, D.D. Bishop of St. Asaph. pp. vi. 46, 4to Lond. 1688

C H. Answer to Vox Cleri &c. examining the reasons against making any alterations and abatements in order to a Comprehension.

pp. 36, 4to Lond. 1690

See Macaulay, vol. iii. p. 495.

S.C. Vindication of the Church of England in answer to a Pamphlet, *B.L.* entitled, A new Test of the Church of England's loyalty. By Mrs. Eleanor James. 4to Lond. 1687

Answer to a Paper entitled, A new Test etc. By Bp. Burnet. *C* 1L. See his Six Papers, *infra.*

The trial and examination of a Libel intitled, A new Test of the Church of England's loyalty; with some Reflections upon the additional Libel, entitled, An Instance of the Church of England's loyalty. 4to. By the Rev. Sam. Johnson. s.a.v.l. C H. In the ninth volume of Somers Tracts. In his Works, p. 9.

Some Considerations about the new Test of the Church of England's loyalty, in a letter to a Country Gentleman on the occasion of the present Invasion, s. 1. s. a. 4to 1688

In Somers Tracts, 1750, vol. i. p. 226. Scott's edition, ix. 198.

The Church of England's complaint in vindication of her loyalty.

England's present Interests discovered with honour to the Prince and safety to the People; submitted to the consideration of superiors. By William Penn. 4to Lond. 1675

A Defence of the Duke of Buckingham's Book of Religion and C 3L. Worship from the exceptions of a nameless author. By the Pensylvanian W. Penn. 4to Lond. 1685

See Wood's Atb. Oxon. *ut supra*. The Duke's discourse gave rise to a considerable controversy, which is comprised in the following political rather than theological pamphlets.

A short Discourse upon the reasonableness of men's having a religion or worship of God. By the Duke of Buckingham. 4to Lond. 1685. In the second volume of The Phenix.

A short Answer to his Grace the Duke of Buckingham's Paper (£. concerning religion, toleration, and liberty of conscience. 4to Lond. 1685.

The Duke of Buckingham his Grace's Letter to the unknown Author of a Paper entitled, A short Answer etc. Lond. 1685. (In Somers Tracts, 1748, vol. i.) A Reply to his Grace the Duke of Buckingham's Letter to the Author of a Paper entitled, A short Answer &c. 1685. A Reply to the Answer of the Man of no name £, to the Duke of Buckingham's Paper. By G. C. 4to Lond. 1685. An Apologie for the Church of England, against the clamours of the (P. 1L. men of No-Conscience, or the Duke of Buckingham's Seconds. By Efdmund Bohun Esq. 4to Lond. 1685.

Some reflections on a Discourse called Good Advice to the Church of England, &c. In State Tracts, 1693, part ii. p. 363.

A Seasonable Discourse shewing the necessity of Union amongst
Protestants in opposition to Popery, as the only means
(under God) to preserve the Reformed Religion. Also the
Charge of Persecution lately maintained against the Established Religion, by W. P. H. C. and other insignificant
Scribblers, detected, proving it to be the Ministers of State and not the Church that prosecuted the Penal Laws on Protestant Dissenters. pp. 14, 4to Lond. 1688
I suppose W. P. H. C. means Wm. Penn, Henry Care.

Heraclitus Ridens Redivivus; or a Dialogue between Harry and
Roger concerning the Times. pp. 8, 4to Oxford 1688
By Harry and Roger are meant H. Care, R. L'Estrange.

C H. A Treatise of true religion, heresy, schism, toleration, and the best means to prevent the growth of Popery. By John Milton. Printed in the year 1673. Works, folio, Amsterdam 1698, p. 807-12.
See also his poem, " On the new forcers of conscience under the
Long Parliament." Irving's Life of Robert Leighton, Archbishop of Glasgow, furnishes an interesting commentary on these lines:
" Men whose life, learning, faith and pure intent
Would have been held in high esteem with Paul,
Must now be nam'd and printed Hereticks
By shallow Edwards and Scotch what d'ye call."

The Burnt Child dreads the fire; or an examination of the merits of the Papists relating to England, mostly from their own
Pens. In justification of the late Act of Parliament for preventing dangers which may happen from Popish Recusants
(25 Ch. ii. c. 2, A.d. 1672). And further showing that whatsoever their merits have been, no thanks to their Religion, and therefore ought not to be gratified in their Religion by toleration thereof. By William Denton M.D.
4to Lond. 1675

The Established Test, in order to the Security of His Majesties CfL
Sacred Person, and Government, and the Protestant Religion.
Against the malitious attempts and treasonable machinations of Rome. pp. 54, 4to Lond. 1679

England's Grievances in times of Popery, drawn out of the Canon
Law, Decretals, Epistles and Histories of those times; with
Reasons why all sober Protestants may expect no better dealing from the Roman Catholics, should God, for their sins,
suffer them to fall under the Pope's tyranny again.
4to Lond. 1679

The Laws of Q. Elizabeth, K. James, and K. Charles the First, C 2. concerning Jesuites, Seminary Priests, Recusants, &c., and concerning the Oaths of Supremacy and Allegiance, explained by divers judgments and resolutions of the Reverend Judges. Together with other Observations upon the same Laws. To which is added the Statute xxv. Car. II. cap. 2, for preventing dangers which may happen from Popish Recusants. And an Alphabetical Table to the whole. By William Cawley, of the Inner Temple, Esq. Fol. Lond. 1680

Some interesting documents relating to Lancashire Recusants are given in Peck's Desiderata Curiosa, vol. i., and in the first volume of Baines's Lancashire, pp. 241-45.

A Discourse concerning the Laws, Ecclesiastical and Civil made against Hereticks by Popes, Emperors and Kings, Provincial and General Councils approved by the Church of Rome. Shewing, 1. What Protestant subjects may expect to suffer under a Popish Prince according to those Laws; 2. That no Oath or Promise of such a Prince can give them any just security that he will not execute these Laws upon them. With a Preface against persecuting and destroying Hereticks. By Daniel Whitby, DD.

4to Lond. 1682. Repr. 8vo Dublin 1723

In Reading's Catalogue of Sion College Library ascribed to Bp. Barlow. See an interesting notice of Whitby in Worthington's Diary, vol. ii. part i. p 202. " A full account of this learned and voluminous writer will be found in the Biog. Brit."

©t In A Letter from a Gentleman in the Country to his Friend in London on the subject of the penal laws and tests. 4to Lond. 1687. A second Letter, &c., 1687. A third Letter, 1687.

Remarks on the several sanguinary and penal laws made in Parliament against Roman Catholics. With some reasons humbly offer'd in order to obtain a Repeal of those Laws for the better advancement of His Majesty's Service and the ease of many of his most loyal subjects. pp. 24, 4to Lond. 1687

Advice to Freeholders and other Electors of members to serve in Parliament, in relation to the Penal Laws and the Test.
4to 1687

The good old Test revived and recommended to all sincere Christians. 4to 1687

A Letter concerning the Test and Persecution for Conscience sake, to a member of the House of Lords. 4to 1687

A Letter in answer to a City Friend shewing how agreeable Liberty of Conscience is to the Church of England. pp. 10, 4to Lond. 1687

A Discourse for taking off the Test and Penal Laws about Religion. 4to 1687

The reasonableness of Toleration and the unreasonableness of
Penal Laws and Tests. 4to 1687

How the Members of the Church of England ought to behave ©, JL. themselves under a Roman Catholick King with reference to the test and penal laws. In a letter to a friend by a member of the same Church. pp. 221, 12mo Lond. 1687

Three Letters tending to demonstrate how the security of this
Nation against al future Persecution for Religion, lys in the
Abolishment of the present penal Laws and Tests, and in the Establishment of a New Law for universal Liberty of Conscience, pp. 27, 4to, Lond. 1688

Some necessary disquisitions and close expostulations with the Clergy and People of England touching their loyalty. Written by a Protestant. 4to, 1688

Old Popery as good as New; or the unreasonableness of the Church of England in some of her doctrines and practices, and the reasonableness of liberty of Conscience. 4to, 1688

The Project for repealing the penal laws and tests, with the honorable means used to effect it. Being a Preface to a Treatise concerning the penal laws and tests.. 4to Lond. 1688

A New Test in lieu of the Old one by way of Supposition, or a satisfactory answer to that great and common question, viz.
If the penal laws and tests should be abolished, how shall the
Protestant Religion and interest be secured. By G. S.
pp. 34, 4to Lond. 1688
See Mackintosh's History of the Revolution, p. 224.

Pax Redux, or the Christian Reconciler. In three parts. Being a project for reuniting all Christians into one sole communion. Done out of French into English, by Philip Ayres, Esq. pp. 106, 4to Lond. 1688

The famous Bull in Ccena Domini, published at Rome every Maunday-Thursday against Hereticks and all Infringers of ecclesiastical Liberties. 4to Lond. 1689

An Historical Account of making the Penal Laws by the Papists against the Protestants, and by the Protestants against the Papists. Wherein the true ground and reason of making the laws is given, the Papists most Barbarous usage of the Protestants here in England, under a colour of law, set forth; and the Reformation Vindicated from the Imputation of being Cruel and Bloody, unjustly cast upon it by those of the Romish Communion. By Samuel Blackerby, Barrister of Grays-Inn. Summa est ratio, quae Religioni facit.
Fol. Lond. 1689.

Epistola ad clarissimum Virum T. A. R. P. T. O. L. A. i.e. Theologian apud Remonstrantes Professorem, Tyrannidis Osorem,
Limburgium, Amstelodamensem scripta a P. A. P. O. J. L.
A. i.e. Pacis Amico, Persecutionis Osore, Joanne Lockio,
Anglo. 12mo Tergon 1689
. 1L. " This piece was so highly approved of in Holland and England, that it was translated immediately into Dutch and English. It was translated likewise into French by Monsieur Le Clerc, who inserted it in the collection of *miscellaneous discourses* of Mr. Locke, printed in 1710." An abstract of the English Letter was inserted in the nineteenth volume of the Bibliotheque Universelle, p. 170 et seqq. " This letter was attacked by Mr. Jonas Proast in a piece intitled, The argument of the letter concerning toleration briefly considered and answered. Oxford, 1690, 4to. Upon this Mr. Locke published A second letter concerning toleration, Lond. 1690, 4to. Mr. Proast replied in A third letter, &c. Oxford 1691, 4 to. Mr. Locke published in answer to this A third letter for toleration, 4to 1692, containing 350 pages. Mr. Proast made no reply for twelve years, but at last published a pamphlet of 18 pages against the long letter of Mr. Locke, who, though in a very declining state (for he died the same year) determined to reply in a *fourth letter concerning toleration,"* &c. Bayle, 1738, vol. vii. A deficiency in this letter has been supplied in C J,, Lord King's Life of John Locke. See ibid. On the Difference between Civil and Ecclesiastical Power, indorsed Excommunication. Dated 1673-4: pp. 297-304. And, Defence of Non Conformity, an unpublished work, in which he animadverts on The Unreasonableness of Separation, by Dr. Stillingfleet: pp. 341-54. Extract from Locke's Common-Place Book, art. Sacerdos, 285-91. See also Tracts on Allegiance, pp. 3-9.

CHAP. IV. *Of the discourses written on occasion of the King's most gracious letters of indulgence.*

C 1L, 39-A Letter to a dissenter, upon occasion of his majesty's late gracious declaration of indulgence. pp. 7, 4to 1687

By George Savile, Marquis of Halifax, born about 1630, died 1695. In the State Papers, 1693, part i. p. 294. Somers Tracts.

" The Marquis of Hallifax, whose dexterity had been the active cause of throwing out the Bill of Exclusion, was in active opposition to King James ere he had held the throne two years, on which Ralph has the following sensible remarks: ' It is no uncommon thing for statesmen to look one way and row another: and yet there is scarce any circumstance of this reign more worthy of remark than the inconsistent parts now acted by two such eminent men as the Marquis of Hallifax and the Earl of Sunderland, and the inconsistent behaviour of his majesty towards them. The latter, who had gone warmly into the exclusion, under a seeming conviction of the many evils likely to bef'al the public under a catholic king, and who was now the oracle of the cabinet, laboured with all his might to introduce those very evils, if not to entail them on posterity. The Marquis, on the contrary, who had been indefatigable to shew that exclusion alone was a greater evil than all those put together, and yet was now out of place and favour, for that reason probably, took as much pains to convince the world that his former triumph was but a lucky mistake, and rather owing to the superiority of his parts than the goodness of his cause.'" Ralph's History, vol. i. p. 9j3.

" Hallifax's object in the present tract is to prevent that dissension between the protestant non-conformists and the church of England, which the declaration was so likely to produce, and to unite them firmly against the papists." The Somers Tracts, vol. ix. p. 50; vol. ii. p. 364 of the original edition (first collection).

" Of the numerous pamphlets in which the cause of the Court and the cause of the Church were at this time eagerly and anxiously pleaded before the Puritan, now, by a strange turn of fortune, the arbiter of the fate of his persecutors, one only is still remembered, the Letter to a Dissenter. In this masterly little tract all the arguments which could convince a Nonconformist that it was his duty and his interest to prefer an alliance with the Church to an alliance with the Court. were condensed into the smallest compass, arranged in the most perspicuous order, illustrated with lively wit, and enforced by an eloquence earnest indeed, yet never in its utmost vehemence transgressing the limits of exact good sense and good breeding. The effect of this paper was immense; for as it was only a single sheet, more than twenty thousand copies were circulated by the post; and there was no order of the kingdom in which the effect was not felt.

Twenty-four answers were published, but the town pronounced that they were all bad, and that Lestrange's was the worst of the twentyfour. The government was greatly irritated, and spared no pains to discover the author of the Letter; but it was found impossible to procure legal evidence against him. Some imagined that they recognised the sentiments and diction of Temple. *Note.* The letter was signed

T. W. Care says, in his Animadversions, This Sir Politic T. W. or

W. T.; for some critics think that the truer reading). But in truth that amplitude and acuteness of intellect, that vivacity of fancy, that terse and energetic style, that placid dignity, half courtly half philosophical, which the utmost excitement of conflict could not for a moment de'range, belonged to Halifax, and to Halifax alone." —

Macaulay, vol. ii. p. 217.

" Lord Halifax published, on the same occasion, a Letter to a Dissenter; the most perfect model, perhaps, of a political tract; which,

although its whole argument, unbroken by diversion to general topics,

is brought exclusively to bear with concentrated force upon the question, the parties, and the moment, cannot be read, after an interval of a century and a half, without admiration of its acuteness, address,

terseness, and poignancy." — Mackintosh's History of the Revolution, p. 174.

40. *i* Answer to a Letter to a Dissenter, upon occasion of His C H. Majesties late Gracious Declaration of Indulgence.

pp. 6, 4to Lond. 1687.

In the Bodleian Catalogue is " An Answer to the Letter to a Dissenter, detecting, the unjust insinuations which highly reflect on his majesty, as likewise the many false charges on the dissenters." " It is justly observed by Sir Walter Scott that the object of the poem (The Hind and Panther) shews that Dryden was not in the secret of James the Second, as the purpose of the monarch was to introduce a free exercise of the catholic religion, not by an union between its adherents and the members of the established church, but by uniting the dissenting congregations in a common interest against the exclusive power and privileges of the panther and her subjects."—Butler's Memoirs of the English, &c., Catholics.

(£. H. 41. Animadversions on a late Paper entituled,,A Letter to a Dissenter, upon occasion of his Majesties late Gracious Declaration of Indulgence. ByH.enry C.are. pp. 40, 4to Lond. 1687 See No. 24 *supra.* A. Wood gives this account of Henry Care: " He is several times reflected upon by Roger L'Estrange in his *Observation,* for a poor snivelling fellow; who after he had wrote several things in behalf of the church of England and the presbyterians, and had reflected on both the Universities in several of his writings as popishly affected, was at length prevailed upon in the time of James II. to write for the Roman Catholics, against the Church which he before had eagerly defended; whereby it was made manifest that what he wrote was not for religion, or conscience' sake, which he before did pretend, but for interest." Peck gives the title, "Animadversions on a late *pamphlet"* &c., but the original reads "paper," as above.—*J. H. T.* CH.

42. An Answer to a Letter to a Dissenter upon occasion of His Majesties late Gracious Declaration of Indulgence. By Sir Roger L'Estrange. pp. 50, 4to Lond. 1687

Born 1616, died 1704. The Letter is incorporated. "This," concludes L'Estrange, " is enough for my present purpose; and if it be not so for common satisfaction, my Third Volume of Observators has fifty times as much upon this Subject" (the King's Prerogative, and the Duty of a Subject).

" The most just principles of unbounded freedom in religion' were now the received creed at St. James's. Even Sir Roger L'Estrange endeavoured to save his consistency, by declaring that though he had for twenty years resisted religious liberty as a right of the people, he acquiesced in it as a boon from the King. — Mackintosh, p. 174.

43. An Answer from the Country to a late Letter to a Dissenter C1L. upon occasion of his Majesty's late Gracious Declaration of
Indulgence. By a member of the Church of England. 4to1687

44. A modest Censure of the immodest Letter to a Dissenter, & 2.. upon occasion of His Majesty's late Gracious Declaration for Liberty of Conscience. By T. N. a true member of the Church of England. pp. 24, 4to Lond. 1687 45. A second Letter to a Dissenter upon occasion of his Ma-C 3L jesty's late Gracious Declaration of Indulgence.
Not from a Romanist, but a member of a Congregational Church.

46. $f The Lay-man's Opinion, sent in a Private Letter to a con-C 5.. siderable Divine of the Church of England. By W.m 47. The Lay-man's Answer to a Lay-man's Opinion. In a Letter C. 1L

48. The Reasons of the Oxford Clergy against addressing.
In the ninth volume of the Somers Tracts will be found — "A Copy of an Address to the King by the Bishop of Oxon, to be subscribed by the clergy of his Diocess; with the Reasons for the Subscription to the Address, and the Reasons against it." With the following note: " That the declaration might be so much the less unpalatable, and that those of the legal church might not be rendered desperate, his majesty had been advised to open it with a clause that seemed to be in their favour, viz.: In the first place we do declare pp. 18, 4to Lond. 1687 to a Friend.
pp. 12, 4to Lond. 1687 that we will protect and maintain our archbishops, bishops and clergy, and all other our subjects of the church of England in the free exercise of their religion as by law established; and in the quiet and full enjoyment of all their possessions, without any molestation or disturbance whatsoever.' Now there wanted not undertakers, even among the bishops themselves, to procure addresses of thanks from the clergy of their respective dioceses to his Majesty, for the instances of his gracious regard towards them. Those of Durham, Chester, Lincoln, Litchfield and Coventry, and St. David's had their endeavours countenanced at least, if not fully answered; for after the form which had been set by the first of those right reverend fathers, the rest, at different times, made their compliments to the throne. But Samuel Parker, Bishop of Oxford, not satisfied with this simple mode of proceeding, insisted upon his clergy joining him in the address, which produced the following controversy."

See also Ralph's History, vol. i. p. 947, where are enumerated some of "the varieties of adulation that steam'd up to the Throne from every corner of the Kingdom, on this occasion." — Mackintosh's History of the Revolution, p. 176.

C1L. 49. b A Reply to the Oxford-Clergy against addressing.
pp. 20, 4to Lond. 1687 The clergy having decidedly the better in their contest with the bishop, Sir Robert L'Estrange, the Coryphaeus of his party, was invoked to the prelate's support, and produced this defence of the proposed address. 50. An Answer of a Minister of the Church of England to a seasonable and important Question, proposed to him by a Loyal and Religious Member of the present House of Commons. £. 1L. Viz. What Respect ought the True Sons of the Church of England, in point of Conscience and Christian Prudence, to bear to the Religion of that Church, whereof the King is a member. pp. 63, 4to Lond. 1687

How vast the contrast between the autonomic independency inculcated in the writings of De Foe, (see A New Test of the Church of England's Loyalty; or Whiggish Loyalty and Church Loyalty compared; in the ninth volume of Somers Tracts, p» 569, in the original edition, vol. iii. fourth collection, pp. 1-15,) and the suicidal extravagances of loyalty scattered through the pages of the most eminent Divines of the seventeenth century, e.g. Sanderson, South, Kettlewell. These champions of Divine Right, not content with the limited obedience advocated hy Grotius and Puffendorf, ut mpra, p. 39, and Barclay, De Regno, et Regali Potestate, 4to Parisiis 1600, were ready in their impolitic and servile speculations to sacrifice the redemption of the whole world to the Juggernaut processions of their Sovereign Lord, or Vicarius Dei. " No conjuncture of circumstances whatsoever, can make that expedient to he done at any time, that is of itself and in the kinde unlawful. For a man to blaspheme the holy name of God, to sacrifice to idols, to give wrong sentence in judgement, by his power to oppress those that are not able to withstand him, by subtilty to overreach others in bargaining, to take up arms (offensive or defensive) against a lawfull Soveraign: none of all these, and sundry other things of like nature, being all of them simply and de toto genere unlawful, may be done by any man, at any time, in any case, upon any colour or pretension whatsoever; the express command of God himself only excepted, as in the case of Abraham for sacrificing his son. Not for the avoiding of scandal; not at the instance of any friend, or command of any power upon earth; not for the maintenance of the lives or liberties either of ourselves or others; not for the defence of Religion; not for the preservation of Church or State: no nor yet, if that could be imagined possible, for the salvation of a soul, no nor for the redemption of the whole world." Sanderson's twelfth Sermon ad Aulam, p. 232, fol. 1656. See also De Foe's New Test; Edinburgh Review, vol. lv. p. 51, (Bowles's Life of Bishop Ken); and Mackintosh's History of the Revolution, pp. 153 and 294. This is perhaps an instance of the solidity of sense and matter being outweighed by high-sounding Ciceronian sentences, in which, as has been observed by Bacon, many absurdities have originated, and which often mislead writers who are over studious of the fascinations of diction. " How many false thoughts has the desire of maintaining a nicety produced?... Who would not laugh to hear Bembo cry that the Pope was elected by the favour of the Immortal Gods"? Port Royal Logic. I have said perhaps an instance, because Burnet states that Bishop Parker had exalted the King's authority in matters of religion in so indecent a manner that he condemned the ordinary form of saying the King was under God and Christ as a crude and profane expression; saying, that though the King was indeed under God, yet he was not under Christ, but above him. Burnet, vol. iii. p. 1186; (fol. 1724, vol. i. p. 696.) In the reign of James I. Bishop Parry "made an apology in the preface to his Welsh version of the Bible, for preferring the Deity to his majesty, after which we cannot be surprised at any instance of adulation."—Barrington's Observations on the Statutes.

C. H. Reflections on his Majesty's Proclamation for a Toleration in Scotland. by Gilbert Burnet. 1687 The Proclamation is given here, and in Echard's History, vol. iii. p. 814. " He had determined to begin with Scotland, where his power to dispense with Acts of Parliament had been admitted by the obsequious Estates." Macaulay, vol. ii. p. 205. Cf. Woodrow's History of the Sufferings of the Church of Scotland from the Restauration to the Revolution, vol. ii. bk. iii. ch. xi. s. ii. " Of the various Acts of Indulgence granted this year (1687) and particularly that Liberty in July, which Presbyterian Ministers fell into, with some remarks." Fountainhall's Historical Notices, 1661-1668. Balcarras's Memoirs touching the Revolution in Scotland, 1688-90. Printed for the Ban natyne Club, 1841. Echard's History, vol. iii. p. 817. Hallam's Constitutional History, vol. ii. ch. 17.

His Majesties most Gracious Declaration to all his Loving Subjects for Liberty of Conscience. Fol. a single Sheet. In State Tracts, 1693. Part ii. p. 287.

His Majestie's Gracious Declaration for Liberty of Conscience in which his Majesty says his " intentions are not changed since the 4th of April 1687." Folio 1688 CH. Six Papers containing I. Reasons against the Repealing the Acts of Parliament concerning the Test. Humbly offer'd to the consideration of the Members of both Houses at thf ir next Meeting, pp. 7. II. Some Reflections on his Majesties Proclamation of the Twelfth of February 168, for a Toleration in Scotland, together with the said Proclamation. pp. 9-15. Proclamation 16-19. III. A Letter, containing some Reflections on His Majesties Declaration for Liberty of Conscience, Dated the Fourth of April 1687. pp. 21-30.

" Theso Reflections appear now too late to have one effect that was designed by them, which was, the diverting men from making Addresses upon it; yet if what is here proposed makes men become so far wise as to be ashamed of what they have done, and is a means to keep them from carrying their Courtship farther than good words, this Paper will not come too late." (In State Tracts, 1693, vol. ii. p. " 292, 293.) In reference to this tract Mackintosh observes: Burnet the historian, then at the Hague, published a letter of warning to the Dissenters, in which he owns and deplores " the Persecution," acknowledging the " temptation under which the Nonconformists are to receive every thing which gives them present ease with a little too much kindness"; and blames most severely the members of the Church who applauded the Declaration, but entreats the Nonconformists not to promote the designs of the common enemy. The residence and connections of the writer bestowed on this publication the important character of an admonition from the Prince of Orange. He had been employed by some leaders of the Church to procure that Prince's interference with the Dissenters, to prevent their being misled by the King; and Dykvelt the Dutch minister, assured both the Church and the Dissenters of his Highncss's resolution to promote union between them, and to maintain the common interests of Protestants. History of the Revolution, p. 174. See also Ralph's History, vol. i. p. 949.

IV. An Answer to a Paper, printed with Allowance, Entitled, A new Test of the Church of England's Loyalty, pp. 31-39.

V. Remarks on the two Papers (ut supra, p. 19). pp. 41-48.

VI. The Citation of Gilbert Burnet, D. D. To Answer in Scotland on the 27th June O'd Stile, for High Treason: Together with his Answer; and Three Letters, writ by him upon that Subject, to the Right Honourable the Earl of Middletoune, his Majesties Secretary of State. pp. 67. By G. Burnet. Hague Jun. 27 Old St. 1687.

M

An Apology for the Church of England with relation to the Spirit of Persecution for which she is accused. By G. Burnet.

In Somers Tracts, vol. ix. p. 174, with a note on the important share this active politician had in the Revolution. First collection, vol. ii. p. 532.

A plain Account of the Persecution, now laid to the charge of the Church of England.

In Somers Tracts. First collection, vol. ii. pp. 525-31. " The stand which the bishops and clergy of the church of England made against the indulgence was ascribed by their antagonists, whether catholics or dissenters of the more violent sort, to a spirit of intolerance and persecution. Dryden, whose Hind and Panther appeared about this time, charges this arbitrary and tyrannical temper upon the church in the following lines:

' If you condemn that prince of tyranny Whose mandate forced your Gallic friend to fly, Make not a worse example of your own.' This was not a charge under which the church of England could remain with safety, at a period when the king was seeking to unite against the establishment dissenters of every persuasion. Various papers were therefore published to take off the edge of that imputation, and to propitiate the minds of protestant nonconformists." — Sir W. Scott's edition, vol. ix. This tract is also in the State Papers, part ii. p. 322, 1693.

Notes upon Mr. Dryden's Poems, in Four Letters. By M. Clifford, late Master of the Charter House, Lond. To which are annexed Some Reflections upon the Hind and Panther. By another Hand. pp. 35, 4to Lond. 1687

A Representation of the threatening dangers impending over Protestants in Great Britain; with an Account of the arbitrary and Popish ends, unto which the Declaration for Liberty of Conscience in England, and the Proclamation for a Toleration in Scotland, are designed. By Robert Ferguson.

In State Tracts, part ii. 380-419. Soraers Tracts, vol. ix. 315-67, which gives a memoir of the author. See also The Jacobite Trials at Manchester in 1694; edited by William Beamont, Esq. 1853.

Their Highness the Prince and Princess of Orange's opinion about a general Liberty of Conscience, &c., being a Collection of four C iL. select Papers, viz.

I. A Letter writ by Mijti Heer Fagel, Pensioner of Holland, to Mr. James Stewart, Advocate, giving an Account of the Prince and Princess of Orange's Thoughts concerning the Repeal of the Test and the Penal Laws. pp. 8, 4to Lond. 1688. Written in 1687.

" The eyes of all men were at this time turned on the Prince of Orange, whose opinions respecting James's proceedings were very likely to crush the opposition made to them, or to blow it into an irresistible flame. ' Complaints,' says Burnet, then resident at the Hague, ' came daily over from England of all the high things that the priests were every where throwing out. See a remarkable Letter from a Jesuit, of the state of England, in Echard's History, vol. iii. pp. 811-13. Penn the quaker came over to Holland. He was a talking, vain man, who had long been in the king's favour, he being the viceadmiral's son.... He undertook to persuade the prince to come into the king's measures, and had two or three long audiences of him upon the subject; and he and I spent some hours together on it. The prince readily consented to a toleration of popery as well as of the dissenters, provided it were proposed and passed in parliament; and he promised his assistance, if there was need of it, to get it to pass; but for the tests he would enter into no treaty about them. He said it was a plain betraying the security of the protestant religion to give them up. ... To all (Penn's promises in the name of the king) the prince replied that no man was more for toleration in principle than he was; he thought the conscience was only subject to God; and as far as a general toleration even of papists would content the king, he would concur in it heartily. But he looked on the tests as such a real security, and indeed the only one, that he would join in no counsels with those that intended to repeal those laws that enacted them. Penn said the king would have all or nothing; but that if this was once done, the king would secure the toleration by a solemn and unalterable law. To this the late repeal of the edict of Nantes, that was declared perpetual and irrevocable, furnished an answer that admitted of no reply. So Penn's negociation with the prince had no effect.' — Burnet, vol. iii. p. 1182. It became necessary to apprize those who opposed James's measures, *i.e.* almost all his protestant subjects, of the sentiments of the prince of Orange concerning the penal laws and dispensing power. This was through the medium of the letter from the grand pensioner of Holland, which was industriously dispersed through England." Somers Tracts, vol. ix. p. 183. First Collection, vol. ii. pp. 540-45. C.i. II. Reflexions on Monsieur Fagel's Letter. In State Tracts, 1693, part ii. pp. 338-42. III. Fagel's second Letter to Mr. Stewart. IV. Some Extracts out of Mr. Stewart's printed Letter, 4to 1689.

Answer to Mr. Fagel's Letter concerning the Penal Laws and Tests. By James Stewart. 4to Lond. 1688. The same in French, 4to Lond. 1688.

"A Scotch Whig, named James Stewart, had fled some years before to Holland, in order to avoid the boot and the gallows, and had become intimate with the Grand Pensionary Fagel, who enjoyed a large share of the Stadtholder's confidence and favour When the Indulgence appeared, Stewart conceived that he had an opportunity of obtaining not only pardon but reward. He offered his services to the government of which he had been the enemy: they were accepted: and he addressed to Fagel a letter purporting to have been written by direction of James. In that letter the Pensionary was exhorted to use all his influence with the Prince and Princess, for the purpose of inducing them to support their Father's policy. After some delay Fagel transmitted a reply, deeply meditated and drawn up with exquisite art. No person who studies that remarkable document can fail to perceive that although it is framed in a manner well calculated to reassure and delight English Protestants, it contains not a word that could give offence, even at the Vatican. It was announced that William and Mary would assist in abolishing every law which made any Englishman liable to punishment for his religious opinions. But between punishments and disabilities a distinction was taken. To admit Roman Catholics to office would, in the judgment of their Highnesses, be neither for the general interest of England, nor even for the interest of the Roman Catholics themselves. This manifesto was translated into several languages, and circulated widely on the Continent. Of the English version carefully prepared by Burnet,

near fifty thousand copies were introduced into the eastern shires, and rapidly distributed over the whole kingdom. No state paper was ever more completely successful. The Protestants of our island applauded the manly firmness with which William declared that he could not consent to entrust papists with any share in the government. The

Roman Catholic princes, on the other hand, were pleased with the mild and temperate style in which the resolution was expressed, and by the hope which he held out that under his administration no member of their Church would be molested on account of religion."—

Macaulay, vol ii. pp. 201-262.

Animadversions upon a pretended Answer to Mijn Heer Fagd'sC! Letter, pp. 30, 4to Lond. 1688. In State Tracts, 1693. Part ii. pp. 343-362.

The Anatomy of an Equivalent. By George Savile, Marquis ofC3L Halifax. In State Tracts, 1693, Part ii. pp. 300-309.

" Even Penn, intemperate nnd undiscerning as was his zeal for the Declaration, seems to have felt that the partiality with which honours and emoluments were heaped on Roman Catholics might not unnaturally excite the jealousy of the nation. He owned that if the Test Act were repealed, the Protestants were entitled to an equivalent, and went so far as to suggest several equivalents." — Macaulay, vol. ii. p. 238. " This project," says Echard (Hist of England, vol. iii. p. 850), " was soon shattered, and the word efficiently dissected by the admirable pen of the Marquiss of Hullifax, in a pamphlet etc. in which are many notable passages, but that towards the conclusion is worthy of a place in History, and of the remembrance of all Princes and great Ministers." Barclay, in his Argenis, presents some political counsels equally appropriate, lib. i. cap. xviii. The king declared that he would maintain his loving subjects in their properties and possessions as well of church and abbey lands as of any other. In opposition to the doctrine of resumption founded on the Council of Trent, was published, by his Majesty's command, The Assurance of Abbey and other Church Lands in England to the Possessors, cleared from the doubts and arguments raised about the danger of Resumption etc. By Nathaniel Johnston M.D. 12mo Lond 1687. On the other side appeared, Abby and Church-Lands, not yet assured to such Possessors as are Roman Catholicks: dedicated to the Nobility and Gentry of that Religion. In State Tracts, Part ii. pp. 326-330, and the ninth volume of Somers Tracts, p. 68. See also Burnet's History of the Reformation, part ii. fol. 297, and A Letter written to Dr. Burnet giving some Account of Cardinal Pole's secret Powers; from which it appears that it never was intended to confirm the Alienation that was made of the Abbey-lands. To which are added Two Breves that Cardinal Pole brought over, and some other of his Letters that were never before printed, 1685. In the seventh volume of the Harleian Miscellany, pp. 258-270.

Mr. Massey's Licence, Dispensation and Pardon, 1686.

The Editor of the State Letters and Diary of Henry Earl of Clarendon observes, But of all the papers which enrich the Appendix, the Dispensation to Massey, Dean of Christchurch, is the most remarkable; as the existence of any such Dispensation seems to have escaped the enquiries of every Historian of James's reign. When Bishop Burnet tells us that the Deanery of Christchurch was given to Massey, one of the new converts; who at the first went to prayers in the Chapel, but soon after declared himself more openly; by this lame account the Bishop allows his readers to believe that some appearances were saved, and that Massey had not absolutely disclaimed Protestantism till after he was in possession of his Deanery. But we now know the contrary; and future Historians will justly treat the Dispensation granted to this Popish Dean of Christchurch as the most alarming of all the attacks made by King James the Second on the Constitution. It will be found also in Gutch's Collect. vol. i. pp. 294-29.0. "This dispensation to Massey contained an ostentatious enumeration of the laws which it sets at defiance."—Mackintosh. Sec also Macaulay.

An Instance of Queen Elizabeth's Power of dispensing with Acts of

Parliament, offered to the consideration of the Gentlemen of the University of Cambridge: together with some Queries thereupon. Printed by Henry Hills, Printer to the King's most excellent Majesty for his Household and Chapel, 1687.

This paper is in Ralph's History, vol. i. p. 259. £.

The Trial of Sir Edw. Hale, Bart., for neglecting to take the Oaths of Supremacy and Allegiance, with his Plea thereto, upon the King's dispensing with the Stat. 25 Car. II., and the Opinion of the Judges thereupon.

" Armed with the sanction of the law, the king was resolved to push the advantages of victory, and to exercise in a wider range that branch of the prerogative which had hitherto been palliated with the pretence of gratitude; and confined to those officers, who had meritoriously served him during the rebellion of Monmouth." Somervile's

History of Political Transactions, &c. Cf. Jus Regium Coronte. Accordingly he made an attempt to exercise this unlicensed and obnoxious power in the University of Cambridge and at Magdalen College, Oxford. The history of these disputes will be found in the following works, relating to the Court of Commissioners.

A short Account of Sir Edward Hale's Case. By Sir Edward

Herbert. pp. 39, 4to Lond. 1688

It will be found in the second volume of the Collection of State (Jf, 5L

Trials, 1735.

The King's Visitatorial Power asserted; being an impartial Relation of the late Visitation of St. Mary Magdalene College, Oxford; as likewise an Historical Account of several Visitations of the Universities and particular Colleges: together with some necessary remarks upon the King's Authority in Ecclesiastical Cases, according to the laws and usages of this Realm: written by direction. By Nath. Johnston, M.D.

Dr. J. was employed by the Commissioners to vindicate their proceedings.

An Enquiry into the power of dispensing with Penal Statutes, together with some Animadversions upon a Book writ by Sir Edw.

Herbert, entitled, A Short Account, &c. By Sir Robert

Atkyns. Folio, Lond. 1689

Lord Chief Justice Herbert's Case of Sir Edward Hale examined,

where it is shewn that his Authorities are very unfairly stated and as ill applied.

Examination of Sir Edward Herbert's Account of the Authorities in

Law, whereby he could excuse his

Judgment in Sir E. Hale's Case. 4to, Lond. 1689

The arguments on this question are contained in the Tracts of Sir Edward Herbert, Sir R. Atkyns, and Mr. Attwood, published after the Revolution. State Trials, vol. xi. That of Attwood is the most distinguished for acuteness and research. Sir Edward Herbert's is feebly reasoned, though elegantly written.—Mackintosh.

A Vindication of the Proceedings of his Majesties Ecclesiastical Commissioners against the Bishop of London, and the Fellows of Magdalen College. 4to Lond. 1688

A Letter to the Author of the Vindication, etc. 4to, Eleutheropoli.

£, 3L. The Legality of the Court held by his Majesties Ecclesiastical Commissioners defended. Their proceedings no Argument against the taking off Penal Laws and Tests. pp. 39, 4to Lond. 1688 " No argument against," but rather incentive to this measure. When liberty of conscience is established, there will be no such Court; but now " the King can either muzzle all the Clergy, or ty up the hands of Protestant Dissenters, and get a Parliament that shall set up Popery."

C. 1L The King's Power in Ecclesiastical Matters truly stated. In State Tracts, 1693. Part ii. pp. 331-334.

On the origin of the High Commission Court during the reign of Queen Elizabeth, King James the First, and King Charles the First, see Sanderson's Episcopacy not Prejudicial to Regal Power, 1661. " The main point of the Act of 1st of Elizabeth, by which the Queen had power given her to punish all that she should think fit, by any free born subject to whom she should delegate her power was repealed by Charles I., and the repeal confirmed lately by Charles II So that without seeing the last Acts of Parliament, no man can tell what the religion of England is." — Martin Green's Letters, 1664, ns quoted in Dr. Oliver's Collections towards illustrating the Biography of the Scotch, English and Irish Members, of the Society of Jesus. Lond. 1845.

A Letter from the Bishop of Rochester to the Right Honourable the Earl of Dorset and Middlesex, Lord Chamberlain, concerning his sitting in the late Ecclesiastical Commission. pp. 20, 4to Lond. 1688 See Echard's History of England, vol. iii. p. 876.

Au Exact Account of the whole Proceedings against Henry Lord Bishop of London before the Lord Chancellor and the other Ecclesiastical Commissioners. 4to Lond. 1688.

Burnet, vol. i. p. 677. Barillon, Sept. 1686. The public proceedings are in the Collection of State Trials. (Macaulay.) See also Lingard, Buckle's History of Civilization, p. 369. " The insane and almost incredible attempt of James II. to set up a High Commission Court by his pretended right at common law or by his prerogative to do so, is familiar to all "readers, through the exquisite pen of Lord Macaulay." (The Acts of the High Commission Court within the Diocese of Durham. Printed for the Surtees Society. Durham, 1858.)

Lawfulness of the Oath of Supremacy and Power of the King in Ecclesiastical Affairs vindicated, with Queen Elizabeth's Admonition, &c. By Philip Nye. 4to Lond. 1683-87-88

Considerations touching the Great Question of the King's Right in dispensing with the Penal Laws; written on the occasion of his late Blessed Majesty's granting the Free Toleration and Indulgence. By Richard Langhorn. Fol. Loud. 1687

The King's Dispensing Power explicated and asserted.

In Somers' Collection. See Ralph, who describes it as written in the style and printed in the manner of Lestrange, vol. i. p. 948.

Compare A Speech against the Suspending and Dispensing Prorogate, 1L. tive, &c. in A Collection of Scarce and interesting Tracts, written by Persons of Eminence; upon the most important political and commercial subjects, during the years 1763-1770. Lond. 1787. Vol. ii. pp. 225-305. "The argument upon this great and interesting question was fully stated in the above pamphlet; which was by many ascribed to Lord Mansfield: but this was not true, for it was written or sketched out first by Mr. Mackintosh, and afterwards corrected and great additions made by Lord Temple and Lord Lyttleton."

Jus Regium Coronae, or the King's supreme Power in dispensing with Penal Statutes, more particularly as it relates to the two

Test Acts, in two Parts. By John Wilson. pp. 79, 4to 1688

See Numbers 26, 27, 30.

The King's Right of Indulgence in Spiritual Matters with the Equity thereof Asserted by a Person of Honour and Eminent C 1L. Minister of State lately deceased Arthur Annesley, Earl of Anglesea. Printed by Henry Care.

pp. 75, 4to Lond. 1688 The rights vested in the Crown are marked out, in a great measure, by the titles which the early law writers give the King, as will be seen in this tract and in Dr. Pusey's publication, " The Royal Supremacy not an arbitrary Authority but limited by the Laws of the Church, of which Kings are Members, Oxford 1850," in which the legitimate authority of Christian Princes has been shewn from ancient Precedents. " The word consecrated King occurs first in the Saxon Chronicle in the reign of Offa, King of Mercia, the contemporary of Charlemagne about 1000 years since; and it is very probable that the ceremony of Ethelred was then used. From the peculiar and mixed authority conveyed by this ceremony to the head of the government, it has become a sacred fountain which has poured from its elevation similar streams on all lesser powers. The chief reason why it is now pointed out to the observation of the reader is to shew this ancient service of the consecration of our Kings, as furnishing in reality such a social contract, such proper origin of government, as the politicians and philosophers of modern times think ought to exist, and without which it is asserted power is an usurpation Similar ceremonies have long been used in the great kingdoms of Christendom; and notwithstanding, by a strange fatality, no author writing on the origin of power in states, has ever turned his eye to it, to read the plain declarations laid down in it."— The Coronation Service, or Consecration of the Anglo-Saxon Kings, as it illustrates the Origin of the Constitution. By the Rev. Thomas Silver. Oxford 1831.

A Letter in answer to two main Questions of the first Letter to a Dissenter. T. Whether Protestant Dissenters ought to refuse the proposed legal Toleration including Catholick Dissenters. II. Whether Protestant Dissenters ought to expect the said Toleration, until the next Succession upon the suggested hopes of excluding Catholicks. By T. G. 4to 1687 % An Answer to the Letter to a Dissenter detecting the many unjust insinuations which highly reflect on his Majesty, as likewise the many false charges on the Dissenters.
4to Lond. 1687

A Letter to a Friend in answer to a Letter to a Dissenter upon occasion etc. , half-sheet folio.

What Manner of Men the Clergy of the Church of England and their Creatures are, briefly and fairly shewn in a Letter occasioned by a Postcript in the above. 4to Lond. 1687

C3L. An Answer to a Scandalous Pamphlet, entitled, A Letter to a
Dissenter concerning His Majesties late Declaration of
Indulgence. By Henry Payne. pp. 8, 4to Lond. 1687

An Answer to Mr. Payne's Letter etc. Writ to the Author of the
Letter to a Dissenter subscribed T. T. By Gilbert Burnet.
4to Lond. 1687

C L. In his Collection of Eighteen Papers, 4to Lond. 1689, pp. 38-44.

Very laudatory of William and Mary, as is also, Reflections on a
Pamphlet, entitled, Parliamentum Pacificum, licensed hy the Earl of
Sunderland, and printed at London in March, 1688. Ibid. pp. 65-82.

Remarks upon a Pamphlet, entitled, A Letter to a Dissenter in another Letter to the same Dissenter.
pp. 12, 4to Lond. 1687 *T. C. D.* Some queries concerning Liberty of Conscience, directed to Wm. Penn and Henry Care, s. 1. v. a. 4to.

T. C. D. Some free reflexions upon occasion of the public discourse about Liberty of Conscience. 4to Lond. 1687. The Dissenters Jubilee: as it was sounded in the audience of a solemn assembly at the Public Meeting place in Spittle Fields near London, on Tuesday May 17th 1687, being a day of Thanksgiving to praise the Lord for his wonderful appearance and overruling Providence in the present Dispensation of Liberty of Conscience. By Charles Nicholets, Preacher of the Gospel and Pastor of a Congregation there.
4to Lond. 1687

Reasons why the Church of England as well as Dissenters should make their address of thanks to the King's Majesty for his late Declaration for Liberty of Conscience. 4to Lond. 1687

Some Free Reflections upon occasion of the Public Discourse C H.
about Liberty of Conscience, and the consequences thereof,
in the present conjuncture. By one who cordially imbraces whatsoever there is of true Religion in al Professions, and hates everything which makes any of them hate or hurt one another. 4to Lond. 1687

Some sober and weighty Reasons against persecuting Protestant
Dissenters for Difference of Opinion in Matters of Religion.
Humbly offered to the Consideration of all in Authority.
" This tract seems designed to reconcile the church of England to the toleration as if it were chiefly intended for the benefit of the protestant dissenters. But the truth is that tho protestant dissenters were at the first publication of the indulgence so elated with their victory over the church of England, so irritated at the remembrance of past severities, and so dazzled with the unexpected and unusual blaze of royal favour, that they were for a time ready to throw themselves into the arms or at the foot of the monarch." — Somers Tracts, vol.
ix. As is manifested by The Dissenters' Jubilee, *ut supra,* and by
A Letter from a Dissenter to the Petitioning Bishops *ut infra.* See also
Brethren in Iniquity: or, The Confederacy of Papists with Sectaries, for the destroying of the True Religion, as by Law Establish'd, plainly detected. Wherein is shewn a farther Account of the Romish Snares and Intrigues for the destroying of 'the True Reformed Religion, as professed in the Church of England, and established by Law, and for the Introducing of Popery or Atheism among us; clearly shewing from very anthentic Writers and Testimonies. That the principal ways and methods whereby the Papists have sought the ruine of our Religion and Church, from the beginning of our Reformation to the present
Times, and by which they are still in hopes of compassing it, are by promoting of Toleration, or pretended Liberty of Conscience; and that for above these sixscore years the Papists have so craftily influenced our Dissenters, as to make them the unhappy Instruments of effecting their most pernicious designs, which they contrived for the Subverting our Church and State. 4to Lond. 1600. And,
A Representation of the threatening dangers, etc. *ut supra* p. 82.

The Toleration Act, which was passed in 1689, was considered as having given to the Dissenters the possession of all they had a right to claim; but the Act by which Dissenters were kept out of Corporations was not repealed till the year 1828, although their claims were in 1787, 1788 and 178.9 so maturely considered and thoroughly understood that, but for the indisposition of the King, their applications for redress would perhaps even at that time have been successful. See I. The Substance of the Speech delivered by Henry Beaufoy Esq., on his Motion for the Repeal of the Test and Corporation Acts, &c. Lond. 1787. II. A Letter to the Bishops on the application of the Protestant Dissenters., including Strictures on some passages in the Bishop of Gloucester's Sermon, on January 30, 1788. Lond. 1789. III. The Debate in the House of Commons on Mr. Beaufoy's Motion for the Repeal of such parts of the Test and Corporation Acts as affect the Protestant Dissenters, on Friday the Eighth of May 1789. Lond. 1789. IV. The Right of Protestant Dissenters to a compleat

Toleration asserted; containing an Historical Account of the Test Laws, and shewing the injustice, inexpediency and folly of the Sacramental Test, as now imposed with respect to Protestant Dissenters; with an answer to the Objection from the Act of Union with Scotland. By a Layman. Lond. 1789. V. Two Speeches delivered in the House of Commons on Tuesday the 2nd of March 1790, by the Right Honourable Charles James Fox, in support of his Motion for a Repeal of the Corporation and Test Acts. Lond. 1790. In the time of George the First a clause was introduced for repealing certain parts of these Acts into a bill introduced into the House of Lords, but failed, although it was supported by some men most eminent for loyalty and public spirit, and likewise by some of the most learned among the Bishops, but more especially by Hoadley, bishop of Bangor, and Kennet, bishop of Peterborough. See a list of Tracts written by Bishop Hoadley in the Bangorian Controversy, as it was afterwards called, Works, vol. ii. p. 379. A defence of these Acts by Warburton, Sherlock, Ellys and Horsley will be found in the *Churchman armed against the Errors of the Time*. It is stated above that the indisposition of the king arrested the progress of the repeal of these acts; but it must be remembered that it was the boast of George the Third that he would bequeath the government to his successor in the same state as that in which he received it. See Buckle, p. 422.

A Letter from a Gentleman in the City to a Friend in the
Country. By William Sherlock, D.D., 1688.

In Baldwin's Farther State Papers, 309-16. — See Mackintosh, ©. *fL* p. 245.

An Answer from a Country Clergyman to the Letter of his
Brother in the City (Dr. Sherlock). June, 1688

A Letter of several French Ministers fled into Germany upon fit. 1L.
the account of the Persecution in France, to such of their
Brethren in England, as approved the Kings Declaration touching Liberty of Conscience. Translated from the Original in French. 4to, no date or place.

A Letter from a Clergy-Man in the City to his Friend in the Country containing his Reasons for not reading the Declaration, 22 May 1688. 1 sheet 4to, 1688

A Letter from a Clergy-Man in the Country to the Clergy-Man in the City etc. shewing the insufficiency of his reasons therein contained for not reading the Declaration. By a Minister of the Church of England, pp. 40, 4to Lond. 1688

An Answer to the City Minister's Letter from his Country Friend. 4to 1688

Letters about reading King James's Declaration of Indulgence to *S. C.* Dissenters in 1688. With Answers to Replys.
4to Lond. 1688

The Minister's Reasons for not reading the King's Declaration, friendly debated. By a Dissenter. Allowed to be Published this 21st day June 1688. pp. 24. 4to Lond. 1688

An Expedient for Peace; persuading an agreement amongst
Christians from the impossibility of their agreement in matters of religion. Also shewing the nature and causes of the present differences; the unreasonableness of persecution, the equity of toleration, and the great benefits of a Pacific Charter. pp. 40, 4to Lond. 1688

Pax Redux, or the Christian Reconciler. In three parts. Being a project for reuniting all Christians into one sole communion. Done out of French into English by Philip Ayres.
pp. 106, 4to Lond. 1688 ML. The Petition of William Sancroft, Archbishop of Canterbury and six other Bishops to his Majesty touching their not distributing and publishing the Declaration of Conscience. 4to 1688
"The dispute between the King and the Church was now drawing to a crisis. The King renewed his declaration of indulgence upon 27th April 1688, and upon the 4th May following enjoined the bishops to disperse it through their several dioceses for the purpose of its being read by the clergy in all the churches. The six bishops were St. Asaph, Ely, Bath and Wells, Peterborough, Chichester and Bristol. They laid before him the reasons that determined them not to obey the order of Council that had been sent them. This flowed from no want of respect to hi3 Majesty's authority, nor from any unwillingness to let favour be shewed to Dissenters, in relation to whom they were willing to come to such a temper as should be thought fit, when that matter should be considered and settled in Parliament and Convocation."—Burnet's History. The Declaration of Charles II. in 1662 and 1672, which was pronounced unconstitutional in Parliament, dispensed only with penal laws. Sec Marlow's Account of the Growth of Popery. In State Tracts, part ii. p. 80, 1689. Matter of Fact, by the Earl of Cflarendon concerning the King's Dispensing Power, etc. Iu Gutch, part i. p. 309. Minutes for his Grace of Canterbury: prepared by Mr. Hanses, to have been spoken at the Triall. In Gutch, ibid. 363-69. A Speech prepared by the Bishop of St. Asaph, to have been spoken at the Trial!, ibid. 369-74. The Petition is in the ninth volume of the Somers Tracts; and, " with some Proceedings thereupon," in the first volume of Qutch's Collectanea Curiosa, 335-02.

Case of Reading King James's Declaration in 1688. Question whether a Divine of the Church of England may, with a safe Conscience, read in the Church the K's D—n for Liberty of Conscience without expressing his consent to the Matter contained in it? By Edward Stillingfleet, D.D. Bishop of Worcester, in his Miscellaneous Discourses. 8vo Lond. 1735 At the consultation of the London clergy Tillotson, Patrick, Sherlock, Stillingfleet and Fowler were the minority against the Declaration. The majority yielded to the authority of a minority 60 respectable.

The Lord Bishop of Rochester's Letter to the Right Honourable the Lords Commissioners of his Majesty's Ecclesiastical Court.

In Somers Tracts. Fourth Collection, vol. ii. p. 221. Harl. Miscell. vol. vii. p. 427, 4to. Fourth Collection of Papers relating to the Present Juncture of Affairs in England. 4to Lond. 1688.

Although he complied with the King's command in reading his Declaration, Bishop Sprat resigned his office as Commissioner. — See Macaulay; Burnet's Memoirs, vol. i. p. 675, vol. ii. p. 620; and Doyly's Life of Sancroft, vol. i. p. 229.

A Short Discourse concerning the Reading his Majesty's late Declaration in the Churches. Set forth by the Right Reverend Father in God, Herbert Lord Bishop of Hereford.
pp. 15, 4to Lond. 1688 In Somers Tracts. First Collection, vol. ii. pp. 361-3. " I should never doubt of God's merciful pardon in it, seeing I did it otit of pure obedience to my King upon God's command, and to so good an end as the preserving of Truth and Peace among us."

A Letter from a Dissenter to the petitioning Bishops.

In the ninth volume of Somers Tracts. " It was too much to expect that all the oppressed dissenters could be won by the reasoning o of Halifax and Burnet. Many there doubtless were who, like the author of this Tract, saw, or wished to see, nothing in the present national crisis, save the exaltation of dissenters of every description over their old enemies of the church of England." Here it will not be out of place to notice The Protestant Reconciler, by Daniel Whitby, 1683, whose "piety, learning, and extensive charity will not be disputed, but his judgment, sagacity, and reasoning powers do not appear to have borne a due proportion to his extensive acquirements." (Note in The Diary and Correspondence of Dr. Worthington, vol. ii. part i. p. 202.) What a violent storm this performance drew upon its author will be seen in Biog. Brit. and Chalmers.

J An Answer to a Paper importing a Petition of the Archbishop of Canterbury and six other Bishops to his Majesty touching their not distributing and publishing the late Declaration for Liberty of Conscience. 4to Lond. 1688

In the ninth volume of Somers Tracts, pp. 119-31. "The bishops had no sooner taken their ground in direct opposition to James's measures, than pamphlets and libels of every description were published against them with unreserved hostility, under the authority of government. They had sedulously avoided the appearance of giving publicity to their petition; but that to which they themselves seemed decently averse, was privately managed by others, for the petition was scarce presented before it got into print, and was dispersed over the whole Kingdom by the clergy instead of the Declaration of Indulgence. The King therefore resolved no longer to keep terms with the church of England but to publish the petition in his own way, and with his own comments. Accordingly the following piece which appears to have been printed by authority, is a sort of casting the gauntlet by the crown to the church." It is inserted, with some Proceedings thereupon, in the first volume of Gutch's Collect. Cur. pp. 335-62. The calumny insinuated in this "Answer" (p. 122) in the Life of James II. vol. ii. p. 158, and Macpherson's Original Papers, vol. i. p. 151, is refuted by Mackintosh, p. 248.

An Address to his Grace the Lord Abp. of Cant. and the Right Rev. the Bps upon account of their late Petition by a true Member of the Church of England. 4to Lond. 1688.

Some Queries to the Archbishop of Canterbury and to the Six other Bishops concerning the English Reformation and the 39 Articles of the Church of England. By P. M. D.D.
4to Lond. 1688 I suppose P. M. D. D. means Peter Manby, Dean of Deny. Cf. The Rubric of the Common Prayer declared by the Act of Uniformity to be a part of that statute which directs that nothing shall be published in church by the minister, but what is prescribed by this book, or enjoined by the King. i The Examination of the Bishops upon their refusal of reading his M ajesty's most gracious Declaration; and the Nonconcurrence of the Church of England in Repeal of the Penal Laws and Test fully debated and argued. 4to Lond. 1688.
In the ninth volume of Somers Tracts, pp. 134-51, and Fourth Collection, vol. ii. pp. 222-43. After having traced the progress of the penal laws and the test, the author remarks: — "Jealous as the founders of that test were (or pretended to be) of the danger of popery, they very well knew the church of England had two impreg« nable bulwarks, the two great acts of Uniformity, that themselves sufficiently alone established, guarded and preserved the church of England in all points without any fortification from the test, nor indeed was the test wanted in the ecclesiastic administration, those very statutes being a greater and stronger test before: for by those statutes is the whole liturgy, the administration of the sacraments, and indeed all the canons and articles of the church supported. For by the fence of those laws first no Romanist can possibly be admitted into the clergy Secondly, no other divine service as the mass or the like can be introduced into our churches already constituted or assigned for the divine service of the church of England." Our author's memory must have failed him, when he asks — " Wherein and what have our churchmen or our non-dispensing churchmen suffered by all this toleration? Have they lost the least particle of their government, discipline, rights, privileges, or professions whatever?" p. 150. "Doubtless," observes Hallam, "the administration of James II. was not of this nature (an extreme case of intolerable tyranny.) Doubtless he was not a Caligula, or a Commodus, or an Ezzelin, or a Galcazzo Sforza, or a Christiern II. of Denmark, or a Charles IX. of France, or one of those almost innumerable tyrants whom men have endured in the wantonness of unlimited power. No man had been deprived of his liberty by any illegal warrant. No man, *except in the single though very important instance of Magdalen College,* had been despoiled of his property. " The Constitutional History of England. vol. ii. p. 242.

Melius Inquirendum, or an impartial Enquiry into the late proceedings against the Seven Bishops, wherein the King's Supremacy is vindicated. By W. E. 4to Lond. 1688

Compare Buckle's History of Civilization in England, p. 367.

Ten Modest Queries humbly offered to the most serious consideration of the Right Reverend Father in God, Thomas Lord Bishop of St. Davids, and that they may be communicated to the rest of the Clergy at his Primary Visitation now held for that Diocese. By a true and sincere Member of the Church of England, and a wellwisher to his Lordship in all things that are good and honest. pp. 4.

Has reference to his reading the Declaration. Thomas Watson appointed 1687 and deprived for simony, May 1699, is here intended. " He was one of the worst men in all respects, that ever I knew in Holy Orders: passionate, covetous, and false in the blackest instances, without any one vertue or good quality, to balance his many bad ones. But as he was advanced by King James, so he stuck firm to that Interest; and the Party, tho' ashamed of him, yet were resolved to support him, with great zeal: he appealed to a Court of Delegates; and they about the end of the year confirmed the Archbishop's sentence." — Burnet's History.

Among tho various localities from which addresses " steamed up to the Throne" on this occasion (see Ralph, Mackintosh, and the Somers Tracts), Chester may be mentioned as very conspicuous for its adulation and servility. In the Political History of the City of Chester, the Charter of King Henry VII. &c., Chester, 1814, there is a circumstantial account of the preparations made by that corporation during the royal progress of James II. in 1CH7, with the address presented by the dissenters. " The Corporation," said the recorder Levinz, " is your

Majesty's creature, and depends merely on the will of its creator, and the sole intimation of your Majesty's pleasure shall ever have with us the force of a fundamental law." Cf. Ormerod's History of the

County Palatine and City of Chester, vol. i. p. 211. Nor in the diocese of Bishop Cartwright (of whose character see p. 27 *supra*)

were obedient clergymen wanting to acknowledge the King's supremacy, and their duty to publish in their churches whatever was enjoined by the King or by their Bishop. See Echard, vol. iii. p. 876. "James thought himself secure of the Tories, because they professed to consider all resistance as sinful — and of the Protestant

Dissenters, because he offered them relief. He was in the wrong as to both. The error into which he fell about the Dissenters was very natural. But the confidence which he placed in the loyal assurances of the High Church party was the most exquisitely ludicrous proof of folly that a politician ever gave." Macaulay's Review of Sir James

Mackintosh's History of the Revolution.

Parliamentum Pacificum: or, The Happy Union of King and Peo-C 1» ple in an Healing Parliament: heartily wish't for and humbly recommended, by a true Protestant and no Dissenter. 4to Lond. 1688 This tract contains severe animadversions on Pensioner Fagel and

Dr. Burnet.

A Letter of several French Ministers fled into Germany upon the account of the Persecution in France, to such of their Brethren in England as approved the King's Declaration touching Liberty of Conscience. pp. 7, 4to Lond. 1688

CHAP. V.

Of the Discourses ivritten in the representing controversy. 51. *k* A papist misrepresented and represented, or a twofold character of popery. The one containing a sum of the superstitions, idolatries, cruelties, treacheries, and wicked principles of that popery which hath disturhed this nation above 150 years; filled it with fears and jealousies, and deserves the hatred of all good christians. The other laying open that popery which the papists own and profess; with the chief articles of their faith, and some of the principal grounds and reasons which hold them in that religion. Narraverunt mihi iniqui fabulationes: sed non ut lex tua. Psal. 119 sic v. 85. By J

L, pp. 128 and R. C. Principles, pp. 1-8, s.l. 4to 1685.

To which is annexed, Roman-catholic principles, in reference to God and the King. And note, there are two more parts of this book. See Nos. 63, 72, *infra*. And four defences of this part. See Nos. 53, 56, 58, 60, *infra*.

Dodd attributes this book to John Gother, or Goter. I suppose the initial letters stand for Joannes Lisboensis. " John Goter: born in Southampton, educated a member of the church of England compare the Introduction to No. 51, p. xi. but afterwards becoming a catholick was sent over to the English College at Lisboe; where he was ordained priest and returned back into England upon the mission. He resided for the greatest part of his time in London; aud appeared at the head of the controversial writers, all king James Second's reign." vol. iii. p. 482. The date 1665 found in some copies was probably intended to mislead his adversaries, because, as Dr. Todd observes, the author says expressly in the Pref. to part iii. (No. 72 *infra*) that the work was not published until 1685: "This book was not publish'd till after the adjourning of the first sitting of Parliament 1685, and at the opening of that Parliament the assault was given by Dr. Sherlock in his Sermon before the two Houses," (sheet a, p. 8.) " Gother's work has always continued to be in great repute among Papists. It was republished in an abridged and expurgated form by their great champion Bishop Challoner, who was Vicar Apostolic of the London district from 1741 to 1780. It has often been reprinted since, and the twenty-eighth edition was published at London in 1832." Cunningham's Preface, etc. *ut infra*.

On the tract, Roman Catholic Principles, see page 6, *supra*.

The declaration of indulgence was both preceded and followed by one of the most fierce polemical controversies between Romanists and Protestants which ever agitated England. Burnet, who was deeply engaged in it, gives the following account of the manner in which it was carried on by the church of England: " Many of the clergy acted now a part that made good amends for past errors. They began to preach generally against popery, which the dissenters did not. They set themselves to study the points of controversy; and, upon that, there followed a great variety of small books that were easily purchased and soon read. They examined all the points of popery with a solidity of judgment, a clearness of arguing, a depth of learning, and a vivacity of writing, far beyond anything that had before that time appeared in our language. The truth is, they were very unequally yoked; for, if they are justly to be reckoned among the best writers that have yet appeared on the protestant side, those they wrote against were certainly among the weakest that had ever appeared on the popish side. Their books were poorly, but insolently writ, and had no other learning in them but what was taken out of some French writers which they put into very bad English; so that a victory over them might have been but a mean performance.

" This had a mighty effect on the whole nation; even those who could not search things to the bottom, yet were amazed at the great inequality that appeared in this engagement. The papists who knew what service the Bishop of Meaux's book had done in France, resolved to pursue the same method here, in several treatises, which they entitled, ' Papists Represented and Misrepresented;' to which such clear answers were writ, that what effect soever that artifice might have where it was supported by the authority of a great king, and the teiTor of ill usage and a dragoonade in conclusion, yet it succeeded so ill in England, that it gave occasion to enquire into the true opinions of that church, not as some artful writers had disguised them, but as they are laid down in the books that are of authority among them, such as the decisions of council received among them and their established offices, and as they are held at Rome, and in all those countries where popery prevails without any intermixture with hereticks, or apprehension of them, as in Spain and Portugal. This was done in so authentical a manner, that popery itself was never so well understood by the nation as it came to be upon this occasion. The persons who managed and directed this controversial war were chiefly Tillotson, Stillingfleet, Tennison, and Patrick; next them were Sherlock, Williams, Claget, Gee, Aldrich, Atterbury, Whitby, Hooper; and, above all these, Wake, who, having been long in France chaplain to the Lord Preston, brought over with him many curious discoveries that were both useful and surprising. Besides the chief writers of those books of controversy, there were many sermons preached and printed on those heads that did very much edify the whole nation. And this matter was managed with that concert, that, for the most part once a week, some new book or sermon came out which both instructed and amused those who read them." Fol. 1724, p. 673-4. See Cat. 4. Contin. p. 10.

C IL. 52. The doctrines and practices of the church of Rome truly represented, in answer to a book intitled a papist misrepresented and represented. By Edward Stillingfleet, D.D. Works, fol. vol. vi. (Gibson, vol. xvi. fol. iii.) pp. 164, 4to Lond. 1686 See Cat. No. 17. Contin. p. 10. Fasti Oxon. vol. ii. col. 118. Reprinted, with a preface and notes, by William Cunningham, D.D., Professor of Divinity and Church History, New College, Edinburgh. A new edition, revised. Edinburgh, 1845.

Cl« 53. Reflections upon the answer to the papist misrepresented; directed to the answerer. pp. 119, 4to, sans date

See State, p. 11 Contin. p. 10. The Bodl. Cat. gives the date and imprint. Lond. 1686.

C H. 54. A papist not misrepresented by protestants; being a reply to the reflections upon the answer to a papist not misrepresented and represented. By William Sherlock, DD.

See Cat. No. 18. State, p. 11. Contin. p. 10. Born about 1601, died 1707. "While sermons in defence of the Roman Catholic religion were preached on every Sunday and holiday within the precincts of the royal palaces, the church of the state, the church of the great majority of the nation, was forbidden to explain and vindicate her own principles. The spirit of the whole clerical order rose against this injustice. William Sherlock, a divine of distinguished abilities, who had written with sharpness against Whigs and Dissenters, and had been rewarded by the government with the Mastership of the Temple and with a pension, was one of the first who incurred the royal displeasure. His pension was stopped, and he was severely reprimanded." — Macaulay.

55. Remarks upon the reflections of the Author of Popery Misre-C H. presented &c. on his Answerer; particularly as to the Deposing doctrine. In a letter to the Author of the Reflections. Together with some few Animadversions on the same Author's Vindication of his Reflections. pp. 68, 4to 1686

See Cat. No. 19. Ath. Oxon. vol. ii. p. 1000. Edit. Bliss, vol. iv. col. 563. This book is anon., but was written by Abednego Seller, rector of Combeintinhead, Devon. Neither Gee nor Peck appear ever to have seen this work, for both give the title incorrectly, Peck copying from Gee, who calls the author Mr. A. Seller " of Plymouth," whence Peck styles him " minister of Plymouth. " The title is correctly given above. This book is an answer to the Reflections (No. 53) and to the Vindication of the Reflections (No. 56.) J. H. T.

56. »I Papists protesting against Protestant-Popery. In answer to C fL, a Discourse intitled, A Papist not Misrepresented by Protestants, being a Vindication of the Papist Misrepresented and Represented, and the Reflexions upon the Answer. Anon.

By the Author of No. 51. pp. 38, 4to Lond. 1686

See State, p. 11. Contin. p. 10. Gee and Peck not having seen this tract, or the former, have given the title in an abridged form, and

Peck has placed it after instead of before 55, not knowing that 55

was a reply to it. J. H. T.

p d,i, 57. An answer to a Discourse intitled, Papists protesting against Protestant-Popery; being a vindication of Papists not Misrepresented by Protestants; and containing a particular examination of Mons. de Meaux late Bp. of

Condom his exposition of the doctrine of the church of Rome, in the articles of invocation of saints and the worship of images, occasioned by that discourse. By William Sherlock, D.D. pp. 131.4to Lond. 1686 See Cat. No. 20. State, p. 11. Contin. p. 10.

C %. 58. 5 An amicable accommodation of the difference between the misrepresenter and the answerer; in return to the last reply against the papist protesting against protestant popery. Permissu Superiorum. By the Author of No. 51. pp. 40, 4to Lond. 1686

C3L. 59. An answer to the amicable accommodation of the difference between the representer and the answerer. By.William Sherlock, D.D. pp. 31, 4to Lond. 1686

See Cat. No. 21. State, p. 12. Contin. p. 10.

C 1L. 60. "i A reply to the answer of the amicable accommodation, being a fourth vindication of the first part of the Papist misrepresented and represented; in which are more particularly laid open some of the principal methods by which the Papists are misrepresented by Protestants in their books and sermons. By the Author of No. 51. pp. 46, 4to Lond. 1686

See State, p. 12. Contin. p. 10.

61. A view of the whole controversy between the representer aud the answerer, with an answer to the representees last reply; in which are laid open some of the methods by which protestants are misrepresented by papists. By William Claget. pp. 123, 4to Lond. 1687 See Cat. No. 22. State, p. 12. Contin. p. 10. Ath. Oxon. vol. ii. col. 327. Edit. Bliss, vol. iii. col. 040. 62. A catechism, truly representing the doctrines and practices of CIL the church of Rome. With an answer thereunto. By John Williams, M.A. The second edition corrected. With a Vindication of a passage in the said catechism from the exceptions made against it, in a reply to the answer of the amicahle accommodation. pp. 82, 8vo 1687

See Cat. No. 23. State, p. 30. Ath. Oxon. vol. ii. p. 1119.

Edit. Bliss, vol. Iv. col. 769.

63. i The catholic representor, or the papist misrepresented and represented. Part II. published weekly in 16 single sheets,

with a title and contents. By the Author of No. 51. Fifteen parts. pp. 88, 4to Lond. 1687

This came out in weekly parts, each part called a chapter. Chaps, i.—vi. are in single sheets of eight pages each. Chaps, viii.—xvi. are in half sheets. A titlepage and table of contents 4 pp. were added.
J. H. T.

64. The papist represented and not misrepresented; being an CD..1L. answer to the first sheet of the second part of the papist misrepresented and represented; and for the farther vindication of the catechism truly representing the doctrines and practices of the church of Rome..By John Williams, M.A. pp 14, 4to Lond. 1687

See Cat. No. 24. State, p. 31. Ath. Oxon. vol. ii. p. 1121.

Edit. Bliss, vol. iv. col. 769.

65 The papist represented and not misrepresented; being in answer C. IL. to the second sheet of the second part of the papist misrepresented and represented. in the point of their praying to the cross, and for a further vindication of the catechism truly representing the doctrines and practices of the church of Rcme. By John Williams, M.A. pp. 14, 4to 1687

See Cat. No. 25. State, p. 31. Ath. Oxon. vol. ii. col. 1119.

It is curious that Wood, although he gives Nos. 04 and 69, in his list of John Williams's works, omits No. 65. This must have been a

mere oversight; but Dr. Bliss has not supplied the defect. The clause in brackets in the title as above has been omitted by Gee and Peck. It is added here from the original. J. H. T. t. 1L 66. Transubstantiaticm no doctrine of the primitive fathers, being a defence of the Dublin letter herein against the papist misrepresented and represented, Part II. cap. 3. By John Patrick, M.A. preacher at the Charterhouse. pp. 72, 4to Lond. 1687

See.Cat. No. 26. Contin. p. 22 and p. 70.

I cannot find any copy of " the Dublin letter," nor can I tell who was its author. Dr. Wake, Contin. (p. 22) says, " The next that gave occasion to the revival of this controversy" i.e. the next after the author of a Discourse of Transubstantiation (Tillotson, 1685), see No. 125 "was the author of the Dublin Letter, who being answered by the Representer in his second part, cap. 3, a learned man of our communion viz. John Patrick made good his party in an excellent discourse," &c. The Representer (loc. cit.) quotes what these authors call "the Dublin letter," under the title of " The Papists doctrine of Transubstantiation not agreeable to the Primitive Fathers." But I can find no title answering to this title in the Catal. of the Dublin Univ. or of the Bodl. Libraries; nor does it appear in Abp. Marsh's Library, or in the large collection of these tracts in the Library of Christ Church Cathedral, Dublin. J. H. T. t. 3L 67. Wholesome advices from the blessed Virgin to her indiscreet worshippers. Written by one of the Roman Communion, and done out of the French into English, by a Gentleman of the Church of England, with a Preface shewing the Motives to the Translation. Anon. By James Taylor, Gent. pp. 20, 4to Lond. 1687 See Cat. No. 27. State, p. 27. Contin. p. 53.

This tract is by Mr. Adam Widenfelt, "a person of high employment under the Prince of Suarzcmburgh." (Translator's Pref.) It is alluded to, and the Preface attacked, by the Representer (No. 63) part ii. cap. 4, p. 29, and therefore comes into this controversy, as its object was to shew that authors of the Romish Communion made the same repre sentation of abuses of which Protestants complain. Taylor is the translator of the book and the author of the Preface. J. H. T.

The original work is mentioned in " A Catalogue of Books exclusively relating to the Church of Home: her doctrines, worship, discipline, controversies and annals; including the Histories of her various

Religious Orders; their peculiar Missals, Breviaries, &c.: the Tracts published during the reign of James II.; and a set of Canonizations from 1800 to the present time. On sale by Howell and

Co., 295, Holborn, London, 1829."

" Widenfeldt, Avis Salutaires de la bienheureuse Vierge Marie a ses Devote Indiscrete, fidelement traduit en Francois, avec le Latin ensuite (par Gerberon) a Lille 1674. Monita vere salularia Marise Reginffi Sanctorum omnium, authore Cremerio, Antverpise 1764. Lettre Pastorale de M. l'Evesque de Tournay aux Fidelles de son Diocese sur le Culte de la tres Saincte Vierge et des Saincts, a Lille 1674, &c. &c. The curious work which forms the first in the above Collection is an attack on the worship of the Virgin, in which the author puts into her mouth, that she detests the worship because God alone ought to be honoured and loved. It created a great noise at the time of its publication, and was the cause of no less than forty-seven writings being published on both sides of the question. Its end however was being strictly prohibited, first by the Inquisition and then at Rome. The two next in the volume were published in favour of it." 68. A Letter to the Misrepresenter of Papists. Being a Vindica-CIL. tion of that part of the Protestant Preface to the Wholesome Advices from the blessed Virgin &c. which concerns the Protestants' charity to Papists, and a Layman's writing in it. In answer to what is objected against it in the 4th Chapter of the second part of the Papist Misrepresented &c. By the same Layman i.e. James Taylor who translated the Wholesome Advices &c., and made the Preface to them.

pp. 16, 4to Lond. 1687 See Cat. No. 28. State, p. 28. Contin. p. 53. It seems as if Dr. Clagett, State, p. 28, imagined this tract to have been written by the Representer, and written on the popish side; but this error Dr. Wake corrects. Contin. p. 53. J. H. T. CIL. 69. The Papist represented and not misrepresented, being an answer to the fifth and sixth chapters of the second part of the Papist misrepresented and represented, as far as concerns praying to images and the cross. And for a further vindication of the Catechism truly representing the Doctrines and Practices of the Church of Rome. Anon. By John Williams, M.A. pp. 14, 4to Lond. 1687 See Cat. No. 29. State, p. 31. Ath. Oxon. vol. ii. col. 1121. Bliss, vol. iv. col. 771.

C/1L 70. The peoples right to read the Holy Scripture asserted. In answer to the 6th, 7th, 8th, 9th and 10th chapters of the second part of the Popish Representer. Anon. By Nicholas Stratford D. D. afterwards Bishop of Chester pp. 88, 4to Lond 1687 See Cat. No. 30. Contin. p. 39. Ath. Oxon. vol. ii. col. 1067. Born 1633, died 1707. From the year 1667 to 1683 he was Warden of Manchester. " August 29th (Thursday) Mr. Stratford, the new Warden, was this day installed. A stranger, unthought of, unknown of, unsought for; and of all that we thought of, none so likely to he a mercy to this place. A good man, of a sweet temper, hrave scholar and preacher; and one that hath an estate of his own, and seems to resolve to settle in the place and to reside. This we thought then; and then, it was so." — Autohiography of Henry Newcome, vol. i., printed for the Chetham Society, 1852.

ClL. 71. The present State of the controversie between the Church of England and the Church of Rome; or an account of the books written on both sides. In a letter to a friend. Imprimatur. Guil. Needham, May 7, 1686. (Anon.) By William Clagett, DD. pp. 36, 4to Loud. 1687

See Contin. vol. i. pp. 10, 11. Ath. Oxon. vol. ii. p. 327.

The state of the controversy on the Popish side will be found in the Preface to the Reply to the defence of the exposition of the doctrine of the Church of England No. 79 infra. J. H. T.

72. The Papist misrepresented and represented; with a Preface, containing reflections upon two treatises, the one the State No. 71 the other the View No. 61 of the Controversie between the Representer and the Answerer. Third Part. Published with allowance. By the author of No. 51. pp. 63 (inch Index), 4to Lond. 1687 See Nos. 61, 71 supra, and No. 82 infra.

See Postscript, being a full answer to a Pamphlet published last night, called, " A third part of a Papist Misrepresented," at the end of a second Defence of the Exposition of the doctrine of the Church of England (No. 80 infra). J. H. T.

An answer to the eighth chapter of the Representer's second part, in the first dialogue between him and his Lay-friend. Licensed, March 1, 1686. Anon. By James Taylor.

pp. 10, 4to Lond. 1687 This tract is on the same subject as No. 70, viz. the right of the Laity to read the Scripture. But it is not mentioned by Gee or Peck. J. H. T. CHAP. VI. *Of the Discourses in the expounding controversy.*

C i. 73. x An Exposition of the doctrine of the Catholic Church in matters of controversie. By the Right Reverend James Benigne Bossuet, Counsellor to the King, Bishop of Meaux, formerly of Condom, and Preceptor to the Dauphin; first Almoner to the Dauphiness. Done into English from the 5th edition in French, by Joseph Johnston, O.S.B. pp. 48, Advertis. pp. 22, 4to Lond. 1685 The Advertisement prefixed to this work is hy Bossuet himself. It was first printed with the French edit of 1679. We learn from it that two answers had at that time appeared in France; one anonymous (by M. De la Bastide) approved by the ministers of Charenton; the other by M. Nougier, vol. xviii. CEuvres de Bossuet, Versailles, 1816. The Exposition is followed by a " Remarque," intended as an answer to the accusation (made by Dr. Wake, in *fiie* Pref. to his answer — see No. 74) of having suppressed the first edition, and materially altered several passages in it. This is followed by some letters relative to the Exposition. And these by " Fragmens sur diverses matieres de controverse, pour servir de reponse aux ecrits faits par plusieurs ministres, contre le livre de l'Exposition de la Doctrine Catholique."

The Bodl. Cat. attributes this translation to John Dryden; and the Hist de Bossuet says that it was translated into English by the Abbé de Montaigne in 1672 (vol. i. p. 280, note.)

The first French edit. Paris (Chamoisy), 1671, 12mo., consisted of about twelve copies only, privately printed, and sent by the author to some friends, whom he requested to return them with their remarks. It is supposed that not more than three or four copies of this edit, remain. Another, which is the first *published* edit., was printed in December of the same year 1671 in 12-mo., also printed by Chamoisy in Paris, pp. 189, and it is said there was a second issue in the same month, which differed in some respects from the former (Hist. de

Bossuet, vol. i. p. 278). See the Pieces Justificatives, ibid. p. 467.
The Exposition was translated into Latin by Fleury, Hist, de Bossuet (vol. i. p. 289.) Cardinal dc Bausset, author of the Hist de Bossuet (vol. i. p. 280 note) says that it was translated into Irish by Father Porter O.S.F. superior of the Convent of S. Isidore at Rome, which translation was printed at Rome 1675 at the press of the Propaganda,

a high sanction to the work. It was also translated into Italian, and printed at the same press. I have not seen either of theso versions.

Twelve editions of the Exposition were published in French during the lifetime of Bossuet. But the sixth, issued in 1686, was the last which he himself corrected, and all subsequent editions were reprints of this. (Hist de Bossuet, vol. i. p. 291, note.)

See State, p. 14, 15-18, where a particular account is given of the occasion for which this book was written. Contin. p. 12. J. H. T.

It is extracted below. In Howell's Catalogue, already mentioned, it is stated that in an 8vo edit. 1685, there is "prefixed a very entertaining history of this famous work by the translator." 74. An exposition of the doctrine of the Church of England in the C&, several articles proposed by Mods, de Meaux, late Bishop of Condom, in his Exposition of the doctrine of the Catholic Church. To which is prefix'd a particular account of Monsieur de Meaux's book. The 3rd edit. Anon. By Wm. Wake, M.A. pp. 87, and Pref. pp. xxxviii. 4to Lond. 1687

See Cat. No. 39. State, p. 15. Contin. p. 13. Ath. Oxon. vol. ii. p. 1059. And No. 22 *tupra*, note.

75. "i« A vindication of the Bp. of Condom's Exposition of the C 3L, doctrine of the Catholic Church. In answer to a book, entituled An Exposition of the doctrine of the Church of England, etc. With a letter from the said Bishop. *Permissu superiorum.* pp. 222, with Contents and Henry Hill's Catal. of books, pp. 4. 4to Lond. 1686

See Contin. p. 16. This is no doubt by Jos. Johnston, an English
Benedictine, of the King's Chapel, who is the translator of the Exposition. The letter from Bossnet which is appended to it was addressed to J. Shirburne, superior of the English Benedictines, who had written to Bossuet, enclosing a letter from Johnston, which asked for information to enable him to reply to Wake and others. The whole correspondence is given in the Versailles edit. of Bossuet's works, vol. xviii. p. 169. J. H. T.

C1L. 76. *t* A pastoral letter from the Lord Bishop of Meaux to the new Catholies of his Diocese, exhorting them to keep their Easter, and giving them necessary advertisements against the false Pastoral Letters of their Ministers. With reflections upon the pretended persecution. Translated out of French, and published with allowance. pp. 37, 4to Lond. 1686

See Contin. p. 16. CEuvres de Bossuet, Versailles 1817, tome xxv. A Paris 1748, tome v. This was probably translated by the Benedictine Jos. Johnston. J. H. T.

C1L. 77. An answer to the Bishop of Condom (now of Meaux) his Exposition of the Catholick Faith &c. Wherein the doctrine of the Church of Rome is detected, and that of the Church of England expressed from the publick acts of both Churches. To which are added reflections on his Pastoral Letter. Anon. By John Gilbert M.A. Vicar of S. John Baptist's Church in Peterborough. pp. 128, Pref. iv., 4to Lond. 1686

See Cat. No. 40. State, p. 14. Contin. p. 13. Ath. Oxon. vol. ii. col. 1132. Fasti Oxon. vol. ii. col. 213. An advertisement prefixed to this work states that it was laid by as useless when Wake's answer (No. 78) appeared — the imprimatur of Wake's book is March 1, 1685-6, that of Gilbert's is June 4, 1686, — "till upon an after view it was thought it might be serviceable; because of a more particular explication of the Church of England's sentiments in it, and likewise of a more full expression of the Romish doctrines from the publick acts of that Church, and its direct answering M. Condom's reasons, which the other author" viz. Wake " does not propose to himself." J. H. T.

78. A defence of the exposition of the doctrine of the Church of & 2,.

England against the exceptions of Monsieur de Meaux, late
Bishop of Condom, and his Vindicator. The contents are on the next leaf. Anon. By Will. Wake MA. (Gibson, vol. xii. fol. iii.) pp. 166 and errata 2 pp. , 4to Lond. 1686

See Cat. No. 41. State, p. 19. Contin. p. 13. Ath. Oxon.

vol. ii. col. 1059. The Appendix, p. 105, to this work contains some valuable pieces, on the question of idolatry, and particularly an account of the suppressed sheets of the Epistle of St. Chrysostom to Csesarius,

cut out of M. Bigot's edit. of Palladius. Paris 1680.— This book was published a couple of months before No. 77, and ought to have been placed before it. J. H. T.

79. A reply to the defence of the exposition of the doctrine of £. 3L.
the Church of England; being a further vindication of the
Bishop of Condom's exposition of the doctrine of the Catholic
Church. With a second letter of the Bishop of Meaux. *Permissu Superiorum.* pp. 190, with Pref. and catal. of Authors
(at the beginning of the book) pp. 30, and at the end, Index pp. 6. 4to, Lond. 1G87

It is probable that this book is also by Johnston, the translator of the Exposition; but the letter from Bossuet, annexed to it, does not occur in the correspondence appended to the Exposition in the Versailles edit, of his works, vol. xviii., already referred to. J. H. T.

80. A second defence of the exposition of the doctrine of the Church of England against the new exceptions of Monsieur de Meaux, late Bishop of Condom, and his vindicator. The first part. In which the account which has been given of the Bishop of Meaux's Exposition, is fully vindicated; the distinction of old and new Popery historically asserted; and the doctrine of the Church of Rome in point of Image-worship more particularly consider'd. Anon. By Will. Wake. (Gibson, vols. xii. and xiii. fol. iii.) pp. 100, with Postscript, pp. 2, being a full answer to a pamphlet published the last night, called A third part of a Papist misrepresented, and Table pp. 8, 4to Lond. 1687

See Cat. No. 42. Contin. pp. 14, 15. Section iii. (p. 94) of this tract contains a list of the books published in this controversy on the Protestant side which had not been answered by the Papists. J. H. T.

C1L. 81. A full answer to the second defence of the exposition of the doctrine of the Church of England, in a letter to the defender. pp. 12, a sheet and a half.

See Contin. p. 15. This is also probably by J. Johnston. In answer to the list of books on the Protestant side remaining unanswered this author says (p. 12), "Your third section is taken up by giving us a Catalogue of books *unanswered;* but you should first have told us whether they were worth answering in particular or no, when all that is said in them is obviated in many Treatises. There are several also of ours that remain ttwanswered; the Guide in Controversie see Nos. 189 — 193 incl. especially, which for anything that I see must remain so, unless some such bold attempter attack them as attack'd the other Discourses see No. 167 of the same author lately published at Oxford, with the like misfortune." J. H. T.

£. IL 82. An answer to the Representees reflections upon the State and View of the Controversy. With a reply to the Vindicator's full answer; shewing that the Vindicator of the Bishop of Meaux has utterly ruined the *new* design of expounding and representing popery. Anon. By Nicholas Claget, M.A. pp. 130, with Pref. and Contents 8 pp., and Rich. Chiswell's list of books at the end, 2 pp. 4to Lond. 1680

See Cat. No. 43. Contin. pp. 11, 12. Ath. Oxon. vol. ii. col. 327. Dr. Bandinel's Bodl. Catal. attributes this book as well as No. 6 to Nicholas Clagett, D.D. of Christ's Coll. Camb., archdeacon of Sudbury; but Abp. Wake (Contin. p. 12) a contemporary, one engaged in the same controversy, and the intimate friend of Wm. Clagett, could scarcely have been misinformed; and he clearly attributes this to the Dr. Clagett who died in the beginning of 1688. J. H. T.

83. A second defence of the Exposition of the doctrine of the C H.

Church of England against the new exceptions of Monsieur de

Meaux and his Vindicator. The second Part. Anon. By

Wm. Wake, M.A. pp. 198, and Rich. Chiswell's list of hooks, 2 pp. (Gibson, vol. xiii. fol. iii.) 4to Lond. 1688

See Cat. No. 44. Contin. p. 15. Ath. Oxon. vol. ii. col. 1059.

See Part i. No. 80 *supra.* Wake (Contin. loc. sit.) gives the following summary of this second part, which Gee and Peck have copied as if it was on the title-page. Part ii. In which the Romish doctrines concerning the nature and object of religious worship of images and reliques are consider'd, and the charge of Idolatry made good against those of the Church of Home upon the account of them. J. H. T.

84. See also, An Answer to the Bp. of Condom's book, intitled an

Exposition of the doctrine of the catholic church upon matters of controversy. Written in French, and translated into

English by Joseph Walker, and by him dedicated to Michael,

Lord Archbishop of Dublin. 12mo Dublin, 1676

The Canons and Decrees of the Council of Trent, celebrated C1L. under Paul III., Julius III., and Pius IV., Bishops of Rome. Faithfully translated into English. With a list of the names, sirnames, countries and dignities of the Legates. 4to Lond. 1687 " There is much artifice in the general list, subjoined to the editions of the Canons and Decrees of the Council, of the Prelates and others who attended it. The last column designates the country of each.

That of Italy is subdivided into almost the minutest portions imaginable; evidently for no other purpose than to disguise the disproportionate and extravagant superiority in number of the Italians. —

Mendham's Memoirs of the Council of Trent. Lond. 1834.

Another translation. The Canons and Decrees of the Council of

Trent. With a Supplement, containing the condemnations

of the early Reformers, and other matter relating to the Council; literally translated into English, hy T. A. Buckley, B.A. Sm. 8vo Lond. 1851

" I will not," says Bossuet, "meddle with any thing but the Decrees of the Council of Trent, because in them the Church has given her decision upon these matters now in agitation." See No. 97, *infra.* (JT.1L. Two short discourses against the Romanists. 1. An account of the fundamental principle of popery, and of the insufficiency of the proofs which they have for it. 2. An answer to six queries proposed to a gentlewoman of the Church of England, by an emissary of the Church of Rome. With a new preface particularly relating to the Bp. of Meaux and other modern complainers of misrepresentation. By Henry Dodwell, M.A. late of Trinity College, near Dubliu, now Camden professor of Oxford. pp. 32, pref. xii. 4to Lond. 1688

On the fundamental principle of popery, as to which there can be "no pretence of misrepresentation, and on which depend all other disputes betwixt the Romanists and the other Communions of Christendom," see Chaps, xvii. and xix.

" You must understand that the project of Converting the FrenchProtestants, which has been more or less carried on ever since Henry the Fourth's time, was more especially agitated at the conclusion of the Pyrenean Treaty almost 30 years since; the Spaniards being apprehensive of the French Power, and willing to divert it by an undertaking, which they thought might find them work at home, and not leave them at leisure to disturb their neighbours. It was resolved then at the same time that the Civil Power began to oppress them, the Church should offer some Terms of a Reunion to them, and all possible endeavours be used to encline them to accept it: to this end Money was secretly given to several of the Ministers, to favour this project: but the design being discover'd by a Minister of BasLangue'doc, the Synod of Nismes, Ann. 1662, and that of Cevennes being assembled not long after, appear'd so vigorously against it, that they were forc'd to lay aside the design for some time. About ten years after it broke out again, but the Ministers of Languedoc and the

Synod of the Isle of France opposing it, as those of Nismes and

Cevennes had done before, it came to nothing.

" Now this second attempt was dated precisely at the same time that the Bishop of Condom's Exposition began to see the light: and that which convinces me that it was purposely contriv'd for the advancing this design is this, that the Marshal de Turenne, who was this Bishop's Convert, and the principal Defender of this Exposition, was also at the same time the great Undertaker for this project. Tis well known how to this end he sent a Person through the several Provinces of France, with private Instructions to those Ministers, which he thought he could most influence to close with it: and in effect he did obtain several of their Subscriptions, whom when the Protestant Synods would afterwards have censur'd for their so doing, the Kings Commissioners took their parts, and would not suffer them to do it." The Present State of the Controversie etc. by Will. Clagett, D.D. pp. 15-17.

Preservatif contre le changement de Religion, ou Idee juste et veritable de la Religion Catholique Romaine, opposee au portraits flatez que l'on en fait, et particulierement a celui de Monsieur de Condom, 1682. Suite de Preservatif, ou Reflexions sur l'adoucissement propose par M. Brueys, Advocat de Montpellier, 1683, par Pierre Jurieu, La Haye.

It is observed by Jurieu in the latter work: " Bossuet's Exposition was condemned by some in his own churchand Father Maimbourg 6aid of Bossuet's work, " Has the church required him to make an Exposition of her doctrines?" Jurieu's Pastoral Letters, Rotterdam 1686-89, the first volume of which was translated, Lond. 1689, were intended to furnish arguments against the publications of Bossuet, Brueys and other defenders of the persecution. Bayle's " Commentaire Philosophique" upon those words of Scripture, " Compel them to come in," was written by way of reflection upon the compulsory conversions effected in France. See also his Dict., art. Ferrier.

A Preservative against the change of Religion, &c., translated out of the French Original by Claudius Gilbert, T. B. and Minister of Belfast. Lond. 1683 An Examination of the Reasons which have occasioned the Separation of Protestants. By M. de Brueys. 16S3 De Brueys was born of Protestant parents, and in 1682 published an answer to Bossuet's Exposition of the Doctrine of the Church, but afterwards became a convert and cast himself at the feet of the author, whose doctrine he had attacked. In Traite de l'Obeissance des Chretiennes aux Puissances tetnporelles, Montpellier, 1709, he attacked Professor Noodt's eloquent discourses on Sovereign Power and Liberty of Conscience; and in the following works he describes the Protestants as having been influenced only by rebellious motives in refusing to yield to the measures of the king for their conversion. " An Examination etc. An Answer to Claude's Complaints of the Protestants against the means which are employed to reunite them to the Church. 1686." "The History of the Fanaticism of our Times, and the Design of the Protestants to cause Rebellion, 1692," which was continued by a second volume in 1709, and a third in 1713. His apologies for persecution were answered in Considerations Generales sur le livre de M. Brueys intitule, Examen des raisons qui ont donne lieu a la Separation des Protestants. Rotterdam 1684. Le Proselyte abuse, ou fausses vues de M. Brueys dans l'Examen de la Separation des Protestants, ibid, 1684.

CIL. Actes of the General Assembly of the Clergy of France Anno Domini 1682, concerning Religion. Translated into English for the satisfaction of Curious Inquisitors into the present French Persecution of Protestants..With Memoirs containing the different Methods (15) which may very profitably be us'd for the Conversion of those who profess the pretended Reformed Religion. 4to Lond. 1682

The Letter writ by the last Assembly General of the Clergy of

France to the Protestants, inviting them to return to their

Communion, translated and examined by Gilbert Burnet

D.D. 1683.

A Pastoral Letter of the Lord Cardinal le Camus, Bishop and

Prince of Grenoble, to the Curates of his Diocess, touching the methods they ought to take, and in what manner they should behave themselves towards their new converts.
4to 1687

Cardinal Camus was opposed to the method of conversion by dragooning. He was not of the society of Jesuits.

A Pastoral Letter from the four Catholic Bishops to the Lay Catholics of England, touching the methods they ought to take and iu what manner they should behave themselves towards their new converts. 4to 1688

The answer of the New Converts of France to a Pastoral Letter fiom a Protestant Minister. pp. 31, 4to Lond. 1686

Acts of the General Assembly of the French Clergy in the year (£. fL. 1685, concerning Religion, together with the Complaint of the said General Assembly against the calumnies, injuries and falsities which the Pretended Reformed have and do every day publish in their books and sermons against the doctrines of the Church. Presented to the King by the Clergy in Body, July the 14th, 1685. pp. 43, 4to Lond. i685

This tract contains a Petition to the King. The King's Edict forbidding all Ministers and other persons whatever of the Pretended Reformed Religion to preach or compose any books against the Faith and Doctrine of the Church; or to use injurious terms or such as tend to calumnie, by imputing to Catholicks those tenets which they condemn: or to speak directly or indirectly against the Catholick Religion. The Doctrine of the Church, contained in our Profession of Faith, and in the Decrees of the Council of Trent. Opposed to the calumnies, etc. pp. 43, 4to. Lond. 1685.

Another edition, entitled, The Proceedings of the General Assembly ©. 3L, of the Clcrgie of France Assembled in the year 10 82 at Paris and in the year 1685 at S. Germains in Lave, concerning Religion. Translated out of French into English by N. N., 4to Lille 1686. Containing also A Pastorall Advertisement by the Church of France Assembled at

Paris by authority of the King; to Those of the Pretended Reformed Religion for their Conversion, and Reconciliation to, the Catholick

Church. And, A Speech made to the Most Christian King, at

Versailles the 21 of July 1685. By the most Illustrious and most

Reverend Lord James Nicholas Colbert, Archbishop and Primate of

Carthage, etc.

CI. In lEuvres de Bossuet, a Paris 1747, is inserted (vol. iii. p. xxvij)

Extrait des Notes de l'Assemblee Generate du Clerge de France de Mclxxxii, concernant la Religion, Monseigneur l'Archevesque de Paris President. Imprimes en la meme annee chez Leonard, Imprimeur du Clerge. Titre: Memoire contenant les differentes Methodes dont on peut se servir tres-utilement pour la conversion de ceux qui font profession de la Religion Pretendue-Reformee, dresse dans cette Assemble, et envoye par toutes les Provinces avec l'Avertissement Pastoral de l'Eglise Gallicane. In this will be found " The Approbation of the Right Reverend the Archbishops and Bishops," which is prefixed to Bossuet's Exposition (No. 73.)

C IL. An Edict of the French King, prohibiting all publick exercise of the pretended reformed religion in his kingdom; wherein he recalls and totally annuls the perpetual and irrevocable edict of K. Henry IV. his grandfather, full of most gracious concessions to Protestants: to which is added the French King's letter to the Elector of Brandenburg, containing several passages relating to the foregoing Edict; as also a brief and true account of the persecution carried on against those of the foresaid religion for to make them abjure and apostatize; together with the form of abjuration the revolting Protestants are to subscribe and swear to: and a declaration of his Electoral Highness of Brandenburg, in favour of those of the reformed religion, who shall think fit to settle themselves in any of his dominions. 4to 1686

An Account of the Persecutions and Oppressions of the Protestants in France. 4to s.l. 1686

Complaints of the cruel treatment of the Protestants in France,
By John Claude. 8vo Lond. 1686
" This day was burnt in the old Exchange, by the common hangman, a translation of a booke written by yc famous Mons' Claude,
relating onely matters of fact concerning the horrid massacres and barbarous proceedings of yc French King against his Protestant subjects, without any refutation of any facts therein; so mighty a power and ascendant here had the French Ambass' who was doubtlesse in greate indignation at the pious and truly generous charity of all the nation, for y reliefe of those miserable sufferers who came over for shelter. About this time also the Duke of Savoy, instigated by yc
French King to extirpate the Protestants of Piedmont, slew many thousands of those innocent people, so that there seem'd to be an universal designe to destroy all that would not go to masse, throughout Europe. Quod avertat D.O. M! No faith in Princes! " Evelyn's Memoirs, 1819, vol. i. p. 627. " Unheard of cruelties to y" persecuted

Protestants of France, such as hardly any age has scene the like, even among the Pagans." Ibid. p. 623.

Triomphe de la Religion sous Louis le Grand, representee par des
Inscriptions et des Devises, avec une Explication, par Pere Le
Jay, de la Compagnic de Jesus. Plates. Paris 1687

An Account of the late Persecution of the Protestants in the C3L.
Vallys of Piemont; by the Duke of Savoy and the French
King, in the year 1686. 4to Oxford 1688

Histoire Apologetique, ou Defense des Liberies des Eglises Re-©.I. formecs de France. Par M. Gautier. Amsterdam 1688

The Life and Death of John Claude, done out of French, by G. P.
4to 1688

Histoire de l'Edit de Nantes, contenant les choses les plus re-CfL, marquables qui se sont passees en France avant et apres sa publication, a l'occasion de la diversite des Religions, jusq'au l'Edit de Revocation. Par Elias Benoit. Oct. 1685.
5 vols. 4to Delft 1693 Of the first two volumes of the translation, all that was printed, the. 1L. publisher, John Dunton, in his " Life and Errors," observes: " It was a wonderful pleasure to Queen Mary to see this history made English, and it was the only book to which she gave her Royal License."

Origine progressi e ruina del Calvinismo nella Francia, ragguaglio istorico, dedicato all' emin. Cardinale Corsi, da D. Casimir Freschot. 4to Parma 1693

An ultramontane history of the Reformed Church of France, composed in the form of Annals from 1517 to 1686. The author relates that " to second the zeal of Louis XIV. in his endeavours to complete the conversion of the Huguenots, the various Religions Orders of France offered the assistance of New Preachers. The Oratory supplied one hundred and fifty; the Jesuits two hundred; the Capuchins above one hundred, and other Religious Societies to the extent of their ability." Page 346. Quoted in " The Witnesses in Sackcloth; or a Description of the Attack made upon the Reformed Churches of France in the Seventeenth Century; with a Bibliographical and Literary Appendix, including Notices of the subsequent history of the French Protestants." Lond. 1852, 12mo.

A Specimen of Papal and French Persecution, exhibited in the Sufferings of eminent Confessors and Martyrs who have signalized their faith and patience within the long and dismal reign of Louis XIV.: particularly of Louis de Marolles, etc. By Thomas Bray, D.D. Fol. Lond. 1712

Arcana Gallica; or, The Secret History of France for the last Century, shewing by what steps the French Ministers destroyed the Liberties of that Nation in general, and Protestant Religion in particular. By David Jones the Author of the Secret History of Europe. 1714 Compendious History of the Reformation in France and of the Reformed Churches, in that Kingdom, from the first beginning of the Reformation to the Repealing of the Edict of Nantes. By Stephen Abel Laval. 3 vols. 8vo 1737-41

An enumeration of Authorities giving a descriptive account of the persecutions of the French Protestants would be imperfect, if reference were not made to Burnet's Memoirs of his Own Times, and his Letters during his travels in the years 1685-6; to Quick's Synodicon in Gallia Reformata; or the Acts, Decisions, Decrees and Canons of the National Councils of the Reformed Churches in France, 2 vols. fol. 1692; and Voltaire's Siecle de Louis XIV. ch. 36. The Roman Catholics must not indiscriminately be charged with this crusade: it was through the instrumentality of the Jesuits, Louis became the " Scourge of God," of whom it has been said: " It will be difficult to select from the whole course of history a single mortal whose follies have been so injurious, and whose faults have been so fatal to his fellow creatures as were those of Louis XIV."—Lectures on the French Revolution by Professor Smyth. See the Pref. and Append. to Burnet's Hist. of the Rights of Princes. In the disgraceful reign of Louis XV. the " dragonnndes" were again exercised. The benevolent projects of Louis XVI. were denied opportunity for development. " The work of Rulhiere, Eclaircissemens sur les causes de la Revocation de l'Edit de Nantes (Giuvres v.) is no other than a perpetual commentary on a State-Paper sufficiently evincing the profound attention which Louis XVI. would have devoted to Ecclesiastical peace, if the hurricane of the Revolution had not swept away all Ordinances Divine and Civil." — Smedley's Hist of the Reformed Religion in France, vol. ill. p. 321.

CHAP. VII. *Of the Discourses written on the occasion of Mr. Thomas Godden's Conference with Dr. Edward Stillingfleet, the Dean of St. PauTs.*

85. A Letter to Mr. Thomas Goddeu giving a true account of the late conference at the dean of S. Paul's. Imprimatur Guil. Needham, Martii 12, 168?. pp. 8, 4to Lond. 1687

See Cat. 47. Contin. p. 40. Ath. Oxon. voL ii. col. 1070. This letter is signed E. S. i.e. Edward Stillingfleet, and dated March 7, 168f. Tbos. Godden was president of the English College in Lisbon, where he took the degree of D.D. in 1656. In 1678 his servant Hill was executed for the murder of Sir Edmundbury Godfrey (Burnet, Own Times, vol. i. 445, sq.) After this he was almoner and chaplain to the queen dowager, and died about Dec. 1688. Ant. Wood says (Ath. Oxon. loc. cit.) " We may here take notice that Dr. Tbo. Godden before mentiou'd who (as Dr. Stillingfleet saith Pref. to the Defence of his Discourse and against a Book called Catholics no Idolaters was the most considerable adversary that had appeared against him) was born, as I have been informed in London of the same family with Sir Adam Browne of Surrey (his right surname being Browne) bred in S. John's Coll. in Cambridge, where he was bach, of arts, but leaving the English church he went to Lisbon in Portugal, where spending some time in the English coll. he was sent on the mission to England," &c. I believe however that his real name was Tilden, see Ath. Oxon. ed. Bliss vol. iv. col. 93.

Gee calls him Mr. Peter Gooden (Cat. p. 9) which I believe is a mistake; and tells us that he had a conference with Dr. Claget about Transubstantiation, Feb. 21, 1686, which was published under this *B.L.* title, The sum of a conference on Feb. 21, 1686, between Dr. Claget and father Gooden about the point of transubstantiation, 8vo Lond. (C. 3L 1689. Also published at the end of Dr. Clagett's Seventeen Sermons preached on several occasions. This was Dr. W. Clagett of Eman. Coll. Cambr. J. H. T. 86. *b* A letter to the D.ean of P. S. Paul's in answer to the £. 1L. arguing part of his first letter to Mr. G odden. Anon. By Mr. John Sergeant, or Sargeant. pp. 36, 4to Lond. 1687

See Contin. p. 40. Ath. Oxon. vol. ii. col. 1009. This Sergeant, alias Smith, was a secular priest, see Ath. Oxon. vol. ii. col. 247 and 1068. But he seems to have also gone hy the name of Holland, and he wrote his book called "Sure Footing in Christianity Examined" under the name of George Hughes. He was a native of Lincolnshire and had been a Sizar of S. John's Coll. Cambr. and A.B. of that University, and was for some time secretary to Dr. Tho. Morton Bp. of Durham. In 1042 he seceded to Romanism and went to the English Coll. of Lisbon; and was in 1652 sent back to England as secretary to the secular clergy of the Mission: in which employment lie remained to his death in 1707. He was accused of heretical opinions by Peter Talbot, tit. Abp. of Dublin. See Stillingfleet's nature and grounds of the Certainty of Faith (No. 95 *infra*) p. 4 sq. against which charge he defended himself in a book entitled Vindicite contra Pet. Talbotum &c. 8vo 1678. John Sergeant wrote against Bramhall under the initials S. W. from which some have given him the Christian name of William, but Wood (loc. cit.) and Dodd (Ch. Hist. vol. iii. part viii. bk. ii. art. 5, pp.

472 sq.) call him John. And in this controversy with Stillingfleet his initials are J. S. See the new edition of BramhaU's Works (Anglo Cath. Libr.) Life p. xxviii vol. ii.
p. 358 note. J. H. T.
Other works of this voluminous Roman Catholic author will be noticed hereafter.

87. A letter to a Friend reflecting on some passages in a letter of ffi, 2,.

Mr. John Sargeant to the D. of P. in answer to the arguing part of his first letter to Mr. G. Anou. By Clement Ellis M.A. Rector of Kirkby in Com. Notting. pp. 31, 4to Lond. 1687
See Cat. No. 49. Contin. p. 40. Ath. Oxon. vol ii. col. 970.
See No. 86.

88. "i A second Catholic Letter against the reflections of Dr. Stil lingfleet's defender. By Mr. John Sargeant. 4to Lond. 1687
See Ath. Oxon. vol. ii. col. 1069.

89. The Reflecter's defence of his letter to a friend, against the furious assaults of M. J. S. in his second Catholic Letter. In four dialogues. pp. 72, 4to Lond. 1688

See Cat No. 53. Contin. p. 42. Ath. Oxon. vol. ii. col. 1069. This is anon, but is evidently by Clement Ellis, the author of No. 87. J. H. T.

CT.1L 90. A second Letter to Mr. G. iu answer to two Letters lately published concerning the conference at the D. of P. Imprimatur Guil. Needham. April 22, 1687. Anon. By Edw. Stillingfleet, D.D. pp. 44, 4to Lond. 1687
See Cat. No. 48. Contin. p. 40. Ath. Oxon. vol. ii. col. 10G9, where however there is nothing about this second letter of Stillingfleet, which was written not against Sargeant (Nos. 86, 88 *supra* as Peck states) but against Mr. M. who had been present at the conference with Godden, and who seems to have published two letters in defence of Godden, of which Peck makes no mention. But Wake (Contin. p. 40) notices them thus: " In return to this *i.e.* to Stillingflcet's first letter, No. 85 *supra* Mr. M. who was with Mr. G. at the conference returned a letter or two to Dr. Stillingfleet concerning the conference; and these produced a second from the Dean of S. Paul's, called &c. A copy of one of these letters, under the initials E. M. *i.e.* Edw. Meredith is in Trin. Coll. Library, Dublin, with this title, *T.C.D.* A letter to Dr. E. S. concerning his late letter to Mr. G., and the account he gives in it of a conference between Mr. G. and himself. 4to, Lond. 1G87.

There must also have been another letter, as Stillingfleet distinctly speaks of two in his title-page, and in his book more than once, as p. 36, " The Author of the first letter desires information," &c.; p. 40. For as the Author of the first letter well observes, " I love to spare my own pains. But I took the opportunity of your Absence. Herein Mr. M. did me injury;" which words seem to make Mr. M. author of this letter also. And yet in his opening sentence p. 3, he speaks of " two gentlemen who have appeared in print so lately." At all events it is evident that the second letter to Mr. Godden (which is dated April 21, 1087) had no reference to Sergeant's letters; which Stillingfleet afterwards answered in a distinct book. See No. 95 *infra*. J. H. T.

91. i A third Catholic letter in answer to the arguing part of Dr.

Stillingfleet's second letter, &c. Anon. By John Sargeant.
4to Lond. 1687

See Contin. p. 40 Ath. Oxon. vol. ii. col. 1069, from whence this title is copied, for Peck does not appear to have seen any of Sargeant's letters. Wake speaks of a fourth and fifth Catholic Letter, and says expressly (Contin. p. 41) that the fifth was so called. They are not given by Wood under that name; and hence Peck suggests that the two tracts, Nos. 93 and 94, although not called "Catholic letters" in the title he has given, may nevertheless be those referred to by Wake. See his note after No. 94. J. H. T.

I have been furnished with the following titles, which prove Peck's suggestion to be groundless: " The fourth Catholick letter in answer C1L. to Dr. Stillingfleet's Sermon (as *infra*) addrest to his Auditory," 1688, 4to. "The fifth Catholick letter in reply to Dr. Stillingfleet's pretended Answer about the 40th part of J. S.'s Catholick letters, addrest to all impartial readers," by John Sargeant. 1688 4to. " Your second falshood is that Dr. St. has reply'd to my first Four Letters: and this is a most notorious Banger. For, first, it is shown in my fifth Letter Page by Page to every Examiner's Eye, from Page 154 to Page 173, that he has omitted so much as to *take notice of* (much more to *Answer*) Thirty Nine parts of Forty of my First and Third Letters.'' A Letter to the Continuator of the Present State of our Controversy. Laying open the Folly of his extravagant Boasting, and the Malice of his Willfull Forgeries. By John Sergeant. (Ad. calc. Continuation, see No. 438 *infra*.) 92. Scripture and Tradition compared; in a Sermon preached at C S.,

Guildhall Chapel, Nov. 27, 1687. By Edward Stillingfleet,

D.D. and Dean of St. Paul's. pp. 32, 4to Lond. 1688

See Cat. No. 50; Contin. p. 40; Ath. Oxon. vol. ii. col. 1069. In the preface to this Sermon, Stillingfleet says: " I intend, God willing,

to publish in a little time a full answer to J. S. his Catholick Letters,

so far as I am concerned in them." See No. 95. Works, vol. i.
p. 393. J. H. T.

See also Sermon xiii. vol. i. p. 176, The Reformation justify'd,
Acts xxiv. 14.
s

C IL. 93. "i" An answer to Dr. Stillingfleet's sermon at Guildhall Chapel, 27 Nov. 1687. By Mr. John Sargeant. 4to See Contin. p. 40; Ath. Oxon. vol. ii. col. 1069; where Wood says: " This was going to press the latter end of January the same year viz. 168£, and I think it was printed in qu. but I have not seen it. " I have not seen any copy of it, nor do 1 know whether it was ever published. J. H. T.

" He owes me a full Answer to my Fourth Letter laying open the vanity of his insignificant Guildhall Sermon; to which he has hitherto said nothing." In A Letter to the Continuator, p. 12. The original title is as follows, " The Fourth

Catholick Letter in Answer to Dr. Stillingfleet's Sermon, Preach't at Guild-Hall, November 27th, 1687. Entituled, Scripture and Tradition Compared, Addrest to his Auditory, pp. 35, Pref. v. 4to Lond. 1688.

94. f The nature and grounds of the certainty of faith. By Mr. John Sargeant.

See Ath. Oxon. vol. ii. col. 1069. These two last pieces, I conceive, make up Mr. Sargeant's fourth and fifth Catholic Letters to Dr. Stillingfleet, spoken of in the Continuation of the present Controversy, p. 41. However quaere.

I know not where Peck got the title of this last book, for which I can find no authority. It is not mentioned in the place of Ath. Oxon. to which he refers; and I think it must have been taken from the title of No. 95, on the presumption that J. S. had written a book with a corresponding title. But this I believe is a mistake. J. H. T.

The following works of Sergeant relate to the subject here under consideration, the Rule of Faith: Sure-Footing in Christianity, or Rational Discourses on the Rule of Faith. With short Animadversions on Dr. Pierce's Sermon (viz. The Primitive Rule of Reformation, pp. 341-90 in his Collection of Sermons, 4to Oxford 1671); also on some passages in Mr. Whitby and Mr. Stillingfleet which concern that Rule: (viz. Whitby's Romish Doctrines not known from the Beginning. Lond. 1662, 4to. Stillingfleet's Rational Grounds of the Protestant Religion, &c. Lond. 1665.) A Discovery of the groundlessness and insincerity of my Lord of Down's Dissuasive, being the fourth Appendix to Sure-Footing. 8vo Lond. 1665. Errour Nonplust, or Dr. Stillingfleet shown to be The Man of no Principles.

With an Essay how Discourses concerning Catholick Grounds bear the highest Evidence. 8vo 1671, 1673. A Letter of Thanks from the Author of Sure-Footing to his Answerer, Mr. John Tillotson.

8vo Paris 1666. Faith Vindicated from a possibility of Falshood (against some part of a Sermon of Mr. TillotKon on Job xxviii. 28), printed 1667, 8vo. The publications of his adversaries will be found in Dodd and the British Librarian, col. 1080, 1081. See also chaps, xx., xxi., xxii. *infra,* and compare Sergeant's Rule of Faith with that of Thomas White, or the author of those Dialogues which pass under Rushworth's name, 1640. Reprinted 1654. And Chillingworth's Answer (subjoined to the best editions of his works, as the folio, 1704, and the new edit. Oxford, 1838, three vols. 8vo.), of whose Conference with White on Tradition an account is given in An Historical and Critical Account of the Life and Writings of William Chillingworth. By Peter Des Maiseaux, 1725.

"Sergeant was the very genius of controversy, and there was no great English Protestant writer of his own time that he did not encounter. As if it were not sufficient to be pitted against Hammond, Bramhall, Jeremy Taylor, Stillingfleet, Tillotson, Whitby, Pierce and Tenison, he got into fierce conflict with Talbot, the Catholic Archbishop of Dublin, who endeavoured to represent his doctrine as heterodox, especially concerning the Rule of Faith. A very curious account of the proceedings in relation to Talbot's charges against him is contained in Sergeant's ' Clypeus Septemplex' (Duaci 1677, 12mo), his Vindicise alterse (12mo), and in a later work of his, of great scarcity, which appears to have escaped Dodd and other historians altogether, entitled, ' Raillery defeated by calm reasoning' (Lond. 1699, 12mo), in which he gives an interesting narrative of the whole transaction." — Worthington's Diary, vol. ii. part i. p. 193, note.

95. A discourse concerning the nature and grounds of the certainty C H. of faith in answer to J. S. his Catholick Letters. By Edward Stillingfleet D.D., Dean of St. Paul's, London, pp. 116, and Cat. of Books printed for Henry Mortlock, 2 pp. 4to Lond. 1688

See Cat. No. 51; Contin. p. 41; Ath. Oxon. vol. ii. col. 1069; Stillingfleet's Works, vol. vi. p. 361. He published in 1673 A Second Discourse in vindication of the Protestant Grounds of Faith, against the pretence of Infallibility in the Roman Church: in Answer to the Guide in Controversies, by R. Holden; Protestancy without Principles; and Reason and Religion, or the Certain Rule of Faith, by E. Warner. With a Particular Enquiry into the Miracles of the Roman Church.

In this he replies also to Cressy, who had published, in a Collection of several Treatises, Stillingfleet's Principles, giving an account of the Faith of Protestants, considered by N. O. Paris 1671, 12mo. E. Worsley also was an Anti-Stillingfleet in The Infallibility of the Roman Catholick Church and her Miracles, defended against Dr. Stillingfleet's Cavils, unworthily made publick in two late Books. The one called An Answer to Several Treatises, &c. The other, A Vindication of the Protestant Grounds of Faith, &c. Antwerp 1674, 12mo.

96. An historical discourse concerning tradition in answer to Mr. John Sargeant. By John Williams M.A. afterwards Bishop of Chichester.

See Cat. No. 52; Contin. p. 41; Ath. Oxon. vol. ii. col. 1119. Although this book is mentioned under the above title (omitting the words in brackets) by Wood and Gee, yet I much doubt if it ever was published. It does not exist in the Dublin Univer. or Bodl. Libraries. I believe the only reason for supposing it to have been published is the following passage in Wake's Contin. p. 41, speaking of John Sergeant's "Fifth Catholic Letter." He says: "There is a very learned person hath undertaken to answer not only that fifth letter, but the other discourses of the Romanists about Tradition in an Historical Discourse concerning Tradition. This we may expect to have published very shortly." If Bp. Williams ever designed such a work, it is probable that he has given us the principal part of his collections for it in his " Examination of the texts cited in proof of the insufficiency of Scripture and necessity of tradition." See No. 376 *infra.* J. H. T.

97. The Council of Trent examin'd and disprov'd by Catholick C 1L

Tradition in the main points in controversie between us and the Church of Rome; with a particular account of the times and occasions of introducing them. Part I. To which a preface is prefixed concerning the true sense of the Council of

Trent, and the notion of Transubstantiation. Anon. By

Edw. Stillingfleet, D.D. Gibson vol. xi. fol. ii. Works vol. vi.

pp. 147, 4to Lond. 1688

See Cat. No. 54; Contin. p. 42. Quaere, if Part ii. was ever published?

There can be no doubt that Part ii. never was published. It does not appear in the collected edition of Stillingfleet's works, where this first Part is given, vol. vi. p. 423. Bp. Gibson, in his Preservative, vol. ii., Append. p. 103, has printed a portion only of this work, viz. to the end of the fifth point, (pp. 1-74 of the orig. edit.,) but without ' any intimation of having omitted anything.

The first Part was intended by the author to prove that there was no Catholic Tradition for the Tridentine doctrines: the second, to give an account by what steps and degrees and on what occasions those doctrines and practices came into the Church.

A second edition of this book was published in London the same year. Stillingfleet's works are edited in a most unsatisfactory manner; the titles of his controversial tracts abridged without notice, often with the omission of essential particulars, and not a word of note to record the circumstances under which they were written. It is a disgrace to the Church that the works of such a man have not yet been collected under a competent editor. J. H. T.

The pagination i3 very incorrect. One of the treatises in vol. v. is paged irregularly 1-54, and 333-576. In vol. vi. there is a chasm from page 224to 361.

98. An appendix to the Council of Trent examin'd, Part I. in C3L. answer to some passages of J. W. of the Society of Jesus,

concerning the Prohibition of Scripture in vulgar languages,

in the Council of Trent. By Edward Stillingfleet, D.D.

2 sheets 4to

This appendix appears at the end of the second edition of the book, 4to Lond. 1688. There is a copy in Trin. Coll. Library, Dublin; and see Stillingfleet's works, vol. v. p. 511. J. H. T.

The subject of the first Part had already been elaborated by Bishop Hall in *The Peace of Rome proclaimed to all the World by her Famout Cardinal Bellarmine*, &c. Lond. 1609. Reprinted by the Rev. Peter Hall, Oxford 1838. That of the second Part — the theological history of the Tridentine doctrines — by Chemnitius in his *Examen Concilii Tridentini*, fol. Genevte, 1641. Translated into English, and entitled A Discourse and Batterie of the Great Fort of unwritten Traditions; otherwise called an Examination of the Counsell of Trent. Lond. 1582, 4to.

C Xh A reply to Mr. Sergeant's Third Appendix, containing some animadversions on A rational account of the grounds of Protestant Religion; (being a vindication of Abp. Laud's Relation of a Conference.) By Edward Stillingfleet, D.D. Works, vol. iv. 626.

©.i. A letter to the Continuator of the Present State of our Controversy. William Wake. See No. 438 *infra*. By John Sergeant.

M.L. A letter desiring information of the conference at the Dean of St. Paul's, mentioned in the letter to Mr. G.

A single half-sheet, 4to 1687

A Relation of a Conference held about Religion at London by Edward Stillingfleet D.D. and Gilbert Burnet with some gentlemen of the Church of Rome. pp. 64, 4to 1687

From Kennet's MSS. additions.

T.CD. Protestant Certainty; or a short treatise, shewing how a Protestant may be well assured of the Articles of his Faith. *Let every man be fully assured* &c. Bom. xiv. 5. pp. 34, Mortlock's Cat. of Books, pp. 2. 4to. Lond. 1689

This is not mentioned by Gee or Peck, but in the Bodl. Cat. is attributed to William Dillingham, D.D. J. H. T.

CHAP. VIII. *Of the discourses written on occasion of the conference between fa-*

ther Andrew Pulton and Dr. Thomas Tenison. 99. A true account of the conference between Dr. Thos. Tenison and Andrew Pulton. By Andrew Pulton.

See Contin. p. 61. " They met on the account of a Boy whom Mr. Pulton had perverted from our Religion. Great things were presently talked, as usual on such occasions, concerning this Conference; and the Papists fail'd not to boast of a mighty conquest made over the Doctor. This forced him to resolve on a Publication of what passed, tho' otherwise as little fit, as designed, to be communicated to the world."—Contin. p. 61. See also a Letter from Dr. Horneck in Tenison's Account, p. 79.

The same with that in Tenison's account, pp. 59-71.

C H. 100. A true and full account of a conference held about religion between Dr. Thomas Tenison and Andrew Pulton, one of the masters in the Savoy. pp. 18, Pref. 4

See Contin. p. 61. No books under these titles are in the Bodl. Cat., nor are they in the Trin. Coll. Library, Dublin. Dr. Tenison's account of the conference contains a Paper entitled, "The account written by Mr. Pulton, a true account of a conference had about Religion between Dr. T. and A. P. on the 29th of September 1687 in Long-Acre London" (pp. 59, see No. 101 *infra*); and there is a reference (p. 78 *ibid*) to a more full account which is spoken of as " Mr. Pulton's second Narrative," but which is not given. J. H. T.

The account referred to is this No., in the beginning of which is this Advertisement: — " A. P. having been eighteen years out of his own country, pretends not yet to any Perfection of the English Expression or Orthography, wherefore for the future he will crave the favour of treating with the Dr. in Latine, since the Dr. finds fault with his English." On which Macaulay remarks: " His orthography is indeed deplorable. In one of his letters wright is put for write, wold for would. He challenged Tenison to dispute with him in Latin that they might be on equal terms." In a contemporary satire, entitled

The Advice, is the following couplet:

"Send Pulton to be lashed at Busby's school,
That he in print no longer-play the fool.
"

101. A true account of a conference held about religion at London, C1L Sept. 29, 1687, between A. Pulton, Jesuit, and Tho. Tenison, D.D. as also of that which led to it, and followed after it. By Tho. Tenison, D.D. The third edition corrected, pp. 83, list of books 1 page. pp. 83, 4to Lond. 1687

See Cat. No. 168. Contin. p. 61. Ath. Oxon. vol. ii. col. 1056.

102. Remarks on a late conference between Andrew Pulton Jesuit and Thomas Tenison, D.D. By Edward Meredith. 4to Lond. 1687

See No. 351 *infra*. Ath. Oxon. yol. ii. col. 1056. I do not understand the double date given by Wood, and copied by Peck, unless the second (1688) refers to No. 106 *infra*. J. H. T.

103. The Vindication of A. Cressener, school-master in Long-C J, Acre from the aspersions of A. Pulton Jesuit and schoolmaster in the Savoy; together with some account of his discourses with Mr. Meredith. Imprimatur Oct. 24, 1687. pp. 14, 4to Lond. 1687 See Cat. No. 170. Contin. p. 62, 63. This Vindication refers to some passages in Dr. Tenison's account of the conference with Pulton, wherein Cressener was alluded to, he having been present, and taking some part, at the conference. See No. 101 *supra*, p. 63. J. H. T. 104. *i* Remarks of Andrew Pulton, Master in the Savoy, upon C 3,. Dr. Tenison's late narrative; with a confutation of the doctor's rule of faith, and a reply to A. Cressener's pretended refutation. pp. 42, 4to Lond. 1687

See Contin. p. 61.

T CI, 105. Mr. Pulton considered in his sincerity, reasonings, and authorities; or a just answer to what he hath hitherto published in his true account; his true and full account of a conference, &c. His Remarks; and in them his pretended confutation of what he calls Dr. Tenison's Rule of Faith. By the said Tho. Tenison. pp. 100, and books printed for R. Chiswell 4 pp. pp. 100, Dedic. &c., pp. 8, 4to Lond. 1667 See Cat. No. 169. Contin. p. 62.

106. *i* Some farther remarks on the late account given by Dr. Tenison of his conference with Mr. Pulton wherein the doctor's three exceptions against Edward Meredith are examined, several of his other misrepresentations laid open, motives of the said Edward Meredith's conversion shewed, and some other points relating to controversy, occasionally treated. Together with an appendix, in which some passages *T.C.D.* of the doctor's book entitled, Mr. Pulton considered, are reconsidered; and in the close the best means of coming to the true faith proposed. To all which is added a postscript, in answer to the pamphlet put forth by the school-master of Long-acre. By Andrew Pulton. 4to Lond. 1688

See Contin. p. 62. Peck ascribes this, as above, to A. Pulton. But it is evidently by Edw. Meredith, as distinctly stated by Wake, Contin. loc. cit., and as appears from the book itself, a copy of which is in the Trin. Coll. Library, Dublin. Meredith had been proposed by Pulton as a witness of the conference; Tenison's three objections were 1. That Meredith had not acted fairly in the conference between Stillingfleet and Godden. 2. That he had in a Coffeehouse pitied the state of St. Martin's (of which Dr. T. was rector) as being under one man, although it was capable of maintaining 30 friars. 3. That he was a convert from the Church of England, and therefore (was as usual with converts) possessed with a spirit of fiercer bigotry. J. H. T.

C %, 107. The Missionaries arts discovered; or an account of their ways of insinuation, their artifices and several methods of which they serve themselves in making converts. With a letter to Mr. Pulton, challenging him to make good his charge of disloyalty against Protestants. And an historical Preface, containing an account of their introducing heathen Gods in their processions, and other particulars relating to the several chapters of this Treatise. Jer. xii. 6, *Believe tftem not, though they speak fair words unto us.* Tertull. adv. Valent. *Habent artificium fyc.* Pers. Sat. v. *Jronte politi fyc.*

By H. minister of the Church of England, pp. 96, Letter to Mr. Pulton, 4 pp. Pref. xxiv. 4to Lond. 1688

See Cat. No. 173. Contin. p. 59. Gee tells us, and is copied by Peck, that this book is " by Mr. H., a Divine of the Church of England." I know not whether it was any additional information that made Peck alter the word " Divine" into " Minister," but I have not been able to learn who Mr. H. was. There is nothing in the book itself to guide us even to the amount of information that Gee has communicated. The title page makes no mention of Mr. H. The letter to Mr. Pulton is signed " Anonymous." Bp. Gibson, who has reprinted this book (Preserv. against Popery, vol. iii. tit. xiii. p. 3) attributes it to " Dr. Hicks" (Titles of the Treatises in vol. iii. p. 6), meaning I presume the celebrated Dr. George Hickes, but it is not in the list of his works given in Bayle's Diet. by Bernard, Bird, and Lockman, nor in that given Ath. Oxon. vol. ii. col. 1002 sq. , nor can I find any other authority besides Gibson's for attributing it to Hickes.

J. H. T.

That this and the following tract were not written by George Hickes is certain, because in a Catalogue which he presented to Thoresby in 1708 of his own Books, Sermons and Tracts, these are not mentioned. See Thoresby's Diary and Correspondence, vol. iv. pp. 115-20, 208, 209.

" That the gentlemen of the Church of Rome may have all the help in the world to convince me of falsifications, if they can; and to spare them that trouble which they put us to, by careless and ignorant quotations, I have here given a Catalogue of the Books 180 cited in the ensuing Treatise, with their Editions." pp. xxii-xxiv.

108. A defence of the missionaries arts,

wherein the charge of *C %.* disloyalty, rebellions, plots and treasons, asserted p. 76 of that book, are fully proved against the Members of the Church of Rome, in a brief account of the several plots contrived, and rebellions raised by the papists against the lives and dignities of sovereign princes since the Reformation. By the Author of the Missionaries Arts. pp. 96, Pref. 6 pp. Advert. of books 2 pp. 4to Lond. 1689
A total Defeat of the Protestant Rule of Faith, by A. Pulton against Dr. Tenison. 4to 1687

A Vindication of Protestant Charity, in Answer to some passages in Mr. E. M's Remarks on a late Conference. Printed with H, Some Reflexions upon a Treatise call'd Pietas Romana et Parisiensis, lately printed at Oxford. By James Harrington.
4to Oxford 1688

See Ath. Oxon. vol. ii. col. 1059, and No. 352 *infra.* A copy of this is in Trin. Coll. Library, Dublin. It is Anon., but was written by James Harrington, A.M., Stud. of Ch. Ch. Ath. Oxon. vol. ii. col. 909 and 1056, where Wood informs us that Mr. E. M. was Edward Meredith, "son of a father of both his names, minister of Landulph in Cornwall," who had been Stud. of Ch. Ch. in 1666, but left without taking a degree, and afterwards became secretary to Sir Wm. Godolphin, when he was ambassador in Spain, and a strict Roman Catholic. See No. 102 *supra.* Mr. Meredith is mentioned by Tenison in his Account of a Conference with Pultou (No. 101 *supra),* where there are some notices of the Conference with Stillingfleet. The late Conference here spoken of is not that between Stillingfleet and Godden, but that between Tenison and Pulton. See Nos. 102, 106. J. H. T.

"i Some remarks upon the author and licenser of " The Missionaries Arts discovered," with a reply to a challenge made him. By Andrew Pulton, in a letter prefixed to the said Pamphlet.
4to Lond. 1688 CHAP. IX. *The sequel of the conference between father Andrew Pulton and Dr. Thomas Tenison; or an account of the* Speculum Ecclesiasticura *and the discourses written thereupon.*
The conference and dispute between father Pulton and Dr. Tenison produced another, which opened with
109. Speculum Ecclesiasticum; or an ecclesiastical prospective glass. By T. Ward, a Roman catholick soldier.

See Contin. p. 63. The Bodl. Cat. attributes this work to the Thomas Ward, who was the author of the " Errata of the Protestant Bible" and other works. I have not seen the original edition which is in folio, a single sheet. It did not however contain the name of T. Ward, as Peck's mode of transcribing the title might lead one to suppose. Wake (Coutin. p. 62) says, "written, we are told, by a souldier of that party, T. Ward." J. H. T.

Note, this Roman catholick soldier was soon after followed by " The protestant Footman." And each party boasted much of their particular champion. See chap. x. *infra.*

The Speculum Ecclesiasticum was reprinted with No. 115 *infra,* d. Peck.
110. Six conferences concerning the Eucharist; wherein is shewed, £, 1L. That the doctrine of transubstantiation overthrows the proofs of christian religion. Imprimatur Jo. Battely, Sept. 12,1687.
Anon. By Monsieur de la Placette. Translated and published by Thomas Tenison, D.D.
pp. 120 and 2 pp. Cat. of Books, 4to Lond. 1687

See Cat. No. 77; Contin. p. 24. This work is a translation from a French writer, M. Jean de la Placette, as we learn from Gee and
Peck, who add to the above title, as if it had formed part of it,
" Written by M de la Placette, and translated and published by Dr. Tenison. This latter statement, that it was published (not that it was translated) by Tenison is evident from the following advertisement prefixed to the work Nov. 5, 1678. Mr. A. Pulton, Jesuit, having in his remarks (published Nov. 4) declared in effect (in pp. 29, 30) that the principles of philosophy which contradict the doctrine of Transubstantiation are to be renounc'd, and that Christians have the same ground to believe Transubstantiation as the blessed Trinity, and demanding *how great the confusion of Dr. TiUoison will be at the Day of Judgment, when he shall find that tenet true;* the said Dr. Tenison, the Publisher of this book does so far as concerns these particulars, refer Mr. Pulton to it, and for the rest of his remarks he will in due time give a very just answer to them."

I have thought it worth while to transcribe this, as it exhibits the rise of a subsequent controversy, "the Doctrine of Transubstantiation and the Trinity compared." J. H. T.
111. Of the incurable scepticism of the church of Rome. Imprimatur Guil. Needham, Oct. 20, 1687. pp. 160 and Cat. of Books 4 pp. 4to Lond. 1688

See Cat. No. 103. Contin. p. 7.
This work by the same Johannes de la Placette was first published in Latin at Amsterdam in 1596, 4to under the title, "De insanabili Romans ecclesise scepticismo dissertatio." The present translation is by the learned Henry Wharton, who when a very young man was employed by Dr. Tenison to make it. See Life of Wharton, in the Appendix to D'Oyly's Life of Sancroft, vol. ii. p. 119, where it is said that he completed the translation in a fortnight. J. H. T.

John de la Placette, born in 1639, died in 1718. Another work of this eminent French Protestant minister ought here to be mentioned, Traite de la Foi Divine. 1697 12mo, and 1716 4to.
112. *fr* A full answer to Dr. Tenison's conferences concerning the Eucharist.
Peck does not profess to have seen this book; he probably inferred its existence from the following which was in his collection. I have never seen either. J. H. T.
113. Of transubstantiation; or a reply to a late paper called a full answer to Dr. Tenison's conferences concerning the eucharist.

A single half sheet, fol. 1688 114. *Jj* A letter to the author of the reply to a late paper called *B.L.* a full answer to Dr. Tenison's conferences concerning the *T.C.D.* eucharist. A single sheet,

4to 1687

Peck marks this as having been written on the Popish side, although from the title as he gives it it would seem as if it had been written in defence of Tenison. He has omitted, however, the words in brackets. The Bodl. puts this under W. D. Who was W. D.? J. H. T.
115. The pamphlet entitled Speculum Ecclesiasticum, or an eccle-C 5L. siastical prospective glass considered in its false reasonings and quotations. There are added by way of preface two farther answers; the first, to the defender of the Speculum; the second to the half sheet against the six conferences.
Anon. By Henry Wharton, M.A.
pp. 72 and Cat. of Books 4 pp. 4to Lond. 1688
See Cat. No. 171. Contin. p. 62. Ath. Oxon. vol. iii. col. 874.

This begins by a letter from Thomas Tenison to Mr. A. B. i.e. Henry Wharton communicating to him certain papers written in defence of the Speculum by its author, which had in some way, as he says, "by a very strange Providence of God," fallen into Tenison's hands. Then the answer from A. B. to Tenison (page 7) in which Wharton examines the references to the Fathers, made by the author of the Speculum, proving them to have been either quoted from spurious writings, or containing nothing to the purpose. Then (page 22) the answer to the half-sheet (see No. 112 supra). Then follows (page 25) a reprint of the Speculum itself " according to the copy bought of the woman in the Savoy, to whom Mr. Pulton directed." At the end of which is " Per T. W." i.e. Thomas Ward the only intimation of the author's name which the Tract contains. Then follows another title page (included, however, in the pagination as page 45) exactly the same as the former with the omission of the clause, " There are added by way of preface," &c. and page 47-72 Wharton's admirable exposure of the gross dishonesty of quotations, citing of forged writings, &c. of the author of the Speculum. J. H. T.

Born in 1664, died in 1694. "Conspicuous amoDgst the recruits whom Cambridge sent to the field was a distinguished pupil of the great Newton, Henry Wharton, who had, a few months before, been senior wrangler of his year, and whose early death was soon after deplored by all parties as an irreparable loss to letters. See the preface to Henry Wharton's Posthumous Sermons." Macaulay.
116. The Roman catholick soldier's letter to Dr. Thomas Tenison.
This letter was reprinted with the next number.

I know not if it was ever printed elsewhere, although Peck says it was *reprinted*. It occurs page 9 of the next number, and is there subscribed T. Ward. In the answer the original edition of the letter is alluded to thus: " Now in your absence the author of the Ecclesiastical Prospective Glass has wrapt up your Speculum examin'd in a little bit of coarse paper." The letter (which makes but two pages) was therefore probably printed originally on coarse paper for sale in the streets, or cheap distribution. J. H. T.

C1L. 117. An answer to the letter of the Roman catholic souldier as he calls himself. In a letter from C. D. to A. B. the examiner of his Speculum. The souldier's letter is added at the end. Imprimatur H. Maurice. Anon. By Thomas Tenison, D.D. pp. 10. 4to 1688

See Cat. No. 172. Contin. p. 62.

Although Gee and after him Peck expressly attribute this tract to Tenison, I have no doubt from the style that it was by Henry Wharton. The Bodl. Catal. also attributes it to Tenison. J. H. T, 118. ℅ *Monomachia*; or a duel between Dr. Thomas Tenison, pastor of St. Martin's, and a Roman catholick soldier, wherein the Speculum Ecclesiasticum is defended against the frivolous cavils, vain objections and false aspersions of Dr. Tenison; the doctor also put to defend his form of ordination and to prove himself priest and pastor of St. Martin's, and lastly to hear the confessions of his parishioners, and give them absolution. pp. 48, 4to 1687 See Contin. p 63.

This is probably by Thomas Ward. See the Answer (No. 117) page 7, where it is called "your mannerly and learned pamphlet called the Duel." Two copies of it in the Trin. Coll. Library, Dublin. J. H. T.

Dodd mentions it in his list of Ward's works. Of his Hudibrastic poem, England's Reformation, see Retrospective Review, iii. 329.

" Before *The Speculum Ecclesiasticum considered* was published, the Doctor obtained a copy of the Defence which the Soldier had prepared of his Quotations, hut was not yet come from the Press; and to finish all at once, an Answer was set forth to that too at the same time, ere it could appear abroad in the world. This the Soldier resented, and expressed his sense of it in a Letter to Dr. Tenison; which, together with a Reply to it, were published under the title of An Answer to the Letter, &c. However, not long after this, the Defence was publish't with a dreadful name, viz. , *Monomachia*, &c. And so I think this worthy Controversie ended." Contin. p. 63.

The author of the *Speculum Ecclesiasticum* divides it into eight parts or columns; and in them undertakes to prove the doctrines of the Church of Rome from Scripture, and the testimonies of the Fathers of the Church for the first 500 years. I. The Succession of the Church. II. The Primacy of the Pope. III. The Infallibility of the Church. IV. The Unity of the Church. V. Transubstantiation. VI. Auricular Confession and Absolution. VII. Invocation or Prayer to Saints, &c. VIII. Purgatory and Prayer for the Dead. Lastly, that Apostolical Tradition is the true Rule of Faith.

A full discovery of the false evidence produced by the Papists against the most reverend and learned Dr. Tho. Tenison.

One sheet, 4to 1688 The soldier's letter is added at the end. N.B. In the note to No. 116 the Editor neglected to suppress the sentence " I know not," &c.
u CHAP. X. *Of the Discourses written in the dispute between Dr. William Sherlock and father Lewis Sabran, about the doctor's*
Preservative against Popery.
119. A preservative against popery; be-

ing some plain directions to unlearned protestants, how to dispute with Romish Priests.
The first part. By Will. Sherlock, D.D. Master of the
Temple. pp. 90, 4to Lond. 1688
See Cat. No. 174. Contin. p. 2.

On the use of Church authority and tradition, as compatible with private judgment, see Daille on the use of the Fathers, Laud's Conference, Taylor's Liberty of Prophesying, John White's Way to the True Church see an account of this interesting folio of the learned Vicar of Eccles, Lancashire, in Humphrey Chetham's Church Libraries, and Newman's Lectures on the Prophetical Office of the Church, viewed relatively to Romanism and Popular Protestantism: Lect. v. On the use of private judgment.

C I 120. *§f* An answer to Dr. Sherlock's preservative against popery. Anon. By Lewis Sabran, Jesuit.
One sheet, 4to Lond. 1688
See Contin. p. 3.

Born in 1652, died in 1732. A memoir of the Chaplain to James II. will be found in Dr. Oliver's Memoirs of the Members of the Society of Jesus.

This Catalogue contains Sabran's other works.

£. 1L. 121. A defence of Dr. Sherlock's preservative against Popery; in reply to a Jesuit's answer. Wherein the R. Father's reasonings are fully confuted. By William Giles, a protestant footman, living with Madam H. in Mark-Lane. The third edition, pp. 27, and the publisher to the reader pp. 110.
4to Lond. 1688 See Cat. No. 176. Contin p. 3.

I know not who was the real author of this book, for William Giles, I presume, is a feigned name. It is evidently the work of a scholar. Three editions at least appear to have been called for the year of its publication. J. H. T.

122. The second part of the preservative against popery; shewing (£.fL. how contrary popery is to the true ends of the christian religion, fitted for the instruction of unlearned protestants. By William Sherlock, D.D. Master of the Temple. pp. 91, 4to Lond. 1688

See Cat. No. 175. Contin. p. 3.
123. Dr. Sherlock's preservative considered; first part, with its defence by William Giles in two letters. By Lewis Sabran, of the society of Jesus.
See Contin. p. 4.
124. A vindication of both parts of the preservative against ©,2,, popery, in answer to the cavils of Lewis Sabran, Jesuit. By William Sherlock, D.D. pp. Ill and Catal. of Books pp. 3, 4to 1588 See Cat No. 177. Contin. p. 4. Peck, by an error of the press, has marked this book as if it had been on the popish side. J. H. T.

Another edition of No. 123, Dr. Sherlock's preservative considered; the first part, and its defence proved to contain principles which destroy all right use of reason, Fathers, Councils, undermine divine faith and abuse moral honesty; in the second part forty malicious calumnies and forged untruths laid open; besides several fanatical principles which destroy all church discipline and oppose Christ's divine authority. In two letters of F. Lewis Sabran, of the Society of Jesus. With a third letter to Mr. Needham. pp. 86, 4to 1688
See Dr. Oliver's Memoirs.

CHAP. XI. *Of the discourses written about the conversions of several persons to the Church of Home, with their motives; and the churchmen's replies.*
©.1L 125. A discourse against Transubstantiation. Anon. By John Tillotson, D. D.
pp. 43 and Catalogue of Books pp. 3, 4to Lond. 1685 pp. 36, 8vo 1687
See Cat. No. 4 State p. 8. Contin. pp. 6 and 8.

This discourse is placed in tlns section because it was attacked by the following, which it seems to have occasioned, but of course not in the sense of having occasioned Mr. Basset's conversion to Romanism, which is a mere pretence. J. H. T.

" Though some of their greatest wits, as Cardinal Perron, and of late Monsieur Arnaud, have undertaken the defence of it (Transubstantia tion) in great volumes; yet it is an absurdity of that monstrous and massy weight, that no humane authority or wit are able to support it: It will make the very pillars of St. Peter's crack, and requires more volumes to make it good than would fill the Vatican." p. 42.

CH. 126. *§t* Reason and Authority; or the motives of a late protestantfs reconciliation to the Catholick Church. Together with remarks upon some late discourses against Transubstantiation. Publisht with allowance. pp. 130, 4to Henry Hills, Lond. 1687 See Contin. p. 8. This work is attributed in the Bodl. and Dublin Catalogues to Josh. Bassett, Master of Sidney Coll. Cambridge. Dodd (Church Hist. vol. iii. p. 483) attributes it to Gother, which can scarcely be true; for the writer of this work represents himself as having been converted to Romanism *after* the publication of Tillotson's discourse against Transubstantiation, which was published in 1685. "At least (he says) I was recommended to a late discourse against Transubstantiation. I read it over and over with great attention," &c. p. 43. It is very possible, however, that Gother may have written the matter of the book or supplied it to Bassett, who was probably a mere instrument in the hands of the party. The main object of the work is to attack this Discourse of Tillotson (pp. 43-113) and that by Dr. Wake (pp. 113 et seq.) See No. 280 *infra*. Joshua Bassett, S.T.B. Caius Coll. made master of Sidney, regiis Uteris Jac. II. 1686. Amotus regiis literis Jac. II. 1 Dec. 1688. Cooper's Annals, vol. iii. pp. 614, 616, 636, 642. Mr. Cooper refers to Bodl. Catal. vol. i. p. 198, and to Bassett's verses on the death of the Duke of Albemarle 1700, on the accession of James II. 168t, and on the birth of the Prince of Wales 1688. For the dates of his degrees see the Graduati Cantabr. J. H. T.

. An answer to a book entitled, Reason and Authority, &c. C1L. together with a brief account of Augustine the Monk, and of the conversion of the English, taken out of Bede's Ecclesiastical History. In a Letter to a Friend. Anon, By Thomas Bambridge, D.D. Fellow of Trinity College, Cambridge. pp. 96, 4to Lond. 1687 See Cat. No. 133. Contin. p. 35. Fasti Oxon. vol. ii. col. 177. Gee calls the author Dr. Bembridge; the name is Bambridge in Wood (loc. cit.), but the true name is Thos. Bainbrigg, as he is called in the Reg. of Cambr. He graduated B.A. 165£. He was Proctor 1678. See Hardy's Le Neve. Graduati Cantabr. and Blomfield Collect. Cantabr. p. iii. Bainbrigg was made A. M. per Regias literas 1661, and S.T.B. per Reg. lit. 1684. He died suddenly August 16, 1703.— Baker's note ib. ed. Bliss. See also Cooper's Ann. of Cambr. vol. iv. p. 64. J. H. T.

Compare Archbishop Parker, De Antiquitate Britannics e Ecclesise, fol. 1572, 1605. Ussher's Discourse of the Religion anciently professed by the Irish and British, 4to Lond. 1631, Works, vol. iv. Basire on the Ancient Liberty of the Britannick Church and the Legitimate Exemption thereof from the Roman Patriarchate &c. &c., 12mo Lond. 1661. Of the Heart and its right Sovereign: and Rome no Mother-Church to England, Or an historical Account of the title of an English Church; and by what Ministry the Gospel was first planted in every county. By Thomas Jones, of Oswestry, 8vo Lond. 1678. See Wood's Ath. Oxon. ed. Bliss. iv. col. 711. Stillingfleet's Origines Britannicse, or The Antiquities of the British Churches, fol. Lond. 1685. Works 1710, vol. i. A new edition with additional notes, hy the Rev. Tho. Pinder Pantin, M.A., 2 vols 8vo Oxford 1842. Bp. Lloyd's History of the Government of the Church, as it was in Great Britain and Ireland when they first received the Christian Religion, 12mo Lond. 1703, and in Pantin's Stillingfleet, vol. ii. With a list of Authors referred to. The Britons and Saxons not converted to Popery, containing an Answer to all material in a hook, " England's Conversion and Reformation compar'd." By George Smith. 8vo. Lond. 1748. On the other side consult A Treatise of Three Conversions of England. from Paganisme to Christian Religion, 3 vols. 12mo. 1603. By

Roh. Parsons. See Wood's Ath. Oxon. vol. ii. col. 67 Cressy's Church History of Brittany, fol. 1668; and Dr. Lingard's History and Antiquities of the Anglo-Saxon Church, 2 vols. 1845.

C IL. 128. *i* The considerations which obliged Peter Manby, Dean of Derry, to embrace the Catholique Religion. Humbly dedicated to His Grace the Lord Primate of Ireland. Ps. xlii. Judica me Deus, et discerne causam meam, &c. Dublin Castle the 11th of March 1686-7. This following Discourse is allowed to be printed. Tho. Sheridan. pp. 19, to the Reader pp. 6, 4to Lond. 1687 See Contin. p. 36. P. Manhy had been a scholar of Trin. Coll. Dublin in 1660, Chaplain to Abp. Boyle, and Dean of Derry, September 17th, 1672. It is said that having been disappointed in obtaining a bishoprick, which he had hoped for from the influence of the Primate, he joined the Church of Rome. This is alluded to in Dr. King's answer to the present work, see No. 129. In 1686 he had a dispensation under the Great Seal to hold the Deanery notwithstanding his having declared himself a Roman Catholic, and therefore it will be observed that in the title page of the present work he styles himself " Dean," not late Dean, " of Derry." In 1688 the king made him an alderman of Derry. After the battle of the Boyne he retired into France; and died in Laiden in 1697. It is said that his brother, also a clergyman, was by his means converted to Romanism, and left two sons who both became Jesuits. Ware, Writers of Ireland (Harris's ed. p. 2.i?), Cotton's Fasti, vol. iii. p. 332.

It is worthy of remark that the " Queries to Protestants, concerning the English Reformation, by T. W. Gent" (see No. 173 *infra*) are the same as those given in Latin, by Peter Manby, at the end of No. 128. J. H. T.

129. An answer to the considerations which obliged Peter Manby, C.1L. Late Dean of London-Derry in Ireland (as he pretends) to embrace what he calls the Catholick Religion. By William King, Chancellor of St. Patrick's Dublin. Isaiah i. ii. I have nourished and brought up children, and they have rebelled against me. pp. 104, 4to Lond. 1687

Cat. No. 130. Contin. p. 35. An edition was printed in Dublin (or with a Dublin title page) the same year. William King had been a scholar of Trin. Coll. Dublin; was Chancellor of St. Patrick's 1679, Dean of St. Patrick's 168f, Bishop of Deny 16!)£, Archbishop of Dublin 1703. He died May 8, 1729. His Answer to Manby gave rise to the following controversial tracts in Ireland.

J A reformed catechism in two dialogues, concerning the English Reformation, collected for the most part word for word out of Dr. Burnet, John Fox, and other Protestant Historians, published for the information of the people, in reply to Master William King's Answer to Dean Manby's Considerations. The first Dialogue. 4to Dublin 1687. Here again, it will be observed, that the author styles himself
" Dean Manby." The second Dialogue never appeared. To this Mr. King replied in
A Vindication of the answer to the Considerations, which obliged Peter Manby, Dean of Derry, to embrace what he calls the Catholick Religion: being an answer to the first Dialogue, already printed, of his reformed Catechism. 4to Dublin 1688. In the same year Manby published *i* A letter to a friend, shewing the vanity of this opinion, that every man's sense and reason is to guide him in matters of faith. 4to Dublin 1688.

And to this King again replied in
A vindication of the Christian Religion and Reformation against the attempts of a late letter wrote by Peter Manby, Dean of Derry, pretending to show that all religions have a like plca, and that there can be no such sins as heresy and schism if every man's sense and reason are to guide him in matters of faith. 4to Dublin 1688. J. H. T.

C1L 130. *i* Consensus Veterum; or the reasons of Edward Sclater, Minister of Putney, for his Conversion to the Catholic Faith and Communion. Jer. vi. 16. Thus saith the Lord, stand you in the ways, &c. Ecclesia Romana principem in ecclesias locum semper tenuit, et antiquarum traditionum tenacissima fuit. Dr. Walton, Prolegom. 10, non procul ah initio.

pp. 100, to the Reader pp. 6, 4to Lond. 1686

See Contin. p. 43. Ath. Oxon. vol. ii. col. 1083. Edward Sclater was of St. John's Coll. Oxford; M.A. 1647: a schoolmaster and afterwards minister of Putney; having joined the Church of Rome on the accession of James II. he had a licence to retain the income of the cure, employing a curate to do the clerical duty. See an allusion to the numerous scandalous cases of this kind that occurred at that time in "Some Dialogues between Mr. G." a clergyman in exactly the same circumstances as Sclater "and others." No. 254 *infra*. On Rogation Sunday, May 5th, 1689, he made a public recantation of the Roman Catholic Religion, and was received into the Communion of the Church of England in the Savoy Church, after which he lived privately near Exeter House or Change Wood. J. H. T.

" The dispensing power was, at the same time, employed for the purpose of enabling Roman Catholics to hold ecclesiastical preferment. The new Solicitor readily drew the warrants in which Sawyer had refused to be concerned. One of these warrants was in favour of a wretch named Edward Sclater, who had two livings which he was determined to keep at all costs and through all changes. He administered the sacrament to his parishioners according to the rites of the Church of England on Palm Sunday 1686. On Easter Sunday, only seven days later, he was at mass. The royal dispensation authorised him to retain the emoluments of his benefices. To the remonstrances of the patrons from whom he had received his preferment he replied in terms of insolent defiance, and, while the Roman Catholic cause prospered, put forth an absurd treatise in defence of his apostasy. But, a very few weeks after the Revolution, a great congregation as sembled at Saint Mary's in the Savoy, to see him received again into the bosom of the Church which he had deserted. He read his recantation with tears flowing from his eyes, and pronounced a bitter invective against the Popish priests whose arts had seduced him.
See the letters patent in Gutch's Collectanea Curiosa. The date is the 3rd of May, 1686. Sclater's Consensus Veterum; Gee's Reply, entitled Vcteres Vindicati; Dr. Anthony Horneck's account of Mr. Sclater's recantation of the errors of Popery on the 5th May, 1689; Dodd's Church History, part viii. book ii. art. 3. — Macaulay, vol. ii. p. 85.

His other Reasons, besides Transubstantiation, are the unity of the Church, St. Peter's supremacy, &c.
131. Veteres Vindicati, in an expostulatory letter to Mr. Sclater C1L. of Putney, upon his Consensus Veterum; wherein the absurdity of his method, the weakness of his reasons are shewn,
his false aspersions upon the Church of England are wiped off, and her faith concerning the Eucharist proved to be that of the Primitive Church. Together with animadversions on
Dean Boileau's French translation of and Remarks upon
Bertram. King Charles the Martyr to the Prince. *Eik. BacriK.* 27. " But if you never see my face again and the meanness of fantastic anarchy." Anon. By Edward
Gee, M.A. pp. 107, 4to Lond. 1687
See Cat. No. 46. Contin. p. 43. Ath. Oxon. vol. ii. col. 222.
This reference ought to be Fasti vol. ii. col. 222. For another answer to Sclater see No. 240 *infra*. J. H. T.

" Mar. 4, 1G83. Edw. Gee, M.A., of St Joh. Coll. in the said univ. Cambridge was then incorporated. This learned divine, who is of the Gees of Manchester in Lancash., is now rector of St. Benedict's church near Paul's Wharf in London, and chapl. in ord. to their majesties king William and queen Mary. He hath written and published several books, mostly against popery, which came out in the reign of king James II., the titles of which I shall now for brevity's sake omit." Edw. Gee Lancastr. de Manchester ubi natus et Uteris institutus, Alius Georgii Gee sutor calcearum, annos natus 17 adm. subsiaator pro magistro Alport: tutore et fidejussore ejus magistro Leech, Maii 9, 1676. Reg. Coll. Jo. Cant. Baker." Fasti Oxon. col. 222. All his 1 irroks against popery are enumerated in this Catalogue.

132. *i?* Transubstantiation defended and proved from Scripture: in answer to the first part of a Treatise intitled, A Discourse against Transubstantiation. The first Part. S. Ignatius Ep. ad. Smyrnseos. *Evj(a.purrLas real irpoaexjrp airoOvriaicovai.*

They abstain from our communion die questioning the matter among themselves. pp. 64, with introduction (at the beginning) pp. 22 and contents (at the end) 2 pp.
4to Lond. 1687
See Contin. p. 8. This, with the following tracts Nos. 133 and 135, were in answer to No. 125 *supra*. There is no other reason why they should be placed in this chapter. J. H. T.
£. 1L. 133. "i A answer to a discourse against Transubstantiation. Hie est Filius meus dilectus. Ipsum audite. This is my beloved son. Hear ye him. Matthew xvii. 5.
pp. 80, 4to Lond. 1687 Contin. p. 8.
Dodd, in his Church History, vol. iii. p. 483, attributes this tract to John Goter or Gother. J. H. T. 134. A reply to a treatise entitled Transubstantiation defended, &c., as No. 132 *supra*.
Contin. p. 8. Qusere if ever printed? An answer to No. 132 is promised by Wake, Contin. p. 3, and is said to have been then prepared. J. H. T.
135. *h* Transubstantiation defended. Part ii. of No. 132 *supra*.
Contin. p. 8. Quaere if ever published? There is no reason to suppose that this work was ever printed. Wake (Contin. p. 8) says that (in 1688) it had not appeared. J. H. T.

ADDENDA ET CORRIGrENDA.
No. 119. Daille or Daltaus; on the merits of this work see Des Maiseaux's Life of Chillingworth.
No. 124. 1688 *pro* 1588. Supplem. Wm. Needham was the Chaplain of the Abp. of Canterbury, who signed the Licence or Imprimatur to Dr. Sherlock's books. J. H. T.
No. 126. At last *pro* At least.
No. 128. After Dean of Derry, — a circumstance which is thus alluded to in Dr. King's Answer: — " Why did

you defer publishing this paper (such as it is), which was ready some time before, till you thought you might be sure of keeping the profits of your Deanery? Either you are a Day or Clergyman. If a Layman are you not abominably sacrilegious to hare possessed, and still retain the Rovenue of a Clergyman? Why do you retain the Title of Dean in the Frontispiece of a book, which is designed to prove you to be no Priest, and consequently incapable of it? If your orders had yielded you as much *per annum* as your Deanery doth, have we not reason to believe you would no more have renounced the one than the other? For shame, — resign our church her own, since you have deserted her, or never talk of conscience." — Answer to the Considerations, &c., p. 13. J. H. T.

After France, — but afterwards returned to England, and died in *London* in 1697. J. H. T.

Vindicue Calvinisticse: or some impartial reflections on the Dean of Londonderry's Considerations, and Mr. Chancellor King's Answer thereto, in which he no less unjustly than impertinently reflects on the Protestant Dissenters. In a letter to a friend, by W. B., D. D. 4to Dublin 1688.

This Tract has been printed among the works of the Rev. Joseph Boyse, of Dublin, an eminent and learned Dissenting Minister, vol. ii. p. 45, Lond. fol. (two vols.) 1728, with a Prefatory Epistle (in which this Tract is particularly alluded to), signed by E. Calamy and five other ministers. J. H. T.

The Romish Priest turn'd Protestant, with the reasons of his conversion. Wherein the true church is exposed to the view of Christians, and derived out of the holy scriptures, sound reason, and the ancient fathers. Humbly presented to both Houses of Parliament. By James Salgado, formerly a priest of the Order of the Dominicans. pp. 31, 4to Lond. 1679

A Confession of Faith of James Salgado, a Spaniard and sometime a priest in the Church of Rome. Dedicated to the University of Oxford. With an account of his life and sufferings, by the Romish party, since he forsook the Romish religion. pp. 15, 4to 1681

A letter to a Lord upon his happy conversion from Popery to the Protestant Religion. By T. Burnet, D.D. Half sheet, 4to 1688

An account of the arguments which moved the author to turn papist; with his confutation of the same, appended to William Chillingworth's Religion of Protestants, abridged (by John Patrick). 4to Lond. 1688

See No. 441 *supra*.

Motives and Reasons for dissevering from the Church of Rome and her Doctrine, by C. hristopher Musgrave after he had lived a Carthusian Monk for 20 years, wherein after the declaration of his conversion he openeth diverse absurdities practised in that Church, being not matters of Report, but such Things whereof he was an Eye and Ear Witness. 4to Lond. 1688

In the second volume of Fronde's History of England from the Fall of Wolsey to the Death of Elizabeth, there is a truthful description by "an Eye and Ear Witness" of the religious life of the monks of the London Charterhouse at the time of the Reformation.

An historical relation of several great and learned Romanists who have embraced the protestant religion &c. See No. 218 *infra*.

Motives of Conversion to the Catholick faith, as it is professed in the Reformed Church of England. By Neal Carolan, formerly Parish Priest of Slane and Stacallan, &c. in Meath. 4to 1688 See an account of Neal Carolan or O'Carolan in Ware's Writers of Ireland by Harris, p. 204..T. H. T.

The declaration of Francis Briber Gent. which he publickly made before the Lord Bishop of Waterford, in the Cathedral Church of Waterford, in the kingdom of Ireland, June 17th, 1688, containing the reasons for his renouncing the Roman Catholic and embracing the Protestant religion; together with what the Lord Bishop of Waterford returned upon that occasion. Half sheet, 4to Lond. 1688

Exomologesis; or, a faithful Narrative of the Occasion and Motives of his Conversion unto Catholic Unity. By Hugh Paulin de Cressy. 18mo Paris 1647-1653

Cressy was a native of Yorkshire, but became Dean of Leighlin in Ireland. See Cotton's Fasti Eccl. Hibrn. (Prov. of Dubl.) pp. 77, 174, 390. He afterwards joined the Benedictines in the English College of Douay, and took the name of Serenus (in religion). See Ware's Writers of Ireland by Harris, p. 356. J. H. T.

"This Exomologesis was the golden calf which the English papists fell down and worshipped. They brag'd that book to be unanswerable, and to have given a total overthrow to the Chillingworthians, and book and tenets of Lucius Lord Falkland." — Wood's Athenre, ed. Biiss. vol. iii. col. 1014. The book and tenets of Lord Falkland will be found in the first volume of Dr. Hammond's works, fol. 1674. Compare Des Maiseaux's Life of Chillingworth.

The noble historian of the Revolution, in his Animadversions upon a book, entitled Fanaticism fanatically imputed to the Catholick Church by Dr. Stillingfleet, and the imputation refuted, by S.erenus C.ressy), 8vo Lond. 1674, answers the arguments which are there adduced from the Catholic Unity of the Church, and charges the author with very different motives from those assigned in the Exomologesis for his conversion. In his dedication to Dr. Stillingfleet he speaks of Cressy as "a person whom he had long known and familiarly conversed with before he was perverted in his Religion, and had often seen since;" and (in p. 86) he asserts that " he never thought of entering the Religion he now professes till the same rebellious power that drove the King out of the kingdom, drove him likewise from the good preferments which he enjoyed in the Church, and then the necessity and distraction of his fortune, together with the melancfaolick and irresolution in his nature, prevailed with him to bid farewel to his own reason and understanding, and to resign himself to the conduct of those who had a much worse than his." His life may be seen in the third volume of Dodd. Cf. Dr. Oliver's

Biography, p. 43.

Memoirs of Mr. James Wads worth, a Jesuit that recanted, discovering a dreadful prospect of impiety in the blasphemous doctrines or Gospel of the Jesuits, with their Atheistical Lives and conversations. 4to 1679 CP. H. The Copies of Certain Letters which have passed between Spain and England in matter of Religion, concerning the general motives to Roman Obedience, between Mr. James Waddesworth, a late Pensioner of the holy Inquisition in Sevill, and W. Bedell, a Minister of the Gospel of Jesus Christ in Suffolk. Appended to The Life of William Bedell, D.D., Lord Bishop of Killmore in Ireland. Written by Gilbert Burnet, D.D. Lond. 1685-92

Besides the English Spanish Pilgrime (see p. 63 *supra*) Wadsworth was the author of other works, e.g. a translation of Sandoval's Life of Charles the Fifth, a documentary work of authority much relied on by Robertson.

Farewell to Popery, in a letter to Dr. Nicholas, by W. H., shewing the true motives that withdrew him to the Romish Religion, and the reason of his return to the Church of England. 4to 1679

The Proselyte of Rome called back to the communion of the

Church of England, in a private letter thought very fit and seasonable to be made public. 4to 1679

Conversion and persecution of Eva Cohan, now called Elizabeth

Verboon, a person of quality of the Jewish Religion.

4to 1680

A Relation of the Fearful Estate of Francis Spira after he turn'd C H. Apostate from the Protestant Church to Popery. To which are now added sundry the like dreadful examples of God's Judgments, on persons of all degrees, that have for fear of worldly interest forsaken the true Religion which once they professed. Together with that incomparable Lamentation of the Great Origen, for his Fall, when he was again received into the Church. By Nath. Bacon, Esq. pp. 81, preface and to the reader pp. 16, 18mo Lond. 1683 CHAP. XII. *Of the discourses written by the country Parson and the Romish Missionary.*

136. The Country Parson's admonition to his Parishioners. Malachi ii. 7: "The Priest's lips," &c. Heb. xiii. 17: "Obey them that have rule," &c.

Single sheet, pp. 14, 8vo Lond. 1686

Cat. No. 112. Contin. p. 29. Ath. Oxon. vol. ii. col. 1026. William Assheton, D.D., Prebendary of York Cathedral and Rector of Beckenham in Kent, the son of the Rev. William Assheton, Rector of Middleton, Lancashire, was born in the year 1641, died in 1711. He was the first projector of a scheme for providing a maintenance for clergymen's widows and others. See Baines's History of Lancashire, vol. ii. p. 606-10.

I have given the title above as I find it in my copy. But Peck (who had also a copy of the book) seems to describe a different edition. He gives the title thus:
—

" The country parson's admonition to his parishioners, with directions how to behave themseives when any one designs to seduce them from the Church of England. By William Ashton, D.D., Rector of in Surrey." 12mo Lond. 1686.

And this is also the title given by Gee and Wake. Ant. Wood (loc. cit.) gives a title differing from both, in these words:
—

"The Country Parson's admonition to his Parishioners, in two parts, persuading them to continue in the Protestant religion, with directions how to behave themselves when any one comes to seduce them." 24mo Lond. 1689.

In the Library of Trin. Coll. Dublin, there is no printed copy of this book, but there is a MS. copy in the hand-writing of Dr. Claud. Gilbert, transcribed from a printed book, and evidently most accurately copied by him, for the purpose of completing his set of this class of works. In this MS. the title is given thus:
—

" The Country Parson's Admonition to his Parishioners, persuading them to continue in the Protestant religion, with directions how to hehave themselves when any one designs to seduce them from the Church of England. By Dr. Asheton, Minister of Beckenham in Kent. Lond. Printed for R. Wilde."

On the whole it seems prohable that there were several editions of this tract, which varied in the title page, but otherwise agreed in substance. It was necessary to give this explanation, lest it should be inferred from the foregoing great discrepancies that there had been published different books, agreeing nearly in the title. The " two parts," mentioned in Wood's title, evidently include the next tract (No. 137) as part ii. J. H. T.

137. The plain man's reply to the catholic Missionaries, pp. 38, and "Books by the same author, pp. 2-12." 12mo Lond. 1688

" It is agreed by Catholicks that the church is an infallible witness and guide. And Protestants profess, that if this could be made evidently appear they would hold out in no controversy at all. This, therefore is to be made evident unto Protestants. This is the task of Catholicks, especially of Catholic Missionaries."—Cressy's Append. to Exomol. Cap. 4, ff. 6.

See Cat. No. 113 (State; p. 34.) Contin. p. 29. A copy of this book, London 1686, 12mo, is in the Library of Trin. Coll. Dublin. J. H. T.

138. The plain man's answer to his country parson's admonition; together with the missionaries answer to the plain man's reply. (Anon.) Lond. 1686

See Contin. p. 30. A copy of this tract in MS., in the handwriting of Dr. Claud. Gilbert, is in the Library of Trin. Coll. Dublin. J. H. T.

139. A Defence of the plain man's reply to the Catholick Missionaries. Being a further examination of the pretended Infallibility of the Church of Rome. Imprimatur, Guil. Needham,

Y

&c., March 29, 1688. By the Author of the Plain-man's reply to the Catholick Missionaries William Ashton, D.D. pp. 44. Title and Argt. pp. 4. 12mo Loud. 1688 See Cat. No. 114. Contin. p. 30. Ath. Oxon. vol. ii. Col. 1026. A copy of this, in MS. in the hand-writing of Dr. Claud. Gilbert, from the edit. Lond. 1687, reprinted 1704, is in the Library of Trin. Coll. Dublin. J. H. T.

140. A defence of the Country Parson's admonition; against the exceptions of the plain man's answer. (Anon. By William Ashton, D.D.) pp. 22, Lond. 1688

See Cat. No. 115. Contin. p. 30. Ath. Oxon. vol. ii. col. 1026.

This tract ought to have been placed before No. 139, as it was published before it. See "The Argument" prefixed to No. 139, in which an account is given of the occasion of the controversy. A copy of this book, in MS. in the hand-writing of Dr. Claud. Gilbert, from the ed. of London 1687, is in the Library of Trin. Coll. Dublin.

It would seem that these tracts were highly valued, and that they must have become very scarce at the beginning of the last century, since Dr. Gilbert took the trouble of transcribing them in his own hand, in order to complete his set. Dr. Claud. Gilbert was elected a Fellow of Trinity College in 1693, Senior Fellow 1698, Vice Provost 1716, Regius Professor of Divinity 1722. In 1735 he accepted the living of Ardstrnw, and at the same time gave to the College Library his splendid collection of books, consisting of upwards of 13,000 volumes; which he saw arranged and placed on the shelves of the library as they now stand before he retired to his living. His bust in marble is preserved in the library, and there is a picture of him in the provost's house. J. H. T.

141. The child's monitor against popery. Written at first for the private use of a child, who hath Popish parents, and now made puhlick for the benefit of others. 24mo Lond.

See Ath. Oxon. vol. ii. col. 1026. Peck and Wood give only as the title of this book, " The child's monitor against popery." Wood adds, but not as part of the title, " written to preserve the child of a person of quality from being seduced by his popish parents." I do not know who were the popish parents of this child of a person of quality; nor have I ever seen a copy of this tract. I have taken the title as given ahove from the list of books at the end of No. 137. J. H. T.

These tracts were all reprinted in 1751, Lond. 4to., with the following advertisement: —

" It may he necessary to observe that, since the time of their *C* iL original editions mentioned in,their respective title pages, each of these pieces (the Child's Monitor only excepted) was reprinted in the year 1706. Which edition, like the former, is now very difficult tobe met with. No apology, therefore, need be offered for introducing these papers into a new acquaintance with the world, as this will be a means the better to promote their dispersion into the hands of unlearned readers, for whose benefit they were principally designed. But a particular reason for their present appearance from the press is, to recover them from an obscurity, in which they have lain so long as to become, in a manner, lost to the world; in order to assist such persons who are collecting these tracts, which have done such honour to the Protestant cause, to make their sets as complete as possible. The four first of them are exactly reprinted according to their original editions, but a printed copy of the Child's Monitor, being too scarce to be obtained, this impression is taken from a transcript of it, communicated by a worthy clergyman."

In the Hist, and Crit. Diet. fol. 1735, there is an analysis of these tracts, art. Assheton.

142. A caution to protestants not to forsake the Communion of ©. 3.. the Church of England. 12mo 1687 143. The plausible arguments of a Romish priest answered by an CH. English Protestant. Seasonable and useful for all Protestant families. Licensed, May 24, 1686. (Anon. By Thomas Comber, D.D. , Pra;centor of York.) pp. 54, with title and pref. &c., pp. 8. List of Books at the end, pp. 2. 8vo Lond. 1686

See Cat. No. 187. Reprinted 1725, 8vo, pp. 47. " The plausible arguments of a Roman priest from antiquity, answered by the Author of the answer to the plausible arguments from Scripture." Of the author of the " Companion to the Temple," and of his writings, Memoirs were published by his great grandson Thomas Comber, A.B., 8vo Lond.

1799.

A protestant's resolution shewing his reasons why he will not be a papist, directed to the meanest capacity. Sixth edition.

12mo Lond. 1684

Friendly and seasonable Advice to the Roman Catholics of England. By Tho. Comber, D.D. Fourth edition.

12mo Lond. 1685 CHAP. XIII. *Of the popish discourses written by way of advice to the*

Protestant pulpits; with the churchmen's replies.

144. *i* Good advice to the pulpits, delivered in a few cautions for fL.

keeping up the reputation of those chairs, and preserving the nation in peace. Published with allowance.

pp. 70. Title and to the Reader pp. 6. 4to Lond. 1687 Contin. p. 10. Dodd, in his Church History, vol. iii. p. 483, ascribes this tract to John Gother; and Wake (Contin. loc. cit.) attributes it to the author of the " Papist misrepresented and Represented," No. 51, *supra;* from which the Bodl. Cat. places it under J. Leybourn. J. H. T.

" In which lie rakes together out of the Sermons publish'd in the last years of the late King's Reign, whatever he thought would serve to make them odious. The Design was well enough laid; and the Circumstances of the Times consider'd, it were not to be wonder'd if some things should have pass'd more hot against those of the Church of Rome, than was to have been wish'd," &c. Contin. pp. 16, 17. The Preachers cited are B. Smith, Dr. Burnet, Jane, Dr. Sharp, Dr. Tillotson, Dr. Stillingfleet, Pelling, Hesketh, Okes, Th. Smith, Johnson, Standish, Turner, Wray, James, Bisby, Tennison, Orme, Hickeringil, Fowler, Hooper, Wallis, Calamy, Butler, South, Sherlock.

145. An apology for the pulpits; being in answer to a late book, £. %.

intituled, Good advice to the Pulpits, together with an appendix, containing a defence of Dr. Tenison's Sermon about Alms: in a letter to the author of this Apology. Imprimatur

&c. H. Maurice, January 12, 1687. Anon. By John

Williams, A.M., afterwards Bp. of Chichester.

pp. 58. Defence, &c., pp. 25. 4to Lond. 1688 Sec Cat. No. 121. Contin. pp. 11 and 17. Ath. Oxon. vol. ii.

col. 1121. After p. 58 follows the Defence of Dr. Tenison's Sermon, with a new pagination and the following title: " A defence of Dr. Tenison's Sermon of discretion in giving alms, written in a letter to the author of the Apology for the Pulpits." The letter is signed "Tho. Tenison," and dated "S. M." (i.e. St. Martin's) "Jan. 11, '87." J. H. T.

CH. 146. *fc* Pulpit sayings, or the characters of the Pulpit-Papists examined. In answer to the apology for the pulpits, and in vindication of the Representer against the Stater of the Controversie. With allowance, pp. 58, pp. to the Reader 14, and contents at the end 2. 4to Lond. 1688

See Contin. p. 17, where this hook is attributed to the Representer, i.e. according to Dodd *(ubi supra)* John Goter or Gother; and according to the Bodl. Cat. John Leybourn. See No. 51 *supra*. "The Stater," mentioned in the title-page, is evidently Dr. Clagett, author of the "State of the Controversy," see No. 71 *supra*. J. H. T.

C 3L. 147. Pulpit popery, true popery; being an answer to a book intituled Pulpit sayings: aud in vindication of the Apology for the Pulpits, and the Stater of the controversie against the Representer. Anon. By John Williams, M.A., afterwards Bp. of Chichester.

pp. 72, Title and contents pp. 6, 4to Lond. 1688 Cat. 122. Contin. p. 17. Ath. Oxon. vol. ii. col. 1121.

A Sermon preached at S. Margaret's Westminster, May 29th, 1(585, before the Honourable House of Commons, by William Sherlock, D.D. 4to 1685

N.B. This Sermon to the House of Commons was the occasion of our following controversies, as being the first thing that appeared in Print against Roman Catholics. See Reply to the Defence of the Exposition of the doctrine of the Church of England, Preface. Cf. No.."'1 note. It is mentioned in Good Advice to the Pulpits, p. 64.

A Vindication of a passage in Dr. Sherlock's sermon as above from the remarks of a late pretended remonstrance, by way of address from the Church of England to both Houses of Parliament. 4to 1685 CHAP. XIV.

Of the Romanists charge of schism and heresy upon the Church of England; with the churchmen's replies. 148. A vindication of the Church of England from the foul aspersions of Schism and Heresie unjustly cast upon her hy the Church of Rome. Anon. By Michael Altham, M.A. Gibson, vol. i. fol. 1. Part i. pp. 30. 4to Loud. 1687. Part ii. pp. 40. 4to Lond. 1687

See Cat. No. 134. Contin. p. 35. Fasti Oxon. vol. ii. col. 220. The Imprimatur of Part i. is dated November 30, 1686; that of Part ii. March 2, 1686, i.e. 168£. Michael Altham was vicar of Latton in Essex. J. H. T.

149. An address to the Ministers of the Church of England. pp. 31, 4to 1688

This seems to be the same tract which is given by Peck again, No. 248.

150. An Answer to a late printed Paper, given ahout by some of the Church of Rome. In a letter to a Gentleman. The second edition. Rev. ii. 5. Remember from whence thou art faln, &c. Anon. By John Williams, M.A. pp. 18, 4to Lond. 1686 See Cat. No. 135. Contin. p. 35. Ath. Oxon. vol. ii. col. 1121.

"The Popish Paper," to which this book is an answer, is given on the back of the title page. J. H. T.

" The same word for word with No. 5. I have compared them."

Dolman. Another edition, 1688, 12-mo pp. 24.

151. Lucilla and Elizabeth, or the Donatist and Protestant Schism parallel'd. 4to 1686

See Contin. p. 36. My copy of this tract has no title, and I think never had: it consists of 4 pp. only in 4to, and at the end of the last page we have " Published with allowance, London, printed by Henry

Hills, printer to the King's most Excellent Majesty, for his Household and Chappel. 1686. J. H. T.

152. A Protestant of the Church of England no Donatist. Or E, H.

some short Notes on Lucilla and Elizabeth. Licensed December 8, 1686. Anon. By William Sherlock, D.D. pp. 6, 4to Lond. 1686

See Cat. No. 136. Contin. p. 35.

153. An apologetical vindication of the Church of England: in C 1L. answer to those who reproach her with the English heresies and schisms, or suspect her not to be a Catholick Church upon their account. (Anon. By George Hickes, D.D.) Gibson. vol. ii. fol. vol. i. pp. 96, with the title and introd.,

pp. 4. 4to Lond. 1687

See Cat. No. 45. Contin. p. 35. Ath. Oxon. vol. ii. col. 1004.

A second edition of this valuable book was published in 1706, with the following title: "An apologetical vindication of the Church of

England: in answer to her adversaries who reproach her with the

English heresies and schisms. With an Appendix of Papers relating to the Schisms of the Church of Rome. By George Hickes, D.D.

The second edition, revised by the Author. London (Walter Kettilby), 1706." 8vo. Besides the appendix this edition has a large and learned Preface. In the interval between the two editions the author, who had been Dean of Worcester, was deprived of his church preferments, for refusing to take the oaths to King William and

Queen Mary. In the second edition he admits the genuineness of the papers attributed to King Charles II. (see No. xii.) which in the first edition he had quoted without expressing any opinion as to their author, — King James II. (as he states) having in the mean time shewn him the originals " interlined with the King's (Charles's) own hand." J. H. T.

A Nonjuring divine of uncommon abilities and universal learning, born at Newsham, Yorkshire, 1642, deprived on refusing to take the z oaths 1689, consecrated Bishop of Thetford hy the Nonjurors 1694, died 1715.

£.&, 154. i The Schism of the Church of England, &c., demonstrated in four Arguments formerly propos'd to Dr. Gunning and Dr. Pearson, the late bishops of Ely and Chester, by two Catholic

Disputants in a celebrated conference upon that point.
pp. 10, 4to Oxon. 1688 See Contin. p. 37, where we read, "This little paper with a large title was the other day reprinted at Oxford by the converts there." And Peck says, " Beprinted at Oxford." It originally appeared in the falsified account of the conference between Drs. Gunning and Pearson, on the one side, and two Romish disputants on the other, held in 1657. This account bears the following title:—Schisme unmask't, &c., *ut infra*. J. H. T. 155. The sum of a Conference had between two. Divines of the Church of England, and two Catholic Lay-Gentlemen, at the request, and for the satisfaction of three persons of quality, August 8, 1671. Publisht with allowance. pp. 40, 4to Lond. 1687
See Contin. p. 36. Peck, doubtless by an error of the press, has omitted to mark this book as being on the popish side.

In the Preface from " The Publisher to the Reader," we are told that " in the year 1676, there happen'd a conference about points of Religion, between some Protestant Divines and some Roman Catholic Gentlemen, which, after a long silence, has been now lately set out the second time, in a fine Dress and with a long Preface: this (the publisher says) gave me the curiosity to seek further into those matters, and meeting accidentally with the copy of another conference held in 1671, wherein some of the same persons were concern'd, I thought good to present you with it." It does not appear, however, who the "two divines of the Church of"England," engaged in the conference of 1671, or who the "three persons of quality" for whose satisfaction it was intended, were. The other conference alluded to is thus described in the margin: "A relation of a Conference, Apr. 3, 1676," and is doubtless that which Thomas Burnet, in his Life of the Bishop, published at the end of the second volume of Burnet's Own Times (vol. ii. p. 685), thus notices: " As the apprehensions of popery grew daily stronger, the most eminent divines of the Church of England signalized themselves in the Romish Controversy: nothing of that kind was more taken notice of than the Account our author printed, in the year 1676, of a Conference, which himself and Dr. Stillingfleet were engaged in with Coleman and the principal of the Romish priests: this made him considered as one who stood in the very front of the opposition to popery."

I have not seen the original edition of this conference, but I have a copy of it, which I doubt not is the same which the publisher of the Conference of 1671 speaks of (in the words just quoted) as having been " lately set out the second time." Neither Peck nor Wake have noticed the Conference of 1676, published by Bishop Burnet, nor does it occur in the Bodl. Cat. I have a copy of the second edition of it, although it is not so called in the book itself, nor any hint given that it was published before.

The first edition of this Conference was printed in 8vo, 1676, under the title: " A relation of a conference held about religion at London, 3 April, 1676, by Edward Stillingfleet D.D. and Gilbert Burnet," &c. See chron. account of Burnet's Works, Own Times, vol. vi. p. 336, (Oxford ed.), fol. vol. ii. p. 727. J. H. T.

156. The Reformation of the Church of England justified, according to the canons of the Council of Nice, and other general councils and the traditions of the Catholick Church. Being an answer to a paper reprinted at Oxford, called the Schisme of the Church of England demonstrated in four arguments, formerly proposed to Dr. Gunning and Dr. Pearson, the late bishops of Ely and Chester, by two Catholic disputants, in a celebrated Conference upon that point. In which answer the unworthy and false dealings of the Papists are shewed, and the charge of schisme returned upon them, and the Church of England proved truly Catholick and Apostolick in her doctrine and constitution. Anon. By William Saywell D.D., Master of Jesus College, Cambridge (afterwards Archdeacon of Ely). pp. 33, with title and pref. pp. 6, 4to Camb. 1688 Cat. No. 142. Contin. p. 37. See above No. 154. Wake (loc. cit.) tells us that Dr. Saywell " was particularly related to one of the abused bishops." I believe Bishop Gunning is meant, to whom Saywell was chaplain, (Fasti Oxon. vol. ii. col. 177,) this being the relation spoken of, not any consanguinity. J. H. T. *N.S.* — The Nos. 148-150 ought to have been marled as being in the CI, An answer to the address presented to the Ministers of the Church of England. pp. 31, 4to Lond. 1688
The same as No. 248 *infra.*

C 1L The English case exactly set down by Hezekiah's reformation in a Court Sermon (on 2 Kings xviii. 22) at Paris. By Dr. Richard Steward, the Dean of Westminster, and of his Majesty's Chappel. Published for the brief but full vindication of the Church of England from the Romanists charge of Schism. And commended to the consideration of the late Author of The Grotian Religion Discovered, pp. 71, 18mo. Lond. 1659. pp. 30, 4to 1687-88

The difference of the case between the Separation of Protestants from the Church of Rome and the Separation of Dissenters from the Church of England. pp. 71, 4to Lond. 1683 & Schisme unmask't: Or A late conference betwixt Mr. Peter Gunning and Mr. John Pierson, Ministers, on the one part, and two disputants of the Roman Profession on the other: wherein is denned both what schisme is, and to whom it belongs. With a brief Recapitulation; wherein at one view may be seen the whole drift of this Conference, for such as want either learning to reach or leisure to read the whole Tract. And all is concluded with a decision of the main question, whether Protestants or those of the Roman Church be schismatiques. Also an Index is drawne pointing at the principal matters. Paris (cum privilegio), 8vo 1658

We learn from the Preface to this production that the conference began a little before Whitsuntide (May) 1657. See an account of the book (which it appears was disavowed by one of the Romish disputants) in the preface to the answer to it (No. 156 *supra),* and in the Engl, transl. of Bayle's Dictionary by Bernard, Birch and Lockman: art. Pearson, John; where we are informed that one of the Roman disputants went under several names, as Spencer, or Tyrwhitt, or Hatcliffe; and that the other was a Physician.

But " The Schism of the Church of England demonstrated" (No. 154) is not a reprint of this account of the Conference (as the translators of Bayle assert, note (a) loc. cit.) but only a Paper added at the end of it, and which (as Dr. Saywell remarks in the Preface to his answer, see No. 156 *supra*) " the authors do not so much as say that it was a part of their dispute, but a pure addition of their own," &c. See also Ath. Oson. vol. ii. col. 766, where we read, "Upon the title of this book bishop Barlow wrote: — "1 am told that John White (author of a Letter to a person of Honour, in vindication of himself and his doctrine, printed 1659, Oct.) was he who did principally manage and put out this disputation." To which he afterwards added this note: " Others say his name was Spencer (the same who answered Dr. Laud's book), and Dr. Lenthal was his associate, who was first of Christ's Coll. *in* Cambridge, then Fellow of Pembroke Hall, a preacher and in orders; afterwards turning papist, would have professed the civil law, and a physician now he is in 1663. This Dr. Breton, master of Emanuel Coll. (who was at the debate), assures me. A Jesuit, who went by the name of Spenser, a Lincolnshire man, is said to be the author of Questions propounded for resolution of unlearned pretenders in Matters of Religion, to the doctors of the prelatical, pretended reform'd Church of England. Paris (alias Lond. as it seems) 1657, 8vo, 4 sh." In a note in Bliss's ed. of the Ath. Oxon. (loc. cit.), on the authority of Baker, who refers to Baxter, Of the True Church, vol. iii. p. 1, we are told that "one of the disputants of the Romish persuasion was Wm. Johnson, alias Terret." This was one of the aliases of the person above spoken of as White, Spencer, Tyrwhitt (Terret?), or Hatcliffe. J. H. T.

"Spencer John — (the account of this great polemical writer is anything but circumstantial in p. 52 Florus Anglo Bavaricus) — sometimes called Vincent Hatclife, was born in Lincolnshire in 1601.... Died 1671. F. Spencer ranks amongst the ablest polemical writers

F. N. Southwell p. 504 of the Bibliotheca, &c., says that he was the Author of an 8vo work published in London, intitled, ' Aut Deus aut Nihil,' also ' Schism detected; see Floras Anglo Bavaricus." From Dr. Oliver's Biography, who mentions two other works he has seen written by Spencer. This publication, "Schism Unmaskt," is ascribed by Dolman to John Sergeant.

A relation of a conference held about religion, at London, by Edward Stillingfleet, D.D. &c., with some gentlemen of the Church of Rome.
pp. 64, and preface with title pp. 8, 4to Lond. 1687

The preface states that this conference was undertaken at the request of Lady T. for the satisfaction "of her husband and some others of the Church of Rome, as well as for clearing such scruples as the perpetual converse with those of that religion had raised in the Lady." This conference took place April 3, 1676. The divines on the side of the Church of England are mentioned in the conference as D. S. and D. B. i.e. Dr. Stillingfleet and Dr. Burnet. The divines on the other side were M. C. (i.e. Mr. Coleman, a Jesuit, secretary to the Duchess of York), and a person called N. N., who did not take any part in the discussion until towards the end. This is no doubt the personage whom Thomas Burnet calls " the principal of the Romish Priests," and I think he must have been either John Gother or John Leyburn. The letters N. N. are the last letters of the Christian and Surname of John Leyburn. The other parties whose initials appear in the narrative are M. L. T. and her husband, S. P. or S. P. T. i. e. My Lady Tyrwhit or Terwhit and Sir Philip Terwhit. M. W. appears to have taken an active part on the Romish 6ide, but I do not know who is designated by these letters; possibly Mr. Woodhead; see No. 189 *infra*.

The Relation of the Conference was drawn up by Burnet, and is subscribed (with their names in full) by Gilbert Burnet, Edward Stillingfleet, and Will. Nailor, a gentleman whom they brought with them to be a witness on their side. See Burnet's account of this conference, Own Times, vol. i. p. 395. "Sir Philip Terwhit (he says) had married a zealous Protestant, who, suspecting his religion, charged him with it. But he denied it before marriage, and carried it so far that he received the sacrament with her in her own church. After they were married, she found that he had deceived her; and they lived untowanlly together. At this time some scruples were put in her head," &c. Then follows (p. 11) " The relation which N. N. desired might be subjoined to the Relation of the Conference," with the answer. Then (p. 16) "The Letter which we promised, wherein an account is given of the doctrine of the church for the first eight centuries demonstrated to be contrary to Transubstantiation in a letter to Lady T." signed by Stillingfleet and Burnet. Also (p. 2D) "A discourse shewing how unreasonable it is to ask for express words of Scripture in proving all articles of faith," by Burnet: and lastly (p. 44) "A discourse to shew that it was not only possible to change the belief of the church concerning the manner of Christ's presence in the sacrament; but that it is very reasonable to conclude both that it might be done, and that it was truly changed."

With respect to the Conference of 1671 (No. 155) it is evidently a report drawn up on the side of the Roman Church. The publisher tells us that " some of the same persons" were engaged in it, as were afterwards in a similar way "engaged" in the conference of 1676. This is sufficiently vague. But it is all the information I possess as to the dramatis personte of the conference in 1671, the subject of which was schism. The dialogue seems to imply that two doctors on the side of England were engaged against one on the side of Rome: they are designated as Dr. 1, Dr 2, and Cath., and the Protestant doctors are sometimes made to speak together, when their words are given as coming from Drs. There'was also a "Company" present who are more than once addressed by "Cath." (p. 10, 16) and who on some occasions took a part in the discussion, where they are called Gentlemen (p. 9), Gentlem. and Gent. (pp. 36, 37, 39), and who always spoke together and on the Popish side. There is also a mysterious personage who made two pretty long speeches, and who is called Narr. (p. 15) and Nar. (p. 28), both on the Romish side. Or perhaps this does not mean any individual present, but rather a Narrative of something which did not take place at the conference. J. H. T.

i Twenty-one conclusions further demonstrating the schism of the Church of England, formerly offered in confutation of Dr. Hammond and Bp. Bramhall. Oxon. 1688

The publications here referred to are Schism Dispatched; or a Rejoinder to Dr. Hammond and the Lord of Derry, 1657, 8vo; Schism Disarmed, against Dr. Hammond and the Bp. of Derry, by J. W. i.e. J. Sergeant. Paris 1665, 8vo.

C iL The True Catholic and Apostolic Faith maintained in the Church of England. Being a Reply to several Books published under the names of J. E., N. N., and J. S., &c. By Andrew Sall, D.D. 8vo Oxford 1676

This very interesting volume, written in reply to Nicholas French's " Bleeding Iphigenia," and his " Dolefull Fall of Andrew Sall," also to the " Unerring Unerrable Church," commences with a Dedication to the Enrl of Essex, Lord Lieutenant of Ireland; followed by a Letter from J. Free, the Superior of the Jesuits in Ireland, with Sall's Reply; the Licence granted to Sall, when Rector of the Irish College at Salamanca, to keep and read Prohibited Books, by the Bishop of Valencia in 1652; then a Letter of Nicholas French, Bp. of Ferns, and his Elogium upon Sall. In " The Literary Policy of the Church of Rome exhibited in an account of her Damnatory Catalogues of Indexes, both prohibitory and expurgatory," by the Rev. Joseph Mendbam, M.A., Lond. 1830, will be found a Papal revocation of the licence of reading heretical works, on the ground of the apprehended conversion of those who were to confute the heretics. "Ferraris, Piompta Bibl. under Fides, will show with what alarm Rotate beheld the discussions of her sons with heretics, and how carefully the Propaganda provided against mischief." Addit. Suppl., p. 16, *ibid.* With what chains the human intellect has been shackled in Papal countries is evinced by the precautions of revision, correction and expurgation, which have been used in the most orthodox books, as will be seen in the licenses prefixed to the second and later editions of the Historia Pontifical by Yllescas. See Southey's Vindicite Ecclesiae Anglicanae, p. 392. Concerning this book, which is the most rare of all Sall's publications, see also No. 218 *infra.*

" The Bleeding Iphigenia" of Dr. French has long been known as a book of uncommon rarity, and has been eagerly sought after by book collectors. Whenever it or the ' Sale and Settlement of Ireland' have appeared at an auction room, crowds of bidders have attended, and the contents of this little volume, in the reader's hands, have sold for no less a sum than £40." Advertisement to the Bleeding Iphigenia in the "Historical Works of the Right Rev. Nicholas French, D.D., Bishop of Ferns, &c. &c. Now for the first time collected." James Duffy, Dublin, 18mo 1846.

'As for the Bleeding Iphigenia there came three copies to this townc, sent by Bp. French. The people are so taken with it as, in my opinion, if 20,000 volumes of it had come over, they would all have been bought up." From a letter from a friar in Connaught, in Dr. O'Connor's Catalogue of MSS. in Stowe Library, vol. i. p. 264. An account of this author is given in Ware's Irish Writers, by Harris, p. 166 et seq. The Bleeding Iphigenia is really the suppressed Preface to the Doleful Fall of Andrew Sall, as appears by comparing the printer's signatures in the original editions. The Bleeding Iphigenia was reprinted Dublin 1829, in Fac Simile so far as the lines go and pages, but not as to type. This edition has a preface signed O. Rev. Ciesor Otway giving an account of the Author, etc. A copy of this reprint on vellum is in the Library of Trin. Coll. Dublin. We have also the orig. edit. without a title page.

The person who wrote against Sall under the initials J. S. was Ignatius Brown (Ware's Writers of Ireland, by Harris, pp. 186-7.) N. N. was Nicholas French, tit. bishop of Ferns. I do not know who J. E. was, but his book is in the Library of Trin. Coll. Dublin. J. H T.

We have, says Dr. Oliver, from the sprightly pen of Ignatius Brown, " The Unerring and Unerrable Church," 8vo. 1675, pp. 310. "An Unerrable Church or None," 8vo. 1678, pp. 342.

The command of God to his People to come out of Babylon, Rev. xviii. 4, demonstrated to mean the coming out of the present Papal Bome, with a most earnest Persuasive to all to come out who are in it, and a Dissuasive from looking back if come out, or entertaining any alliance with that Communion, and herewith a Calculation of the time that the Papacy can according to this Prophecy continue, is given, etc. 1688 CHAP. XV.

Of the Romanists charge of an Agreement between the church of England and the church of Rome; with the churchmens replies. 157. An agreement between the Church of England and Church .1. of Rome, evinced from the concertation of some of her sons with their brethren of the Dissenters. Published with allowance. pp. 88, and pref. and title pp. 8, 4to Lond. 1687

See Contin. p. 18, where this tract is attributed to the Representee but it is not mentioned among his works by Dodd. See No. 51 *supra.* In p. 61 there is a paper, which the preface tells us was drawn up by another hand, entitled, " The Necessity of an Agreement between the Church of England and the Church of Rome, evinced from the nature and constitution of a National Church episcopally established." J. H.T.

" I must observe, by the way, that though the Prefacer does ascribe this learned Piece to another Author, yet he has concealed the true Father: His other Author was a good Roman Catholick, who disputes in good earnest from the Subordination of Pastors in the Church to prove the Supremacy of an Oecumenic or Universal Pastor; but the true Author was an Independent Protestant, from whom this honest Romanist borrows every argument, and almost every word, excepting such little variations as a Papist must of necessity make in an Independent's writing, without ever confessing his Benefactor, or owning from whence he had it. The title of the Book is, The Catholick Hierarchie, or the Divine Right of a Sacred Dominion in Church and Conscience, truly Stated, Asserted, and Pleaded. Printed for Sam. Crouch at the Princes Arms in Pope's Head-Alley in Cornhil, & Tho. Fox at the Angel in Westminster-hall, 1681. In the XIV. Chap, of which Book, p. 76, being a Digression concerning the Subordination of Pastors; whoever has the curiosity may find this entire Treatise of the Necessity of Agreement between the Church of England and the Church of Rome, onely with this difference, that the Independent disputes against the Subordination of Pastors by this very Argument, That the Asserting the Subordination of Pastors in the Church, doth by all good consequence infer the Supremacy of an Oecumenical or Universal Pastor." Sherlock's Vindication, &c., p. 63.

158. A vindication of some Protestant principles of church unity and Catholick communion, from the charge of Agreement with the Church of Rome. In answer to a late pamphlet intituled, An Agreement between the Church of England and the Church of Rome, evinced from the concertation of some of her sons with their brethren the Dissenters. By William Sherlock, D.D., Master of the Temple, pp. 128, title and advert. pp. 6, Rogerson's List of Books pp. 2, 4to. Lond. 1688 See Cat. No. 123. Contin. p. 18. At the end of the advertisement " To the Reader," the author states that he had intended a preface to explain some notions about the Church, but has reserved it for a distinct treatise. See No. 196 infra. J. H. T.

T. 1,159. The difference between the Church of England and the Church of Rome, in opposition to a late Book intituled An Agreement between the Church of England and the Church of Rome.

Imprimatur H. Maurice, Oct. 6, 1687. Anon. By John Williams, M.A. (afterwards Bp. of Chichester).
pp. 81 incl. title, 4to Lond. 1687 See Catal. No. 124. Contin. p. 18. Ath. Oxon. vol. ii. col. 1121. This ought to have been placed before Sherlock's book, as it was published first. The Imprimatur of Sherlock's having been Nov. 16, 1687. Peck followed the order in which they were given by Gee. J. H. T.

The doctrinal Theses and Anti-Theses of the two Churches have more recently been stated in Bishop Marsh's Comparative View of the Churches of England and Rome. Second edition, with some Explanatory Notes on Church Authority, the character of Schism, and the Rock, on which our Saviour declared that he would build his Church. 8vo Lond. 1816.

Papists no Catholicks and Popery no Christianity. Anon. By C 2.,
W. Lloyd, Bp. of St. Asaph, pp. 12, to the reader, &c., pp.
2. Printed for the Author. 4to Lond. 1677
A second Ed. much enlarged. pp. 56, was printed 4to Lond. (for
Henry Browne at the Gun in St. Paul's Ch. yard), 1679. J. H. T.

A Short and True Account of the several advances the Church of CSL.
England hath made towards Rome, or a Model of the
Grounds upon which the Papists for these hundred years have built their hopes and expectations, that England would ere long return to Popery. By Dr. Du-Moulin, some time
History Professor of Oxford. Veritas Odium parit.
pp. 118, 4to Lond. 1680 Also, A Confirmation of the precedent Discourse, drawn from several Passages out of the Irenicum, A Weapon-Salve for the Churches Wounds, written by Edward Stillingfleet, D.D., Dean of St. Paul's, Canon of Canterbury, and Chaplain in Ordinary to His Most Sacred Majesty. The Postscript. A True Report of a Discourse between Monsieur De L'Angle, Canon of Canterbury, and Minister of the French Church in the Savoy, and Lewis Du Moulin; the 10th of February

167§, Lond. 1679. Declaratory Considerations upon the Present State of the Affairs of England. By way of Supplement. Lond. 1679. A New Essay towards a true Ecclesiastical History, which may serve as a key to the Annalls of Baronius. " Jortin observes on this great cardinal and advocate of the Roman See, that he breathes nothing hut fire and brimstone, and accounts kings and emperors to be catchpolls and constables, bound to execute with implicit faith all the commands of insolent ecclesiastics." Disraeli's Curiosities of Literature. For an account of Du-Moulin see Wood's Fasti Oxon. ed. Bliss, vol. iv. col. 113.

CHAP. XVI. *Of the discourses written by the Romanists reflecting upon the Reformation of the Church of England; with the Churchmen's replies.* 160. 41 The Church of England truly represented according to Dr. Peter Heylin's history of the Reformation. See Contin. p. 36. And No. 181, *infra*.

" Sanderson, in bis History of the Life and Reign of King Charles, layeth a scandal upon the Doctor that he was an Agent for the See of Rome. The Doctor indeed in all his writings did ever assert the King's Prerogative, and the Churches Rights, for which he incurr'd the Odium of the opposite Party, with whom 'tis ordinary to brand such persons with the ignominious name of Papists, or being Popishly affected, as abhor the other extreme of Puritanism, in which kind of Calumnies the Doctor hath sufficiently had his share, though no man hath written more sharply against the Church of Rome, as appears from most of his Books, and particularly in his Theologia Veterum, and his Sermons upon the Tares: but though these have not been able to secure him from the malicious Tongues and Pens of ill men, yet his innocence hath found very worthy Advocates. Among whom I thank particularly the Reverend and Learned Dr. Stillingfleet in his Answer to T. G. see No. 85 *supra* who would have made use of the Puritans accusation for the Papists purpose, but the worthy Doctor quickly refuted him out of the fourth Sermon of Doctor Heylin upon the Tares, where he lays at the door of the Papists the most gross Idolatry, greater than which was never known among the Gentiles.

" But against these things 'tis commonly said, and as commonly believed, that some persons, and those of most illustrious quality, i.e. the Duchess of York have been perverted from the Protestant Faith to Popery, by reading some of the Doctors Books, and particularly that which he writ about the History of the Reformation, called Ecclesia Restaurata This Objection having many particular charges contained in it, will require as many distinct Answers, which I shall give in short. And first, if it be true that any have embraced the Roman Faith, by means of that Book, he may conclude them to be very incompetent Judges in the matters of Religion, that will be prevailed upon to change it upon the perusal of one single History; and especially in the Controversies between us and the Papists, which do not depend upon matter of fact, or an Historical Narration of what
Occurrences happened in this Kingdom, but upon doctrine of Faith,
what we are to believe and disbelieve, in order to our serving God in this life, and being Eternally blessed with him in the next." — Life of Heylin, prefixed to his works, pp. 24, 25. The charge above referred to is not confirmed by his other work published in 1657, viz.,
Ecclesia Vindicata; or, the Church of England Justified; I. In the C1L.
Way and Manner of Reformation. II. In Officiating by a Public
Liturgy. III. In prescribing a Set Form of Prayer to be used by
Preachers before their Sermons. IV. In her Right and Patrimony of
Tithes. V. In retaining the Episcopal Government, and therewith,
VI., The Canonical Ordination of Priests and Deacons. By Peter
Heylin, D.D. (Compare Woodhead on Church Government, part v.,
pp. 250-54,) Nor by that published in 1(545, The Parliament's Power in Lawes for Religion, or an Answer to the Calumny of the Papists,
nicknaming the Church of England by the name of a Parliamentary Religion, 4to Oxf. 1645.

161. The State of the Church of Rome when the Reformation C 2,. began; as it appears by the advices given to Paul III. and Julius III. by creatures of their own. With a Preface leading to the Matter of the Book. Anon. By Will. Clagett, D.D. pp. 34, and pref. pp. 8, 4to Lond. 1688

See Cat. No. 137. Contin. p. 35.

It is scarcely possible that Dr. Clagett could have been the author of the translation of the documents which he has published in this tract. For in one place the well known theological phrase, ex opere operato, is translated (p. 24) "by the works done," and there are several other errors of ignorance or of carelessness. It is probable, therefore, that Dr. Clagett only wrote a hasty preface to the publication, and that the translation was executed by some inferior hand, and yet he apparently adopts the translation as his own when he says in the Preface, " I thought a few hours spent in translating them into our language would not be thrown away." It is most unfortunate, however, that one of the documents thus put forth, viz., " the advice to Julius III. " (which the Preface tells us was " the most fatal thing that ever happened to the reputation of the Roman cause") is a manifest pasquinade, the production of the celebrated Peter Paul Vergerio, bishop of Capo d'Istria. How any one could read it, and believe it to be a serious document, addressed by three bishops to a Pope is very surprising; and even Dr. Clagett seems to think some apology to be necessary, for he says in the Preface, " that the nine" (who wrote the first letter) " were serious and seemed to be so: the three (who wrote the second letter) were serious and seemed not to be so; which makes the advice of the former look like sincerity and that of the latter to look like wit," &c.

Nevertheless the Consilium was published as a serious document by John Wolfius in his Lectiones Memorabiles (vol. ii. p. 549), by W. Crashaw (from a different copy); and afterwards by Edw. Browne (who reprinted Crashaw's edition) in his additions to the Fasciculus of Orthuinus Gratius. In Wolfius the Consilium is addressed to Paul III., not Julius III., and a passage at the end relating to England and queen Mary (Clagett's ed. p. 33) is omitted, we may therefore perhaps infer that the first edition of the Pasquinade was put forth in the time of Paul III., and that another edition which Crashaw reprinted, addressed to Julius III., with the allusion to queen Mary's persecution of the Protestants in England, came out afterwards. At all events it does not appear to have deceived anybody when first published, nor to have been intended to deceive, for Vergerio has given it as his own in his works; a fact which Crashaw endeavours to explain by telling us that Vergerio inserted it in his works because he had found it in the Pope's private study — " Hoc Vergerius in conclavi privato (pessimarum Musarum Musaeo) Papse, inter secretiora et sacratiora papalis Imperii arcana inventum, amicis primo privatis communicavit, deinde suis inseruit operihus." And yet the document so far from being communicated only to his private friends had been printed and published in 1549, and afterwards in 1553, whereas the works of Vergerio, in which it appears, bear date Tubingen, 4to 15G3, two years before the author's death. The other document, viz., the " Advice" given to Paul III. by nine bishops is probably genuine; or at least it cannot be suspected of a protcstnnt origin, as it appeared in Crabbe's edition of the Councils, 1551; and in the Acts of the first Council of Pisa, Paris 4to 1612. See Mendham's Literary Policy of the Church of Rome, pp. 48, 49, and Index of Greg. XIV. pp. 75-83. Also an Article in the British Magazine (vol. xxxv. for 1849, pp. 538-42), on Dr. Cumming's edit, of Gibson's Preservative against Popery.

It is curious as showing the haste with which Dr. Clagett's tract was got up, that although he entitles this latter document " An Advice given to Paul III. by four Cardinals and five other Prelates," and speaks of it in his preface as signed by nine, yet he has printed the names of eight only of the subscribers, having omitted one name, and transposed the title of the omitted name to another bishop. The names of the prelates, as he gives them, are these: Frederick Archbishop of Brundusium, which ought to be Frederick Archbishop of Salerno. He then omits the name of " Jerome, Archbishop of Brundusium," but gives the remainder correctly, viz., " Joh. Matthew Gibet Bishop of Verona, Gregory Cortese Abbat of St. George at Venice, Fryar Thomas, Master of the sacred palace." And yet he seems to have taken some pains in the matter, as he inserts the surnames of Gibet and Cortese, which do not appear in Brown's reprint. Fascic. vol. ii. p. 236. In the signatures of the three bishops, at the end of the Advice given to Julius III., there are also mistakes of carelessness: — " Giles Talceta" ought to be " Giles Falceta," and " Gerards Burdragus" ought to be " Gerhard (or Gerhardus) Busdragus." The author of the paper in the British Magazine, above referred to, has shown that " Gerhardus Busdragus" was a name assumed by Vergerio in some of his similar pieces of ironical controversy. A good account of this singular man will be found in the English translation of Bayle's Dictionary, by Bernard, Birch and Lockman. J. H. T.

The title of the genuine Consilium is as follows: Consilium Delec-C JL. torum Cardinalium et aliorum Pralatorum, de emendanda Ecclesia. S. D. N. Papa Paulo 3 ipso jubente conscriptum et exhibitum an: 1538. Libellus vere aureus. Ante annos 70 in Concil. Tridentino primum editus; deinde Romani Antichristi tyrannico jussu in juste suppressus. Nunc autem ab interitu vindicatus et renuo recusus. Ex Bibliotheca W. Crashawi. 4to Londini 1609. "This little-known but often-mentioned work was the result of the Consultations of the

B B

Cardinals and other divines appointed by Pope Paul III. to report on the state of the Church, and what necessity there might be for a Reformation. At the end of the volume is appended a list of those appointed to the important undertaking, and it includes the most learned and respected churchmen of the age, as Cardinals Pole, Contareni, Sadolct, &c. It produced an animated discussion between Schelhom and Cardinal Quirini in the last century, the latter at first maintaining that the book was not authentic, but was put forth primarily by the Protestants; but he afterwards convinced himself of the contrary. This *Adoice* is appended to Carranza's Summa Conciliorum, 1546 and 1551. This *Counsel* is transformed into a Council in Foster's translation of Ranke's History of the Popes, vol. i. p. 3, note, Lond. 1853, Bohn, vol. i. p. Ill, and the same mistake appears twice in the Christian Remembrancer for July 1856, pp. 80, 92, where mention is made of the Council of Cardinals." Gibbing's Trial and Martyrdom of Carnesecchi. It will be found also in Durandus de Modo Concilii, etc. ad calc. 105-12. The title of the supposititious Consilium is: Consilium quorundam Episcoporum Bononiae congrcgatorum quod de ratione stabiliendae Romano) Ecclesia; Julio III. Pont. Max. datum est. Quo artcs ct astutiae Romanensium et Arcana Imperii Papalis non pauca propalantur. Ex Bibliotheca W. Crawshawi, 4to Lond. 1613. For the history of this " Conciliabulum" consult Notes and Queries, first series, vol. ix. Schelhorn's remarks on these two documents are in the seventh volume of his Amoenitates Literariae, p. 276 et seq.

The true title of the original and excessively rare edition is as follows: " Consilium Delectorum Cardinalium & aliorum Praelatorum de emendanda Ecclesia, S.D.N.D. Paulo III. ipso iubentc conscriptum & exhibitum, M.d.xxxvii." It has no place of printing, but has the arms of Paul III. on the title, and was printed 1538, the year after its being " Conscriptum et exhibitum." See Reprint of the Roman Index, by Rev. R. Gibbings, Pref. p. 20.

In some copies we find Concilium for Consilium.

Trin. Coll. Dublin has one with this title: —

Concilium delectorum Cardinalium et aliorum Prajlatorum de emendanda ecclesia, S.D.N.D. Paulo tertio ipso iubente conscriptum, et exhibitum Anno M.d.xxxviii. Accessit sequitatis Discussio super Con«'Iio sic Delectorum Cardinalium, &c., ad tollendam per Generale concilium inter Germanos in religione discordiam. Antwerpise. In scuto Burgundiss per Joannem Steelsium Anno a Christo nato ll.S.XXXIX.

The author of the zEquitatis discussio was Joannes Cochlseus.

There were two editions of Crashaw's reprint of this: one with the title as given *supra*, " Londini excudebat Felix Kvnston sumptibus

Richardi Boyle, 1609."

The other with some slight variations in the title, as " S.D.N.D.

Paulo III." and "anno 1538," "Londini Excudebat N. O. sumptibus

Richardi Boyle." This consists of a single sheet, with signature A.,

containing twelve leaves, and is therefore properly 12mo.

The short note, " Lectori," which follows the address to the Abp.

of York in the 4to, does not occur in the 12mo. edit.

In both these editions the document is called Consilium. But it is Concilium, p. 130 of the Apologia sacri Pisani Concilii Moderni, at the end of the "Acta primi Concilii Pisani," 4to Lut Paris, 1G12, where the whole document is given. J. H. T.

162. Catholic Theses, on several chief heads of controversy. £,1L. Anon. By Abraham Woodhead, fellow of Univ. Coll. Oxford. 4to Oxford 1689

See Ath. Oxon. vol. ii. col. 617 where Wood expresses a doubt whether the work was ever completed. And the same doubt is repeated in the Cat. of the Bodl. Libr. J. H. T.

For a notice of Woodhead and his writings see No. 218 *infra*. 163. b Church Government. Part V. A Relation of the English Reformation,.and the lawfulness thereof examined by the Theses delivered in the four former parts. Ailon.'S By Abraham Woodhead. pp. 260, with title, contents and address pp. 12. 4to Oxford 1687

See Contin. p. 36. Ath. Oxon. vol. ii. col. 616-17. The title-page has a woodcut ornament with a medallion head of King Alfred. The prefatory letter begins, " Sir, well knowing your fidelity and loyalty to your prince," &c. But there is nothing to show to whom this epistle was addressed. There is no doubt that the author was Abraham Woodhead, fellow of Univ. Coll. Oxford, one of the most zealous con-. verts to the Church of Rome of that period, who died May 4, 1678 (at. 70), leaving behind him a great number of works in MS. on the controversial questions at issue between the Roman and English Churches. Many of these, and the present amongst the number, were afterwards printed, at a private printing press which he had set up in his lodgings, by Obadiah Walker, Master of Univ. Coll. , for which press (as the books printed by him could not have been licensed in the ordinary way) he had obtained the special licence of James II. This circumstance is the cause of the mistake committed by many and even by contemporary writers, that this, and some other of Woodhead's works, were written by Walker. Burnet, in the first part of his Reflections (No. 172 *infra*) on this treatise, says in the introduction, " We have been long in expectation of some extraordinary productions of the eminent convert of Oxford. His age Walker was then, 1688, about 77 years of age, his learning, and the present conjuncture hath raised that expectation very high; and though the ill success of his discourses concerning the presence in the Sacrament and the adoration of it see Nos. 279, 282 *infra,* which are also by Woodhead, although printed by Walker, hath sunk his reputation to a great degree," &c. Here it is evident that Walker must have been intended; for his being a head of a house in Oxford, his having avowed himself a Romanist in 168$, and his attempt to set up a chapel for the celebration of Mass in his College, all gave him a notoriety, which accounts for his being styled by Burnet "the eminent convert of Oxford." Moreover in 1688 Woodhead was dead, and therefore could not have been the person alluded to. Nevertheless it is clear that Burnet must have known very well that Walker was only the reputed author, for he adds (p. 4) " I am, I confess, much inclined to believe, he who hath published this book could not have writ it."

This book is styled " Part V.," and " four former parts" are alluded to in the title. These were also by Abr. Woodhead, and had reference to the Presbyterian controversy. They were published together C IL under the title, " A brief account of ancient Church-Government, with a reflection on several modern writings of the Presbyterians (the assembly of divines, their Jus Divinum ministerii Anglicani, published 1654, and Dr. Blondel's Apologia pro sententia Hieronymi, and others) touching this subject. Anon. Lond. 1662 4to (in four parts) reprinted in 1685. In the first ed. of the Ath. Oxon. Wood had stated, on the authority of " a certain R. Catholick, who was originally of Univ. Coll.," that this book was written by Obad. Walker. But in his second edit. he cancels this statement, and says, " Some say it was written by R. Holden, a Sorbon Dr., but falsely; for Abr. Woodhead was without doubt the author of it." Ath. Oxon. vol. ii. col. 614 ed. Bliss, vol. iii. col. 1159. For an account of Obad. Walker, see Ath. Oxon. vol. ii. col. 933 sq. J. H. T.

Walker had a license granted to him by the King, dated May 1686, for the exclusive sale of certain books for twenty-one years. The list of them was printed in the second volume of Gutch's Miscellanea Curiosa; they are all in favour of the Roman Catholic Religion.

The Contents of the four former parts are — I. The Apostles the successors of Christ. II. Bishops the successors of the Apostles. III. The Presbyterians plea against Bishops. IV. An answer to this their plea. Cf. Bentley's Phileleutherus Lipsiensis. " It was agreed over all Christendom at once in the very next generation after the Apostles to assign and appropriate to them the word *Eiriaicoriros* or bishop. From that time to this that appellation, which before included a Presbyter, has been restrained to a superior Order. And here's nothing in all this but what has happened in all languages and communities in the world. See the Notitia of the Roman and Greek Empires; and you'll scarce find one name of any State Employment, that in course of time did not vary from its primitive signification. So that should our Lutheran Presbyters contend they are Scripture Bishops, what would they get by it? No more than lies in the syllables. The time has been when a commander even of a single regiment was called Imperator: and must every such now a days set up to be Emperors? The one pretence is altogether as just as the other." Remark, xxxiv. Also Jer. Taylor's Episcopacy Asserted § 21 (Polemical and Moral Discourses, fol. 1657, p. 157, 8), Du Moulin and Andrews in Wordsworth's Christian Institutes, vol. iii., Pearson (Vindic. Ignat. part II. ch. iii. quoted ibid. p. 196.) "We shall find that the Dissenters in this Kingdom, usually passing under the title of ' the Three Denominations,' that is the Presbyterians, the Independents, and the Baptists (or more correctly, Anabaptists), declare for the parity of the ministers of the Gospel in matters of Church government. But we have seen that the Universal Church and our ancient Church, as a portion of it, was from its beginning established in Episcopacy. Our judicious Hooker asserts, 'A thousand five hundred years and upwards the Church of Christ hath now continued under the sacred regimen of bishops.' Salmasius of France, one of the most learned of all Presbyterians, admits, concerning Episcopal government: ' The thing itself is most ancient; for, if the times of the Apostles are excepted, those two orders of bishops and presbyters have been distinct in the church.' If this be conceded, then Salmasius gives up the contest; for it is evident, as has been already observed, that the Apostles themselves, as shewn in the New Testament, exercised this supervision, which, as an abiding part of their office, has descended to the bishops of the Church. Blondel, another very learned Frenchman and Presbyterian, singularly enough admits,' By all that we have said to assert the rights of the Presbytery, we do not intend to invalidate the ancient and Apostolical constitution of Episcopal pre-eminence. ' And the three leading Reformers,

Luther, Melancthon, and Calvin, were all in favour of Episcopacy, as their works, if examined, will shew. If any doubt this assertion, especially as it regards Calvin, let such consult the 'Life and Correspondence of Parker, Archbishop of Canterbury,' as written and published by Strype, and they may be satisfied." *The Church of England apostolical in its origin, episcopal in its government, and scriptural in its belief. Wherein, also, its claims, in opposition to Popery and Dissent, are considered and asserted.* By the Rev. Tho. P. Pantin, M.A. (The references are not given, because the tract itself, pp. 48 12mo., may easily be obtained from Mr. Stewart, King William-street, Lond.)

St. Hieronom himself when out of his anger against John Bp. of Jerusalem he endeavoured to equal the Presbyter with the Bishop, though in very many places he spake otherwise, yet even then also and in that heat, excepted ordination, acknowledging that to be the Bishop's peculiar." Jer. Taylor's Sermon preached at the Consecration of two Archbishops and ten Bishops, Dublin 16G1. "I shall say one thing more, which indeed is a great truth, that the diminution of Episcopacy was first introduced by Popery, and the Popes of Rome by communicating to Abbots and other mere Priests special graces to exercise some special offices of Episcopacie, hath made this sacred order to be cheap, and apt to be invaded." — Ibid.

Of Tracts against Episcopacy there were, in Milton's words, " Numbers numberless." " Never did men so ply their adversaries with the hail-shot of Libels as Martin Marprelate and his followers plied upon the Bishops." — Heylin's Pref. to Ecclesia Vindicata. They were finally put down at Manchester by the Earl of Derby. See Baines's Lancashire, vol. ii. p. 263. Copious notices of them will be found in Fuller, Collier, Strype (Ann. vol. ii. p. 261), Wood by Bliss, Ames by Herbert, and Bcloe. See also Maskell's Hist. of the Marprelate Controversy during the reign of Elizabeth. The Smectymnuans, viz. Marshall, Calamy, Young, Newcoraen, and Spurstow, who wrote a celebrated book called Smectymnuus (a title made up of their initials, Christian and surname), although they were " undertaken" by Bp. Hall in The Humble Remonstrance, and by Heylin in his Hist of Episcopacy and his Hist of the Presbyterians, had a powerful effect, and, as Calamy affirms, gave the first deadly blow to Episcopacy. In this struggle to render Episcopacy, in Baillie's words, "a poor plucked craw," Milton joined the side of the Puritans, and in coming forward with his Apology for Smectymnuus and other tracts he may have been influenced by his regard to Thomas Young, one of the writers, who for some years had been his preceptor. — See Robert Baillie's Letters and Journals. Edited by David Laing for the Bannatyne Club. Baillie or Baylie, Principal of the University of Glasgow, and the most learned champion of Presbyterianism, was the author of Laudensium ΑυτοΚαΤαxpiai';, the Canterburians Self-Conviction; or an evident Demonstration of the avowed Arminianisme, Poperie and Tyrannie of that Faction, by their own Confessions, &c, 1640, 4to, 1641-1643. The Unlawfulnesse and Danger of limited Episcopacie, whereunto is subjoined a short Reply to the Modest Advertiser of that Treatise; as also the Question of Episcopacie discussed from Scripture and the Fathers, Lond. 1641, 4to. An Historicall Vindication of the Government of the Church of Scotland, from the manifold base calumnies which the most malignant of the Prelats did invent of old, &c. Lond. 1646, 4to. Of the celebrated Rutherford's writings an account will be found in " Bibliographical Notices of the Church Libraries bequeathed by Humphrey Chetham." The sentiments of Stillingfleet and other irenical writers are given in David Irving's Life of Leighton, and in the Rev W. Goode's Vindication of the Doctrine of the Church of England on the Validity of the Orders of the Scotch and Foreign Non-Episcopal Churches. 1852. The reader who desires to examine impartially both sides of the question will be satisfied with An Inquiry into the constitution, discipline, unity and worship of the Primitive Church, that flourished within the first three hundred years after Christ. By Lord Chancellor King. In two Parts. 1712. Partl. With Remarks and an Appendix, the whole comprising an Abridgment of an " Original Draught of the Primitive Church," in answer to the above-mentioned Discourse. By a Clergyman of the Church of England. Lond. 1843. The Editor, the Rev. T. J. Whittington, late Curate of Winwick, Lancashire, " not merely confined himself to that able work" (the Original Draught, &c.), "but occasionally had recourse to the learned and useful labours of Potter, Pearson, Wheatly," &c. Sec also Bishop Sage's Principles of the Cyprianic Age, &c., with Memoir and Notes, and his Fundamental Charter of Presbytery, as it hath been lately established (1688) in the Kingdom of Scotland, Examin'd and Disprov'd, &c., together with a Preface. Printed for the Spottiswoode Society, Edinburgh, 1844, 46.

CSL, 164. Of the authority of Councils and the Rule of Faith. By a Person of Quality. With an answer to the eight Theses laid down for the trial of the English Reformation, in the book that came last week from Oxford. pp. 113, Pref. pp. 1-6, 4to Lond. 1687 See Cat. No. 96. Contin. p. 31. Instead of "last week," Gee and Peck have it " the Book that came lately from Oxford." The Imprimatur is dated "March 22, 1686" (i. e. 1684); so that Woodhead's Church Government, Part v., containing the eight theses (see No. 163) must have come out a week before that date, although it is dated 1687. Peck, copying Gee, says, "The first part (about councils) by — Hutchinson (Gee spells the name Hutchison) Esq., the rest by Dr. Clagett." But the book is in three parts; the first p. 1, " Of the authority of Councils;" the second, p. 63, " Of the Rule of Faith;" and the third, p. 101, "Postscript," in answer to Woodhead. It is this last that is by Dr. Wm. Clagett. The two former parts are by " a person of quality," i.e. Mr. Hutchinson.

See Pepys's Diary March 23, 1669 (vol. ii. p. 321), where a Mr. Hutchinson is mentioned, whose " vein" lay in matters of religion. J.H.T.

On the Tria Capitula referred to in the former tract, see Crakanthorp's Vigilius Dormitans, Romes Overseer Overseene. Or a Treatise of the Fift Generall Councell held at Constantinople, anno 553, under Justinian the Emperour in the time of Pope Vigilivs: the occasion being those Tria Capitula, which for many yeares troubled the whole Church. Wherein is proved that the Popes Apostolicall Constitution and definitive sentence in matter of Faith was condemned as hereticall by the Synod. And the exceeding frauds of Cardinall Baronius and Binius are clearely discovered. Fol. Lond. 1631.

The story of the Council of Rimini or Ariminum, anno 359, also referred to in the former tract, is very elegantly told by Sulpitius Severus, and by Jerome in his Dialogues agninst the Luciferians. See also Palmer's Treatise on the Church on Arianism in connexion with synodical action. — Historical Collections concerning Church Affairs. By a Presbyter of the Church of England. Lond. 1696 4to.

" Here I had been obliged to shew some part of that Cloud of Witnesses wherewith we are encompassed in maintaining that the Fathers took the Holy Scriptures for the Rule of their Faith; but that this point is made out so learnedly and so plainly in the late Vindication of the Answer to some late Papers No. 17 *supra* from pag. 40 to pag. 50," &c. Rule of Faith p. 80.

165. Animadversions on the eight Theses laid down, and the ML inferences deduced from them, in a Discourse entitl'd Church Government, Part v. lately printed at Oxford. They went out from us, &c., 1 Joh. ii. 19. Anon. By George Smallridge, B.A., of Christ's Church. pp. 68, and to the University Reader pp. 2. 4to Oxford (printed at the Theater), a wood-cut of the Theater on the title page. 1687

See Cat. No. 141. Contin. p. 35. Ath. Oxon. vol. ii. col. 1065. Gee says that this book is in two parts; meaning, I presume, the next article (No. 166) as the second part, but this last I think is not by Smallridge. Both are in answer to No.

163 *supra*. J. H. T.

Compare the King's Right of Indulgence in Spiritual Matters, p. 90 *supra*. Peter Walsh in his Hist. and Vindic. of the Loyal Formulary or Irish Remonstrance, 1674 fol., admits that ecclesiastical constitutions are not independent of the Prince's sanction. To the Title of c c

Supreme Head over the Church, given to King Henry VIII. hy the Parliament, the learned Jackson devotes a Chapter in his Treatise of Christian Obedience, being the Second Part of his Twelfth Book, concerning the Holy Catholick Faith and Church, vol. iii. pp. 920-30. For an account of Jackson, one of the greatest of English Theological Writers, see Worthington's Diary and Correspondence, vol. i. p. 282-3.

The following extract from the Advertisement to this treatise relates to the subject under consideration, whilst it is an interesting supplement to a note in p. 60 *tupra*. " Whereas one, either the true or a personated Roger Widdrington and some others of Romish persuasion, had so much conscience and loyalty, He to write for the lawfulness of taking the Oath of Allegiance, and they to take the same: this J. E. Matthew Kellison in his fifteenth chapter (of the Right and Jurisdiction of the Prelate and the Prince, &c.) strives to prove that the Oath can neither be proposed nor taken without sin. Against this bold Author on the one hand, and on the other against such amongst us as yield not due obedience either to Laws Civil or Ecclesiastical, to their Prince or to their Prelate, doth our good Author level much of his Discourse. The Reader may (perhaps) be content to be advertised of one particular more, viz. That there be two Books which pass under the name of Roger Widdrington. One called Disputatio Theologica de Jurament. Fidelitatis, quoted often by J. E. in his fifteenth Chapter: the other, Responsio Apologetica, cited by J. E. pag. 295. But I have heard a very ancient and most learned Man, Mr. Herbert Thorndike of Happy Memory, say that the reputed Author (at least of one of those Books) was a Priest of the Church of Rome,

called Father Preston, who was prisoner in the Clink in Southwark, and being afraid of hard usage, chose to continue so, rather to enjoy a dangerful liberty, esteeming his Prison a Castle or Sanctuary rather than a Gaol." Of Dr. Matthew Kellison, Dodd says, in The Secret Policy of the Society of Jesus, p. 180: "It speaks his worth enough to say he was President of Douay College, Royal Professor and Rector of the University of Rheims, and Parent to many excellent Pieces in defence of the true Religion." They are enumerated by Watt CIL 166. Reflections on the historical Part of Church Government.

Part v. He that is first in his own cause, &c., Prov. 18, 17. pp. 99, 4to Oxford (printed at the Theater), a wood-cut of the Theater on the title page. Ifi87 See Contin. p. 35. This is attributed to Smallridge in the Bodl. Cat., probably on the authority of Gee (see last art.) But Smallridge, wbo is undoubtedly the author of No. 165, says (p. 65 of that tract), " I should now proceed to consider the Historical part of this Discourse; but *that* I understand is already under the consideration of another hand, from which the reader may shortly expect a satisfactory account." And the Introduction to the " Reflections," speaks of the "Animadverter," i.e. the author of the "Animadversions" (No. 165) which seems to imply that the " Animadverter" was not the author of the " Reflections." It was probably for this reason that Peck separated this tract from the preceding; without attributing it to Smallridge. And that the author of No. 165 was not the same as the author of No. 166, is further evident from the preface to Atterbury's Answer to the discourse concerning the spirit of Martin Luther" (see No. 168 *infra*) where he says: "In the Defence of our Reformation to come 'twill be found that the Considerer i.e. the author of No. 167 is no good historian; the Replyer see No. 281 *infra* has proved him no good Catholic; the Animadverter see No. 165 no good subject; and all together no good Disputant; so that I have no new side of him left to entertain the reader with." Here the author of the defence of the Reformation is apparently distinguished from the "Animadverter," who was certainly Dr. Smallridge. Nevertheless it is possible that Dr. Smallridge may have written the Reflections, with a design to pass for a different person from the author of the Animadversions: this, however, I think is not very likely, when we consider the language he has used, as quoted above, in reference to the Reflections.

Atterbury's tract, (No. 168), received its Imprimatur July 29, 1687, whereas "the Defence of the Reformation" (No. 166) was not licensed until October 19, 1687. It was therefore still "to come," when Atterbury wrote. The Replyer (No. 281) was before both, having been licensed May 19, 1687. J. H. T.

There is another passage in the Reflections more convincing than that in the Introduction. " The Question here discust has already been debated in the Animadversions, and if the Reader desires to be farther satisfied I can not more oblige him than by sending him to the Most Reverend and Learned Author," p. 24.

"As long as the Sacred History of Hezechiah's and Josiah's Reformation shall be preserved, this prerogative of Godly Princes (of Reforming in extraordinary cases without or against a major part of their clergy) will need no other defence. The particulars of the Parallel have been so exactly drawn in a Discourse lately reprinted (Dr. Steward's Sermon, see p. 172 *supra)* that any farther attempt would be a presumption," &c, p. 96. Compare Steph. Grardineri Oratio de Vera Obedientia in Brown's Fasciculus, vol. ii. pp. 802-20. On the other side see Woodhead's Catholick Theses, Head ix.

C1L. 167. %? Two discourses. The first concerning the spirit of Martin Luther, and the original of the Reformation. The second concerning the celibacy of the Clergy. Anon. By Abraham Woodhead. 4to, printed at Oxford (with the same head of K. Alfred as on the title of No. 163.) 1687 See Contin. p. 36. Ath. Oxon. vol. ii. col. 616. Published by Obadiah Walker, at his private printing press, see above No. 163. The two discourses are separately paged, and have also separate titles, besides the general title above given. The first is entitled " Considerations concerning the spirit of Martin Luther, and the original of the Reformation." pp. 104, whence the author of this tract is sometimes called " The Considerer," by writers on the other side (see note to No. 166); the second part is entitled "A Discourse concerning the Celibacy of the Clergy," pp. 39. This has an imprint which the first has not, " At Oxford printed, anno 1687." Under this it is given separately by Peck, No. 267 *infra.* J. H. T.

C 1L. 168. An Answer to some considerations on the Spirit of Martin Luther, and the original of the Reformation; lately printed at Oxford. "The fierceness of man,' &c., Ps. 76,10. Anou. By Francis Atterbury, student of Christ Church (afterwards Bp. of Rochester). pp. 68, and Preface pp. 2, 4to Oxford, printed at the Theater, with a wood-cut of the Theater on the title page. 1687 See Cat. No. 140. Contin. p. 35. Ath. Oxon. vol. ii. col. 1064.

"By the same Authority he sentenc'd the Canon-Law consisting of the former decrees amass'd, as well those of Councils as those of Popes to the fire; and assembling the University solemnly burnt it at Wirtemberg." The matter of fact is true, but 'tis frivolous to say he assum'd to himself any particular Authority in the doing it. The reasons he publish'd declare that 'twas done by virtue of the Commission he had as Preacher of God's word: and the Oath he took at his going out Dr. *of confounding all pernicious doctrines as much as in him lay,* &c. p. 35. Compare Baker's Reflections upon Learning. " If any thing can be said worse of them (some Books of Grration's Decree) than they have said themselves, it may be had in Luther (Oper. tom. ii. p. 120 Wit.), who began the Reformation with burning the Canon Law, and in vindication of what he had done made a Collection of such Articles as were most liable to give offence. I have not yet compared his Quotations with the Text, and therefore do not put them down, but if they be faithful I am sure there is enough to give a Man a hard opinion of the Canon Law," p. 166. I find that the Articles selected by Luther refer not to the Decree but to the Decretals, and declare the Pope's dispensing and absolute Dominion. " The total abrogating (by Henry VIII) of that course Compilation of the Canon-Laws, which never was founded on any good Authority was so just a thing, that there are very few learned men in the Roman Communion at present, that will not say it were well for the Church if it were quite laid aside, since now all men but such as our Author are ashamed of it." Burnet's Reflections on the Oxford Theses, p. 73 (No. 172 *infra.)*

" It was perhaps more to the credit of the reigning pontiff that he gave charge to his master of the Sacred Palace, T. Manrique, to prepare a reformed edition of the Canon Law. And the task was performed with some real integrity — indeed too much for Rome; for in the reign of his successor (he himself escaped the disgrace) the proposed improvements were generally rejected, and the Decretals reedited with the greater portion of their original corruption." Mendham's Life and Pontificate of Pius V., p. 173.

169. The Religion of Mar. Luther neither Catholick nor Protestant; proved from his own Works. With some Reflections in answer to the Vindication of Mar. Luther's spirit, printed at the Theater in Oxon. His Vindication being another argument of the Schism of the Church of England. pp. 24, 4to Oxou. (Henry Cruttenden) 1688

See Ath. Oxon. vol. ii. col. 940. Wood attributes this tract to Thomas Deane of Univ. Coll., one of the converts of Obad. Walker, in 1685 (see above No. 163). But it is probable that Wood had never seen the book. He calls the first part of it " a thing reprinted," and erroneously gives the other two paragraphs of the title as if they were two additional tracts appended to " The Religion of Mar. Luther, &c." thus:

"Some Reflexions in Answer to the Vindication of Martin Luthers spirit, &c.

" His Vindication; being another argument of the Schism of the Church of England.

" These two were printed in Oxon, &c They were printed at the end of a thing reprinted, and entitled 'The Religion of Martin Luther,'" &c. Ath. Oxon. *ubi supra.*

This statement, erroneous in itself, Peck has made still more so. For he splits the book into three, which he numbers 169, 170, 171. Thus — 169. *i* The religion of Martin Luther neither Catholick nor Protestant; proved from his own works. An old thing reprinted.

See Ath. Oxon. vol. ii. col. 940.

170. *h* Some reflections, in answer to the vindication of Martin Luther's spirit, &c. By Thomas Deane. 4to Oxon. 1688

See Ath. Oxon. vol. ii. col. 940.

171. % A vindication of Thomas Deane's forsaking the Church of England; being another argument of the schism of the Church of England. By Thomas Deane. 4to Oxon. 1688

"See Ath. Oxon. vol. ii. col. 940. Note, these three last pieces are all printed together."

The title thus given to the imaginary No. 171 is a preposterous blunder, not warranted by anything that Wood had said, and still less by the original tract; where " His vindication" is not Deane's Vindication, but Martin Luther's. It means in fact Atterbury's Tract in Vindication of Luther, No. 168 *supra.* The author intended to say that the Vindication of M. Luther, " printed at the Theater at Oxon,"

was so great a failure that it only furnished an additional argument of the Schism of the Church of England; and the whole of what he says on this point, after a long examination of Atterbury's tract (pp. 9-24),

occupies a paragraph of only eight lines, with which the pamphlet concludes. This is an instructive instance of the danger of describing books at second hand, which is the source of such strange mistakes,

even in the hands of men of real learning.

I do not know what was Wood's authority for stating that the first part of this tract was " a thing reprinted." J. H. T.

In his book " Of Education, especially of young Gentlemen," Oxf. 1687, Obad. Walker gives this precept: "The same cautions prescribed in speaking, or greater, are to be observed in *writing.* The neglect of their pens hath ruined very many; and particularly the great Master of Civility, the Author of Galateo. For going to present to the Pope a petition, by mistake he delivered a copy of licentious Verses writ by him; whereby he lost the Pope's favor, his own reputation, and all hopes of future advancement." 172. Reflections on the Relation of the English Reformation, ©,5., lately printed at Oxford. In two Parts. Anon. By Gilbert Burnet, D.D. pp. 56, with app. pp. 14, 4to Amsterdam, (printed for J. S.) 1688 See Cat. No. 138. Contin. p. 35. Another edit (probably the same with a new title page) appeared, Lond. 1689. The first part of this Tract is entitled " Reflections on the Relation of the English Reformation," &c., and is an answer to No. 163 *supra.* The second part (p. 39) is headed " Reflections on the Oxford Theses, relating to the English Reformation." And then follows a paper, with separate pagination within brackets, and new signatures A. and B. (pp. 14) entitled "The History of the Divorce of Henry VIII. and Katharine of Arragon, with the defence of Sanders. The Refutation of the Two first Books of the History of the Reformation of Dr. Burnett. By Joachim le Grand. With Dr. Burnett's answer and vindication of himself." This is the title page of Le Grand's work, which was printed in French, Paris, 1688, 8vo. The article which follows, entitled Dr. Burnett's answer and vindication, is a short review or censure of the work, followed p. 4 by Dr. Burnet's vindication, entitled " A Letter to Monsieur Thevenot, being a full refutation of Mr. Le Grand's History of Henry VIII's Divorcing Katharine of Arragon. With a plain indication of the same by Dr. G. B." This letter is dated " Hague, 20 of June." *T.C.D.* The Tract on the Divorce of Henry VIII. is evidently no part of

Burnet's " Reflections," and is only by accident found bound up with the copy above described. It is printed in double columns, which the " Reflections," &c. is not, and on a larger page and paper. The letter to M. Thevenot was publ. in 4to 1689, with this title: "A Letter to Mr. Thevenot, containing a censure of M. Le Grand's History of King Henry the Eighth's divorce. To which is added, a censure of Mr. de Meaux's history of the variations of the protestant churches; together with some further reflexions on Mr. le Grand." Chronol. account of the works of Bp. Burnet. (Own Times, Oxf. edit. vol. vi. p. 346.) J. H. T.

173. Some queries to the Protestants, concerning the English Reformation. By T. W. Gent. Published with allowance. pp. 8, 4to Lond. (Nath. Thompson) 1687 See Contin. p. 37. These are the same queries which Dean Manby has given in Latin at the end of his " Considerations," No. 128 *supra.* T. W. is Thomas Ward. See No. 174. And see also King's Answer to Manby, ch. vi. p. 86 (No. 129 *supra.)* The same are found under the title, Some queries to the Archbishop of Canterbury, *ut supra,* p. 99. J. H. T.

£.&. 174. The Queries offered by T. .W. to the Protestants concerning the English Reformation reprinted and answered. Anon. By Wm. Claget, D.D. Imprimatur Nov. 23, 1687.

pp. 48, 4to Lond. (H. Clark) 1688 See Cat. No. 143. Contin. p. 36. Ath. Oxon. vol. ii. col. 327. Qusere, if this Mr. T. W. was not one Mr. Webster of Lynne. See No. 184 *infra.*

I know not why Peck has made this suggestion as to T W., except that Wehstor hegins with W.; there is no allusion in the Tract No. 184 to the queries of T. W. , nor anything to identify T. W. with Mr. Webster of Linne. It seems much more probable that the initials T. W. stand for Thomas Ward, " the Roman Catholic soldier" (see above No. 10.0), and it is worthy of note, in confirmation of this conjecture, that the concluding queries speak of errors in the English Bible, a subject upon which Thomas Ward wrote a special treatise this same year, entitled, The errata to the Protestant Bible, or the truth of their English translations examin'd, &c. 4to Lond. lb'88. Reprinted Lond. 1737, and 4to Dublin

1807.

This book is taken altogether from Gregory Martin's " A discoverie of the manifold corruptions of the holy scriptures by the heretikes of our daies, specially the English sectaries, and of their foule dealing herein," &c. Khemes 1582, 8vo, a book which was completely answered before Ward was born, by Dr. W. Fulke (whose defence of the English Translations was reprinted by the Parker Society in 1843). The republication of Ward's book in Dublin, in 1807, with the sanction of the Irish Roman Catholic bishops, produced two answers, both respectable, viz., I. An Analysis of Ward's errata of the Protestant Bible. By Rich. Ryan, D.D. Dublin, Svo 1808. II. An Answer to Ward's errata of the Protestant Bible. By Rich. Grier, D.D. Dublin, 4to 1812. J. H. T.

175. A Dissertation concerning Patriarchal and Metropolitan C fL authority, in answer to what Edw. Stillingfleet, Dean of St. Paul's, hath written in his book of the British Antiquities. By Eman. a Schelstrate, S.T.D.C.L. i.e. Sacrse Theologiaj Doctor, Canonicus Lateranensis and Prefect of the Vatican Library. Translated from the Latin. With allowance. pp. 128, with Title and Dedic. to James II. pp. 10, Preface pp. 22, and at the end Index, Postscript and list of books authoized by his Majesties letters patent. pp. 8, 4to Lond. (Matthew Turner) 1G88 See Contin. p. 36. In the Dedication, which is subscribed " Emmanuel of Antwerp in the Low Countries," James II. is styled " Defender of the Faith, Conqueror, Triumphant, Peacemaker." At

D n the end is a curious list of Popish books, which Matthew Turner of Holborn, bookseller, and his assigns only, had licence to publish by his Majesty's letters patent. The original Latin of this work was printed at Rome 1687, 4to. Emanuel a Schelstrate, or Scheelstrate, of Antwerp, of which town he was a native, and chanter of the Cathedral there, was afterwards promoted to be Librarian of the Vatican and Canon of St. John of Lateran and of St. Peter at Rome, where he died in 1692, aged 44. His works prove him to have been a man of eminent industry and learning.

Of his answer to Stillingfleet Wake says, Contin. loc. cit., " As to this Book, since Mr. Schelstrate's Friends have ventured to expose it in a Translation here, the Reverend and most worthy Dean of Paul's will not fail, if God continue him health and opportunity, to give an Answer; and I am sure the world will not be angry with me for raising their expectations of the Dean's Answer, since they are satisfied that he will make them sufficient amends for them. " Upon this Peck has put into his Catalogue the answer, as if it had been published adding, however, a quaere, thus: 176. An answer to a dissertation concerning patriarchal and metropolitical authority, &c. as above. By Edw. Stillingfleet, D.D., Dean of S. Paul's.

He promised such a thing. But quaere if ever published? See Contin. p. 36.

It does not appear that Stillingfleet ever promised such a thing, although Wake promised for him. No such thing appears to have been ever published. J. H. T.

The title of Stillingflcet's work here referred to is as follows: " Origines Britannicse; or, the Antiquities of the British Churches." Reprinted at Oxford, at the University Press, 1842, in 2 vols. 8vo. To which is added, An Historical Account of Church Government as first received in Great Britain and Ireland. By W. Lloyd, D.D., Bishop of Worcester. A new edition, with additional Notes, by the Rev. Tho. P. Pantin, M. A. Of the Origines Britannicse and of Schelstrate's Dissertation in the original Latin, a review will be found in the fifteenth volume of the Bibliotheque Universale. " I shall not here answer," says Schelstrate (Pref. p. 2), " all the objections he hath thought fit to make; for since he hath written against those things which I had deduced from ancient Testimonies concerning the Patriarchal Power of the Roman Bishop over the West, in my Book intitled, Antiquitas illustrato, I will refute what he hath writ in answer to it, when I publish my Book de Antiquitate, &c, with the addition of three or four Ages to it." The enlarged edition of this, his greatest work, was printed

2 vols. fol. 1690-97. The student will find full information on the respective limits of the Patriarchates in Bingham's Orig. Eccles., book ix. chap, i., illustrated with maps. In the seventh volume of Usher's works will be found The original of Bishops and Metropolitans briefly laid down. See p. 3 *supra*.

177. A discourse concerning the necessity of Reformation, with C.l. respect to the errors and corruptions of the Church of Rome.

The first part. pp. 60, including title. Imprimatur, H.

Maurice, &c. Feb. 8, 1686. The second edition. London

(Rich. Chiswell) 16S7, 4to. Anon. By Dr. Nich. Stratford,

Dean of St. Asaph, afterwards (1689) Bp. of Chester.

See Cat. No. 1. Contin. p. 5. Ath. Oxon. vol. ii. col. 1067. The first ed. was dated 1685. J. H. T.

Reprinted in Gibson's Preservative, vol. i.

" This pretended Infallibility of the Church of Rome hath as little support from the Doctrine of the Autient Christian Church, as it hath from Scripture and Reason," p. 11. Compare The Search after Infallibility. Remarks on the Testimony of the Fathers to the Roman Dogma of Infallibility. By James Henthorn Todd, D.D. Lond. 1848. They will be found also in the British Magazine from April to November 1848, inclusive.

The necessity of Reformation is made evident by taking a particular view of the Corruptions. I. In Doctrine. II. In Worship. III. In

Manners. IV. In Discipline. Compare No. 5 and No. 161. For corruptions in discipline our Author refers the Reader also to the

History of the Council of Trent by Father Paul; the Review of the

Council of Trent by Ranchin, transl. by Langbaine; Espencajus's

Comment on the first Chap, of the Epistle to Titus; Richerii Historia Conciliorum. To these may be added the declamations in Von der

Hardt's Concilium Constantiense by

Peter d'Ailly, etc.

(T. 1L. 178. The necessity of Reformation, with respect to the errors and corruptions of the Church of Rome. The second part. Wherein is shewed the vanity of the pretended reformation of the Council of Trent: and of R. H.'s Vindication of it, in his fifth discourse concerning the Guide in Controversies. Anon. By Nich. Stratford, D.D. pp. 119, Pref. and Contents pp.4. Imprimatur Car. Alston Martii 6, 168J. 4to Lond. 1686.

See Cat. No. 2. Contin. p. 5. Ath. Oxon. vol. ii. col. 1067. Wake says, Contin. 1. c., that the author designed a third part, which however does not appear to have heen ever published. R. H. (the initials of the second syllables of his names) is Abraham Woodhead, who published his Guide in Controversies, under those initials. See Nos. 189-193 *infra*. J. H. T.

This part contains also The Authority of Father Paul's History of the Council of Trent asserted, pp. 29-61.

179. A discourse concerning the necessity of Reformation, &c. Part III. By Nicholas Stratford, D.T). 4to 1686

See Cat. No. 2. Contin. p. 5. So Peck gives the title and date of this imaginary third part. But there is no evidence that it ever existed; for Wake (I. c.) only says, " We have hopes that it will be published ere long," and Gee (following Wake) that from the same learned hand "we expect ere long the third and last part." But as Gee's Cat. was printed 1G89 it is evident that Peck drew upon his imagination when he dated this supposed third part 1686. J. H. T.

C H. 180. A discourse about the charge of novelty upon the reformed Church of England, made by the Papists asking of us the question, Where was our religion before Luther? Anon. By Gregory Hascard, D.D., Dean of Windsor.

pp. 36, 4to Lond. (Robt. Horn) 1683 See Cat. No. 8. Contin. p. 4.

" This is the common and trite Objection against our Religion, very frequent not only in the mouths of their more ordinary Disciples, hut also of their more learned Writers, Bellarmine, Campian, Smith." p. 4. ' The Popish Faith is Pius Quartus his Creed at Trent, so that we may justly demand of Papists, where was their Religion before

Trent, which was since Luther." Lloyd's Papists no Catholicks. See also Nos. 209, 355, 371, 372 *infra*.

England's Independency upon the Papal Power, historically and judicially stated, hy Sir John Davis and Sir Edward Coke.

4to Lond. 1674

Historical Vindication of the Church of England in point ofC 1L. Schism, as it stands separated from the Roman, and was reformed by Elizabeth. By Sir Roger Twysden.

4to Lond. 1675

The Pillars of Rome broken, wherein the several Pleas for the Pope's authority in England, with the material defences of them that have been made by the Romanists, are revised and answered. By Fr. Fulwood, D.D. 4to Lond. 1679

The Protestant Religion vindicated from the Charge of Singularity £. IL. and Novelty, in a Sermon Preached before the King by J.

Tillotson, D.D., Dean of Canterbury. Works, fol. 1696, vol.

iii. pp. 308-18. Lond. 1680

Sure and Honest Means for the Conversion of all Hereties; and Wholesome Advice and Expedients for the Reformation of the

Church. 4to Lond. 1688

A Discourse concerning the Church in these following Particulars.

I. Concerning the Visibility of the true Church. II. Concerning the Church of Rome. III. Concerning the Protestant Churches. IV. An Answer to this question, Where was your

Church before Luther. By the Rt. Revd. Father in God

Rcbt. Sanderson, late Ld. Bp. of Lincoln. 1688

CHAP. XVII.

Of the Discourses written by Romanists reflecting upon the validity of the orders of the Church of England; with the Churchmen's replies. 181. £« The Church of England truly represented.

See Contin. p. 55. Is not this the same as No. 160 *mpral* See Contin. p. 36. Wake appears to be mistaken when lie says that " the occasion of reviving this matter," of the validity of English ordination, " was given by a little scurrilous libel that went abroad," under the name of " The Church of England truly Represented," in answer to whose Calumnies three discourses were published, meaning Nos. 182, 186, and 184 *infra*. For the "little scurrilous libel" was quite different, and is printed in Burnet's answer (No. 182 *infra)*, and is there entitled "Arguments to prove the Invalidity of the orders of the Church of England." It appears also from what Burnet says (Pref. p. 27) that it had not been printed, but only given about in MS. to such persons as were known to be wavering. No. 186, however, was avowedly written in answer to No. 160; and No. 184 professes to be a reply to "some scattered objections of Mr. Webster of Linne," but makes no mention of No. 160, or any other tract on that side. Wake says that of these three discourses "two are new, and the other only reprinted," which probably means that a second edition of Burnet's tract (the first ed. having appeared in 1677, 8vo) was brought out in consequence of the publication of No. 160. J. H. T.

The arguments of the Romanists are briefly recapitulated in No. 154 *supra*. CI. 182. A vindication of the ordinations of the Church of England, in which it is demonstrated that all the essentials of ordination, according to the practice of the primitive and Greek Churches are still retained in our Church. In answer to a paper written by one of the Church of Rome to prove the nullity of our orders; and given to a Person of quality. The second edition. Anon. By Gilbert Burnet, D.D., afterwards Bp. of Salisbury. pp. 94, with title and Pref. pp. 30, Chiswell's list of books at the end pp. 4, 4to Lond. (Ric. Chiswell) pp. 94, Pref. xxviii. 4to Lond. 1688 (Gibson, vol. iii. fol. 1.)

See Cat. No. 161. Contin. p. 54. The first edition of this book was printed in 8vo 1677. The " Paper" is printed at length, p. 1. The " Person of quality" to whom it was given was Lady Terwhitt, at whose house Burnet and Stillingfleet had the conference with Coleman, 3 April, 1676, see pp. 174-6 *supra*. Speaking of this conference Burnet says (Own Times, vol. i. p. 39.5); " Soon after that, the lady, who continued firm upon this conference, was possessed with new scruples about the validity of our ordinations. I got from her the paper that was put in her hand, and answered it; and she seemed satisfied with that likewise. But afterwards the uneasiness of her life prevailed more on her than her scruples did, and she changed her religion." J. H. T.

183. Concio ad clerum, habita coram Academia Cantabrigiensi, £,1L, Junii 11 A 1687, pro gradu Baccalaur. in S. Theologia. Ubi vindicatur vera et valida Cleri Anglicani, ineunte Reformatione, ordinatio. Cui accessit concio habita Julii 3, 1687, de canonica Cleri Anglicani ordinatione. Latine reddita et aucta a Thoma Browne, S.T.B. Coll. D. Joh. Evang. Soc.

OuTca? T)fias XoytecrOa avOparKo;, &c. 1 Cor. iv. i. Annexum est Instrumentum consecrationis Matth. Parker, Archiepiscopi Cantuariensis, ex MS. C.C.C. Cant. First sermon pp. 38, with Pref. and title pp. 14. Second sermon pp. 66, 4to Cantabrigian (Jo. Hayes) 1688. (Reprinted 8vo Lond. 1731.)

See Cat. No. 162. Contin. p. 55. Fasti Oxon. vol. ii. col. 220.

The second sermon has this separate title: " Concio habita coram Academia Catabrigiensi Julii 3 A" 1687, ubi vindicatur canonica Cleri Anglicani ineunte Reformatione ordinatio: a T. Browne, S. T. B. Coll. D. Joh. Evang. Soc. *Xap-qcrare fifias,* &c. 2 Cor. vii. 1." 4to Cantabrigise (Jo. Hayes) 1688. J. H. T.

" The validity of the consecration of Archbishop Parker is a matter of much importance to the English Church. For if it could be proved, as the old Papists endeavoured to bring it about, that he was no true Archbishop or Bishop," by reason of the want of, or irregularity of consecration, then "as a sequel all the Bishops that he afterwards consecrated should be no Bishops, because he was none himself, and therefore could not consecrate nor give order to others," &c. An Account of the Rites and Ceremonies which took place at the Consecration of Archbishop Parker, with an Introductory Preface and Notes. Communicated to the Cambridge Antiquarian Society by the Rev. James Goodwin, B.D. Cambridge, 1841. See also The Succession of Bishops in the Church of England unbroken; or the Nag's Head Fable refuted, &c., by the Rev. E. C. Harington, B.D., 1852, and No. 2 *supra*. It is rejected by Lingard himself as a palpable forgery.

C1L. 184. A short defence of the orders of the Church of England, as by law establish'd: against some scatter'd objections of Mr. Webster of Linne. By a Presbyter of the Diocess of Norwich i.e. Luke Milburne, minister of Yarmouth.

pp, 36, 4to Lond. (Randal Taylor) 1688 See Cat. No. 163. Contin. p. 55. I do not know who was the Mr. Webster of Linne, against whom this tract is written, nor where his "scatter'd objections" are to be found. J. H. T. 185. A plain answer to a Popish priest, questioning the orders of the Church of England, drawn up for the satisfaction of his parishioners, by a minister of that Church. The second edition, from the author's own correct copy. To which is now annext, An answer to the Oxford Animadverter's Reflections upon it. By the same Author. pp. 32, 4to Lond. (Sam. Smith) 1689 See Cat. No. 164. Ath. Oxon. vol. ii. col. 1000. This tract is by Abednego Seller, who although he left Oxford without a degree, was a man of deep and real learning. He was Rector of Combeinton Head in Devonshire, and ejected as a nonjuror at the Revolution. The first edition was published 1688, 4to, and was soon after answered by Thos. Fairfax, a Jesuit of St. Omers, of the Fairfax family in Yorkshire, one of the persons forced upon Magd. Coll. as a fellow by James II. This answer appeared at the end of a book printed at the licensed press of Obadiah Walker, Univ. Coll., entitled Twenty one questions further demonstrating the Schism of the Church of England, &c., 1688. Where Fairfax's answer has been printed with this title: " Some reasons tendered to impartial people why Dr. Henry Maurice, Chaplain to his Grace of Canterbury, ought not to be traduc'd as a Licenser of a Pamphlet entitled, ' A plain answer to a Popish Priest,'" &c. J. H. T.

" Fairfax was appointed in the reign of James II. professor of Philosophy in Magdalen College, Oxford. When the revolution burst forth in all its horrors, he was attacked in the streets of that city, dashed on the ground and trampled upon, and narrowly escaped being murdered outright." — Dr. Oliver.

The first edition of " A Plain Answer" contains 10 pp. 1688. C1L.

The second edition concludes with the doctrine of Intention. This C 3L. subject is fully discussed not only by Marsden, but in Mason's Vindication of the Church of England. See Index in Lindsay's Translation.

186. A defence of the ordinations and ministry of the Church of ©.l. England. In answer to the scandals raised or revived against them, in several late pamphlets, and particularly in one intituled The Church of England truly represented, &c. *ToXfirjTal avffdBei';,* &c. 2 Pet. ii. x. Anon. By Edmund Whitfield, B.D. , fellow of Kings Coll. Cambridge. pp. 64, Title and "To the Reader" pp. 6, 4to Lond. (Brab. Aylmer) 1688

See Cat. No. 165. This Tract is in answer to No. 160 or No. 181 *supra*. J. H. T.

From which is cited (p. 3) the passage referred to by Macaulay.

" Another Roman Catholic treatise begins by informing us that the ignis fatuus of reformation which had grown to a comet by many acts of spoil and rapine had been ushered into England, purified of the filth which it had contracted among the lakes of the Alps." — Vol ii. p. 110.

This defence relates to the whole contest, and takes in both the old and new objections already answered by Usher, Mason, Bramhall, &c.

" Allowing that all the Christianity which these after ages can pretend to here in Britain ows its original either to Pope Eleutherius and his Legates in the reign of King Lucius, or else to Pope Gregory the First and Austin the monk his deputy, in that of King Ethelbert, I say allowing all this, and letting them take their choice which of these two Popes they will make the source and Fountain of this Succession, we are able to derive ours through this channel as well as themselves." It is remarkable that Pope Eleutherius sent only presbyters for the conversion of the Britons, and consequently they could not have derived episcopal succession from Rome. Most probably they found bishops here, as this institution came down from the first planting of Apostolical Churches, and Lucius, like Constantine, only confirmed the Christian religion by a national establishment. Bishops of British Churches were present at the Councils of Arles, Nice, Sardica and Ariminum, in which canons were passed by metropolitans and other bishops without the confirmation of the Patriarch of Rome. It is also remarkable that Augustine was consecrated bishop by Etherius, Archbishop of Arles, and that his predecessors had aspired to raise that metropolitan seat into a kind of Pontificate of Gaul. " Under Leo the Great, A.d. 445, the supremacy of the Roman See was brought to the issue of direct assertion on his part, of inflexible resistance on that of his opponent Hilarins, the Archbishop of Arles, inflexibly resisted all the authority of the Pope and of St. Peter; and confronted the Pope with the bold assertion of his unbounded metropolitan power." (Milman's Hist. of Latin Christianity, vol. i. pp. 192-3.) Thus had the British Church not been Metropolitan, it would have been under the jurisdiction of Arles not of Rome, subject not to the Roman Supremacy but to the Gallic Liberties. Notwithstanding that Augustine and his successors acknowledged the primacy of the bishop of Rome, " it does not yet appear that, for above 600 years after, any of them were required at their consecration to take an oath of fidelity and obedience to their lord pope." — Burnet's Vindication of the Ordinations of the Church of England, p. 87; Lewis's Life of Dr. Reynold Pecock, p. 122; Mendham's Life of S. Pius V. ad calc.

Stillingfleet's Origines Britannicae contains a learned history of the antiquity of our church, which was probably founded by St. Paul, according to bishops Stillingfleet and Burgess, Williams and other divines.

187. The validity of the Orders of the Church of England, made out against the objections of the Papists, in several Letters to a Gentleman of Norwich, that desired satisfaction therein. By Humphrey Prideaux, D.D., Prebendary of Norwich, pp. 128, 4to Lond, (John Richardson, for Brab. Aylmer) 1688

See Cat. No. 166. Ath. Oxon. vol. ii. col 25, and 1058. The reference to col. 25 is an error of Peck. I can find nothing there relating to this hook or its author. The Preface tells us that the " Gentleman of Norwich, who desired satisfaction, was Mr. Anthony Norris, late a justice of the peace for the County of Norfolk." The book begins by an Account of the Conference between Mr. Earbery and Mr. Kipping on the Anglican side, and Mr. Acton a Jesuit and Mr. Brown on the other, concerning the validity of English orders. Mr. Norris having been present at this conference sent Dr. Prideaux an anonymous paper, containing his " Summary of the Conference." This led to a correspondence between him and Dr. Prideaux, which occupies the remainder of the pamphlet. J. H. T.

This learned divine was born in 1648, died 1724. A second edition of.this treatise was printed, with other ecclesiastical tracts by the same author, 8vo Lond. 1716.

188. Roman Catholicks uncertain whether there be any trueCiL. Priests or Sacraments in the Church of Rome; evinced by an argument urg'd and maintain'd (upon their own principles) against Mr. Edward Goodal of Prescot in Lancashire. By Thomas Marsden, Vicar of Walton in the same County. The Treatise divided into two parts. The first being explicative of terms. The second Argumentative. pp. 136, Title, Pref. and Contents pp. 8. 4to Lond. (Walter Kettilby) 1688

See Cat. No. 167. Con tin. p. 57. Ath. Oxon. vol. ii, col. 1025.

Fasti Oxon. vol. ii. col. 141. "Tho. Marsden, of Brazen. Coll., was afterwards Chaplain to the English merchants trading at Lisbon in Portugal He is now living and able to publish other matters." He

was *able* to draw the weapons of controversy from the armoury of

Scholastic Philosophy.

In this treatise the author insists on the insecurity and absence of faith produced in the mind of the Romanist by this uncertainty.

" Anxiety would oppress the soul, were it left to fluctuate about the weighty matters of Religion, such as the truth of our Sacraments is acknowledged to be. And it hath been shewn that the truth of these can not be known, unless the Minister's Intention be so too." His adversary, Goodall, had evidently been a Protestant. " Pray tell me, how it happens, that in your Study of Theology, for full twenty years in our Communion, you were not able to find one of their distinguishing Articles defensible: and now in one years time see them all perspicuous and surely founded Pray then tell us, how, all at once, you hapned to find out all those Points we call Popery, to be warranted by Divine Authority." p. 136. Cf. Fowler's Discourse of Christian Liberty, sect. 3, chap. 16, Lond. 1680.

A Treatise of the Vocation of Bishops and other Ecclesiastical Ministers; proving the Ministers of the Pretended Reformed Churches in general to have no calling, against Monsieur du Plessis and Mr. Doctour Field, and in particular the pretended Bishops in England to be no true Bishops, against Mr. Mason. By Anthony Champ or Champney. 4to Douay 1616

See Mason's second Dedication.

A Treatise of the nature of Catholic Faith and Heresie, with Reflexions upon the Nullitie of the English Protestant Church and Clergy. By Peter Talbot. 8vo Rouen, 1657

He published this whilst a Father of the Society of Jesus. He was afterwards Archbishop of Dublin. " Dodd, p. 284, vol. iii. Church History, might have improved his article, had he paid more attention to the spirit of Father Southwell's Narrative, which lay open before him." Dr. Oliver, p. 268. " Peter Talbot, brother to Richard Talbot, Duke of Tyrconnel; born in Ireland, but originally from a noble family of that name in England." Dodd. " Under the name of Erastus Senior (sic?) he docs not rely on the Nag's Head Consecration Story." Dr. Oliver. For an account of Peter Talbot see Ware's Writers of Ireland, by Harris, and D'Alton's Memoirs of the Archbishops of Dublin.

P Erastus Senior scholastically demonstrating this conclusion, that (admitting their Lambeth records for true) those called Bishops here in England, are no Bishops either in order or jurisdiction, or so much as legal, in answer to Mason, Heylin, and Bramhall. By John Lewgar. 12mo 1662

" Notwithstanding what bad been said, there was some one or more of them still hardy enough to publish a book (pretending to prove the Nullity of the Prelatic Clergy) about the year 1657, in 8vo *tit supra* I have now before me another, of the like sort, intituled, Erastus Junior, or A Fatal Blow to the Clergies pretensions to Divine Right; in a solid Demonstration by Principles, Forms of

Ordination, &c., that no Bishop nor Minister, &e., hath any right or authority to preach, &c., in this Nation from Christ, but only from the

Parliament; in two Parts, 4to. Bearing the name of Josiah Webb,

Gent., a furious Detester of the Dregs of the Anti christian Hierarchy yet remaining among us; but written indeed by John Lewgar, a

Revolter to Popery There is also a second part of Erastus

Senior Junior? pretending to demonstrate by Forms of Ordination

&c And now I shall proceed to that other performance (of the same Author) with the following title, Erastus Senior, Scholastically demonstrating, &c I may be allowed to observe what

an Author of great learning and reputation assures us, of both these doughty performances under the titles of Erastus," etc. See Prideaux's

Valid. of the Orders, &c, p. 23, 1688. There is no copy of Erastus Senior in the Bodl. nor in Dublin

Library except the reprint published in " The English Catholic

Library," vol. ii. Lond. (Dolman) 1844, 8vo. J. H. T.

A Vindication of a Sheet concerning the Orders of the Church of C1L. England against some Reasons, etc., printed at Oxford. pp. 10, 4to Lond. 1688

" Christ instituted no form of words (in the institution of Orders) as absolutely necessary; those which he used in the Mission of the Apostles we think the fittest, and therefore as such, use them in our Ordination; but for that form which the Church of Rome uses, there is no shadow of proof in Scripture or Antiquity. The delivery of the vessels is so far from being instituted by Christ that it is by the Romanists themselves acknowledged a Novelty." See Morinus, &c.

Compare Sall's " Catholic Religion Maintained in the Church of England," chap. viii. " How far the Church of England agrees with the Romish in matter of Ordination; wherein they differ; and how absurd the pretension of Romanists is, that our difference herein with them should annul our Orders." And Burnet's Vindication, Append.

Canonica Successio Miasterii Ecclesise Anglicanae tam contra Pontificios quam Schismaticos vindicata Authore Sam. Fuller S.S. Th. Prof. Cappellano Regio &c. 4to Cantabr. 1690

The Controversy of Ordination truly stated, as far as it concerns the Church of England by law established; being an exposition of the Thirty-Sixth Article. With a full Account of what both Roman Catholics and Protestants have delivered upon the subject of Ordination. Especially the Attempt of Dr. Burnet, late Bishop of Salisbury, in order to clear that point, is impartially considered, &c. By Thomas Ward. 8vo Lond. 1719

See Mason's Vindication by Lindsay, p. 112. This was answered in Elrington's Clergy of the Church of England truly ordained, and not obliged to subscribe to damnable Contradictions, in reply to Ward's Controversy of Ordination, 8vo Dublin 1808.

Amongst the Romanists, Courayer, Canon Regular of St. Genevieve, distinguished himself by a Dissertation sur la Validite des Ordinations des Anglois, Brux. 1723, and by a masterly "Supplement" to the same work, in which he overthrows triumphantly all the objections of Pere le Quien, Father Hardouin, and other Romanists, to our Ordinations. These were translated by Daniel Williams, and published Lond. 1728, 8vo, under the titles, A Defence of the Validity of the English Ordinations, and of the Succession of the Bishops in the Church of England: together with Proofs justifying the Facts advanced in this Treatise (1 vol. 8vo), and a Defence of the Dissertation (2 vols. 8vo). "Besides which," says Mason, "there is another Book in English, come out by Owl-light," intituled, & Remarks upon Le Courayer's Book in defence of the English Ordinations, wherein all his arguments are answered, and the invalidity of the English Ordinations is fully considered and fully proved, by Clerophilus Alethes, (John Constable.) — Without place or date.

" It is," observes Dr. Oliver, " a work of considerable research, and was much admired by the Rev. Robert Manning, an excellent judge in such matters." According to Chancellor Harington (Notes and Queries, second series, vol. i. p. 135), Constable did not respond to any portion of Courayer's Defence of his Dissertation. These " Remarks" and another popish publication by John Trapp — (England's Conversion and Reformation compared, Antwerp 1725, 8vo) — are noticed in Lindsay's Pref. to Mason pp. 114-16.

Besides Courayer several Romanists have allowed the Orders of the Church of England to be good and valid, *e.g.* Father Walsh, Father Davenport, alias Sancta Clara and Cudsemius; see

Prideaux p. 45 (quoted by Lindsay). Bossuet made the same admission in his letter to Mabillon, quoted in the Appendix of Courayer's Defence, &c. Barnes, the Benedictine, went so far as to write a book (CatholicoRomanus Pacificus, see Brown's Fasciculus, vol. ii. p. 826-70) to induce the Roman patriarch to receive the English church into his communion, and to justify us from the charge of schism and heresy. See Basier On the Ancient Liberty of the Britannic Church and the legitimate exemption thereof from the Roman Patriarchate: three chapters concerning the Priviledges of the Britannic Church, &c. selected out of a Latin Manuscript, entitled Catholico-Romanus Pacificus: translated by Rich. Watson, Loud. 1661, 8vo. In Ussher's Opuscula, ad calc. will be found, Sententia de Ecciesise Britannicse Privilegiis, ex Cathol. Rom. Pacif. sect. 3. This learned and candid man (Barnes) was, in consequence of his liberal notions, seized at Paris, carried prisoner to Rome, immured in the dungeon of the Inquisition, and ere long thrust into a madhouse, where he died. On his melancholy end see also the authors referred to in Walch, Bibl. Theol. vol. ii. p. 355. Basier's opusculum appears to have been unknown to ©«1L. Bingham; see Antiq. of the Christian Church, chap. ix.

Detection of the Forgery of the Nag's Head Consecration: or a modest Vindication of the Clergy of the Church of England, both as to their Orders and Succession. By Matthew Earbery.
8vo Lond. 1722

Sec No. 187 *supra*. He makes use of Leslie's four famous marks.

The Succession of Protestant Bishops asserted; or the regularity of the ordinations of the Church of England justify'd. Wherein the first Protestant Bishops are cleared from the aspersions lately cast upon them by Mr. Thomas Ward, &c. By Daniel Williams. 8vo Lond. 1721

The first edition of the celebrated work of Francis Mason, "from which it appears," says Wood, vol. i. col..546, " that the author was a general-read-scholar, thorough-pac'd in the Councils, and all sorts of Historie, whether divine, civil or profane," was in English, published Lond. 1613, fol., but greatly enlarged in the second, which the author C1L wrote in Latin. The last edition is as follows: A Vindication of the Church of England, and of the lawful ministry thereof: that is to say, of the succession, election, confirmation and consecration of bishops, and also of the ordination of priests and deacons. In five books. Wherein the Church of England is defended against the calumnies and reproaches of Bellarmine, Saunders, Bristow, Harding, Allen, Stapleton, Parsons, Kellison, Eudsemon, Becanus, and other Romanists. Now faithfully translated from the Author's Latin edition (much enlarged and corrected). Whereunto is added a new edition of a Sermon of the same author's concerning the authority of the Church in making Canons and Constitutions in things indifferent. On 1 Cor. xiv. 40. Also printed in Wordsworth's Christian Institutes, vol. iv. p. 444. A copy of the first reformed Ordinal. A Translation of some fragments of Letters written to Father Le Courayer; in an Appendix. Together with an exact Index of the principal matters, and marginal Notes upon the whole Book. To all which is prefixed A full and particular Series of the Succession of our Bishops, through the several Reigns since the Reformation; an Historical Account of the Rise and Progress of the present Controversy, and of the several Writers on both sides; and particularly of our Learned Author Mason, and of all his Works, in a large Preface. By John Lindsay, a Priest of the Church of England. Fol. Lond. 1728.
Liudsay considers the pamphlet spurious, which was published under Mason's name entitled, The Validity of the Ordination of the C1L.
Ministers of the Reform'd Churches beyond the Seas, maintained against the Romanists, printed at Oxford 1641, 4to, for divers reasons,
as " 1. With respect to the time of its appearance in the world. 2.
With respect to its Editor; viz. John Duree, a Scotsman, and a
Preacher, though whether he had taken Orders according to the Form of the Church of England, which it seems he always scrupled, it doth not appear. However he was a great pretender towards the making a reconciliation between the Calvinists and Lutherans beyond the
Seas; but so far from being a friend to the Church of England, that he sided with the Presbyterians, when they became prevalent in
1641, was one of the zealous Preachers before the Rebellious Parliament, and by them, amongst other employments, made one of their pious Assembly of Divines, to reform away the Church of England
(Root and Branch) as they themselves reform'd the State," &c. An account of John Dury, or Durseus, will be found in Worthington's
Diary and Correspondence. Cf. Lindsay in Byrom's Remains, vol. ii. part ii. p. 532.

Professor Hey, in his admirable Lectures on Divinity, Cambridge, 1798, in reference to a succession of Bishops among Protestants, cites "Baxter on Councils, p. 471, Sect. viii., and page 484, Prop. vi.— Burnet on the Validity, etc. — Neal, vol. i. p. 502, bottom, 4to. — Heylin's Hist. of Episcopacy. — Archbishop Bramhall has a work on this subject, which may be good: see the account in his Life, Biogr. Britan. note *(u)* : or his works in folio." To avoid repetition I must here refer to page 2, and conclude with , The story of the ordination of our first Bishops in Q. Elizabeth's reign at the Nag's Head Tavern in Cheap-Side thoroughly examined; and proved to be a late invented, inconsistent, self-contradictory and absurd fable. In answer to Le Quien and to Remarks on Le Courayer. By Thomas Brown, B.D.
8vo Lond. 1731

F *r* CHAP. XVIII.
Of the discourses written of the unity, authority and infallibility of the Church.
d. 189. *i'* The guide in controversies; or a rational account of the doctrine of Roman Catholicks concerning the ecclesiastical guide in controversies of religion; reflecting on the later writings

of Protestants, particularly of Archbp. Laud and Mr. Stillingfleetj on this subject. By R. H. pp. 85, Pref. vii. 4to s. l. 1673

Sic in Catal. Bodl. This is by Abraham Woodhead, of Univ. Coll. Oxford. (See what has been said of him No. 163 *supra.*) He appears to have chosen the letters R. H. because they were the initials of the second syllables of his names. Peck gives the title of this book erroneously, and I have therefore corrected it, as above. It consists of five parts, with an appendix. Peck (following Wood) mentions only four; and yet Wood, although he says that the work consists of four parts, gives afterwards the title of the fifth. Ath. Oxon. vol. ii. cols. 614, 615. The first and second parts were published in London in 1666, 4to; the third and fourth, London 1667, 4to. So says Ant. Wood; but the Bodl. Catal. (which library contains only Parts III. and IV.) gives the date 1668, and says that no place of printing is mentioned. Parts I. and II. are of extreme rarity, the whole impression having been burnt in the fire of London, with the exception of a very few copies. Parts II. and III. were published Ci, in London 1667 i.e. 166J), and all four parts together, with some additions and alterations, were printed again in London 1673, 4to.

The words " rational account" shew an evident allusion to Stillingfleet's " Origines Sacrse, or a rational account of the grounds of the Christian faith," &c. , and to the same author's Rational Account of the grounds of the Protestant religion, &c.

Peck ought to have placed these books by Woodhead in Chap. I,, as they were connected with Stillingfleet's controversial writings published in the reign of Charles II. But as they were again brought into the controversy about an infallible guide, &c., in the reign of
James II., he has placed them out of chronological order here; and
I have not thought fit to change their place, although I have been, in consequence, obliged to introduce here a notice of several tracts that ought to have had a place in Chap. I. J. H. T.

190. The Guide in Controversies. Part II. Proceeding uponClL. the Concessions of Learned Protestants that the Pastors of the Church, some or other, in all Ages, do guide their subjects infallibly in Necessaries to search which, in any Division happening among these Pastors, are those to whom Christians ought to adhere, and yield their obedience, pp. 87-152.

191. The Guide in Controversies. Part III. pp. 153-373.

See Ath. Oxon. vol. ii. col. 614. Part of this third discourse was refuted by Dr. Edw. Stillingfleet, in his work entitled

A second (see No. 193 *infra*) discourse in vindication of the protestant grounds of faith, against the pretence of infallibility in tho Roman Church, in answer to the Guide in Controversies, by R. H. Protestancy without principles, and Reason and Religion, by E. W. 8vo Lond. 1673.

See Stillingfleet's works, vol. v. p. 117, where the initials R. H. are erroneously attributed to R. Holden, and E. W. to E. Warner. For R. H., as we have seen, denote AbRaham WoodHead; and the other two tracts are known to be by the Jesuit Edward Worseley; they are not mentioned by Peck, but were published with the following titles: Protestancy without principles; or sectaries unhappy fall from infallibility to fancy; in four discourses. 4to Antwerp 1668. Reason and Religion; or the certain rule of faith; where the infallibility of the Roman Catholic Church is asserted, against Atheists,
Heathens, Jews, Turks and all sectaries, with a refutation of Mr.
Stillingfleet'8 many gross errours. 4to Antwerp 1672.

And soon after, the same author published a reply with this title:
The infallibility of the Roman Catholick Church and her miracles, C S» defended against Dr. Stillingfleet's cavils, unworthily made publick in two books; the one called An answer to several treatises, &c. (see Stillingfleet's works, vol. v. p. 220); the other, A vindication of the protestant ground of faith, &c. 2 parts, 4to Antwerp 1674.

We learn also from Ant. Wood (loc. cit.) that Stilliugfleet's tract was answered by Abr. Woodhead himself in a pamphlet entitled,

Exercitations concerning the resolution of faith, against some exceptions, 4to s. 1. 1674. This book 1 have never seen; neither is it in the Bodleian Library. I give the above title on AVood's authority. J. H. T.

" Edward Worsley, born in Lancashire in 1604, admitted at the age of 22, and Professor 29 Sept. 1641. For many years taught Philosophy and Theology at Liege, of which College he became Rector from 1658 to 1662. E. W. must ever rank among the ablest controvertists of this or any other country, as the following works will prove: ?. i. ' Truth will out,' in answer to Dr. Jeremy Taylor's ' Dissuasive from Popery,' 4to, Lond. 1065, &c. &c. A posthumous work of his appeared, entitled, Anti-Goliah, or an Epistle to Mr. Brevint, containing some Reflexions upon his Saul und Samuel at Endor." 8vo, 1678. Dr. Oliver. In Chap. XVII. of the former treatise, he charges Taylor with wronging the Canon Law by quotations unworthily corrupted.

£. 3L. Dr. Oliver has omitted in his list of Worsley's works A Discourse of Miracles wrought in the Roman Catholic Church, or, A full refutation of Dr. Stillingfleet's unjust exceptions against Miracles, together with a large discovery of the Doctors unreasonable frauds, manifest in his many false, perverted and impertinent Quotations, 8vo Antwerp, 1676.

C3L. 192. The Guide in Controversies. Part IV. pp. 374-448.

Containing the Socinian's Apology for the believing, and teaching, his doctrine against former Church-Definitions, and present ChurchAuthority, upon the Protestant's Grounds (not holding anything contrary to the Holy Scriptures).

It may here be remarked that Smallridge, in his Animadversions, etc. (No. 165 *supra*) writes: — "I may not omit for the Reader's diversion a Grammatical Criticism which our author hath made upon the little particle *as*. It is enacted the 32nd Henry VIII. 26 c.: 'That all such Determinations, Decrees, Definitions, and Ordinances *as*, according to God's word and Christ's Gospel, shall at any time be set forth by the Arch-Bishops, Bishops, and Doctors in Divinity appointed by his Majesty, or else by the whole Clergy of England, in and upon the matters of Christ's Religion, &c., shall be by all his Grace's subjects fully believed, obeyed," &c. Upon which he makes this learned note. Whereas under the Reformation private men are tied only to obey and believe the Definitions of Councils when they are set forth according to God's word, i.e. when private men think them to be so, yet here this Liberty was thought fit to he restrain'd, and private men tyed to believe these Definitiens when set forth *as* according to God's word,

i.e. when the setters forth believe them to be so. To obey a thing defin'd, according to God's word, and to obey a thing defin'd, *as* being according to God's word, are Injunctions very different. Now a little skill in *Honest Walker's* particles would have clear'd this point, and a

School-boy that was to turn this passage into Latin, would have known that *as* is put for *which*. Accordingly Keble, abridging this statute,

makes it run thus: All Decrees and Ordinances *which* according to

God's word, &c. But this it is for people to meddle in Controversie at an age when they have forgot their Grammar. Notwithstanding,

therefore, this Aristarchus, we still retain the Liberty of believing and obeying only such thiugs which be defined according to God's word.

For which we are much blamed in the conclusion of this Discourse."

193. f An appendix to the four discourses concerning the Guide Cf.lL.

in controversies; further shewing the necessity and infallibility thereof, against some contrary Protestant principles.

pp. 246, Pref. and Contents 25. 4to s. 1. 1675 Some copies of this book have the title, " A discourse of the C H, necessity of Church-Guides, for directing Christians in necessary faith; with some annotations on Dr. Stillingfleet's answer to N. O. By R.H." 4to s. I. 1675. See Ath. Oxon. vol. ii. col. 614. A copy with this title is in the Bodleian Library. The initials N. 0, were also adopted by Woodhead (being perhaps the letters following the initials UNiversity COllege), in his book entitled, " Dr. Stillingfleet's principles, giving an account of the faith of protestants, considered by N. O." 8vo Paris 1671. This was an answer to Dr. Stillingfleet's book entitled, " A rational account of the grounds of the protestant religion; being a vindication of the Archbishop (Laud) of Canterbury's Relation of a Conference, &c., from the pretended answer by T. C." fol. Lond.

1665. T. C. (i.e. Thos. Carwell, whose real name is said to have been Spencer) wrote " Labyrinthus Cantuariensis; or Dr. Laud's labyrinth; being an answer to tho late Archbishop's relation of a conference between himself and Fisher. " Fol. Paris 1658. This was the first discourse, of which E. W.'s discourse was the sequel or second discourse. " Annotations on Dr. Stillingfleet's Answer to N. O.'s consideration of his principles." This is the second part of No. 193 *supra*, and printed with it. Ath. Oxon. vol. ii. col. 614. "Dr. Stillingfleet *B. L.* against Dr. Stillingfleet; or the palpable contradictions committed by him in charging the Roman Church with idolatry," &c. 8vo s.!. 1671. Bodl. This is by John Williams, a Roman Catholic writer. "The *B. L.* new way of answering examined; in a reply to two pamphlets, entituled, Dr. Stillingfleet against Dr. Stillingfleet, and Dr. Stillingfleet's principles considered," &c. 8vo Lond. 1672. " Dr. Stillingfleet still *B. L.* against Dr. Stillingfleet; or the examination of Dr. Stillingfleet against Dr. Stillingfleet examined." Anon. By John Williams. 8vo, s. 1. 1675.

C 3L. " Considerations on the Council of Trent; being the fifth discourse concerning the Guide in Controversies;" by R. H. i.e. Abraham Woodhead. 4to s. 1. 1671, No. 208. See Ath. Oxon. vol. ii. col. 615, where Wood says: " 'Tis said there is a sixth pnrt concerning the alienation of church lands, but Quaere?" J. H. T.

Meric Casaubon, the adversary of Sergeant, defended Stillingfleet against Carwell or Spencer, in his treatise " Of the Necessity of Reformation in and before Luther's time, and what hath visibly most hindered its progress. Occasioned by some late most virulent books written by Papists, but especially by that entitled Labyrinthus Cantuariensis." Paris 1658. 4to Lond. 1664.

By Dolman "Stillingfleet still against Stillingfleet" is ascribed to J. Keyns, who wielded, says Dr. Oliver, his powerful pen against Dr. Stillingfleet, pointing out his contradictions and blunders. His controversy with the Doctor continued with little interruption from 1671 to 1675. He published also in London "A Rational Compendious Way to convince without any dispute all persons whatever dissenting from the True Religion." 12mo 1674.... It is well known that this polite scholar was the principal compiler of the " Florus AngloBavaricus." 4to Liege 1685. This history of the Jesuits comprises the eventful crisis of Oates's plot.

Of Cressy, whose replies to Stillingfleet have been noticed *supra*, pp. 132, 157, Butler in his Memoirs of Catholics, vol. iv. p. 423 remarks: " His conversion did not deprive him of his protestant friends. The learned Dr. Henry Hammond having received from him a copy of his Exomologesis declined, in the language of friendship, to become his antagonist, " that he might give no disturbance to a person for whom he had, as he expressed himself, so great a value, and who could have no humane consideration in the exchange he had made. ... A new edition of the Exomologesis, with a succinct view of the controversy between Cressy and his two great opponents (Lord Clarendon and Dr. Stillingfleet), would form an interesting manual of Catholic controversy." In those days the spirit of charity, thus exercised by Dr. Hammond, was not diffused through society, but "a cruel and false opinion prevailed that as Protestantism and Christianity are inseparable, so Romanism and Christianity are incompatible." (See Gladstone on the State in its Relations with the Church, chap, vi. , where there is an historical sketch of the policy of the State respecting religious differences down to the Revolution in 1688, and a similar outline from the Revolution to the present time.) Consequently no controversialist is more entitled to be heard in vindication of the Reformation and in the defence of the Church of England against the objections of the Romanist, that by casting out the authority of the Bishop of Rome she cast off the head of all Christian unity, and so must needs be guilty of Schism. See his Works, fol. Lond. 1684, vol. i. pp. 526-531. Lib. of Angl.-Cath. Theol., Oxf. 1847, vol. ii. An account of Hammond is given in Worthington's Diary and Correspondence, vol. i. p. 222.

Having already mentioned most of the treatises constituting the controversy between Cressy and his two great opponents, I shall here give a complete list. " The Sancta Sophia" of Father Baker, a Benedictine monk, in the abridgment given of it by Father Cressy of the same order, and " Philotheus's Pilgrimage to Perfection, in a practice of ten days solitude," Bruges 1668, were once popular among English Roman Catholics. The Sancta Sophia was severely animadverted upon by Dr. Stillingfleet in his " Idolatry practised by the Church of Rome." Cressy replied to it by his "Answer to part of Dr. Stillingfleet's book," &c, and his " Fanaticism fanatically imputed to the Catholic Church by Dr. Stillingfleet." See his Collection of several Treatises in answer to Dr. Stillingfleet, viz. 1. "Fanaticism," &c.; 2. "The Roman ChurcR's devotions vindicated from Doctour Stillingfleet's misrepresentation," by 0. N., a Catholick; 3. "The Roman Doctrine of Repentance and of Indulgences vindicated," &c.; 4. Dr. Stillingfleet's "Principles," &c., by N. O., 1671-2. In answer to this work Lord Chancellor Clarendon published a vindication of Dr. Stillingfleet, entitled, " Animadversions," &c. Mr. Cressy answered by an " Epistle apologetical of S. C. to a person of honour, touching his vindication of Dr. Stillingfleet," which contains many notices of a personal kind which deserve to find a place in his biography. His Sancta Sophia is extracted from forty small treatises of Father Baker, and printed Douay 1657, 2 vols. 12mo. Worthington's Diary and Correspondence, vol. ii. part i. p. 196. To this Dr. Stillingfleet replied by his Answer to Mr. Cressey's Epistle apologetical, &c. All these controversial works are ably written and deserve an attentive perusal; not so much, however, for their mystic lore as for the important facts and observations which they communicate respecting the grounds on which the penal laws, in the English code against the Roman Catholics, can be best attacked or defended." The Retrospective Review, vol. i. part ii. On Mystical Devotion, by Ch. Butler.

Ci. 194. A Discourse concerning a Guide in matters of faith. With respect, especially, to the Romish pretence of the necessity of such a one as is infallible. The second edition, corrected. Anon. By Thos. Tenison, D.D., Vicar of St. Martin's, afterw. Abp. of Canterbury. pp. 50, Title and Contents pp. 6, Cat. of Books by Tooke (at end) pp. 2. 4to Lond. (T. Basset and Benj. Tooke) 1687 In Gibson's Preservative, vol. iv. fol. 1.

C1L. 195. A fair and methodical discussion of the first and great controversy between the Church of EDgland and the Church of Rome, concerning the infallible guide; in three discourses. Anon. By George Hooper, D.D., afterwards Bp. of St. Asaph, then of Bath and Wells. Works, fol. Oxf. 1757, pp. 27-126. 4to Lond. 1689

See Atb. Oxon. vol. ii, col. 1041). "The title has three Discourses but two only appear." " They were begun before the Revolution,
and that event put an end to the controversy." Works, p. 12G.
Born 1640, died 1727.
196. A discourse concerning the Nature, Unity, and Communion CtL.
of the Catholick Church, wherein most of the controversies relating to the Church are hriefly stated. Part I. By William Sherlock, D.D., Master of the Temple.
pp. 60, 4to Loud. (Wm. Rogers) 1688 See Cat. No. 105. Contin. p. 29. In Gibson's Preservative, vol. iii. fol. i. The following tracts of the same author, which are all in the tt. iL., are in Gibson: No. 119, No. 122, vol. xi. fol. 2; No. 158, vol. xiv. fol. 3; No. 196, vol. iii. fol. 1; No. 246, vol. xi. fol. 2; No. 306, vol. iv. fol. 1; No. 337, vol. vi. fol. 2; No. 353, vol. iii. fol. 1; No. 370, *ibid*.

Compare the second Part of " A Discourse of the Visible and Invisible Church of Christ." In which it is shewn, That the Powers claim'd by the Officers of the Visible Church, are not inconsistent with the Supremacy of Christ as Head; or with the Rights and Liberties of Christians, as Members of the Invisible Church. By John Rogers, B.D., Lond. 1720. " Respecting the great distinction between the Visible and Invisible Church, on which most of the controversies concerning its Divine Institution principally depend, see Dr. Rogers's Discourse, &c., and a Review of that Discourse, published soon afterwards, and entering more largely into a discussion of the controverted points; both of them masterly Treatises." Van Mildert's Bampt. Lect. viii. Append. p. 406.

197. A discourse concerning the nature, union, and communion of the Catholic Church. Part II. *By* William Sherlock, D. D.

See Cat. p. 17. It does not appear that this second part was ever published. Gee (loc. cit.) says: "The author did intend, and we hope will ere long gratify the world with the second part of this Discourse concerning the Church." So that it had not appeared in 1689, and I can find no evidence that it ever appeared. J. H. T.
198. The Pillar and Ground of Truth. A Treatise shewing that C1L GG the Roman Church falsly claims to be *that* Church, and the pillar of *that* Truth, mentioned by St. Paul in his first Epistle to Timothy, chap. iii. v. 15. Which is explained in Three Parts. Anon. By Simon Patrick, D.D., afterwards Bp. of Ely. Imprimatur Jo. Batteley, May 9,

1687. pp. 126, to the reader with title pp. 10, list of books at the end pp. 4. (Gibson, vol. v. fol. 1.) 4to Lond. (Bic. Chiswell) 1687
See Cat. No. 106. Contin. p. 30. Fasti Oxon. vol. ii. col. 166. The Bodl. Cat. says that this book is by some attributed to Dr. Wm. Sherlock, Master of the Temple. See "Autobiography of Bp. Patrick," 8vo Oxford 1839, and Cat. Bodl. tom, iv., where this book is ascribed to Bp. Simon Patrick. J. H. T.

Simon Patrick born 1626, died 1707; was one of the most learned men as well as one of the best writers of his time.

Compare Van Mildert's Sermon above referred to, Preservation of Scripture-Truth a sacred charge committed to the Church, Inquiry how far it has hitherto fulfilled that trust, Conduct of the Church of England in this respect, Her principles of Scripture-interpretation, &c.

5ML. 199. A short discourse concerning the Churches Authority in matters of Faith, shewing that the pretenses of the Church of Rome are weak and precarious in the resolution of it. Licensed March 8, 1686. pp. 27, Title and Pref. pp. 4. 4to Lond. (Randal Taylor) 1687 See Cat. No. 108. Contin. p. 31. Gee tells us that this tract is " by Ignotus," as if it were so said on the title page. He meant only that he himself knew not the author. Peck gives it without the author's name. But it is ascribed to John Williams, afterwards Bp. of Chichester, in the Bodl. Catal. although not mentioned by Wood in the list of that author's works. See Ath. Oxon. vol. ii. col. 1020. J. H. T.

Compare Leslie's Tract entitled, Of Private Judgment and Authority in matters of Faith, Oxford 1832, vol i. p. 378, fol. vol. i. p. 180, and his other Tract, The Case Stated between the Churches of Rome and England, vol. iii. and fol. vol. i. " A small volume by the Margaret Professor of Divinity in Cambridge (Marsh) under a similar title, A Comparative View of the Churches of England and Rome, comprises within a short compass so much extensive research, forcible reasoning and perspicuous illustration of the subject, as almost to supersede the necessity of further investigation. If to this work, however, be added a careful perusal of the two pieces of Leslie just mentioned, together with his Case of the Regale and of the Pontificate stated in the same volume, a clearer view may perhaps be taken of some points, upon which it did not fall within the scope of Dr. Marsh's design to dilate."

Van Mildert's Bampton Lectures, Append, p. 328, who quotes Leslie's happy illustration of the whole subject, in the case of a Traveller and his Guides.

200. A plain and familiar discourse by way of dialogue betwixt a (E.fL. Minister and his Parishioners, concerning the Catholick Church. In three parts. I. Shewing what's the Nature of the Catholick Church. II. That the Church of Rome is not the Catholick Church. III. That the Scriptures, and not the Church, are the rule of Faith. Which may serve as an answer to some late Tracts upon that argument. By a Divine of the Church of England, pp. 70, Title and Pref. pp. 4. (Gibson, vol. iii. fol. 1.) 4to Lond. (R. Clavel and B. Tooke) 1687
See Cat. No. 109. This Tract is by Samuel Freeman, D.U., Dean of Peterborough, as Gee and Peck tell us. J. H. T.

Eusebius Paget or Pagit wrote Christianography; or a description of sundry sorts of *Christians in the World not subject to the Pope*, &c., 4to Lond. 163,3. Often reprinted; with a Treatise of the Religion of the Ancient Christians in Britany, in some editions. (Watt.) An edition with the date 1674 bears his name in the title page. Cf. T. P. Pfantin in Baxter's Key for Catholics, by Allport, p. 16, in which the Nature of Catholicity is explained, as in ancient writers, (see Suiceri Thesaurus) to be synonymous with orthodoxy. See also Raynoldes's Conference with Hart (Third Conclusion), 4to Lond. 1584.

201. A few plain reasons why a Protestant of the Church of Eng-d. land should not turn Roman Catholick. By a real Catholick of the Church of England. I Thess. v. 21. Prove all things, &c. Imprimatur, Jo. Battely, Sept. 15, 1687.
pp. 53. 4to Lond. (R. Clavel) 1688
See Cat. No. 110. Contin. p. 35. Ath. Oxon. vol. ii. col. 878. This Tract is by Thomas Barlow, Bp. of Lincoln. It is in the form of a Letter, addressed to a clergyman, who consulted Bp. Barlow on the best mode of meeting the arguments of the emissaries of the Church of Rome. Wood says (loc. cit.) that " Dr. J. Battely, the licenser, would not suffer several sheets to pass, and therefore they were omitted." Dr. Bliss, in his ed. of the Ath. Oxon. (vol. iv. col. 338) has published a curious letter of Abp. Sancroft to Barlow, in which the Abp. says of this Tract: " There is no man versed in your books, but in reading a tenth part of this will as plainly discover it to be yours, as if Thom. Lincoln, were tested in the title page, literis uncialibus." This remark is most just; but nevertheless the Tract is anon. The author, at the end of the Postscript, subscribes himself, " N. N.;" perhaps taking the final letters of the two syllables of Lincoln. In Bp. Barlow's " Genuine Remains," London (John Duuton), 1603 8vo. there is a paper (p. 454) on the claimed "Infallibility of the Church of Rome," which contains a great deal of the same matter as the present tract. J. H. T.

C 1L. 202. Good and solid reasons why a Protestant should not turn Papist; or Protestant prejudices against the Roman Catholick religion; propos'd in a letter to a Romish priest. By a Person of Quality. The third edition. pp. 37, title and contents pp. 4, Taylor's Cat. of Books pp. 3. Imprimatur July 9, 1687. 8vo Lond. (John Taylor) 1688 See Cat. No. 111. Contin. p. 30. Neither Gee nor Peck appear to have seen this book, and they have given the title very inaccurately. Gee says by Ignotus," meaning that he did not know the author. It is attributed to the Hon. Robert Boyle in the Bodl. Catal. The first C1L. edition was printed 1687 in 4to, entitled " Reasons why a Protestant," &c. J. H. T.
The first edition, pp. 32. Taylor's Cat. of Books, pp. 2.

£. 1L. 203. *b* A conference with Mr.

Claude, minister of Charenton, concerning the authority of the Church. By James Benigne Bossuet, Bishop of Meaux, councillor to the most Christian King and formerly preceptor to the Dauphin; first Almoner to the
   Dauphiness. Faithfully done into English out of the French
Original. Publisht with allowance, pp. 126, title, advertisement, &c,, pp. 8. 4to Lond. (Matthew Turner) 1687
See Contin. p. 31. The Conference ends p. 55. Then follows
" Reflexions on a writing of Mr. Claude," (pp. 57-126.) The "Writing of Mr. Claude" is No. 204 sq. The original edition is entitled " Conference avec M. Claude, ministre de Charenton sur la matiere de l'Eglise. Paris 1682, 12." And it will also be found in Bossuet's Works (Versailles, 1815) toni. 23, p. 233 sq. I know not by whom the translation was made. J. H. T.
204. Mr. Claude's answer to Monsieur de Meaux's book, intituled, A C H. Conference with Mr. Claude, with his Letter to a Friend,
wherein he answers a Discourse of M. de Condom, now Bishop of Meaux, concerning the Church. Imprimatur, Guil. Needham, Jun. 18, 1687. 4to Lond. (T. Dring) 1687
See Cat. No. 116, where Gee says; "Translated and published by
Ignotus." This only means that he did not know who translated and published it. This book is paged thus: Author's Preface; and Translator to the Reader, &c., pp. i-xxvi; Relation of the Conference, pp.
1-30; Answer to M. de Condom's Discourse concerning the Church,
pp. 1-67. See the account of this conference, in the " Life and Death of Mr. Claude," p. 32 (No. 205 *infra*).
Reponse au livre de l'evesque de Meaux intitule Conference avec
M. Claude. 8vo. Queville, 1683. 2 parts. This is the original of
Nos. 204 and 206.
A relation of the famous conference held about religion between
M. Bossuet and M. Claude at the Countess of Roye's house; translated from the French copy as it was lately published by M. Claude. Fol.
Lond. 1684. J. H. T.
See an account of the theological conferences held between the doctors of both churches in Mosheim's Institutes of Ecclesiastical
History, cent. xvii. sect ii. p. 12, &c. He has here assembled Roman,
German, French, Dutch and English peace-makers both Protestants and Roman Catholics. The Author Townsend of " Historical Col-©, fL,
lections out of several grave Protestant Historians, concerning the
Changes of Religion, and the strange confusions following from thence:
in the Reigns of King Henry the Eighth, Edward the Sixth, Queen
Mary, and Elizabeth," 8vo 1674, in chap. vii. Append. produces the
Assertions of some Protestants concerning Church Authority, some of which he considers as concessions to the Dignity and Authority of the
Church of Rome; viz. Sir Edw. Sandys, Dr. Jer. Taylor, Grotius, Dr.
Field, Dr. Hammond, Dr. Jackson, Dr. Ferne. Ab Uno Disce Omnes.
See Dr. Field's Appendix, contayning a Defence of svch partes and passages of the former Foure bookes (of the Church) as haue bin either excepted against, or wrested to the maintenance of Romish errours (fol. Oxford, 1628.)
— " Concerning Grotius's opinion, design and great endeavours for reducing the Churches to Popery," see
Baxter's Key for Catholics, edited by Allport, and The Grotian Religion Discovered against Mr. Thomas Pierce, 8vo Lond. 1658. In a note, pp. 371-4, vol. 1, of Worthington's Diary and Correspondence there is an admirable vindication of Grotius, from which I cannot refrain from quoting in part the noble portrait originally sketched by
Grotius for Arminius: —

"Damnatus aliis, ipse neminem damnat
Modestiseque limitem premens, donat
Nunc verba vero, nunc silentium paci."
CIL. 205. The Life and Death of Monsieur Claude, the famous Minister of Charenton in France. Done out of French by G. P.
Imprimatur, G. Needham, Sept. 13, 1687. pp. 58, Title and
Pref. pp. 14, Dring's list of books at the end, pp. 2.
4to Lond. (Thomas Dring) 1688
An " Abrege de sa vie" by Mr. de la Deveze, Pastor at the Hajnie, is quoted in Bernard, Birch, and Lockman's transl. of Bayle's Dictionary. Article Claude (John). And an extract there given note (E) agrees so nearly with the corresponding passage of the present Tract, that I have no doubt M. de la Deveze Abel Rodolph de Ladevcze, or de la Devese is the author of this Life " Done out of French by G. P." But who G. P. was I do not know. J. H. T.
Born 1619, died 1687. His "Historical Defence of the Reformation," one of the ablest vindications of protestantism, was published in English by T. B. Lond. 1683, 4to, and his " Essay on the Composition of a Sermon" which he wrote about the year 1676, for the use of his son, was translated and published in English in 1778 by the late Rev. Robert Robinson, of Cambridge, 2 vols. 8vo, with a Life of the Author, and notes, "all which, as displaying an implacable and unprovoked hostility to the established church, have been very properly omitted in a new edition of the translation, published in 1796, by the Rev. Charles Simeon of King's College, Cambridge." Chalmers.
206. The second part of Mr. Claude's answer to Monsieur de Meaux's Book, intituled, A Conference with Mr. Claude, &c., containing an examination of M. de Meaux's thirteen reflections on a writing of Mr. Claude's, pp. 200, Title, to the Reader, and Contents, pp. 6.
4to Lond. (T. Dring) 1688
Gee does not mention this second part. See 204. J. H. T.
" The Protestants have not," says Bossuet, " the consolation which the Catholics have, to see Jesus Christ's promise visibly accomplisht, and maintain'd during so many ages. They can not shew a Church which has ever been since Jesus Christ came to build it on the Rock; and to save his word, they are obliged to have recourse to a Church of the Predestinate, which neither them-

selves, nor any one else can shew." " While the Reformed deny the perpetuity of Christ's presence with the Church of Rome, they may fairly be called upon to establish the perpetuity of a Church or Churches, which by the maintenance of their own doctrine in all grand essentials, shall connect them with the Primitive Church, and thus shew that, in their case, neither of the promises of Christ has failed of its accomplishment." Faber's " Inquiry into the History and Theology of the Ancient Vallenses and Albigenses; as exhibiting agreeably to the Promises the perpetuity of the Sincere Church of Christ." Lond. 1838. But the most satisfactory solution of this difficulty on the part of Protestants is given in Baxter's Key for Catholics (chap, xxiv., Visibility). Compare Allix's Remarks upon the Ecclesiastical History of the Ancient Churches of the Albigenses, Bp. Ussher, de Success, et Statu Eccles. and in his Answer to the Jesuits and the Ancient Religion of Ireland, Mornay's Mystery of Iniquity, Dr. Field of the Church, Flacius Illyricus, Sir Humphrey Lynde's Via Devia, sect. 24 (in Gibson's Preservative, Suppl. vol. iv.) See also No. 5, p. 9, *supra*.

£. IL. 207. An historical examination of the authority of general Councils, shewing the false dealing that hath been used in the publishing of them; and the difference amongst the Papists themselves about their Number. The second edition corrected. pp. 76, Title, Pref. and Contents pp. 18.

Lond. (H. Mortlock) 1688 See Cat. No. 97. Contin. p. 31. Gee attributes this book to " Mr. Jenkins," and Peck to " Robert Jenkin, M.A., Fellow of S. John's College, Cambridge." The Bodleian Catal. has it under " Jenkins" (—) probably from Gee.

Roman forgeries, or a true account of false records, discovering the impostures and counterfeit antiquities of the Church of Rome. Anon. By Thomas Traherne. 8vo. Lond. 1673.

See Ath. Oxon. vol. ii. col. 531. This book having been published before the reign of James II. does not properly come within the period to which this Catalogue is confined. But I have inserted it as having been the first tract on the forgeries in the Councils; and mentioned by Dr. Comber as being the work that set him upon the design of conti- nuing the subject. For Traherne died in 1674 without completing his book, which does not go much beyond the Nicene Council. The subject is one which is far from being exhausted, and for the sake of those who may desire to pursue it, I. mention here the following books of an earlier date: —

Problema de Romanic fidei ementito Catholicismo, contra Cocceium. By William Perkins. 4to Cantab. 1604. £, 3L Censura quorundam scriptorum quse sub nominibus sanctorum et veterum auctorum a pontificiis passim in eorum scriptis, citori solent; in qua ostenditur scripta illa vel esse supposititia, vel dubiae saltem fidei. By Robert Cooke; (Robertus Cocus;) Fellow uf Brasenose Coll. Oxford. See Ath. Oxon. vol. i. col. 396. 4to Lond. 1614; 4to Lond. 1623; 8vo Helm. 1655. t, 1L. A treatise of the corruption of Scripture, Councils, and Fathers, by the prelats &c. of the Church of Rome, for maintenance of poperie. Bp Thomas James, D.D., first keeper of the Bodleian Library. 4to Lond. 1611; 8vo Lond. 1688. See Ath. Oxon. vol. i. col. 538.

Roman Forgeries in the Councils during the first four centuries. Together with an Appendix concerning the forgeries and errors in the Annals of Baronius. By Thomas Comber, D.D., Prebend of York, pp. 175, and introd. matter pp. 14. (Robt. Gavel!.) 4to Lond. 1689. Divided into two parts, part i. containing centuries I.-III.; part ii. containing century IV.

The Church History clear'd from the Roman Forgeries and corruptions found in the Councils and Baronius: from the year 400 till the end of the fifth General Council An. Dom. 553. Being the third and fourth parts of the Roman Forgeries. By Thomas Comber, DD., Dean of Durham. "For wo have not followed," &C. 2 Pet. i. 16. pp. 335, and pref. matter pp. 14. (Robt. Clavell.) 4to Lond. 1695.

The foreign writers Junius, Daille, and Rivet, although caute legendi, ought to be consulted; and I hope I may be excused for recommending also the following work of a living author. " Roman Forgeries and Falsifications; or an examination of Counterfeit and corrupted records, with especial reference to Popery. Part I. By the Rev. Richard Gibbings, M.A." 8vo Dublin 1842. It is to be regretted that the little encouragement now given to works of deeper learning than ordinary, has prevented the appearance of more than Part I. of this valuable work. J. H. T.

The author " designs two things: first, To shew the false dealing that has been used in putting forth the Councils. Secondly, To shew that Papists are not agreed in the Authority of them as they are put forth." For a reference to notices of forgeries of Canons and Decretal Epistles see Baxter's Key for Catholics, edited by Rev. J. Allport, Lond. 1839. For a complete body of information upon this point, the reader may consult Mendham's Literary Policy of the Church of Rome. Lond. 1830. Of James's treatise above mentioned there is a large analysis in Oldys's Britisli Librarian.

" As the Authority of Apostolical Traditions," says our Author, " could reach no farther than the first Ages, so in succeeding times we have little reason to think that the Holy Ghost had much to do in their Councils; Christ himself seems to have been almost excluded, since Christ's Vicar, as he styles himself, has had such an absolute sway in Councils. If any one shall say, says Gerson (apud Richer, 1. 2, p. 262) there must be recourse to the See and Court of the High Priest, we will not deny it, if Divinity shall have there two impartial H B

Doctours, not seduced, not proud, not covetous or envious, not favourers of the temporal and spiritual Power, more than of the Truth; otherwise it would be more tolerable to have none than to endure such." p. 71. Compare Hallam (Constitutional History of England, chap, iv.) in reference to Hooker's Ecclesiastical Polity: "It may justly be objected to some passages that they elevate ecclesiastical authority, even in matters of belief, with an exaggeration not easily reconciled to the protestant right of private judgment, and even of dangerous consequence in those times; as when he inclines to give a decisive voice in theological controversies in general councils; not indeed on the principles of the church of Rome, but on such as must end in the some conclusion, the high probability that the aggregate judgment of many grave and learned men should be well founded..

.. Hooker's mistake was to exaggerate the weight of such men's judgment; and not to allow enough for their passions and infirmities, the imperfection of their knowledge, their connivance with power, their attachment to names and persons, and all the other drawbacks to ecclesiastical authority.

" It is well known that the Preface to the Ecclesiastical Polity was one of the two books to which James II. ascribed his return into the fold of Rome; and it is not difficult to perceive by what course of reasoning on the positions it contains it was effected." .1. 208. *b* Considerations on the Council of Trent, &c., being the Fifth Discourse concerning the Guide in Controversies (with a Digression against Claude on Transubstantiation). By Abraham Woodhead. pp. 335 and 24, 4to Lond. 1675 This Tract has already been described No. 193 in connection with the other publications of the author, forming parts of the same series, and the pamphlets to which they gave rise. J. H. T.

209. Pope Pius his Profession of Faith vindicated from novelty in additional articles. Published with allowance. pp. 40, 4to Lond. (Henry Hills) 1687 See Contin. p. 57. Dod, in his Church History, vol. iii. p. 483, attributes this tract to John Gother. J. H. T. 210. The creed of Pope Pius the IV., or a Prospect of Popery, CiL taken from that authentic record, with short Notes. Anon.
By Michael Altham M.A. Imprimatur Guil. Needham,
Jun. 29, 1687. pp. 10, 4to Lond. (L. Meredith) 1687

See Cat. No. 183; Contin. p. 58. And No. 10 *supra*. 211. The additional articles in Pope Pius's Creed, no Articles of

ML
the Christian faith. Being an answer to a late Pamphlet intituled Pope Pius his profession of faith vindicated from novelty
in additional articles. And the Prospect of Popery taken from that authentick record, with short notes thereupon defended.
Anon. By Michael Altham, M.A.
pp. 88, 4to Lond. (L. Meredith) 1688
See Cat. No. 184; Contin. p. 58. Michael Altham was of Christ's Coll. Cambr., and Vicar of Tatton in Essex. J. H. T.
212. A brief Examination of the present Roman Catholick Faith contained in Pope Pius his New Creed, by the Scriptures, Antient Fathers, and their own modern writers, in answer to a letter, desiring satisfaction concerning the visibility of the Protestant Church and religion in all ages, especially before Luther's time. Imprimatur Guil. Needham, Oct. 26, 1688. pp. 123, Title and introd. pp. 4, 4to Lond. (James Adamson) 1689

Peck erroneously attributes this book to Mr. Altham, confounding it with Gee's No. 183 (which is No. 210 *supra),* and referring also to Contin. p. 57 (which ought to be p. 58), where we find only mention of Nos. 210 and 211 *supra*. Neither Gee nor Wake mentions this book. Bp. Gibson has reprinted it in his Preservative against Popery, vol. iii. tit. x. p. 7, and attributes it to Mr. *Samuel* Gardiner. There is a copy in the library of Trin. Coll. Dublin, which is in every respect the same as the anon, one, except that it has a new title page, giving the author's name thus: — "By Samuel Gardiner D.D., late Rector of Eckinton in Derbyshire." J. H. T.

Compare No. 206 *supra*. 213. A sermon preached on St. Mark's Day Mdclxxxvi. in the parish Church of St. Paul's, Covent Garden. By Symon Patrick, Rector there afterwards Bishop of Ely.
pp. 48, 4to Lond. (R. Royston) 1686 See Cat. No. 119; Contin. p. 31.

CiL. 214. Doubts concerning the Roman Infallibility: I. Whether the Church of Rome believe it. II. Whether Jesus

Christ or his Apostles ever recommended it. III. Whether the Primitive Church knew or used that way of deciding controversie. Anon. By Henry Maurice D. D., Domestic Chaplain to Archbishop Sancroft.
pp. 39, 4to Lond. (James Adamson) 1688
See Cat. No. 132; Contin. p. 31; Ath. Oxon. vol. ii. col. 873.

" May I be allowed to ask, on what authoritative decision of *what* Ecumenical Council do Bossuet and Trevern and other Popish Ecclesiastics claim for their Church this same prerogative of Infallibility?

" In the eleventh century, during which no Ecumenical Council was sitting, the famous Hildebrand, who played the part of Pope by the style and title of Gregory VII., decided indeed that the Roman Church has never erred, and never will err under the conviction that ' were the talisman of infallibility broken the magic edifice of the Papal dominion would crumble to ruinsWhately; hut this can only serve the turn of those who hold the individual Infallibility of the Pope; nor will it serve even their turn, who hold the individual Infallibility of the Pope, unless they can produce the infallible decision which infallibly assigns to the Pope the privilege of individual Infallibility Where does there exist the canon of an Ecumenical

Council, in which the possession of Infallibility is decreed to the
Church of Rome?" Faber, *ubi supra.*
215. "i Seek and you shall find: or a search into the grounds of Religion: together with some queries in order to a particular satisfaction, upon account of the various opinions in this present age. Quseritis me et invenietis &c. " You shall seek me and you shall find me," &c. Jer. 29, 13. Permissu superiorum. pp. 26, To the Reader pp. 10, Hills's Catal. of books pp. 2. 4to Lond. (Henry Hills) 1686

See Contin. p. 31. I know not who the author was. J. H. T.
216. A Discourse shewing that protestants are on the safer side, notwithstanding the uncharitable judgment of their adversaries; and that their religion is the

safer way to heaven. pp. 43. 4to Lond. (Richd. Chiswell) 1687

See Cat. No. 117; Contin. p. 58. Gee, and after him Peck, tell us that this tract is " by Mr. Bolieu, chaplain to the Lord Chancellour Jeffreys," meaning Luke Beaulieu prebendary of Gloucester, of whom see an account Ath. Oxon. vol. ii. cols. 1065-6.

He wrote also, Take heed of both extreatns; or plain and usefull cautions against popery and presbytery, in two parts. 8vo Lond. 1675.

The holy Inquisition; wherein is represented what is the religion of the Church of Rome. 8vo Lond. 1681. J. H. T.

Compare No. 457 *infra*.

The Jesuit Peter Talbot, in his " Treatise of Religion and Government," 4to 1670, discusses the argument whether Protestantcy be less dangerous to the Soul than the Roman Catholic Religion? In the Appendix to Townsend's Historical Collections, chap, ii., are Testimonies of Scripture evidently convincing, that there can be no hope of Salvation for such as are separated from the Church by Heresie or Schism. Laud speaks out (Conference with Fisher § 38): "All Protestants unaimously agree in this, 'that there is great peril of damnation for any man to live and die in the Roman persuasion.'" On the difference between Protestants and Romanists on this subject see Stillingfleet's Doctrines and Practices of the Church of Rome, chap, xxxv., with a Preface and Notes by W. Cunningham, D.D., 12mo. Edinburgh 1845, and his Rational Account of the Grounds of the Protestant Religion. Part iii., chaps. 4 and 5. " Chillingworth," remarks Mr. Hallam, " well redeemed any censure that might have been thrown on him by his great work in answer to the Jesuit Knott, entitled the Religion of Protestants a Safe Way to Salvation. See No. 441. In the course of his reflections he had perceived the insecurity of resting the Reformation on any but its original basis, the independency of private opinion. This too he asserted with a fearlessness and consistency hitherto little known, even within the Protestant pale; combining it with another principle, which the zeal of the early reformers had rendered them unable to perceive, and for want of which the adversary had perpetually discomfited themi namely, that the errors of conscientious men do not forfeit the favour of God. This endeavour to mitigate the dread of forming mistaken judgments in religion runs through the whole work of Chilling worth, and marks him as the founder in this country of what has been called the latitudinarinn school of theology. In this view, which has practically been the most important one of the controversy, it may pass for an anticipated reply to the most brilliant performance on the opposite side, the History of the Variations of Protestant Churches; and those who from a delight in the display of human intellect, or from more serious motives of inquiry, are led to these two masterpieces, will have seen perhaps the utmost strength that either party, in the great schism of Christendom, has been able to put forth." Hal lam's Constitutional History of England, vol. i. p. 486. Compare Chillingworth'8 "Thoughts of Peace" in Book iv. p. 16, and The Principles and Practices of certain Moderate Divines of the Church of England, &c, by Edward Fowler, D.D., Bishop of Gloucester, p. 314.

217. Thirty plain but sound reasons why Protestants dissent from Popery. To which is added, Thirty-four points, held by many Papists, which were never yet rationally proved by any one of them. Therefore Protestants expect a reasonable proof of them, before they can be satisfied of the truth of them, so as to become their converts. Written in a plain and familiar style, for the instruction of the common people, that they may be able to give a reasonable answer to any Popish emissary when he assaults them. pp. 28, 4to London, printed in the year 1688

See Cat. No. 181. Contin. p. 58. Gee says that this is "By Ignotus," meaning that he did not know the author. Peck has numbered this work 216 by a mistake of the press, instead of 217. J. H. T.

d, 218. An historical relation of several great and learned Romanists who did embrace the Protestant religion, with their reasons for their change, delivered in their own words. Collected chiefly from the most eminent Historians of the Roman perswasion. To which is added a catalogue of sundry great Persons of the Roman Catholick Religion, who have all along opposM the Tenents of the Church of Rome. With allowance, April 20, 1688. pp. 34, 4to Lond. (Rich. Baldwin) 1688

See Cat. No. 188; Contin. p. 59. Gee says that this is "By Ignotus," i.e. he did not know by whom. This is 217 in Peck, by amistake of the press. J. H. T.

Instead of describing this very interesting tract here, I shall notice it iu the Supplement, to be inserted in Part II., in the hope of devoting to the subject the consideration it deserves.

219. Veritas Evangelica; or the gospel truth asserted in sixteen useful questions, which being seriously searched into, will open the way to find out assuredly the true and saving faith of Christ, which is but One, as the Apostle affirms, Eph. 4; One Lord, one Faith, one Baptism. Written by T. K. and now published by R. C. Read; Understand; and then Censure. Published with allowance, pp., 4to Lond. (N. Thompson) 1687

See Contin. p. 57. " The Epistle Dedicatory," subscribed R. C., is " To the most serene and supreme Nursing Mother of the Holy Catholick Church, Mary, by the Grace of God Queen of England, Scotland, France and Ireland." The preface is signed T. K. I know not who are R. C. and T. K. J. H. T.

220. A brief account of the first rise of the name Protestant; and what Protestantism is: with a Justification of it, and an earnest exhortation to all Protestants to persist in that Holy Religion. By a Professed enemy to Persecution. pp. 40, 4to Lond. printed in the year 1688 See Cat. No. 196. Contin. p. 59. On the title-page is an extract from the " Lord Bishop of Cork's Protestant Peacemaker," p. 128: — " I am and must be in mind, that the strength of the Protestant Cause, both here at Home, and throughout Christendom, lyes in the Union of Protestants; and the Glory, Purity, and

Power of Christianity in the world, stands or falls with Protestantism." The Bodl. Catal. (under *Protestant)* attributes this book to Samuel Bolde. The author was evidently of the school favorable to Protestant Dissent; but the Bodl. Cat. does not give this work under Bolde, perhaps because when the article Bolde (Sam.) was printed, it had not been ascertained that it was by him.
Samuel Bolde was Vicar of Shapwicke, Dorsetshire. To which is added, " A plea for moderation towards Dissenters. " It was probably in allusion to this that he calls himself "a *professed* enemy to Persecution." J. H. T.

C 2.. 221 The Protestant Resolved: or a discourse shewing the unreasonableness of his turning Roman Catholic for Salvation. Anon. By Clement Ellis. (Gibson, vol. iv. fol. 1.) pp. 91, 4to Lond. 1688 See Cat. No. 197. Contin. p. 59. Ath. Oxon. vol. ii. col. 970.

£. 5 222 The Protestant Resolution of Faith, being au answer to Three Questions. I. How far we must depend ou the Authority of the Church for the true sense of Scripture? II. Whether a visible succession from Christ to this day makes a Church, which has this visible succession, an infallible interpreter of Scripture: and whether no Church, which has not this succession, can teach the true sense of Scripture. III. Whether the Church of England can make out such a visible succession. Anon. By Will. Sherlock, D.D. (Gibson, vol. v. fol. 1.) pp. 26, Pref. iv. 4to Lond. 1686 In reply to the first two questions see Cbillingworth, chap. iii.

A Sermon in confutation of R. H., the author of the Guide in
Controversies, shewing that his most plausible arguments produced against Protestants do more effectually conclude for
Judaism against Christianity. By Dan. Whitby. 8vo 1679.

See No. 277, 346, by the same author, who subjoined some Reflexions on a late Popish book called The Guide of Controversies t his work on Host-worship. 8vo Lond. 1679.

The Church of Rome no safe Guide, or Reasons to prove that no rational Man who takes due care of his eternal Salvation can give himself up unto the conduct of that Church in matters of Religion. By John Owen. 1679

A Letter to a Priest of the Romish Church, wherein the grounds of their pretended Infallibility are called for and examined in some Queries. 4to Lond. 1675 i Dr. Stillingfleet's Principles of Protestancy cleared, confuted and retorted; and the Infallibility of the Roman Catholic Church asserted; and that the same Church alone is the whole Catholic Church. By Peter Talbot, Archbishop of Dublin.
4to 1673

See Stillingfleet's Rational Grounds of the Protestant Religion, part ii. chap. 5. Of the Roman Church's Authority, chap. 7. The Pope's Authority r,ot proved from Scripture, or Reason, part iii. chap. 1. Of the Infallibility of General Councils, &c. A Reply to Mr. J. Sergeant's Third Appendix, containing some Animadversions on the Book intituled, A Rational Account, &c. In p. 222 I have mentioned Meric Cosaubon as defending Stillingfleet, against Carwell or Spencer. Wo find him again associated with Stillingfleet in his tract, The New Way of Infallibility lately devised to uphold the Roman Cause; the ancient Fathers and Councils laid aside: against J. S. (the author of Sure Footing) his Letter lately published, 4to Lond. 1665. See also p. 131 *supra.*

Popish Labyrinth: shewing the Errors of the Papists in that opinion that the Church can not Err. By Simon Episcopius. Done into English by J. K. (Opp. Theolog. fol. Amst., 1650, tom. ii. pp. 148-53.) 8vo Lond. 1673

The same, translated from the Latin. By R.Watson. 8vo Lond. 1826

Roma Mendax: or the Falsehood of Rome's high pretences to Infallibility and Antiquity evicted. By John Menzies, S.T.P.

Lond. 1675
The Infallibility of the Church of Rome examined and confuted. In a Letter to a Roman Priest. By Gilbert Burnet, D.D.
pp. 35, 4to 1680 4« I. Question. Why are you a Catholic? The answer follows, &c. (No. 432 *infra.)*
Why are you not a Roman Catholick? A discourse occasioned by the pamphlet, intituled, Why are you a Catholick? pp. 54, 8vo 1679

A vindication of the answer to some late papers, &c. *(ut supra,* No 17), by Edward Stillingfleet, D.D.

" A discourse so learnedly and clearly written, that we ought to thank our adversaries for their importunity that has produced us so excellent a Treatise in a point of such importance." State, p. 25.

A Conference between John Lewgar and Mr. Chillingworth, whether the Roman Church be the Catholic Church, and all out of her Communion Heretics or Schismatics. Lond. 1687 See No. 441 *infra.* "The arguments on both side3 are set down with the Answers and Replies to them. This Method hath the advantage of bringing a Controversy within a narrow compass, and of shewing at one view the weight of the arguments, the closeness of the answers, and the justness of the conclusions; and thereby it was the most suited to Mr. Chillingworth's clear, impartial and strong way of arguing.

" We have in the same manner the substance of a dispute he had with Mr. Daniel, wherein he disproves the Infallibility of the Church of Rome, by an argument taken from the Contradictions which are contain'd in the Doctrine of Transubstantiation No. 441. He had another with a gentleman he does not name, in which he confutes the same Infallibility by proving that either the present Church of Rome errs in offering Tapers and incense to the Virgin Mary, or that the ancient Church of Rome did err in condemning as Heretics the Collyridians for offering a Cake to her No. 441. Besides the pieces already mentioned, Mr. C. wrote one to demonstrate that the doctrine of Infallibility, the main point of Romish votaries, is neither evident of itself, nor grounded upon certain and infallible reasons, nor warranted by any passage of Scripture No. 144. And in two other Papers he shews that the Church of Rome hath formerly erred; first by the admitting of Infants to the Eucharist, and holding that without it they could not be saved; and secondly by teaching the Doctrines of the Millenaries, viz. that before the world's end Christ should reign upon Earth for a thousand years, and that the Saints should live under him in all holiness and happiness; both which doctrines are condemned as false and heretical by the present Church of Rome No. 441. He writ also a short Letter No. 441 in answer to some objections put to him by one of his friends, wherein he shews that neither the Fathers nor the Councils are infallible witnesses of Tradition; and that the Infallibility of the Church of Rome must first of all be proved from the Scripture. He concludes with these words: ' Remember that if we have any infallible way, we have no use (at least no necessity) of an Infallible Guide; for if we may be saved by following the Scripture as near as we can (though we err), it is as good as any Interpreter to keep unity in charity (which is only needful) though not in opinion; and this can not be ridiculous, because they say if any man misinterpret the Council of Trent, it shall not damn him; and why (without any more ado) may not the same be said of Scripture?'" Des Maiseaux, pp. 38-40. Chillingworth was confronted on some of these arguments by E. Hawarden in Wit against Reason: or The Protestant Champion, the great, the incomparable Chillingworth, not invulnerable. 8vo. Brussels 1735.

Two short discourses against the Romanists, &c. See p. 118.

Five snort treatises; 1. Concerning Faith necessary to Salvation. 2. Of Infallibility. 3. Concerning the obligation of not professing or acting against our judgment or conscience. 4. Concerning obedience to ecclesiastical governors and trial of doctrines. 5. Concerning Salvation possible to be had in a Schismatical Communion. 4to Oxford 1688

Among the most zealous defenders of Papal Authority is John Thomas de Rochaberti, who left a long treatise, — De Romani Pontificis Autoritate, 3 vols. fol. esteemed in Spain and Italy, prohibited in France; and Bibliotheca Pontificia, a large collection of all the Treatises which have been written by different Authors in favour of the Pope's Authority and Infallibility; 21 vols. fol. Rome, 1700. Also prohibited by Act of Parliament of Paris.

" Bossuet who denounced the Pope's infallibility was a great orator, a consummate dialectician, and an accomplished master of those vague sublimities by which men are easily affected. All these qualities he employed in the production of what is probably the most formidable work ever directed against Protestantism. This is the opinion of Mr. Hallam respecting Bossuet's History of the Variations of Protestant Churches. Const. Hist. vol. i. p. 486; compare Lerminier, Philos. du Droit, vol. ii. p. 86. Attempts have been made by Protestant theologians to retort against the Catholics the arguments of Bossuet, on the ground that the religious variations are a necessary consequence of the honest pursuit of religious truth. See Blanco White's Evidence against Catholicism, pp. 109-112; and his Letters from Spain by Doblado, p. 127. With this I fully agree; but it would be easy to show that the argument is fatal to all ecclesiastical systems with strictly defined creeds, and therefore strikes as heavily against the Protestant Churches as against the Catholic." Buckle's History of Civilization in England, vol. i. p. 721. I think it right to give, without always adopting, the opinions of this able and learned writer. The limits of church authority are clearly stated in Archbishop Whately's Errors of Romanism, Essay IV. " Scepticism," as his Grace observes, " is not implied by absence of a claim to infallibility" (The Kingdom of Christ, p. 336); and Buckle himself admits that there is a decisive criterion of religious truth, p. 323 et aeqq. Bacon, in his Adv. of Learning, discussing the use of reason in spiritual things, maintains that 'Creeds are safeguards against novelties and theories. Cf. Tatham's Chart and Scale of Truth, vol. ii., and Morell's Philosophy of Religion, 1849.

For an answer to the imputation of divisions among Protestants, and with it the same retorted upon the church of Rome, see Field on the Church, ch. 42 and passim. Stillingfleet's Idolatry of the Church of Rome, c. v. Cf. the Divisions of the Church of Rome. (Works, vol. v. p. 170.) Bp. Hall, *ut supra,* p. 134. Placette on the In curable Scepticism of Rome (No. 3 *supra).* Concerning Salvation possible to be bad in a Scbismatical Communion, see The Protestant

Resolved, *ut supra,* pp. 56-65.

A Discourse concerning the Unity of the Catholic Church main-£. 1L tained in the Church of England No. 9 *supra.* 4to Lond. 1684

Catholick Religion asserted by St. Paul, and maintained in the CIL. Church of England; in opposition to the Errors of the Church of Rome. In a Sermon preached at St. Warbrough's Church in Dublin. By William (King) Lord Bp. of Kilmore and Ardagh. pp. 22, 4to Dublin 1686 Dr. Sherlock sifted from his Bran and Chaff; or a certain Way of finding the true Sense of the Scripture, and discovering who are the true living Members of the Church of Christ No. 415 *infra.* 4to Lond. 1687

Controversial Discourses relating to the Church, being an Answer to Dr. Sherlock's Discourse concerning the Nature, Unitie, and Communion of the Catholick Church. By B. D.
8vo Douay 1697

A Treatise of the Pope's Supremacy. To which is added, A Discourse concerning the Unity of the Church. By Isaac Barrow.
4to Lond. 1688 In the first volume of his Works, the Discourse, p. 293-325. See p. 28 *supra* and chap. xix.
The Pillar and Ground of Truth (on 1 Tim. iii. 15), a Sermon ML
preached before the King at Whitehall, May 7, 1676. By
John Sudbury, D.D., Dean of Durham and Chaplain in
Ordinary to his Majesty. 4to Lond. 1676

Novelty of the Modern Romish Religion sent forth in answer to three Queries propounded by N. G., Priest. By S. Felgate.
8vo Lond. 1682

" The Church of Rome hath changed the Primitive Canon, or Rule of Faith, by adding new articles to it, as necessary to be believed in order to Salvation;

look to the Confession of Faith, according to the

Council of Trent We deny not but that general or provincial Councils may make constitutions concerning extra-fundamental verities, and oblige all such as are under their jurisdiction to receive them, at least passively, so as not openly and contumaciously to oppose them. But to make any of them a part of the creed, and to oblige all Christians under pain of damnation to receive and believe them, this is really to add to the Creed, and to change the ancient Canon or Rule of Faith. But alas, these superadded articles of the Trent Creed are so far from being certain truths, that they are most of them manifest untruths, yea, gross and dangerous errors. To make this appear, I shall not refuse the pains of examining some of the chief of them." The Corruptions of the Church of Rome in Relation to Ecclesiastical Government, the Rule of Faith, and Form of Divine Worship; in answer to the Bishop of Meaux's Queries: with an Appendix containing the Creed of Pope Pius IV. By Geo. Bull, D.D., Lord Bishop of St David's. (In the 2nd volume of the Churchman Armed). Compare BramhaH's Just Vindication of the Church of England, (Works p. 56, vol. i.)

It is stated by Nelson in his Life of Bull, that in a letter addressed to himself the Bishop of Meaux proposed several Queries to Dr. Bull, in order to know the sentiments of so great a man upon those subjects (what is meant by the Catholic Church), which the Bishop expected to receive with no small degree of satisfaction. "But just as Dr. Bull's Answer" adds Nelson "came to my hands, I received the melancholy news of the Bishop of Meaux's Death, which prevented the progress of that controversy; which we might have expected to have seen carried on with great decency, and to good effect, by two such great men, though of different Communions, if the Providence of God had not put a stop to it by taking the Bishop out of the world before Dr. Bull's Letter was sent to him," p. 250. In Spry's Bampton Lectures already referred to, p. 10, one Sermon is devoted to "The Inefficiency and Mischievous Tendency of the Measures which have been taken at different Periods for the Restoration of Unity." The author reviews the "labours for peace" of Cassander, Bossuet, Grotius and Wake. An account of Bossuet's controversy with Wake (see chap, vi.) will be found in the Appendix, pp. 422-25. On the subject of this Sermon the reader is referred to Walchii Bibliotheca Theologica, vol. ii., c. v., sect. 14, § 20; Sazii Onomasticon, vol. ir., sect. 17, &c.

A short Historical Essay touching General Councils, Creeds and Impositions in Religion. By Andrew Marvell. 4to Lond. 1688

In the third volume of his Works. In page 126 he points out the original "good-natured" signification of heresy and heretic. Cf. Hobbes's Dialogue between a Philosopher and a Student. Sect. v.

The Judgment of private discretion, etc., by Richard Kidder (No. 422 *supra*). ' 1687

In Gibson, vol. v. fol. vol. i.

The unreasonableness of the Romanists requiring our communion with the present Romish Church, etc. By William Squire (No 449 *infra*). 1672. Cf. Rose's State of Protestantism in Germany, pp. 8-30.

Fides Ecclesise Anglicanse vindicata ab incertitudine, etc., a Johanne Cudworth (No. 454 *infra*). 1688

De Ecclesia Romana, etc., a Georg. Ash well (No. 455 *infra*). 1688

The Salvation of Protestants asserted and defended, etc., by J. A. Dalhusius (No. 457 *infra*). 1689

I shall not overlay the titles of the Author of the Complete Catalogue with a supplement not synchronical, but nevertheless I shall conclude with a book the date of which is nearer our own times than our predecessors.

An Interesting Controversy with Mr. Ritschel, Vicar of Hexham, by Thomas Ward, Author of The Cantos and The Errata of the Protestant Bible, from a Manuscript written by Himself. " Why shall we hesitate to throw ourselves upon the authority of the catholic church, which has always maintained herself by the succession of bishops, by the faith of the people, by the decision of councils, and by the authority of miracles? Not to acknowledge her doctrine is a proof either of great impiety or extreme arrogance." St. Augustine. 279 pp. exclusive of Pref. and Life. 8vo Manchester, 1819

" The work which is here offered to the public was occasioned by a personal interview between the author see No. 109 *supra* and Mr. Ritschel, vicar of Hexham, on the subject of religion. The particulars of this interview Mr. Ward laid before the world in a book entitled A Conference with Mr. Ritschel, vicar of Hexham. Mr. Ritschel replied: answers were exchanged on either side; and the following pages are what Mr. W. wrote in reply to the second letter of the Vicar of Hexham." Pref. x. iv.

Dodd does not mention the Conference with Ritschel in the list of Ward's works.

Reading the Fathers Chillingworth contemptuously calls travelling on a "north-west discovery," p. 366. (Edit. 1846.) Even to Augustine, who was probably the ablest of them, Chillingworth pays no deference. See what he says at pp. 196, 333, 376; and as to the authority of the Fathers in general see pp, l.2, 346. " After a prodigious waste of industry and erudition, a learned foreigner (M. Daille) at length shewed the inutility and the folly of pursuing the contest any further. In a well£, fL considered discourse, On the use of the Fathers, he clearly evinced that their authority was much less than was generally supposed, in all points of religious controversy; and that their judgment was especially incompetent in *those* points, which were agitated by the two parties This discovery had great effects. It opened the eyes of the more candid and intelligent inquirers; and our incomparable Chillingworth, with some others (Lord Falkland, Lord Digby, Dr. Jer. Taylor, &c.) took the advantage of it to set the controversy with the church of Rome, once more, on its proper foot; and to establish, for ever, the old principle *that the Bible,* and that only (interpreted by our best reason) *is the religion of protestants."* Hurd's Sermons on the Study of the Prophecies, *ad finem* Serm. xii. Cf. Warburton's Preface to his " Julian." CORRIGENDA ET ADDENDA TO PART I.

N.B. Such of the following notes as are by Dr. Todd were not placed in the Editors hands in time, so as to be available for insertion in their proper places: —
Paoe I — *Tract No.* 1. My copy of this book (for I have no doubt it is the same) has this title: — " Four conferences concerning, I. Reading the Holy Scriptures in the Vulgar Tongue. II. Half Communion. III. Worshipping of Images. IV. Invocation of Saints. Imprimatur R. Bathurst, Oxford 1688." J. H. T.

Chap, i., observes Dr. Todd, is very meagre and imperfect; several tracts of Stillingfleet, Burnet, and John Williams (Ath. Oxon. vol. ii. col. 1120), which belong to the succeeding controversy, are omitted in it. Also some of the Sermons in the "Morning Exercises" of the Dissenters might have been included. On the general subject of the controversy see Stillingfleet's Life, p. 17 vol. i. of his Works.

Paob 2 — *Tract No.* 2. The book to which this is an answer, although called "a popish MS.," seems to have been printed in 1633, and to have been the same of which the title is thus given in the Bodl. Cat. under N. N.

" The progenie of catholics and protestants whereby on the one side is proved the lineal descent of catholics for the Roman faith and religion, from the holie fathers of the primitive church, even from Christs verie time until these our dayes, and on the other the never being of protestants during al tho foresayd time." Rouen 1633, 4to.

The author of " Origo Protestantium" (John Shaw) died 22nd May 1689. J. H. T.

K K

The title concludes thus: — " Otherwise then in confessed and condemned Hereticks. And al this is conuinced by the manifold and clearest acknowledgements of Protestant Writers, both forrain and domestick. By thine owne mouth I iudge thee, naughtie seruant Luc. six. 22."

The writer, Lawrence Anderton, was born in Lancashire, educated at Blackburn and Cambridge, became a convert, and entered the Society of Jesus in 1604. " He became a bright ornament to his order: when on the mission, he principally resided in Lancashire, where he died in 1643." Dodd refers to Alegambe p. 294. Athen. Oxon. p. 480 col. 668. Life of Robert Bolton, by Edward Bagshaw, 1633. This work is dedicated to M. Doctour Morton, Superintendent of Litchfield and Coventrie, on account of his " Appeale for Protestants," *Xt* II. made in answer to " The Protestants Apologie for the Roman Church," by James Anderton, alias John Brerely. See p. 58, and Baxter's Key for Catholics, edit. by Allport, p. 426. Page 3 — *Tract No.* 3. This is by Peter du Moulin, Jun. — Peter Talbot, tit. A bp. of Dublin, and brother to the D. of Tirconnel, wrote some books under the signature of N. N. (Harris's Ware's Writers, p. 193, and BramhaU's Works, Oxford 1842, vol. i. p. 30.) But this must be a different person, probably John Leyburn, taking the final letters of his names. J. H. T. Ibid. *Tract No.* 4. William Lloyd, Bp. of St. Asaph, 1690, translated to Lichfield and Coventry, 1692, to Worcester 1699, ob. 1714. J. H. T.

Page 4. On the loyalty of the Papists, see Dodd's Church History of England, part vi. art. 5.

Page 5. The Compendium: or a short View of the late Tryals in relation to the present Plot against his Majesty and Government, &c. By the Earl of Castlemain. 4to Lond. 1679.

Prefatory discourse to a late Pamphlet entitled, A Memento for English Protestants, and being an answer to that part of the Compendium which reflects upon the Bp. of Lincoln's Book. 4to Lond. 1681.

Pagb 9 — *Tract No.* 5. John Williams was Rector of St. Mildred's, Poultry, and Canon of St. Paul's, London, Chaplain to William III., D.D. of Cambr. in 1689 (although originally of Magd. Hall, Oxford), afterwards Bishop of Chichester. J. H. T.

Page 10— *Tract No.* 6. Anon. By Nicholas Clagett, D.D., Archdeacon of Sudbury, of Chr. Ch. Coll. Cambr. This is attributed to Nicholas Clagett in his Life in the Biographia Britannica, which professes to have been drawn up from materials communicated by his son, Bishop Clagett. J. H. T.

Ibid. *Tract No.* 8. As King Charles II. died Feb. 6, 168$, it is evident that this book ought not to have been given among those published *before* the reign of James II. Peck, however, had no copy of it, and he therefore very naturally followed Gee, wh«, however, speaks of it as one of the Treatises published near the end of the reign of King Charles II. J. H. T.

Page 11 — *Tract No.* 11. Compare The Protestant Journal for 1831 and 1832. "The offering of Tapers and incense to the Virgin Mary" (see Chillingworth's Conferences) is illustrated in the Review of Lidgate's poem, "How Candelmesse Day first toke the Name," Oct. 1832, pp. 602-624.

The following tract by Edward Worsley? might here be mentioned on the other side: —" Anti-Haman, or An Answer to M. G. Burnet's Mistere of Iniquiti unvailed. (See No. 429 *infra.)* Wherein is shewed the conformity of the doctrine, worship and practice of the Roman Catholic Church with those of the Purest times. The Idolatry of the Pagans is truly stated, and the imputation of Pagan Idolatry cleerely confuted. And reasons are given why Catholikes avoyde the communion of the Protestant Church. To which is annexed a Letter to R. Cudworth, D.D. With Leave of Superiours. 1679."

No. 11 is not by Thankful Owen. The author was Henry Hallywell, the Platonist. See Worthington's Diary, &c., vol. i. p. 135, and advertisements in Hickes's Jovian. Omitted in Wood's List of Hallywell's Works.

Page 13 — *Tract No.* 12. See Contin. p. 58, where we are told, "To this" (i. e. to the short and plain way, as above), " there is an answer almost finished by a very learned person, who will demonstrate to the world, how little that book had in it to convince." On the authority of this statement Peck puts down the answer as if published, No. 18. But I cannot find that it was ever printed, nor do I know who the " very learned person" alluded to was; probably Stillingfleet.

See Evelyn's account of the death bed of Charles II., Memoirs, vol. i. p. 581-2, and "A true relation of the King's death. To which are added Copies of two papers found in the Strong-Box." Phoenix Lond. 1707, vol. i. p. 566. J. H. T.

Paob 14— Tract No. 13. The Bodl. Catal. mentions this as a single sheet without place or date, in folio; under the title of " Copy of a paper written by the late Duchess of York." I cannot find any edition of it with the title given above by Peck. I conclude, therefore, that he took that title from the words with which Stillingfleet's answer to the Duchess's paper begins. The third letter is said to be written by a Great Lady *for the satisfaction of her friends,* as to the reasons of *her leaving the communion of the Church of England and making herself a Member of the Roman Catholic Church;* but the words in *Italics* are evidently cited by Stillingfleet from the first paragraph of the paper itself as given in p. 18 *supra.* It is curious that Hudleston does not notice the Duchess's paper. J. H. T.

, 3L. The folio sheet is No. 1008 of the Halliwell Collection of Pro clamations, &c. From "St. James's, Aug. 20, 1670." Ed.

The tract given imperfectly by Peck, No. 160 and again No. 181 *infra,* is entitled, The Church of England truly represented, according CD. to Dr. Heylin's History of the Reformation, in justification of the late
Duchess of York's paper, Lond. 1686, 4to. J. H. T.

Page 15. *For* veneration *read* vexation.

Ibid. Tract No. 14. See State p. 24 Stillingfleet's Life, p. 18, prefixed to his works, vol. i. fol., Lond. 1707, and works, vol. vi. p. 641. J. H. T.

Page 16 — Tract No. 15. See State p. 24. Peck had not seen this tract. He gives the title erroneously thus: " A defence of the Papers written by the late King, and found in his strong box." He adds no imprint or date.

Ibid. *Tract No.* 16. See State p. 25. J. H. T.

Ibid. *Tract No.* 17. See State p. 25. J. H. T.

Ibid. *Tract No.* 18. See the note on No. 12. J. H. T.

Pagb 18. *Copies of two papers,* &c. On the authenticity of these papers see Evelyn's Memoirs October 2, 1685, and Dr. George Hickes's Apologetical Vindication of the Church of England (2nd edition) Introduction, who says that he saw the original *interlined* in the King's own hand. But it is certain that the papers themselves were not in the King's hand. See Burnet's testimony, Own Times, vol. i. p. 615 Oxford, 8vo ed. vol. ii. p. 471-2. The King's papers are certified by James II. (p. 8 of this pamphlet) to be true copies, and to have been in his Royal brother's own hand, but the paper by the Duchess is introduced (p. 9) without any heading, and without any certificate. See Burnet's account of the Duchess's death, Own Times, vol. i. p. 309-10. She died March.31, 1672, at which time it was not publicly known even that the Duchess of York had become a Romanist. In another place (vol. i. p. 308) Burnet tells us that the Duke in 1673 shewed him the Duchess's paper, and that " it was all writ with her own hand." Lord Clarendon's letter to the Duchess, mentioned by Burnet, will be found in Speeches, &c., annexed, Sedley's Poetical Works (1707) p. 92, and in Harleian Miscell. vol. iii. See also Monthly Repository (1815) vol. x. p. 294-296, Calamy's Life, vol. i. p. 68. Voltaire, in his Siecle de Louis XIV. (chap. ix. note) say3, L'argent de Louis XIV. gouverna l'Angleterre depuis 1669 jusqu'en 1677; il determino Charles II. a se convertir, puis a differer sa conversion. Cos details de corruption sont honteux, mais il est utile que les peuples les connaissent, et que les princes apprennent qu'ils sont toujours reveles. Page 19. *Remarks on the two Papers.* This letter was written 1685, but £, IL not published till 1688. Note in List of Burnet's works, Own Times, vol. vi. p. 339. It is not in Trin. Coll. Dublin, nor in the Bodl. J. H. T.

Pagh 20. This Letter is not the same as that referred to. The former will be found in A Fifth Collection of Papers relating to the present June-£, ture of Affairs in England. 4to, Janewny, Lond. 1688.

Page 21 —Tract No. 21. There was a Mr. Thomas Goodwin "pastor of a church of Christ at Pinner, Middlesex," who was probably the author of 21. See Bodl. Catal. J. H. T.

Ibid. *Tract No.* 22. See Ath. Oxon. vol. ii. p. 327, where this book seems to be attributed to Dr. Win. Claggett. J. H. T.

Pagb 24 — *Tract No.* 23. This book is a re-issue of two tracts previously published. Burnet's answer to the Bishop of Oxford appeared originally in three parts, viz.: 1. An Inquiry into the reasons, &c. (See p. 65 *supra.*) 2. A second part of the Inquiry into the reasons offered by Dr. Sam. Parker, bishop of Oxford, for abrogating the test; or an answer to his plea for transubstantiation, and for acquitting the Church of Rome of Idolatry. 4to 1688.

3. A continuation of the second part of the Inquiry, &c. relating to the idolatry of tho church of Rome.

These two last pieces (the second part of the Inquiry and the continuation of the second part) were published a few months afterwards in one tract, with the title of " A discourse concerning Transubstantiation and Idolatry," &c, as above.

Paob 25—Tract No. 24. Second edit. The first edit. was in folio, Lond. 1687, and a third edit. in 4to was published in Lond. 1688. See Ath.
Oxon. vol. ii. col. 631, where A. Wood gives this account of H.
Care, (*ul infra,* p. 76.)

Paob 29 — *Tract No.* 28. See Le Neve's Fasti, p. 13.

Page 31. *For* 1685 *read* 1585. Cf. p. 51.

Page 39. Bibliotheca Politica, by James Tyrrel.

Page 45. Of Oliver Carter see also Notes and Queries, 2nd series, vol. iv. p. 130. The Rev. Canon Raines possesses a copy of this rare tract.

Page 60. William Howard, *add,* afterwards Viscount Stafford. C IL« Page 62. *The late Apology, reprinted,* &c., by Dr. Lloyd, afterward Bishop of St. Asaph. See Butler's Memoirs of Catholics, vol. iii. p. 47.

Page 67. *The Church of England's complaint, Sec.* In Somers Tracts, 3rd Collection, vol. iii. pp. 135-401.

Ibid. Considerations moving to a toleration and liberty of conscience, with arguments inducing to a cessation of the penal statutes against all dissenters whatever upon account of religion, occasioned by an excellent discourse upon that subject, published by his Grace the Duke of

Buckingham. Humbly offered to the Parliament at their next sitting at Westminster. Tantsene animis coelestibus irse? pp. 12, 4to Lond.
1685. J. H. T.

Page 72. *The famous Bull,* &c. Translated by H. Wharton. See

D'Oyley's Life of Wharton (Life of Abp. Bancroft), Append. No. 1, vol. ii. p. 125. J. II. T.

fit. IL. ought to have been affixed to this tract. Ibid. Locke's Epistola was translated into English by Mr. Popple. (Watt.)

B. L. ought to have been affixed to this. Mr. Crossley also possesses the rare original.

Page 102. The city we call Lisbon is by the natives called Lisboa as well as Lisbona. See Lasor A Varea, or Coronelli.

Page 104. An account of Gother's second work (No. 53) will be found in Cunningham's Preface to Stillingfleet's Doctrines and Practices, pp. 3840. To No. 51 (ff. 1L. ought to have been affixed.

Pace 112 — *Tract No.* 73. A detailed account of Bossuet's Exposition and of his controversy with Wake is given in Mendham's Literary Policy, pp. 220-32.

Pagb 117. To the note from Mendham's Memoirs, &c., add: This fact is &i» illustrated in "The Council of Trent plainly discover'd not to have been a Free Assemhly," &c. &c. By Michael Geddes. Lond. 1714, 8vo; and in Luzancy's Reflexions on the Council of Trent. Oxford, 1677, 8vo.

Page 137 — *Tract No.* 102. Peck gives the date " 1687, 88." I would now say that the double date probably indicated the old style year 168, the book having perhaps been printed in Jan. or Feb. of what we would now call A.d. 1688. J. H. T.

Pagb 142— *Tract No.* 111. *For* 1596 *read* 1696.

Page 143 — *Tracts Nos.* 115, 117. In reference to the authorship of these see D'Oyley's Life of Sancroft, vol ii. p. 121. J. H. T. Page 157. *For* Revolution *read* Rebellion.

Page 166. This Sermon (by Sherlock) was answered in a Remonstrance by way of address from the Church of England to both Houses of Parliament. Sherlock replied in a Vindication, 1685. After some time "a good man" published A Papist misrepresented and represented, &c. J. H. T.

Page 180 — *Tract No.* 158. tt. H. ought to be affixed to this. In Gibson, vol. xiv. fol. vol. iii.

Ibid. *Tract No.* 159. In Gibson, vol. xiii. fol. vol. iii.

Page 192 — *Trac t No.* 164. Hutchinson in Gibson, vol. v. fol. vol i.

Pagb 199. Insert before " In his book," &c, Deane's master, whose creature and convert he was, was a strong friend to calligraphy as well as to Popish principles.

Page 204— *Tract No.* 180. In Gibson, vol. ii. fol. vol. i.

Page 208. Respecting the consecration of Bishop Barlow, which is an important question on account of the part he took in the consecration of Archbishop Parker, see Notes and Queries, 2nd Ser. vol. vii. p. 48.

Pagb 210—*Tract No.* 186. Compare No. 127. A succinct account of the traditions and legends respecting the introduction of Christianity into England will be found in Collier's Ecclesiastical History of Great Britain, chiefly of England; and in reference to its sister, " the Sacred Island," see Dr. Todd's History of the Ancient Church of Ireland; and The Testimony of St. Patrick against the false pretensions of Rome to Primitive Antiquity in Ireland, by Henry J. Monck Mason, LL.D. Dublin, 1846.

Pagb 230. On the prejudices of Grotius against the doctrine of Antichrist, see Hurd's Sermons on the Study of the Prophecies. On the discrepancies of interpreters in general on this subject, Dr. Todd's Donnellan Lectures, 1840. In Lecture v. he shows that Romanism is inadequately opposed by the application of the prophecy to the corruptions of the Papacy.

Page 231. To Baxter's Key for Catholics, &c, add: and the two following works by the same author: — The Successive Visibility of the Church of which the Protestants are the soundest Members, I. Defended against the Opposition of Mr. William Johnson, 12mo. Lond. 1660. Which is the true Church; the whole Christian World as headed by Christ, or the Pope and his Subjects, in answer to Mr. Johnson. 4to Lond. 1679. See also the Second Part of his Key for Catholics.

Page 233. Comber's Roman Forgeries are in Gibson, vol. xv. fol. vol. iii.

Ibid. 4th paragraph. In this reference to Mendham my memory unaccountably deceived me. The Decrees discussed in his Literary Policy are those issued by the official authorities of Rome against such books as were offensive to the Roman see. The history of the false Decretals, and of their principal object, the exaltation of the episcopal, but more especially of the papal power, will be found in Gieseler's Ecclesiastical History, vol. ii. See also Townsend's Ecclesiastical and Civil History philosophically considered, vol. ii. chap. iii. The Jus novum or Pseudoisidoriau principle that obedience was due to all the papal decrees, was brought in by the Pope, Nicolas I., 836 years after Christ. See Milman's History of Latin Christianity, vol. ii. p. 373.

Page 234 — *Tract No.* 208. See No. 178 *supra.*

Page 236 — *Tract No.* 214. In Gibson. vol. iv. fol. vol. i.

Page 247. *A short Historical Essay: Be Ecclesia Montana: An interesting Controversy.* These three Tracts are in the Chetham Library: the letters ffl. 1L.

were inadvertently omitted.

Ibid. In the 13th line, for *supra* read *infra*.

End Of Part I.

CPSIA information can be obtained at www.ICGtesting.com
Printed in the USA
BVOW06s1005250315

393296BV00012B/157/P

Russian Oil Supply

Russian Oil Supply
Performance and Prospects

JOHN D. GRACE

Published by the Oxford University Press
For the Oxford Institute for Energy Studies
2005

OXFORD
UNIVERSITY PRESS

Great Clarendon Street, Oxford OX2 6DP

Oxford University Press is a department of the University of Oxford.
It furthers the University's objective of excellence in research, scholarship
and education by publishing worldwide in

Oxford New York

Auckland Cape Town Dar es Salaam Hong Kong Karachi
Kuala Lumpur Madrid Melbourne Mexico City Nairobi
New Delhi Shanghai Taipei Toronto

with offices in

Argentina Austria Brazil Chile Czech Republic France Greece
Guatemala Hungary Italy Japan Poland Portugal Singapore
South Korea Switzerland Thailand Turkey Ukraine Vietnam

Oxford is a registered trade mark of Oxford University Press
in the UK and in certain other countries

Published in the United States
by Oxford University Press Inc., New York

© Oxford Institute for Energy Studies 2005

The moral rights of the author have been asserted
Database right Oxford Institute for Energy Studies (maker)

First published 2005

All rights reserved. No part of this publication may be reproduced,
stored in a retrieval system, or transmitted, in any form or by any means,
without the prior permission in writing of the Oxford Institute for Energy
Studies, or as expressly permitted by law, or under terms agreed with
the appropriate reprographics rights organization. Enquiries concerning
reproduction outside the scope of the above should be sent to Oxford
Institute for Energy Studies, 57 Woodstock Road, Oxford OX2 6FA

You must not circulate this book in any other binding or cover
and you must impose this same condition on any acquirer

British Library Cataloguing in Publication Data
Data available

Library of Congress Cataloguing in Publication Data
Data available

Cover designed by Clare Hofmann
Typeset by Philip Armstrong, Sheffield
Printed by The Alden Group, Oxford

ISBN 0-19-730030-8   978-0-19-730030-5

3 5 7 9 10 8 6 4 2

To Debra and my family

CONTENTS

Figures	ix
Maps	x
Tables	xi
Acknowledgements	xii
Preface	xiv

Introduction	1
Chapter 1: The Opening of Russia's Oil Industry	6
Beginnings in Baku	6
From the Revolution through the Second World War	8
Comment	10
Chapter 2: The Volga-Ural Basin	14
Exploration	16
Production	19
The Romashkino Field – Anchor of the Volga-Ural Basin	22
Comment	25
Appendix to Chapter 2: Volga-Ural Basin Geology	28
Chapter 3: West Siberia	34
Exploration	36
Production	45
Samotlor – Russia's Largest Oil Field	47
Comment	52
Appendix to Chapter 3: West Siberian Basin Geology	56
Chapter 4: The Peak, Collapse and Recuperation	65
Всех Сильнее!*	66
The Bigger They Are, The Harder They Fall	73
Stabilization of Output	80
Recovery	81
Comment	85
Appendix to Chapter 4: The Russian Oil Market from 1983 through 2002	89

*[Stronger Than All Others]

Chapter 5: Industry Performance — 104
  Ontogeny Recapitulates Phylogeny — 105
  Lukoil — 109
  Lukoil in Timan-Pechora — 114
  Yukos — 119
  The 'Yukos Affair' — 124
  Sibneft — 130
  Surgutneftegaz — 134
  TNK-BP — 138
  Independents — 143
  State Producing Organizations — 150
  The Division of Spoils — 156
  Comment — 161

Chapter 6: The Outlook for Russian Oil Supply — 178
  Russia's Resource Base — 178
  Future Output from Producing Fields — 183
  Discovered, Undeveloped Oil and Condensate Resources — 189
  Exploration — 195
  Synthesis — 201

Chapter 7: Conclusions — 212
  Russia's Oil Resources — 213
  The Role of Oil in Russia — 216
  The New Russian Oil Industry — 218
  A Chance for Choices — 222

Postscript — 230

Appendix I: Notes for Maps and Figures — 235
  Maps — 235
  Figures — 239

Appendix II: Quantification of Oil Resources — 250
  Crustal Abundance vs. Resources — 250
  The SPE/WPC Reserve Definitions — 256
  What the SEC Definitions Add — 259
  The Soviet/Russian System — 260
  Comment — 266

Bibliography — 272

Index — 281

FIGURES

1.	Russian/Soviet, US and Saudi Oil Production	2
2.	Time Line of the Industrial Development of the Volga-Ural Basin	14
3.	Relationship between Oil Discovery Size and Discovery Date, Volga-Ural Basin	18
4.	Oil Production from the Volga-Ural Basin by Field Generation	20
5.	Cross-Section of Romashkino Field* (Indicated in Map 5)	
6.	Romashkino Field Oil Production and Water Cut	23
7.	Time Line of the Geologic Development of the Volga-Ural Basin	28
8.	Time Line of the Industrial Development of the West Siberian Basin	35
9.	Relationship between Oil Discovery Size and Discovery Date, West Siberian Basin	40
10.	Oil Production from the West Siberian Basin by Field Generation	47
11.	Cross-Section of Samotlor Field* (Indicated in Map 9)	
12.	Maximum, Mean and Minimum Discovery Size Brought Online by Decade in West Siberia	50
13.	Time Line of Geologic Development of the West Siberian Basin	56
14.	Domestic Consumption and Export of Soviet/Russian Oil	68
15.	Relationship between the Number of Producing Wells and Oil Production	71
16.	Relationship between the Number of New Wells, Idle and Producing Wells	74
17.	Relationship between the Number of Idle Wells and Oil Production	75
18.	Oil Prices, Tariffs, Excise Taxes, Operating Costs and Producer Net Income	79
19.	Ruble/Dollar Exchange Rate, 1996–2004	82
20.	Price of Brent Crude, 1998–2004	83
21.	Monthly Russian Oil Production, 1998–2004	84
22.	Russian Oil Supply and Demand in 1983	94

* Located in colour section

23.	Russian Oil Supply and Demand in 1987	95
24.	Russian Oil Supply and Demand in 1993	96
25.	Russian Oil Supply and Demand in 1997	98
26.	Russian Oil Supply and Demand in 2002	99
27.	Russian Oil Production by Industry Sector	104
28.	Lukoil Oil Production by Subsidiary	110
29.	Yukos Oil Production by Subsidiary	121
30.	Relationship of Number of Producing Wells and Well Productivity at Yuganskneftegaz	129
31.	Relationship of Production and Well Productivity at Noyabrskneftegaz	132
32.	Relationship of Drilling Footage and Oil Production at Surgutneftegaz	136
33.	TNK Oil Production by Subsidiary	141
34.	Oil Production by Bashneft, Tatneft, Russian Independents and Joint Ventures	145
35.	Number of Russian Independents and Joint Ventures	149
36.	Oil Production by State Enterprises	152
37.	Distribution of Russian Oil Revenues, 1993–2002	159
38.	Relationship between Domestic Price of Oil and World Parity Prices	160
39.	Proved Oil Reserves of the Top 15 Countries	180
40.	Production Costs in the West Siberian and Volga-Ural Basins	188
41.	Relationship between Pareto and Lognormal Distribution of Field Sizes	254

MAPS

See colour section

TABLES

1. Key Oil Fields of West Siberia by Generation of Discovery and Development — 38
2. Characteristics of Fields in Phased Development of West Siberia — 45
3. Major Sources of Production Growth from 1998–2002 — 85
4. Basic Data for 1983 Soviet Oil Market — 93
5. Basic Data for 1987 Soviet Oil Market — 94
6. Basic Data for 1993 Russian Oil Market — 96
7. Basic Data for 1997 Russian Oil Market — 97
8. Basic Data for 2002 Russian Oil Market — 98
9. Technical and Financial Performance Indicators for Lukoil — 113
10. Technical and Financial Performance Indicators for Yukos — 122
11. Technical and Financial Performance Indicators for Sibneft — 133
12. Technical and Financial Performance Indicators for Surgutneftegaz — 138
13. Technical and Financial Performance Indicators for TNK — 140
14. Technical and Financial Performance Indicators for Rosneft — 154
15. Estimate of Russia's Proved Reserves by Producer — 179
16. Russia's Conventional Oil Resource Base — 181
17. Most Important Post-Peak Fields — 184
18. Most Important Pre-Peak (Growing) Fields — 187
19. Most Important New Field Development Projects — 190
20. Cartographic Data for Maps — 235
21. Regressions of Discovery Sizes versus Discovery Year for Volga-Ural Basin — 241
22. Regressions of Discovery Sizes versus Discovery Year for West Siberian Basin — 242

ACKNOWLEDGEMENTS

The professor who supervised my geologic education, George Hart, said 'you learn geology through the soles of your feet.' Starting in the eighties, the unwearied energy of dozens of Russian geologists, geophysicists and engineers, guided me over the vast territory of Russian oil and gas. These men and women showed me first hand how their science, technologies and economics worked, explained where they did not work and could be improved. Without their spirited dedication to teach, debate and to tolerantly and seriously consider endless questions, my education on the topics of this study would have remained shallow and bookish.

First among them was the late Vladimir I. Shpil'man, founding Director of the Siberian Scientific-Analytic Center and in the Soviet period, a scientist and leader in the famous West Siberian Scientific Research Institute for Oil and Gas Exploration Geology (ZapSib-NIGNI). Vladimir was an exemplar of the best of Soviet science with the foresight to see paths through which the durable intellectual accomplishments of the old order could prosper in a new Russia. He and his colleagues were unstinting in their friendship and efforts that not only schooled me in West Siberian geology, but imparted an understanding of their philosophy of science and how they applied it to exploring and producing oil and gas.

Before the dissolution of the USSR, most of what we learned in the West of Soviet petroleum geology was from their abundant scientific literature. Critical contributors (in the last forty years) included V.I. Shpil'man, I.I. Nesterov, A.E. Kontorovich, V.E. Khain, G.Kh. Dikenshtein, N.V. Lopatin, G.F. Trebin, S.P. Maksimov, N.N. Nemchenko and others too numerous to list.

In the West, the decades of translations and studies by Jim Clarke and the dozens of works by Greg Ulmishek form a core of analysis that brought the Russian geologic literature into English. They also bridged many of the differences between Soviet and Western approaches to oil and gas and made very strong independent contributions to our scientific understanding of the region's hydrocarbon potential. On the quantitative side, the recent vast improvement by IHS Energy in their field and production data bases has substantially enhanced the feasible resolution of analysis on Russian oil and gas resources.

The works of Robert Campbell on the economics of Soviet oil and gas remain the best industry studies anywhere in the world. That he wrote them between the sixties and eighties, when the availability and quality of Soviet data were abysmal, remains an inspiration for rigorous empiricism. The primary source of Western scholarship on the politics of oil and gas in the late Soviet period is Thane Gustafson's 1989 book, *Crisis Amid Plenty*. Chrystia Freeland's *Sale of the Century, Russia's Wild Ride from Communism to Capitalism* provided an excellent, accessible account of 'privatization' during the Yeltsin administration that gave much-needed context to what happened to the nation's oil assets.

I have drawn heavily from twenty years of experience in the oil industry, most immediately from clients of Earth Science Associates and their projects. The present work grew out of a study in 2003 with PFC Energy on the performance of major Russian oil companies. Deep appreciation is extended to PFC Energy and Jerry Kepes for their support and permission to use data and analysis from that study here.

My tenure and former colleagues at ARCO (later subsumed into BP) afforded me a unique opportunity to work in both geologic basin analysis and economic modelling of oil and gas supply and to begin to understand the relationship between them. This, in turn was built on a foundation gained at Louisiana State University, most importantly from George Hart, Jim Hawkes, Tom Owen and Herman Daly.

While still a draft, very generous friends, colleagues and my wife reviewed all or major sections of this work: Emil Attanasi, Greg Ulmishek, Tony Finizza, Richard Strickland, Mara Heikes and Debra Grace. Their collective input, corrections and suggestions were invaluable. At Earth Science Associates, without the patient professionalism of Mara Heikes, the project simply would have never been finished. She carefully shepherded and improved text, maps and figures through countless revisions.

This book is published under the auspices of the Oxford Institute for Energy Studies (OIES). Jonathan Stern, whom I have known for years through his scholarship on Soviet and Russian natural gas, catalyzed the relationship that led to publication. At OIES, Kate Teasdale has expertly coordinated the project. Judy Mabro's editing and Philip Armstrong's composition of the book afforded a wide suite of improvements. Above all, OIES Director, Bob Skinner, through considerable time, critical thought and persistence has guided the book from an overly technical and narrow treatment in the draft to a much more useful and usable final work.

Thanks are due to all of them. The caveat that remaining errors are my own particularly applies.

PREFACE

As the world confronts a new phase in the oil market with prices not experienced since the early eighties, the question on everyone's mind is which countries will dominate future supply? OPEC, certainly capable and willing to develop new productive capacity, must confront the uncertainty of this new market situation. On one side is demand; although over the long term certain to continue to grow, the recent enormous surge in China's consumption surprised many, as did the related growth in US demand. The uncertainty of policy responses to current fiscal and external imbalances in the USA and unreliable statistics on Asian countries' oil consumption compound the short-term uncertainty of oil demand. Inversely, supply − reasonably certain in the short term − appears less certain further in the future. In the past, non-OPEC producers responded to higher prices by increasing production and displaced OPEC, leaving it with costly shut-in capacity. What can and will they do today? The most important non-OPEC exporter by far is Russia. Understanding Russia and its potential to help meet the growth in world oil demand is a key to postulating the future of the world oil market. In the following pages, John Grace provides a very timely and essential analysis for discussing the role Russian oil might play.

Russia's oil resources are not in question. Its conventional oil reserves are the largest of any non-OPEC country. Since the world oil industry began in the 1860s, Russia has produced more oil than any other country, after the United States. During the Soviet era its production rivalled those of the USA and Saudi Arabia. In 1987 Russia was the largest producer in the world. Nine years later in the chaotic wake of the Soviet collapse, production had sunk to nearly half, equivalent to losing almost all of the North Sea's output at the time. Since then Russia's production has steadily increased; by 2004 it again approximated Saudi Arabia's.

What is behind this recovery? Can Russia continue to expand and go on to exceed its mid-eighties levels? And more important, will it and should it? This book provides the essential framework regarding Russia's oil endowment that is needed before one can consider answers to these and other questions. John Grace reminds us of how central oil has been to the modern economic history of Russia, beginning in Baku on the Caspian Sea in the late nineteenth century. Oil has been the engine pulling the country's material production. But like any engine, its future performance depends on its past maintenance and in many ways oil reservoirs are no different. Key to a reservoir's performance is its pressure. This is the energy that drives the motor. Push a reservoir too hard — release its pressure to get out as much oil as quickly as possible — and early decline and foregone oil are assured. The author provides valuable insights into how geological caprice bestowed on Russia its hydrocarbon riches and critical glimpses of how Russia in turn exploited and abused that endowment. This treatment, grounded in the essentials of its geological setting, why the oil is where it is and what encouraged its exploitation, is a refreshing and far more convincing analysis than those that simply graphically project recent increases of output. Understanding past exploitation of fields is critical if we are to begin to speculate on their future performance.

The history of oil is laced with politics. But Russian oil is also dominated by technocratic bullheadedness in the Kremlin. Keeping a mental image of the path of world oil prices since the sixties, the reader will follow John Grace's description of how the central planners in Moscow pushed its industry to produce more and more. As the Volga Urals fields declined, Moscow dispatched its geologists and drillers to more prospective but more remote and vastly more difficult areas in Western Siberia — such was Moscow's relentless, almost frenetic pursuit of higher output. He paints a picture of the Russian system resembling an athlete on steroids, where the steroids — oil — began to control the athlete. Moscow put its star athlete on an accelerating treadmill; when its heart failed, the system failed with it.

The legacy of communist era management and petroleum production practices are imprinted on today's Russian oil industry and in particular its structure. Understanding this aspect helps us comprehend the ranking and geographic focus of the Russian companies that are quickly becoming household names; which fields constitute their core assets; what their upside might be; and where they might sit as a potential target for re-nationalization or merger. The concentration and size distribution of the companies is reflected in the size of the fields under production and development, mirroring to a certain extent a worrisome structural phenomenon among the international oil companies after their mergers and acquisitions during the nineties. Very large oil companies are not sustained by small oil fields. We also begin to understand why the return of Yukos to state ownership might be about more than reprimanding its principal owner for interfering in politics.

The reader with even a passing knowledge of post-Second World War Russian history will be able to see how this physical background of the Russian oil industry, its endowment and management figured in the command economy. We also might appreciate why, during the Yeltsin interregnum, oil was the target of perhaps the most egregious appropriation of a nation's resources by private agents in history (some have called it a give-away; others have called it theft); and then understand the recent methodical and heavy-handed Kremlinesque restoration of those resources to state ownership.

How the Russian leadership uses oil and gas to gain political legitimacy and leverage both at home and abroad will be a force to understand and watch carefully. Just as Vladimir Lenin saw electrification of Russia and Soviet control as defining communism, perhaps Vladimir Putin sees oil and gas as defining post-communist Russia. Subsidized domestic energy prices and hydrocarbon exports underpin the current Russian economy. While this dependence alone might qualify Russia for membership in OPEC, more relevant is whether Russia and OPEC have competing or convergent interests in the oil market. The following analysis by John Grace provides the basis for beginning to understand what position Russia might take should oil prices ever decline to levels that begin to seriously erode its revenues from oil.

Robert Skinner

INTRODUCTION

The ascension of a strong Russian oil industry this decade is the most influential new force in the world oil market since the empowerment of the Organization of Petroleum Exporting Countries (OPEC) in the 1970s. Russia holds more oil resources than any country outside OPEC and vies with Saudi Arabia for world leadership in production and exports (Figure 1). The productive capabilities of Russia's oil industry and the policies of its government clearly move both short- and long-run world oil prices. Russia is at once an ally and opponent of OPEC and stands in the same dichotomous relationship to oil consumers. It is a fulcrum.

Oil and natural gas drive the national economy. Buoyant oil prices after 1999 salvaged Russia from a depression that began before the demise of the USSR. At the same time, the escalating dependence of both the economy and government on oil and gas places the nation's chances for long-run, broad and sustainable economic development at risk. Putting the nation's massive natural resource endowment at the service of its people remains a slippery goal; sought since Russian independence in 1992, but always escaping political grasp.

Yet, the Russians keep trying to get the role of oil right. The structure and function of the industry are at the centre of the national stage. Oil policy both mirrors and enables larger developments in Russian politics. The rise of a more monocratic state under the government of President Vladimir Putin was economically catalysed by oil-driven prosperity. The crackdown on the nation's leading oil producer, Yukos, and its erstwhile chief executive, Mikhail Khodorkovsky, furthered two basic goals of the Putin administration: crushing opposition to its centralization of authority and reversing the privatization of national political power by a small, extraordinarily rich group of men known as the Oligarchs.

Irrespective of their present importance, Russia's oil producers, as all others, operate under the constraints imposed by the geology, technology and the economics of exploration and development. Beyond the natural limitations that shape supply, the Russian oil industry also bears the imprint of engineering decisions made over decades of Soviet management. And since 2003, Russia's oil production possibilities, the character of the industry and the role of oil in the Russian economy also reflect the rising role of state control.

This environment sets the stage for the central conflict examined here. On one side are the natural characteristics and limits of one of the world's largest natural resource bases; on the other are political motivations and the technical and economic mechanisms of its exploitation. This is a contest between oil fields, the location, size, and depth of which determine their economic accessibility and the application of money, technology and human effort to produce them.

That the scene is set in Russia adds considerable complexity. The dynamics of basin depletion are thoroughly mixed with the sea changes that attended the downfall of a Superpower. The Russian oil industry, once insulated from the world market, competition and foreign investment, now must adjust to all of these while recovering from the largest production collapse ever seen. If disarray within the country were not enough, the world oil market that surrounds the new Russian industry has brought prices from less than $10/barrel (bbl) to more than $50/bbl.

Understanding the present and prospective supplies of oil from Russia is intimately tied to not only the geology of its resources, but the history of their development. There is a deep hysteresis in petroleum production that makes future productive capacity dependent on past development decisions. Therefore, the first part of this study is devoted to the evolution of Russia's involvement with oil, which started with its recovery from mud pits on the coast of the Caspian Sea in the nineteenth century.

After revolution terminated the Imperial regime in 1917, the successor Soviet government saw industrialization as the answer to ideological demands and a method for modernizing a resistant rural nation. Energy

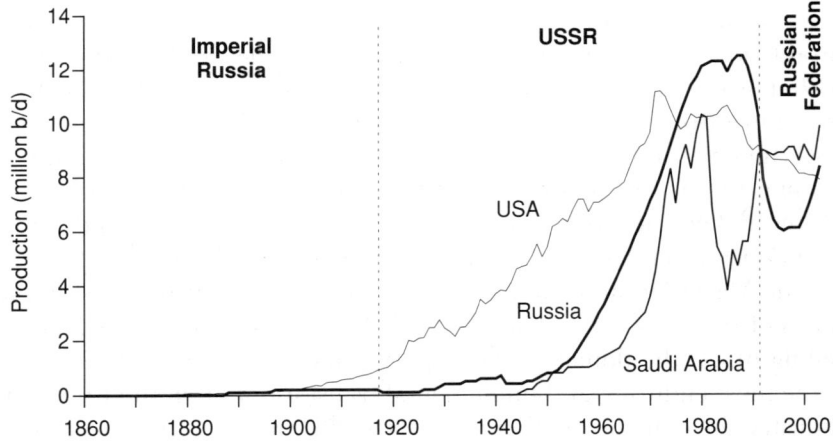

Figure 1: Russian/Soviet, US and Saudi Oil Production[1]

was critical, but initially coal met most of the demand. Russia's big plunge into oil followed the Second World War. It came from a basin that ran between the west flanks of the Ural Mountains and the broad piedmont and plains surrounding the Volga River (Map 1). Volga-Ural oil primed the post-war recovery and the largest economic expansion in Soviet history.

As the Volga-Ural province matured, depletion would have intruded on the USSR had geologists not found vastly more oil and gas on the east side of the Ural Mountains, in West Siberia (Map 1). Starting in the sixties, the new basin ultimately gave the Soviets the world's richest endowment of natural gas and the second greatest volume of recoverable oil. Yet, after West Siberia underwrote the national economy with putatively free energy for another 15 years, inherent inefficiencies and the economics of finite resources brought the industry down.

From the industry's historical development, this analysis turns to the mechanics of the cycle in which the USSR became the world's largest oil producer, its extensive breakdown followed by recovery. What characteristics of its resource base enabled the Soviet Union to produce 12.4 million barrels of oil per day (b/d) and why did output from those same fields crash? What technologies successfully raised output and why could they not sustain it? After hitting bottom, how did the present, striking recovery occur? The rise, and fall, and recuperation of Russian oil production intricately entwine the politics of the Soviet and successor Russian governments with the financial and technical realities of massive engineering operations in the vast Arctic swamp that is West Siberia.

It was on this highly unstable economic and political foundation that the modern, post-Soviet Russian oil industry was formed. State production enterprises became private companies and, in the unruly milieu of the nineties, a large portion of the nation's oil assets fell under the control of a small band of individuals. Russia's first independent government, under President Boris Yeltsin, deserves great credit for leading the nation beyond the dissolution of the USSR. The regime, however, became systemically corrupt. One of the first and largest economic casualties was the loss of the nation's oil assets.

The Yeltsin administration, however, did transform Russia's oil producers from total dependence on state budgets to complete reliance on selling oil on the domestic and export markets for their revenues. This is the most enduring and fundamental transformation in the Russian oil industry since the dissolution of the Soviet Union. It is this institutional innovation that will play the largest role in determining future supplies and the least likely to be reversed.

At the end of the 1990s, forces entirely outside the Russian oil industry's control once more introduced basic economic changes, but this time to producers' advantage. Devaluation of the Russian rouble, kicked off with surprise in August 1998, ignited the transformation. In itself, this converted producing oil in Russia from a money-losing to a profitable enterprise. Then, in 1999, after years of languishing at lows not seen in decades, the world price of oil began a sustained climb to more than four times what it had been before. The financial underpinning of the Russian oil industry moved from feeble to flourishing.

The reduction in costs born of devaluation, and the flush revenues from high world prices, brought a rise of nearly 50 per cent in Russian oil output between 1998 and 2004. The expansion drew on improved performance across all of the nation's fields, but particularly on several large new projects. This mounting dependence on a small number of very large fields makes the structure of supply fragile, exacerbated by the concentration of production under the control of a handful of firms.

As they stand now among their international peers, Russia's major oil companies rank among the top in measures like production and reserves. They are increasingly transparent in their technical and financial operations. This decade has witnessed begrudging improvements in corporate governance and a much better understanding of profitability. But these are still Russian organizations and their corporate strategies weigh some factors differently than is done in Western companies. This includes their relationship to the state, how they view foreign involvement in their industry and how they value natural resources, all of which will also guide the course of Russian oil supply.

Moreover, change is again afoot. A central goal of the Putin administration has been reversal of the chaos of the Yeltsin years. Its pursuit over the last two years has stifled opposition and condensed both political and economic power around the Russian president. In the oil industry, it brought down Russia's largest producer, Yukos. The government has moved to recapture oil assets lost in the nineties and renationalize the natural gas industry.

The Putin administration is not opposed to market economics *per se*, but does not see them as intrinsically beneficial. Markets are potent tools to be used, with strong state guidance, to further the government's national economic strategy. The growing concentration of industry management under state aegis, with all its echoes of the Soviet past, raises a new source of uncertainty on the path of future oil supply.

Yet, as of late 2004, the Russian oil industry has successfully expanded output for six years. Its leading position in world supply seems secure.

The Russian industry and government face a range of technical and political questions in determining, for the next 5 to 15 years, whether oil output will go up or down and how fast. This has ramifications not only domestically, but in its relationship with OPEC and its role in influencing world oil prices. How much Russian oil supply is likely to grow, and whether continued increases are even in the best interest of the nation, are the topics that close this study.

Two practical decisions were made in the development of this study. First, for consistency and because English measurement units are most familiar to English readers, they are used throughout.

Second, the quantification of oil resources is a complex topic, with critically important differences in the standards by which terms like 'reserves' are used in Russia and in the West. Oil quantities in this analysis are almost exclusively quoted using the Soviet standards of reserve analysis, largely held over by the Russian industry. This is known as the $A+B+C_1$ system. It is a highly problematic standard, but extremely useful in providing a consistent measure for gauging and comparing the resources of fields, basins and companies.

However, to allow comparisons between Russian and Western oil companies, and between Russia's resource base and that of other countries, the Western concept of proved, probable and possible reserves is also employed. A comparison of the difference between Soviet/Russian and Western standards of resource and reserve measurement appears in Appendix II.

To the caveats on measurement must be added a warning on time. Russia itself, and its oil industry, are highly dynamic. It has been a constant struggle keeping up with the latest developments over the year during which this study was prepared. To the greatest degree possible, the data and analysis have been made current as of October 2004. However, since this is a fast-moving target, a postscript describing significant last-minute developments has been included.

Notes

1 All sources and technical notes on figures and maps are provided in Appendix I.

CHAPTER 1

THE OPENING OF RUSSIA'S OIL INDUSTRY

Beginnings in Baku

For the hundreds of millions of years oil has been forming in the Earth's crust, some share has always bubbled to the surface. There, it has become a source of attraction and entrapment – first for wildlife and more recently for humans. On the Eurasian landmass, perhaps the most spectacular oil seeps ring the southern rim of the Caspian Sea, particularly on the southwest coast, around the Apsheron Peninsula of Azerbaijan (Map 2).

For centuries, Apsheron seeps supplied illumination and potions for mainly southbound regional trade. Production was in no sense industrial. Oil was skimmed with rags and buckets; some pits were eventually deepened by shovel. Along with the oil comes natural gas, venting through the mud and often igniting – giving a mystical character to the region and Baku, the city that grew among the percolations. From medieval times forward, these pits probably gave up oil at a rate of tens to hundreds of barrels per day.

Azerbaijan spent most of the last millennium as a Turkish, Mongol or Persian vassal. However, in 1723, near the end of his reign, Tsar Peter the Great seized the west coast of the Caspian from Persia. Twelve years later, the Persians got it back. What is now Azerbaijan again fell under Russian control in 1806, formally annexed to the empire by Alexander I in 1813. Yet for the following fifty years, men continued to produce Baku's seeps by hand.

In the 1870s things changed. Liberalization of state production licensing allowed longer lease terms – encouraging investment and drilling for oil. Early wells discovered the first major fields: the Balakhany-Sanbunchi-Ramany complex in 1871 and the Bibi-Eybat field in 1873.[1] Foreign investment and involvement, most prominently done by the Nobel family (of dynamite and Prize fame), catalysed production and spawned local refining of crude oil to kerosene.[2]

In the last quarter of the nineteenth century, kerosene revolutionized illumination, displacing whale oil and competitive liquids in lamps around the world. Because of its much lower cost, kerosene exponentially expanded the market, rolling back darkness in cities and, to a lesser extent, in the countryside. The Russian Empire protected its new industry through tariffs designed to suppress competition by imports of the American monopoly, Standard Oil, already entrenched in Europe.

Critical innovations in transport accompanied advances in production and the introduction of refining. Rather than ship products out in wooden barrels, the Nobels organized a route by tanker across the Caspian from Baku to Astrakhan, up the Volga River by barge and pipeline – then to urban markets by rail. After a short war with the Ottoman Turks in 1877, Russia regained the east coast of the Black Sea. Baku producers launched a second path to market via a system of rail and pipelines across the Caucasus Mountains from Baku to the port of Batumi (Map 2).[3] While also serving the Russian market, the route provided the first true opportunity to export crude oil and petroleum products to Europe, further accelerating development.

Russian production rose from 660 b/d in 1870 to more than 3,000 b/d in 1875 – up to 39,000 b/d in 1885. Between 1898 and 1901, Russia reigned as the world's largest oil producer. At that time, it, and the United States, almost evenly split world production of somewhat more than 500,000 b/d.

Whether *fin de siècle*, the vulnerability of being number one, or decay of the Romanov dynasty, a variety of threats surrounded Russia's leadership in production. In 1896, the Imperial government raised royalty (i.e., tax) rates. In domestic and European markets, aggressive competition from Standard Oil depressed prices and limited profit. The opening years of the twentieth century also presaged the end of Russia's Imperial age. Labour and ethnic trouble in Baku and Batumi, the 1905 Revolution and loss of the Russo-Japanese War arrested domestic demand and oil production tumbled thereafter.

As the industry coped with rising taxes and softened prices, for the first time it faced the impact of resource depletion. Most Apsheron oil came from the two super-giant fields discovered in the 1870s. They contain an estimated ultimate recovery (EUR) now assessed at more than 8 billion barrels.[4] This total volume is enormous, but at both fields most of the oil was deep – beyond the roughly 2,400-foot technologic depth limit of late nineteenth-century wells.[5] Therefore, although only about 1 billion bbls had been produced by 1900, less than 15 per cent of the fields' total resources, the shallow, accessible oil was running out.

The decline spurred new exploration. Some searched in Azerbaijan, but the Russians also widened the geographic base of production. Oil finds spread west along the northern front of the Caucasus Mountains

(Map 2). The most important of the new fields were found in Chechnya, around the city of Groznyy, and further toward the Black Sea, around Maykop. While these discoveries were smaller, and produced less, they dampened the post-1904 decline enough to limp forward until the First World War.

From the Revolution through the Second World War

In 1917, war and revolution finished the Romanov dynasty and oil production crashed. Russia suffered between 1 and 3 million casualties and lost 5,000 industrial establishments in the First World War, substantially reducing demand.[6] On the supply side, the Baku oil fields lost two-thirds of their workforce between 1913 and 1920.[7] Many workers headed off to various armies – some just headed off. The new Soviet government's nationalization of oil in the summer of 1918 was another blow to the industry – particularly its foreign investors. Over the period of the Civil War, from 1918 through 1921, output averaged 81,000 b/d, compared to 206,000 b/d in the last pre-war year, 1913.

In its first four years, the Soviet economic experiment failed miserably. Ruinous organization of both industry and agriculture mired the nation in famine and profound depression. In 1921, Vladimir Lenin, Russia's new leader, pragmatically retreated and introduced the New Economic Policy (NEP). This re-enfranchised some of Russia's small businesses and farms and, significantly for the oil industry, reopened the door for foreign investment.

From the NEP's outset through the early thirties, a wide variety of Western companies re-entered the Russian petroleum market. Some directly operated or served as contractors for field production, refining and transportation. Others became active partners in purchasing Soviet exports and developing downstream relationships in Europe, where the crude oil was refined.

Not until 1928 did the Soviet oil industry regain Russia's 1901 output. Two factors led the recovery.[8] Geographically, the Soviets broadened the production base to include Kazakhstan and Turkmenistan and expanded fields along the Caucasus Mountains.[9] The key, however, was new technology.

In the rush surrounding the first discoveries in Texas at the turn of the century, oil drillers adopted a new technique from water-well drillers called rotary drilling. Russian producers imported it as a vastly superior alternative to nineteenth-century cable-tool drilling. A cable-tool rig drops a heavy pointed metal weight down the hole to break the rock, which is then scooped out. Rotary drilling uses a rock-cutting bit to bore through rock; drilling fluids carry the pulverized rock to the surface. More important than its greater speed and smaller crews, a rotary rig's deeper reach accessed previously unavailable oil.

While rotating bits revolutionized operations underground, at the surface, engineers added the pumps to wells. This not only raised oil faster, but increased recovery. These engineering advances, more than new discoveries, allowed Soviet production to expand in the twenties and thirties.

Economic growth of the young Soviet state steadily raised domestic demand, particularly for transportation fuels. The government also discovered the value of exports. Soviet oil played an escalating role in the European energy balance – accounting for one in seven barrels of West European imports from 1926 to 1935.[10]

As they would again in fifty years, oil export earnings became a vital source of foreign exchange. Having accounted for only 7 per cent of Imperial Russian export earnings immediately before the First World War, by 1932 oil was twice as important, standing second only to timber.[11] Russia's pre-war role as Europe's breadbasket, like millions of peasant farmers themselves, did not survive the Soviet transition.[12]

During the early thirties, Josef Stalin eliminated the last vestiges of the NEP, enlarged rural collectivization and launched the first campaigns of purge and terror. Beyond the enormous human cost, his rule assailed the entire Soviet economy. Oil production rose in the thirties, but more slowly, reaching 622,000 b/d by the Second World War. There was no more innovation in exploration or production; engineers simply squeezed more from the old Azeri and North Caucasus fields.

By the mid-thirties, decelerating production caused the oil industry to miss meeting state plans. The resultant shortages became a bottleneck for the entire Soviet economy. Even oil's share in total Soviet energy consumption fell.[13] Average production costs in the North Caucasus and Azerbaijan were rising as the impact of field depletion overcame the cost savings captured through rotary drilling and pumps.

To reverse these trends, geologists began to explore a new frontier to the northeast – the Volga-Ural basin. Yet a host of factors retarded the shift away from traditional producing areas. Some scientists doubted the prospectivity of the new region. Many feared that costs in such a distant place would exceed those already faced in the south, making the venture a questionable economic gambit. Finally, the Soviet government, for its entire revolutionary ardour, was highly risk-averse.

In June 1941, history once more turned Russia upside down when 175 divisions of German soldiers crossed the western border. In six months, the Wehrmacht blitzed 400–500 miles east into Russia. In the following year, two major German drives targeted Soviet oil. The first pushed directly east to the Volga River to interdict transport routes for Azeri and Central Asian oil. The second thrust was toward Baku and the fields around Groznyy and Maykop that they would encounter on the way.

The Nazis never made it to Baku. Moreover, Soviet forces sabotaged the North Caucasus fields in retreat – denying imperative supplies to the Germans. Still, the 1942 campaign cost the USSR almost one-third of its oil capacity. Although the German drive to the Caspian ultimately failed, gains along the Volga stopped a substantial share of Azeri crude and products still transported along the route established by the Nobels sixty years earlier.

The Red Army turned the tide at Stalingrad, on the banks of the Volga River, in January 1943 and fought steadily westward for the next two and a half years. By the war's end, the USSR had suffered more than 20 million casualties, lost a very large share of its capital base and oil output was down 40 per cent.

Comment

A century ago, as it is today, Russia was a leader in world crude oil production. Very shallow oil in Azeri fields, protectionist tariffs and strong demand for a new product, kerosene, made this happen. Foreign money and management were also central elements, but Baku would have attracted neither had it not been for a billion barrels within 2,400 feet of the surface and Imperial cooperation to exclude American kerosene from the expanding domestic market.

Big success in oil demands big economies of scale. The Baku fields as a source of supply, and the Russian market as a source of demand, were among the greatest in the world. In any such region, the few very largest projects – super-giant fields, pipelines and refineries – dominate the industry. This powerfully encourages both concentration and vertical integration. In Baku, the scale of the leading projects also leveraged the money and management brought by the Nobels, Rothschilds and the top Russian operators.

The Imperial Russian regime allowed a competitive fringe of small producers, refiners and retailers. Yet, from the inception of the modern industry until the Bolshevik Revolution, economic clout remained concentrated in a small number of (disproportionately foreign) hands. Control of transport further distilled power in the industry. While there were many producers and refiners in Baku, the route north into Russia was controlled by the Nobels; export to Europe over the Caucasus required a deal with the company backed by the Rothschilds.

Nationalization and state control under the Soviets was an entirely different arrangement. However, when the Russian industry re-emerged in 1992, it reflected some of its pre-Soviet structure. The state was central, but resources were licensed to private companies. A few very large concerns directed an overwhelming share of production and refining. Transportation is now in state hands, and it is again a principal lever for controlling how much is produced and exported – and by whom.

Some aspects of the industry's organization are, of course, different. The role of foreigners in the present Russian industry is small. In Imperial times, they brought money and technology unavailable in Russia. Today, Russian companies rely on technical experience gained in the Soviet period, record oil prices provide the needed money, and foreign technology (and management, for that matter) can be bought.

Russian production over its first 70 years exposed three fundamental issues reprised in the last two decades: the profit split between producers and the state, the effects of resource depletion and the impact of the political environment on productive capacity.

Since the start, the state has owned the oil below the surface of the Earth. Either government organizations produced it, as in the Soviet period, or companies under state licence found and raised the oil. Liberalization of tsarist licence terms in the 1870s transformed crude production from medieval scavenging into an industrial process. The supply this created coincided with growing demand for a new, widely used product – kerosene. As output skyrocketed over the next three decades, the Russian state angled for an increasing share of the oil wealth.

By 1896, taxes on oil rose to what producers complained of as 'confiscatory' levels.[14] Nevertheless, between 1896 and the peak year of 1901, output rose 68 per cent. As demonstrated in the 1990s, when the cost of delivered oil (including taxes) rises so high relative to price that producers' net income becomes negative, production will decline. Yet the principal causes of the first post-1901 decline were not economic.

If the adversity is limited to prices and costs, established fields and refineries can be maintained in modest decline for years. The capital costs of oil are heavily front-loaded. After wells are sunk, pipelines laid and refineries built, at least for a while, producers need to cover only relatively low marginal costs.

It was depletion and, above all, political instability that collapsed

Russia's first oil peak. These returned as central to the demise of Russian output after 1987, along with a more important role for economics.

Most of the oil from nineteenth-century Baku was produced out of what were later recognized as the shallow reservoirs and seeps of two super-giant fields. These fields alone contained many times the roughly 1 billion barrels produced through the turn of the century. However, within the bounds of extant technology, extracting that first billion largely emptied the shallow, technologically accessible reservoirs. After that point, to restart *growth* required either fundamental advances in production technology and/or big exploration success in a virgin area.

Together, depletion and lower profits should have produced no more than a wobbly plateau or modest decline after the 1901 peak. That is what happened through 1904. But oil production is highly susceptible to a chaotic environment and the political, social and macroeconomic paroxysms of 1905 cost Russia 29 per cent of national output.

After 1905, as the Romanov dynasty stumbled toward the First World War, Russia never regained its previous stability. Output rose for several years after 1905, but again declined. Depletion did not worsen suddenly in the decade between 1905 and 1914 and international oil prices were basically flat. However, in the absence of a stable environment, the industry could not get the traction required to regain the level of production achieved in 1901, never mind growth.

Even more severe was the Bolshevik Revolution and Civil War. Military action swept across the country, the Russian economy was dismembered and Azerbaijan was lost to independence for almost two years. Depletion did not cause the loss of nearly two-thirds of output between 1916, the year before the Revolution, and 1921, when the Civil War ended. The failure of Russia's political, social and economic structure, rather than an adverse relationship between prices and costs, caused the oil industry to crumble. Non-violently, and over a more protracted period, when the national armature shattered again between 1988 and 1995, it created the same effect in the oil industry.

Notes

1   The two fields, particularly the former, were the source of much of the oil found and traditionally produced in the region. Therefore, they were discovered at some distant point in antiquity. What distinguishes the oil recovered from them after their 'official' discovery dates was that production

came from reservoirs that were not accessible from pits on the surface but produced by wells.

2 For a short description of the Nobel story, see Daniel Yergin, *The Prize, The Epic Quest for Oil, Money and Power* (New York: Simon & Schuster, 1991), pp. 57–61. For a fuller history of the development of the Russian industry in the Imperial period, see Marshall I. Goldman, *The Enigma of Soviet Petroleum, Half-Empty or Half-Full?* (London: George Allen & Unwin, 1980), pp. 13–24. Robert W. Tolf, *The Russian Rockefellers: The Saga of the Nobel Family and the Russian Oil Industry*. (Stanford, CA: Hoover Institution Press, 1976) is a book-length treatment of the role of the Nobel family.

3 For a short review of the diplomatic and military history surrounding Russia's southern border in the second half of the nineteenth century, see Nicholas V. Riasanovsky, *A History of Russia*, 5th Edition, (New York: Oxford University Press, 1993), pp. 384–8.

4 The source of the estimated ultimate recovery of the fields is '*International Energy Exploration and Production Database,*' IHS Energy. Data on EUR and reserves provided by IHS report what was carried as the $A+B+C_1$ resources of a field. This concept, and how it differs from the Western concept of oil reserves, is explained in Appendix II.

5 S.P. Maksimov, ed., *Neftyanyye i gazovyye mestorozhdeniya SSSR* [*Oil and Gas Fields of the USSR*], Volume 2, (Moscow: Izdatel'stvo Nedra, 1987), pp. 86 and 88.

6 The number of Russian casualties in the First World War varies by source. However most report numbers in the range of 1 to 3 million. The source of the estimated number of lost industrial establishments is Riasanovsky, *A History of Russia*, op. cit., p. 478.

7 Ya.D. Gurevich, 'Vosstanovitel'nyy period i pervyye pyatletki (1923–40 g.g.)' ['The Period of Reconstruction and the First Five Year Plans (1923–40)'], in V.A. Dinkov, ed., *Neft' SSSR* [*Oil of the USSR*] (Moscow: Izdatel'stvo Nedra, 1987), p. 10.

8 For a description of the new areas put on production and technological advances in the 1920s, see Ibid, pp. 19–23.

9 Production from Groznyy to Maykop went from 26,000 b/d before the war to 74,000 in 1928 and to 172,000 four years later.

10 Goldman, *The Enigma of Soviet Petroleum*, op. cit., p. 26.

11 Ibid., p. 27.

12 During the Civil War, between 2 and 8 million people died.

13 Robert W. Campbell, *The Economics of Soviet Oil and Gas* (Baltimore, MD: The Johns Hopkins University Press, 1968), pp. 121–2.

14 Reportedly the state's share went to 40 per cent. Goldman, *The Enigma of Soviet Petroleum*, op. cit., p. 20.

CHAPTER 2

THE VOLGA-URAL BASIN

The Volga-Ural basin was the first new basin the Soviet regime developed. From the Revolution to the Second World War, they expanded production in the traditional centres and industrialized output in Central Asia. Yet their efforts between the west flank of the Ural Mountains and the middle course of the Volga River pioneered a virgin frontier (Map 3).

The gamble paid off. Under-funded after the initial discoveries in the thirties, and the object of the intense focus of meagre resources during the Second World War, thereafter the basin powered Soviet oil for the next two decades (Figure 2). Today the Volga-Ural basin is no longer the nation's premier producer, but is responsible for nearly a quarter of Russian supply. It is presently a stable, if declining, region favourably situated in the middle of the nation's refining and energy transportation infrastructure.

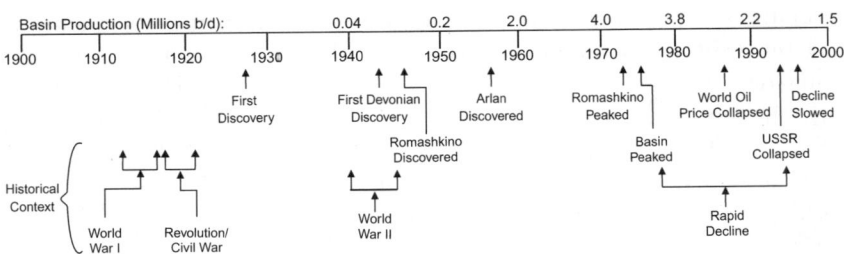

Figure 2: Time Line of the Industrial Development of the Volga-Ural Basin

The Volga-Ural basin exposed the full cycle of Soviet oil development. After the discovery of the super-giant Romashkino field, the organizational power of a command economy concentrated massive resources. That commitment sunk wells and raised oil at an unprecedented rate. Plentiful oil delivered record domestic economic growth and added a strategic new tool to Soviet foreign economic policy.

In a command economy, however, the state giveth and the state taketh. In the mid and late-sixties, planners in Moscow realized the dimensions of oil and gas resources on the east side of the Ural

Mountains in West Siberia. Support for the Volga-Ural basin shrivelled as fast as it had swelled twenty years earlier.

The money did not stop completely. After the Second World War, the refining industry and pipeline infrastructure of the USSR shifted to this new centre, built around the super-giant fields of the Volga-Ural basin. That capital base was fixed and, even under idiosyncratic Soviet economic standards, would not move east. West Siberian oil would be pumped west of the Ural Mountains for refining and export. Therefore, continued funding of Volga-Ural production made sense.

Because of the structure of the Soviet oil industry, however, there was no equivalent tier of independent oil companies to continue aggressive exploitation of the Volga-Ural basin once most of the money, energy and attention shifted to West Siberia. Funding between regions for the Soviet Oil Ministry was a zero-sum game. Moreover, under the Soviet system, the large producing organizations in the Volga-Ural basin did not have access to the windfall they would have enjoyed had they directly sold output at record world oil prices in the mid and late-seventies.

Instead, as Moscow moved the focus of production east, budgets crashed to the point where Volga-Ural producers were themselves ignominiously assigned supplemental geographic areas of operation in West Siberia. Production fell hard, picking up speed until the end of the eighties, when a massive campaign to maintain the Soviet Union's peak oil production temporarily refinanced activities in the basin, just after world prices had crashed!

In the chaos of the early nineties, the output breakdown in the Volga-Ural basin largely mirrored the nation as a whole; precipitous losses were arrested in the middle of the decade.

Since the mid-nineties, the area between the Ural Mountains and the middle course of the Volga River has teased and disappointed. More joint ventures between Western companies and Russian producing and exploration organizations took root there than in any other part of the country. The same is true for establishment of independent Russian oil companies after 1991.

Some of this innovation was the hunger of the region's industry, reflecting two decades of a strict financial diet. Some was the relative insulation provided by the two dominant, ethnically-based local administrations: Tartarstan and Bashkortostan. There was also an attitude engrained in Moscow – which survived the demise of the USSR – that the crown jewels were in West Siberia, so central authorities were more permissive about what happened elsewhere.

The last six to seven years have witnessed a modest revitalization.

The largest producing organizations have not mounted big recoveries, but the medium fields and smaller organizations have sharply raised their contributions to production. Working in the other direction, starting in 1999, some of Russia's largest companies, most notably Lukoil, began sweeping up many of the small firms and projects.

Because of the proximities of refining, pipelines and markets, the Volga-Ural basin enjoys standing cost advantages. With these conditions, more and smaller fields can be profitably produced, and there is a large inventory of discovered, but undeveloped, fields in the basin. Even more than in West Siberia, the future of oil output from the Volga-Ural basin is a function of industry structure.

Along one path is attachment to the region's two dominant producers – Tatneft and Bashneft, which are in turn attached to the basin's two biggest fields, Romashkino and Arlan. On another path is development of scores of smaller fields and medium projects at the bigger fields undertaken by a variety of firms and under various structures. The evolution of the local industry, since the first discoveries sixty years ago, will set the bounds of how that process goes forward.

Exploration

In 1929, on the western edge of the Ural Mountains, a drilling crew looking for potassium salts instead struck oil. The discovery in the forest at Chusovskiye Gorodki confirmed the long-suspected presence of oil and gas in the Volga-Ural basin (Map 3). From tar pits on the surface in the central and northern basin, to exploding peasant outhouses in the south, there was plenty of evidence at the Earth's surface that hydrocarbons had accumulated beneath it.[1]

Nine years earlier, I.M. Gubkin, the 'father' of Soviet petroleum geology, suggested directly to Lenin that the west flank of the Ural Mountains held great promise for oil.[2] Gubkin was ignored. The little exploration that did follow the Chusovskiye Gorodki discovery established around ten fields. All the oil was in reservoirs less than 3,000 feet deep. No one discovery was very big but they were distributed so widely over the basin that they mapped an extensive hydrocarbon system.

Yet what Moscow saw were small fields located hundreds of miles from refineries and industry. Planners kept the investment needed for aggressive exploration of the new basin concentrated instead in the North Caucasus and Azerbaijan.[3] This was a conservative course, although one steered in the face of steadily rising costs for delivered fuel from those traditional producing areas.[4]

The German invasion changed everything. To cope with the loss of the North Caucasus and reduced flows from both Azerbaijan and Central Asia, wartime efforts focused almost exclusively on expanding production from the Volga-Ural basin.[5] Even if initial discoveries there were small, far more importantly, the region was safe – 500 miles east of the fighting.

By the end of the war, basin production reached 55,000 b/d, only 50 per cent higher than in 1940. Yet it was a major wartime accomplishment and critically important to the military effort. Moreover, because national production had fallen so sharply over the war years, the 18,000 b/d addition itself represented 5 per cent of Soviet output in 1945.

From a geologic viewpoint, the basin's big break occurred in the middle of wartime operations. Drillers found shallow (Carboniferous) oil at the Tuymazinskoye field in 1937, although none of the wells tested deeper strata (Map 3).[6] In 1941, geologists proposed that an 'exploration tail' be added to a production well to be drilled at the field. This is deepening a well beyond its primary production target to test for oil in a deeper reservoir. The exploration tail was not pursued and engineers continued drilling only shallow wells. When they finally tapped the deeper Devonian at Tuymazinskoye three years later, it turned the Volga-Ural basin from a middling contributor to Soviet supply into a world-class oil province.[7]

The success in the deep Devonian strata forced geologists to rethink their exploration strategy. Probably one of many prospects initially overlooked because of its depth was only 40 miles to the west of Tuymazinskoye; an exploration target seismically mapped in 1934, but never drilled. With a new view toward the potential of Devonian rocks, in 1948 the engineers drilled deep. In discovering Romashkino, they found a field that was not only the richest one in the basin, but was then the largest oil discovery in the world.

With Romashkino to anchor production, the Volga-Ural basin finally attracted the financial, political and scientific backing to explore both in the prolific structural core of the basin and in other less intensely prospective areas. In the ten years following the Second World War, scores of fields containing nearly half of the basin's oil were added to Soviet reserves. The majority of successes were in the zone from the southern Tatar Arch through the Birsk Saddle to the Perm-Bashkir Arch – most of the oil was in Devonian rocks.[8]

Drillers located more oil in the Volga-Ural basin through the mid-1950s than had been discovered in all the fields found in the country before. But as it happens in nearly all basins, seismic techniques located the largest, most structurally obvious exploration targets first. Therefore, the early discoveries in each part of the basin were the very largest fields in those trends.

The downside of finding the largest fields first is that, after the initial flush, the sizes of subsequent discoveries drop exponentially (Figure 3). This did not result from bad management nor was it a symptom of Soviet command-economy rigidity. It arises in all basins from the interplay of two empirical characteristics of hydrocarbon exploration.

First, in a basin, the distribution of the discovered field sizes (as measured by their recoverable oil and gas) is lognormal.[9] That is, most of the resources are concentrated in a few extremely large fields and the rest is divided between a very large number of small fields. Second, since field area is also lognormally distributed, even random drilling yields the largest fields early in the exploratory process.[10] The more efficient exploration, the greater is the likelihood that the very largest fields will be discovered at the outset.[11]

Figure 3 shows the size of new discoveries over time for the basin's richest structural provinces: the southern Tatar Arch, Birsk Saddle and Perm-Bashkir Arch. Over the last fifty years in the first two areas, the average size of new discoveries fell by half every eight to nine years. On the Perm-Bashkir Arch, the sizes of new fields halved every five years. The scatter in the chart shows that these are high-variance relationships.[12] Therefore, although *average* field size fell dramatically, around

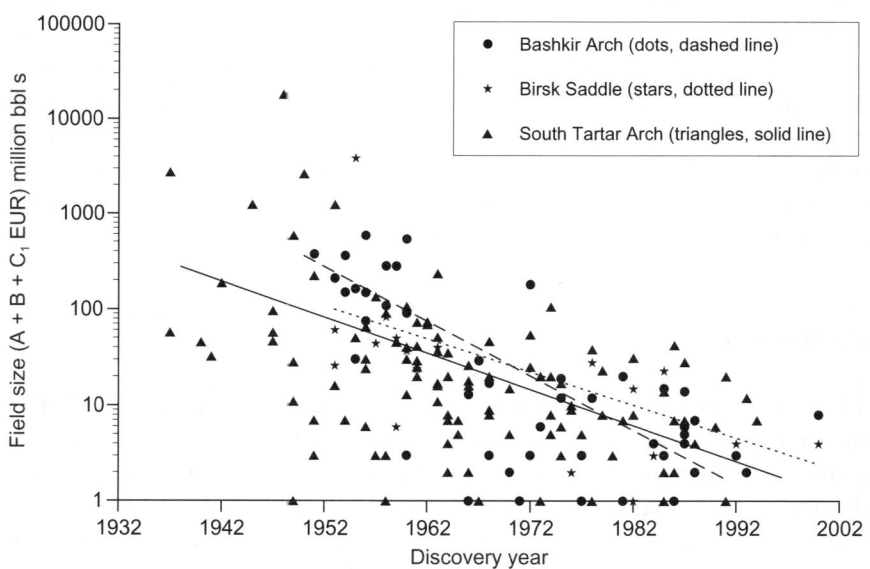

Figure 3: Relationship between Oil Discovery Size and Discovery Date, Volga-Ural Basin

that declining average, the range of discovery sizes for any one year was very wide (although the variance also dropped over time).[13]

As a result of these trends, a few super-giant fields – reliant mainly on Devonian reserves – dominated the basin's resource base. Following these very largest discoveries, there was a second generation of smaller but still major producers. They were the largest fields in the sub-basins and plays established outside the structural core of the basin and/or in strata other than the Devonian.[14] The fields in subordinate plays were smaller and contain much less oil than those with reservoirs in Devonian rocks.

Exploration over the past five decades produced one more generation of discoveries. Some large fields and dozens of medium ones populated the third generation. However, it is mainly composed of hundreds of small fields. While tiny compared to Romashkino or Arlan, it was these smallest fields that helped staunch the sharp decline in production that ended in the mid-nineties (see below and Figure 4).

From an exploration standpoint, the Volga-Ural basin is now highly mature. Since 1960, geologists have found only two fields with more than a billion barrels of recoverable oil.[15] Before 1960, there were seven, with several over 2 billion barrels and the largest, Romashkino, at about 17 billion bbls.

The small discoveries that have dominated exploration results over the last thirty years, despite their very large numbers, are too small to actually reverse the basin's production decline. However, it will be the industry's success in developing medium and small fields that ultimately moderates the rate of decline in basin production. This change in mix from basin output dependent on giant fields to a growing role for medium and small fields is the hallmark of high exploration maturity – meaning the basin does not have much undiscovered oil left to give.

Production

The discovery of the Devonian reservoirs at Tuymazinskoye in 1944 focused the Soviet oil industry and triggered twenty-five years of blistering growth in output. The very largest fields fuelled the first two decades of annual increases (Figure 4). Tuymazinskoye led off, but was soon overtaken by Romashkino (see Box 1 on page 22). Several other super-giant fields emerged in the 1950s to carry the basin to its peak in 1976.

A blend of geologic and technologic factors drove the juggernaut.

Above all, the Volga-Ural basin is, geologically, very prolific. Moreover, once geologists unlocked the roles played by broad structural traps and Devonian reservoirs, exploration was efficient. By the time the basin peaked in the seventies, almost 50 per cent of the oil came from the five largest fields (Figure 4). This allowed the Soviets to concentrate their resources and achieve economies of scale that would have eluded them with a smaller set of fields.[16]

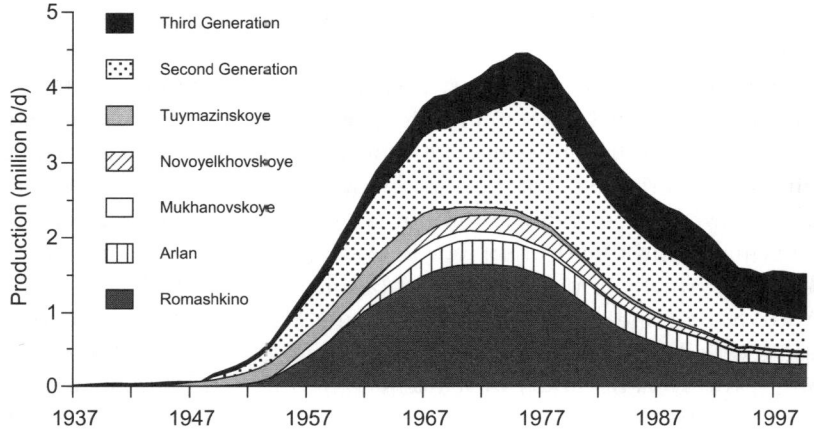

Figure 4: Oil Production from the Volga-Ural Basin by Field Generation

Favourable geology, however, was only half the story. The other half was manmade; namely, the application of so-called 'enabling technologies'. The prevailing drilling method in Azerbaijan and the North Caucasus was rotary, the mechanics of which are fairly simple. A powerful motor on a rig at the surface rotates a steel pipe (drill string) that extends from the surface to the bottom of the well. A rock-cutting bit at the end of the drill string bores through the rock. Rotary drilling has been the leading technology in the West since its introduction at the beginning of the twentieth century.

The early drilling targets in Azerbaijan and the North Caucasus were relatively shallow (< 3,000 feet) and the rocks fairly soft. Therefore, the torque required to rotate the drill string, and turn the bit never grew too high. In this situation, the quality of steel used in Soviet drill strings was sufficiently strong to reach most target depths.

In the Volga-Ural basin, however, particularly after recognition of the enormous potential of the deeper Devonian strata, drilling targets were further below the Earth's surface. Moreover, the older, more lithified rock of the Volga-Ural basin was harder. This required higher drilling torque, which in turn demanded superior strength drill-string steel. The Soviet steel industry was basically unable to provide high-strength drill string in volumes necessary to develop the basin.

Engineers responded with turbo drilling, which does not depend on rotating the drill string.[17] Instead, immediately above the bit, they placed a turbo drilling motor, which itself did the work of turning the bit. This obviated the necessity of twisting the pipe and thereby reduced the required quality of steel.

Turbo drilling radically increased the productivity. Combined with the growing number of rigs available, the total number of feet of development drilling conducted per year nationwide jumped from 1.9 million feet in 1946 to 7.1 million feet by 1950 and 12.1 million feet by 1960.[18] Turbo drilling is not without its engineering and economic liabilities.[19] Nevertheless, without this innovation, the Soviets would have never achieved the increase in output seen between its introduction at the Tuymazinskoye field in 1947 and the late sixties when the rate of production growth in the Volga-Ural basin faded.

A second engineering advance was water flood. The initial natural pressure on oil and gas in reservoirs thousands of feet below the surface is progressively depleted in development by the penetration of wells. Eventually, oil flows more slowly, then not at all. One response is to install pumps. An alternative is to drill more wells on an ever-tighter grid, reducing the distance between the oil and the surface, thereby dropping the reservoir energy required for production. However, both of these approaches, particularly the latter, are very capital-intensive.

Finally, there is water flood. As oil and gas occupy pore space at the top of a reservoir underlain by rock saturated with water, injecting more water from below pushes the oil above toward the wells. The first water flood was launched at Tuymazinskoye the year after the first turbo drilling.[20]

An optimally managed water flood not only maintains higher flow rates, but expels more oil than either natural pressure or pumping. With its introduction, average Soviet producing well productivity went from about 40 b/d in 1950 to nearly 400 b/d ten years later.[21] Geologically superior reservoirs in the Volga-Ural basin, compared to the fields of the North Caucasus and Azerbaijan, generated some of this gain. Most, however, was due to water flood.

The process, however, is not free. Water injection wells must be drilled and tremendous volumes of water must be pumped into the reservoirs and separated from oil after production. Nevertheless, these expenses were small compared to the short-run benefit of maintaining high flow rates and deferring the capital costs of in-fill drilling.

Box 1

The Romashkino Field – Anchor of the Volga-Ural Basin

Soviet historians saw industrial successes in grand and heroic terms. In the case of the Romashkino field, the superlatives were actually apt. The field's 17 billion barrels not only made it the world's largest field when discovered, its two decades of production growth largely fuelled the Soviet economy through its greatest expansion. It established the potential of the Volga-Ural basin and its geologic structure pointed drillers to hundreds of related discoveries, containing billions of barrels of oil.

The field is a roughly circular field, about 35 miles in diameter, centred around a major basement uplift, the Almatyevsk High, on the middle of the southern Tatar Arch (Map 5). Although the structure is large, except on its western edge, it is a broad, gentle uplift. The oil is trapped throughout 6,500 feet of porous interbedded sandstones and limestones (see Figure 5, in colour section).

The shallowest hydrocarbons (offset to the west of the field proper) are in Permian strata, known as the Melekess tar sands (see the Appendix to this Chapter). These highly viscous, heavy oil accumulations are presently uneconomic to produce. Lighter oil from deeper reservoirs leaked over geologic time to charge these shallow reservoirs. The Melekess accumulations are close enough to the Earth's surface that ground water, and the bacteria that live in it, invaded the reservoirs. This degraded the oil, increasing its viscosity. The resistance of the oil to flow is exacerbated by the very low temperatures of the shallow Melekess rocks. While they are not an economic source of production today, future technology may unlock some share of these very large resources.[22]

Below the Permian, there are over 200 Carboniferous and Devonian reservoirs at Romashkino.[23] The shallowest of these (in the Carboniferous) also show some degradation, holding heavier oil (26° API gravity).[24] Almost all of Romashkino's oil, however, is below the Carboniferous, in Devonian reservoirs, contained principally in the sandstones of the Pashiy Formation (Map 4 and Figure 5).

While the Pashiy reservoirs are not simple and homogeneous, they are extensive and have generally high porosity and permeability. The oil is light (32° API gravity), but, like most Volga-Ural basin crude, it is relatively high in sulphur (1.5 per cent).[25] The reservoirs are deep enough to escape both the cold and ground water that degraded the oil of shallower horizons. At its peak, Romashkino, depending almost entirely on the Pashiy reservoirs, produced over 1.5 million b/d (Figure 6).

Given the expansive area of the field, and the large number of reservoirs, development has required nearly 20,000 wells. Although both turbo drilling and water flood were demonstrated first at the neighbouring Tuymazinskoye field, they received their most intensive applications at Romashkino. The water floods at Romashkino were largely responsible for the high sustained rate of growth in the field for over twenty years. They also caused water cut at the field to increase at only a slightly slower rate than that of oil production, although it has plateaued in the past fifteen years (Figure 6).

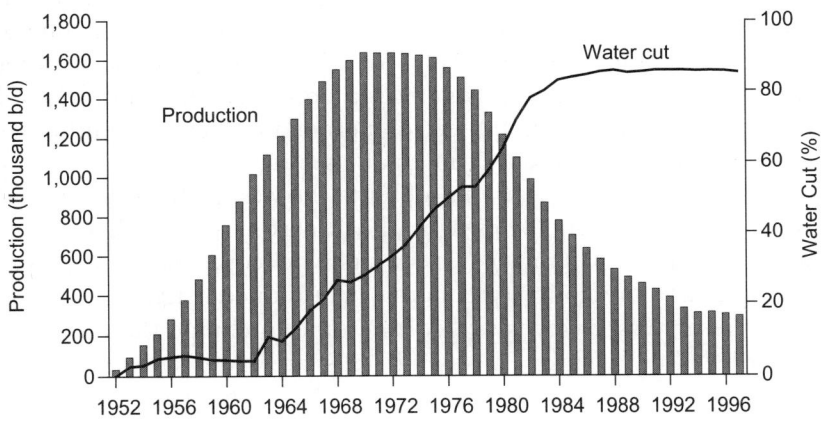

Figure 6: Romashkino Field Oil Production and Water Cut

The Romashkino field is the crown jewel of Tatneft, the main oil-producing company in the Tatar Republic (Tatarstan). Tatneft is the integrated successor of the Soviet producing association of the same name. Its shares are traded on the Russian stock exchange, but its largest single shareholder is the Tatar government. Romashkino is at the centre of the economy of Tatarstan.

The field presently contributes about 60 per cent of Tatneft's output (equal to half of Tatarstan's production) and accounts for slightly less than half of its producing wells. Production has been flat since the mid-nineties. Neither the field, nor the company, participated in the national rally in output after 1998. Tatneft's inability to raise output at Romashkino (or at its other fields) largely reflects the basin-wide problem of escalating production costs in very large, mature fields.

> Over the past five years, Tatneft has reported one of the fastest rates of cost increases in the country. The company has used this to lobby for federal taxation that provides tax credits for producing high-cost fields. Although as much political strategy as analysis, Tatneft's Deputy Director General suggested in 2004 that if they did not get relief, the field would be unprofitable by 2010.[26]
>
> While water cut is high and well productivity is low, Romashkino is so large, and geologically complex, that it is likely to benefit from technologies applied in similar fields in the West. Those with the greatest impact will be long horizontal completions, reservoir fracturing, geologic and geophysical field studies to identify by-passed reservoirs, and higher efficiency pumps and oil-water separation units.
>
> Romashkino, like most Volga-Ural basin fields, will eventually face a price discount on its oil because of its sulphur content. Nevertheless, it is located in the middle of the Russian refining and oil transportation complexes. It could be shut down in the next ten years by costs or a return to low world prices. However, the US experience with very old, super-giant fields with hundreds of reservoirs, like Romashkino, is that they seem to produce almost forever. These highly mature super-giants are often sold (sometimes in pieces) to smaller companies with lower cost structures.

In even the best-managed flood, the water ultimately wins. Water cut inexorably rises and the diminishing volume of oil eventually does not justify the cost of raising and separating the water that comes with it. Figure 6 shows the relationship between oil production and average water cut at Romashkino. Between eight and nine barrels of water are raised in the field's wells for every barrel of oil recovered today. Romashkino's experience broadly represents most of the basin's large fields.

The extreme reliance on the very largest fields in the Volga-Ural basin bore its own costs. Romashkino's decline, which started at a rate normal for a field its size (1−3 per cent annually) rapidly accelerated to four times that level. This meant that, in the mid-seventies, the field started losing 80,000 to over 100,000 b/d of capacity a year. Unless this loss was covered by equal or greater increase in annual production from new fields, the basin's total production would inevitably fall. For a few years, other giants and the largest second generation fields covered the loss, but that could not continue.

By the mid-seventies, the campaign to develop West Siberia was in full swing. The Soviet Ministry of Oil massively diverted resources from the Volga-Ural basin eastward to the new frontier. There was no money to develop the hundreds of medium and small fields. Therefore, there was no cushion of offsetting production when the output of the handful of super-giants, found in the forties and fifties, began rapid declines. Also for want of budget, at the largest fields, further measures (within Soviet technologic reach) to arrest the sharp declines were abandoned. By 1977, three decades of climbing production from the Volga-Ural basin were over.

In the eighties, the basin lost capacity at 100,000 to 200,000 b/d annually. Occasional gasps of money and effort slowed the decline in some years (for instance at the end of the eighties). Yet through the end of the Soviet period in 1991, Volga-Ural output fell 5 per cent annually.

But it got even worse. When Moscow's support disappeared in the first few years of the Russian independence, production plummeted. The basin marked the first year of Russian independence, 1992, with a 6 per cent loss, 10 per cent for the second and 9 per cent for the third. In 1995, however, the situation stabilized. The region's two major producers, Tatneft and Bashneft staunched the haemorrhages at Romashkino and Arlan respectively.

After the mid-nineties, the basin's performance has nourished hope for future success. It has been the medium-sized fields of the third generation of discoveries that fuelled the flattening of Volga-Ural decline (Figure 4). This cohort of discoveries has $A+B+C_1$ EUR of less than 100 million bbls. While 100 million bbls is a large oil accumulation, few fields in this group are that size. The average size in this group of discoveries is 15 million bbls and the median is only 7 million bbls, a very small field by world standards. If this trend can be nurtured, it will substantially soften the long-run rate of decline in the basin.

Comment

Soviet development of the Volga-Ural basin marked one of the regime's largest industrial undertakings. Its accomplishment highlighted a rare strength of a command economy – quick muster and application of resources to a huge task. It also exposed deep faults. Prominent among them was the untempered pursuit of ever greater physical production, irrespective of cost. Ends justify means.

However obtained, the region's oil fuelled the USSR's recovery from the Second World War. It supplied the greatest macroeconomic expansion in Soviet history. Without it, the economic boost of the war reconstruction might well have died with Stalin in the early fifties. At the same time, oil became central to Soviet imperial policy. The economies of the USSR's newly won constellation of East European client states were turned to petroleum and fed by the Volga-Ural basin.

When the size of West Siberian oil discoveries became obvious in the mid and late sixties, economic support for the Volga-Ural basin quickly folded. Very large production organizations dominated in the command economy. There was no second tier of independent companies to exploit extension, or enhanced recovery opportunities, which prolong the lives of the biggest fields or develop smaller ones. Likewise, Moscow did not allow the industry to directly ride the wave of skyrocketing world prices. So, as state funding flowed east of the Urals, even the basin's large producers had no financial alternatives.

From a national command perspective, of course, it made sense to redirect a rig drilling 20-million bbl exploration targets along the Volga River to developing 800-million bbl fields along the Ob River in West Siberia. Yet, it was the inflexibility of the Soviet structure that made it an 'either/or' proposition. Physical output goals at any cost, and rigid attachment to a large centralized industrial structure made the basin's precipitous decline between its peak, and the mid-nineties, almost inevitable.

The post-peak supply of oil from any basin is, by definition, totally a function of its rate of decline. The Western Canadian sedimentary basin in Alberta and Saskatchewan lost oil production after its 1973 peak at an average of 1.1 per cent annually. In contrast, in the Volga-Ural basin, from its 1976 peak through the break-up of the USSR, production fell at 5 per cent annually. A basin declining at 1.1 per cent loses half its output every sixty years; decline at 5 per cent halves every fourteen years. Many factors separate performance between these two areas, but perhaps none more than the firm-size structures of their industries.

The trend in the Volga-Ural basin since the mid-nineties is tantalizing. Stunning losses after Russian independence turned into stable production in the second half of that decade. Capping the freefall at the very largest fields was critical. But, mainly growth in output from the medium and small fields flattened the decline. With so much production and transportation infrastructure in place at this point in time, especially at present (2004) prices, new medium and even small fields in the Volga-Ural basin can be very profitable to develop.

The crucial issue for the province is how the structure of the industry will evolve. The Volga-Ural basin spawned more Russian independent oil companies and joint ventures with foreigners in the nineties than any other part of the country. The region became an incubator for entrepreneurs until about 1998. This could explain why the medium/small-field sector of the industry has contributed the increment of oil that stabilized basin production.

However, starting in 1999, a wave of consolidation, led by Lukoil, washed across the basin. Where there were dozens of small domestic and mixed domestic/foreign oil and gas production firms in the basin in 1998, by 2003, the amount of oil produced by these independents shrank dramatically.

The economics of those selling small firms and projects are clear. They 'flipped' deals to large companies and happily took whatever profit came out. The question is what happens to these projects now in the hands of extremely large corporations, whose stated focus is not little fields and enhanced recovery projects in the Volga-Ural basin. In the West, for example, large companies and small fields do not mix; precisely the reverse restructuring has occurred – large firms have sold out to smaller, lower cost firms.

If Lukoil follows the prevailing model of Western majors, it will eventually close many of these small projects. If it tries to sell some projects, the type of small firm that would pick them up may be absent from the market place, causing even more to shut down. Divesting small fields may well maximize the value for shareholders of major companies like Lukoil. But, it may also eliminate production from many of the smaller fields most likely to retard the basin's decline.

The presence of extensive production and transportation infrastructure in the Volga-Ural basin, and its much shorter distance to domestic and export markets, should make the basin a haven for small, but profitable, projects. The course is not entirely smooth. Volga-Ural basin oil is relatively high in sulphur and will eventually trade at a discount, reflecting that characteristic. The basin has also seen increases in production costs since 2001. Because of the maturity of the basin, this trend will be hard to reverse, although new fields, with low initial water cuts and higher well flow rates, may escape most of this burden.

Although small companies have come and gone in the basin, it remains the domain of Tatneft, and Bashneft. If the trend of federal and local policy opposes developing small companies for small fields, it is the re-engineering of these largely unreformed Soviet-era structures that will make the difference between a slow decline for the basin or a faster demise.

Appendix : Volga-Ural Basin Geology

The Volga-Ural basin is a very large and geologically complex feature. It formed over the course of more than 200 million years (Figure 7). A series of broad tectonic ridges divide the basin laterally, although most major events in its evolution are common to all areas. Vertically, there were four major sedimentary (first-order) cycles of deposition. Hydrocarbons have been found in all of them, although the bulk of conventional oil resources are confined to the earliest.

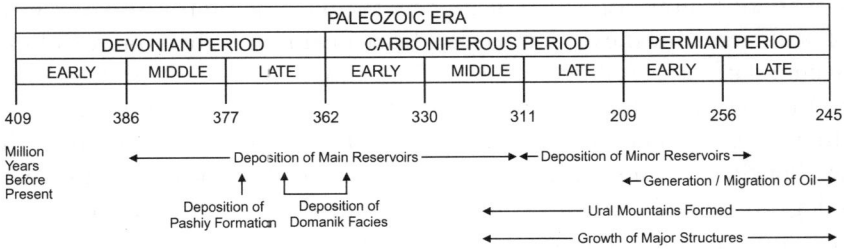

Figure 7: Time Line of the Geologic Development of the Volga-Ural Basin

Geologically, the Volga-Ural basin is much older than either the North Caucasus or the South Caspian basin, which includes Azerbaijan. The region began as the eastern coast of a large tectonic plate called Baltica, which included most of the present-day European continent.[27] The Ural Mountains were absent; in their place was a broad eastern ocean.[28] Moreover, rather than occupying its present chilly latitudes, the region was far closer to the equator – making the eastern ocean warm.

As Baltica drifted, its eastern margin impinged on several large fragments of crust that presaged later, much larger collisions. Erosion of the continental core to the west covered large parts of the basin with sheets of sand. In this dynamic environment, seas from the eastern ocean encroached inland and receded, reworking and redistributing much of the sediments. The sandstones deposited over this first major cycle of sedimentation formed hundreds of reservoirs that now contain the largest share of oil and gas found in the Volga-Ural basin. The most prolific is the Late Devonian Pashiy Formation.

During the Late Devonian, warm interfingered seas along Baltica's eastern coast produced abundant marine biota forming the source of most of the region's oil and gas, the Domanik facies.[29] The Domanik facies are a combination of fine-grain silts, clays and some marls, high in organic carbon (up to 5 per cent) deposited in restricted, shallow water environments. As water depth continued to drop, on regional highs, carbonate reefs and related biologic facies developed.

Map 5 shows two of the fundamental relationships that shaped the distribution of oil and gas fields found in the Volga-Ural basin. First is the distribution of the Domanik's organic-rich, fine-grain source rocks that created most of the basin's oil (diagonal red lines). Specifically, the map outlines that area where the unit's total organic carbon (TOC) exceeds 1 per cent.[30] Second, overlaid on the source rock distribution, is the extent of Devonian sandstones with thickness greater than 320 feet (dark yellow stipple). Within this region, potential reservoirs were of sufficient thickness, porosity and permeability to host large-volume accumulations of oil.[31]

In Map 5, the intersection of the areas of source and reservoir holds the highest chances for finding oil fields. Even better – this is where the *largest* fields are most likely to be found. The fields, shown in Map 5 with a legend reflecting their estimated oil and gas resources, confirms the spatial correlation between optimal source and reservoir rocks and the basin's largest discoveries, including the super-giant Romashkino field.

The second major cycle of deposition lasted through most of the Carboniferous Period. The productive section is principally in the lower part of the unit. In the case of the basin's second largest field, Arlan (and others in this section), drapes on underlying reefs, or other carbonate build-ups from the Devonian cycle, formed the traps. Most sandstone reservoirs are not extensively continuous and rock quality is variable. Most of these accumulations are sealed by the basal portion of thick, basinwide Lower-Middle Carboniferous carbonate rocks. In the shallower part of that unit, limestones are less dense, and often dolomitized, producing a secondary set of reservoirs, usually at fields with deeper production.

Considering the Volga-Ural basin as a whole, the final two first-order cycles contain only a small fraction of the total hydrocarbon endowment.[32] At the end of the Carboniferous and into the Early Permian, the Siberian plate, approaching from the east and the Kazakh plate, coming from the southeast, collided with Baltica. The collision produced compression along Baltica's eastern margin – raising the Ural Mountains. Orogeny and erosion usually go hand in hand; in this case, a massive load of new sediments shed off the west flank of the Urals into the basin. The process was episodic. Sometimes shallow seas covered particular locales; later these areas were uplifted and became dry land – only to be submersed again.

The thick wedge of Uralian sandstones and shales pushed the

Devonian source rocks deeper, exposing them to the heat required to transform buried marine ooze into oil and gas. The orogeny also caused compression to the west of the mountains, creating uplifts and down warps within the sedimentary cover throughout the Volga-Ural basin (Map 6). In the subsurface, these structures focused migrating oil and gas and concentrated them into traps.

The most important of these large uplifts was the Tatar Arch, located in the centre of the basin (Map 6). The Tatar Arch has persisted for hundreds of millions of years and remains a hilly region today. The next most important structure is the Perm-Bashkir Arch, 180 miles to the northeast. Between these two highs lies the Birsk Saddle, shaped as its name implies, with the front high of the saddle leading up to the Perm-Bashkir Arch and the back on the northeast flank of the southern Tatar Arch.

These three features, besides standing high and attracting oil, occupy most of the propitious intersection in Map 5 of the major oil sources and reservoirs of the Volga-Ural basin. Therefore, while this region only covers about 15 per cent of the total basin area, it contains 60 per cent of the discovered oil.

With the reduction of the Uralian orogeny in the Permian Period, and its cessation in the Triassic, the basin's geologic development closed (Figure 7). Some oil and gas, generated in older source rocks migrated up to shallow Permian sandstones, but most of it remained in the deeper strata. It is mainly Permian rocks that cover the Earth's surface across the basin today.[33]

Notes

1 Over what is now the super-giant Orenburg gas field, outhouses sporadically blew up as users' lanterns ignited the slowly accumulating natural gas within them. As it occurs in nature, natural gas has no odour. Therefore, there was no obvious warning that gas had gathered in a structure before it exploded.
2 For a review of the role of I.M. Gubkin in predicting and encouraging exploration of the Volga-Ural basin, see A.V. Valikhanov, 'I.M. Gubkin i razvitiye neftyanoy promyshlennosti Tatarii,' ['I.M. Gubkin and the Development of the Oil Industry of the Tatar Republic'] in *Gubkinskiye Chteniya – K 100 Letiyu so Dnya Rozhdeniya* [*Gubkin Readings – In Honor of the 100th Anniversary of His Birth*] (Moscow: Nedra, 1972), pp. 33–9.
3 In addition to bureaucratic resistance, most geologists at the time believed that the habitat of oil was limited to intermountain and foreland basins and did not include the type of platform setting that covers the main portion

of the Volga-Ural basin (Gregory F. Ulmishek, personal communication, 2004).
4 See Campbell, *The Economics of Soviet Oil and Gas*, op. cit., pp. 121–2 for a discussion of Soviet decision making in the allocation of investments between regions before the Second World War.
5 For the full Soviet description of the oil industry during the Second World War, see A.D. Budkov and L.A. Budkov, 'Gody ispytanii (1941–1945 g.g.)' ['Years of Testing (1941–1945)' in Dinkov, *Oil of the USSR*, op. cit., pp. 31–60.
6 For a short overview of the geologic development of the basin, see the appendix to this chapter.
7 Campbell, *The Economics of Soviet Oil and Gas*, op. cit., p. 128. In relaying this story, Campbell, whose analysis is almost ubiquitously informed by a very good technical understanding of oil and gas operations, blames the failure to deepen the original well on the deep-seated risk aversion often exhibited by Soviet managers. This doubtlessly played a role. However, geologists proposing exploration tails on production wells – only to have them vetoed by the engineering department – is a constant feature in Western oil companies too. Field development is run by engineers, very few of whom willingly gamble budget on new exploration concepts. Geologists are rich in these concepts and highly motivated to spend engineering budget to test them.
8 In what was perhaps more scientifically impressive than his original recommendations on the basin as a whole in 1932, twelve years before the discovery of Devonian oil at Tuymazinskoye, Gubkin proposed that the principal hydrocarbon resources of the basin would be found in that part of the Devonian strata where most of the largest accumulations were eventually discovered. A.V. Valikhanov, in *Gubkin Readings*, op. cit., p. 35.
9 The exact mathematical form of basin-level and play-level hydrocarbon accumulation size-frequency distributions in *nature* is more complex and beyond the bounds of this study. However, the distribution of *discovered fields* has been shown in nearly all basins and plays of the world to be lognormal (see Appendix II).
10 Field area is highly correlated with size as measured by estimated ultimate recovery (EUR) of oil and gas; therefore, because EUR is lognormal, field area is as well.
11 In a 'perfectly efficient' exploration process, fields are discovered in strictly descending order of size: the largest field is found first, second largest second and so on. This has never been actually observed.
12 The high variance in the relationship between field size and discovery order is also reflected in the low R^2s in the regression analysis reported in Appendix I.
13 These relationships are repeated in hydrocarbon-bearing provinces worldwide. What changes between basins (and the plays within them) are the slopes of the regression lines and the variances surrounding them (Figure 3).

14 A 'play' is a collection of discovered and undiscovered oil and gas fields that share common reservoirs, hydrocarbon sources and trapping mechanisms. Generally, fields of a single play adhere to a coherent statistical distribution of field sizes and numbers, such as the lognormal distribution. For example, the basin's largest field, Romashkino, with most of its oil reservoired in the Devonian, is in a separate play than the Arlan field, the second largest in the basin, as its principal resources are mainly in the shallower Carboniferous strata.

15 These were found in 1962 and 1966, both just over one billion bbls $A+B+C_1$ EUR.

16 The skewness, or dominance of very large fields in a basin's total distribution of fields, is related to the basin's tectonic evolution. The Volga-Ural basin, as a craton-accreted margin basin, has a field size distribution of moderate skewness. This still means a very large share of the basin's oil is contained in the very largest fields. Even more highly skewed (more concentrated) distributions are found in rift basins (e.g., in the North Sea); less skewed (more dispersive) distributions are found in delta-dominated basins (e.g., US Gulf of Mexico or Nigeria). See H.D. Klemme, 'Field Size Distribution Related to Basin Characteristics,' in *Oil and Gas Assessment, Methods and Applications*, (AAPG Studies in Geology #21) Dudley D. Rice, ed., (Tulsa, OK: American Association of Petroleum Geologists, 1986), pp. 85–100.

17 Turbo drilling was first used in the southern producing regions before the Second World War, but produced its big effect in the Volga-Ural basin.

18 Campbell, *The Economics of Soviet Oil and Gas*, op. cit., pp. 104–05.

19 In an excellent analysis of the engineering and economic aspects of this technology (that only a drilling engineer could truly love – or really understand), Campbell argues that turbo drilling was employed in the Soviet oil industry in a suboptimal way (Ibid., pp. 108–20). Much of his criticism relies on the Soviets' failure to optimize with respect to total economic costs of drilling, an important component of which is drilling time. While a valid measure, especially for US operations, the situations in the USSR and the USA at that time were vastly different. In the Soviet Union, labour was very cheap and the opportunity cost of labour time low. It appears in retrospect that Soviet planners may have got much closer to a microeconomic optimum than Campbell's conclusion supports.

This does not impeach Campbell's argument that higher quality steel and more flexibility in drilling regimes available to development teams would have produced more oil with a lower combined cost of capital and labour. The optimum, however, requires balancing not only the marginal rates of technical substitution between competing methods (e.g., rotary and turbo drilling), but also the ratio of marginal costs of providing each. In the Soviet oil industry of the fifties and sixties, marginal costs favoured a much higher labour to capital mix than in the West.

20 Ibid., p. 131.
21 Ibid., p. 134.
22 A similar relationship exists at the largest US field, Prudhoe Bay, on the

North Slope of Alaska. There, the West Sak tar sands occupy shallow cold reservoirs several thousand feet above the field's main light oil reservoirs. Like the Melekess deposit, the West Sak heavy oil sands have largely escaped commercial production. Another massive accumulation, known as the Athabasca tar sands, is located in western Canada. In this case, however, the tar sands are so close to the surface that much of the oil is produced through surface mining techniques. After many years of research and development of both surface mining and *in situ* processes, the Western Canadian unconventional deposits now contribute a major share of Canadian liquid hydrocarbon production and are responsible for most of the country's growth in output.

23 Maksimov, *Oil and Gas Fields of the USSR*, op. cit., vol. 1, p. 51.
24 James A. Peterson and James W. Clarke, 'Petroleum Geology and Resources of the Volga-Ural Province, USSR,' *US Geological Survey Circular 885* (1983), p. 21.
25 G.F. Trebin, N.V. Charygin and T.M. Obkhova, *Nefti mestorozhdenii Sovietsogo Soyuza* [*Oils of the Fields of the Soviet Union*] (Moscow: Nedra, 1980), pp. 163–8.
26 'Tatneft Promotes Differentiated Taxation of Oil Production,' *Radio Free Europe/Radio Liberty Tatar-Bashkir Daily Report*, April 12, 2004, www.rferl.org.
27 Baltica is also known as the Eastern European plate and in the Russian geologic literature it is called the Russian plate.
28 Here, and in the appendix to Chapter 3, the discussions of the directions of plate motion are based on the relative positions of the plates today. In other words, when Siberia is described as approaching Baltica's eastern margin, this is the orientation of that margin today. The vector of Baltica's movement during the Permian was to the north and the Urals were oriented east-west, not north-south as they are now. However, this level of geometric fidelity to plate motion is beyond the resolution of this study.
29 The Domanik is also a major hydrocarbon source in the Timan-Pechora basin to the north.
30 For effective transformation of organic carbon to oil to occur, there must be at least a critical minimum concentration – here taken to be 1 per cent TOC. While areas with less than 1 per cent TOC may get charged with oil, the volumes are usually limited.
31 As with source rocks bearing less than 1 per cent TOC, sandstones less than 320 feet thick commonly contain oil and gas fields – but generally smaller in size.
32 The exception is the Orenburg gas/condensate field in the Buzuluk Depression in the southern-most part of the basin, which has principal reservoirs in the Permian section.
33 Most geologic periods are named after locales where the 'type section' or archetypal rocks of that age are exposed at the surface. The Permian Period (a name used worldwide) gets its name from the city (and oblast) of Perm, located in the northern part of the Volga-Ural basin.

CHAPTER 3

WEST SIBERIA

West Siberia is immense by all measures. It boasts the second largest volume of discovered oil in the world and the planet's richest concentration of discovered natural gas. Two out of every three barrels of Russian oil come from the basin and more than 85 per cent of the country's gas. It is the home of Russia's major oil companies and the state gas monopoly. Most of the men who control supply began their careers in West Siberia. It is the heart of the Russian oil and gas industries.

The basin's area equals one-third that of the continental USA, or, about four times the size of France (Map 7). As part of Siberia, naturally, it is cold. In contrast to the remainder of that fabled land, however, West Siberia is unexpectedly wet – the world's largest swamp. Vast distances, bitter climate and a seasonally soggy surface make it one of the most challenging environments anywhere for producing hydrocarbons.

Development of the Volga-Ural basin, including the industrial complex it spawned along the Volga River, was a colossal undertaking. Yet, in many ways, that paled before the subsequent transformation on the east side of the Urals (Figure 8). In 1960, West Siberia was tundra and forest – virtually unpopulated. Thirty years later, it produced one-fifth of the world's oil and gas and was home to over 3 million people.

The economic attraction was not just the total volume of hydrocarbons – it was the enormous size of the largest oil and gas fields. Field size afforded geologists from the Ministry of Geology extraordinary efficiency in exploration. Field size provided engineers from the Ministries of Oil and Gas with economies of scale that, at least initially, powerfully offset the cost burden of settling and working in an Arctic swamp 1,500 miles from consumers.

It was in West Siberia that Moscow struck its Faustian bargain with the Soviet oil and gas industries. As long as the government delivered ever-increasing funding to the basin, its oil and gas men would return ever-increasing production. The economic and political story of the basin's oil juggernaut was the industry wringing every rouble possible out of Moscow and, in turn, squeezing every accessible drop of oil from its new fields beyond the Urals.

Particularly in the seventies, the balance of benefits flowed in

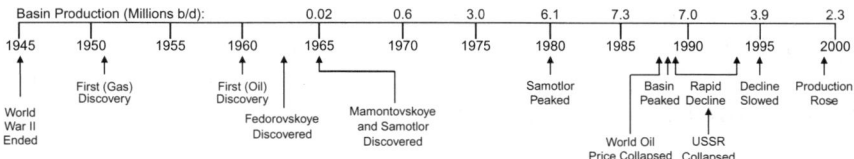

Figure 8: Time Line of the Industrial Development of the West Siberian Basin

Moscow's favour. By 1970, a quarter century of post-war expansion was slowing very quickly. Nearly-free energy had postponed the USSR's macroeconomic reckoning for a decade. Within its empire, Eastern European economies, nursed on Volga-Ural oil in the fifties and sixties, were switched to West Siberian oil and later, heavily, to its gas.

Then, suddenly, in the mid-seventies, when output from the basin was growing at its fastest, the world price of oil quadrupled. Exports to Western Europe brought the USSR a vital infusion of scarce hard currency, providing critical economic flexibility to the Soviet government at a time of mounting need.

Oil prices climbed into the early eighties and so did West Siberian oil output. Yet, as the seventies closed, looming problems foretold the peak of the basin's oil production. A leading indicator was declining exploration performance. More immediate were signs in the fields themselves: declining well flow rates and increasing water cuts.

As the eighties opened, Samotlor, the basin's and the nation's largest field, reached a maximum of 3.4 million b/d – over a quarter of Soviet production. This was the beginning of the end. By the middle of the decade, the balance had shifted. The oil industry was extracting enormously more money from Moscow than it was giving back in increased oil deliveries. Moreover, in 1986, high world prices, which had become an expansive excuse for maintaining the Faustian bargain, broke down. As the USSR fell apart at the end of the eighties, neither the industry nor the government could any longer maintain the maximum oil/maximum funding deal under-girding their relationship. Both production and industry finances fell apart.

What eventually emerged from the collapse of the Soviet oil industry in West Siberia was a powerful new set of actors in the Russian and world oil markets. Industry privatization started in West Siberia and eventually attracted almost all the old Soviet oil-producing associations. These new companies are still heavily shaped by their Soviet patrimony in resources and capital base, and also in outlook on the technology, economics and the politics of oil.

It is nearly impossible to see how any other area of Russia will surpass West Siberia in oil production through the first quarter of this century. It may remain the nation's leading producer indefinitely. The basin's size itself, and a most propitious geologic history, combined in West Siberia to generate and trap hydrocarbons as in no other place in Russia and very few other places in the world. As West Siberian oil goes – so will the Russian industry.

Exploration

I.M. Gubkin, who stood ahead of his time in predicting the potential of the Volga-Ural basin, advanced an even more prescient hypothesis two decades before the first discovery in West Siberia. In 1932, at a conference in Sverdlovsk, he proposed that the Mesozoic coal-bearing facies exposed along the eastern flank of the Ural Mountains continued to the east, under the present-day surface of West Siberia.[1] He theorized that in Mesozoic time, excellent conditions prevailed for the accumulation of the type and extent of organic matter that would generate vast quantities of oil and gas. He didn't exactly produce Map 10 at the time – but he got the main idea precisely right.

As his advice on the potential of the Volga-Ural basin was ignored in the twenties, his proposals on West Siberia received the same reception in the thirties. Systematic exploration in West Siberia did not start until after the Second World War, almost a decade after Gubkin's death. The first successful drilling was on the extreme western margin of the basin where a small gas field was found in 1953. In 1960, oil was discovered.[2] However, it was an amazing series of fields found in the central and northern parts of the basin in the early and mid-sixties that demonstrated the colossal dimensions of West Siberia's hydrocarbon resource base.

Throughout the sixties, more than 75 billion barrels of oil were discovered in the central basin. In the north, after finding the Tazovskoye field in 1962, Soviet explorationists found what was originally estimated to be 400 trillion cubic feet of natural gas. These new fields added roughly 14 per cent to world discovered oil resources and a tremendous 27 per cent to the world's discovered natural gas as of 1970.[3]

Discovery of West Siberia's four largest oil fields occurred between 1962 and 1965.[4] These fields contained over 50 billion bbls of recoverable oil (Table 1). Moreover, with the exception of the Krasnoleninskoye field complex, a single exploration concept guided geologists: drill the crests of the large uplifts along the Middle Ob and expect to encounter oil in Lower Cretaceous rocks.[5] The formula not only led to scores of replicable successes, but the new super-giant finds were conveniently close to each other. The first ones all fronted or straddled West Siberia's only transportation artery, the Ob River (Map 7).

As with the discovery of Romashkino 15 years before, this first generation of West Siberian super-giant fields focused the Soviet government and organized the economic, scientific and technical resources required for a massive campaign. Yet, initially, there were strong forces working against the development of this new, highly promising region.

For Russians, the popular conception of Russia ends in the east at the Ural Mountains. When Volga-Ural basin production began, Soviet bureaucrats assigned it to the 'Eastern' oil trust although it is on the *west* side of the Urals – a mere 600 miles east of Moscow. The Middle Ob region is another 900 miles further east of the Volga-Ural basin – moreover it is за Уралом [beyond the Urals]. Distance opposed a major industrial operation.

The second strike against the region was water. West Siberia is a massive Arctic swamp, with two seasons – flood and freeze.[6] The water problem arises because the Ob River flows from the south to the north (Map 7). Consequently, during the spring thaw, melt waters enter the Ob's hundreds of tributaries in the south while the lower reaches and mouth of the river, 400 miles north, are still frozen. The water backs up south of this ice plug and floods the basin. As West Siberia is physiographically the largest flat land on Earth, even small rises in river levels inundate its expansive plains.[7]

Inertia reinforced the obstacles posed by nature. As the industry was loath to move north into the Volga-Ural basin in the thirties, they were highly reluctant in the sixties to transfer personnel and equipment to this forebodingly remote location. The industry was comfortably entrenched west of the Urals and in a theme that persisted for two more decades – resources for West Siberia were at the expense of local operations.

Exploration drillers nevertheless picked off West Siberia's largest discoveries with relative ease. Their targets were very large, at shallow depths and were clear on seismic. Finding the fields, therefore, required only a modest investment in manpower and wells. As the inventory of enormous discoveries grew, which would take years to put on line, there was little immediate pressure to apply greater resources to West Siberian exploration. Instead, at the outset, Soviet exploratory effort remained concentrated west of the Urals. The slow speed of the move east slaked industry sluggishness. It also met the logical economic requirement to maximize output where infrastructure was dense, already bought and the distance to market short.

Table 1: Key Oil Fields of West Siberia by Generation of Discovery and Development

Field (Numbers in Map 8)	Field Discovery Year	Year of First Production	Per cent Depletion A+B+C1 in 2000
First Generation			
Samotlor (1)	1965	1965	68
Fedorovskoye* (2)	1963	1973	62
Mamontovskoye* (3)	1965	1965	78
Second Generation			
Krasnoleninskoye (4)	1962	1985	10
Sovietskoye (5)	1962	1966	99
Pravdinsko-Salymskoye (6)	1964	1968	24
Bystrinskoye (7)	1964	1974	67
Aganskoye (8)	1965	1973	82
Vakhskoye (9)	1965	1975	29
Lyantorskoye (10)	1966	1978	38
Varyeganskoye (11)	1967	1974	71
Pokachevskoye[1] (12)	1970	1977	24
N. Varyeganskoye (13)	1971	1976	57
Povkhovskoye (14)	1972	1978	54
Sutorminskoye (15)	1975	1982	60
S. Yagunskoye (16)	1978	1982	38
Muravlenkovskoye (17)	1978	1982	79
Third Generation			
Komsomolskoye (18)	1966	1986	18
Malo-Balykskoye (19)	1966	1984	21
Tarasovskoye (20)	1967	1986	33
Vatyeganskoye (21)	1970	1984	26
Tevlin-Russkinskoye (22)	1971	1986	26
Vachimskoye (23)	1971	1987	13
Orekhovo-Yermakovskoye (24)	1974	1986	18
Fourth Generation			
Van-Yeganskoye (25)	1974	1978	7
Kharampurskoye (26)	1978	1990	13
Konitlorskoye (27)	1978	1996	6
Priobskoye (28)	1982	1989	1
Druzhnoye (29)	1982	1985	31
Tyanskoye (30)	1985	1995	5
Sugmutskoye (31)	1987	1995	12
W. Salymskoye (32)	1987	None	0

* Fedorovskoye is defined in the IHS data as Federovo-Surgutskoye; Mamontovskoye is defined as Ust-Balyk-Mamontovskoye and Pokachevskoye as Pokachevsko-Uryevskoye.

Although funding for West Siberian exploration rose consistently through the sixties, by the seventies, the volume of new reserves added in the region annually showed a clear decline. Better funding of exploration would have slowed the fall. But overriding the political dimensions of the process, West Siberia followed the expected pattern. Early drilling found the largest fields. Just as they had in the Volga-Ural basin (and virtually all basins around the world), after the first wave – discovery sizes declined exponentially (Figure 9). The lognormal distribution of field sizes – not Soviet shortcomings – drove this dynamic.

Throughout the Soviet period, Moscow planners strove mightily and confidently against the limits of physics and biology. Their river diversions for transportation and power, irrigating deserts for cotton and an enormous attempt to cultivate the thin soil of the Kazakh steppe all testify to a pointed arrogance toward the constraints imposed by nature on the economy of man. The deterioration of exploration performance in West Siberia, therefore, was credited to insufficient and inefficient effort. The bosses in Moscow did not recognize the falling size of new discoveries as a natural evolution.

West Siberian geologists did not help. Throughout the seventies, while resisting Moscow's most extreme demands, they assured their superiors that there was plenty of oil left to find. They would surely find it in the places they had not yet looked – in the far north and east and in deep strata, under the massive gas discoveries. Grander budgets, new equipment and better technology, they claimed, would rescue the effort and return the salad days of the mid-sixties along the Middle Ob.[8]

There was indeed more oil to be found, but from today's perspective it is clear that the huge oil discoveries of the first few years were not to be repeated. It is likely that some at the top of the West Siberian geologic establishment suspected as much at the time. Soviet petroleum geologists were among the most scientifically sophisticated in the world and made major intellectual investments in assessing the hydrocarbon potential of lightly explored areas.

Advocacy of the 'up-side' of exploration is understandable. Exploration geologists are optimists by nature. The vast majority of exploratory wells are failures, so without a solid core of hope for the next prospect, there is little reason to go to work. Nevertheless, that optimism was surely fuelled by the type of bureaucratic angling that also exists in Western oil companies. If an exploration manager responsible for a region can convince his superiors of the vast untapped potential of his area, money flows to his programme – so it went in West Siberia.

Exploration budgets for West Siberia did increase steadily. Yet, on average, geologists found less oil each year. The rate of decline in the size of new discoveries in West Siberia was roughly the same as it was in the Volga-Ural basin. In both cases, the average size of new fields fell by half about every eight years (Figures 3 and 9). The variance in the size of discoveries made each year in West Siberia remained high.[9] This meant that even with a fast dropping average discovery size, large fields continued to be found.

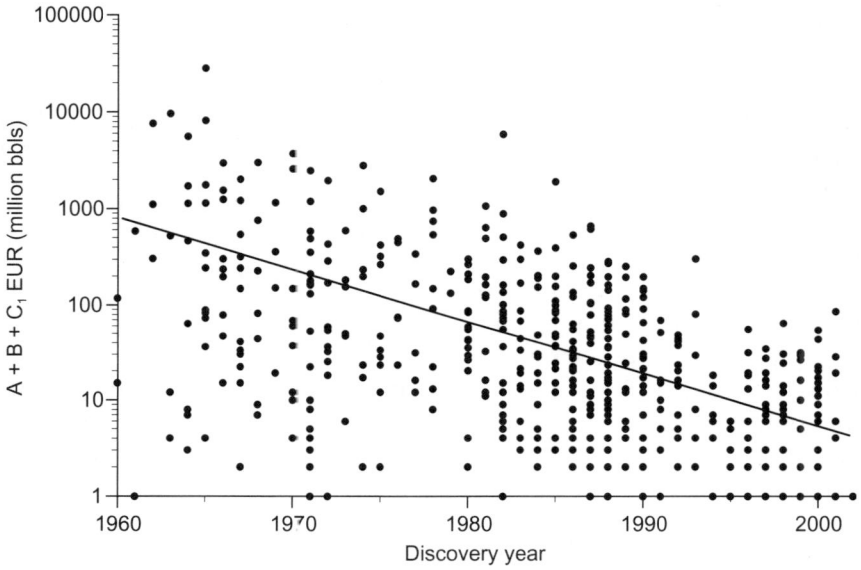

Figure 9: Relationship between Oil Discovery Size and Discovery Date, West Siberian Basin

Exploration Cycles. The processes of West Siberian exploration and development went in phases. The first three biggest finds anchored the basin: Samotlor (1965), Mamontovskoye (1965) and Fedorovskoye (1963). Production from these fields carried the basin and the nation through the sixties and seventies. These fields cover enormous areas, around 1,000 square miles each. They occupied very prominent uplifts on even larger positive regional features. Hence, they were pretty clear, even on sixties-vintage Soviet seismic. The first two fields came on line in 1965; Fedorovskoye started production in 1972.[10]

Born of the same exploration concept, the generation of new fields that followed these first three super-giants tested somewhat smaller structures around and between them. They also moved further north of the Ob River (Table 1 and Map 8).[11] The average discovery year of the second generation was 1969 and the average year of first production was 1977. These were to be the fields that provided incremental production as the first three began to fade in the eighties.

The third generation of discoveries was, on average, even further away from the Ob River – mainly to the north (Map 8). Explorationists successfully searching for gas in the northern basin realized that there was a chain of uplifts, at the Neocomian level, that ran from the Taz Gulf south to the area between Surgut and Nizhnevartovsk along the Middle Ob. It roughly paralleled one of the old tensional rifts in the Permo-Triassic basement of the basin.[12] Along the northern extent of this chain are the world's largest natural gas fields. Further south, these structures trap fields with increasing oil content and relatively small volumes of gas.

The third-generation discoveries were much smaller than the second and, while found over the same period, their development was deferred. With these fields, the Soviet Ministry of Oil intended to fill the gap in the late eighties that would be created after the first generation peaked and increase in the growth of collective output from the second generation started to fall.

There was a final, fourth generation of major fields, discovered in the seventies and eighties, but deferred – to be developed in the nineties. They never got a chance to shine during the Soviet regime. Their real development (beyond test production at some) was left to the new Russian oil industry that emerged after the collapse of the USSR.

Of course, mixed in with the discoveries of the top fields in Table 1, drillers found hundreds of other fields (Map 8). These 'other' oil fields now total over 400, which is 85 per cent of the total number of fields discovered in the basin to date. Nevertheless, collectively, they hold only 15 per cent of the basin's technically recoverable oil. Of these smaller fields, roughly 160 are on line. In 2000, they produced about a quarter of West Siberian output.

Post-Soviet Exploration. The break-up of the USSR savaged the search for new fields. During the Soviet period, the Ministry of Geology funded the search for new fields directly from the federal budget. Production associations within the Ministry of Oil were divorced from exploration – managerially and financially. Therefore, when the private companies emerged from the Soviet production associations, they had no real exploration departments.[13] After some time, centralized financing of exploration was reconstituted under the Russian Federation through an 'exploration tax' on oil production. This process yielded a relatively low volume of new oil in generally small fields.

At the end of the nineties, and more profoundly after elimination of the exploration tax at the beginning of 2002, the large Russian oil companies began to develop genuine, integrated in-house exploration capabilities. This led to a pick-up in activity, although exploratory operations remain principally within the confines of geologic concepts and specific drilling targets identified in the Soviet period.

Over the last decade, most of the exploratory drilling that did occur was 'extension' exploration. This is drilling for new reservoirs within existing fields, or to expand the known boundaries of reservoirs already found. It is not inconsequential work. In mature petroleum provinces (like most in the USA), more oil resources are added through extension exploration than by finding brand new fields (because average new field discovery is so small in mature basins).

Given the economic and political roller coaster of the nineties, extension exploration was perhaps the wisest course. It produces new oil in existing fields, and the exploration risk is low relative to looking for new fields. Production infrastructure is usually already in place. Consequently, although the new oil requires new wells, it is processed and transported through existing facilities, lowering capital costs. Because extension discoveries are new reservoirs within a field, the new wells usually enjoy high flow rates and low water cuts relative to the old wells producing out of the field's old reservoirs. High flow rate and low water cut reduce operating costs.

There are, of course, downsides. The sizes of new reservoir discoveries are almost always smaller than the average of reservoirs already found in the field. So, although new reservoirs will soften a field's decline rate, they rarely reverse it for more than a year or so at best. Moreover, as the field is drilled up, these opportunities simply run out. All the reservoirs are eventually found, fully delineated and produced to their economic limits.

As of 2003, West Siberia's production was again rising. However, within a few years, when it resumes the decline that began in the late eighties, aggressive and successful extension exploration will be central to minimizing the annual drop in production. It is extension exploration, combined with increased recovery factors from producing reservoirs, that allows many of the largest North American basins to decline at between 1 and 3 per cent per year. There are exceptions, but late in the cycle, new field exploration adds little.

Yet West Siberia is much less mature than all but a few US basins. New field exploration in the nineties did yield a few discoveries in the >100 million bbls EUR range. Fields in this size range continue to be found. If there had been more new field exploration over the last decade, these fields would have been found faster. More await discovery.

In the Middle Ob, however, as would be expected after 40 years of looking, only small fields are being found. In some cases, at the company level, this is an acceptable result. For the same reasons as in the Volga-Ural basin, smaller fields can be profitably developed in the Middle Ob because of proximate infrastructure and transportation. The role of these fields, however, is to offset declines at major fields. They will not drive growth in the basin's production (or even that of an individual large company).

The hunt for new fields, as it begins again in earnest, could take several directions. The most obvious is to pursue the tried-and-true 40 year-old concept of drilling Neocomian highs and expecting oil in the Neocomian Megion and Vartov formations. Plenty of smaller highs remain undrilled. However, they are generally in the extreme north of the basin or on its eastern and southern margins. In the north, because of the thermal maturity of the Bazhenov and Neocomian shale source rocks (buried more deeply than in the Middle Ob), hydrocarbons are more likely gas and condensate than crude oil (see the Appendix to this Chapter).[14] There are untested stratigraphic traps throughout the basin.

On the eastern margin, and across the wide southern rim of the basin, there is surely the potential for new fields. These regions are lightly drilled and the Russians have found some large fields there. But in contrast to the centre of the basin, hydrocarbon source rocks were leaner (see Appendix to this Chapter). There, as well, shallower burial transformed a smaller fraction of Bazhenov Formation organic matter to oil than occurred in either the basin centre or north. Compressional structures, the key to focusing and trapping Neocomian oil in the Middle Ob, are generally less dense and smaller along the eastern and southern margins. While the occasional major discovery in this zone could be a company-maker, such finds are unlikely to even temporarily reverse the basin decline (when it returns).

A more promising possibility is in the central and northern basin – in the Achimov Formation. These are highly heterogeneous rocks. Achimov reservoirs are lower quality than the main Megion and Vartov reservoirs above them. Because of their relatively limited lateral continuity and lower permeability, Achimov wells have lower average flow rates and lower recoveries than in the main Megion and Vartov units. A promising exception is Yukos' standout new field development project, Priobskoye, in which most of the oil is reservoired in the Achimov.

With few exceptions, so far, Achimov reservoirs have only been tapped incidentally in fields driven by Megion and Vartov production. As explorationists pursue Achimov targets independently from shallower objectives, they may find more productive regions and accumulations larger than those found to date as secondary targets. The improved drilling and production technology brought from the West to the basin in the last decade will also differentially improve performance in Achimov reservoirs (e.g., 3-D seismic, hydraulic fracturing and long horizontal completions). Because the Achimov sits directly on the Bazhenov shale and is heavily interbedded with shales itself, these should also be charged with oil. The challenge is finding locations where their reservoir quality (as measured by well flow rates) and accumulation size are sufficient for commercial production on a stand-alone basis.

Finally, there is the potential of the Lower and Middle Jurassic section. Like the Achimov, these rocks are more heterogeneous than the classic Megion and Vartov reservoirs. Moreover, because they are stratigraphically below the Bazhenov, they must generally rely on less prolific sources for their oil. Nevertheless, along with the Achimov, the Lower-Middle Jurassic plays are probably the most promising in the basin.

These exploration concepts, while not aggressively pursued to date, are in the geologic mainstream. Further out on the limb would be attempts to demonstrate oil and gas potential in pre-Jurassic rock. This would involve defining and testing those parts of the Permo-Triassic basement not metamorphosed during the very earliest stages of basin formation. Some pre-Jurassic oil was found in the southern basin in Soviet times, but never enough to spark more than mild scientific interest.

Also outside the box of traditional resources is the concept of producing oil directly out of the Bazhenov shale. In some cases, shales, when they are fractured, can reservoir as well as generate oil and gas. The Miocene Monterey shale of California has produced billions of barrels, both generated and hosted in the same rocks. Experimental production from the Bazhenov shale was achieved during the seventies and eighties. Always big fans of nuclear energy, the Soviets even detonated atomic bombs (called 'peaceful nuclear explosions') in the Bazhenov to enhance the natural fractures and increase oil flow (it did not work). One of the interesting projects to watch is the joint venture involving Shell in the Salym group of fields, where the Bazhenov is a principal development target (see Chapter 6).

The key to Bazhenov production will be a combination of careful seismic analysis and modelling the conditions under which the Bazhenov becomes brittle and fractures. These are the formation's 'sweet spots.' If the secrets of Bazhenov production are ultimately unlocked, the potential physical volume of oil available is gigantic. As California producers will attest, however, producing shale is not easy or cheap. While the calculated volume of oil in the Bazhenov totals tens of billions of barrels, the fraction that is presently technologically and economically producible remains very low. Nevertheless, it remains part of the basin's long-run potential.

Production

The Soviet strategy for producing West Siberia's oil resources operated on two levels. First was the order and timing of field development. Second was a largely uniform engineering plan employed at each field. Both elements were deeply entwined with the Soviet political economy. Both had, and continue to have, profound implications for the economics of oil supply from the basin.

Basin Development Strategy. The Soviet Ministry of Oil exploited the resources of West Siberia in phases (Table 2). These were built around fields grouped by their sizes, locations and the order in which they were discovered. Logically, they began with the super-giant fields found along the middle reaches of the Ob River. From that base, they tapped major new fields around the very largest first-producers. As these successors to the first three came on line, two more groups of major fields awaited. Together, there were 32 fields among these four generations of giant and super-giant oil fields. All are presently producing oil.

Mixed in with the 32 largest fields were hundreds of smaller fields discovered since the sixties. Because of their exponentially smaller size than the top fields, the only ones developed were those very close to

Table 2: Characteristics of Fields in Phased Development of West Siberia

Group of Fields	Number of Fields	Number of Producing Fields	Estimated Ultimate Recovery*	Average Discovery Year	Average First Production
First Generation	3	3	46	1964	1968
Second Generation	14	14	34	1969	1976
Third Generation	7	7	10	1969	1986
Fourth Generation	8	8	14	1982	1992
Others	452	165	35	1984	1989

* Oil in billions of barrels of A+B+C_1 EUR.

the large producing fields or along pipeline routes. Presently, about a third of these are online.

The first generation of super-giant fields that propelled Soviet production from the mid-sixties through the seventies consisted of three fields. Their development, and the construction of major oil pipelines to return the crude to refineries in the Volga-Ural basin, almost wholly consumed investment in West Siberia in the sixties. Samotlor was the biggest and the largest field ever discovered in Russia (or the other republics of the former Soviet Union). It is described in the box on page 47. This one field carried most of the entire increase in basin output for over a decade after its first production and when it peaked, Samotlor contributed a quarter of Soviet oil production.

The other two first generation fields, Fedorovskoye and Mamontovskoye, were super-giant finds as well, but much smaller than Samotlor. Fedorovskoye was the more prolific and consistent performer. While contributing to the expansion of production in the early seventies, its big ramp-up in output occurred in the late seventies, increasing by 171,000 b/d in 1979 alone. It held its peak of just over one million b/d from 1983 to 1985. The post-peak decline started at the high end of the range expected of a field that size, 5 per cent, which it maintained until the industry began to collapse at the end of the eighties.

Mamontovskoye, 40 miles down the Ob, proved more difficult. Ultimately, it also topped one million b/d (in 1986), but its rise was more ragged. While Fedorovskoye presented a challenging surface environment, even more of Mamontovskoye straddles the Ob River flood plain, seriously complicating field operations (Map 8). Yet the production association organized around the field was newer (Yuganskneftegaz, now the central subsidiary of Yukos) and a little further removed from the *apparatchiki* of the Middle Ob administrative centre in Nizhnevartovsk. It was recognized as a star performer in the troubled middle stretch of the eighties.[15]

This troika of first generation fields supplied the growth in Soviet oil through the seventies (Figure 10). Nonetheless, by the end of that decade, it was clear that any further growth had to come from the basin's second generation of discoveries.

Moscow had deferred the development of the 14 second-generation fields throughout the sixties and early seventies, as the first generation devoured almost all resources allocated to West Siberia. Yet, by the mid-seventies, Soviet engineers could see a gap in productive capacity that would only widen ten years hence. Therefore, on average, from the mid-seventies through the mid-eighties, West Siberian producing associations brought on a new second-generation field each year.

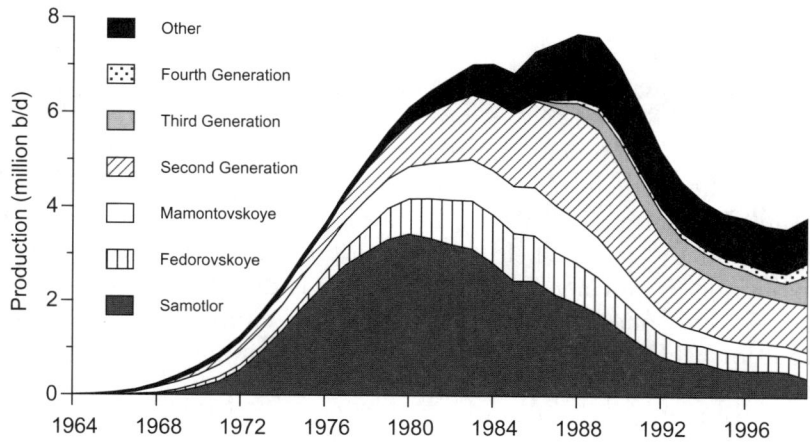

Figure 10: Oil Production from the West Siberian Basin by Field Generation

In the mid-eighties, it was the second-generation fields, even more than Fedorovskoye and Mamontovskoye, which helped edge Soviet production up. Increases in production at Fedorovskoye and Mamontovskoye, between the Samotlor peak in 1980 and their own maximums, were almost entirely consumed to offset the losses at Samotlor. Without the contribution of the second-generation fields, West Siberian, and

---

Box 2

Samotlor – Russia's Largest Oil Field

Because of its size and obvious trapping geometry on seismic, Samotlor was one of the first fields found when exploration began along the middle reaches of the Ob River in the sixties. It was discovered in 1965 on the right bank of the river, 20 miles north of the city of Nizhnevartovsk (Map 8). As one of the largest oil fields in the world, it became the centrepiece of the Soviet oil industry, accounting for one-quarter of national oil production in 1980, when it peaked at 3.4 million b/d.

By geologic structure, it is an excellent model for most of the fields in the Middle Ob region, greatly scaled-up. The field occupies the crest of the Nizhnevartovsk Arch – a vast, low relief positive structure in the central basin (Map 9). It is roughly the same area as Romashkino. Originally oval-shaped, extension exploration in the eighties enlarged the field to the west.

Like almost all West Siberian fields, Samotlor contains multiple reservoirs confined to rocks of the Lower Cretaceous Neocomian

Epoch. There are ten principal producing units. They extend from roughly 5,000 feet deep to about 7,500 feet (Figure 11).[16] Within the Neocomian section, almost all the oil was found in the sandstone and siltstone reservoirs of the Megion and Vartov formations. Although engineers produced oil from all the main reservoirs over the last four decades, the dominant units are the 450-foot thick BV_8 at the top of the Megion and the BV_{10} below it.

Also typical of Middle Ob fields, oil from Samotlor is relatively light – 34° API gravity. Compared to Volga-Ural basin production, it has low sulphur content – 0.9 per cent on average.[17] The field's first round of wells tested at flow rates up to 1,400 b/d, underwhelming by world standards.[18] Initial production entrained only small volumes of water. However, flow rates quickly dropped and water cut rose. Approximately 20,000 wells have been drilled into Samotlor as either producers or water injection wells. Today, its 5,000 active producing wells make an average of 66 b/d.

In the sixties, although the Soviets began development simultaneously at several fields in the middle of the basin, the greatest effort was concentrated at Samotlor. After several years required for the initial round of development drilling and pipeline construction, the field grew at a rate of 100,000 b/d annually. In the seventies, at its peak rate of growth, Samotlor added more than 500,000 b/d capacity in one year. This covered the lion's share of the Soviet increases in domestic oil consumption and oil exports through the entire decade of the seventies.

Samotlor's initial planned goal for peak output was 2 million b/d, anticipated to occur in 1977.[19] Managers in Moscow progressively raised the bar to the 3.4 million b/d mark that the field reached in 1980. In achieving this target, Samotlor's peak became one of the highest in the history of the world oil industry.

Over the first three years after the peak, production dropped at about 3 per cent annually – normal for a field of its size. However, in 1984 and 1985, a crisis hit Samotlor causing the loss of more than 500,000 b/d (for the context of this, see Chapter 4). While other West Siberian fields (most importantly Fedorovskoye and Mamontovskoye) were able to cover Samotlor's losses when they were 3 per cent per year, they could not increase production by the 500,000 b/d lost in 1985, and the output in West Siberia dropped for the first time in its 25-year history.

Production crashed at Samotlor for two principal reasons. First, because of the very aggressive water flood, water cut rose throughout the seventies and very dramatically in the early eighties. Every barrel of oil required raising an ever-increasing volume of water. Pumping and processing requirements became overwhelming. Second, presaging a catastrophic problem to come, the lack of proper well maintenance led to the loss of at least 1,000 producing wells at the field in 1984 and 1985.

The collapse of production at Samotlor was an economic and political debacle of national proportions. The new Soviet leader, Mikhail Gorbachev, came to West Siberia in 1985 to inspect and fire managers throughout the industry. A massive new investment programme in the field followed. This stabilized Samotlor in 1986 at 2.5 million b/d, but it fell hard again in 1987, but less in 1988 – the final year of Soviet peak production.

As the Soviet oil industry began to crumble in 1989, production at Samotlor plummeted. By 1995, when the fall was arrested, output stood at only 750,000 b/d; an unprecedented loss of production from a single field. It represented about a quarter of the total loss in Russian production.

The field has followed a complex ownership path, starting with its division between two Soviet producing organizations as the USSR fell apart. In the nineties, it was the subject of considerable haggling and intrigue. By the beginning of this decade, half the field was in the hands of the Nizhnevartovsk division of TNK. The northern half of the field belonged to Sidanco, which also later joined TNK-BP. Samotlor became the principal asset of TNK when it joined with the British major, BP, to form TNK-BP.

As of January 1, 2003, Samotlor had produced 16.4 billion bbls of oil. Using WPC/SPE definitions, it was credited with proved reserves of 4.09 billion bbls, 320 million bbls of probable reserves and 850 million bbls of possible reserves (see Appendix II).[20] The field accounts for just under half of the proved reserves of the TNK-BP company. Production at the field began to rise (by a small amount) in 2001 and in 2002 was 329,000 b/d.

Although TNK-BP has substantial producing assets besides Samotlor and is involved in promising projects at undeveloped fields – this field is the centrepiece of the company's portfolio. If the combination of Western and Russian expertise embodied in TNK-BP is to thrive, it must succeed at Samotlor. This may involve some increase in production, but much more importantly, it will be in reducing production cost and ensuring that the eventual return of declining production is at a slow rate (see Chapter 6).

total Soviet oil output, would have hit their maximums in the early eighties.[21]

Although the third generation of West Siberian giants did make a contribution to the final gasp that produced the Soviet peak of 12.4 million b/d in 1987 and 1988, it was too little and too late to add much. More was supplied by the 'other' fields of the basin. These fields had been discovered since the outset of exploration in the sixties. The largest were greater than 100 million bbls. EUR – although most were smaller (Figure 12).[22] Over the eighties, there was a concerted push to bring on the smaller fields, with the number producing rising from 38 in 1980 to 128 in 1989.

Figure 12: Maximum, Mean and Minimum Discovery Size Brought Online by Decade in West Siberia

Overwhelmingly, these smaller producing fields were located very close to the giant fields that carried the base load of West Siberian production. The proximity of infrastructure and transportation offset the economies of scale their smaller sizes did not afford. While small by West Siberian standards, at the end of the eighties, as the edifice of Soviet production began to crumble, these fields contributed over one million b/d, reaching a collective maximum of 1.5 million b/d in 1990 (Figure 10).

Field Development Strategy. For industry managers in the USSR, there was nothing more important than the 'Plan.' There were Five Year Plans, annual plans and quarterly plans. Plans were denominated in targets for output, input consumption and disposition of resources within every industrial organization in the Soviet economy. It was a top-down process. At the bottom, in individual producing associations, there were technical plans specifying how each organization's goals were to be accomplished.

With this rigid approach, it is not surprising that engineers conducted the vast majority of field development in West Siberia under a single basic engineering plan followed at each successive field. The process started after a field discovery, when the Ministry of Geology concluded its work by drilling delineation wells designed to document the extent and character of the reservoirs and oil resources of a field. This gave the Ministry of Oil's local production association a fairly clear mapping of the most productive reservoirs.

On the basis of those maps, and the results of tests run on the delineation wells, the producing association designed the first-round of drilling targeted at the largest reservoir in the field. Crews built drilling pads in the West Siberian swamp. From these higher and dryer locations, several dozen wells were drilled in all directions. Drilling multiple wells directionally from centralized pads minimized the costs and logistic difficulty of operating in a wetland.[23]

The intersection of these wells with the reservoir formed a geometric grid. In the first round of drilling, the grid was fairly loose. Pattern drilling (locally called the 'Siberian box') carried the advantage of easy planning, but did not respect the geologic heterogeneity of reservoirs.[24] Mixed in the grid of producing wells were water injectors. Under Soviet practice, water flood usually commenced at the beginning of field development and continued to the field's abandonment.

When the main reservoir was drilled up, a second set of producers and injectors targeted the next largest reservoir(s). Although Soviet drillers sometimes produced multiple reservoirs through a single well bore, each major producing interval usually got its own drilling grid.

Initially, wells typically produced oil from the reservoir to the surface relying only on the natural pressure. Natural reservoir pressure was substantially augmented by water flood. However, even with an aggressive water flood (and to meet Plan-mandated production quotas, Soviet water floods were *always* aggressive), the oil flow rates of wells inevitably declined for two reasons: depletion of reservoir energy and increasing water cut.

In response, Soviet engineers followed a two-prong strategy to boost flow rates: pumps and in-fill drilling. Mechanization, or using pumps and gas lift equipment, was the first step. The most common type used in the USSR was the familiar sucker-rod pump. There are also down-hole pumps, specifically electrical submersible pumps (ESPs), which are more efficient than sucker-rod units. Finally, there was gas-lift. Gas is injected at the bottom of the well, thereby reducing the density of the fluid travelling up the hole and adding energy through the expansion of the injected gas as it rises.

While better at manufacturing gas-lift equipment, the Soviet industry produced only a small volume of ESPs. Domestic models were limited in their service depths and broke frequently. Instead, ESPs were imported, making them a rare and special treat. Most mechanized West Siberian wells sported only sucker-rod units. Although cheap to make and install, they required repairs two to three times as often as the other technologies.[25]

Engineers put pumps on every well they could. Nevertheless, they quickly met the limit of improvements that could be won with sucker-rod pumps. Without the option to upgrade to ESPs, sucker-rod pumps would only soften the wells' decline rates. Moreover, installing pumps meant incurring the cost and management requirements of maintaining them, which proved critical when national production crashed after 1988 (see Chapter 4).

The second line of attack was infill drilling. As the bump in output from mechanization declined, a second geometric grid of wells was planned for the spaces in between the first grid in a reservoir. In theory, infill wells increase the total volume of oil recovered from a reservoir. Whether drilled in the West or the USSR, however, most infill drilling is for production rate acceleration – not increased recovery. When drilled on a pattern, particularly with the reservoir under water flood, infill drilling can actually reduce the amount of oil ultimately recovered. As meeting the current quarter's planned production goal overwhelmed all other considerations, infill drilling became the brute-force instrument of choice.

While ensuring that some growth was eked out of the basin through 1987, the collective effect of mechanization and infill drilling was to sharply increase cost (see the appendix to Chapter 4).[26] There was not only the immense capital cost of wells and pumps, but a massive increase in the required number of men on the ground in West Siberia to drill and repair the tens of thousands of wells on line.

Comment

Oil and gas are so abundant in West Siberia because the basin is just so colossally big. Over such an extensive expanse, geologic processes occurred on a massive scale. The basin's principal oil source rock was not just locally rich, but contained 23 trillion tonnes of hydrocarbon-generating organic matter spread across 800,000 square miles. Magnitude saved the reservoirs too. They are not world class producers per well, but there are just so many of them, occupying such a large rock volume, that the total resource base they contain is immense.

These resources were very disproportionately concentrated in a very small number of extremely large and shallow fields. Without the tremendous economies of scale enjoyed by the early discoveries, West Siberian oil and gas may have remained in the ground. Economy of scale is the great redeemer of oil fields all over the world. In West Siberia, it forgave huge distances, a remorseless climate, low flow-rate wells and the logistic nightmare of operating in an Arctic swamp.

The Soviets did not create the oil resources of West Siberia, but discovered them. So given this enormous natural endowment, how well did they and their heirs do?

Measured by the traditional standard of recoverable hydrocarbons discovered per exploratory well, the process of finding oil and gas in West Siberia was very efficient. Because of the lognormality of the field sizes, this also led to not only incredibly large early discoveries, but to the exponential decline in discovery sizes as exploration continued.

The Soviet government railed against the outcome of this natural phenomenon, but neither a command economy nor a 'communist' ideology could repeal it. It will not be reversed by the magic of markets, either. Additional exploration will find more oil; however, efforts within traditional areas and plays will continue to yield mainly small fields. Carrying these concepts to under-explored parts of the basin will uncover larger fields, but each will bear the burden of remoteness in a land where distance is measured in dollars per barrel.

West Siberia will only enjoy an exploration renaissance in the light of new exploration thinking and even that must be counted as a necessary, but not sufficient, condition for success. Whether it is finding sand fairways for Achimov fans, unlocking the paleogeography of the Lower and Middle Jurassic section, finding the sweet spots in the Bazhenov or a completely new hypothesis, the economics must work, in addition to the science.

An exploration geologist in a big Western oil company may work five years between getting new field wildcats drilled. Collectively, West Siberian geologists, from the sixties to the collapse of the USSR, were testing prospects every few days – and finding hundreds of millions to billions of barrels of oil (and trillions of cubic feet of gas) at a time. Wonderful science at a breakneck speed, but it was in no sense guided by consideration of either the costs to develop and deliver their finds to consumers.

The challenge before West Siberian exploration is not finding hydrocarbons, despite the intellectual satisfaction it gives. It is finding economically efficient energy resources. That will apply whether the basin is dominated directly by the state, a few major companies, or dozens of them.

The burden of supply, however, will not fall on exploration for at least the next two decades. That onus belongs to the fields already discovered in the basin. This obviously includes the 200, or so, that are on line, as well as the hundreds discovered but undeveloped and the scores of liquid hydrocarbon accumulations located with the gas fields in the northern basin.

The Soviet stewardship of its West Siberian fields is a very mixed record. They attained production levels unmatched in the world – that was their goal. However, it was accomplished with tremendous sacrifices. Those costs had four dimensions.

First, was simply the economic resources denied the rest of the Soviet economy to ensure ever-increasing production of oil through the national peak in output in 1987 and 1988. As shown in the next chapter, at the maximum of West Siberian and Soviet production, they were producing oil that cost much more per barrel than its sales price on the world market. The command economic structure of the USSR hid these costs in an elaborate system of cross-subsidies and 'strategic considerations,' like earning hard currency. Freedom from responsibility for costs at the field level led to horribly wasteful decisions, like drilling new wells when much cheaper pumps would have sufficed.

Second, was the long-run damage to the fields. Oil fields suffer hysteresis, or a sensitivity of future performance to past management. The most profound future limitations will be experienced because of the past overdependence on very aggressive water floods in the basin's biggest fields. Billions of barrels of recoverable oil have doubtlessly been bypassed in reservoirs throughout the Middle Ob and are now either inaccessible or only available at water cuts that are too high to economically produce.

Third, was a critical human dimension. When they committed to developing the oil and gas fields of West Siberia, the Soviets also decided to settle the basin. This sparked the immigration of several million workers and their families.[27] Oil and gas production in the USSR was many times more labour intensive than it ever was in the West. So, after the collapse of the Soviet Union, when the industry became constrained by market, it began to massively shed employees.

That process will only continue, ultimately leaving potentially hundreds of thousands of people in cities and settlements over a thousand miles from European Russia with poor local prospects and limited opportunities to move.

Finally, there was the cost to the natural environment. The greatest damage is to surface and near-surface ground waters contaminated mainly by leaking oil field gathering systems. These impacts have been felt and exacerbated by the rising population of people, whose cities grew beyond the carrying capacity of the fragile ecosystems where they sprang up. While it does not have to be, the historical fact is that oil production (much more than gas) is a locally dirty business. Here, scale worked against West Siberia. Because there are tens of thousands of wells and thousands of miles of gathering pipe, the sum of spoiled spots runs to thousands of square miles.

Since the collapse of the USSR, things have changed in West Siberia. While suffering with the nation in the depression of the nineties, oil and gas money shielded a higher portion of the population from destitution than was felt in other places. Moreover, since 1999, the basin enjoyed some of the run-up in world oil prices, although the average improvement has lagged the increase in world prices.

Clearly, for oil, industry structure is fundamentally changed with the advent of private companies and exploration and production financed through market sales instead of state budgets. The flood of money over the last few years has led to better science and engineering in the basin. Some of the boost came from Western technologies – some from Russian know-how. At many, but not all companies, technology and money have improved technical indicators like well flow rates, water cuts and mean time between well repairs.

The influence of integration into the world industry has worked a less obvious effect on the long-run management of the basin's oil resources. As discussed in Chapters 4 and 5, it is very hard to sort out how much of the improvement of the last four to five years has come simply from higher revenues and how much from better management of the resources.

Although there is a scrappy sector of independent oil companies in West Siberia, production and all other oil operations are dominated by the major companies. This thin structure at the top of the industry is both a remnant of the Soviet heritage and a product of economies of scale in oil field production seen worldwide. As attention turns to the vast portfolio of discovered but unproduced fields in the basin, it is highly uncertain that such a top-heavy industry can efficiently exploit these resources. So, as in the Volga-Ural basin, an important component of future production is dependent on state policy toward smaller companies, independent of the majors that presently control West Siberia.

No matter how world oil prices, government policy or foreign investment evolve, the Russian oil and gas industries, for the foreseeable future, will remain based in West Siberia. It is not only a matter of remaining resources and the established capital base in the basin – four decades have created a political, social, scientific as well as economic mass in West Siberia with profound inertial force. Individual or small groups of projects in East Siberia, the Arctic Ocean or on Sakhlin Island will be very important to Russian oil supply, but they will never create the great industrial centre that grew across the middle reaches of the Ob River.

Appendix: West Siberian Basin Geology

By gross structure, the geology of West Siberia is simpler than the Volga-Ural basin. It formed after the Volga-Ural basin, the uplift of the Ural Mountains in the Permian Period that closed the geologic development of that basin and gave birth to the basin in West Siberia (Figure 13).

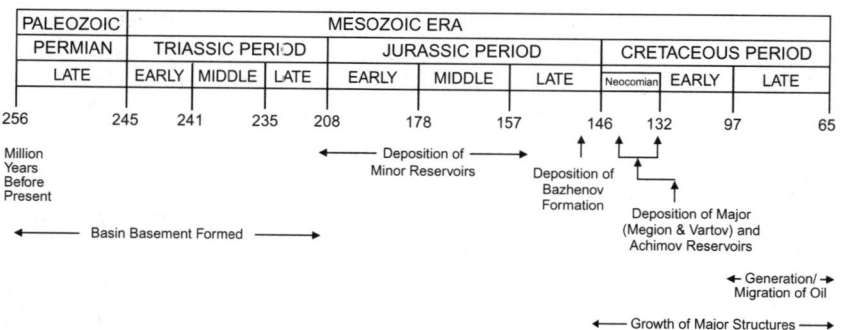

Figure 13: Time Line of Geologic Development of the West Siberian Basin

A great rock mélange stretched a thousand miles east of the Urals from the end of the Permian Period into the Triassic Period. Part of it came from the Ural Mountains on the eastern boundary of Baltica. Some was from the leading western edge of the Siberian plate. The Kazakh plate added a chunk in the south and a scattering of ocean crust, island arcs and tectonic flotsam was caught in between as these three plates converged. This multilithic foundation formed the basement of the West Siberian basin.

In the Early Triassic, as the three plates adjusted to their new positions, sometimes the basement of West Siberia was thrown into tension. This opened rifts in the basement surface with geometries similar to the Red Sea and its southern landward extension, the East African Rift Zone. Later in the Triassic, the plates pressed together, compressing the basement and raising modest highlands throughout the basin.

From its birth at the end of the Uralian orogeny through the Triassic Period, West Siberia was as it is today – mainly land. Seas encroached through the lows caused by earlier rifting. Just as the Kara Sea covers the very northern basin today, throughout the basin's geologic evolution, the further north, the more likely a sea would be found. The Triassic climate was warm (although dry), as the conjoined Baltica, Kazakh and Siberian plates were thousands of miles closer to the equator than their present, decidedly cool latitudes.

Rising global sea level and a wetter West Siberian climate marked the beginning of the Jurassic Period. The influx of water eroded the highlands in and around the basin. Rivers flowed toward the basin centre from the south, east and west. Increasingly through the Jurassic, the broad flatlands of central and northern West Siberia collected this water and sediment in shallow seas. At times, these seas were open to the ocean in the north; sometimes not. Periodically, what is now Novaya Zemlya and the Taymyr Peninsula fused to close off a Mediterranean-like sea.

The sands worn from the peripheral highlands filling the Early Jurassic seas were often mineralogically immature; they contained a high proportion of the sediments directly eroded from older igneous and metamorphic rock. Because of their mineralogic immaturity, the Early-Middle Jurassic sands that became oil reservoirs have greater clay content – which degrades reservoir quality.

Because of the hummocky topography of the Permo-Triassic basement, the seas and lakes of the Early and Middle Jurassic were likely to be isolated from each other, and existed for relatively short periods of geologic time. The irregular topography distributed irregular rock geometries. Shales deposited in shallow Early and Middle Jurassic lakes and seas, therefore, were not extensive across the basin; they formed neither regional hydrocarbon sources nor seals.

This state of neither open-ocean, nor dry land, gave the Early and Middle Jurassic rocks a highly mixed character. This heterogeneous environment hosts some discovered oil and gas – but not very much compared to the rocks deposited in the Early Cretaceous. It is, however, the oldest rock in the basin still carrying a realistic chance of becoming a complex, but potentially rich, exploration frontier. Through the Middle into the Late Jurassic, the environment became increasingly marine. Seas centred on the Middle Ob region became larger and more persistent. Yet, periodically, the water retreated and the basin filled with sands disgorged through the surrounding river deltas.

This progression met its logical conclusion near the end of the Late Jurassic, when the transgression of a single sea covered the entire basin. In the basin centre, the water was deeper than previous Jurassic seas. Moreover, the Late Jurassic sea was largely isolated from the broad sweep of global ocean circulation.

The sediments deposited over the period from 152 to 146 million years ago in this broad, warm and quiescent sea are known as the Bazhenov shale. Water temperature was high enough to support an abundant biologic community of algeas and the types of related microorganisms whose remains form the source of oil and gas. In the basin centre, the water depth was 600 to over 2,200 feet deep.[28] The rich accumulation of total organic carbon (TOC) can be seen in Map 10.

Multiplying the volume of the Bazhenov shale by its percent TOC yields an estimate and map of the total mass of organic carbon available for transformation to oil and gas. The data from that map can be subjected to a more complex mathematical transformation in order to estimate the volume of hydrocarbons generated. The product of this second transformation, which is principally a function of the heat applied to the organic matter during burial, is shown for the Middle Ob area of the basin in Map 11.[29]

As the Late Jurassic closed, the Bazhenov Sea episodically retreated to the north. Greater sand volumes fed in from the elevated periphery. In the centre of the basin, mild tectonic compression renewed the uplift of old Permo-Triassic highs. This further shrank the Late Jurassic seas. They became increasingly disconnected and less persistent. While organic production and its preservation dropped, over the balance of the Late Jurassic and into Early Cretaceous time, source rocks continued to form.

Although the Bazhenov sea ebbed at the beginning of the Cretaceous, most of the basin remained under water. An increasing volume of sand entered this sea, principally from the highlands on the Siberian plate to the east. A broad shelf ran north-south, roughly parallel to the modern course of the Yenisey River. On the shelf itself, the relatively thick reservoirs of the Megion and Vartov formations were deposited. Similar sands, sourced from large rivers and deposited on a broad shelf are the same types of rocks productive on the Gulf of Mexico shelf in the US or the Niger River delta off Nigeria. Although the Megion and Vartov contain the main oil-bearing reservoirs of the basin, they are not exceptional by worldwide standards in thickness, permeability or homogeneity. Compensating that, however, they are present in very bountiful volumes (Map 12).[30]

Like the Gulf of Mexico, or Nigeria, seaward of the broad shelf, there were smaller volumes of sediments deposited in deeper water on and below the slope. These sands form the more complex, but poorly explored reservoirs of the Achimov Formation. While harder to find and produce than shelf sands, deep-water reservoirs have produced a remarkable set of discoveries worldwide since recognition of their potential in the eighties. These include major discoveries in the deep water of the US Gulf of Mexico, Nigeria, Equatorial Guinea and Brazil. In West Siberia, the most important Achimov producer is Yukos' Priobskoye field in the Middle Ob.

As the Early Cretaceous continued, the growth of large structures in the central basin picked up. These large uplifts (shown in the Middle Ob area in Map 11 as yellow polygons surrounded by teeth pointed down-slope) played two critical roles in the trapping of oil in the region. First, the broad, very large positive structures served to focus migrating oil from very large areas (up to thousands of square miles of fetch). This, and the relative absence of shallow, through going faults that would vent oil to the surface, created efficient pathways between the Bazhenov source and Neocomian reservoirs.

Second, smaller uplifts, on the larger positive structures, formed the immediate traps that caught and retained the oil in the Megion and Vartov reservoirs. As in the Volga-Ural basin, West Siberia's major uplifts only cover a fraction of the basin's total area, but trap the vast majority of the discovered oil and gas.

At the close of the Neocomian Epoch, most of the West Siberian basin was again above the water line. When marine incursions occurred, they were generally restricted to the north, fingering southward to shallow bays and estuaries. Another cycle of basin-wide marine transgression did follow in the Late Cretaceous (depositing an important shale that seals the super-giant gas fields of the northern basin), but otherwise, sediments piled on slowly in the Middle Ob region over the last 132 million years.

Other than by adding to the burial that cooked the organic matter in the Bazhenov shale into oil and gas, post-Neocomian sedimentation and basin development had little influence on the oil resources of West Siberia. The region has also remained tectonically quiet, with occasional compression slightly increasing the size of uplifts – trapping even more oil and gas. This quiescence, however, also meant that the oil, once trapped, remained secure in those traps – rather than leaking and being lost to the surface.

One final, partly tangential aspect of West Siberian geology must be addressed. The basin holds the world's largest discovered gas resources. They are almost completely concentrated in 60–100 fields in the northern-most part of the basin (Map 7).

Although the topic of natural gas is beyond the bounds of this study, because of their impact on liquids supply, a few salient facts are included here. Almost all of the northern gas fields belong to a few highly related plays and share very similar geologic structure. In nearly all these fields, about two-thirds of the natural gas is 'dry,' nearly pure methane containing almost no hydrocarbon liquids. The dry gas is reservoired in rocks of Late Cretaceous age, deposited in the Cenomanian Epoch. These rocks are younger by 30–40 million years and stratigraphically higher than the Neocomian oil reservoirs of the Middle Ob.

The smaller volume of hydrocarbon liquids in the Cenomanian reflects the biogenic mechanism by which the methane was formed. This process was different than the thermal cracking of marine organic matter that charged the oil fields to the south.[31] Since the sixties, the Soviets, then the Russians produced more than 300 trillion cubic feet of natural gas from a half-dozen super-giant fields in the northern basin; nearly all of that gas came from the shallow (~3,500 feet deep) dry gas Cenomanian reservoirs.

The gas fields of the northern basin, however, are two-storied. Approximately 4,000 feet below the Cenomanian dry gas reservoirs are Neocomian reservoirs – the same age rock that contains nearly all of the oil in the Middle Ob. The rock strata in West Siberia, from the basement up, generally and gently dip to the north. Therefore, the Neocomian rocks around 6,000 feet deep along the Middle Ob are at 8,000 feet or more than 400 miles to the north where the super-giant gas fields were found.

The deeper burial of the Upper Jurassic Bazhenov and Neocomian shales in the north exposed the marine organic matter to higher temperatures. The organic matter cracked first to oil, as it did along the Middle Ob. Then on deeper burial, and higher temperatures only seen in the north, the crude oil cracked further – producing condensate. Regional changes in the geochemistry of organic matter of these shales also made the north more prone to produce condensate than crude oil.

Since the first discoveries in the sixties, Gazprom, the state natural gas monopoly, has focused its efforts almost exclusively on the shallow, dry Cenomanian gas. Almost completely ignored were billions of barrels of condensate (and some oil) in place at the same fields in the deeper Neocomian reservoirs. Why these resources remained fallow and their prospects for development are discussed in Chapter 6.

Notes

1 The role of I.M. Gubkin in recognition of the hydrocarbon potential of West Siberia is best documented in two papers, A.A. Trofimuk, 'Prognozy I.M. Gubkina v otnosheniye neftegazonosnosti Sibiri' ['The Predictions of I.M. Gubkin in Relation to the Oil and Gas Potential of Siberia'], pp. 40–51 and I.I. Nesterov, N.N. Rostovtsev, M.Ya. Rudkevich, F.K. Salmanov and Yu.G. Erv'ye, 'Otkrytiye Zapadno-Sibirskoy neftegazonosnoy provintsii – pobeda ucheniya I.M. Gubkina' ['The Discovery of the West Siberian Oil and Gas Province – A Victory for the Scholarship of I.M. Gubkin'], pp. 42–6. Both appear in *Gubkin Readings*, op. cit.
2 Nesterov, et al, in *Gubkin Readings*, op. cit., p. 42.
3 According to *Oil and Gas Journal*, a standard industry source, as of 1970 world reserves of oil were 530 billion bbls and world gas reserves were 1,490 trillion cubic feet. Note that these totals were reported under definitions much closer to the Society of Petroleum Engineers/World Petroleum Congress (SPE/WPC) standard than the Soviet $A+B+C_1$ EUR resource definition (i.e., the Soviet numbers are overestimates relative to the SPE/WPC definition). Therefore both percentages are high, but by unknown extents (see Appendix II). *Energy Statistics Sourcebook*, 11th Edition (Tulsa, OK: Pennwell Publishing, 1996), pp. 157 and 171.
4 As in other instances, these are Soviet/Russian-style $A+B+C_1$ estimates of recoverable oil.
5 For an overview of the petroleum geology of the West Siberian basin, see the Appendix to this chapter.
6 While West Siberia is also cold, all of Russia is cold and most of the basin (other than the extreme north) is not drastically worse. In terms of latitude, Surgut, in the centre of the oil-producing region, is about half way between Perm, in the northern part of the Volga-Ural basin and Ukhta, in the southern Timan-Pechora basin. Siberia's renowned cold starts in earnest east of the Yenisey River.
7 Two other serious aspects of the water problem are the impact of permafrost and the corrosive chemical composition of surface waters in some areas. These are, however, only serious problems in the northern, gas-bearing part of the basin. See Benjamin J. Seligman, 'Long-term Variability of Pipeline-Permafrost Interactions in North-west Siberia,' *Permafrost and Periglacial Processes*, vol. 11, no. 1 (January–March 2000), pp. 5–22.
8 For a discussion of the politics of this process, see Thane Gustafson, *Crisis*

Amid Plenty (Princeton, NJ: Princeton University Press, 1989). This is a meticulously researched work on the politics of Soviet oil and gas in the seventies and eighties. It provides abundant insights into decision making and a great volume of useful data. However, parts of the analysis suffer from misunderstanding the technical basics of oil and gas exploration and production. Ironically, like the Soviet managers he criticized, Gustafson concluded that the declining ability to add reserves in West Siberia after the sixties arose principally from poor planning and management. Both were regular features of the Soviet oil and gas industries and surely exacerbated the situation, but did not cause it. More exploration would only have meant that the path travelled down the regression line in Figure 9 would have been at a faster pace, giving it a steeper negative slope – not shallower.

9 This can be seen in the spread of data in Figure 9 and the relatively low R^2 in the associated Table 22 in Appendix I.
10 The discovery date of Fedorovskoye is a little problematic because of its eventual combination with several fields collectively referred to as Surgutskoye (plus locaticnal qualifiers). The earliest of this complex, North Surgutskoye, was discovered in 1963, which is used here for the discovery date of the Fedorovskoye-Surgutskoye complex. It is common all over the world for large fields to amalgamate, as their extents and geologic relationships are uncovered by drilling, but it makes some issues, like discovery date, a little confusing.
11 From a geologic and exploration viewpoint, most of the reservoirs in the Krasnoleninskoye (which is a complex of fields on the Krasnoleninskoye uplift) are part of a different hydrocarbon play. Most of its oil is in geologically older rock, of Early and Middle Jurassic age, and even older weathered and fractured basement highs below. The reservoir quality is much poorer. This is part of the reason why the field, discovered in 1962, did not produce until 1985. Poor reservoir quality and concomitant low well performance, were also a part of the reason Krasnoleninskoye ranked among the worst performers in the nineties.
12 See the Appendix at the end of this chapter for a short review of basin geology.
13 Some of the major Russian oil companies did acquire some of the exploration units of the Ministry of Geology during the nineties. However, obtaining title to the discovered, but undeveloped fields on the balance sheets of the geologic organizations motivated these acquisitions. Organizations previously charged with finding new fields remained largely idle throughout the nineties.
14 Lukoil's curious exploratory programme in the Bolshekhet Depression, to the east of the Taz Gulf, has demonstrated this unsurprising result by finding five fields reportedly containing 22 trillion cubic feet of gas and 759 million bbls of liquids (probably condensate with a small volume of crude oil). Lukoil *2002 Annual Report*. It was nice of the company to show that the concept, proved at scores of fields, was still valid slightly outside the bounds of previous drilling. However, the economic rationale for the

15 Gustafson, *Crisis Amid Plenty*, op. cit., p. 117.
16 Maksimov, *Oil and Gas Fields of the Soviet Union*, op. cit., vol. 2, pp. 197–8.
17 Gravity and sulphur are for the BV_8 reservoir, Trebin, et al, eds., *Oils of Fields of the Soviet Union*, op. cit., p. 559.
18 Maksimov, *Oil and Gas Fields of the Soviet Union*, op. cit., vol. 2, p. 198.
19 Gustafson, *Crisis Amid Plenty*, op cit., p. 87.
20 The reserve audit, conducted by the US petroleum engineering firm of Miller and Lents, is available on the TNK-BP web site, *www.tnk-bp.com*.
21 In 1977, the US Central Intelligence Agency released an analysis of future Soviet oil supply. They forecast peak production from the USSR as early as 1978 and no later than the early eighties at a level between 11 and 12 million b/d. Concern over the growing cost burden of water cut appears to have been an important factor in this conclusion. While water handling and drilling requirements did ultimately do in Soviet production growth, it happened about five years 'late' relative to the high end of their forecast timing range. Their high-end peak rate was approximately 500,000 b/d, or 4 per cent too low.

The errors in calling the timing and level of peak production (both small in oil forecasting terms) were probably due to a failure to fully appreciate the productive capacity added by the second generation discoveries in West Siberia. When viewed from outside the USSR at the time, these fields would have 'come out of nowhere.' The original 1977 study was published under the title 'The Impending Soviet Oil Crisis.' Another slightly less pessimistic analysis was released two years later, J.R. Lee and J.R. Lecky, 'Soviet Oil Developments' in *Soviet Economy in a Time of Change*, op. cit., pp. 581–99.

A recent retrospective analysis by the CIA can be found on their web site, J. Noren, 'CIA's Analysis of the Soviet Economy,' *www.odci.gov/csi/books/watchingthebear/article02.html*. Goldman, *The Enigma of Soviet Petroleum*, op. cit., devoted a large amount of attention to these analyses.
22 In Soviet times, a general rule of thumb appears to have developed that fields with $A+B+C_1$ EUR less than about 50–70 million bbls were not economic to develop. Although that standard fell in the eighties to include a few fields that were smaller, it was not until after the break-up of the USSR that fields less than 50 million bbls EUR played any significant role in West Siberian production.
23 The normal procedure onshore, in both the USSR and the West, is to move the drilling rig for each well and drill vertical holes. However, in a swamp, that would require constructing a new drilling pad for each well – an expensive operation.
24 This type of pattern drilling was also the rule in the West at the time. During the eighties in the West, however, there was an increasing recognition that drilling based on reservoir geology, rather than a geometric pattern, both raised recovery and reduced the number of wells required for development.

Water flood usually exacerbates the losses inherent in drilling producing wells on a grid.
25 For data on mean time between failure by pump type over the seventies and eighties, see Gustafson, *Crisis Amid Plenty*, op. cit., p. 113.
26 For overview of data on costs, Ibid., p. 101. For greater detail, see Matthew Sagers, 'Oil Production Costs in the USSR' in *PlanEcon Long Term Energy Outlook* (Washington, DC: PlanEcon, 1987), pp. 50–51 and Albina Tretyakova and Meredith Heinemeier, 'Cost Estimates for the Soviet Oil Industry: 1970-1990,' CIR Staff Paper No. 20, (Washington, DC: US Bureau of the Census, 1986).
27 For an analysis of this in the broader context of Soviet policy in Siberia generally, see Fiona Hill and Clifford G. Gaddy, *The Siberian Curse – How Communist Planners Left Russia Out in the Cold*, (Washington, DC: The Brookings Institution Press, 2003).
28 S.I. Filina, M.V. Korzh and M.S. Zonn eds., *Paleogeografiya i neftegazonosnost' bazhenovskoy svity Zapadnoy Sibiri* [*Paleogeography and Oil and Gas Potential of the Bazhenov Suite of West Siberia*] (Moscow: Nauka, 1984), p. 26 puts the maximum depth at 1,200 feet. Citing more recent analyses, Ulmishek concludes that the maximum water depth of the Bazhenov sea was as deep as 2,240 feet, Gregory F. Ulmishek, Petroleum Geology and Resources of the West Siberian Basin, Russia (U.S. Geological Survey Bulletin 2201-G, 2003), p. 10.
29 The map multiplication is actually multiplication of the gridded data on thickness and per cent TOC that underlie the maps.
30 For a detailed description of these relationships in English, see Ulmishek, *Petroleum Geology of West Siberia*, op. cit.
31 See John D. Grace and George F. Hart, 'Giant Gas Fields of Northern West Siberia,' *Bulletin of the American Association of Petroleum Geologists*, vol. 70, no. 7 (July 1986), pp. 830–52 for a review of the biogenic generation of Cenomanian gas versus the thermogenic generation of the Neocomian liquid hydrocarbons in both the central and northern parts of the basin.

CHAPTER 4

THE PEAK, COLLAPSE AND RECUPERATION

The cycle of peak, collapse and recovery of Russian oil production over the last 30 years is not, in itself, unique – either in the history of the Russian industry or at large. However, the size of the rise, the level of maximum production and the pace of the precipitous fall that followed all set records. During three smaller, earlier cycles, Russian production reached a pinnacle, fell and then went on to a new and even higher zenith. Is it reasonable to expect this time that Russia is headed for an output that will exceed the 11.4 million b/d reached in 1987?[1]

There are similarities between the most recent cycle and its predecessors. Yet the contexts of extant economics, politics, technology and depletion in Russia's key producing regions sharply differentiate them.

The USSR set the world record in oil production by the force of a state policy that concentrated a wholly disproportionate share of the nation's wealth to attain that goal. They were successful because, in West Siberia, the country enjoyed the resources of a massive new basin that yielded enormous volumes quickly and, initially, at a relatively low cost. Within West Siberia, Soviet strategy relied on a very small number of extraordinarily large fields. While their outputs were growing, these few fields afforded very strong economies of scale.

As the USSR failed between 1989 and 1991, the state funding that sponsored the peak buckled and oil production began to crash. The new government of the Russian Federation that followed rejected the Soviet command-economy for its oil industry. They made producers depend on market sales of oil for required revenues.

Yet a free domestic market for crude oil never developed in Russia; it does not exist today. Since Russian independence, the domestic price of oil has been heavily regulated at levels substantially below parity with world prices. Although regulation over much of that time was necessary for social and macroeconomic reasons, the effect was to tightly restrict the revenues available to the industry from the home market, which consumed roughly two-thirds to three-quarters of production.

For the first four to five years after the collapse of the USSR, export revenues were also systematically drained by government tax and transportation tariff policies. Oil production in Russia through 1998 was a money-losing proposition, which was strongly reflected in the collapse of production. When the loss per barrel stabilized in the middle of the decade, so did output. The industry found a stable bottom in production of around 6 million b/d – nearly half of the 1987 peak.

In 1998, Russia devalued the rouble, providing a strong mechanism to raise the net incomes of oil producers. In 1999, the industry enjoyed its first positive return to production of oil. The run-up in world oil prices beginning in 1999 powerfully augmented the windfall from devaluation. These new revenues renewed investment in fields nationwide, funded consolidation in the industry and, critically for supply, financed several major new field development projects. In response, production between 1998 and 2003 rose 2.4 million b/d, or 40 per cent.

The state of the industry in 2004 is stronger than at any point in the past, even though Russia is presently producing 2 million b/d less than its last peak production. Moreover, in spite of a new zenith in its financial health, it is unlikely to bust its previous record in output.

Although West Siberia is the second richest oil province on the planet, it is now a relatively mature basin. While large, untapped fields abound, there is no new class of ready and accessible super-giant fields waiting. Indeed, much of the recently restored production has ridden on a small number of large fields. These fields are many times smaller than the fields that supported output in the seventies and eighties.

At the same time, there is no indication that the range of 9–9.5 million b/d Russia will achieve in 2004 is all it can produce. Balancing the greater maturity of the resource base are the influences of record oil prices. If sustained, they will continue to generate enormous gross revenues for the industry. A growing share of these funds is being consumed by increased taxes, tariffs and operating costs, all of which separate gross revenues from net income producers receive at the wellhead. It is the latter that counts in oil supply, making the output path as much a function of state policy as world prices.

The mechanics of how the Soviets achieved the high-point of output in the eighties, why and how it fell apart, and the conditions of its present restoration all inform on the course of future supply of oil from Russia.

Всех Сильнее!*

For two decades after the end of the Second World War, steadily climbing Volga-Ural production propelled Soviet economic growth. It took only a few years to recapture national pre-war oil output. Then, for the next 25 years, the USSR enjoyed what was, in retrospect, its economic heyday.[2] From 1955 to 1975, the nation's gross national product (GNP) expanded at more than 5 per cent annually – impressive by any standards. Yet over each successive Five Year Plan, the increase slowed a little more.[3]

In the sixties, just as the surge of Volga-Ural production began to flag, geologists found a new and unexpected source of even greater riches – West Siberia. The new basin not only closed the shortfall between Moscow's dictates and what oil came from west of the Urals, it moved output and expectations to a new and much higher level. Beyond oil, the fresh basin beyond the Urals held what was soon recognized as the world's largest discovered concentration of natural gas.

By 1972, oil had overtaken coal as the country's leading source of energy.[4] Although the economic expansion was slowing, the Soviet Union was becoming ever more oil-dependent. From the end of the fifties to the late seventies, Soviet oil consumption grew at an expanding rate (Figure 14).[5] Yet, every year's larger increment of new oil bought a smaller increase in GNP. Were the growth in oil supply to abate, it might have sparked a recession or worse.

By the seventies, this fundamental connection between macroeconomic growth and rising cheap energy supplies led Moscow into a Faustian bargain with its oil and gas industries. As long as the state shovelled ever-increasing money into West Siberia, the basin's oil and gas producers promised ever-increasing production.

Cheap oil and gas drove Soviet economic policy. They not only fed the domestic economy directly, they also centred foreign trade. Soviet ideology still hewed to the goal of autarchy. However, by the seventies, deficiencies in that plan spurred expanding agricultural imports and Moscow began buying abroad what was needed, but was poorly produced by domestic industries. To cover this shopping, oil, then natural gas became the nation's main hard currency earners.

The great explosion in world oil prices in the seventies and early eighties radically leveraged mounting oil exports.[6] Reflecting their escalating importance, the Soviets sent one out of every four barrels in new production abroad. By the early eighties, 60 per cent of hard-currency earnings came from oil; gas added another 15 to 20 per cent.[7]

Soviet foreign trade, however, was more than just swapping hydro-

---

* *Vsekh sil'neye* [Stronger than all others] – part of a line in a song from the Civil War about the Red Army being stronger than all others. Being number one (at anything and everything) was a persistently deep part of Soviet ideology.

68 Russian Oil Supply

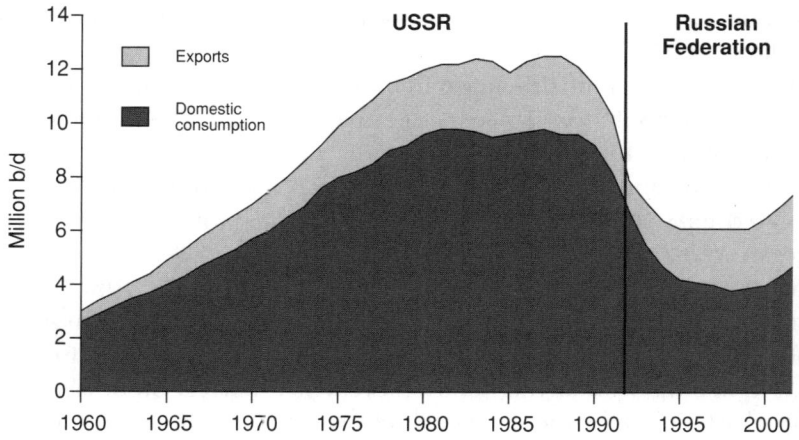

Figure 14: Domestic Consumption and Export of Soviet/Russian Oil

carbons for wheat with the West. There were the Soviet client states. To further bind its empire, the USSR deliberately pushed its satellites into almost complete reliance on Soviet oil, then natural gas. The economics of supplying oil and gas to Eastern Europe were complex. These nations paid for much of what they received in barter of a variety of goods and services, including construction of the pipelines that served them. By some measures, the Soviet Union deeply exploited its vassals in this relationship, viewed by others, the advantage flowed the other direction.[8]

Two facts about Soviet energy trade within its sphere are certain. One is that the absolute volume of Soviet oil and gas delivered to its client states rose sharply through the seventies. The other is that from the mid-seventies into the early eighties, the opportunity cost of those supplies skyrocketed with the combination of surging world prices and an ever-wider hard currency market for Soviet oil and gas.

As Western nations coped for the first time with the economic consequences of oil dependence, the leadership in Moscow blithely assumed their own endowment was endless. They suffered little anxiety over the abilities of their oil and gas industries to meet ever higher targets. In mid-decade, concerns that arose over climbing production costs and sputtering performance in the Volga-Ural basin evaporated in the high heat of attention and possibilities surrounding West Siberia.[9]

The seventies were a wrenching time for the West; many of its troubles rooted in a pervasive reliance on cheap imported oil. In 1970, the price of Arab light at Ras Tanura, the leading world marker crude, stood at $1.80/bbl – a price that had been solid in nominal terms for a decade. By 1976, it shot to $12.38/bbl and, in 1979, to an almost-unbelievable $30.03.[10]

At the decade's end, Russia's arch-rival, the United States, suffered under inflation of 13 per cent and the bank prime lending rate at the same level. The first oil price shock of 1973 sparked a two-year recession; the impending second shock would do the same. The US imported half of its oil needs, much from places where it had sharply decreasing influence.[11]

Moscow regarded this tableau of capitalist turmoil with a smug public face. The USSR, after all, had become the world's largest oil producer in 1975 and was on a clear track to lead the world in natural gas. Rather than importing, one of every five barrels of Soviet crude was exported. Yet, as the seventies drew to a close, below the surface, a new reality was slowly percolating up from the fields toward Moscow.

By 1979, Romashkino, and three of the other five largest fields of the Volga-Ural basin, had peaked. Only Arlan was growing, barely, and it hit its maximum the following year. The basin as a whole reached its zenith in 1976. Viewed on the eve of the eighties, there was little chance it might catch a second wind. The last field over a billion barrels went on line in 1971 and even it was nearing its top. The situation west of the Urals did not look good.

Of course, balancing the bad news, in West Siberia, the picture was far from bleak. Even there though, more quietly and forebodingly, trends portending coming trouble were surfacing. Below the banner headlines, throughout the seventies, exploration yielded progressively lower gross volumes of new reserves. Each year saw the average size of new discoveries slide – despite dramatically increased funding (Figure 9).[12] Average water cut was rising sharply in all but the very youngest fields. Basin-wide, the flow rates of newly drilled wells fell by half between 1975 and 1980. Over the same period, the rate of growth in oil production itself, while still outstanding, also dropped by half of what it was in the first half of the decade.[13]

While engineers pushed output at Samotlor way beyond initial plans, as its rate of growth approached zero, the USSR was desperately dependent on this lone field. The next fields down, Fedorovskoye and Mamontovskoye, were much smaller. Samotlor made 3.4 million b/d in 1980, the other two topped out a few years later at 1 million b/d each.

The lognormal distribution of field sizes dictated that it just deteriorated from there. As the three first-generation fields peaked, the burden shifted quickly to the second generation of discoveries. These 14 fields did make a major contribution to the basin's growth (Figure 10).

However, on average, they were less than one-tenth the size of Samotlor. If the largest three fields declined quickly, the second generation could not fill the gap. Moreover, greater reliance on an ever wider geographic distribution of smaller fields imposed increasingly tough infrastructure and management requirements.

The answer from Moscow was 'Drill!' Drill infill wells at the old super-giant fields; drill at the second and third generation giants; spud more wells at the dozens of 'other,' smaller fields found around the major accumulations. Even drill at the aging and smaller fields west of the Urals. The number of new wells rose in Central Asia and engineers put more wells down in the new offshore province of Azerbaijan.

If 'Socialism + Electrification = Communism' placed the burden of success on *elektriki* in the thirties – from the mid-seventies to mid-eighties, keeping communism's promise fell squarely on *buroviki*, the drillers. This was no surprise. The same *buroviki* who turned the Volga-Ural basin into a pincushion in the fifties and sixties rose to run the Soviet Ministry of Oil twenty years later.

Yet, as long as there were large, fresh fields to drill, the 'Drill!' approach was eminently sensible. In 1976, a 6 per cent increase in the nation's well stock won a 6 per cent increase in production. But by the early eighties, even though the well count rose 6 per cent annually, each year's increment bought less than 1 per cent more oil.[14] Natural resource economics offers few more obvious cases of diminishing marginal returns to the investment of labour and capital (Figure 15).[15]

Moreover, this narrow dependence on drilling left three critical components of sustainable production seriously under funded. Two were technical – well maintenance and mechanization (i.e., adding pumps). Both were stealthy deficiencies. As long as the percentage growth in wells through new drilling exceeded the percentage of wells failing, output could be held roughly level. Drilling new wells was much more expensive than installing pumps. But if the bosses cared only about physical volumes of oil produced and ignored cost, men in the field could hide the failure to meet repair and mechanization goals under the cover of output from new wells.

The third problem, overshadowing the entire West Siberian oil and gas industry, was housing. In typical Soviet fashion, the decision was made in the sixties to settle as well as develop West Siberia. Marshes were drained for new towns, but construction never kept pace with the surging tide of workers. Some crews from west of the Urals flew in as temporary brigades that then rotated out. They stayed in abysmal makeshift housing, with nearly no amenities – dismal even by Soviet standards.

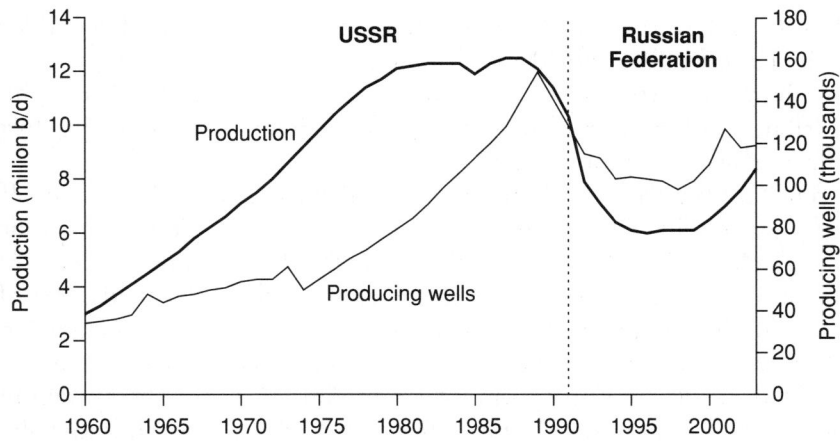

Figure 15: Relationship between the Number of Producing Wells and Oil Production

The result by the eighties was a population of over two million in the Middle Ob and northern basin (for natural gas). Most workers in West Siberia earned more than nearly anyone else in the USSR, but many lived in perhaps the nation's worst poverty. It became progressively harder to attract needed labour, particularly skilled workers. Most of them had the option to remain west of the Urals, do little but live well, albeit with less cash at the end of each month.[16]

Then, in 1984, disaster struck at Samotlor. From its peak in 1980 through 1983, the field had lost about 100,000 b/d of capacity annually. While a large absolute volume, a decline around 3 per cent could be expected from a field that size. Fedorovskoye and Mamontovskoye, still together increasing at about 150,000 b/d annually, filled the gap.

In contrast to the previous four years, in 1984, Samotlor lost 10 per cent of its production and another 15 per cent in 1985 – a total of 673,000 b/d of capacity. This dramatic collapse was a failure with many fathers. Most prominent among them was the loss of wells through mechanical breakdown, which reached 1,000 by the end of 1985.[17] This was the foreseeable outcome of neglecting maintenance and repairs.

Water cut also played a major role. The water injected into the ground with such fervour in the seventies had to be pumped back to the surface in the eighties. Water climbed from 24 per cent of the fluid lifted by Samotlor's wells in 1980, to 68 per cent by 1985 – an extraordinarily quick rise. The field was drowning in water, all of which required pumping and processing to recover any oil. Nizhnevartovskneftegaz, the production association responsible for Samotlor, was in dire need of pumps and expanded oil-water separation facilities.

The trigger for these events may have even been pulled in Moscow. During the brief reign of Yuri Andropov (1982–84), the government made a furtive attempt to rein in the oil industry's colossal spending.[18] The cut was small and only affected the increase in funding. But by that time, the industry had been running at full capacity for years; Soviet oil production had become extremely fragile. In this state, even a hiccup in the rate of ever-increasing investment may have propagated downward and destabilized the most precarious element of the system – production at Samotlor.

While Fedorovskoye and Mamontovskoye covered losses at Samotlor through 1983, by mid-decade, their increases unfortunately, but predictably, gave out. Both fields experienced doubling of water cuts; both were plagued by idle wells. Consequently, much of the 1984–85 shortfall at Samotlor translated directly to the national level. Moreover, under the national plan, output growth in West Siberia was to offset the annual losses from the Volga-Ural basin, which by the early eighties totalled more than 200,000 b/d per year. Because of the failures of 1985, for the first time since the height of the Nazi invasion in 1942, oil production in the USSR fell.

Heads rolled. Drilling superintendents in the swamps of the Middle Ob to the Minister of Oil were sacked. In Moscow, the new Soviet administration of Mikhail Gorbachev promised to re-orient the economy from heavy industry to consumer goods and services. But completely contrary to that goal, with the threat of collapsing oil output, the industry wrested even more money from the state. Gorbachev went to West Siberia in 1985 to personally rally the workers and flay their bosses.

By the end of 1985, a Stakhanovite assault on renewed oil growth was well under way. The languishing Volga-Ural basin was energized, cutting the basin-wide decline from 200,000 b/d annually to about 64,000 b/d in 1989.[19] In Azerbaijan, engineers accelerated development of the new offshore fields. In Kazakhstan, further delineation drilling of the Tengiz field, discovered in 1980 on the northeast coast of the Caspian Sea, demonstrated the presence of billions of barrels of oil. Had there been secret prayers offered in Moscow for a new, virgin exploration frontier to relieve the burden on West Siberia – the North Caspian basin appeared to be the answer.[20]

The development of Tengiz was the most technically challenging of any oil field in the country. Its reservoirs are very deep and bear abnormally high temperatures and pressures. Several thousand feet of salt cap the reservoirs and a deadly high concentration of hydrogen sulphide is mixed in the field's associated gas. Nevertheless, the field offered the industry the hope of salvation. If they could tough out the rest of the eighties in West Siberia, big oil might be won in the south in the nineties.

In West Siberia, the Soviet state pulled all the stops between 1986 and early 1988. The pumps needed at Samotlor were bought from France. They rushed rigs into the surprisingly prolific second-generation fields. Although the third generation of discoveries averaged 15 times smaller than Samotlor, they were drilled too. Even very small fields (by West Siberian standards), located near large ones, were entrained. In fact, as West Siberia reached its peak in 1987 and 1988, it was this last group of about 100 'other' smaller fields in the basin that actually pushed the Soviet Union over the 12 million b/d mark (Figure 10).

This was the last industrial gasp of the Soviet regime. It was a great success, if measured only by the extraordinarily narrow standard of physical oil lifted from the Earth's crust. In that 'success,' however, were more than the seeds of the coming collapse, there were full-grown pathogens waiting to attack.

Yet only irony rewarded their efforts. In 1986, the principal excuse for diverting so much national wealth to ever-increasing oil production was lost in the downfall of world prices. A barrel of crude oil, which went for a high of over $35/bbl in 1980 slid to $27.53 in 1985. But in 1986, the loss of OPEC unity chopped prices by half – gutting the USSR's hard currency income.

Modernization of the Soviet Union, promoting a consumer economy and rationalization of investment in basic industry formed the core of Gorbachev's *perestroika*. Hard currency earnings from oil and gas were vital to these reforms and when oil prices buckled, much of the economic justification of endlessly rising investment in oil went with it.

Nevertheless, the final push carried the industry forward through 1988, which marked the end of the national peak in production. Despite Gorbachev's oft-repeated goal of slipping the bonds of the Faustian bargain made with the oil industry a decade earlier, on his watch, from 1984 through the end of the national peak in 1988, investment in the industry rose 45 per cent.[21]

The Bigger They Are, The Harder They Fall

With over 120,000 producing wells, hundreds of thousands of employees and billions of roubles invested, the Soviet oil industry did not simply peak then die. The force of two decades of focused and fulsome patronage carried production for another year, as in 1989 national output fell by only 300,000 b/d, or 2.5 per cent. That, however, was as far as inertia could take them.

For the next five years, Russian oil production plummeted. The speed was unprecedented and the absolute loss of capacity unequalled in the history of the world industry. The immediate cause was simple – a massive contraction of the stock of producing wells. The algebra of that reduction was also straightforward. Russia lost an exponentially increasing number of wells that had been producing, at the same time that the number of new wells being drilled collapsed (Figure 16).

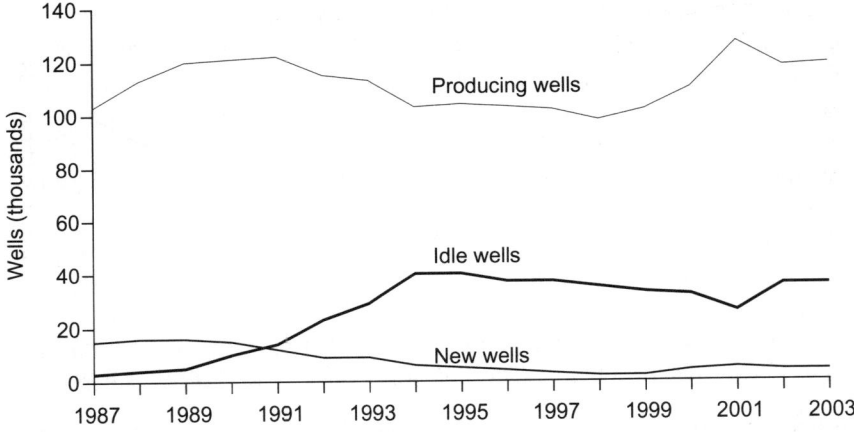

Figure 16: Relationship between the Number of New Wells, Idle and Producing Wells

The much more serious side of the problem was the growth of 'idle wells,' the designation for a well that was producing and stopped. Had only new drilling been affected, Russia would have suffered only a fraction of the capacity it actually lost.

The idle well 'crisis,' as it became known, began immediately after the massive 1986–88 recovery campaign wilted (Figure 17). State budgets for field operations dove in every year thereafter, falling by half as of 1992.[22] Well repair took the hardest hit. By 1991, the number of wells going off line exceeded the number of new wells drilled. In 1992, the number of producing wells in the newly independent Russian Federation was lower than during its last year as part of the USSR (Figure 16).

As budgets shrank, producers deferred maintenance; the backlog of wells awaiting repairs quickly and inexorably accumulated. Whereas idle wells ran at around 3,000 during the eighties, by 1993 there were 29,101. This cost the nation 1.6 million b/d of production, or 23 per cent of national output. A seemingly incredible number of wells remained offline for want of small repairs or lack of routine attention. Wells accounting for nearly 40 per cent of the lost production in 1993 could have been fixed for an average of $55,000 each.[23] If even only half of the extant world price of $17/bbl flowed back to the wellhead, the cost of fixing wells requiring minor repairs could be recouped in three to four months.

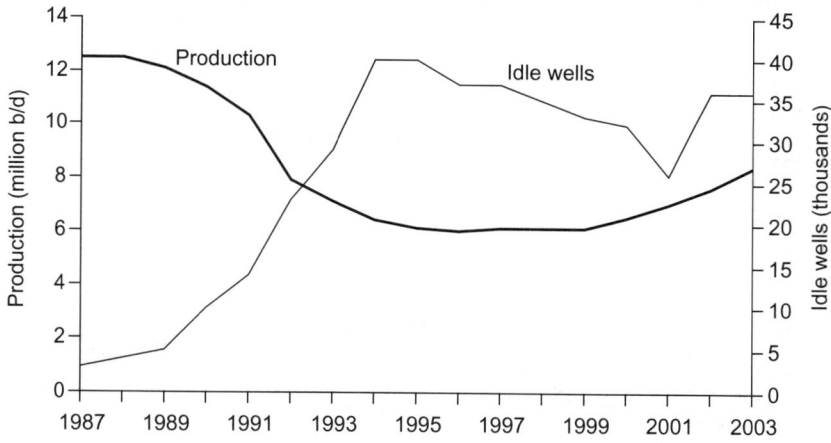

Figure 17: Relationship between the Number of Idle Wells and Oil Production

Beyond wells that could be quickly and cheaply fixed, thousands of others were simply turned off. In some cases it was conservation – shutting down marginal wells while still operable, rather than waiting for them to break. In other cases, because electricity prices started to escalate quickly after the end of the USSR, for low-productivity wells, it cost more in electricity to run the pumps than producers got for the oil.

While sudden poverty was the primary aetiology of the idle well crisis, it was not the only cause. The other major factor was the fracturing of the industry itself. That started in 1989 and 1990. As the twitchy Gorbachev administration increasingly reshuffled ministers and managers, it became impossible to get consistent direction out of Moscow – despite the ever more precarious state of the industry.

Finally, on December 26, 1991, the USSR officially dissolved. Organizationally, this propagated through oil supply in two ways. At the top, the unified Soviet oil industry became disjointed and spread between what had suddenly become several independent countries. The most important connection lost was with Azerbaijan. While the USSR's oil production was more than 80 per cent concentrated in the Russian republic, much of the industry's ancillary support came from Baku. Azeri plants were responsible for a large fraction of oil field equipment, including the gear for drilling and pumps.

After independence, Azeri equipment, previously provided to Russian fields basically for free, at first became unavailable because of disrupted inter-republican rail transit. Then, if a producing organization in Russia could get Azeri equipment at all, their formerly fraternal Azeri comrades wanted cash – US dollars specifically – and they wanted payment in advance.[24] In the first couple of years of Russian independence, this was almost impossible. As a result, while Russian producing organizations had plenty of manpower to drill wells and repair equipment and facilities, they increasingly lacked the parts.

Another, even more momentous organizational rupture occurred within Russia itself. During the Soviet period, producing divisions of the Soviet Ministry of Oil operated over compact geographic domains. There were approximately 30 of these state entities. A few weeks before the collapse of the USSR, three of them, Langepasneftegaz, Urayneftegaz and Kogalymneftegaz, revolutionized the industry in becoming the first private oil company in Russia since the fall of the tsar – Lukoil.

In the late eighties, the Gorbachev administration allowed the formation of small, private service-sector companies. However, the establishment of Lukoil was the conversion of three major state entities at the centre of the national economy. After independence, several more state oil-producing associations also made the transition to 'private stock companies.'

In principle, the *quid pro quo* between these new entities and the new Russian government was simple. While the federal government initially retained a majority stockholding in each company, the state essentially transferred title to reserves and equipment to the new private firms. In return, these companies took the responsibility of self-financing. The sale of oil on domestic and export markets would finance operations and (hopefully) provide profits to the firms' stockholders, including the state itself.

The elimination of state funding occurred as promised. However, the other side of that bargain, allowing producers to earn required revenue from the sale of oil at home and abroad quickly derailed and stayed off the track for several years. Both components of revenue

– domestic and export – failed. Of the two, however, the biggest and most enduring impediment to a true market-based Russian oil industry was domestic price controls.

In 1992, 77 per cent of crude oil production was consumed within Russia.[25] On a purely volumetric basis, therefore, the majority of the industry's revenues would be expected from domestic sales – but that did not happen. Immediately after the dissolution of the USSR, the Russian Federation government moved to maintain the extreme Soviet price controls on crude oil. The 1992 controlled price (including value added tax of 28 per cent) was approximately \$0.50/bbl compared to \$19.37/bbl for Brent, the standard world price marker crude.[26]

Inflation that was to savage the country for several more years had begun. To allow domestic oil prices to suddenly fly up to parity with world prices might have utterly destroyed the brand new Russian economy – already badly weakened by systemic congenital defects. Moreover, the government argued, the industry only 'needed' \$1.50–\$2/bbl.[27] Therefore, the \$10 to \$15 gap between the price really 'needed' to maintain production and parity would have gone only to the privileged few catapulted to the top of the emerging oil industry. Even without 70 years of Soviet ideology, it was politically easy to oppose sudden and far-reaching price deregulation.

Nevertheless, the embryonic market imposed imperatives and the International Monetary Fund made its demands. Over the first three years of Russian independence the domestic price of crude oil did rise, although never close to world price parity. The domestic controlled price climbed to the \$4/bbl range in 1993; \$5/bbl the following year and up to \$8/bbl in 1995. There was also an increasing volume of 'free market' domestic sales that exceeded the controlled price. Some of the increase in domestic prices reflected government manipulation of taxes and transportation tariffs, but some increased flow of money did make it back to producers.

Even as the price of domestic oil rose, however, producer revenues were assaulted by another entirely new economic phenomenon – non-payment. The Soviet system of clearing accounts between economic entities disappeared with the USSR. For several years, no real banking system supplanted it. It was extremely hard for a customer to pay, even if he were so disposed.

Yet most were ill-disposed. Major industrial enterprises and local governments consuming oil products shared a very strong inertial sense of entitlement to get theirs paying little or nothing in return. Realizing that basic heating, transportation, and what employment there was, desperately depended on energy supplies, the government took no measures to enforce payment of producers' receivables. In fact, they often intensified the problem by mandating deliveries of crude to important domestic customers – irrespective of arrears.

The non-payment problem was central to the crash of Russian oil starting in 1993, and very influential in 1994 and 1995. As much as 30 per cent of receivables for domestic sales were either not paid at all or paid in barter. The bartered goods were usually of questionable value and always required additional costs to liquidate. By the end of 1994, approximately $10 billion was owed to the industry, but by the end of the third quarter of 1995, that had doubled.[28] Non-payment by customers in the other former Soviet republics compounded it.

The combination of tight domestic price controls, and non-payments, drastically elevated the importance of export sales between 1992 and 1998. Foreigners paid in hard currencies and just as importantly, they actually paid. The problem with revenues from export sales was not with the buyers at Russia's borders, it was the route the money had to take from the border back to the wellhead.

In principle, money followed the same route to the wellhead whether the oil was sold on the domestic or export markets. Ignoring the problem of non-payment, the starting point was the price for oil paid at the sales point.[29] For the domestic market, that was the refinery gate, usually in the Volga-Ural basin. For export sales, it was the point where the oil crossed the Russian border, either at the ports on the Baltic and Black Seas, or where the export pipelines leave the country.

From the sales prices, producers must pay the cost of transportation from the fields to the sales points. In virtually all cases, the transportation was provided by the state pipeline monopoly Transneft, which charged state-determined tariffs. Further, the amount of excise taxes levied directly on the volumes of oil sold must also be subtracted.[30] Finally, there were the operating costs of producing oil in the fields.

Although the export oil sale price was much higher than the domestic price, this margin became the main target for government entities to extract revenue. From 1992 through 1995, the Russian federal government constantly manipulated both the transport tariffs and taxes to reap as much as they could of export earnings. Moreover, all manner of local government entities imposed taxes and fees on domestic and export oil for an amazing array of causes. Between all levels of government, there were at times over a dozen levies: severance taxes, road taxes, surface use taxes, environmental taxes, social welfare taxes, excise taxes, taxes to support exploration and nearly as many others as idle and impoverished bureaucrats could imagine.

Russians at all levels saw their oil industry as ridiculously moneyed and chiefly a mechanism for grotesquely enriching a clique of top insiders. Therefore, it was quite deliberately milked. Every entity that could do so dipped into the stream of cash flowing between export sales points and the wellhead. To varying degrees, the money that did make it back to the wellhead was further depleted by mismanagement and to swell the personal wealth of a small coterie of industry managers and their allies.[31]

The money left over (when there was any) constituted the producer's net income at the wellhead. This money was available for capital investment (Figure 18). With those funds, companies could invest in fixing idle wells, drilling new ones or exploring for new fields. They could also distribute the funds to shareholders or make investments or pay people that did not contribute to Russia's capacity to produce oil.

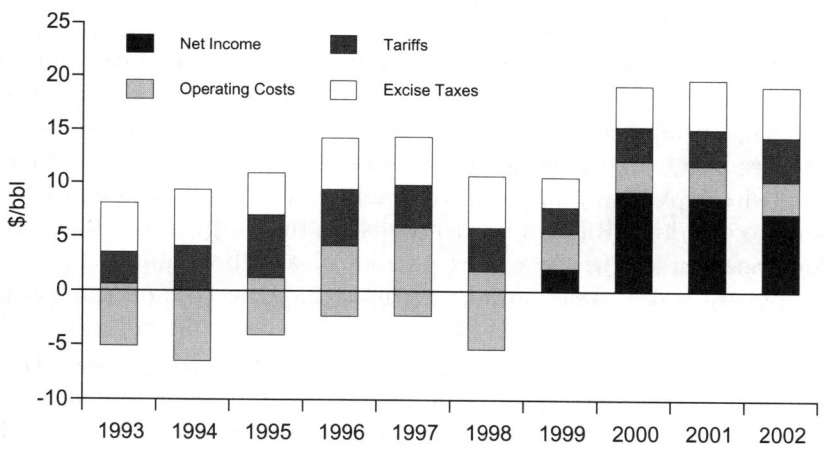

Figure 18: Oil Prices, Tariffs, Excise Taxes, Operating Costs and Producer Net Income

Restricting attention to the flows from sales point to wellhead, Figure 18 shows the relationship between the average sales price of oil, tariffs, excise taxes and operating costs and what was left over. Between 1993 and 1998, the combination of low domestic and world prices, and the high deductions drawn from sales revenues, produced annual losses on the production of oil in Russia.

The industry's nadir occurred in 1994 when from an average sales price of less than $10/bbl, Russian producers lost more than $6 on each barrel produced. Although this was not the empirical bottom of

80 *Russian Oil Supply*

production, 1994 was generally considered as the low point of the Russian oil industry. Throughout the nation, producers were simply shutting off well pumps as they lost less money by not producing thousands of wells.

In February 1995, the Federal Board of Bankruptcy Affairs found that all of Russia's oil production organizations, with one exception (Surgutneftegaz), were insolvent.[32] As measured by share prices, between September 1994 and March 1995, 80 per cent of the value of equity in Russian production companies disappeared.[33]

Stabilization of Output

The situation improved slightly in 1995 due to firming export prices, limited domestic price decontrol and small rollbacks in both taxes and tariffs. Rising operating costs did, however, offset some of these gains (Figure 18). Even though producers lost money on each barrel, they were losing less. The progress was enough to slow the collapse of the previous five years. Production in 1995 was only 3 per cent below 1994 – a stunning victory in terms of the industry's recent history.

In 1995, the big wave of privatization hit the Russian oil industry. The firms that did not go private immediately after Russian independence were held in an odd trust arrangement by the Russian Ministry of Fuels and Energy. In 1995, in a procedure described in greater detail in Chapter 5, the government divested a large part of their equity holding in producing organizations.

While privatisation removed the state from a controlling position in many companies, Moscow remained very involved in the oil industry. Reflecting increased sophistication in regulation, starting in the mid-nineties, the federal government began to rely more on the levers of taxes, transportation tariffs, export quotas and to a lesser extent, licensing of subsurface mineral rights.

Because of smaller economic losses at the wellhead, and loans from international organizations, such as the World Bank and European Bank of Reconstruction and Development, the number of idle wells in Russia stabilized in 1995 and 1996. The improvement meant Russia lost less than 2 per cent of output between 1995 and 1996. Fixing wells, better maintenance and a minimal level of new drilling kept the number of producing wells constant from their 1994 low through 1998.

Steadying the stock of producing wells stabilized production in the mid-nineties. The re-election of Boris Yeltsin as Russian President in 1996 ensured that the industry would not be returned to state hands.

The Communist Party candidate proposed this and he lost. Unfortunately, Yeltsin's victory also meant that the nation would continue to muddle along, politically and economically.

For the oil industry in a second Yeltsin administration, the privatization processes begun in 1995 continued in various forms in 1996 and 1997. In some instances, this expanded the position of industry outsiders; in others, the transfers strengthened the position of management teams held over from Soviet days (see Chapter 5).

Financial jeopardy returned to Russia in 1998 when world oil prices again collapsed with the Asian Crisis and OPEC's counter-cyclical decision to increase oil output. The price of the Brent marker crude, which held at around $20/bbl in 1996 and 1997, fell to an average of $13.11/bbl for 1998. The slide began in late 1997 and accelerated in 1998.

By the beginning of 1998, even exporting oil became unprofitable in spite of government roll-backs of taxes and transportation tariffs.[34] The situation in the industry once more became dire. Between October 1997 and August 17, 1998, the share prices of Russian oil companies dropped by over 70 per cent.[35] That this was in line with the slide in all Russian equities was scant comfort.

Reduced taxes and tariffs mitigated some of the producers' losses and shifted some of the incidence in falling oil prices to the state. However, the loss of state revenues from tariffs, excise and corporate income taxes pushed the shaky Russian federal government into an untenable fiscal situation. To firm Russia's position, in July 1998, the World Bank and International Monetary Fund committed more than $22 billion to the government.[36] It was to no avail.

On Friday, August 14, with his own matchless bluster, Boris Yeltsin promised the world 'there will be no devaluations of the rouble ... I say it firmly and clearly. It is not just my fantasy. Everything has been calculated.'[37] Fantasy or not, by the following Monday morning, the numbers did not add up; Russia unpegged the rouble. It followed that with a default on sovereign debt making the 'loans' essentially worthless, the upside for the dollar-denominated oil assets was immense.

Recovery

In late August 1998, it was hard to be optimistic about Russia's situation. Although oil production had been stable since 1995 at around 6 million b/d, there were no signs of growth. Foreign direct investment had largely bypassed Russia since independence, and after devaluation and default there was no reason to expect any inflow at all. The August events pummelled the young and thin domestic capital markets.

Yet in retrospect, rouble devaluation was central to the recovery of Russia's oil production. When the rouble's value came to rest in 1999, it was worth between one-fifth and one-sixth of its pre-August 1998 value (Figure 19). Change in the value of the rouble had no direct effect on the rouble price of oil sold on the domestic market, nor on most transportation tariffs, taxes or operating costs, which were all denominated in roubles.

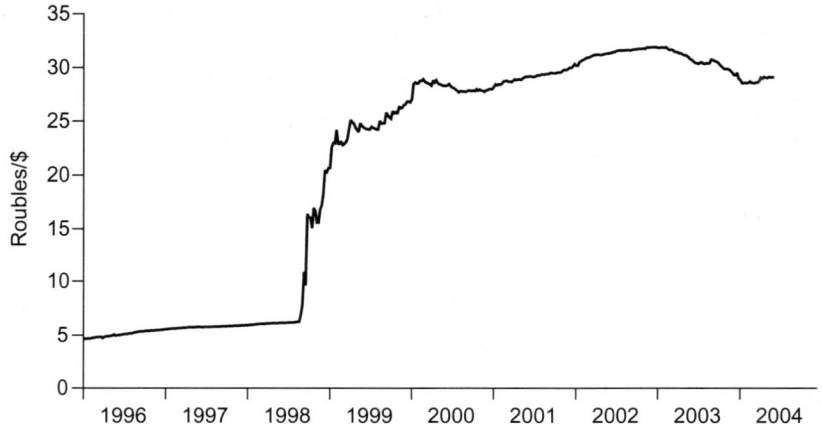

Figure 19: Ruble/Dollar Exchange Rate, 1996–2004

However, measured in dollars, the taxes, tariffs and operating costs paid by the companies all fell dramatically, mirroring the devaluation. Even though export prices remained low through the end of 1998 and into 1999, every dollar received covered five to six times more taxes, tariffs and operating costs. Moreover, the crisis atmosphere accelerated measures to cut operating costs, mainly through reductions of the companies' very large labour forces.[38] The combined effect was to radically raise both the rouble and dollar net incomes of Russian oil producers. Suddenly in 1999, companies that had struggled with losses on production since 1992 were actually making money producing oil (Figure 18).

Primarily because of devaluation, instead of a $5/bbl loss suffered with each barrel produced in 1998, producers received $2/bbl in net income in 1999 (Figure 18).[39] As the economy was still reeling macroeconomically from the devaluation, insignificant production growth in 1999 was not surprising. But the stage was set for a new economic regime in the industry and there was more good news to come.

The next big wind to fill the sails of Russian oil was price. Low world oil prices, which in part precipitated the Russian financial crisis in the summer of 1998, persisted for the rest of that year. Between December 1998 and February 1999, Brent oil traded at daily lows below $10/bbl – levels not seen in two decades. Yet over the following 12 months, the Brent marker crude reached more than $30/bbl – the largest sustained increase in 20 years (Figure 20).

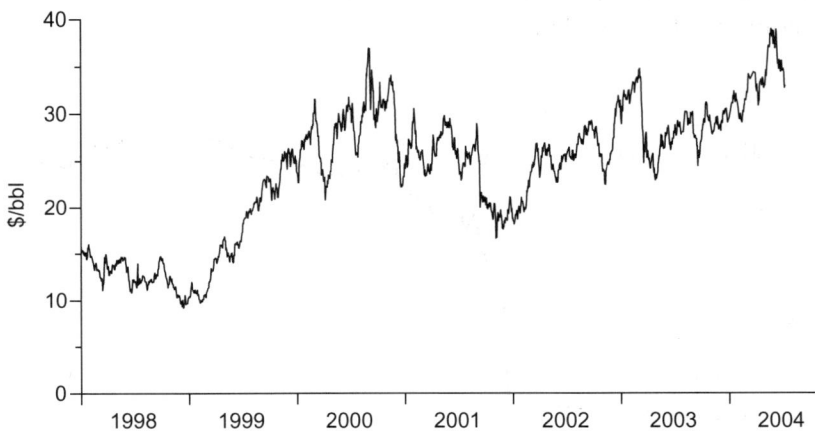

Figure 20: Price of Brent Crude, 1998–2004

The initial run-up in prices did not directly boost the companies' bottom lines. The first part of the increase merely provided enough revenue to cover the loss on every barrel lifted. Domestic oil price controls also slowed the recovery. In fact, in 1999, domestic prices fell. Because two-thirds of Russian production was destined for the domestic market, lower revenues from the home market decelerated the rising tide of money flowing toward company coffers. Yet, the increases in price and rouble devaluation combined to make a major contribution to the profitability of Russian oil production in 1999 (Figure 18).

By the beginning of 2000, the surge in export prices and a significant increase in domestic prices substantially raised the volume of income heading back to producers. They, in turn, began to plough back into the fields much of the net income received at the wellhead (over $9/bbl in 2000). The number of idle wells fell, and for the first time in a decade, the number of new wells rose. Output went up a bracing 6 per cent (Figures 16 and 21).

The same trend continued through 2002. The increases not only fuelled drilling in general, they supported the initial development of

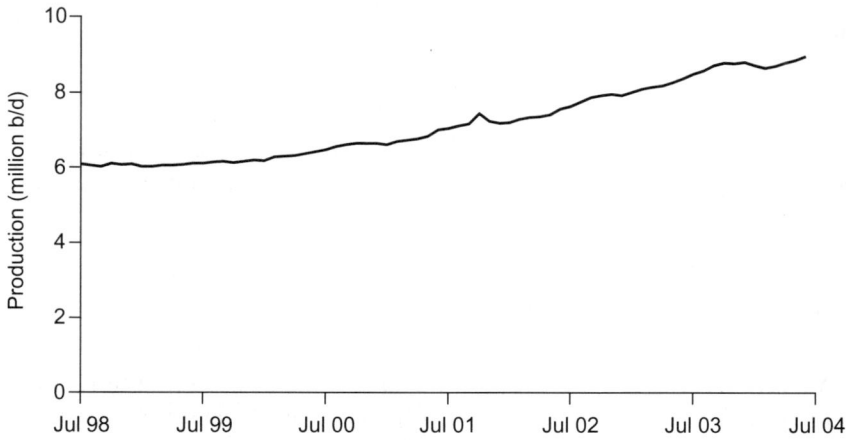

Figure 21: Monthly Russian Oil Production, 1998–2004

a handful of major new fields. The windfall also built war chests within several of the largest companies, which covered the beginning of the most recent round of corporate acquisitions and industry consolidation.

Oil prices fluctuated, but around $25/bbl – a fundamental change from the $12/bbl-world of 1998. The government did, as expected, enlarge its percentage take, raising taxes and tariffs in 2001, 2002 and 2003, but at extant sales prices there was more than enough money to go round and still support significant investment in new productive capacity.

A critical insight into the resurrection of Russian production after 1998 comes from its composition by field. The rising tide of producer net income raised all boats; output increased across nearly all producing organizations in the country. Companies accomplished this by minimizing the decline rates at old fields, through better management and by more drilling. Bringing a relatively large number of small new fields on line between 1999 and 2003 also helped.

While there were perhaps a dozen large fields whose increases powered the post-1998 rise, the five highest-growth fields stand out among them (Table 3).[40] All are located in West Siberia, three in the Middle Ob region and two to the north. With the exception of the smallest, these were fields that had been discovered in the Soviet period. Their sizes and good productive characteristics were long known by the companies that held their licences since Russian independence. There simply had not been the money to develop them.

Table 3: Major Sources of Production Growth from 1998–2002

Field	Production (1,000 b/d) 1998	2002	Operator
Tevlin-Russinskoye	210	247	Lukoil-Kogalymneftegaz
Priobskoye	26	238	Yukos-Yuganskneftegaz
Sugmutskoye	24	160	Sibneft
Sporyshevskoye	8	79	Sibneft
Tyanskoye	46	143	Surgutneftegaz
Total	314	867	

All are divided among four of the five major oil companies in the country, with Sibneft holding two. One of them, Tevlin-Russinskoye, was a third-generation West Siberian discovery, put online in 1986; it was never brought up to capacity before the money ran out. Three are fourth-generation discoveries that experienced no commercial production in the Soviet period. Sporyshevskoye, discovered in 1993, is the only field with major production growth discovered after the collapse of the USSR, and it is the smallest of the group.

Collectively, these five fields increased output by approximately 553,000 b/d between 1998 and 2002, 35 per cent of the 1.6 million b/d growth in Russian production over that period. So, although recovery in Russian production came from scores of fields producing more, and, hundreds losing less, the output from just a few fields capped the tip of the nation's output growth. This, in a sense, was a return to the narrow base of very large fields that drove the increase in Soviet production in the seventies.

Perhaps more importantly, with the exception of Sporyshevskoye, the Soviets discovered these fields two decades ago. What the post-1998 recovery has lacked is broad support for growth coming from fields found and developed *after* Russian independence and the formation of the industry's raft of new private companies.

Comment

In basing fundamental policies on the assumption of limitless resources, Moscow slid into a Faustian bargain with its oil industry: ever-more money for ever-more oil. Like any such deal, it was bound to fail. But in its pursuit, from the seventies through the mid-eighties, Soviet dogma turned the production of physical oil into an end in itself. The result, by the close of the Soviet period, was a system in which no rational relationship existed between the quantity of national wealth devoted to oil and the value of oil brought to the nation.

If Soviet supply strategy was quixotic, they balanced it with a demand policy an equal distance from reality: free oil for the people. For decades, however, they got away with it. As long as delivered cost was very low and the world prices stayed at a low level (< $3/bbl until the first OPEC embargo in late 1973), there was actually little distortion. In fact, from the Second World War to the mid-seventies, the Soviets put their nation's resource base at the service of their own national economic development as few other nations did.

Yet, to everything, there is a season. In the case of depletable natural resources, particularly lognormally distributed deposits of oil and gas, what is feasible, even easy, early in development becomes impossible later. In exploring and producing the Volga-Ural basin, then West Siberia, the Soviet industry rode two successive incoming tides – each large, long lasting and perfectly timed. But tides always retreat. Production always falls: from the well, to the field, to the basin.

As a basin peaks, the average size of producing fields drops, reservoirs are often deeper and fields located further from existing infrastructure. Concomitant is increasing cost. Costs began to rise sharply at the end of the sixties in the Volga-Ural basin, which in itself would have applied pressure to raise domestic oil prices or increase government subsidies.

West Siberia saved Moscow from that decision by allowing the country to switch supply to a basin still in the initial low-cost phase of growth. At exactly the same time, the world price of oil first quadrupled and then nearly tripled again from there. This generated revenues that not only covered higher costs, but provided a powerful incentive to raise output at any cost.

A decade later, it was West Siberia's turn to face the economic consequences of an impending peak. There was no third tide to ride.[41] The industry had only West Siberia's fields, the most volumetrically important of which were at, or beyond, their engineering maximums. This led to what might be called a 'second derivative spiral'. In relying on ever-more drilling and aggressive water floods to raise output, producers had become addicted not only to the levels of annual support, but to the idea that each year's budget would be larger than the previous one. In return, each year the industry produced more oil, but each year's increment was smaller than the one before. Marginal investments up and marginal returns down is an unsustainable dynamic.

Unlike the mid-seventies, when skyrocketing world oil prices forgave rising Volga-Ural basin costs, in the mid-eighties the world price of oil crashed. Export earnings collapsed, petroleum products were still given away domestically and there was no end to the oil industry's appetite for funds. Even if the USSR had not disintegrated, it is very hard to see how a major decline in oil production, and increases in domestic petroleum prices, would not have ensued.

Because of the contradictions of a command economy and for a myriad of other good reasons, the USSR ignominiously entered the dustbin of history. It left, however, a vast and complex legacy.

Its oil industry, despite leading world oil production for over a decade, was morbidly obese. The highest-cost end of supply supported millions of barrels per day of capacity that could not cover its costs at extant world prices (see the appendix at the end of this chapter). This included many fields, the technical impediments of which perversely became reasons to produce them, rather than leave them in inventory. It included oil wrung from wells that trickled only a few cups of oil for every barrel of water pumped and wells drilled so densely that initially they flowed only a few tens of barrels per day.

Moreover, while the USSR produced more oil than any other nation, its industry led from within a bubble of isolation that protected a very brittle structure. Oil-producing associations, as state entities, performed a wide variety of social and economic functions, only indirectly related to oil and gas exploration and production. That created a cost structure that would have been highly uncompetitive in the world market, had they been required to face it.

Moreover, Soviet oil-producing associations depended only on state budget, which bore no direct relationship to world oil prices, or the value of their product to the domestic economy. Their institutional goal was simply to produce more in the short run. This translated into an extraordinary reliance on aggressively developing the few very largest West Siberian fields to meet quarterly targets. Short horizons exacerbated the impact of field size lognormality, which made the next fields below the top group exponentially smaller and more expensive to develop. Balancing so much industrial weight on literally a handful of operations is inherently precarious.

On the demand side, feeding the home market with virtually free petroleum not only created demand for patently uneconomic uses, but made lavish consumption central to the national economy. Refineries were accustomed to paying nothing for the crude they consumed and receiving nothing for the products they produced. All revenues for all major industrial enterprises came from state budgets.[42]

The new Russian government's mandate in the nineties to producers to get their funding from oil sales, therefore, squarely opposed the interests of consumers and the oil industry. The stage was set for a mighty and inevitable collision. But once the collapse was under way – what was the reform-minded administration of Boris Yeltsin to do?

Had the Russian government, on independence, rejected Soviet price controls and prohibited non-payments, oil production would not have fallen as far as it did. But to take a commodity as basic as energy from oil, in a very cold nation, and allow its price to rise suddenly by 30 or 40 times would have further impoverished millions of people, and to what end?

While the 'gradualist' approach 'distorted' the economics of the Russian oil industry for a decade, it was the only, although perhaps needlessly messy, alternative. Through the dialectic of learning by repeated error, a compromise oil market evolved in the mid-nineties. Domestic prices did rise, although not to world parity, the non-payment problem receded, the state rolled back tariffs and taxes and enough money finally flowed as far as the wellhead to arrest the production crash.[43]

An equilibrium level of around 6 million b/d described a band of output consistent with average losses in upstream operations around a few dollars per barrel. Had things not changed in and after 1998, production would have declined somewhat raggedly from there. In this counterfactual case, Russia today, nearly a decade after the collapse stopped, would be producing in the 5–6 million b/d range.

Things, however, did change. The devaluation of the rouble provided a dollar and rouble windfall to producers which moved them from a loss on each barrel to healthy profits. Devaluation itself provided the means to recapture many of the wells simply turned off in the nineties because income at the wellhead did not cover costs. The rapid and sustained escalation of world oil prices that followed in 1999 and 2000 transformed the industry from financially viable, but limp, to swiftly strong. If happiness is the recession of pain, by the start of the new millennium, the Russian oil industry was ecstatic.

This new financial muscle funded the 2.4 million b/d, or 40 per cent increase in production between 1998 and 2003. It also sponsored the latest round of industry consolidation that brought big changes in several of the top Russian oil companies (as described in the next chapter). While producers' net income has fluctuated since its big leap in 2000, its range is far above the levels that jeopardize output.

It should not, however, be assumed that the Russian oil industry has found the key to perpetual motion. The very strong and sustained boost of the 1998 rouble devaluation to Russian oil production economics was a one-shot deal. Every year since, macroeconomic inflation eroded more of the advantage it brought. From 1998 through 2002, the increase in the producer price index (the inflation measure most relevant to industrial processes) grew by 30 per cent annually, albeit at a falling rate. The increase in the price of electricity, a major component of production costs with so many wells on pump, was 23 per cent per year – with no downward trend.[44]

The influence of high world oil prices is not a one-time effect but a continuous one – as long as prices remain high. As of the autumn of 2004, world prices are, in nominal terms, at record levels. But even if a floor of $25/bbl Brent can be assumed for the next few years, it would be dangerous to rely on Russia for the production performance afforded by recent $35–$50/bbl oil.

Perhaps as important, high world oil prices are only a necessary, but not a sufficient, condition for the continued vigour of the Russian industry. It is not gross revenue, but the money that makes it back to producers after tariffs, taxes and operating costs, that counts. Stricter domestic price controls (or lower world prices) could bring down gross revenue, but the greater risk for net income is in the subtrahend – increases in tariffs, taxes and operating costs.

Central to consideration of future supply, it should also be kept in mind that a very small number of large, new field development projects led the restoration of production this decade. There was no other way to add millions of barrels of capacity quickly without relying on new, very large fields. This re-emergence of a narrow armature also brings back some of the fragility of the last Soviet drive to increase production.

The dependence on a small number of very large fields is being mirrored more and more in the structure of the industry itself. The tendency since 2000 has been to increasing concentration of oil resources in the hands of a shrinking number of firms. Overwhelming all of these factors, in the last two years there has been a strong drive to re-assert the federal government directly in the management of oil and gas production. Taken together, it sounds familiar – large state-run (or heavily state-influenced) producing organizations and reliance on a very small number of large fields.

Appendix: The Russian Oil Market from 1983 through 2002

The objective of this appendix is to show, using the supply and demand graphs of classical microeconomics, the changes in Russian oil markets between 1983 and 2002. Five annual short-term snapshots are presented for 1983, 1987, 1993, 1997 and 2002.[45] In the first two, Russia is defined as the Russian Soviet Federated Socialist Republic (RSFSR) of the USSR. In the last three, Russia is the Russian Federation (which is geographically conterminous with the RSFSR). Because of scant and often ambiguous data, some of the values of economic variables shown are approximate and embody a number of assumptions. They do, however, show the general relationships central to Russian oil supply and demand over the last twenty years.

Domestic demand includes all oil consumption by Russian refineries, whether the resulting products were consumed within Russia or exported. This is because – throughout the Soviet period and since – the price paid by domestic refiners for oil was the same whether the resultant product was sold on the export or domestic market. Moreover, production of petroleum products by Russian refineries is an activity of the Russian domestic economy, whether the product is intended for domestic or export consumption.[46]

The same very low elasticity of demand for oil was used in all instances. It was based on the estimate of short-run price elasticity of demand of -0.06 for oil in 23 countries (not including Russia), made by Cooper.[47]

During the Soviet period, Russia was one of fifteen constituent republics of the USSR. Therefore, for 1983 and 1987, there are three components of demand represented by separate functions: demand in the RSFSR, total Soviet demand for Russian oil (which includes Russian exports to other Soviet republics) and total demand (which also includes export demand from outside the USSR). In the post-Soviet period, there are only two demand functions: for domestic consumption within the Russian Federation and total demand (which includes all exports).

The area under the supply function to the point of annual production represents the total delivered cost of Russian oil. For all five years, total costs include operating and transportation costs. For the post-Soviet period, they also include excise taxes levied on oil production and transport. The shapes of the supply functions for each of the five years reflect the author's judgment; they were governed by consideration of the distributions of fields by size and geography and of wells by flow rate, water cut and geography. Costs were estimated for the Soviet period from a variety of sources. For the Russian Federation period, they come from reports by producing companies and the Russian Ministry of Fuel and Energy.

Definitions of Terms

Average delivered cost is an estimate of the cost of oil delivered to domestic refiners or export points, which is the sum of operating cost, transportation and, during the post-Soviet period, excise taxes, in current dollars per barrel.

Consumer surplus is an estimate of the difference between the domestic revenues that producers would have received if sales in the domestic market had taken place at prices in parity with world prices and the amount of domestic revenues actually received from sales at the regulated domestic prices. Note that the estimates of consumer surpluses graphed and reported here include only that fraction captured by consumers because of Soviet and Russian government regulation of domestic oil prices.[48] The consumer surplus is measured in billions of current dollars and is indicated by the cross-hatched area in Figures 22–26.

Domestic consumption is the total quantity of oil consumed within Russia (oil production minus oil exports) in millions of barrels per day. This includes the volumes of oil consumed by Russian refineries in making petroleum products for export as well as for the domestic market.

Domestic price is an estimate of the average Russian refiner's acquisition cost for oil at the refinery gate in current dollars per barrel. The domestic price in 1983, 1987 and 1993 also applied to Russian oil sold to refiners in other Soviet republics. In the Soviet period, domestic prices were purely symbolic.

Domestic revenues are estimates of the revenue received for the sale of oil in the domestic market (domestic price times domestic consumption) in billions of current dollars. Particularly in 1993, and to a progressively smaller extent in both 1997 and 2002, actual domestic cash revenues received by producers were less than the revenues used here. This is because of the problem of non-payment by refineries and the use of under-value barter payments. Because these effects could not be quantified, they were not included. However, the reader should keep in mind that this necessary assumption brings a positive bias to estimates of domestic revenues and by extension, net income. The estimate of consumer surplus has a negative bias for the same reason.

Net income is the income available to producers at the wellhead. It is total revenue minus total cost, in billions of current dollars.

Oil exports are the total volume of oil sold in export from Russia in millions of barrels per day. Imports for all years represented were less than 300,000 b/d, so they did not affect the analysis. In 1983 and

1987, the exported volume did not include the delivery of Russian oil to other republics of the USSR; after that, it did.

Oil export revenues are estimates of the revenues received for the sale of oil in the export market (world price times oil exports) in billions of current dollars. It was assumed that exports to Soviet East European client states in 1983 and 1987 were made at world prices. That probably was not the case, in which case export revenue would have been less than given here, but it is unknown by how much.

By 1993, the Russian Federation was charging world market prices to its former East European clients. However, it was still exporting oil to former republics of the USSR (mainly Ukraine and Belarus) at prices that were less than the world market price, but greater than domestic price. Moreover, non-payment by former-Soviet export customers was a serious, but unquantified revenue drain in 1993. Therefore, the domestic price was applied to exports from Russia to other republics of the former Soviet Union in 1993. By 1997, apparently all export customers paid prices in parity with world oil prices, or very close to it; the non-payment problem had sharply diminished by then as well.

Oil production is the total volume of oil produced in millions of barrels per day.

Oil to other USSR is the total volume (in 1983 and 1987 only) of Russian oil delivered to refineries in other republics of the USSR, in millions of barrels per day. After the collapse of the USSR, these volumes were included in exports.

Revenues from other USSR are the amounts paid by consumers in other republics of the USSR for Russian oil in 1983 and 1987. The same purely symbolic prices used for the domestic markets were used for these volumes, in billions of current dollars.

Total cost is an estimate of the delivered cost of oil, including operating costs, transportation costs and, in the post-Soviet period, excise taxes, in billions of current dollars. Total costs are indicated in Figures 22–26 as areas covered by grey.

Total revenue is an estimate of the revenue derived from the sale of all Russian oil production (domestic revenues plus export revenues) in billions of current dollars. Total revenues are indicated in Figures 22–26 as areas covered by a vertical dash.

World price is an estimate of the average price for oil sold in export at the Russian border in current dollars per barrel.

The Russian Oil Market in 1983

During the Soviet period, under its command economic system, oil production associations were required to produce as much as possible, given the budgets provided by the government (Table 4 and Figure 22). Oil was priced in the domestic market without regard to either the delivered cost or world prices. Typically, over the period, it was estimated at between $0.20 and $0.50/bbl (the latter is used here).

Table 4: Basic Data for 1983 Soviet Oil Market

Variable	Value	Variable	Value
World Price	$25.39/bbl	Total Delivered Cost	$12.8 billion
Domestic Price	$0.50/bbl	Domestic (RSFSR) Revenue	$1.1 billion
Average Delivered Cost	$3.07/bbl	Other USSR Revenue	$0.3 billion
Oil Production	11.4 mb/d	Export Revenue	$33.7 billion
Oil Exports	3.7 mb/d	Total Revenue	$35.1 billion
Oil to Other USSR	1.4 mb/d	Net Income	$22.4 billion
Domestic (RSFSR)		Consumer Surplus	
Consumption	6.3 mb/d	(RSFSR)	$50.9 billion

Costs over a very large volume of production were low because of the dominant role of very large fields. The high end of the short-run marginal cost/supply function was composed principally of output from two types of fields. One class included fields located in environments that were harsh and distant from infrastructure (e.g., Timan-Pechora), highly depleted fields (e.g., North Caucasus and some in the Volga-Ural basin) or fields with very poor oil or reservoir characteristics (e.g., some fields in Timan-Pechora). The other source of high-cost production was the final increment of oil squeezed from the largest, most mature fields in West Siberia, obtained as a result of infill-drilling and very high-injection-rate water floods.

As long as export prices were very high, total revenues covered not only producing the high-cost volumes at the right-hand end of the supply function, but also the subsidy that provided oil to Soviet refineries at prices several times less than the average delivered cost. Because the Soviet rouble was not a convertible currency, export income also attracted a premium in the eyes of the Soviet government, as oil exports became a critical source of hard currency earnings.

94 Russian Oil Supply

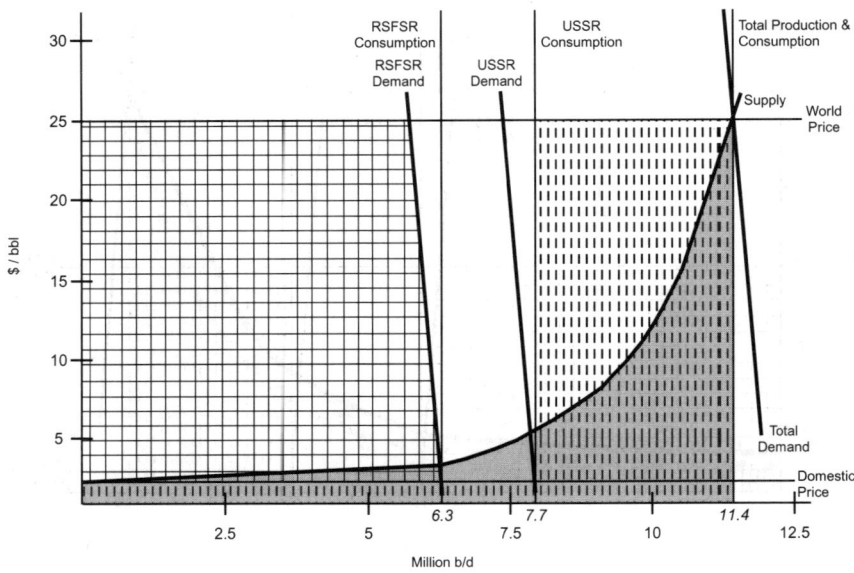

Figure 22: Russian Oil Supply and Demand in 1983[49]

Pricing oil at a purely symbolic level, from a microeconomic perspective, constituted an extreme form of price regulation. As a consequence, an enormous consumer surplus was captured by Russian refineries purchasing oil on the domestic, regulated market.

The Russian Oil Market in 1987

Between 1983 and 1987, the world price of oil crashed. The Soviets did not respond by reducing production (Table 5 and Figure 23). At the same time, oil production costs rose significantly as Russia hit its peak production. Although production was essentially flat between

Table 5: Basic Data for 1987 Soviet Oil Market[50]

Variable	Value	Variable	Value
World Price	$15.04/bbl	Total Cost	$21.3 billion
Domestic Price	$0.50/bbl	Domestic(RSFSR) Revenue	$1.1 billion
Average Delivered Cost	$5.12/bbl	Other USSR Revenue	$0.4 billion
Oil Production	11.4 mb/d	Export Revenue	$14.9 billion
Oil Exports	2.7 mb/d	Total Revenue	$16.5 billion
Oil to Other USSR	2.4 mb/d	Net Income	-$4.8 billion
Domestic (RSFSR)		Consumer Surplus	
Consumption	6.2 mb/d	(RSFSR)	$29.5 billion

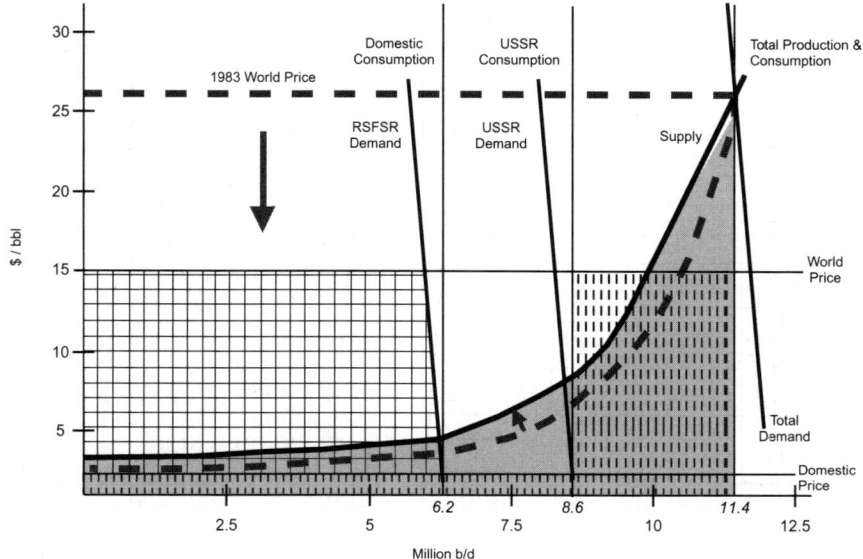

Figure 23: Russian Oil Supply and Demand in 1987

1983 and 1987, delivered oil cost rose by two-thirds. Costs increased across the board, as producing associations followed more and more expensive strategies to increase output as much as possible from nearly all fields.

As a consequence of the radical drop in export prices, increasing costs and Moscow's failure to reduce production in response, oil was produced at a significant economic loss in 1987. The Soviets subsidized both domestic consumption and exports. Some of the subsidy for exports could be explained by the premium attached to hard currency earnings compared to rouble expenses of production and transport. However, the overwhelming cause was the tunnel-vision of Soviet planners – focused on physical production targets – rather than the economics of production.

Even though the world oil price dropped over 40 per cent by 1987, a very large consumer surplus still accrued to Russian consumers because of the radical regulation of domestic prices.

The Russian Oil Market in 1993

The collapse of the USSR fundamentally changed the system for funding oil production. Producers were required to cover costs through oil sales on the domestic and export markets. Although the domestic price was still regulated to be less than one-third of the world price, it rose significantly (Table 6 and Figure 24). Because the regulated domestic price was less than the delivered cost, the domestic market was still served at an economic loss. This was partially compensated by export revenues.

Table 6: Basic Data for 1993 Russian Oil Market

Variable	Value	Variable	Value
World Price	$13.69/bbl	Total Cost	$21.0 billion
Domestic Price	$4.47/bbl	Domestic Revenue	$7.6 billion
Average Delivered Cost	$8.09/bbl	Export Revenue	$9.2 billion
Oil Production	7.1 mb/d	Total Revenue	$16.9 billion
Oil Exports	2.4 mb/d	Net Income	-$4.1 billion
Domestic Consumption	4.7 mb/d	Consumer Surplus	$14.4 billion

Producers' economic losses precipitated a major drop in production. They mainly shut-in the high-cost, right-hand side of the 1987 supply function; this brought total production down by 4.3 million barrels per day. Of that drop, approximately one-third of the volume lost was oil that was uneconomic to produce given prevailing costs and

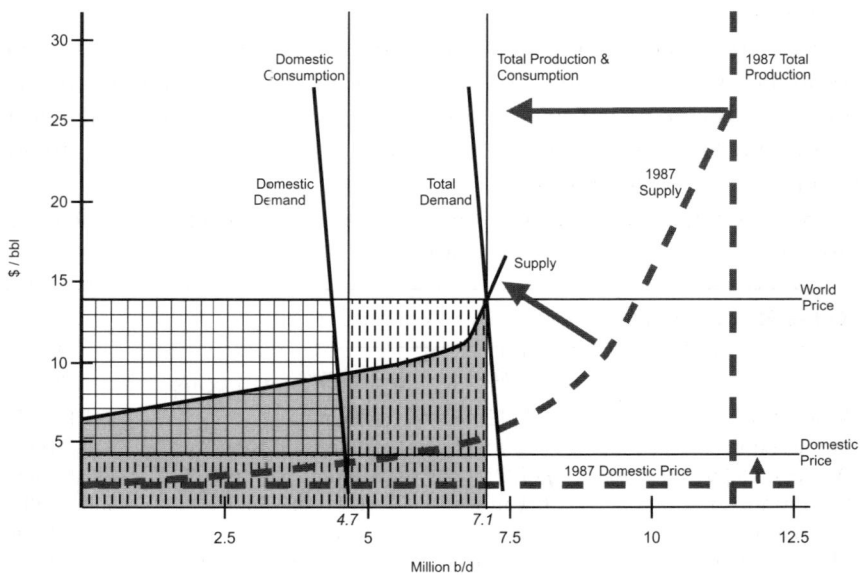

Figure 24: Russian Oil Supply and Demand in 1993

prices; this amount had been produced at a loss since the world price crash of 1986. The other two-thirds of the loss was due mainly to the economic chaos that attended the early post-Soviet period and revenue 'leakages' due to non-payment of producers and under-value barter payments for oil.

As shown above, production of oil in Russia in 1993 was at an economic loss. Note that, in addition to an economic loss on a variable cost basis, the industry also incurred capital costs. Although these were radically lower in 1993 relative to 1987, the capital investments that were made deepened producers' loss on every barrel produced.

The consumer surplus remained fairly large because of the considerable gap between world oil prices and the regulated prices of the domestic market.

The Russian Oil Market in 1997

By 1997, Russia's macroeconomic freefall abated and oil production had stabilized. World prices appreciated slightly, but domestic prices rose dramatically, approaching parity with world prices (Table 7 and Figure 25). However, a large share of the higher revenues went to cover significantly higher delivered costs. The increase in costs was across the board: higher wages and increased supplier prices raised operating costs; transportation tariffs and excise taxes both rose significantly compared to 1993.

The net effect of price and cost movements was largely (but not completely) to eliminate the losses on production suffered in the first five years of the post-Soviet period. Nevertheless, because of high costs, there was little money available for the volume of capital investments required for production growth.

Because the gap narrowed between world and domestic prices, the consumer surplus reached its minimum.

Table 7: Basic Data for 1997 Russian Oil Market

Variable	Value	Variable	Value
World Price	$15.92/bbl	Total Cost	$31.8 billion
Domestic Price	$12.50/bbl	Domestic Revenue	$18.7 billion
Average Delivered Cost	$14.29/bbl	Export Revenue	$11.6 billion
Oil Production	6.1 mb/d	Total Revenue	$30.3 billion
Oil Exports	2.0 mb/d	Net Income	-$1.5 billion
Domestic Consumption	4.1 mb/d	Consumer Surplus	$4.8 billion

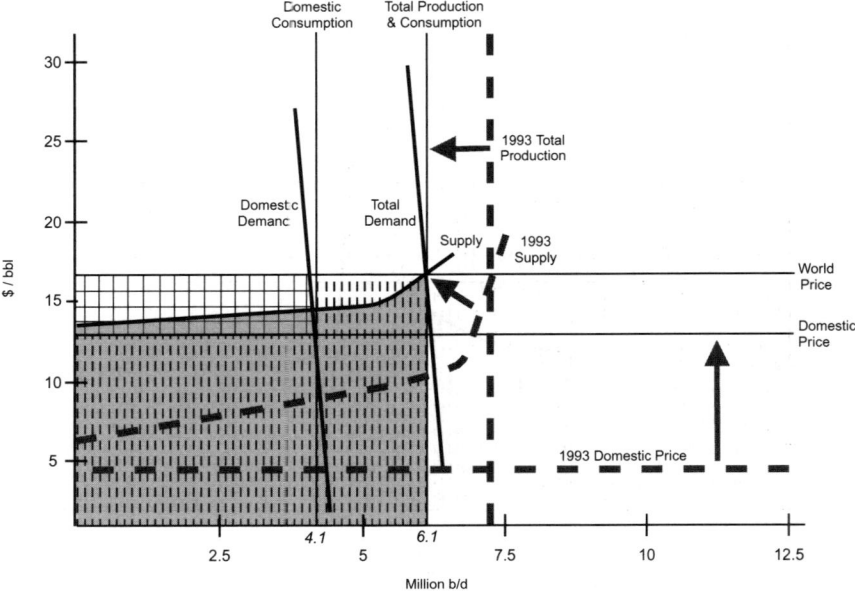

Figure 25: Russian Oil Supply and Demand in 1997

The Russian Oil Market in 2002

The situation in the Russian oil market in 2002 was fundamentally different from that in 1997 in three ways (Table 8 and Figure 26). First, because of the 1998 rouble devaluation, costs dropped substantially, producing a major increase in supply. Even four years after the devaluation, average delivered cost was still 17 per cent lower than in 1987. Second, starting in 1999, the world price of oil began a rapid escalation; by 2002 it was one-third higher than in 1997. Finally, because of the large inflows of net income beginning in 1999, by 2002 Russian production had risen by more than one-quarter.

Table 8: Basic Data for 2002 Russian Oil Market

Variable	Value	Variable	Value
World Price	$21.55/bbl	Total Cost	$33.3 billion
Domestic Price	$15.37/bbl	Domestic Revenue	$20.5 billion
Average Delivered Cost	$11.84/bbl	Export Revenue	$31.6 billion
Oil Production	7.7 mb/d	Total Revenue	$52.2 billion
Oil Exports	4.0 mb/d	Net Income	$18.9 billion
Domestic Consumption	3.7 mb/d	Consumer Surplus	$7.7 billion

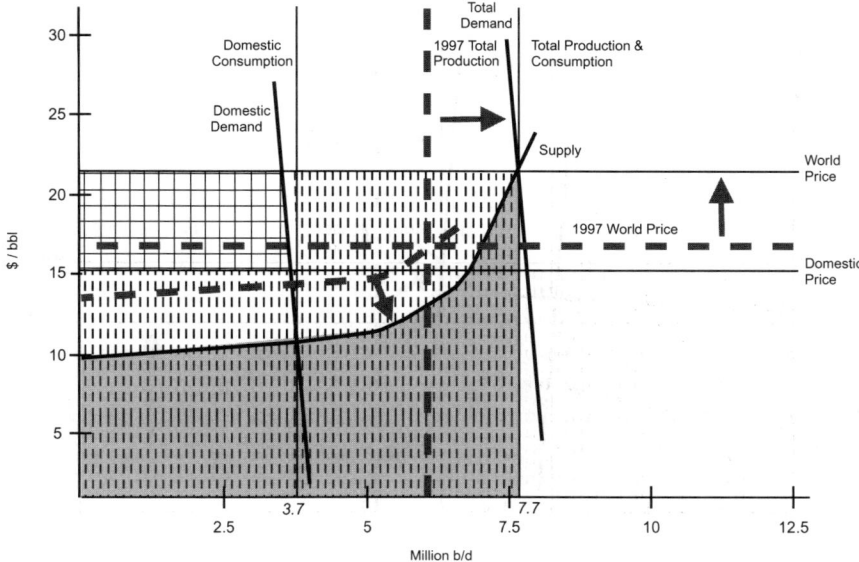

Figure 26: Russian Oil Supply and Demand in 2002

Notes

1 While the Soviet oil production peak in 1987 and 1988 was at 12.4 million b/d, the peak in output from the Russian Federation at the same time was 11.4 million b/d.
2 Imogene Edwards, Margaret Hughes and James Noren. 'US and USSR: Comparisons of GNP,' in Joint Economic Committee, Congress of the United States, *Soviet Economy in a Time of Change*, vol. 1, (Washington, DC: US Government Printing Office, 1979), pp. 369–400.
3 Machiko Nissanke, 'Oil Exports and the Soviet Economy' in Margaret Chadwick, David Long and Machiko Nissanke, *Soviet Oil Exports, Trade Adjustments, Refining Constraints and Market Behaviour* (Oxford: Oxford University Press, 1987), p. 71.
4 Marshall I. Goldman, *The Enigma of Soviet Petroleum*, op cit., p. 52.
5 Over the period, it increased an average of 300,000 b/d per year. This is the total output of a new, very large oil field each year.
6 Chadwick et al., eds, *Soviet Oil Exports*, op. cit. is the most comprehensive treatment of the economic role oil exports played in the late Soviet period. Its orientation is toward Soviet trade with the West.
7 Jonathan P. Stern, *Soviet Oil and Gas Exports to the West* (Hants, England: Gower Publishing Company Limited, 1987), p. 123.

8 This fundamental historical question reflects on the currently important issue of the economics of imperialism and remains in need of research.
9 For a review of the lax attention and attitude of the Soviet political leadership to oil supply in the seventies, see Gustafson, *Crisis Amid Plenty*, op. cit., pp. 63–76.
10 Nominal prices are from the annual statistical reports produced by BP, available in spreadsheet format through the US Department of Energy, Energy Information Administration web site at *www.eia.doe.gov/pub/international/iealf/BPCrudeOilPrices.xls*.
11 Data on inflation is based on the Consumer Price Index, US Bureau of Labour Statistics, *ftp.bls.gov/pub/special.requests/cpi/cpiai.txt*; interest rates are from the US Federal Reserve, *www.federalreserve.gov/releases/h15/data/a/prime.txt* and the relative volume of imported oil from US Department of Energy, Energy Information Administration, *Annual Energy Review 1997*, DOE/EIA-0384(97), (Washington, DC, July 1998), Table 5.1.
12 For discussion of exploration funding, see Gustafson, *Crisis Amid Plenty*, op. cit., p. 78.
13 Ibid., p. 91.
14 There were two immediate reasons for the diminished return to investment in wells. First was that an increasing share of new wells did nothing more than offset the losses at wells whose oil production rates had declined that year, including those that stopped flowing altogether. From 1970–75, 64 per cent of new wells did nothing more than offset declines, from 1976–80, that percent rose to 76 per cent, by 1981–5, virtually all new wells drilled were required to simply hold the production level. M.M. Sattov, 'Nadezhda i Sversheniya' ['Hope and Accomplishments'] in Dinkov, *Oil of the USSR*, op. cit., p. 143.

The second reason was that the average flow rates of new wells each year, while higher than the average of all wells, was dropping (i.e., the marginal physical product of each new well was falling). Therefore, while in 1979 it may have required one well to increase gross capacity by 100 b/d, by 1980 the average new well flow rate might have dropped to 90 b/d, so 1.1 wells would be required to make a 100 b/d capacity addition.
15 In the Appendix to this Chapter, five snap shots, using traditional supply and demand graphs, are described for the Russian oil market in 1983, 1987, 1993, 1997 and 2002.
16 By 1985, the Central Committee of the Communist Party of the Soviet Union and the Council of Ministers of the USSR (neither much remembered for their concern for people's living standards) officially identified improvement of workers' living conditions as one of the top priorities to be addressed by the nation's oil and gas complex. Sattov, 'Nadezhda i Sversheniya' ['Hope and Accomplishments'] in Dinkov, *Oil of the USSR*, op. cit., p. 137.
17 Gustafson, *Crisis Amid Plenty*, op. cit., p. 104.
18 Ibid., p. 107.
19 The main strategy was to ramp-up the basin's intermediate and small

fields, although there was also success at staunching the annual losses at the biggest fields.
20 Production from the North Caspian basin by traditional recovery from surface seeps goes back to antiquity in the Emba region of Kazakhstan. That oil, and all of the historical production in the basin that followed, was drawn from shallow fields. These were located above a massive regional Permian age salt strata formed during part of the regional tectonic collisions of plates that also raised the Ural Mountains. Salt is notoriously difficult to image through with seismic techniques (particularly extant Soviet methods) and is equally complex to drill through because of its plastic properties under the stress of deep burial.

Therefore, while the North Caspian was an old, mature basin in the Mesozoic and Cenozoic section above the salt, the establishment of Tengiz as a super-giant oil field below the salt opened a massive new play within the basin. In the 1990s, after the collapse of the USSR, a foreign-Kazakh consortium extended that play offshore below the Caspian Sea with the discovery of the Kashagan field. Between the estimated ultimate recovery of 8–19 billion barrels at Tengiz and 7–9 billion estimated from Kashagan, the sub-salt North Caspian basin would have become the next Soviet exploration frontier (the 'Fourth Baku'). It came too late. Moreover, the geologically important portions of the North Caspian basin ended up on the Kazakh side of the boundary with Russia after the end of the USSR. The Tengiz and Kashagan reserve ranges were found in *Alexander's Oil and Gas Connections* (www.gasandoil.com).
21 Gustafson, *Crisis Amid Plenty*, op. cit., p. 119.
22 Matthew J. Sagers and John D. Grace, 'Observations on the Russian Oil Sector in 1992 and 1993,' *International Geology Review*, vol. 35, no. 9 (September 1993), p. 857.
23 John D. Grace, David I. Heather and Vladimir I. Shpil'man, *Oil Potential from Idle Wells in Russia* (Dallas, TX: Troika Energy Services, 1993), pp. 9–10. For additional economic analysis (built in part on the Grace, Heather and Shpil'man work), see James L. Smith, 'On the Cost of Lost Production from Russian Oil Fields,' *The Energy Journal*, vol. 16, no. 2 (1995), pp. 25–57.
24 The alternative was to buy the needed equipment in the West. There, however, the relationships generally did not yet exist, parts often differed in details from Soviet standards, they were more expensive and, naturally, these suppliers also wanted dollars up front.
25 As in all instances in this study, references and data for domestic consumption of oil in Russia include all deliveries to Russian refineries, whether the resultant petroleum products were consumed in the domestic market or exported.
26 For two opposing views of the impact of price decontrol in the first year of Russian independence, see Mikhail Surtsukov, 'The Cost of Doing Nothing' (for decontrol) and B. Lagutenko and A. Sakovitch, 'A Step Toward Hyperinflation' (against) both in *Russian Petroleum Investor*, April 1992, pp. 38–41.

102 *Russian Oil Supply*

27 Surtsukov, 'The Cost of Doing Nothing,' op. cit., p. 39.
28 'Quick Fix,' *Russian Petroleum Investor*, December 1995/January 1996, p. 13.
29 Non-payment by oil company customers is ignored in this analysis because of the extreme difficulty of empirically measuring the problem over time and by producer. Moreover, the problem was not limited to non-payment for oil sold. Oil companies passed some of these losses on by not paying taxes, suppliers and workers. The problem was economy-wide. There is an implicit assumption here that non-payment *to* oil companies may have been balanced by non-payment *by* oil companies.
30 The taxes referenced here are those applied to volumes of oil produced and sold. They are, therefore, excise taxes. It does not include income or profit taxes that are calculated on a corporate basis after deductions of expenses and amortization.
31 It should be noted that the greatest portion of wealth redistributed to industry managers and financial insiders did not happen in the 1992 to early 1995 period, but in the Loans for Shares programme at the end of 1995, through the government 'tenders' of its shares in 1996 and 1997 and most dramatically when the value of the companies vaulted up after the events of 1998 and 1999. See Chapter 5.
32 'On Borrowed Money,' *Russian Petroleum Investor*, March 1995, p. 12.
33 'Lost Innocence,' *Russian Petroleum Investor*, April 1995, p. 64.
34 'Picky, Picky,' *Russian Petroleum Investor*, April 1998, p. 10.
35 'Taking Stock of Russia's Energy Sector,' *Russian Petroleum Investor*, September 1998, p. 8.
36 'Damage Control,' *Russian Petroleum Investor*, August 1998, p. 5.
37 Chrystia Freeland, *Sale of the Century – Russia's Wild Ride from Communism to Capitalism* (New York: Crown Books, 2000), p. 318. See also Joseph E. Stiglitz, *Globalization and Its Discontents* (New York: W.W. Norton & Co., 2003) pp. 133–65. Professor Stiglitz, an eminent economist and Nobel Laureate, said that from his perspective as chief economist of the World Bank, the devaluation was visible substantially in advance of mid-August. Market indicators, such as the divergence of the rates paid on dollar-denominated and rouble-denominated Russian sovereign debt (called GKOs), certainly evidenced a big impending change based on first principles of macroeconomics. However, even as Stiglitz admits, the senior management at the International Monetary Fund rejected his analyses and proceeded with disbursement of the July facility.
   Freeland's and Stiglitz's analyses provide excellent bookends to the story of the August devaluation. Freeland tells the inside story from Moscow and Stiglitz from the perspective of academic economist and world banker sitting at the top of the World Bank/International Monetary Fund in Washington, DC.
38 'From the Ashes,' *Russian Petroleum Investor*, October 1998, p. 17.
39 The devaluation produced a collateral benefit. Although the industry only imported a relatively minor share of required equipment, services and

supplies from abroad, as it always does, devaluation radically raised import costs. This provided a significant boost to Russian oil service companies. Also, some Western service companies, which would typically import foreign goods and services, were induced to produce more of what they sold within Russia. Producers raised imports of Western production technology in the years that followed devaluation, but they placed even more orders with their domestic service industry. It also in a sense 'Russified' some of the new Western technology that had made small penetrations into exploration and production since the late 1980s.

40 This discussion of the sources of supply at the field level does not include 2003 because as of this writing, in September 2004, field-level data for 2003 are still unavailable.

41 Possibly the deep North Caspian basin could have been the third tide, but it was beyond Soviet technology at that time. Moreover, when the USSR split up, most of the good areas ended up on the Kazakh side of the border.

42 The budget money itself was not even 'real' Soviet roubles, but something called *beznalichnyye den'gi* – roughly 'non-personal' money that could only be used in settling inter-enterprise balances.

43 From 1995 through 1997, the industry also experienced a highly idiosyncratic phase of privatization, discussed in the next chapter. However, while this process continues to influence the industry today, it actually had little impact on oil supply at the time it was happening.

44 International Monetary Fund, Country Report No. 3/145 (May 2003), Russian Federation: Statistical Appendix, available at *www.imf.org/external/pubs/ft/scr/2003/cr03145.pdf*.

45 Because these are short-run analyses for each year, capital costs are not included.

46 This is not to exclude the value of the same type of analysis of the refined products markets. That, however, is beyond the scope of this study.

47 John C.B. Cooper, 'Price Elasticity of Demand for Crude Oil: Estimates for 23 Countries,' *OPEC Review* (March 2003).

48 There is additional consumer surplus above the world price. However, the shape of even the short-run demand function outside the domain of world prices seen over the last twenty years is not known (presumably it becomes more elastic). This component is not addressed here.

49 Note that the demand functions in this appendix are not drawn as constant elasticity due to limitations in the drawing software and because it would make little difference, visually, given the low level of estimated elasticity.

50 Production and disposition of oil do not balance in Table 5 because of rounding error (0.1 million b/d).

CHAPTER 5

INDUSTRY PERFORMANCE

The contemporary Russian oil industry developed from the collapse of a state ministry in a command economy. From that inauspicious beginning, within a decade after the dissolution of the USSR, a handful of private, major oil companies emerged to dominate the nation's supply (Figure 27). Yet the most basic and enduring economic change in the industry is not the organization of companies, or even their size or ownership. It is that oil production in Russia is now funded by selling output on domestic and export markets, rather than from the state budget.

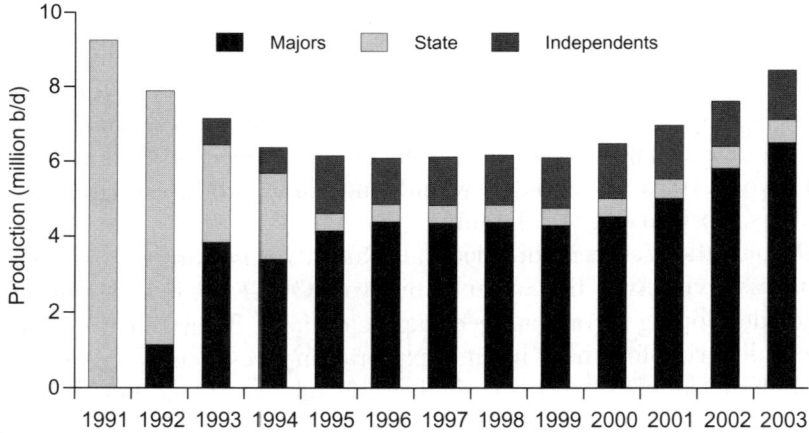

Figure 27: Russian Oil Production by Industry Sector

This rewriting of the rules of the game imposed a sweeping set of micro changes on how oil was produced within the companies themselves. But, perhaps more importantly, the formation of private firms changed the balance of power between the industry and the state in ways that are still very much in flux. This struggle is basic to the economic policy of the government and a source of considerable uncertainty and risk to the industry.

Although Russia's major oil companies are now privatized, they bear the deep imprint of their Soviet past. Subsidiaries of major producers remain nearly exclusive franchisees in the geographic domains of their predecessors (Map 13).[1] More importantly, for the successful ones, there is a relationship to the Russian state that still reflects a Soviet light on the actions and strategies of the firms' senior managements. They have adopted many Western technologies to excellent effect and, to a lesser extent, absorbed some corporate management principles from abroad. But, throughout the industry there is an immiscible mix of fundamental changes in reaction to sudden immersion into a mainly market environment and strong elements inherited from a statist upbringing, protected by historical inertia and a new, powerfully conservative national politic.

Ontogeny Recapitulates Phylogeny

The passage of the Russian oil industry to its present structure has been, as Winston Churchill once famously said of Russia itself, a 'riddle wrapped in a mystery inside an enigma'. The route was tortuously complex and many of the details are still unknown outside a small circle. What resulted was in no sense monolithic. Had a Russian Rip Van Winkle nodded off as oil production peaked in 1987 and 1988, and awoke 16 years later, he would find some producers unchanged – others most jarringly different.

Despite their current diversity, all Russia's upstream organizations started as divisions of the Soviet Ministry of Oil.[2] Each held responsibility for developing a compact geographic domain. They relied on other state ministries for their inputs (exploration prospects, construction, equipment, supplies) and provided crude oil to yet another ministry to be refined and distributed to consumers. In the Soviet economy, all money and power flowed from the top down and economic variables, like prices, costs and production rates were unrelated to each other.

As the USSR fragmented at the end of the eighties, and the reality of declining production set in, Moscow began to allow very modest economic experimentation. More than a planned grant of latitude to local managements, innovation sprang in the empty space created by the weakening control of the moribund central government. In this increasingly fluid environment, a month before the USSR officially dissolved, Moscow ratified a radical proposal. The managements of three West Siberian producing associations, Langepasneftegaz, Urayneftegaz and Kogalymneftegaz, asked to secede from the Oil Ministry and form a 'joint stock company' – Lukoil.

How a 'private' company was to operate in an otherwise command economy we will never know, as the Soviet colossus survived only a few more days. However, after Russia's independence, more producers followed suit. Upstream units that went private quickly amalgamated with many of the nation's refineries. Usually, these combinations recast old relationships. Producing association A, which in Soviet times sent most of its crude oil to refinery B, absorbed B into its new corporate structure. So, in becoming private, several at the same time became vertically integrated oil companies.[3]

Within six months of Russia's independence, the young economic reformers who President Boris Yeltsin brought into government devised a plan to distribute to the Russian people the industrial wealth inherited from the USSR. They intended to accomplish this by giving citizens shares in the nation's industrial enterprises.

The initial issue of stock in privatized firms, at least in the case of oil companies, was divided between three groups. The government held a majority of shares in each firm. The second tranche was to be issued to each new company's workers, management and, in some cases, the local population where the company operated. Therein was the first rub.

The distribution of this second portion of stock was wholly opaque. While workers occasionally received shares, it was usually a token amount or nothing at all. Company management, particularly those at the very top, were the foremost beneficiaries. They received large stock disbursements directly from Moscow; they bought shares from their workers at bargain prices; sometimes they held workers' shares in 'trust' through newly formed, non-state pension funds.

The private companies' bosses, called the 'Red Directors' in the West, were the ones sitting atop Russia's oil-producing associations when the Soviet music stopped playing.[4] They were a combination of very competent engineers and Communist Party hacks, but above all, they were men who owed their positions to mastery of an economic and political system that no longer existed. Suddenly, not by dint of entrepreneurship, but largely by luck of timing, they commanded the resources of the largest national component of the world petroleum industry.

The third fraction of company stock was the wild card, the strangest of all. Yeltsin's reformers intended these shares to go directly to the Russian people at large. Therein was the second rub.

The millions who were to become the shareholders, the populist capitalists of the New Russia, had no cash. Therefore, the government issued vouchers, each with a face value of 10,000 roubles ($25 in 1992) to every citizen, including children.[5] People could use the vouchers to buy shares of the freshly privatized firms.

The vouchers were liquid; they could be bought and sold between individuals, as well as exchanged for stock. Their value on nascent exchanges fluctuated wildly. With no experience in either stocks or ownership, billions of roubles in vouchers were traded for vodka, food and other necessities of life. They were the objects of swindles; many probably ended up in the trash. But as time passed, a small class of entrepreneurs amassed vast voucher holdings and systematically traded them for equity positions in Russian companies.

A large, but unknown fraction of stock in oil companies, originally exchanged for vouchers, also made its way into the hands of the Red Directors. Once the dust had settled on the voucher scheme and the direct and indirect distributions to company managements were completed, a wave of firm consolidation in the oil industry set in.

In Darwinian fashion, larger producers bought smaller ones. Some were economically logical amalgamations; some were managers cashing out; others procured just because they were available. By the beginning of 1995, of the roughly three dozen original Soviet-era producers in Russia, over 20 were still wholly in state hands and 13 were listed as private companies (or subsidiaries of private companies). The most important of these were Lukoil, Yukos, Surgutneftegaz, Slavneft, Sidanco, Komineft, Eastern Oil and Onako. To these must be added the two top organizations of the Volga-Ural basin, Tatneft and Bashneft, which were different because of the roles played by their respective local governments – Tatarstan and Bashkortostan.

The year 1995 was a watershed. Macroeconomically, although the calamitous slide was slowing down, the cumulative effect of years of depression pushed the national government toward bankruptcy. Politically, the accelerating deterioration of peoples' living standards threatened defeat for Yeltsin in the 1996 elections and a return of the unreformed Communist Party to power. The oil industry had lost nearly half of its peak production – and its best hope was merely to staunch the haemorrhage.

Into this quagmire came a few men with energy, initiative and a common plan. These audacious plotters, less than a dozen at the core, were to become Russia's infamous 'Oligarchs.' They were a varied lot, from the ranks of the Soviet *nomenklatura* to street-level capitalists who prospered in the loosened but hardscrabble milieu of Moscow in the late eighties.[6]

By the time the USSR collapsed, most of them had made their way into the previously unimagined sphere of private banking. In the early nineties, the term 'bank' in Russia covered a very broad sweep: from loan sharking and money laundering to legitimate foreign exchange operations and actually holding deposits for the few Russians who did not keep their money under the mattress. They performed some clearing and factoring roles for inter-enterprise transactions, filling part of the void left by the disappearance of the Soviet system. A few connected banks rose on state business, managing the accounts of ministries and particularly agencies like Customs, with access to hard currencies.

The formal part of the Oligarchs' 1995 offer to the Kremlin was this: their banks would loan to the state money desperately needed to close the fiscal chasm between tax receipts and government expenditures. In turn, the state collateralized these loans by transferring to the banks the management rights of large blocks of government-owned stock in some of the nation's most important, newly private firms.[7] Much of the stock was oil, but large parts of the communications, transportation and mining industries were also included. The scheme was known as 'Loans for Shares'.

The government had a year to repay the loans. If they did not, with modest additional costs, the shares became the property of the banks. There were second-order details that also benefited the creditors. For instance, the fraction of a company's equity gained through the loans could be leveraged by the bank's promise to further invest in the acquired firm. These investment pledges were flimsy, more often observed in the breach, but would come back to haunt a few selected principals a decade later.

Its designers introduced two egregious and complementary flaws into Loans for Shares. First, the government secretly evaluated its shares pledged in collateral at a tiny fraction of their worth on any open market – even given the extreme extant risk discount on Russian assets. Should the government default on the loans in a year (which, in 1995, was a very good bet), a tremendous windfall would immediately befall the creditors at the state's expense. Second, of course, rigging such a massive devaluation of the collateral shares made no sense unless the scheme was closed to all but the small circle of men who proposed it and extended the credit.

Not only did a feeble, corrupt and fiscally panicked Yeltsin administration agree to the plan, they let the Oligarchs administer it and use the one-year loan term to soften up their impending acquisitions to the realities of new ownership.

Informally, the rest of the Oligarchs' bargain was this: in return for state permission to swindle Russia out of tens of billions of dollars of its industrial and natural resource bases, the Oligarchs largely bankrolled and managed Yeltsin's successful re-election campaign in 1996.

Lukoil and Surgutneftegaz, where the Red Directors were strongest, muscled into the scheme to protect and enlarge the equity positions they already enjoyed coming out of the voucher process.[8] But for three other top oil companies, Yukos, Noyabrskneftegaz (which became Sibneft) and Sidanco (now part of TNK-BP), Loans for Shares ultimately stripped the sitting West Siberian ex-Soviet managers of their positions and transferred control to the new Oligarchs from Moscow.

As rising net income filled the coffers of Russian oil companies across the board after 1998, another wave of consolidation swept over the industry. Lukoil, Yukos, and what has become TNK-BP, all acquired smaller producers – some with deliberation, others willy-nilly. This narrowed the industry's structure to a few very large firms at the top – five major oil companies and two regionally important firms. They were surrounded by a shrinking number of small producers and a small, but restive, state sector.

In the fall of 2004, the state sector of the industry, consisting of Rosneft and Gazprom, began to contest the attention being given to Russia's private oil companies with a merger announcement. Powered by the strong statist wind blowing across Russia since mid-2003, the intention was clearly to raise the profile and direct intervention by Moscow in the detailed operation of the oil industry. If not a retreat to the Soviet model, the Putin administration is back-peddling from control largely by using the more sophisticated levers of taxation, tariffs and licensing.

Although at the same time more nationalistic and interventionist, only during the Putin administration, which began eight years after the fall of the USSR, have foreign firms gained an appreciable role in the Russian oil industry. In ironically Soviet style, the largest projects that have been given the nod this decade include several expensive and complex multinational ventures in the relative isolation of the Pacific Ocean off northern Sakhalin Island, a multibillion dollar investment by BP in TNK and in September 2004, a smaller, but significant equity position for the American major, ConocoPhillips, in Lukoil.

Lukoil

In 2004, Lukoil, Russia's first private oil company, returned to leadership of the nation's oil industry. In the last two years, it had lost production and financial pre-eminence to Yukos. While Lukoil still remains in second place by several leading measures, it is today strong and standing, if not a stellar company; Yukos, eviscerated by a year of government attacks, is not.

The secret to its survival, as well as lacklustre technical performance, can be found in a management team with deeper roots in its Soviet past than its ambitiously Westernized rival. 'We at Lukoil know how to act in our limits,' replied company president Vagit Alekperov to a reporter's question on the differences between himself and former Yukos chairman, now-jailed, Mikhail Khodorkovsky.[9]

Knowing limits made Lukoil's board solidly, but not completely, Russian. Knowing limits has slowed, but not stopped, company layoffs, lowering the adverse social and political impacts of privatization. It has made the company proudly assertive about being one of Russia's largest taxpayers and very circumspect in lobbying for release from obligations to the state. Knowing limits kept Alekperov, and his technically oriented cadre of senior managers, out of Russian politics and on the good side of the Putin administration.

Yet, the same conservatism that steeled Lukoil, while Yukos fell, denied the company much of the performance boost that should have come from five years of steadily rising prices. Company oil output has grown, but only through producing asset acquisition, rather than better management of its own fields (Figure 28). In fact, among major oil companies, only Lukoil has failed to secure higher output from its legacy assets.

Lukoil was born bold, a revolutionary idea in the closing days of the Soviet state. While initially brash in public, the company quickly settled into doing what it knew best, nose-to-the-grindstone engineering to halt

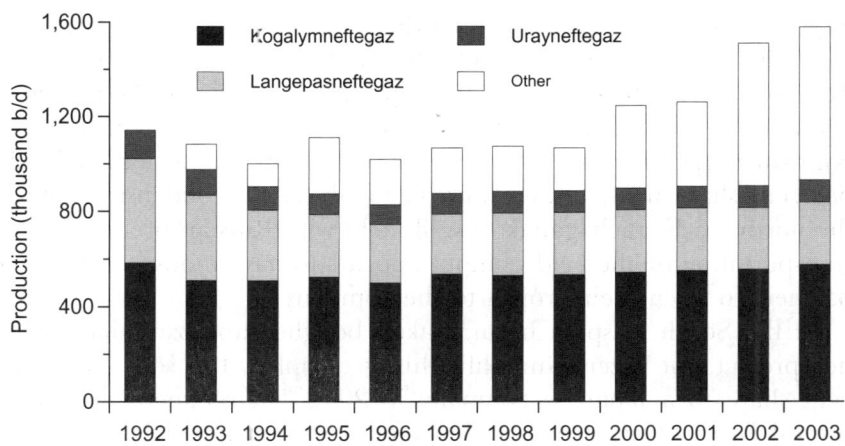

Figure 28: Lukoil Oil Production by Subsidiary

the production haemorrhage that opened the decade. If ordinal rank counts most, its plan succeeded. Measured by production, revenue or capitalization, Lukoil was Russia's number one oil company for more than a decade.

The original Soviet producing-association partners, Langepasneftegaz, Urayneftegaz and Kogalymneftegaz, each gave an initial letter to form the company name. The first and last of these were senior producers of the Middle Ob region; Urayneftegaz covered the very small discoveries made in the fifties and sixties on West Siberia's western margin (Map 13). The company made the downstream refining and marketing acquisitions typical of the early nineties. By the middle of the decade, they had gathered a few relatively small to medium producing associations west of the Urals.

From the start, Lukoil took the Western oil and gas majors as its model. Those mega-companies were integrated, from exploration and production, through refining and marketing; they made petrochemicals and presided over great international operations. While the natural gas business, which is an integral part of the likes of Shell and ExxonMobil, was ignored by Lukoil for ten years, that component recently entered the company's planning. In 2002, Lukoil was the first Russian oil company to list its shares on a Western exchange (London).

Two strategic pursuits distinguish Lukoil from other Russian majors: its international interests and, fuelled by the post-1998 revenue rush, a shopping binge that brought dozens of small oil companies into its fold.

Operations abroad have led the company to the distant corners of Columbia and Iraq, but most of its interests are closer to home. Its largest commitment is in neighbouring Kazakhstan. Invited largely to ease oil pipeline transit through Russia, Lukoil joined the Chevron-Texaco consortium developing the super-giant Tengiz on the northeast coast of the Caspian Sea, with a 2.7 per cent stake. It took half of the Kumkol project in the central part of the country and obtained a 15 per cent share in the giant Karachaganak oil-gas-condensate field in the north. At Karachaganak as well, help with Russian processing and transportation of the field's output appears to have motivated Western partners to open their project to the company.

In the South Caspian basin, Lukoil bought into Azerbaijan's banner project, the Azeri-Guneshli-Chirag complex, but sold its 10 per cent share to a Japanese company in 2002.[10] It retained interests in several Azeri offshore exploration blocks. The company's forays into Egypt, Columbia and pre-invasion Iraq seemed more in pursuit of the bragging rights of 'worldwide operations' than a coherent economic rationale. The Lukoil gas stations in the eastern United States fall into the same bundle of business safaris.[11] Nevertheless, the company expects the contribution from projects outside Russia to rise from the 2003 level of 58,000 b/d to 280,000 b/d by the end of the decade.[12]

Even before the money became easy after 1998, Lukoil was the most acquisitive of the Russian majors. It has added a random variety of small oil charms to the corporate bracelet since the beginning. The first logical acquisitions, however, were in the Volga-Ural basin, complementing its refineries there. Fired with new revenues after 1998, and finally at least a rudimentary vision for buying companies, Lukoil launched a comprehensive move to corner upstream and downstream operations in the Timan-Pechora basin.

It was acquisitions that gave Lukoil its production growth and masked a performance that otherwise would have been starkly disappointing (Figure 28). Unfortunately, it also created an organizational behemoth. By January 1, 2003, 47 separate entities under the Lukoil umbrella held licences to explore and produce oil and gas in Russia.[13] That year, company management recognized the administrative burden of such unwieldiness and began consolidation.

As in oil companies worldwide, some of the restructuring was just redrawing organizational charts and tomfoolery by the men at the top. However, in announcing in spring 2004 that it would sell 100 million bbls of 'unprofitable fields,' Lukoil opened the door to jettison assets that it probably should have never acquired.[14] There are growing demands from Moscow that companies no longer simply sit on production licences without moving toward development. This sale will relieve some of that pressure. It will also allow Lukoil to focus energy and resources where the expected return is in concert with corporate goals.

Acquisitions bought corporate-level production increases between 1999 and 2003. But for the medium and long term, the company's planned growth rests on two different, far more sustainable supports: offshore, in the Russian sector of the Caspian Sea, and in the Timan-Pechora basin.[15]

In the offshore Russian sector of the Middle Caspian basin, Lukoil won licences in the mid-nineties. Drilling with their own jack-up rig since 1999, the company has already made five commercial discoveries in its licence area.

While they doubtlessly longed for oil, based on test data, the new Caspian fields appear disappointingly gassy. Two fields did test initial well flow rates of over 2,000 b/d, but the volumes of oil discovered pale before the Kashagan discovery in the Kazakh sector of the North Caspian basin.[16] The company reported 2003 estimated proved plus probable (SPE/WPC) reserves in these fields as 542 million bbls and 16.1 tcf of gas.[17] Plans call for first production in 2006 and 250,000 b/d from the Caspian by 2010.[18]

On a higher level, the company's decision to explore the Russian Caspian was corporately courageous because Lukoil is the only company in the post-Soviet Russian oil industry to open a major new exploration frontier. While the Lukoil acreage is unlikely to be as prospective as they hope (over 14 billion barrels of oil equivalent), it is a province of serious geologic potential that is very convenient to both the export and domestic markets.[19]

Obtaining a dominant position in the Timan-Pechora basin was the second, and more important, part of the company's medium- to long-term plan to raise oil production. Although Lukoil now dominates the basin, its original plans were twice as large, but had to be reined in due to a drop in profits in 2001 and 2002 (Table 9).[20] Lukoil's operations in the Timan-Pechora basin are outlined in Box 3.

Table 9: Technical and Financial Performance Indicators for Lukoil[21]

Indicator	Units	2000	2001	2002	2003
Oil Reserves	Billion bbls	12.9	14.6	15.3	16.0
Gas Reserves	Trillion cubic feet	3.6	13.2	24.2	24.5
Oil Production	Million b/d	1.4	1.5	1.5	1.6
Gas Production	Billion cubic feet	127	116	126	133
Oil Reserves / Production	Years	25	27	28	28
Total Assets	Billion US$	17.1	19.9	22.0	26.6
Revenues	Billion US$	13.4	13.6	15.4	22.3
Income Before Income Taxes	Billion US$	4.1	2.8	2.6	4.6
Income Taxes	Billion US$	0.8	0.7	0.7	1.0
Net Income	Billion US$	3.3	2.1	1.8	3.7
Basic Earnings per Share	$/share	4.83	2.68	2.26	4.52

Beyond raising oil production, Lukoil seeks to improve corporate profitability.[22] This goal often appears at odds with the production-growth objective. Given little control on the prices of its products, profitability can only be increased through reductions in cost, such as their plan to halve their workforce of 180,000 by 2010.[23]

The other major push is shutting-in low-profitability wells. The company did shut-in 1,130 low-oil/high-water wells in 2002. A good start, but far less than the goal of 5,000 loudly proposed at the beginning of that year. Beyond these measures, there are the calls for 'cost containment' and 'greater efficiency' that decorate corporate vision posters worldwide.

> **Box 3**
>
> *Lukoil in Timan-Pechora*
>
> Timan-Pechora is a paradoxical place – geologically, geographically and politically (Map 1). The rocks hold large oil resources, though much smaller than either the Volga-Ural or West Siberian basins. A big fraction of the oil is light and sweet; some of these same fields boast among the highest initial well flow rates in Russia. While the Soviets developed some of the 'good' fields, for reasons still not understood, they also took on a number that became technical nightmares. In the latter, the oil is heavy and very waxy. Some wells are surrounded by hundreds of tonnes of what is basically very dirty candle wax, scraped from the wells to keep small volumes of oil trickling through.[24]
>
> Geographically, direct access to the ocean strongly favours the basin, even though tanker access is restricted to impossible in winter. The advantage of ocean entrée is the ability to evade the morass of the Transneft pipeline system when exporting crude. Although plans for major loading terminals abound (both in the Pechora Bay and 600 miles to the west at Murmansk), this advantage remains unexploited.
>
> Geography also dealt the basin a very severe climate. It is substantially north of the oil-producing area of West Siberia and its proximity to the Arctic Ocean makes it snowier and windier. With the exception of the Yamburg gas field in northern West Siberia, nowhere in Russia is a substantial volume of oil or gas produced from a worse place to work. From shortly after the 1917 Revolution, the basin was a big island in the Soviet GULAG archipelago.[25]
>
> This mix generated the lowest productivities and highest production costs in the Soviet oil industry. The situation just got worse after the collapse of the USSR. Because marginal production costs were so far in excess of the revenue making it back to the wellhead, Timan-Pechora production plummeted.
>
> Yet into this scene flocked droves of Western companies in the early nineties. They were drawn by ocean access (enhanced by advertised assistance from nuclear-powered icebreakers) and the high flow rates at some of the fields. Moreover, Soviet then Russian government officials, actually encouraged foreign investment in the basin, whereas Western oil executives traipsing about West Siberia were basically tourists.
>
> As the nineties closed, many of the foreigners were gone. A few

stalwarts survived the weather, Transneft intransigence, contentious local politicos and persistent opposition in Moscow to production sharing agreements (PSAs). One of the three operating PSAs nationwide is in Timan-Pechora (TOTAL's project at Kharyaginskoye). Lukoil joined the Kharyaginskoye PSA as part of its occupation of the basin in 2002, but withdrew the following year, citing unacceptably high costs.[26] One of the most successful joint ventures (JVs) nationally, 'Polar Lights,' managed by ConocoPhillips, is centred on the Ardalinskoye group of fields, also in the basin. In late September 2004, ConocoPhillips bought the last government-held shares in Lukoil, leveraging their joint experience in the basin (see below).

Despite individual successes, by the beginning of this decade, all but a few of the region's joint ventures, Russian independents and the successor of the region's Soviet producing association, Komitek, were ripe for acquisition. From 1999 through 2002, with a little strong-arm work and money, Lukoil pocketed most of the basin's important assets.

Timan-Pechora is Lukoil's biggest gamble. While exploration risk attended its move into the Russian sector of the Caspian, operations in Timan-Pechora added a whole different scale of political and technical jeopardy. The region did not become the basket-case of the industry just because of obstreperous locals.

Operating costs, even at the good fields, will possibly always be very high relative to other parts of the country. On the other hand, transportation bottlenecks (if not tariffs) improved considerably with the commissioning of the Baltic Transport System pipeline in 2001.[27] A major Arctic Ocean loading terminal could be a big help in offsetting high production costs.

Lukoil's Timan-Pechora strategy sports a considerable upside. Most importantly, there is a very large inventory of discovered and delineated, but undeveloped fields from Soviet times that holds hundreds of millions to billions of barrels of technically recoverable oil. Many of them enjoy high flow rates and good oil quality.

Additionally, although it remains unexploited, the opportunity for direct export by sea from the basin holds significant potential advantages.[28] The basin also extends offshore, into what is one of the more promising, large and relatively accessible exploration frontiers in the country. Finally, if the company is economically successful in the basin, it will be a powerful stimulation to the economy of an otherwise stranded, remote, far-northern region – which will please the all-important men in the Kremlin.

> On balance, the risk of low wellhead netback is a very durable feature of operation in Timan-Pechora. The company must control operating and transportation costs (and hope prices don't fall). If these factors align propitiously, the basin could reasonably support the gross increase implicit in Lukoil's corporate goal of 4 to 5 per cent annual growth in output. The plan calls for approximately 650,000 b/d from the basin in 2010, more than three times the production in 2003.

The company's success in the Middle Caspian, and its evolving strategy for Timan-Pechora, provide a foundation for optimism about prospects in the next five to ten years. Yet all this planning for growth and economy is predicated on successful field management. In this, the performance of Lukoil's core, legacy assets, waves a big caution flag.

To its credit, Lukoil has reduced production costs somewhat; well productivity, which fell throughout the nineties, has also modestly rebounded. But faced with rising prices and strong (post-1998) net income, Lukoil failed to get a significant bump in old fields and was able to accelerate development at only one big and important field, Tevlin-Russinskoye. Flat output from its main subsidiaries is uniquely bad among industry majors since the beginning of the decade.

The performance of its two principal producing units, Langepasneftegaz and Kogalymneftegaz, best measures Lukoil's ability to run fields. In 2003, these two units made 53 per cent of Lukoil's total output. In 1992, they were 72 per cent of company production (Figure 28).

Langepasneftegaz operates a dozen fields located along the right (north) bank of the Ob River between Samotlor (operated by Samotlorneftegaz, a division of TNK-BP) and Fedorovskoye (operated by Surgutneftegaz) (Map 13). Langepasneftegaz's fields are old, but still, the subsidiary contributed 17 per cent of the total corporate output in 2003.[29]

Between its 1988 peak production of 600,000 b/d and 1996, Langepasneftegaz lost half of its production output. This was not because of a single major field, but was a systemic collapse spread across all fields. While the decline was checked in mid-decade, since then output has been flat.

Langepasneftegaz's failure to raise output could be because the corporation underfunded it, problems with poor local management or because the productivity of its field stock was so low that it could not compete for investment funds with other subsidiaries. The region is very mature, so the prospects for new field development, beyond the extension of the Pokachevskoye field to the North Pokachevskoye structure, are slim.[30]

In 1999, Lukoil split Langepasneftegaz, perhaps in response to disappointing performance. It appears they carved out the Pokachevskoye and perhaps North Pokachevskoye fields – leaving the rump of Langepasneftegaz with a miserable resource base. The probable outlook for the combination of the two organizations is continued decline, flat production with luck and a bump from North Pokachevskoye in the very best instance. Like most corporate reorganizations in the oil industry worldwide, the 1999 split did nothing for output.

A happier light shined on neighbouring Kogalymneftegaz. The Soviets organized it to exploit the fields found north and northwest of the area run by Langepasneftegaz (Map 13). These include three of the most prolific second-generation giant fields discovered in the basin: Povkhovskoye, Vatyeganskoye and South Yagunskoye. Moreover, Kogalymneftegaz holds one of the most promising of the third-generation finds: Tevlin-Russinskoye (Table 1).

By comparison with Langepasneftegaz, Kogalymneftegaz enjoys a robust resource base. Fields are less depleted, well flow rates are higher and water cuts lower. Therefore, when Russian production collapsed in the early nineties, Kogalymneftegaz never fell as far as the others. From its peak in 1990–91, it lost about 20 per cent in two years – but production has grown steadily, if very slowly, ever since.

The dynamics of Kogalymneftegaz's performance had two components. The predicate to progress was arresting the short, sharp declines at Vatyeganskoye, South Yagunskoye and Povkhovskoye – then holding them in a slow steady decline. These three giant fields still have considerable remaining resources and the capability of increasing production over short periods. However, they are more likely to follow the gentle, well-behaved declines established in the mid-nineties.

The complement to stable base-load production was developing the Tevlin-Russinskoye field. By not having to cover big losses at other fields, a very large share of the gross increase in output at Tevlin-Russinskoye fell to the subsidiary's bottom line – raising total production. Tevlin-Russinskoye production is still (as of 2003) rising, and this will probably continue for several more years. Kogalymneftegaz has successfully managed low decline rates at its three largest fields over the last eight years. It is reasonable to assume, unless economic conditions worsen appreciably, that when Tevlin-Russinskoye starts down, it will fall slowly. Discovery of significant new fields within Kogalymneftegaz's patch is also unlikely. Total production growth will move in lock step at a rate somewhat below that of Tevlin-Russinskoye.

Beyond its new acquisitions in the Timan-Pechora basin, the other Lukoil unit that is volumetrically important is Permneft. This is a mid-sized producing organization of the Volga-Ural basin. It has roughly 100 fields on its books, of which about one-third are producing. After losing capacity in the early 1990s, Permneft production has stayed virtually flat since. Although Lukoil has acquired independent companies in the area, it apparently has decided against much investment in this division.

The balance of Lukoil's dozens of other producing units, outside Timan-Pechora, does not make much difference. Some of the Russian independents and joint ventures, acquired in the 1999–2002 buying sprees, harbour the potential for large percentage increases in production, because they are built around new fields. But in general, these are small fields and will not make a large contribution to a company producing 1.6 million b/d.

In a change that could have a major impact on the company, in the summer of 2004 the Russian government decided to sell its last 7.6 per cent equity stake in Lukoil. This is a revenue opportunity for the state treasury; the auction starting price of $29.83 per share would raise $1.93 billion.[31] On September 29, 2004, ConocoPhillips bought the government's shares for slightly more than the original minimum price, paying $1.988 billion. ConocoPhillips immediately followed with a planned purchase of another 2.4 per cent of Lukoil stock.

The agreement between the two companies is extensive, but not now on the scale of the BP position in TNK. ConocoPhillips will be permitted to obtain up to 20 per cent of Lukoil's stock at a cost that will likely be over $5 billion. While the American firm also has received a side agreement strengthening its management rights in Lukoil beyond what 20 per cent would normally entitle it to, the fact remains that ConocoPhillips does not enjoy blocking rights, which obtain at 25 per cent plus one share.[32]

ConocoPhillips has carefully crawled out on a limb before in Russia – to find success. Its Polar Lights project, in Timan-Pechora, has been a relatively small but consistently valuable project that afforded the company one of the most effective entries into Russia of any Western oil major. As part of the Lukoil deal, the two companies formed an ambitious joint venture in the northern part of Timan-Pechora (where Polar Lights is located). The American firm has not only leveraged its experience into a significant role in a very prospective region, but gained a solid perch in Russia's leading oil company.[33]

The question central to the decision by Lukoil to invite ConocoPhillips in is, how welcome will it make its new partners? If ConocoPhillips is allowed to influence how the company manages its existing fields and provides balance to Lukoil's acquisition programme, the combination may, as the announcements claim, bring together the best of two worlds. At the other end of the spectrum, Lukoil could limit cooperation to specific projects. Even if these are large ventures, like that envisioned for the northern Timan-Pechora basin, the impact will not be any more significant than the purchase by ARCO, in the early nineties, of 8 per cent of Lukoil – which led to nothing for either side.

Yukos

In October 2004, it is impossible to call Yukos the leader of the Russian oil industry, but by several traditional measures, it is still number one. While the company produces more oil than any other, the chief executive officer that presided over its ascendancy is in jail. Yukos developed the big new field, Priobskoye, that led Russia's oil production resurgence, but the corporation faces legal charges that could carry penalties of $10 billion or more. Of course, being on the verge of legal dismemberment pokes a large hole in the image of 'leadership'.

Yukos, the company that highlighted the run-up in Russian production, became the darling of Western investment circles. As the company moved to the forefront of technical performance this decade, it was also in the vanguard of improving corporate transparency in reporting financial and reserve data. In development of their star field, Priobskoye, as well as in re-engineering legacy assets, Yukos demonstrated the best of what combined Russian and Western technology and management practices could bring.

Despite these accomplishments, the dissolution of the corporation, at least in its present structure, appears almost certain and imminent. Yukos' political and legal troubles overshadow every aspect of its business. For the purposes of explanation, however, they are separable from its technical and financial accomplishments, and are explained in Box 4 on page 124. Yukos' performance as an oil company is reviewed here.

Yukos was born second into the new Russian oil industry of the early nineties. The company began with just one of West Siberia's major production associations, Yuganskneftegaz. It acquired an obligatory downstream asset quickly, and made an early merger with one of the Volga-Ural basin's smaller organizations, Samaraneftegaz.[34] The company was not very acquisitive, adding only a medium-size West Siberian producer, Tomskneft, at the end of the decade (Figure 29).

Although it was founded as a private company, in April 1993, as was the case with most pre-1995 privatizations, the Russian government retained a majority interest in the company. Therefore, Yukos became one of the biggest prizes of the Loans for Shares scheme. In an auction on December 8, 1995, 45 per cent of Yukos' shares were offered in exchange for a loan to the government; another 33 per cent of the stock was offered in a related 'investment tender.' The state's asking price was $300 million for the two blocks of shares, plus the promise by the winner to invest another $200 million in the company.

As occurred with most of the Loans for Shares deals, the prospective buyer, Mikhail Khodorkovsky's Menatep Bank, organized the auction. Although there was competition offered by other Oligarchs, Khodorkovsky's access to cash and top officials of the Yeltsin administration, trumped all other offers. He paid only $9 million more than the opening price on the block of 78 per cent of Yukos' shares.[35] At that time, Yukos had roughly 14 billion barrels of Soviet/Russian $A+B+C_1$ resources.[36] If even only half of those were proved reserves in the SPE/WPC sense, Khodorkovsky and his partners paid only 6 cents per barrel for Yukos. Brent oil, in 1995, was $17/bbl. Worldwide, the acquisition price of 'in-ground' oil ranged from $1 to $6/bbl.

There were additional machinations in 1996 that further consolidated Menatep's position in Yukos. Yet the changes did little to the technical performance of the company. Production, which had stopped declining in 1995, remained fairly stable through 1998 (Figure 29). However, the company was particularly well poised to exploit the rise in income that began in 1999.

Its ace in the hole was a major discovered and undeveloped field, Priobskoye. Although it posed some special operational challenges, it contained very large volumes of technically recoverable oil. During most of the nineties, Yukos tried to get others to finance the field's development. Amoco (now part of BP) reportedly spent $100 million pursuing the field.[37] At one point, Yukos approached Lukoil with a plan for joint development. None of these efforts bore fruit, but as of 1999, the rising tide of income made partners unnecessary, and Yukos began development of the field on its own.

In 2000, driven by the initial increases at Priobskoye, Yukos' output began a major, sustained increase. It was on its way to becoming the country's largest producer. More than just rising production, over the period of 2000 through the beginning of 2003 the company made a very broad accession to leadership of the Russian oil industry.

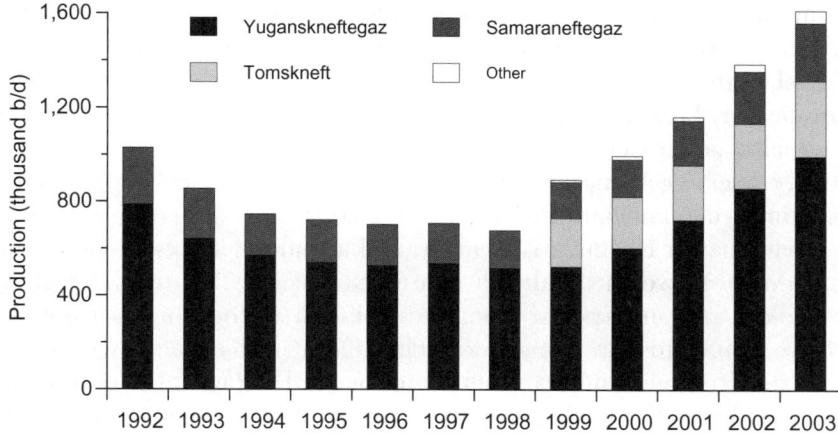

Figure 29: Yukos Oil Production by Subsidiary

In 2001, it began reporting financial results using the Generally Accepted Accounting Principles (GAAP) standards (and restating previous years back to 1997). In 2002, it revealed the structure of its share ownership.[38] While it is amazing that this took a decade, it marked an important step toward corporate transparency. In addition to assessing its oil and gas resources using the Soviet/Russian $A+B+C_1$ standards, the company reports not only reserves under SPE/WPC definitions, but the even more strict system accepted by the US Securities and Exchange Commission (SEC) (see Appendix II). By 2003, its board contained roughly half Russian and half directors from outside Russia.[39]

While the stain of Loans for Shares perhaps never went away, during this decade Yukos emerged from a shady corporate adolescence, publicly aspiring to become the Russian exemplar of sound, even progressive management. Its efforts were rewarded technically as well as financially (Table 10). Consistently behind Lukoil throughout the 1990s, by the beginning of 2003 it had become the nation's largest oil producer.[40]

Technical measures of the company's performance have risen across the board. Mainly through Priobskoye, they have reduced oil production costs, raised well productivity and even lowered average water cut. The company appears aggressive about applying Western technology, not only to new projects like Priobskoye, but to re-engineering some of their major, old West Siberian fields.

The company has focused on Russia, with foreign upstream involvement limited to a position in a low-profile Kazakh exploration block.

In addition to investing in its own fields, it began (for the second time) courting Sibneft, one of the most technically aggressive and successful oil companies in the country. Not only would the merger have significantly augmented reserve and productive capacity but would have also added leveraging experience in contracting and managing Western service company relations. As a result of the 'Yukos Affair,' the companies unwound the merger in 2004.

Downstream in 2002, Yukos acquired a major refinery in Lithuania and threw its weight behind a consortium of Russian majors seeking to build a private pipeline from West Siberia to the northern port of Murmansk. This project could help relieve the capacity constraint on exports, diminish Transneft's monopoly leverage and potentially ease access to the North American market. The company raised (rail) exports to China and vocally lobbied for a pipeline connecting East Siberia to the Pacific market. Perhaps angling for exposure to eventual electricity deregulation, perhaps hedging a major cost component (or both), in 2002 Yukos took positions in four regional electric distribution companies.

Yukos is part of the pack beating a path to natural gas. While presently an insignificant gas producer, by 2003 the company had bought controlling interests in three independent gas producers in the northern part of West Siberia. Plans, as of 2003, called for raising gas production over six times by 2005, although these have probably changed as the company sought, in 2004, to sell some of the gas assets to raise the money to settle its tax problems.[41]

Until its recent problems, from a Western viewpoint Yukos had 'done

Table 10: Technical and Financial Performance Indicators for Yukos[42]

Indicator	Units	2000	2001	2002	2003
Oil Reserves	Billion bbls	11.7	12.6	13.7	14.7
Gas Reserves	Trillion cubic feet	2.6	4.5	7.8	7.9
Oil Production	Million b/d	1.0	1.2	1.4	1.6
Gas Production	Billion cubic feet	56	60	84	122
Oil Reserves / Production	Years	32	29	26	25
Total Assets	Billion US$	8.5	10.5	14.4	18.5*
Revenues	Billion US$	9.1	9.5	11.4	12.2*
Income Before Income Taxes	Billion US$	4.9	3.9	3.8	4.3*
Income Taxes	Billion US$	0.7	1.2	0.7	0.8*
Net Income	Billion US$	3.7	3.2	3.1	3.5*
Basic Earnings per Share	$/share	1.68	1.49	1.41	1.65*

* As of the 3rd quarter only.

it all right' and the company's financial position is orders of magnitude better than before 1999. Yet, putting aside its legal and political problems, there is evidence on the technical side that the juggernaut has begun to slow down.

The company's reduction in production costs, loudly touted, will soon begin to reverse. Increasing output from high-productivity wells at Priobskoye drove most of the operating costs to decline. As the rate of its growth slows in mid-decade, there is no successor new field of that size to exploit for the same effect.[43] The flush of virgin production at Priobskoye, as well as better management of the old fields, brought corporate average water cut down. This too is a fleeting redoubt in a war that is always won by the water. Water cut will start a brisk climb within a few years at Priobskoye. While shutting in high-water/low-oil wells at Mamontovskoye and other large old fields is laudable and improves efficiency, this is also generally a one-time gain. The growth of water cuts, and with them water handling costs, is inevitable.

Forced to switch more of its exports to rail, transportation costs have risen (in part because it was exporting more oil to China, to which there are no pipeline options). Taxes are up (exclusive of the consequences of alleged evasion). There is little reason to expect that operating costs, tariffs or taxes will fall any time soon.

The centre of the company's assets is its Yuganskneftegaz subsidiary. This is the division that drove the company's exceptional rise in production; it is also apparently the prize in the sights of Russian tax authorities presently focusing legal problems on the corporation (see Box 4).

Yuganskneftegaz's operations are concentrated on the left (south) bank of the Ob River (Map 13). Production hit its maximum in 1986 as part of the mid-eighties peak from the Middle Ob region. However, after being the favourite of the Soviet oil industry in those years, it was hit hard after its zenith.[44] The organization lost half of its output within the next decade – a loss caused by the demise of its first generation, anchor field, Mamontovskoye.

The collapse at Mamontovskoye, which contributed about half of the association's peak production, did not stabilize until the end of the nineties, later than most. Nevertheless, output began growing again in 2000. Yukos credits new drilling based on reservoir geology and production simulation modelling to guide the location of wells, rather than drilling a simple grid.[45]

Halting the decline at the unit's largest field provided a stable foundation to capture the gains made at Priobskoye. Its discovery in 1982 was late, given that it straddles the Ob River only 70 miles downstream from

> **Box 4**
>
> *The 'Yukos Affair'*
>
> The Yukos Affair is rooted in two separate problems that intertwined to surround the company and the man who sat atop its corporate structure – Mikhail Khodorkovsky. One source of the trouble is very clearly political. The second, which would probably not have arisen in the absence of the first, taps fast dealing during the Loans for Shares programme. Together, these currents have engulfed Russia's largest oil producer, and will most likely destroy it, at least in its present form. They also make it almost certain that Khodorkovsky, Yukos' former Chief Executive Officer, will be stripped of his wealth and may ultimately face the choice of jail or exile.
>
> The criminal indictments that Khodorkovsky, and his partner Platon Lebedev, face are actually the easier part of the affair to understand. Of the range of charges filed by prosecutors against the two men, most boil down to actions taken by the Menatep Bank ten years ago. Khodorkovsky was its chairman and Lebedev, its president. As explained above, at that time a broad scheme, which became the Loans for Shares programme, evolved for exchanging government-held shares in privatized firms for loans to the government. In some situations, the resulting equity position of the lender in the acquired company could be leveraged by a pledge from the bank to further invest in the firm.
>
> Menatep, a bank central to the Oligarch ring, used this investment leverage option to gain a 20 per cent stake in one of Russia's largest chemical fertilizer plants – Apatit.[46] However, ultimately Menatep did not make the required investment in Apatit. Consequently, the state alleges that it obtained the 20 per cent stake by fraud. Prosecutors further charge that in management of Apatit, Khodorkovsky and Lebedev used Yukos-controlled offshore shell companies in transfer pricing schemes to further defraud the company's other shareholders, including the state, which retained 20 per cent of Apatit's shares.
>
> There is a second set of charges against the men personally for tax evasion. Here again, their actions as individuals have entwined with the Yukos corporation. The state claims they used the corporation, its assets and even staff, to create personal tax dodges. The tax case has many detailed facts, but most appear to arise out of the state's conclusion that Khodorkovsky and Lebedev knew they had specific

tax obligations on income received and employed instruments of the Yukos corporation to avoid paying them.

After the arrest of Lebedev in July 2003 and Khodorkovsky three months later, momentum grew around the case, accelerated by the national Duma elections in December and upcoming presidential contest in March 2004. In this electric environment, in January 2004, federal tax authorities charged that Yukos, as a corporation, had also defrauded the state by failing to pay $3.4 billion in tax owed for 2000. Since authorities acted on Yukos' 2000 corporate return, charges have been made and/or investigations have begun concerning the corporation's 2001 and 2002 filings.

The corporate tax charges are much more complex than the personal, criminal complaints against Khodorkovsky and Lebedev. Part of the corporate tax case rests on a conclusion by the Tax Ministry that Yukos stretched provisions in the tax code to the point of illegality. In other words, they are denying, *ex post*, use of tax loopholes that Yukos invoked in its 2000–2002 returns to reduce its taxes. The provisions exploited by Yukos involve accounting assignments of income to 'domestic offshore zones,' which enjoyed lower marginal tax rates than would obtain had the income been credited in the localities where it was actually earned.

The resulting tax liability, growing out of the 2000 and 2001 returns, totals between $6.8 and $8 billion. Adding the results of investigating Yukos' 2002 and now, possibly its 2003 return, it is likely that penalties and interest will raise the amount due to over $10 billion.

The more complex part of the Yukos Affair is not the detailed nature of legal problems facing Khodorkovsky, Lebedev and Yukos, but why their actions got them into trouble. If Russian prosecutors were to pursue all who committed fraud, even multi-million dollar frauds, during the mid-nineties, they would have to reopen the GULAG. Equally, Yukos was by no means the only company, even major company, to exploit the domestic tax havens, created at their behest to avoid federal taxes. Khodorkovsky and his company ran foul of more than legal norms.

Khodorkovsky's immediate political offence was a direct, and increasingly open, challenge to the presidency of Vladimir Putin. In July 2000, six months after Putin became Russian president, a conclave was convened at the Kremlin that included most of the Oligarchs who made out so infamously under the lax regime of Boris Yeltsin. At this meeting, Putin purportedly made the assembled super-rich an offer they could not refuse. They could keep their wealth if, and only if, they kept out of Russian politics.

At least two, Boris Berezovsky and Vladimir Gusinsky, whose empires included major media outlets, quickly chafed under the new strictures. Their continued public opposition to Putin and his policies immediately brought criminal investigations and the two fled the country (leaving much of their wealth behind). The new Russian government was not as pliable and buyable as the old one and showed that they would not brook powerfully rich men extending their sway beyond the bounds of business.

Khodorkovsky's course took a shallower path than Gusinsky and Berezovsky. As a result, it was longer before his activities rose to the level of visible opposition to the Kremlin that had triggered the disposition of the two media magnates. However, Khodorkovsky personally, and with the use of Yukos' corporate philanthropy, began to financially support liberal causes and parties, most importantly Yabloko and the Union of Right Forces. This political block was voicing increasing criticism of what they saw as the Putin administration's undermining of democratic pluralism in the name of the 'rule of law.'

In 2003, with Duma elections approaching in December, Khodorkovsky further ratcheted his attacks on the Kremlin. He and his allies usually cast their opposition in the cloak of democracy and freedom, determined to check the retreat (perceived and actual) to the days of centralized authority, the KGB and rule by unalloyed power.

Less publicly, Khodorkovsky's candidates for the coming legislative elections were, not coincidentally, also actively involved in securing the same tax loopholes and legislative advantages that are now central to several of the fraud charges against Yukos. So, while Khodorkovsky was publicly singing the praises of a participatory democracy and tolerant pluralism, less obviously he was moving to privatize the Russian legislature to protect and further his personal and corporate economic interests.

The Putin administration, long before its September 2004 revanchist proposals on centralization of power, was progressively closing avenues for political competition – always in the names of security, efficiency and order. An increasingly high-profile, uncowed opponent, with infinitely deep pockets, and perhaps only partly inspired by the national good, became an intolerable danger. The government fired a warning shot by arresting Lebedev in July 2003, but Khodorkovsky apparently believed his status, and the moral correctness of his putative goals, insulated him. He was wrong.

Why, then, with Khodorkovsky in jail, did the state directly attack Yukos as a corporation? Yukos played, and continues to play, an absolutely central role in the Russian economy. To destroy it seems, at least from abroad, to be enormously short-sighted and spiteful. Russia's macroeconomic recovery this decade, which is no small part of Putin's fabled popular support, rests directly on the contributions made by the nation's oil industry, and Yukos, in many ways, was not only its leader, but its future.

Yet it should be no surprise that the economic consequences even of dismembering Yukos would be ranked as less important to the government than its own hold on power. In addition, because Khodorkovsky mixed so deeply what he did personally and corporately, Yukos came to be seen by the Kremlin as the instrument of his threat. That the company was allegedly escaping massive tax obligations through loopholes born of corruption made Yukos a co-conspirator of Khodorkovsky, vitiating any corporate right to exist arising out of its contribution to the national economy.

For his part, the Russian president has been publicly clear: 'I can say just one thing, Russian state officials and the government are not interested in a bankruptcy of such a company as Yukos'.[47] Either, things had changed between the beginning and end of the summer of 2004, or there was at least a little dissembling by President Putin. In October 2004, it seems almost certain that Yukos will be dismembered, officially, for the purpose of settling its tax claims.

The idea receiving widest circulation is that Yukos' leading subsidiary, Yuganskneftegaz, will be seized and sold by the state to satisfy the tax judgment (whatever it ends up being). One variant of this general scheme envisions Yuganskneftegaz bought by Gazprom, which is about to be enlarged by the absorption of Rosneft. This would both renationalize a key oil asset privatized through the Loans for Shares programme, and make Gazprom a major player in Russian oil supply. Neither Gazprom nor Rosneft has demonstrated any special skills in managing the type of legacy assets Yuganskneftegaz has. It is also highly uncertain that either could sustain the type of growth Yukos got out of its big new field – Priobskoye.

Another scenario has the Yukos subsidiary going to neighbouring Surgutneftegaz, a company that clearly has the technical competence and financial resources for the stewardship of the assets. The transfer would reward the corporate fealty of Surgutneftegaz to the Putin administration. It would also plug a gaping hole in that corporation's growth strategy – the need for new fields to drill. Surgutneftegaz

128 *Russian Oil Supply*

> management of Yuganskneftegaz's fields is the course most likely to have the least adverse impact on supply.
>
> The least likely alternative is that the assets go to a Western oil company. It is not politically palatable and neither financially nor technically necessary.
>
> In the Yukos Affair, the Putin administration has drawn a bright line around the activities of major Russian corporations and those who run them. At least as things stand now, the financial resources that a market economy affords corporations and individuals will not be allowed to be used against the political interests of the present administration. Moreover, one of the consequences that might be expected for crossing that line is expropriation of the economic means supporting anything the Kremlin sees as a threat. Finally, as part of reversing the excesses of the nineties, companies should expect not only to be more rigorously held to legal obligations, like taxes, but increasingly required to play a broader role in supporting national policies than they have in the past, or may in other countries.

Mamontovskoye (which was discovered two decades earlier). It was not so much hard to find (it occupies a very big structure) as hard to get at. The Ob River flood plain is particularly soggy there and the logistics of surface operations unusually difficult. Therefore, development was deferred throughout the Soviet period.[48]

After its 1997 low of 526,000 b/d, two years of engineering measures restarted growth at Yuganskneftegaz. Since then, however, Priobskoye powered the drive to 995,000 b/d in 2003. The company is employing 'new' methodologies to develop their top field. The drilling strategy recognizes the considerable heterogeneity of the field's reservoirs – rather than poking down wells on a grid. They widely employ extended reach directional wells to minimize the number of surface locations requiring drainage and construction of drilling pads in the river flood plain.

This transition from Soviet-style extensive pattern drilling is a large part of why Priobskoye can be developed at all. The company has claimed the strategy paid off in new well flow rates that average 1,788 b/d. Their data place the field's average well production in 2001 at 293 b/d, four times the basin-wide average.[49]

It is easy to see the impact on efficiency of improved engineering and particularly the flush of high-rate new-field wells at Priobskoye. Figure 30 shows the number of producing wells and average well productivity for Yuganskneftegaz. The former has remained nearly flat since 1995. The latter has escalated sharply since 1999, initially because of its

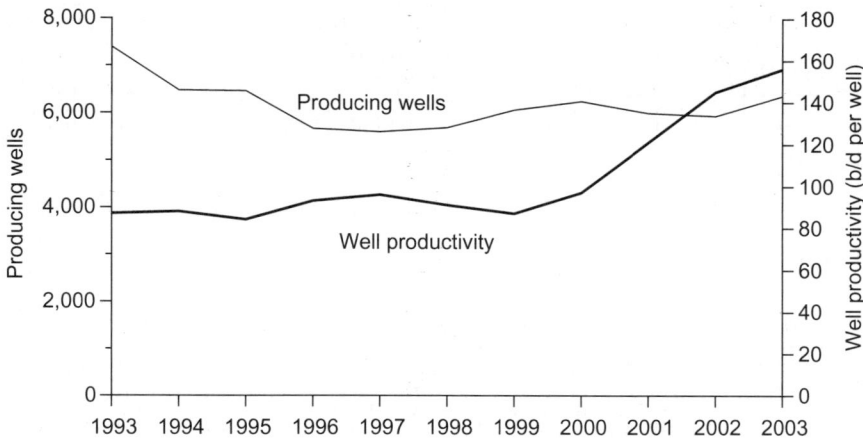

Figure 30: Relationship of Number of Producing Wells and Well Productivity at Yuganskneftegaz

operations at older fields and most profoundly from 2001 through 2003 due to Priobskoye.[50]

If the Yukos Affair leads to the dismemberment of the corporation, the most likely scenario is that the Yuganskneftegaz division will be stripped out and sold. This would leave Yukos with a shadow of its present structure. The corporation's other major producing divisions, Tomskneft and Samaraneftegaz, contributed only 35 per cent of 2003 output.

Tomskneft is a mid-sized West Siberian producer responsible for fields in the Tomsk Oblast, which occupies most of the south-eastern part of the basin. It is a mixed bag of several very old fields, located relatively close to the Samotlor field in the Middle Ob region, a scattering of smaller producing fields and substantial exploration/new field development potential. While it dipped somewhat in the mid-nineties, output stayed relatively flat through the end of the decade. However by 2002, the organization turned in a 19 per cent increase in production and followed this in 2003 with a 16 per cent rise. This is probably the result of new field development begun at the beginning of this decade.

Samaraneftegaz is a small Volga-Ural basin producer. Although it has a far less robust resource base than Tomskneft, it achieved an impressive 16 per cent output rise in 2002 and 12 per cent in 2003. Both junior divisions of Yukos share potential for good percentage growth as long as investment continues, but the long-run potential of Tomskneft is much greater. Neither organization contains the same type of potential as Yuganskneftegaz (because of Priobskoye).

The loss of Sibneft from Yukos' future has already sharply lowered its long-run outlook. If the corporation's present woes lead to the loss of Yuganskneftegaz, not only will its present productive capacity be savaged, but its reserve base and future growth potential will also disappear.

Sibneft

In 2003, before the wave of trouble swamped Yukos, Sibneft was to merge with the industry leader. In combining, the two companies would have attained a commanding presence in the industry, with a good chance of holding a pre-eminent position for years. Perhaps it was that very prospect that prevented it from happening. If Moscow's intention was to deflate Yukos, it could not afford to allow a merger that would have secured that company's position at the top of Russian oil.

Even viewed from Sibneft's perspective, as the legal problems of Platon Lebedev became the legal problems of Mikhail Khodorkovsky, and then of the Yukos corporation itself, its perfect union quickly soured. By the third quarter of 2004, the deal which was all but consummated a year earlier, came apart.

The upstream assets of Sibneft consist almost completely of what was the Soviet Noyabrskneftegaz producing association (Map 13). It was the second-most-northern oil producer in West Siberia, so it was explored only in the seventies.[51] As a result of distance and timing, the Soviets had only developed a few fields in this rich zone before the USSR collapsed. This gave Noyabrskneftegaz a large inventory of discovered, undeveloped fields when the modern Russian industry started forming.

While in the care of the state in the first half of the nineties, Noyabrskneftegaz lost one-third of its output. This did not happen for lack of fresh fields to develop. Most of the reason, of course, was money. However, some of Noyabrskneftegaz's problems arose literally from being one of the last stops on the rail line that supplied it out of the main depots along the Ob River. Supplies bound northward would 'fall off the train' in the distance between the Ob and the company's headquarters in the Arctic settlement of Noyabrsk.

Being a state ward, Noyabrskneftegaz was a prime candidate for the Loans for Shares programme in 1995. Its 'privatization' stands as perhaps the most overtly fixed in a programme that was itself the essence of perfidy and contrivance. As 1995 closed, and the Yeltsin administration was wrapping the last gems of the nation's resource and industrial bases, one of the Oligarchs who helped frame the programme, Boris Berezovsky, began to feel that he had not received his share.[52]

The presidential decree authorizing Loans for Shares required its completion by year-end and its regulations specified at least 30 days between the initiation of an auction process and its conclusion. At the end of November, days before the deadline, Berezovsky proposed to the government that, rather than taking shares in an existing firm, the state allow him to combine Noyabrskneftegaz with the oil refinery in Omsk, to form a new company for him to control – Sibneft.

With rapidity perhaps never seen in the Kremlin before or since, all of the paperwork to auction two major assets of the Russian oil industry was completed within three days. Berezovsky, whose media empire had always been at Yeltsin's service, was able to obtain 51 per cent of the newly formed Sibneft for $100.9 million, $900,000 above the reservation price.[53] At that time, Noyabrskneftegaz had Soviet/Russian $A+B+C_1$ oil resources of 6.1 billion bbls. As was the case with the acquisition of Yukos by Khodorkovsky and his partners, even if only half of that volume was proved in the SPE/WPC sense, Berezovsky got Noyabrskneftegaz's oil for 6 cents per barrel.[54] In 1995, Brent oil was $17/bbl. Worldwide, the acquisition price of 'in-ground' oil ranged from $1 to $6/bbl.

The transfer of ownership did nothing for the company. Production at Sibneft, which had bottomed in the mid-nineties, remained flat through 1999. The following year, however, things did change. On the last day of the millennium, Boris Yeltsin suddenly retired, turning over the reins of the Russian government to Vladimir Putin.

The new president's patience with the Oligarch's freewheeling role in government was short and, by the summer of 2000, he demanded that it stop. Berezovsky, whose influence was enforced by media holdings (most importantly, a TV network), quickly and publicly ran afoul the new Russian president and was driven into exile. On his way out, Berezovsky sold his interests in Sibneft (among other holdings) to one of his original partners in the Loans for Shares deal, Roman Abramovich.[55]

Coincident with Berezovsky's departure, and Abramovich's succession, Sibneft's management and performance both perked up. Output in 2000 rose, but only by 5 per cent, reflecting the rouble devaluation and increasing export prices. Yet in 2001, the company's oil production jumped a stunning 20 per cent. This was followed by 28 per cent growth in 2002 and 19 per cent in 2003 (Table 11). Even as oil production bounded upward nationally, Sibneft's performance stood out, making it the fastest growing oil company in the country.

Importantly, Sibneft achieved these accomplishments not by brute force (i.e., massive drilling), but by better engineering. Between 2000 and 2003, production per well doubled from 87 b/d to 173 b/d and water cut fell from 67 to 62 per cent (Figure 31). In addition to stabilizing the decline at the company's older fields, Sibneft ramped up two new fields that started production originally in the mid-nineties. The more important was Sugmutskoye, one of the fourth-generation giant fields of the West Siberian basin (Table 1).

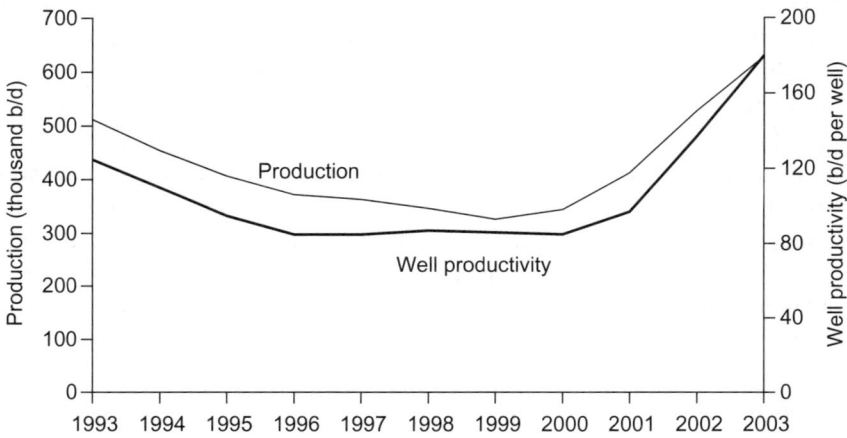

Figure 31: Relationship of Production and Well Productivity at Noyabrskneftegaz

No small part of this success arose from a rich, largely undeveloped resource base. Some share came also from a novel level of openness at Sibneft to Western technology and management. Around 2000, the company began extensive relationships with Western oil service firms. These contractors provided the company with the latest technologies in reservoir modelling, horizontal completions and hydraulic fracturing.[56] Sibneft also took foreigners directly into top project management positions. These decisions not only paid off in higher production and productivity, they gave the company experience in managing Western service-company relationships that are perhaps the best developed in the Russian industry.

If technical prowess was not enough, fed by revenue growth, the relatively small Sibneft did a little shopping. In 2001, it bought a 10 per cent stake in Slavneft, which had an odd structure involving ownership by the Russian and Belarus governments. In 2002, Sibneft and TNK together bought another 75 per cent of the shares in Slavneft, splitting them 50–50. This gave Sibneft at least a 42 per cent stake in an entity, which while plagued with its own problems, nevertheless produced 294,000 barrels per day.

By the time Sibneft again caught the attention of Yukos in 2002, its output was skyrocketing, it was technologically and managerially sophisticated and had begun to augment its original endowment with acquisitions. Moreover, the company's principal shareholder, Abramovich, had displayed possibly useful political acumen by installing himself as the governor of Chukotka, a barren peninsula on the extreme northeast tip of Russia, across from Alaska. While Chukotka itself added nothing, it placed the Oligarch in the upper house of the Russian legislature, and therefore, made him a much more powerful man.

Table 11: Technical and Financial Performance Indicators for Sibneft[57]

Indicator	Units	2000	2001	2002	2003
Oil Reserves	Billion bbls	4.6	4.6	4.6	4.8
Gas Reserves	Trillion cubic feet	1.5	1.4	0.9	0.9
Oil Production	Million b/d	0.34	0.41	0.53	0.63
Gas Production	Billion cubic feet	50	58	50	70
Oil Reserves / Production	Years	37	31	24	21
Total Assets	Billion US$	4.6	5.7	7.5	8.1
Revenues	Billion US$	2.4	3.7	4.8	6.7
Income Before Income Taxes	Billion US$	0.8	1.4	1.3	2.5
Income Taxes	Billion US$	0.1	0.1	0.2	0.2
Net Income	Billion US$	0.7	1.3	1.1	2.3
Basic Earnings per Share	$/share	0.21	0.32	0.23	0.48

Sibneft's domain contains an enviable set of fields. However, in spite of the income brought by higher oil prices, the company may not have the capital depth to develop its patrimony at a rate high enough to sustain its recent performance. While the 19 per cent growth in output in 2003 was in itself stellar, it was less than the company had planned.[58] Corporate distraction by its deteriorating relationship with Yukos was part of the cause, but the production plan was also probably shorted by the investment budget.

Sibneft had much to offer in its annulled marriage to Yukos, but what *it* was looking for was finance. The company can carve a secure niche in the industry on its own. Yet, its capital asset base is only half of the next largest company (TNK-BP). It remains ripe for a relationship that picks up where the disappointing courtship of Yukos left off. It could take a foreign partner, perhaps not at the level of TNK-BP, but closer to the recently announced investment of ConocoPhillips in

Lukoil. The impending break-up of Yukos itself may also redistribute assets and power within the industry that suggests a wholly novel path to the firm.

Surgutneftegaz

In the middle of the seventeenth century, the hierarchy of the Russian Orthodox Church undertook reforms to bring its practice and liturgy in line with the rest of the orthodox world. While the Tsar supported the changes, and the patriarchs of the great eastern sees blessed them, the adjustments produced a schism among Russia's faithful. Those who refused to accept the innovations were known as *starovery*, or Old Believers. The *starovery* became isolated and insular in their retention of the old practices, but were never extinguished.

When the Yeltsin administration dismantled the Soviet Ministry of Oil and imposed the market-oriented revolution of the early nineties, a new core of Old Believers rejected the reforms and the direction in which the new orthodoxy was taking the economy and country. To say Surgutneftegaz became one big monastery for the oil industry's *starovery* perhaps pushes the metaphor too far, but not by much.

For a decade after the collapse of the USSR, Surgutneftegaz remained proudly out of step with much of the change that surrounded it. It spurned upstream alliances and has only a single refinery, with a compact marketing domain. It eschews foreign projects, favours Russian technology and remains the least transparent of the majors. Its board and management are solidly Russian. It even retained its original Soviet name!

Yet, in its confident traditionalist way, Surgutneftegaz showed that a less radically modified variant of the old Soviet production association could succeed in market-oriented Russia (Table 12). And in the last two years, as the Putin administration charted an increasingly nationalist and conservative course for the country, much of what once seemed quaintly schismatic has become the centre of industry fashion. The union of strong state and strong company is no longer an Old Belief.

The Soviets built Surgutneftegaz to exploit West Siberia's second largest field – Fedorovskoye. It was also endowed with other very large fields: Lyantorskoye, one of the largest second-generation giants, and Tyanskoye, one of the most prolific of the fourth-generation giants (Table 1).

The organization lost nearly half of its production between its mid-eighties peak and the middle of the nineties. Since its low of 662,000 b/d in 1998, however, its output has grown by an extraordinary 63 per cent to 1.08 million b/d in 2003. There were two causes.

The foundation of its success was to arrest the precipitous rates of decline at the corporation's three old major fields: Fedorovskoye, Bystrinskoye and Lyantorskoye. All three bottomed out in 1994 and have stayed flat since. Had they failed to halt the collapse at these fields, because they are so large, all efforts at new fields would have been consumed just filling the shortfall created by the collective decline of the largest fields.

On this stable base, Surgutneftegaz built its growth in production on the development of three major new fields: Vachimskoye, Tyanskoye and Konitlorskoye. Tyanskoye is among the handful of new fields that tipped the extraordinary climb in national output over the last five years; it drove the company's post-1998 recovery. While this field was discovered in Soviet times and presents no special engineering impediments, from what little information they release, the company's development of it appears to be exemplary.

Bringing on large new fields was the proximate cause of Surgutneftegaz's resurrection, but on a more fundamental level the company drilled its way to success, another echo of its Soviet past. It is not necessarily the wrong strategy. However, the company faces a mature resource base, occupying the centre of the densely drilled Middle Ob region; it does not have a significant inventory of new large fields to tap. Production moved nearly in lock-step with development drilling, and without new fields it will ultimately reach sharply diminishing returns to adding new wells to established fields (Figure 32). Well productivity has grown since 1998, but was responsible for less than a third of the increase in output.

While relying on the drill bit, at least the company focused its efforts on the development of new fields. In its ability to bring major new fields online in the nineties, Surgutneftegaz led the Russian oil industry. Perhaps its insularity gave it the managerial and financial focus that escaped its more distracted competitors.

Surgutneftegaz has not balanced all its success on drilling alone. In a deft move, the company also developed substantial power-generation facilities at a handful of key fields. With electricity costs so important to a company critically reliant on pumps, self-generated power provides a substantial shield to increases in production costs that would otherwise be beyond its control.

The company now also makes wider application of higher performance electrical submersible pumps, which are responsible for 80 per cent of total output. Further, they set 144 horizontal completions in

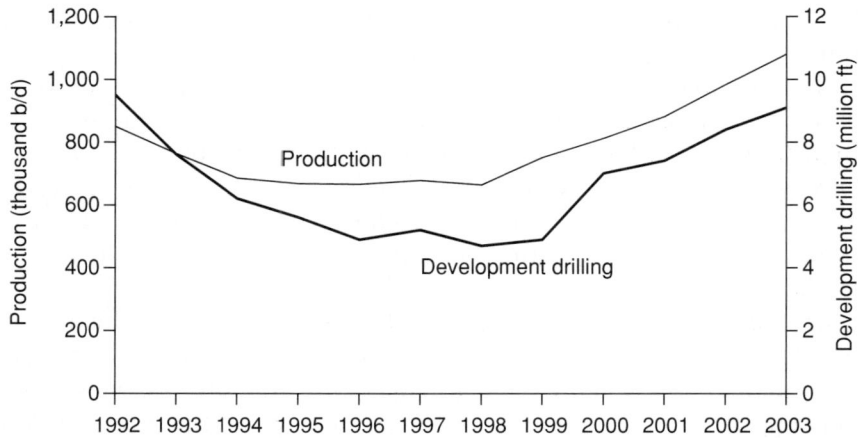

Figure 32: Relationship of Drilling Footage and Oil Production at Surgutneftegaz

2003, 16 per cent of new wells. Compared to the company's total well stock, horizontal completions produce four to five times more oil than conventional completions. There has been an active fracing programme, involving approximately 200 wells per year.[59] Finally, about one-third of the addition to the number of producing wells was through repair of formerly idle wells.

It is assumed, in the absence of major funding changes, that the company's old major fields will continue well-behaved declines at the 3–4 per cent per year level into the indefinite future. The exception to this could be Lyantorskoye, which is sufficiently large and less mature, giving it the capacity to increase production over short periods. It is, however, fundamentally a field in decline. Growth will be centred on the development of Tyanskoye and to a much less extent, Konitlorskoye, Vachimskoye and smaller new fields.

From Old Believer to bellwether, Surgutneftegaz now presents a strong alternative model to structuring a Russian oil company in the image of the Western majors. It is one where the division between corporation and state is purposefully indistinct. The company's chief (who still goes by the Soviet title General Director), Vladimir Bogdanov, was the West Siberian campaign manager in President Putin's first election campaign. Putin, comparing the physical conditions and amenities between Surgutneftegaz headquarters' city of Surgut, with that of Yukos, Nefteyugansk, described the difference as between 'night and day.'[60] A strong complementary connection between company and state has become central to success in today's Russia.

This is a firm with a reputation for taking care of its own, and for an authoritarian approach to employees – both recalling a time before 1992. Nevertheless, workers at Surgutneftegaz reportedly make twice as much as those in Yukos, which buys a lot of patience with rules about the colour of work overalls. A production growth strategy that relies so heavily on drilling also ensures greater local employment at a time when others, like Lukoil, are counting on layoffs for cost savings. Bogdanov and his colleagues may not be creating a proletarian paradise on the right bank of the Ob River, but the company's view and record of social responsibility is received with approval in the capital, as well as in Surgut.

Surgutneftegaz's narrow focus on its local fields, not distracted by acquisitions and foreign investments, has also left it with massive retained earnings, between $5 and $8 billion. Being in the good graces of the Kremlin, and having cash in hand, the company stands perhaps uniquely ready if, or when, the state sells off the Yuganskneftegaz division of Yukos to satisfy its tax judgement.

The opportunity to acquire Yuganskneftegaz, which is located across the Ob River, would quench the biggest concern about the company's long-term technical performance – its lack of new fields to drill. It would add Yuganskneftegaz's Mamontovskoye field, West Siberia's third largest, but it would also give Surgutneftegaz Yukos' grand prize – Priobskoye. This field, which led the nation's production run-up, has perhaps hundreds of locations left to drill and the potential to increase production for several more years.

If Yukos is not dismembered, or if Surgutneftegaz decides not to enter the fray, it faces a serious challenge in securing the foundation for long-term growth. Working the intensive margin of field development can be very profitable, but cannot be continued indefinitely. The company has made forays into East Siberia. Some plans include the soon-to-combine main state entities, Rosneft and Gazprom. But these are high-cost, high-risk and, more importantly, years from realization. At a minimum, they need a plan to bridge the inevitable peaking of their traditional field base and what might be gained in the remote wilds to the east.

The company also faces some of the contradictions at the corporate level on which the Putin administration must reflect at a national scale. Market forces have provided enormous financial gains, but winning at the market game requires observing some basic rules. For a corporation capitalized on domestic and foreign exchanges, this includes respecting minority shareholder rights.

In the summer of 2004, Harvard University, an owner of Surgutneftegaz's American Depository Receipts, initiated legal proceedings to recover dividends they claimed the company owed. The company, in order to accumulate the billions of dollars it now has in cash, set among the lowest dividends in the industry. While Harvard's case is detailed, and remains to be adjudicated, the company's initial response was to assert that the Russian company would act in its interests as perceived by its management. It offered little beyond advising minority shareholders to read prospectuses more carefully and to better understand the context in which Russian companies operate.[61]

Table 12: Technical and Financial Performance Indicators for Surgutneftegaz[62]

Indicator	Units	2000	2001	2002	2003
Oil Reserves	Billion bbls	6.9	6.6		
Gas Reserves	Trillion cubic feet	12.5	11.8		
Oil Production	Million b/d	0.81	0.88	0.98	1.1
Gas Production	Billion cubic feet	395	392	470	491
Oil Reserves / Production	Years	23	21		
Total Assets	Billion US$	10.2	12.1	15.8	
Revenues	Billion US$	6.1	5.6	5.9	
Income Before Income Taxes	Billion US$	2.5	3.3	4.0	
Income Taxes	Billion US$	0.8	0.5	0.4	
Net Income	Billion US$	2.7	1.8	1.6	
Basic Earnings per Share	$/share	0.06	0.04	0.04	

Perhaps the snub was only bad public relations. Another possibility is that Surgutneftegaz sees outside stockholders as ticket holders to an event they are allowed to watch, but in which they do not participate. If the latter is the case, it may limit the company's access to the capital markets that have treated it quite well this decade. If all the company's future investment needs can be met out of cash flow, in the end, its rebuff to shareholders will cause it little harm, but that is probably not a sustainable strategy for corporate development.

TNK-BP

Before its 2003 merger with the British major, BP, TNK was much better known for corporate intrigue than excellence in oil production. Yet from its chequered past, the new entity, TNK-BP, emerged as a wholly novel model for Russian oil companies. Company leaders received the requisite political approval and, with surprising alacrity, quickly got down to improving both technical and financial performance (Table 13).

Previously, TNK (standing for the Russian initials of Tyumen Oil Company) boasted the least stable and most confusing history of any in the industry. One of its two original companies started as the rump descendent of the top tier of the Soviet Oil Ministry in West Siberia, Glavtyumenneftegaz. This organization was a pure bureaucracy: it actually produced no oil itself, but only oversaw the basin's production associations. When the Soviet music stopped at the end of 1991, a new organization, called Tyumenneftegaz, somehow ended up with a dozen or more fields, which were almost all undeveloped.[63] Tyumenneftegaz was resource rich, with no cash and, as they had little production, meagre income with which to drill its undeveloped inventory.

At the birth of the Russian Federation, the production associations not included in the first few private conglomerates were assigned to a government holding entity that became Rosneft. Tyumenneftegaz was among them, along with the two producing associations responsible for the Samotlor field – Nizhnevartovskneftegaz and Chernogorneft. In the 1995 'great escape,' TNK emerged from the Rosneft structure with majority positions in both Tyumenneftegaz and Nizhnevartovskneftegaz, which ran the older, southern sector of Samotlor (Chernogorneft went to another major, Sidanco).

The new TNK structure simply continued the performance of its constituent parts, which remained under their previous, Soviet-era managements. In 1997, however, in a process that in many ways (except in publicity) paralleled the Loans for Shares programme, a group of outside investors acquired 40 per cent of TNK stock held by the Russian government. They were a combination of a US-based investment concern, Access/Renova, and the investment arm of the Alpha Bank, run by two of the Oligarchs, Pyotr Aven and Mikhail Friedman. They gained a majority position in the company the following year.

The TNK transactions were more complex than those of the Loans for Shares programme, they were spread over a longer period and the composition of TNK itself was fluid while the Access/Renova-Alpha group completed its acquisition. However, it appears that approximately $260 million was paid for about 90 per cent of the company's stock. In 1993, the Soviet/Russian $A+B+C_1$ resources of Nizhnevartovskneftegaz and Tyumenneftegaz were roughly 14.6 billion bbls.[64] If only half that volume had qualified as proved reserves, in the SPE/WPC sense, the investors obtained the oil for approximately 4 cents per barrel. Brent oil averaged between $13 and $19/bbl from 1997 through 1999, when the purchases were made. Worldwide, the acquisition price of 'in-ground' oil ranged from $1 to $6/bbl.

From the beginning of the Access/Renova-Alpha take over, TNK was in and out of court, and associated with a wide variety of schemes to acquire production assets, mainly in West Siberia. It fought a rearguard action by the Soviet-era management of Nizhnevartovskneftegaz, and increasingly became entangled with its neighbour, Sidanco.

Although Sidanco was formed in May 1994, it came to life in the Loans for Shares programme at the end of 1995. Vladimir Potanin, one of the core Oligarchs, obtained 51 per cent of its shares in return for $130 million.[65] At that time, using the Soviet/Russian $A+B+C_1$ definitions, the company had about 22 billion bbls in reserves.[66] Even if only half that amount was actually proved reserves, in the SPE/WPC sense, Potanin paid about 1 penny per barrel at a time when Brent averaged $17/bbl. Worldwide, the acquisition price of 'in-ground' oil ranged from $1 to $6/bbl.

Table 13: Technical and Financial Performance Indicators for TNK[67]

Indicator	Units	2000	2001	2002	2003
Oil Reserves	Billion bbls	7.7	7.3	8.4	9.0
Gas Reserves	Trillion cubic feet	3.9	4.1	3.6	0
Oil Production	Million b/d	0.6	0.8	0.7	1.2
Gas Production	Billion cubic feet	94	166	129	240
Oil Reserves / Production	Years	35	25	33	20
Total Assets	Billion US$	9.6	9.2	12.6	15.3
Revenues	Billion US$	4.3	5.2	8.1	10.3
Income Before Income Taxes	Billion US$	2.6	1.5	2.1	3.0
Income Taxes	Billion US$	0.3	0.1	0.2	0.2
Net Income	Billion US$	1.7	1.1	1.5	2.7
Basic Earnings per Share	$/share	34,000	22,000	30,000	54,000

Two years after its 'privatization,' BP made Sidanco the first significant investment by a Western major in a large Russian oil company, taking 10 per cent.[68] At first, it seemed to have no effect, as the company continued to muddle along. By 1999, it had lost its main subsidiary, Chernogorneft, to TNK in a suspicious bankruptcy proceeding.[69] In a related transfer during 2000, what had been Sidanco's KondPetroleum division (formerly the Krasnoleninskneftegaz producing association in the western part of West Siberia), also began operating under TNK as TNK-Nyagan.

Undaunted by these Byzantine dealings, in 2000 BP increased its investment in Sidanco to the blocking position of 25 per cent, plus one share, and actually took over management of the company. Sidanco and BP then filed suit to recover Chernogorneft and, in 2001, a court stripped it from TNK and returned it to them.

As part of the settlement of the Chernogorneft litigation, TNK took a majority position in Sidanco. In 2001, TNK also picked up a medium-size producer from the extreme southern Volga-Urals basin, Onako. In 2002, TNK and Sibneft split up the approximately three-quarters equity interest in Slavneft, the upstream assets of which consisted of the Middle Ob producing organization, Megionneftegaz (Map 13). If this was not enough instability, reorganization within TNK in 2000 took Samotlor operations out of Nizhnevartovskneftegaz, and created a new organization, Samotlorneftegaz.[70] The net effect is to make Figure 33, showing TNK production by division over time, rather confusing.

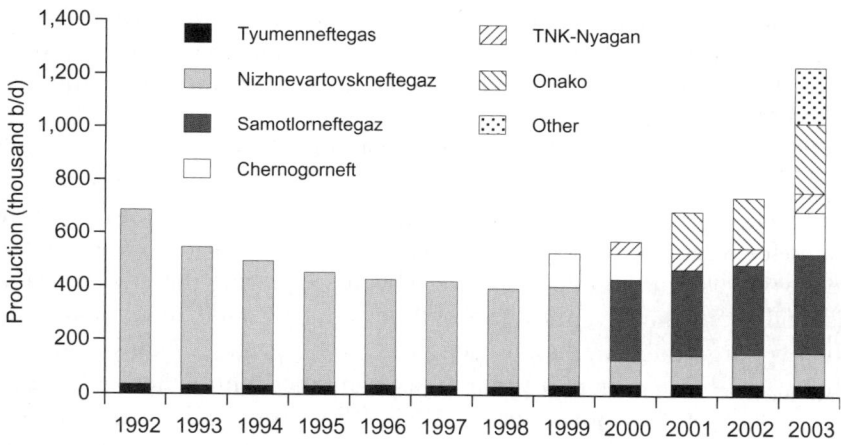

Figure 33: TNK Oil Production by Subsidiary[71]

Apparently inspired by settling the Chernogorneft mess, BP and TNK managements began constructing a far larger plan. In February 2003, they announced the creation of TNK-BP, a new corporation capitalized by the assets of TNK and Sidanco and most of the Russian interests of BP. The British major also kicked in over $6 billion in cash and securities.[72]

The principal asset of what is now TNK-BP is Russia's largest field, Samotlor. When it peaked in 1980 at 3.4 million b/d, it contributed 28 per cent of the output of the USSR, which at the time was the world's largest producer. Post-peak decline for the first three years averaged 3 per cent, but increased abruptly in 1984 to 10 per cent and 15 per cent in 1985 (Figure 10). As explained in Chapter 4, because of Samotlor's importance, the Soviets applied massive investment in 1986 to arrest the fall. This, though, was followed by a precipitous decline that did not end until the mid-nineties. From that point, until the turnaround, beginning in 2001, the field went into a slower, but erratic decline (see Box 2 on Samotlor in Chapter 3).

Despite 40 years of production, Samotlor remains rich in petroleum resources. In their April 3, 2002 report, the American petroleum engineering firm Miller and Lents, Ltd., under contract to TNK, performed a reserves evaluation of the field.[73] It lists proved reserves (in the SPE/WPC sense of the term, see Appendix II) at Samotlor of 3.7 billion bbls.[74]

This volume credited to Samotlor is greater than the proved reserves of any single field in the United States. Yet, with appropriate conservatism, the Miller and Lents production forecast showed a continued decline, with only a short plateau requiring investment in reserve volumes below the proved level. Under new management, Samotlor has done considerably better than that. BP-TNK raised production at the field in 2003 and anticipates a 14 per cent gain in 2004.[75]

Unquestionably, there is a large volume of oil at Samotlor only requiring better pumps, smarter water injection programmes, fracing and well workovers. Application of technologies well established in the West for years promises to be relatively cheap. Moreover, there are reservoirs within Samotlor that were bypassed during the Soviet period, as drilling in the seventies and eighties concentrated most heavily on the two largest accumulations (see Box 2 in Chapter 3). Many reservoirs that were thinner, or had small areas, remained untouched. This is an enormously rich opportunity for TNK-BP to apply 3-D seismic to find the accumulations and then set horizontal completions to produce the thinner of them and frac the tighter ones.

On the other hand, Samotlor's present renaissance must be put in perspective. It should not be assumed that TNK-BP's ability to raise production by 30,000–50,000 b/d in a year presages a sustainable climb. Many of the field's initial 20,000 production and injection wells are still idle because of water cuts that simply make them uneconomic, even at $30/bbl oil.[76] Moreover, a very large share of the remaining oil in place in the largest and oldest reservoirs is probably forever lost because of poorly executed water floods around the time the field peaked in 1980.

Nevertheless, if TNK-BP can raise the field's recovery factor by just 1 per cent, another 200 million bbls in reserves would roll to the company's books and around 25,000 b/d would be added to production. The question for oil supply is how much it will cost to raise recovery by 1 per cent and how many 1-per cent increments they can squeeze out of a 40-year-old field.

Beyond Samotlor, the newly consolidated TNK-BP is a hodgepodge of fields. There are large, untapped accumulations in the undeveloped inventory originally deeded to Tyumenneftegaz at one end. At the other is the Krasnoleninskoye field, which has been the engineering problem child of West Siberia since the Soviet days. Onako is a medium-sized, but steady Volga-Ural producer and TNK-BP holds several other medium and small units. All these resources will support building production for several years and then hold a plateau for several more – from existing assets. However, without sustained incremental improvement in productivity at Samotlor, it is difficult to see the diamond-in-the-rough BP sought in its big Russian acquisition.[77]

The other low hanging fruit in the TNK portfolio that attracted BP was its position in East Siberia. These projects represent the company's long-run assets and a significant upside. The lead times and uncertainties surrounding East Siberian development projects, however, are considerable. They are also under political pressure. Moscow is leaning on the industry generally either to develop areas under licence, or forfeit them. The imminent merger of state organizations Rosneft and Gazprom, exacerbates this, as they claim to have precedence in operations east of the Yenisey River. This may force TNK-BP to liquidate parts of its position, unless it raises its investment budget to accommodate not only its active engineering programme in West Siberia, but also to begin one or more major frontier development projects to the east.

Despite the dislocation of a major, multi-national merger, TNK-BP turned in a 14.8 per cent production increase in 2003 and anticipated another 10 per cent in 2004 (although slower growth thereafter).[78] It plans capital investments of $1 billion annually in 2004 and 2005.[79] If this kind of growth can be maintained and mirrored in its financial performance, all parties to the deal will be more than pleased. However, if the boost fades, the union may memorialize mindsets on both sides that reflected distraction by physical volumes of oil rather than the economics of their profitable extraction and sale.

Independents

In countries with market-based oil and gas industries, the role of medium and small 'independent' companies is critical to supply. Although they usually do not establish new basins or initially produce the largest fields, as a region matures, it is the independent companies that keep most of the oil flowing.

Some smaller companies take over the big old fields after they peak, exploiting secondary reservoirs and, with lower costs than the majors, keeping wells online longer than their larger cousins could have afforded. It is the independents who discover and develop the medium and smaller fields, and thereby reduce the rate of decline in basins through their long waning leg of development. Outside of countries with national oil companies, independents, collectively, are central to oil supply.[80]

If the concept of 'private' oil companies was tough to accept in Russia after 70 years of Soviet rule, the notion of a private small to medium independent oil company, neither under state control, nor part of a huge conglomerate, has never really gained momentum. In the first year or so of the Russian Federation, there was Lukoil and either state enterprises or joint ventures (JVs). JVs all began as projects between state enterprises and foreign firms (Figure 34).[81] Later independent Russian oil companies emerged.

Joint Ventures. Initially JVs took two forms, of which the first was purely an expedient. Russian organizations knew from their own experience that hydraulic fracturing ('fracing') of reservoirs could stimulate higher well flow rates. Western service companies offered to perform this work, but in the first few years the Russians did not have the hard currency to pay. This gave birth to the modality of 'service joint ventures' whereby Western contractors took physical oil in payment for fracing services. At first this was a significant share of the JV production. but later there was a return to the standard model of cash for services.

The second form of cooperation between foreign and Russian producers took the more classical form of a joint venture. Typically, a foreign oil company made an agreement with either an oil producer or one of the exploration organizations previously subordinate to the Soviet Ministry of Geology.[82] The foreign company contributed cash for operations. The Russian side contributed some or all of its ownership interest (i.e., state licences) covering one or more fields, the existing capital equipment (if any) and all the manpower desired. When discounted from Soviet reserve estimates to SPE/WPC standards, most of these discovered fields were not very large.[83]

The majority of JV projects involved undeveloped fields, or fields where development had just begun but had become financially stalled. A few JVs took on field-rehabilitation projects or programmes to improve the efficiency of production and/or surface processing. Most arrangements provided for state-granted accelerated recuperation of costs and some initially involved preferential access to export and transportation. In cases where the JV took over a producing field, the foreign party's economic interests were usually restricted to the amount

MAPS

1. Russia and its Principal Oil Provinces
2. Major Oil and Gas Fields of Azerbaijan and the North Caucasus
3. Oil and Gas Fields of the Volga-Ural Basin
4. Oil and Gas Reservoirs and Source Rocks of the Volga-Ural Basin
5. Structural Contour Map of the Devonian Pashiy Formation, Romashkino Field
6. Principal Structural Features of the Central Volga-Ural Basin
7. Oil and Gas Fields of the West Siberian Basin
8. Oil Fields of the Middle Ob by generation, West Siberia
9. Structural Contour Map of the Alym Formation, Samotlor Field
10. Oil Field Size and Organic Richness of the Bazhenov Formation, West Siberia
11. Oil Generation, Field Size and Structural Elements of the Middle Ob, West Siberia
12. Oil Field Size and Thickness of Neocomian Interval, West Siberia
13. Fields of the Middle Ob Region by Producing Company

FIGURES

5. Cross-Section of Romashkino Field (Indicated in Map 5)
11. Cross-Section of Samotlor Field (Indicated in Map 9)

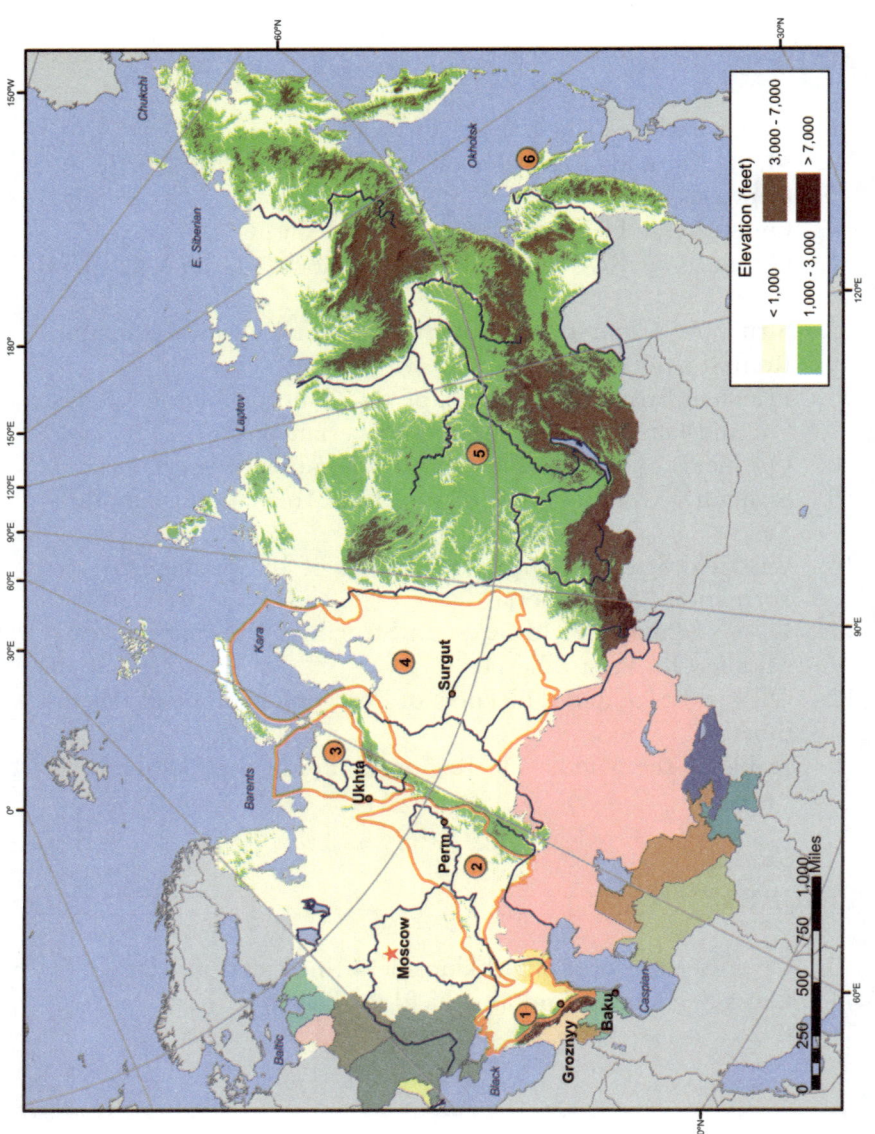

Note: 1. North Caucasus; 2. Volga-Ural; 3. Timan-Pechora; 4. West Siberia; 5. East Siberia and 6. Sakhalin Island. Republics of the former USSR are shown around Russia in pastel colours.

Map 1: Russia and its Principal Oil Provinces

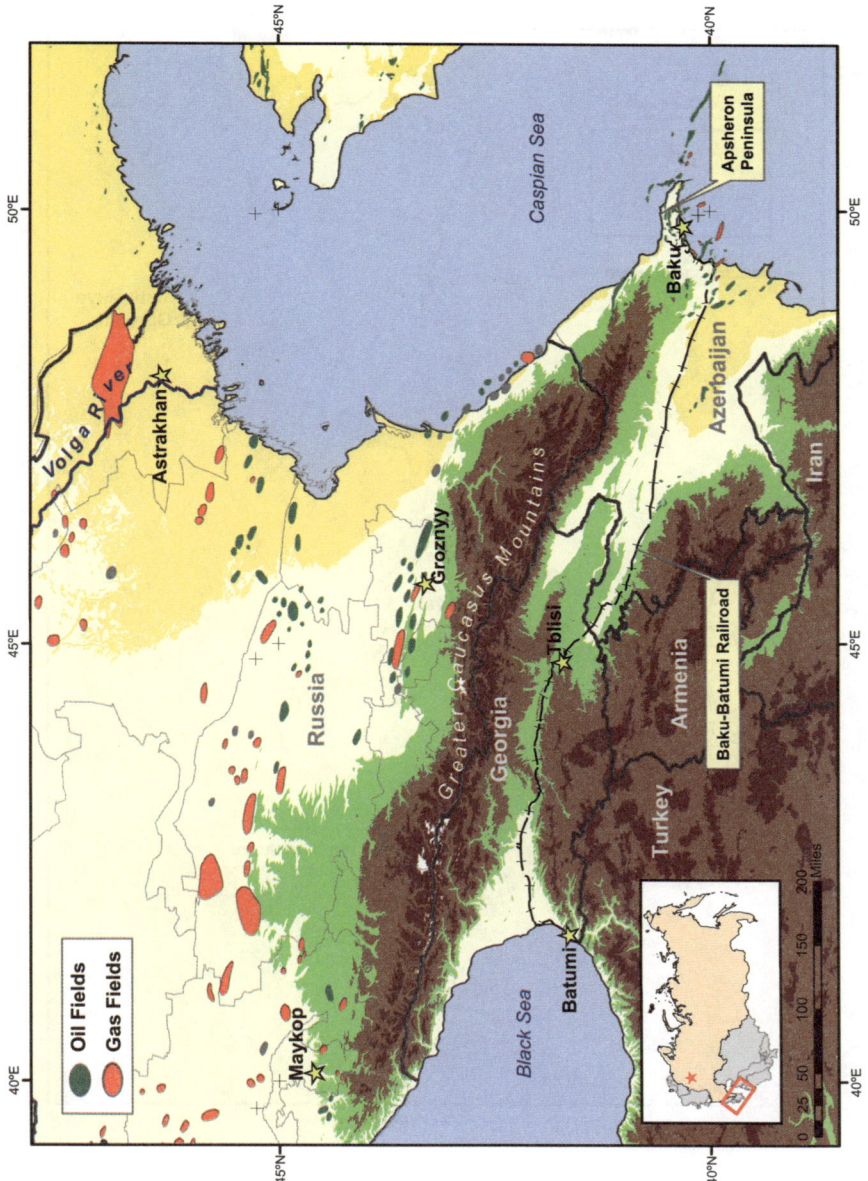

Note: Elevation, in this and following maps, follows Map 1.

Map 2: Major Oil and Gas Fields of Azerbaijan and the North Caucasus

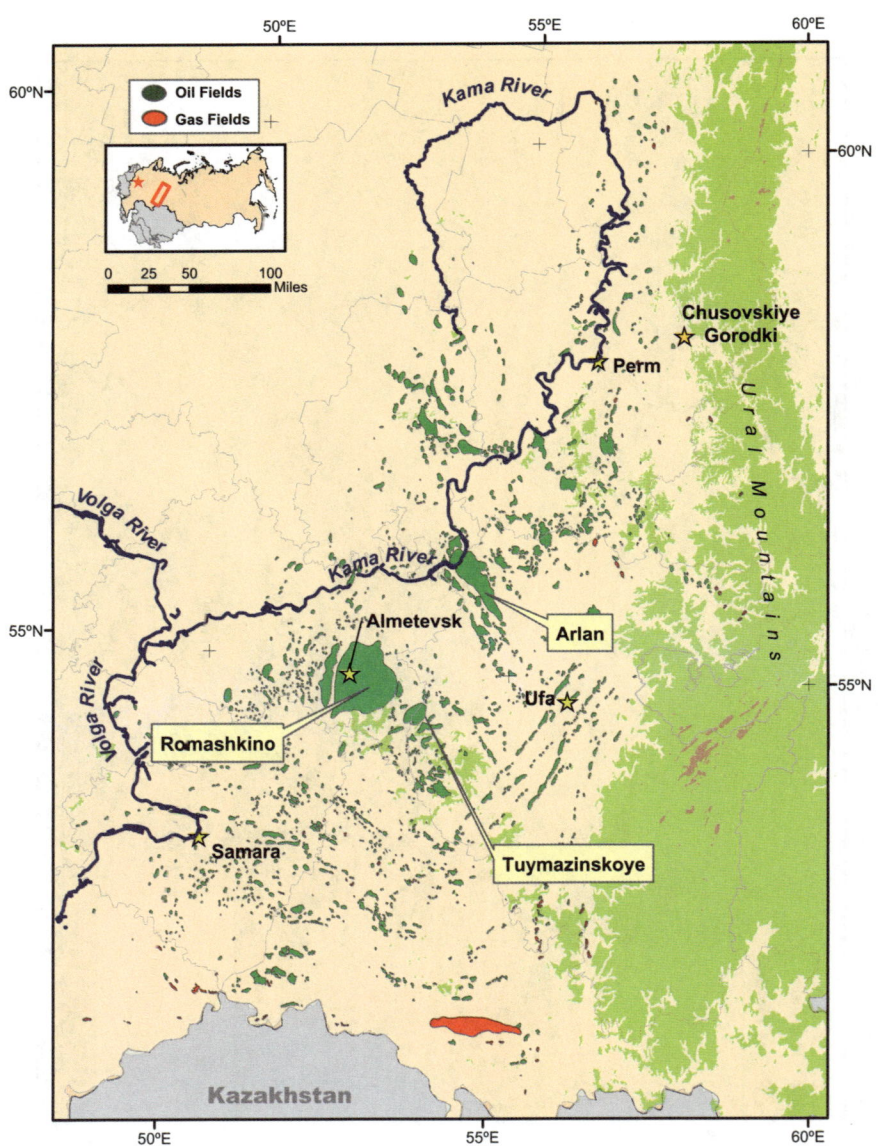

Map 3: Oil and Gas Fields of the Volga-Ural Basin

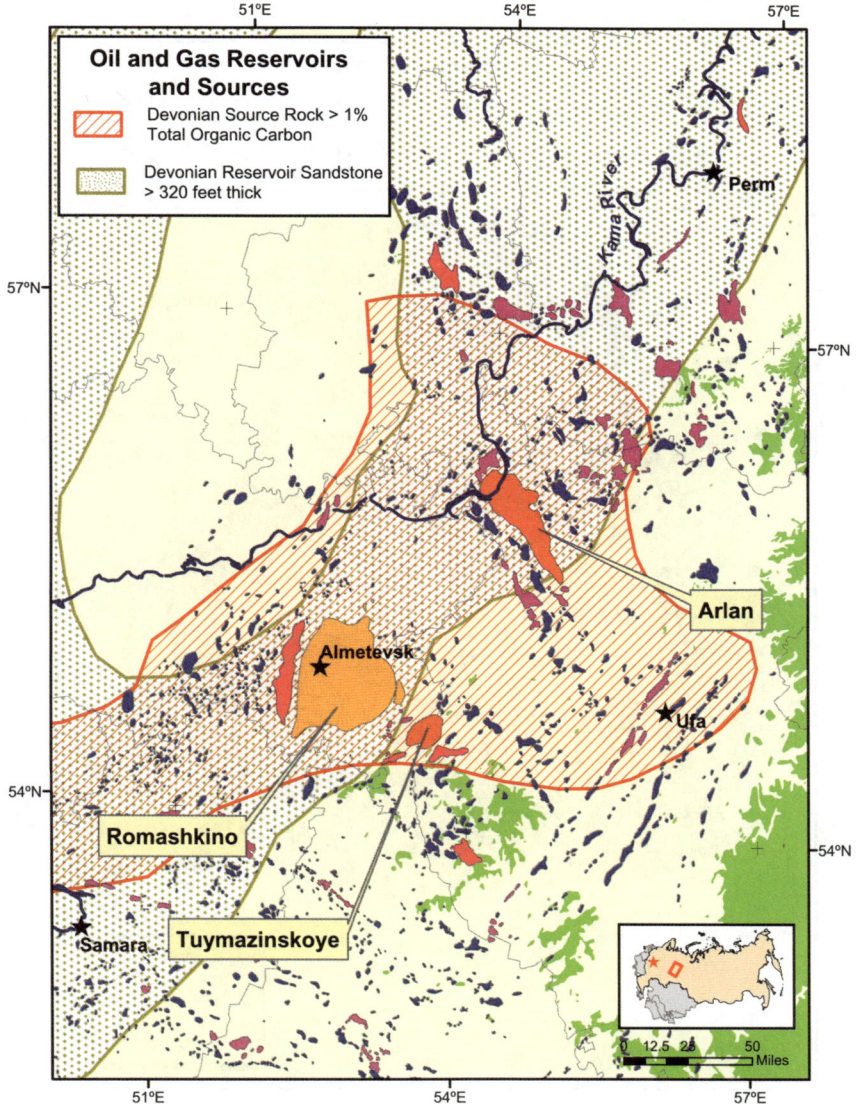

Note: Shows the relationship between field location and size and the distribution of two of the principal geologic controls on the formation of oil and gas accumulations. The distribution of source rock (red stripe) controlled where oil and gas were generated. The distribution of thick sandstones (dark yellow stipple) shows where the best opportunities are for finding reservoirs. The intersection of these two areas holds the highest probabilities of large discoveries. Field colours reflect field size, which follow the legend of Map 6.

Map 4: Oil and Gas Reservoirs and Source Rocks of the Volga-Ural Basin

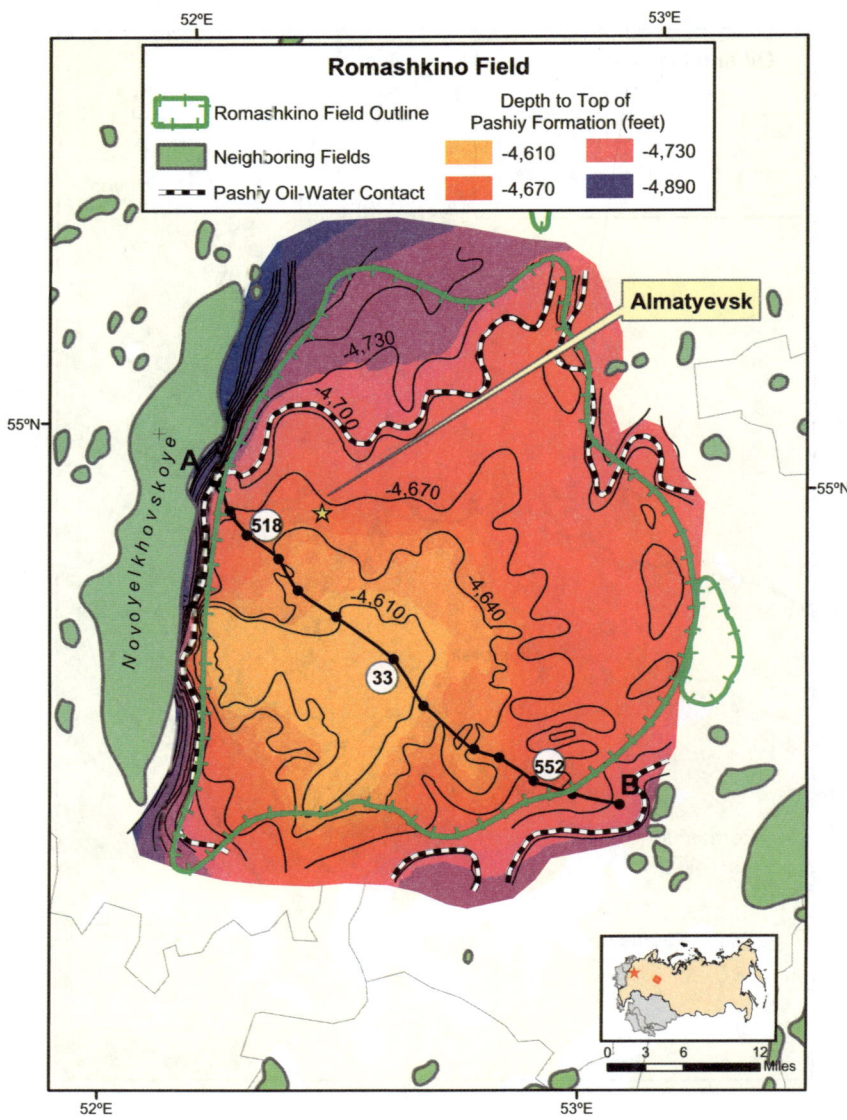

Note: The line A-B marks the location of the cross-section in Figure 5. The numbers in circles show the location of reference wells in Figure 5.

Map 5: Structural Contour Map of the Devonian Pashiy Formation, Romashkino Field

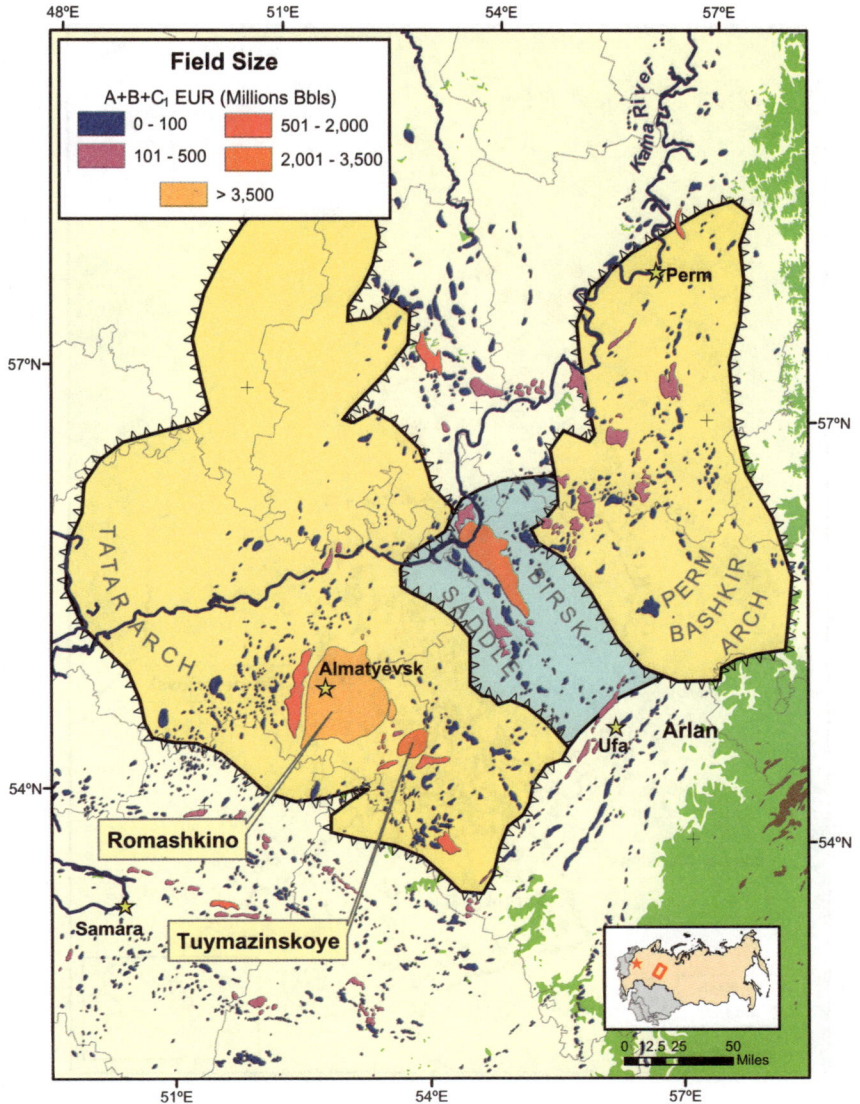

Note: Shows the Tatar Arch and Perm-Bashkir Arch (yellow, outlined in teeth pointing down-slope) and the Birsk Saddle between them (blue). These three zones contain approximately 60 per cent of the discovered oil and gas of the basin, including almost all of the largest fields. The measure of field size is $A+B+C_1$ EUR (see Appendix II).

Map 6: Principal Structural Features of the Central Volga-Ural Basin

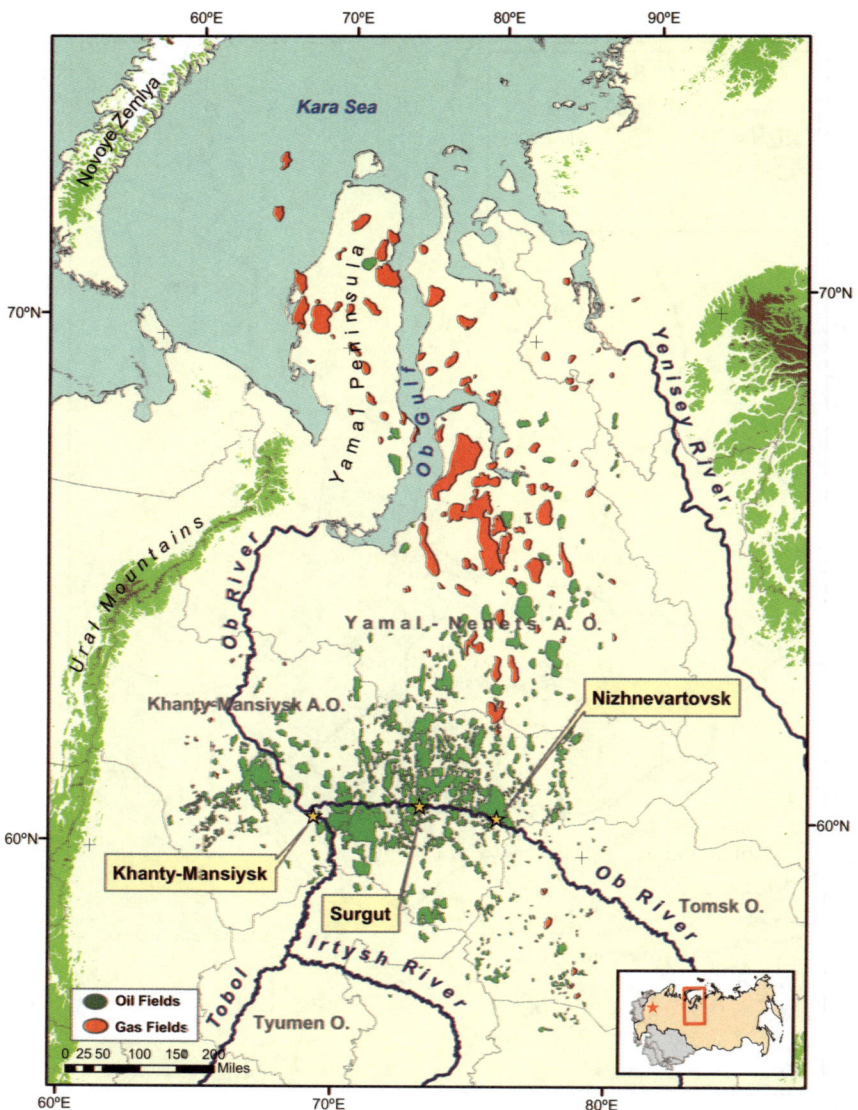

Map 7: Oil and Gas Fields of the West Siberian Basin

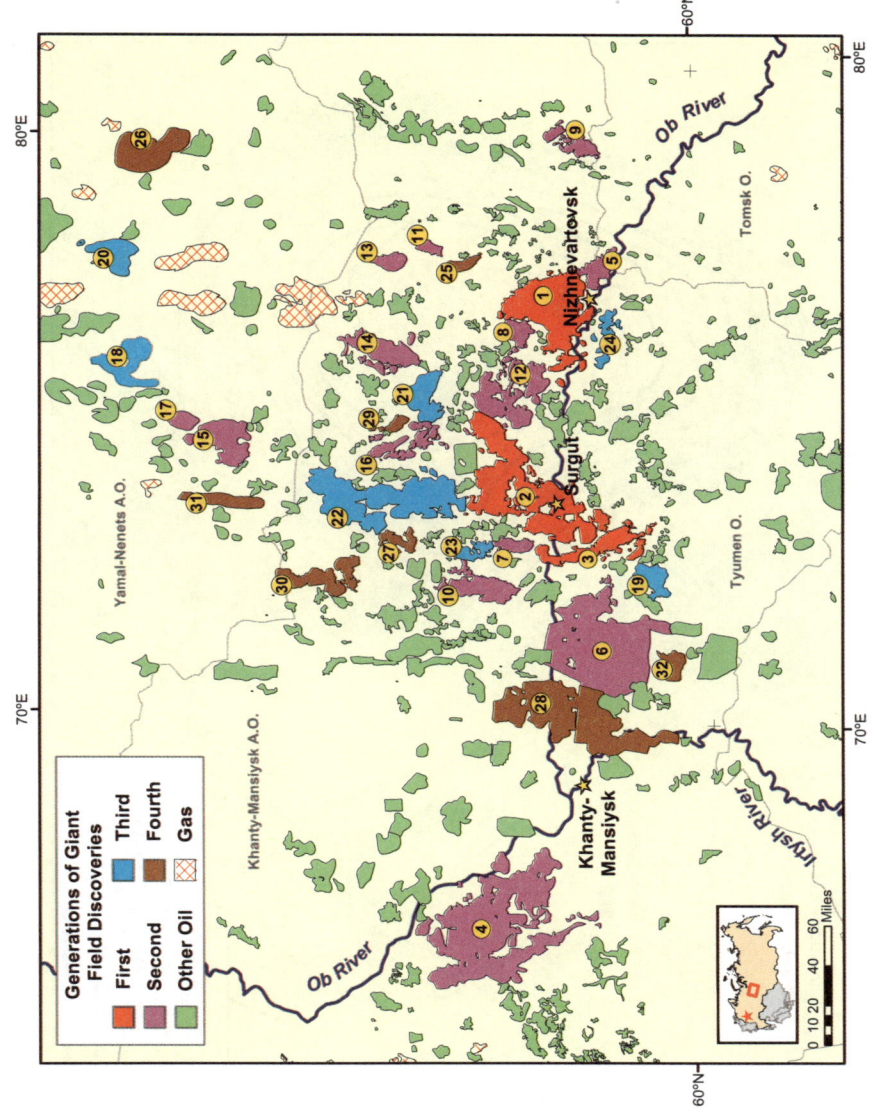

Note: Numbers identifying the fields correspond to the fields listed in Table 1.

Map 8: Oil Fields of the Middle Ob by generation, West Siberia

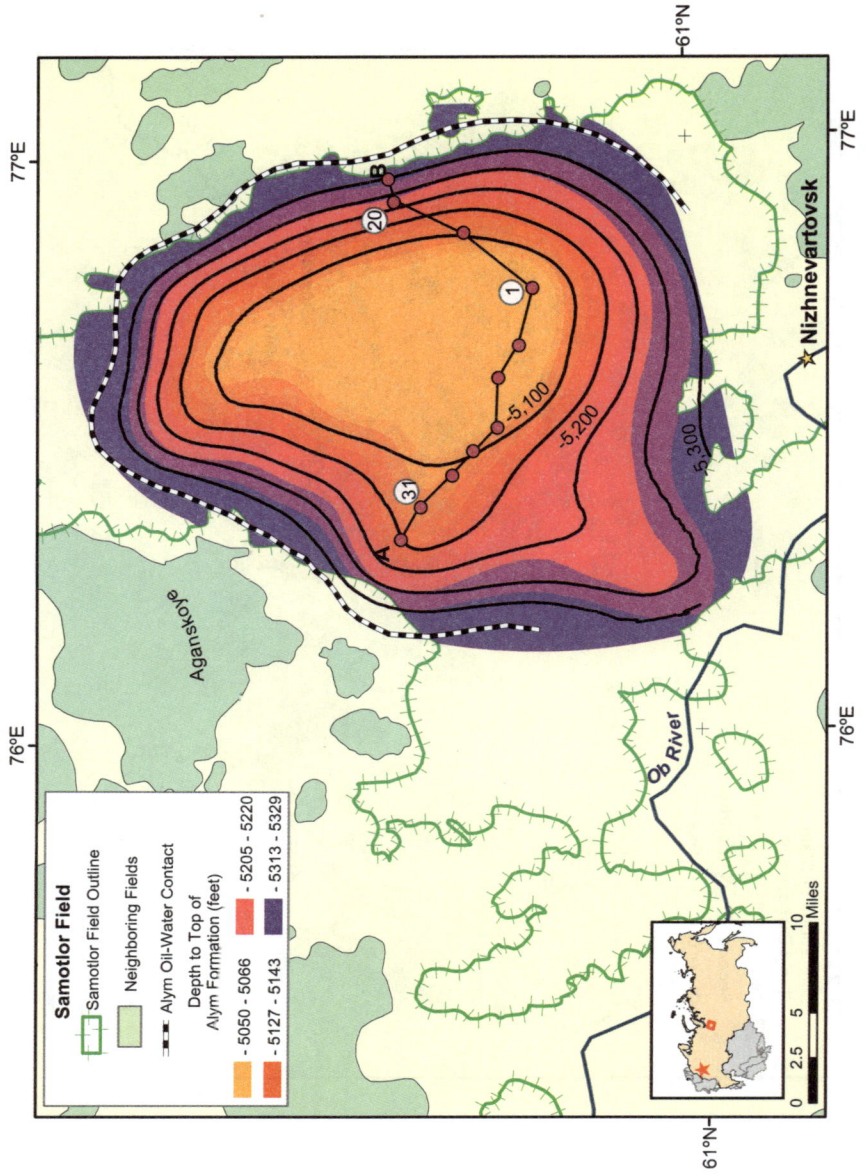

Notes: The line **A-B** shows the location of the cross-section in Figure 11. The field's outline exceeds the structure map area because of field growth, particularly to the west, since the date of the original construction of this structure map and cross-section.

Map 9: Structural Contour Map of the Alym Formation, Samotlor Field

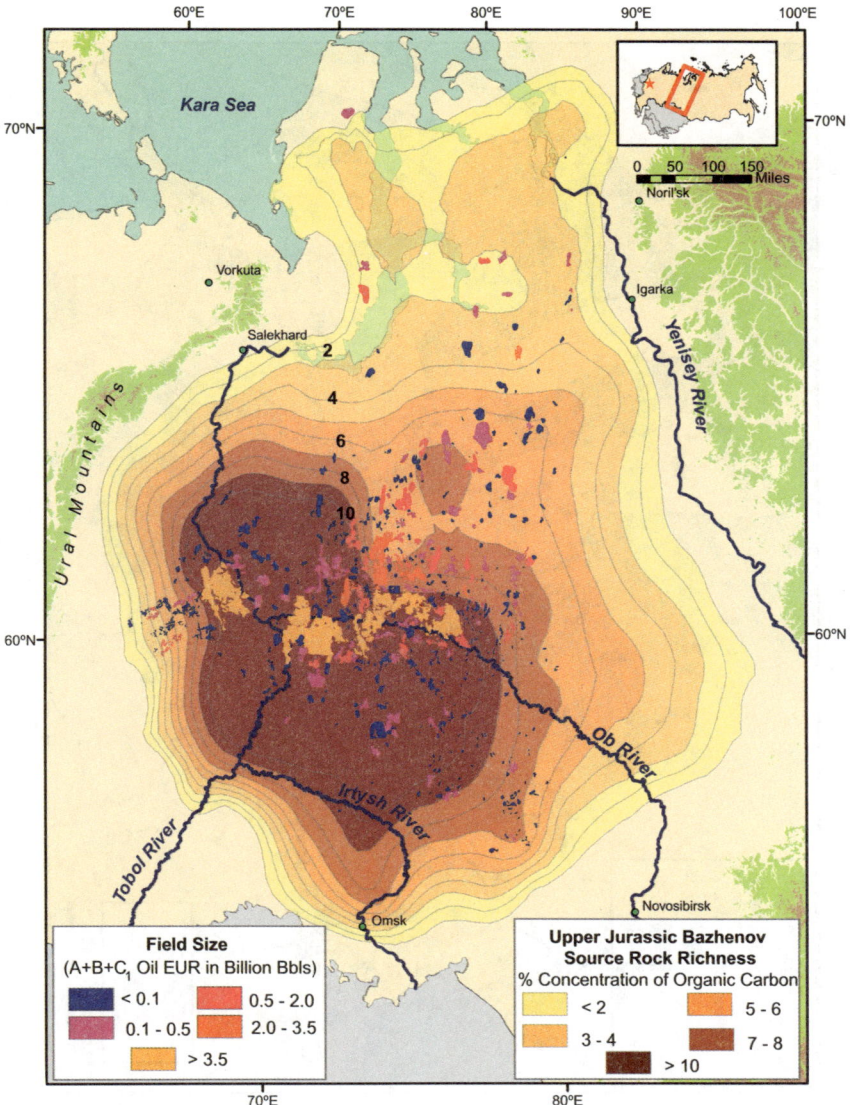

Note: Shows the richness of the Late Jurassic Bazhenov source rock (tan to brown filled contours in percent total organic carbon content) and the sizes of discovered oil fields in the West Siberian basin (coloured polygons) as measured by their A+B+C$_1$ oil EUR.

Map 10: Oil Field Size and Organic Richness of the Bazhenov Formation, West Siberia

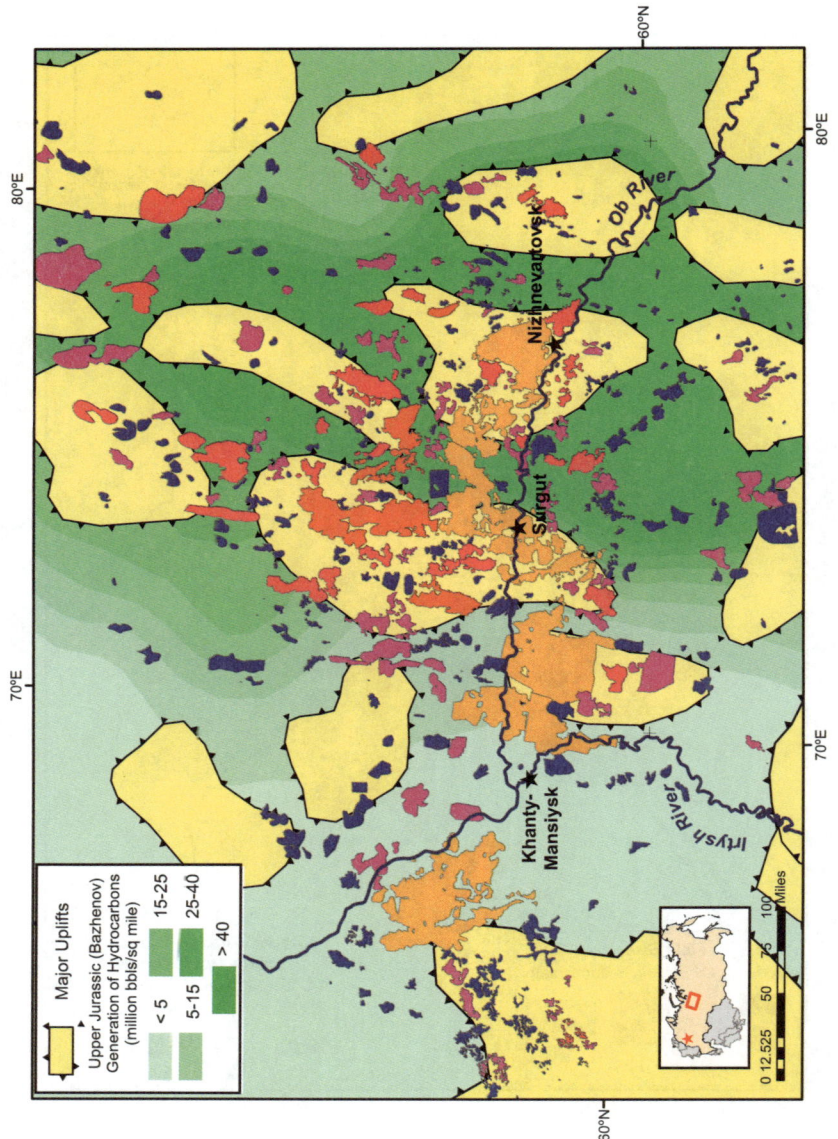

Note: Shows the relationship between the volume of hydrocarbons generated in the Bazhenov shale (ramped greens in the background), the location of major uplifts (pale yellow polygons with teeth pointed down-slope) and the location and size of fields. The legend of field size follows Map 10. The Krasnoleninskoye field, northwest of the city of Khanty-Mansiysk, is sourced mainly by the Lower and Middle Jurassic rocks, not the Upper Jurassic Bazhenov.

Map 11: Oil Generation, Field Size and Structural Elements of the Middle Ob, West Siberia

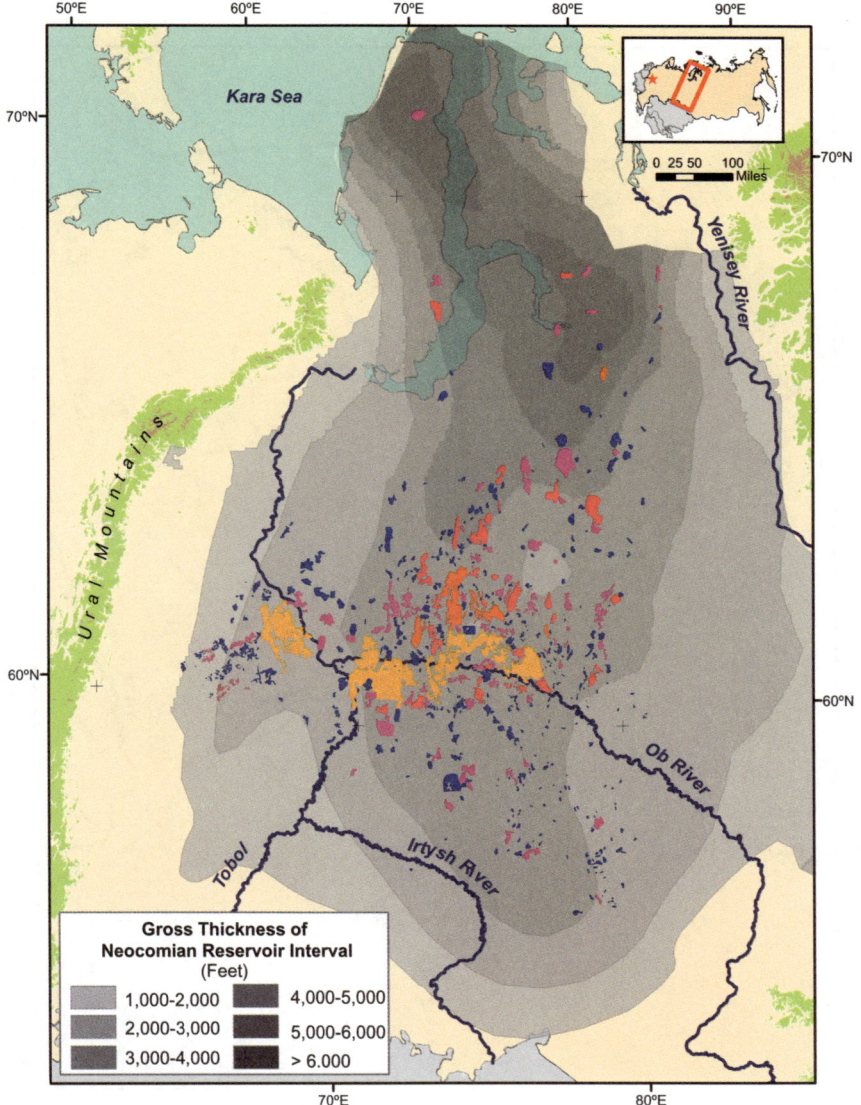

Note: Shows rocks that contain most of the oil reservoirs in the fields of the West Siberian basin. The field sizes follow Map 10.

Map 12: Oil Field Size and Thickness of Neocomian Interval, West Siberia

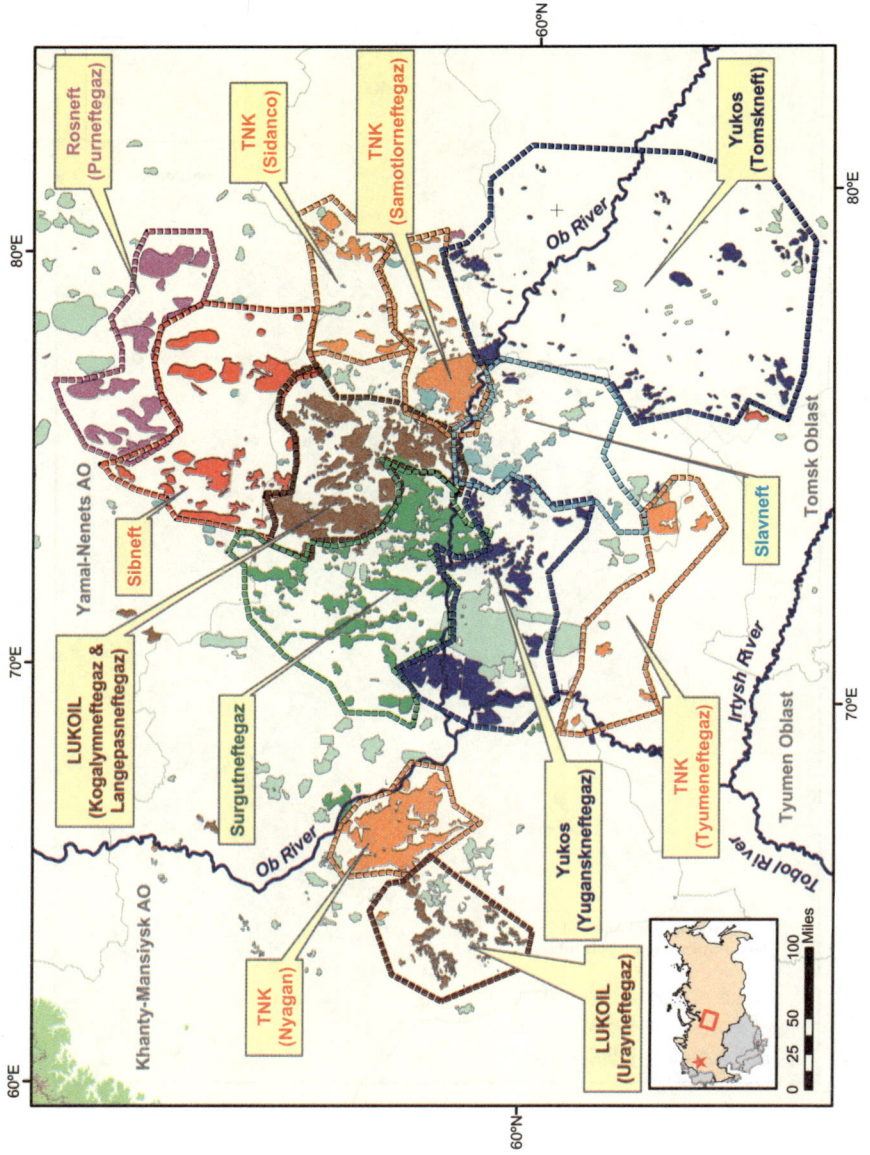

Note: Shows locations of the principal West Siberian areas of operations of the major Russian oil companies. The fields are coloured by their company, which is also reflected in the colour of the company label (fields not assigned to these companies are light green).

Map 13: Fields of the Middle Ob Region by Producing Company

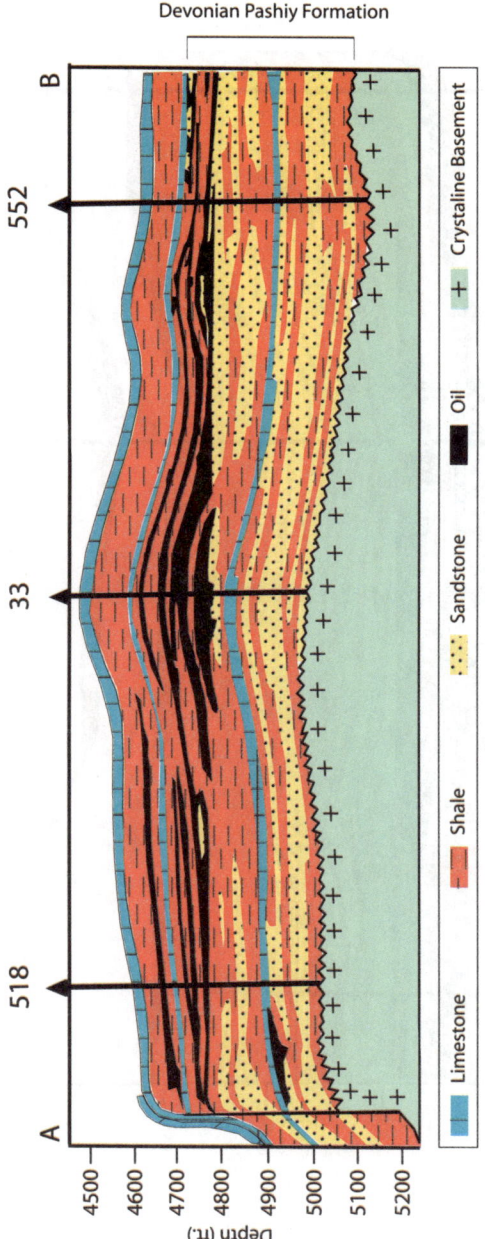

Note: The top of the figure shows the locations of three wells identified in Map 5. The vertical exaggeration is 1:300.

Figure 5: Cross-Section of Romashkino Field (Indicated in Map 5)

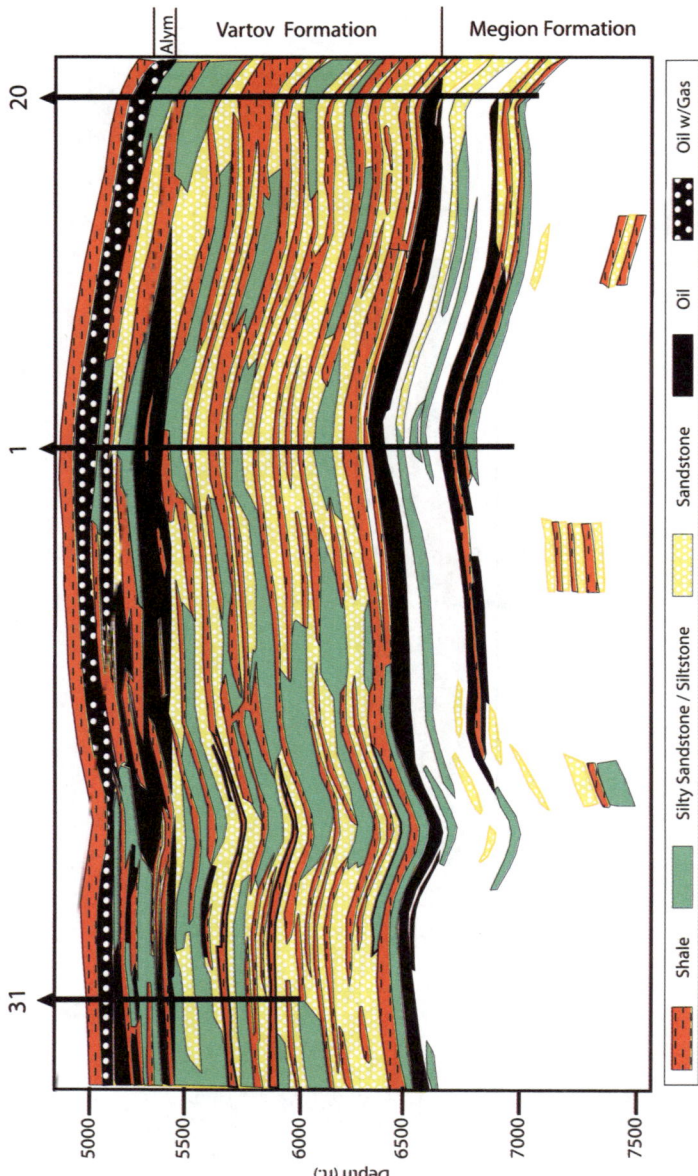

Note: The location of the cross section is shown in Map 9 along line A-B. The numbers in the map correspond to the wells identified by number in this cross section. The field's largest reservoir, the BV_8, is at the top of the Megion Formation. The vertical exaggeration is 1:150

Figure 11: Cross-Section of Samotlor Field (Indicated in Map 9)

of production *added* by the JV project over what would have been produced in its absence.

The foreigners who entered the Russian market in the nineties (particularly the first half) ran the gamut. There were shifty and inspired individuals (with and without oil experience) and many small, principally American, independent oil and gas companies confident that their entrepreneurial spirit was just what Russia needed. Medium-sized firms came and, of course, there were the Western majors. Most in this last group immediately angled for what would have been extremely large projects – nearly all of these grand ambitions failed.

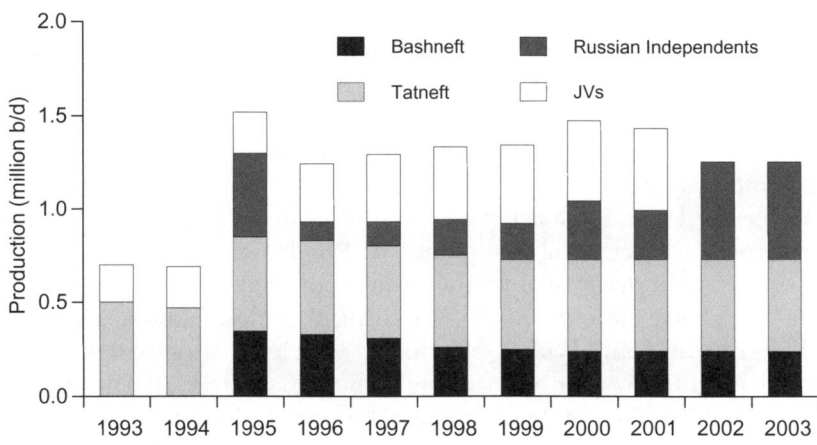

Figure 34: Oil Production by Bashneft, Tatneft, Russian Independents and Joint Ventures

Nonetheless, even though the vast majority of proposals were never realized, they exposed the Russian industry to Western technology, the best and worst of Western management and the lively wildcatter fringe that has always orbited the Western industry. In the impoverished first few years of Russian independence, that these visitors dropped several hundred million dollars passing through did not hurt either. Earlier hoards had done much worse.

Only three to four dozen joint ventures have produced oil in Russia since 1992. Some Western partners have left, others entered – usually buying the interests of those on their way out. Details of these sales were rarely publicized; therefore, it is unknown in which direction the arbitrage of positions in Russian JVs has gone. It is likely that many of the original entrants who sought exit through the mid-nineties sold at a discount to their entry price. The long-run value of participation over the last few years, however, has doubtlessly attracted premiums.

The contributions of JVs to Russian oil supply have grown very slowly from about 200,000 to about 500,000 b/d. A long list of disappointments for both sides explains why foreign direct investment in Russia's oil industry languished. Some of it was due to the general political and economic morass of the Yeltsin years; some to the lack of a sufficiently 'protective' legal structure (usually crystallized in the desire for broad PSA legislation) and some to the incessant problems with transporting oil out of the country for sale. Russians complain of promises never kept and of many foreigners who simply wanted to rob them.

A small number of JVs have consistently led the group in longevity and volume of oil produced. They are geographically diverse, covering projects in West Siberia, the Volga-Ural basin and Timan-Pechora. Of the 516,000 b/d made by independents (including JVs), the top ten JVs were responsible for 36 per cent in 2002.

While the JV sector has been lacklustre from the start, the very small direct role of foreign oil companies in Russian production may soon grow. The main driver will be the projects off Sakhalin Island. Two of these are PSAs, the others, while desiring that designation, are not.

The ExxonMobil PSA, Sakhalin I, which is anticipated to ship first oil in 2005, is planned to reach 250,000 b/d in 2010 out of an estimated 2.2 billion bbls of recoverable oil. Although it is mainly a liquefied natural gas project, Shell's Sakhalin II PSA will also produce hydrocarbon liquids before the end of the decade from an estimated 1.2 billion bbls of estimated ultimately recoverable liquids. In early October 2004, a joint BP-Rosneft exploration project, known as Sakhalin V, discovered a field with 4.4 billion BOE of liquids.[84] As they were quick to note, this is the first major new field discovered in the Sakhalin area since Soviet times. Onshore, there are finally signs of life at Shell's West Salym project in West Siberia; it should be able to produce tens of thousands of barrels per day before 2010.

Collectively, these projects could eventually double the present contribution of JV (including PSA) projects to Russian oil supply. Outside of Sakhalin, and Lukoil's project with ConocoPhillips in northern Timan-Pechora, however, there is no inventory of big JV projects awaiting a final green light. The American oil company, Marathon, has struck a new and interesting partnership in West Siberia and TOTAL's Kharyaginskoye PSA in Timan-Pechora could be expanded. The other joint ventures (as distinguished from foreign equity investment in Russian companies, like the formation of TNK-BP) appear to be stuck in the evolutionary path that led to the present contribution of about 500,000 b/d.

In addition to the belated rise of several major projects, since the beginning of this decade smaller JVs have undergone a significant change. Because of the fundamental changes in oil production economics in Russia, a rising number of Russian and foreign investors are seeking opportunities. Money from both sources is increasingly mixing in what were historically regarded as JVs and Russian independents. This homogenization of the sources of capital investments reflects increasing financial maturity.[85] Financial maturation may also reflect arriving at a long-run equilibrium level of penetration for JV projects in the Russian industry.

Russian Independents. Among the (non-JV) Russian independents, there are two divisions. At the top are Tatneft and Bashneft. Then there are scores of small Russian companies, most of which were 'true' independents, in the Western sense of the term. They are unaffiliated firms, financed by investors; some trade on organized Russian exchanges, others are privately held. In this group, however, there are a few companies that were actually subsidiaries of major Russian oil companies, but viewed as independents.

Tatneft and Bashneft, are and always have been, the senior producers of the Volga-Ural basin, because they sit atop the Romashkino and Arlan fields, respectively. They also hold neighbouring fields and command a dominant share of the basin's resources.

Both companies have strong downstream components that distinguish them from the balance of Russian independents. Because of that, at times over the nineties, these two companies were considered majors, like Surgutneftegaz. However, recently, the stable Bashneft and Tatneft, non-acquisitive and very firmly rooted in their home republics, became increasingly distant from the evolving models of 'major Russian oil companies' and more like large, specially situated, independents.

Both Tatneft and Bashneft went through the same production cycles over the last two decades. Because of the final Soviet campaign to save production in the late eighties, decline rates, which had been increasing for years, were arrested. However, when the rug was pulled out as the Soviet Union collapsed, faster declines resumed. Although a little later than in West Siberia, during the nineties both Bashneft and Tatneft suffered their own idle well crises and even more output was lost.

The post-1998 market for Russian oil has treated Tatneft and Bashneft kindly. They enjoy the advantage of better proximity to export markets than does West Siberia. While domestic price regulations are no different, as their fields surround the nation's principal refineries, at least it costs less to transport oil for sale at controlled prices. These factors have stabilized production. In 2002, Bashneft enjoyed its first increase in output, but in 2003 managed a 0.3 per cent rise. Production from the larger Tatneft has been flat since the mid-nineties.

In 2002, the Tatarstan government announced a long-run strategy simply to hold production steady. It recognized both the impact of rising production costs, and the fact that smaller fields will play an increasing role in the republic's output. Production from Tatneft, based around Romashkino and several other very large fields, was presumed to show slow annual reductions.[86]

However, almost unbelievably, at the end of 2003 Tatneft made a stunning announcement. Despite an 11 per cent drop in profits for the first half of that year, the company proposed a $6.6 billion investment programme for 2004–2008. A major goal of the plan is to *double* production. This seems a far less sober assessment than that offered the year before by the Tatarstan government.[87] Tatneft enjoys proved reserves (in the SPE/WPC sense) of 5.5 billion bbls.[88] While that volume, if located in a single *new* field, could theoretically support more than 500,000 b/d of production, Tatneft's 5.5 billion bbls are distributed largely over hundreds of old, well-drilled, highly water-saturated reservoirs. To imagine that it will double output within the next three years is fantasy.

The government of Bashkortostan is the principal stockholder in Bashneft, although its equity composition is rather opaque.[89] Although it lists 2003 Russian A+B+C_1 reserves of 2.6 billion bbls, a realistic outlook for Bashneft (and its home republic) is for flat to declining production.[90] Both Bashneft and Tatneft could increase output over relatively short periods, and sustained high export prices certainly make that easier to accomplish. They will also benefit, more in profitability than production, from the application of both Russian and Western technologies that were unavailable in the 30 years the basin has existed in the shadow of West Siberia.

Because of their locations and integration into petrochemical production and refining, both companies will continue to enjoy good comparative advantages economically (although higher sulphur content in their crude will be a slowly increasing drag on the prices they get). These factors all combine to form a foundation for optimism, but not so much as to think that either of the largest units of the Volga-Ural basin industry will recapture the glory of forty and fifty years ago.

The balance of Russian independents, around 300 since the mid-nineties, is composed of generally small operations. Most are centred on a single field, some as little as a part of a single field, while others involve projects to increase production at fields where most of the oil belongs to another organization. A number of the independents developed out of the fields discovered in the Soviet period by exploration organizations of the Ministry of Geology and retained by them after the demise of the USSR.

While some of the independents have remained atop of the fields that spawned them, many companies have left the fold. Some simply failed, but it appears the majority leaving the industry sold their assets – occasionally to other small firms, but, increasingly in recent years to major oil companies. This consolidation reached a highpoint in 2002 as the total number of Russian independents plus JVs in the county fell by over 40 firms (23 per cent, see Figure 35). Many of these companies went to Lukoil, although some joined Yukos and Rosneft (TNK had bigger fish to fry and Surgutneftegaz doesn't date).

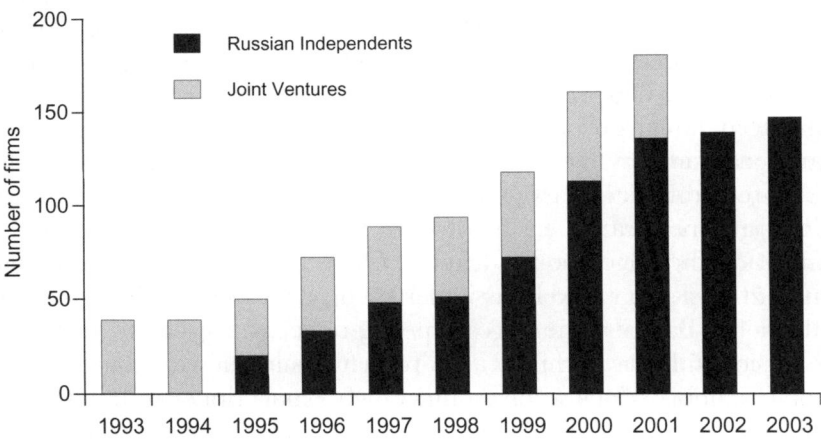

Figure 35: Number of Russian Independents and Joint Ventures

The typical Russian independent produces several hundred to several thousand barrels of oil per day. It often has a 'special' relationship with the major oil company generally responsible for the area in which it operates. This affords the independent some of the advantages of infrastructure and access to transportation required for sales. The owners vary from oil and gas institutes, to local governments, to the cashiered managers shed from the old exploration organizations. Increasingly, they have been formed by investment funds seeking direct exposure for foreign and Russian investors to Russian oil production.

Just as the greatest share of production by the JVs is concentrated in the top projects, so it is with the Russian independents. Like the JVs, these are spread over West Siberia, the Volga-Ural basin and Timan-Pechora. However, it should be noted that a number of these top producers were among those harvested almost exclusively by Lukoil between 2000 and 2002. Two of the big independents (Lukoil-Perm and Lukoil-Aik) were actually subsidiaries of the company all along and were rolled back into the corporation. The balance was purchased. This moves the average profile of the Russian independents to an even lower level of production and sphere of operation.

State Producing Organizations

As the Yeltsin administration came to a close at the end of the nineties, it appeared that the Russian government's direct role in oil and gas production operations would almost completely wither. Rosneft, the state holding company for the Soviet producing associations that never found homes in the market, was heading for a small, although sustained, caretaker role. Gazprom, the state gas monopoly, was under increasing international pressure to split vertically (production from pipeline transport) and, among other changes, to liberate its upstream units.

Now, in mid-decade, the situation is squarely reversed. The Putin administration clearly sees for itself a much larger, not smaller, direct control over oil and gas production. Over the last two years, the government has progressively assigned a bigger strategic role to Rosneft in some of the nation's largest up-and-coming projects. Moscow has also successfully beaten back European pressure to 'reform' Gazprom in anticipation of closer integration of Russia into the continental economy.

To consolidate the state's position, in September 2004 Moscow announced that Gazprom would acquire Rosneft as a subsidiary, to be called Gazpromneft. The transaction is to be structured so that the government (which owns 100 per cent of Rosneft) will return to majority equity ownership in Gazprom (of which it presently owns 38 per cent). Although Gazprom has occasionally fancied itself as a private company, irrespective of the division of shares, it has been a state entity from its inception. This part of the merger will burnish Gazprom's 'private' veneer, while at the same time formally renationalizing the gas industry, but through the mechanism of stock ownership.[91]

Theories abound on the immediate implications of Gazprom's purchase of Rosneft. At the highest level, it parallels, in the economic domain, the Putin administration's radically increased centralization of political power in the hands of the executive branch of the federal government. Even within that narrow structure, placing top Putin aides in board and executive positions in the state sector of the oil and gas industries further concentrates economic power in the hands of a very few men surrounding the Russian president.

The move also reflects a growing sentiment, expressed at the top in Moscow, that Russia must have a strong, state-run energy company to gain its deserved position in world energy markets, particularly in oil, where it faces the national companies of OPEC. At the same time, the combined state oil and gas company also creates wider opportunities to project Russian commercial power abroad through the direct investment and operational activities.

At the next level down, folding Rosneft into Gazprom may be in preparation for the dismemberment of Yukos through the sale of its main subsidiary, Yuganskneftegaz. Adding Yukos' most productive unit into the newly enlarged Gazprom would recapture for the state a large share of the nation's oil resource base privatized in the nineties. Combining the 2003 Gazprom and Rosneft liquids production yields 611,000 b/d or 7 per cent of national output. Adding the output of Yuganskneftegaz would give 1.6 million b/d, or almost one-fifth of Russian oil production – a major expansion.[92]

At an operational level, the acquisition provides Gazprom with a ready source of oil production and new net income. Gaining existing liquids capacity benefits Gazprom in two immediate ways. First, oil is usually more profitable to export than gas. Second, the domestic price controls on natural gas are even more severe than on oil, so oil can be more profitable to sell into the domestic market. Both these propositions can be project specific, with profitability depending on the cost of production and transportation. However, having oil is always better than not having it, and for Gazprom to have Rosneft's oil opens up a set of commercial possibilities it would not enjoy otherwise.

While the union of Rosneft and Gazprom must be viewed in its wider political context, one of the factors that will fundamentally affect its utility as an instrument of state policy is whether its technical performance moves forward. Herein, the record is decidedly spotty.

In 1992, when the Russian state succeeded to ownership of the assets of the Soviet Ministry of Oil, all of the nation's oil producers, with five exceptions, passed to the Russian Ministry of Fuels and Energy.[93] The arrangement was loose and poorly organized. The state funded some organizations; others formed 'private' companies under the umbrella of the state trust. Between 1992 and 1995, several, mainly stronger producers, left the state fold, although the government initially held majority positions after their birth into the market.

The equity composition of oil companies in the first few years of Russian independence did not make much economic difference in any case. Through domestic price controls and state skimming of export earnings, the new companies could not make any money producing oil. So, while there was a private stock float in a handful of oil companies, the *de facto* dominance of the state in oil and gas production remained unchanged. Oil production crashed through the mid-nineties, and the government, as a majority shareholder in the private companies, and director of state companies, went along for the ride.

In 1995, principally through the Loans for Shares programme and related actions, a raft of new companies escaped the state structure (Figure 36). After the effect of government defaults in Loans for Shares, state holdings in the new oil companies in most cases dropped to less than 50 per cent. Some of the producers graduated to form their own companies (e.g., Onako) or combinations between themselves (e.g., TNK); others became subsidiaries of Lukoil, Yukos or Sidanco.

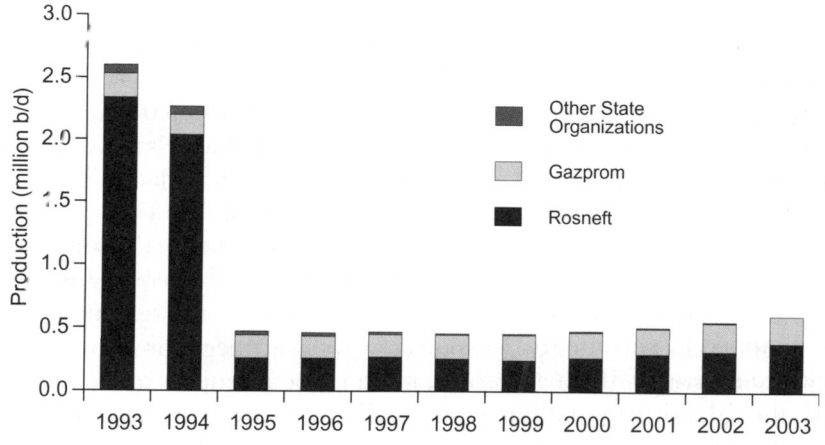

Figure 36: Oil Production by State Enterprises

The entities left in the state nest were organized under the Rosneft structure. Until the end of the Yeltsin administration, Rosneft remained a caretaker. Like all parts of the Russian oil industry, its fortunes rose with the devaluation of the rouble in 1998 and the run-up in world prices starting in 1999, but that merely made Rosneft a better-appointed halfway-house for the state wards it contained.

Under the Rosneft umbrella, at one extreme is Grozneft (by various names), the producing organization responsible for oil in the Chechen Republic – a highly problematic asset. In addition, there are the units covering neighbouring Dagestan Republic, Krasnodar Kray and Stavrapol Kray – extending across the North Caucasus. Beyond the political instability and violence, these units contain the oldest oil-producing region of the USSR left in Russia.[94] While it is not without resources, the North Caucasus basin enjoyed its moment in the sun in the first half of the twentieth century.

At the other extreme is the exception in Rosneft's portfolio, Purneftegaz. This is the northern-most of the old Soviet oil-producing associations of West Siberia (Map 13). Because oil development in the basin started along the middle course of the Ob River, and later moved north, exploration of Purneftegaz's region began last among the oil areas. As a result, the fields of Purneftegaz are only slightly depleted, which gives the organization high growth potential.

Purneftegaz's fields are not as large as those to the south. The subsidiary's operations area also marks the geologic transition (going north to south) between the basin's gas and oil zones. Nevertheless, in its resource base, Purneftegaz shares many of the technical characteristics of Sibneft (the old Noyabrskneftegaz) immediately to the south – a highly successful operator over the last four years. At times since the mid-nineties, it seemed that Rosneft simply held Purneftegaz to retain a showcase producer and give it legitimacy. It contributed over 60 per cent of Rosneft's output in 2002.[95] In 2003, Purneftegaz's share of the total slipped to 50 per cent, as its production remained flat and that of the company grew substantially by acquisitions (Table 14).

At the outset of the Putin administration, little changed for Rosneft that did not arise from higher oil prices and a cheaper rouble. Yet, even in the first three years of the decade, the company was more often tapped to become the Russian partner in strategic projects. These included several of the high-profile, multinational projects offshore from Sakhalin Island; negotiations with the Kazakhs over the Kurmangazy prospect that straddles the international border in the middle of the Caspian Sea and development of the first major field, Prirazlomnoye, in the Pechora Bay, the offshore extension of the Timan-Pechora basin.

Since 2002, Rosneft's profile has continued to rise, with its most frenetic activity coming in 2003. That year, it began competing against Lukoil in the latter's bid to control the Timan-Pechora basin. In so doing, it raised its position in the ConocoPhillips project, Polar Lights, and acquired a major independent in the basin, Northern Oil. During the same year, it also secured the Vankorskoye field in the extreme north-eastern part of West Siberia.

Table 14: Technical and Financial Performance Indicators for Rosneft[96]

Indicator	Units	2000	2001	2002	2003
Oil Reserves	Billion bbls	9.5*		9.5*	6.7*
Gas Reserves	Trillion cubic feet	56.5*		45.9*	119.7*
Oil Production	Million b/d	0.3	0.3	0.3	0.4
Gas Production	Billion cubic feet	199	216	228	248
Oil Reserves / Production	Years				
Total Assets	Billion US$	3.7	4.3	5.2	6.5**
Revenues	Billion US$	2.5	2.3	2.7	1.7**
Income Before Income Taxes	Billion US$	0.8	0.7	0.5	0.3**
Income Taxes	Billion US$	0.4	0.2	0.2	0.1**
Net Income	Billion US$	0.5	0.5	0.3	0.2**
Basic Earnings per Share	$/share		23,134	24,330	16,451 10,164**

* These are Soviet/Russian A+B+C_1 resources and not comparable to the reserve estimates made on the basis of SPE/WPC definitions as reported for other companies in this chapter.
** Through June 30, 2003.

In fact, a bit like Lukoil, while Rosneft proudly claims a 55 per cent increase in production between 1998 and 2003, over two-thirds of that increase is attributable to acquisitions (most of it in 2003). Less than one-third of the increase came from better management of its legacy assets. Of the fraction that did come out of its previously owned subsidiaries, almost all of the increase came from its flagship West Siberian unit, Purneftegaz. But even there, given the inventory of fresh fields they could have developed, a 19 per cent improvement since 1998 is disappointing.

Before being subsumed into Gazprom, Rosneft was destined to enter major projects almost always as a partner, being too small to carry the entire investment burden. This apparently was by design, pushing one of the state's clearest agents into small roles in a string of large projects regarded by Moscow as strategic. Theoretically, Rosneft, as the Gazpromneft division of Gazprom, would have greater access to go it alone. However, its access to capital may in the end be restricted, not enlarged in its new little niche within the very much larger Gazprom structure.

Until the merger is complete, the other player in the state sector of the Russian oil industry is Gazprom itself, the immediate and largely unchanged successor to the Soviet Ministry of Gas. The economics of Russian gas supply are beyond the bounds of this study. However, two points relative to its supply of condensate and oil must be made.

First is that the liquids Gazprom produces are largely incidental to gas production. When gas production rises, liquids production rises. Since 1998, the company's production of liquids has risen faster than the percent growth in gas. However, the bottom line is that over a period during which oil prices had risen dramatically, Gazprom only produced 31,000 b/d more in 2003 than in 1998. This is an insignificant part of the growth in Russian oil supply.

The second concern over Gazprom's liquid supply strategy is a reflection of the first, and one of the deep enigmas of the Russian hydrocarbon industry. Gazprom faced even stricter domestic price controls on gas than existed on oil. Moreover, because a greater share of gas is sold domestically than oil, Gazprom has endured far more financial distress than did oil producers. Its export earnings were likewise diminished and a bigger share of exports (than oil) went to other former republics of the USSR at distressed prices and terms. In part, because of the perception that the nation's endowment is virtually endless, gas has been assigned a low economic value, even after the end of the Soviet period.

If gas has been such bad business, why has Gazprom sat on literally billions of barrels of hydrocarbon liquids? Most of these resources are deeper (Neocomian age) condensate horizons in their super-giant gas fields in northern West Siberia, but there are also liquids resources in the North Caucasus and in Timan-Pechora (see Appendix to Chapter 3). These liquids would fetch high returns relative to gas, yet Gazprom chugs along at just over 200,000 barrels of liquids per day.

The company's production is as much as a single, very large oil field. However, with systematic exploitation of the Neocomian condensate (and oil) reservoirs at the four largest fields in northern West Siberia, Gazprom could attain three to five times that level.[97] That would be enough to make an important business difference to Gazprom. To significantly increase their liquids production and transport capacity would require big investments. But at first blush it would seem to be a far wiser direction than building a gas pipeline under the Black Sea to feed an abundantly oversupplied Turkish market.

Gazprom is staffed by *gazoviki* – 'gas men.' There has never been a liquids orientation in Gazprom; in the Soviet period, they studiously avoided producing them. Its present failure to exploit its liquids opportunities at a time of rapidly rising prices demonstrates that little has changed. The company's liquids resources will remain largely untapped until either the inherited 'gas-only' culture of the organization is expelled or the licences to the liquids accumulations are stripped by the state for failure to develop them. Given Gazprom's present perch in the economic vision of the Putin government, the latter is extremely unlikely to happen.

The resultant question is: with the absorption of Rosneft as a minor subsidiary, will the oil company's presence in the corporate structure be a strong enough force to reverse the gas-only mentality? Perhaps the larger question flowing from the Gazprom-Rosneft merger is: will this union enlarge hydrocarbon liquids supply, or in the end contract it?

Gazprom has demonstrated little ability to increase liquids production supply from its own resources. Rosneft has raised its production, but this was only accomplished by acquisitions. While acquisitions bring more production under the state flag, they do nothing to expand the Russian supply as a whole. Moreover, unless Rosneft is more successful at raising output in acquired firms than it has been in its top producing unit, Purneftegaz, this move also bodes poorly for the impact of the union on national output.

For its part, the management of Rosneft is saluting smartly at the Kremlin's plan for its absorption by Gazprom. It is not, however, going without expressing reservations. In a statement on the company website, management asserted a defence of its performance over the past six years (particularly in its quickly ascendant last two years). It declared that, whatever happens, its asset value and management structure should not be eroded.[98] Perhaps the company's management realizes that its outlook for growth, as a company, was brighter as an increasingly agile small operator than it will be as a very small part of an organization with little interest in oil.

The Division of Spoils

So, where did all the money go?

Where it came from helps understand where it went. The biggest source of money in the Russian oil industry has been the hundreds of billions of dollars that have passed through as revenues. A share of that went to pay workers, to buy electricity for pumps, drill new wells and repair old ones. It cost money to move crude oil from Russia's fields to its refineries or to be exported. The government, at various levels, took a big piece. In principle, these components of cost are simple to compute, even if estimates are surrounded by considerable uncertainty.

Yet when Russians and Westerners ask where the oil money went, the question does not refer so much to the disposition of revenues. The question is how a small number of men at the pinnacle of the Russian industry became incredibly wealthy. Between a half dozen and a dozen made over a billion dollars, scores more pocketed millions of dollars each. Some of these men still command the firms that made them prosperous beyond their wildest imaginations. Some cashed-out, others were driven out, but all left with enormous rewards.

These beneficiaries did not get their fortunes through the revenues made by producing companies selling oil. They became super-rich by obtaining equity positions in those producers. This source of wealth – the asset values of the companies – was, and is, ultimately based on the nation's natural endowment of oil and the accumulated investment in exploration and production made by the USSR.

These assets at first belonged to the Russian state, as successor to the Soviet Ministry of Oil. They were Russia's inheritance. The government could have retained the oil, which is what it did with the nation's natural gas industry and resources. Instead, the Yeltsin administration decided to 'privatize' its oil. In so doing, they granted control of, and most importantly, ownership in, a significant share of Russia's oil asset base to men who were the top local industry bureaucrats when the USSR fell apart (e.g., Lukoil's Alekperov and Surgutneftegaz's Bogdanov). Most of the balance was turned over for pennies on the dollar to the Oligarch cabal in the mid and late nineties (e.g., Yukos' Khodorkovsky, Sibneft's Berezovsky and Abramovich, TNK's Vekselberg, Aven and Friedman; Sidanco's Potanin).

Had those who became rich only been given licence to siphon off revenues from producing companies, the loss would have been much smaller and of short duration. In gaining the nation's oil *assets*, the Red Directors, Oligarchs, and their allies won power, a durable foundation of wealth, and the capacity to enlarge their riches on a scale that would not happen if they had only gained a high level of income.

It is also important to recognize the distinction between enrichment through acquisition of equity assets and mere access to revenues. The fact of holding their wealth through Russian oil company stock has exposed, and continues to expose, the Yeltsin-era beneficiaries to state action. If their assets were more fungible, or held abroad, they would be less subject to the seizure and impairment that Moscow can easily visit on the equities of a Russian firm.

It is likely that no one will ever know exactly how much of Russia's resource wealth ended up in the pockets of the scores of people who were in the right place at the right time, or who exploited the deep corruption of Russia's feeble first post-Soviet government. *Forbes Magazine*, which compiles such information, lists Russia's 100 richest men.[99] Of these, approximately 40, who control over half of the wealth of the group, are partially or wholly tied to the oil industry.

Together, their riches total over $80 billion. Many, in addition to oil, have large holdings in banking and minerals, communications and basic industries, so only a fraction of their net worths derive from oil. At the same time, the market capitalization of Russia's top oil companies as of the spring of 2004 was approximately $120 billion. Subjectively, probably 15 to 30 per cent of the value of the top five Russian oil companies went into the hands of individuals whose holdings derived from 'special' relationships with the Russian government when it distributed the equity originally held in the nation's oil industry.

With the exception of Berezovsky (Sibneft), Lebedev and Khodorkovsky (Yukos), the Putin administration has not interfered with the extraordinarily skewed distribution of Russia's oil patrimony made in the nineties. Indeed, the holdings of all the beneficiaries of Yeltsin's give-away have appreciated more since 2000 than before (although as a result of prices, much more than policies). As of 2004, it seems that an equilibrium has developed that not only protects the original allotments, but creates opportunities to expand the value of holdings of firms deemed most cooperative by the present administration in Moscow.

The division of revenues derived from the sale of oil is less twisted, but also illuminates an important aspect of what happened after independence. As discussed in Chapter 4, revenues from the sale of oil on domestic and export markets are taken as equal to the average price on each market times the volume of oil sold annually. Prices were evaluated at the refinery gate for the domestic market and at export points for that fraction of oil that left the country. What were not considered were the effects of non-payment, and payment with barter, that occurred in varying degrees throughout the 1990s.

Following the short-run annual analyses in the Appendix to Chapter 4, the total revenues received by producers for the sale of domestic and export oil can be assigned to three expense categories: operating costs, transportation tariffs and excise taxes. For the period 1993 to 2002, covering field operations was the upstream industry's greatest variable cost (Figure 37). The next largest component was excise taxes levied by government organs on the production and transportation of crude oil. Finally, there were the costs of transportation itself.

The money left over at the wellhead, after paying tariffs, excise taxes and operating costs, was the producer's net income. This was the amount of money that was available to companies for capital investments, profits and uses that may not have contributed to Russian oil supply. This amount does not include income taxes, as those were calculated after capital expenditures and on a consolidated basis over each corporation (i.e., considering downstream and non-oil production activities).

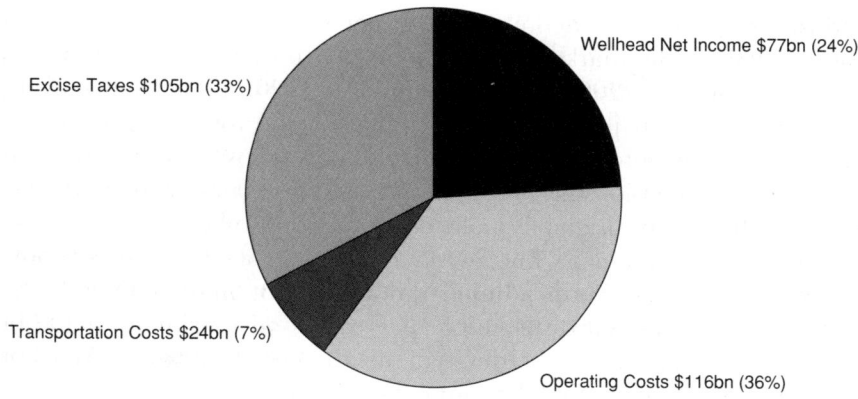

Figure 37: Distribution of Russian Oil Revenues, 1993–2002

Looking at the relationship over time of wellhead income to production, production fell while net income was strongly negative, and rose when it was positive (Figure 18). So, while the asset division which was justified as necessary to form a market may not have succeeded, the response of Russian producers to market signals through the revenue side worked as one would expect.

The sum of net income, from the years when it was positive, was $77 billion. Some of this sum was depleted for the enrichment of individuals, although, as mentioned above, the primary mechanism for that was on the asset, not the revenue side. A fraction of the money left to producers in wellhead net income was also lost through mismanagement. Additionally, these funds supported some of the expenditures for recent mergers and have swelled retained earnings.

As far as it goes, and within the limits of very uncertain data, the accounting above is fairly complete. The asset side of Russia's oil wealth was divided between the government (acting as a very poor trustee for the Russian people), hundreds of top insiders who profited boundlessly from the corrupt Yeltsin administration's plan to privatize oil and thousands of common stock holders in the nation's oil companies.

There was a final component of Russia's oil wealth, however, normally not considered and unaccounted in either the distribution of equity or revenues – consumer surplus.

When the Russian Federation government succeeded that of the USSR, it maintained the stringent domestic price controls on oil of the Soviet command economy. In the beginning, the controlled price was enormously below what would have prevailed in the absence of state action. A domestic price in parity with world price would have been approximately equal to the price of Russian oil sold in export at the border, minus the cost of transportation between the border and an average domestic refining point, like Ufa in the Volga-Ural basin.

Figure 38 shows the relationship from 1993 through 2002 between the average domestic sales price for Russian oil and the domestic price that would have been in parity with the world oil price. Omitting the exceptional year of 1998, the world parity price for oil in Russia was an average of $7/bbl higher than the actual domestic price under state price controls.[100] Russian consumers paid an average of about $10/bbl for oil from 1993 to 2002, where they would have paid nearly $17/bbl had the world and domestic markets been in equilibrium.

Figure 38: Relationship between Domestic Price of Oil and World Parity Prices

The difference between what was paid under price controls and what would have been paid without them is called 'consumer surplus.' It is the savings consumers gain by paying less than they would have been willing to pay (or would have had to pay) for a good or service.[101] In the case of Russian oil between 1993 and 2002, approximately $100 billion of consumer surplus was enjoyed broadly by Russian consumers of products made from Russian oil.[102]

Although the $100 billion consumer surplus was not distributed in cash or equity in oil companies to the Russian people, neither is it just a theoretical construct of economists. Had the Russian government completely decontrolled oil prices in 1992 and let world prices determine them, billions of additional dollars each year would have gone from the nation's firms, governments and individuals consuming petroleum to Russia's oil producers. The private oil companies would have been up to $100 billion dollars richer and the populace equally poorer.

A massive collapse in macroeconomic demand drove Russia into depression in the nineties. To withdraw an extra $100 billion would have further impoverished tens of millions of people when many were already living at or beyond the edge. As the consumer surplus was money directly saved by consumers, this also spared the government what it would otherwise have had to pay to consumers as state income subsidies for energy.

The existence of the consumer surplus arising out of state price controls is separate from, and in no way compensates for the Yeltsin administration's massive transfer of Russia's oil assets to a tiny group of industry insiders and financial sharpies. Nor was it part of the revenues that flowed from domestic and foreign oil buyers to the government and oil industry in the nineties. It was, however, a largely democratic way to transfer at least a share of the endowment Russia received from the USSR to the Russian people at large. It was a more effective mechanism than the voucher programme of the early nineties which had that very goal.

Comment

Russian oil producers now operate under rules that are fundamentally different from those in force 15 years ago. Over that same period, Russia's role in the world oil market also profoundly changed. That this was a costly transition for the industry was to be expected. It was but a small share of the overall economic and human expense borne by the nation in its post-Soviet evolution. The industry largely survived its nadir, several years of fibrillation and emerged into a strong recovery which has already lasted half a dozen years. For organizations producing oil today in Russia, the environment remains dynamic but much more stable and with a far brighter outlook than even five years ago.

At the root of most of the changes was the decision to privatize oil. When made early in the Yeltsin administration, this was, and remains, very controversial. Putatively part of a national policy to bequeath the industrial assets inherited from the USSR to the Russian people, it mutated into a highly concentrated industry divided between a few tenacious Soviet-era managers and Oligarchs. While Yeltsin's team successfully moved oil producers from the state budget to the market for funding, the parallel plan to democratically privatize the asset value of Russia's oil legacy failed.

Majors and Lesser Oil Companies. The greatly condensed industry, with a very small number of firms dominating supply, was not just the result of political intrigue. The lognormal distribution of field sizes favours skewness in firm size, as do economies of scale (to a point). There was also historical momentum coming from seven decades of the Soviet maxim that bigger was always better. If the Russians wanted a capitalist citation for their decision, then just look to the Western oil industry, in which the only constant for five decades has been combination.

The result, by 2003, was that over 80 per cent of Russian supply came from the five major private companies (Lukoil, Yukos, TNK-BP, Surgutneftegaz and Sibneft) and two major regional producers (Tatneft and Bashneft). However, no robust tier exists below them. There are scores of independent oil companies which produce about 10 per cent of national output. Yet this sector, so important to the supply of oil from mature basins in market economies, enjoys the support of neither the industry nor the government. This failure to nurture a second tier of oil and gas firms is one of the structural threats to long-run Russian oil supply.

Barriers to entry for independent oil companies are a big reason why there is still, twelve years after Russian independence, a vast Soviet dowry of discovered, but undeveloped fields. Most of the Russian majors (with the exception of Surgutneftegaz) are over-endowed with physical oil assets relative to management capabilities and even to their greatly expanded access to cash. That is, they stand astride far more fields and physical oil than they have capital and management resources to develop. Without a second tier of companies to buy these assets from them, they will languish. Moreover, because of this inventory, the majors themselves are deterred, for good economic reasons, from serious exploration for new fields. More discoveries might simply compound their problems.

The small and intermediate fields, and large fields on their last legs, which were spun off to small firms, have been important contributors collectively to non-OPEC oil supply outside Russia. Western majors have repeatedly learned that the cash from selling small and intermediate fields is almost always more valuable than the risked present value of future net income streams that would accrue if, and only if, these fields were developed or kept online.

While the market that emerged in Russia tolerates independent oil companies, it is not an encouraging environment. The majors might persuasively argue that there is no dynamic sector of small and medium firms out there to take up these fields and produce them. This is a chicken-and-egg problem that only state policy can change. With its powers to control exploration and production licences, access to transportation and tax policy, Moscow could easily foster an aggressive generation of companies that could successfully exploit this large inventory of discovered, but undeveloped fields. While these are not the projects that will raise production, they are the difference between a decline after the next peak of 1 to 3 per cent instead of greater than 5 per cent or even more. That difference is worth billions of dollars to the Russian economy and Russian government annually. Yet that is not the present direction of flow.

Rising State Role. The other most potent trend in the industry is the dramatic rise in the role of the federal government in the direct management of oil production. The first phase, which began quietly in the early Putin administration, but very visibly after 2002, was the empowerment of the state oil company – Rosneft. Using state muscle, Rosneft insinuated itself into several strategic high-profile projects, including those with major Western oil and gas companies. Using Rosneft as a proxy, Moscow has extended a new channel of direct influence in the management of exploration and major new field developments (with substantial financial leverage).

The second phase began in 2003 with the move against Yukos. This action is more complex than its oil-industry ramifications. As it seems nearly certain that Yukos' central subsidiary, Yuganskneftegaz, will be stripped from the corporation, it will effectively renationalize one of Russia's foremost oil assets privatized in the nineties. Even if Yuganskneftegaz is ultimately sold to a private company, like Surgutneftegaz, its fields will move from a very independent management structure, to one in very close orbit around the Putin administration's vision of the economy and the role of Russia's natural resources and private companies in it. Moreover, on a cash basis, whether it's called a sale price, tax judgement, or whatever name, Moscow will recover a major share of the loss it suffered in Loans for Shares, when these same assets originally went to Khodorkovsky's group for pennies per barrel.[103]

The latest step in re-inserting the state into the industry is the impending absorption of Rosneft by Gazprom. One objective, through equity acquisition, is to renationalize the gas industry. Another is to give Gazprom, already a major economic instrument of state policy, a larger direct entrée into the nation's oil production. Finally, a unified state oil and gas company will also move forward Moscow's external relationships in the world oil market and with leading foreign actors.

These recent state initiatives must be taken against the background of continued domestic price controls on oil (and gas), firm command of the nation's oil transportation system and successful defence against forces seeking to bring the nation's natural gas industry up to market standards. Common to this array of policies is the Putin administration's central goal to raise and sustain Russia's economic growth. The Russian energy industry is to be put directly in the service of that aim (as it was in Soviet times). In fact, market mechanisms are only valuable to Moscow as tactical instruments of national policies and are by no means seen as intrinsically good.[104]

A growing share of national production coming from state organizations quickly focuses attention on the relative efficiencies of state versus private Russian companies both in developing legacy assets and in bringing new fields on-line. If the past records of Gazprom and Rosneft are indicative, there is little reason to believe that a greater state role in production will in fact lead to greater production. If Moscow's intent is to progressively shift assets back to direct state management, it may well have to trade production to achieve that end. This is the second, growing, structural limitation on supply.

The Role of Foreigners. As the Putin administration's philosophy of a larger state role in natural resource management evolved, so an official line on foreign involvement in Russian oil gelled. By the beginning of the decade, two courses carried most of the potential for significant foreign involvement in the industry.

One was to take distant, expensive and technically complex projects, like those off the northern end of Sakhalin Island. There was no downside to approving and even encouraging these projects. Russian companies, until perhaps the last year or so, would not have been able to do them technically or financially. Better still, they were over 4,000 miles away from Moscow. The likes of even super-giant companies like Shell and ExxonMobil, whose Sakhalin projects are the most advanced, look much smaller when viewed from the capital at such a distance. Important as well is that economic success on Sakhalin (by any means) would serve a remote and stranded local population and project Russia into Asia and the Pacific in ways that would not happen otherwise. A true win-win situation.

Sakhalin remains on track for significant contributions to both liquids and gas supplies by the end of this decade and bright performance over the next twenty years. However, apparently success cannot be left to its own devices under the newly interventionist oil policy of the Putin administration. Both Gazprom and Rosneft have either wriggled into otherwise closed Sakhalin deals or are threatening to. Moreover, other state organs, responsible for licensing, have already started to chip away at the security of ExxonMobil's Sakhlin III project for failure to follow an aggressive investment schedule. Perhaps a new Russian partner would help motivate ExxonMobil's expenditures?

While Moscow will in all likelihood continue to invite foreign major oil companies into tough projects in remote areas, they will restrict the number and ensure that the projects fit an increasingly comprehensive national plan. The projects themselves will usually come with a ready-made partner in the form of Gazprom, or its new oil subsidiary – Gazneftprom.

BP blazed the other trail into the industry. In taking 10 per cent of Sidanco in 1997, even as things were still falling apart for that company and the industry at large, BP put down a marker. Although it was interested in projects, it also wanted to build a major equity position in one of the significant privatized Russian companies that emerged after 1995. Through rather dogged persistence, BP enlarged and defended its minority position, then came to manage a major, albeit troubled company (and what 'troubled' meant by the wildly expansive standards of Russia in the late nineties must have been a most rude shock to the straight-laced British firm).

In 2002, BP parleyed resolution of one of Sidanco's many entanglements, with equally scrappy TNK, into negotiations for a merger that would win them a position in the Russian industry aspired to, but not attained by any other foreigners. But by the official commemoration of the 50:50 deal in February 2003, the tide had begun to turn. International oil prices continued an unabated climb – revenues strengthened Russian oil companies, the Russian economy and the Russian government.

The need for foreign capital shrank, affording greater nationalism. When ExxonMobil took its shot at acquiring 40 per cent, or more, of Yukos in the summer and fall of 2003, both the Russian government and ExxonMobil recoiled from a union that would have injected America's largest oil company into a bottomless political quagmire. ExxonMobil left with its Sakhlin I project intact, but was perhaps a little rattled to learn that their timing (and choice of targets) would not allow them the type of position rival BP had gained only months before.

By the time ConocoPhillips, long quietly successful in Timan-Pechora, came to court Lukoil, the bar had dropped to a 20 per cent stake – less than a blocking position – with no explicit encouragement that it would be raised later. Moreover, ConocoPhillips and Lukoil could demonstrate practical business synergies in Timan-Pechora, another remote, economically desperate region – a big plus for Moscow. ExxonMobil buying into Yukos was undoubtedly promoted as providing future advantages for everyone in sight; it was, however, a pretty purely financial deal.

Moscow's present tolerance for foreign involvement is way below the high-water mark of the TNK-BP merger. Sibneft remains the only candidate in the short run for a significant equity acquisition by a foreign buyer. It is the smallest of the five national majors and the only one in any need of cash (and then only for expansion of production, not maintaining the status quo). A block sale of Sibneft shares to foreign investors is probably on the cards, but more on the order of the ConocoPhillips investment in Lukoil, not the ExxonMobil run at 40 per cent (plus) of Yukos or the record-holding TNK-BP merger of equals.

If the truth be known, almost no Russians ever wanted to see Russian natural resources sold to, or controlled by, foreigners. In part, this is from centuries of historical momentum favouring collective ownership and management of land. A part of it comes straight from the immediately preceding 70 years of state ownership and ideological enmity to private property. There was no small measure of xenophobia and a parallel recognition that plenty of the foreigners came only to cheat Russians of their nation's resources.

Perhaps above all, a core of national pride in the industry survived from having been the world's largest oil producer – without any foreign involvement at all. So, having the technology and manpower and experience to accomplish that, why was it necessary to sell out to the Europeans, Japanese and Americans? During the nineties, Russian resistance was steeled in the hope that somehow the financial *status quo ante* could be at least partially restored (state intervention, bank loans, selling small blocks of stock?). Then Russian companies could get back to producing oil and, where necessary, buy Western technology and services, but they need not trade their patrimony away. Since 1999, the economic pressure to allow outsiders in has largely disappeared, leaving only relationships of choice.

The initial success of TNK-BP and the self-evident progress in three of the Sakhalin licence blocks (Shell's Sakhalin II liquefied natural gas and hydrocarbon liquids project; ExxonMobil's Sakhalin I oil development and now a major new discovery announced by BP and its partner Rosneft, on the Sakhalin V block) demonstrate there are niches in political and economic ecology of Russian oil for foreign firms to exist and even prosper.

Firm Performance. The tide of increased world oil prices (and initially, the devaluation of the rouble) has benefited everyone. Although the government is taking a higher share in excise taxes and transportation tariffs and operating costs are rising, net income has climbed steadily for the entire Russian oil industry. Therefore, it is not really news that the nation's companies are doing quite well.

Against this background of overall success, there are some important differences within the five major oil companies. The veil of rosy performance is probably most deeply refuted by examining how much increased production has come from acquisitions and how much has come from improvement in the performance of either legacy or acquired assets. This puts the performance of Yukos, Sibneft, Surgutneftegaz and TNK-BP in a positive light and Lukoil in a poor one. Both Lukoil, and the state firm Rosneft, have increased output overwhelmingly by buying it. While probably good for the respective firms, this is just a rearrangement of assets on a national scale and provides no net increase in Russian oil supply.

A second beam through the fog of euphoria illuminates output growth potential through the end of this decade. Considering its programmes in the Caspian and Timan-Pechora, Lukoil probably casts the best light. The success of intensive engineering at legacy fields at TNK-BP holds the potential to improve production for several years.

Surgutneftegaz probably faces the most serious resource constraint, although it is more likely to bind after 2010. The imminent distribution of Yukos' assets may enlarge Surgutneftegaz's opportunity set. If the company does not acquire any of Yukos' assets, it has the industry's largest pot of retained earnings, and can buy new opportunities.

Sibneft is healthy, but may be capital-constrained below its performance potential, based strictly on resources in place. It is unlikely that the company will remain in today's form for another five years. It is large enough to be a very healthy regional producer, like Tatneft with young fields, but is more likely to be subsumed or join with another Russian or foreign company. Its assets could also be sucked back into the state fold if that trend accelerates.

Yukos must be considered in isolation. While in its present structure it is well positioned for short- and long-term growth, its impending dismemberment cannot be ignored. Surgutneftegaz, Lukoil and TNK-BP appear to have mastered the political skills vital to operation in post-Yeltsin Russia. Together, these three companies form the industry's long-run core. In 2003, they produced just under half the nation's oil. It is a share they are likely to retain.

Among all firms, as the role of the state in the industry has grown sharply over the last two years, the pressure for greater corporate transparency and fair dealing has suffered some reversals. Both Surgutneftegaz and TNK-BP are under fire from minority stockholders.

168   *Russian Oil Supply*

The former has yet (in October 2004) to release an annual report for 2003. Moscow, perhaps with some companies' approval, intermittently makes ominous sounds about resurrecting Soviet-era secrecy rules on oil reserve data, furthering the obfuscation it supposedly opposes. On the other side, the Putin administration's treatment of Yukos has brought fervour to paying taxes and demonstrating that they are correctly and openly calculated, improving the flow of information to the government and investors alike.

All producers are facing rising costs, but these are not yet rising at a rate close to that of world-price driven revenues. Financial performance of Russia's oil companies has and will remain very closely tied to world prices (and the extent of domestic price liberalization). Costs will make a difference, but the type that are measured per barrel are largely exogenous; the ones that can, and should be controlled, are those racked up in poorly thought-through acquisitions.

Performance of independent Russian oil companies is likely to decline. Individual projects may be very profitable, but as a sector, there is presently no reason their lot will improve over the next few years. The recently fed and newly oiled Gazprom is ascendant, which is perhaps the darkest cloud in an otherwise sunny environment (if you don't hold any Yukos stock).

Notes

1. Compare Map 13 with the map of Soviet West Siberian producing organizations as of 1991 in Sagers and Grace, op. cit., p. 860.
2. The exception to this was hydrocarbon liquid production by Gazprom, which before 1992 was the Soviet Ministry of Gas.
3. The middle step, transportation of oil through pipelines, has always remained under the control of the state organ – Transneft. The refineries that in Soviet times were divisions of the Ministry of Oil Refining and Petrochemicals, also controlled 'marketing' of petroleum products. These geographically compact domains followed the refineries into the new corporate structures.
4. In Russian, they were still referred to as 'Generals,' reflecting the title of 'General Director' that they had in Soviet times.
5. Freeland, *Sale of the Century*, op. cit., p. 59.
6. Chrystia Freeland's *Sale of the Century*, op. cit. provides an excellent review of the process generally, although it does not concentrate on the oil industry.
7. The Loans for Shares programme started with a trial balloon floated in late 1994 by one of the central Oligarchs, Vladimir Potanin, (who eventu-

ally obtained the oil company, Sidanco) when he offered to 'manage' the nation's largest metallurgical combine, Norilsk Nickel, in return for a loan to the government. The programme's scope broadened into the Loans for Shares programme the following year. Freeland, *Sale of the Century*, op. cit., pp 172–3.

8 The roles the Lukoil chief, Vagit Alekperov, and Surgutneftegaz's Vladimir Bogdanov played in securing the positions of their management teams, while not as tawdry as the Oligarchs', were not models of openness and fairness either. For instance, when the auction for the government's Surgutneftegaz shares was held, it was in the city of Surgut, in West Siberia. If a trip to Surgut were not discouraging enough, to further exclude unwelcome outsiders from attending, the Surgut airport was inexplicably closed on auction day. David E. Hoffman, *The Oligarchs, Wealth and Power in the New Russia*, (New York: Public Affairs, 2002), p. 318.

9 Peter Maass, 'The Triumph of the Quiet Tycoon,' *New York Times Magazine*, August 1, 2004, p. 29.

10 'Lukoil Sells Azeri Assets to Shift Focus to Russia,' *Nefte Compass*, November 21, 2002, p. 8.

11 In 2000, the company acquired the marketing arm of the American independent Getty Petroleum and thereby came to operate 1,300 gas stations in the northeast USA. See *www.lukoil.com/about/history.htm*.

12 For 2003 international production, Lukoil, *2003 Annual Report*, (English), p. 19. For 2010 estimate, Lukoil, 'Lukoil: Efficient Growth' (PowerPoint investor presentation in English), June 2002, p. 21, *www.lukoil.com/pdf/240602.pdf*.

13 Lukoil, *2002 Annual Report* (English), p. 12.

14 'Lukoil to Sell Some Oil Reserves Amid Industry Shift in Russia,' *Wall Street Journal*, April 19, 2004, p. A8.

15 That the company bought producing assets to raise its corporate productive capacity is not a unique strategy – it is done in the West all the time. Neither is it necessarily a bad strategy from the viewpoint of the company's shareholders to buy production, rather than explore for it, or further develop owned fields. However, when one Russian company buys existing productive capacity of another Russian company, it does nothing to raise the capacity of the nation as a whole. It merely changes the legal title to already productive fields.

16 Lukoil, *2001 Annual Report* (English), p. 11.

17 Lukoil website, *www.lukoil.com/static_6_5id_252_.html*. These estimates represented a 53 per cent increase in proved and probable oil reserves on Lukoil's North Caspian leases between 2002 and 2003. However, the gas-oil ratio still makes these principally gas resources.

18 The most recent presentation from Lukoil on the production plans for the Caspian fields quotes the target of 250,000 as barrels of oil equivalent (BOE) per day, which leaves the door open for gas production to be included. Lukoil, '2002 Financial Results (US GAAP)' (PowerPoint investor presentation), June 2003, p. 20. Earlier forecasts had couched the outlook

only in terms of oil.
19 Lukoil estimates that the resources of the Russian sector of the Middle Caspian as a whole are 33 billion BOE, of which 9 billion bbls of oil is expected. 'Wag the Dog, Companies Question Russian Rules Over Oil Search,' *Nefte Compass*, June 27, 2002, pp. 1–2.
20 'Half and Half, Lukoil Halves Timan-Pechora Investments,' *Nefte Compass*, April 11, 2002, p. 4.
21 For financial data, the 2001 and 2003 Lukoil *Annual Reports*, Consolidated Balance Sheets and Income Statements, as audited by the international accounting firm KPMG. Net income may not sum due to rounding. Reserves are year-end, SPE/WPC definition proved. Over the period, Lukoil reserves have been audited by the American petroleum engineering firm, Miller and Lents. Production data for 2004 are from Energy Intelligence Group, *The Almanac of Russian and Caspian Petroleum 2004*, Lukoil worksheet.
22 Not included in this discussion is the corporation's strategy for gas production, increasing exports or improving refining margins. For this information, see Lukoil's annual and financial statements at *www.lukoil.com/report/year_reports_all.htm*.
23 Energy Intelligence Group, *The Almanac of Russian and Caspian Petroleum 2003*, Lukoil worksheet (2003).
24 At the Yarega field, which is almost unique in the world, oil is actually recovered through mining methods. Vertical shafts were sunk through the shallow reservoirs and lateral shafts dug below them. The oil slowly drips into troughs lining the lateral shafts below them and is pumped out of the 'mine.'

Soviet engineering logic placed a very high premium on being *able* to do things – whether they *should* be done or not. The absurdly expensive mechanism for recovering oil at Yarega was advertised at the time with considerable pride – because it worked at all. The fact that titanium is recovered from this unique hydrocarbon accumulation may ultimately make its oil production a profitable co-product.
25 Prisoners in the GULAG camps were more likely assigned to the region's coal mines and forests than to oil development. However, Ukhta, the oil industry centre, was solidly populated with lesser offenders living there under administrative exile. They and their children were, and remain, heavily represented in the region's oil industry work force.
26 For the story of Lukoil's entry into the Kharyaginskoye project, see 'French Kiss: Lukoil Joins Total in Kharyaga,' *Nefte Compass*, October 31, 2002, p. 3. For its exit, see 'Through, Lukoil Quits Kharyaga Project in Blow to Total,' *Nefte Compass*, September 25, 2003, p. 1.
27 The initial system opened in 2001 with a capacity of 240,000 b/d. A 2003 expansion brought it to 600,000 b/d. It is scheduled to increase to 840,000 b/d in 2004. 'Transneft Increases Baltic Pipeline Capacity,' *Alexander's Oil and Gas Connection*, vol. 8, no. 23 (November 27, 2003).
28 In 2000, Lukoil built an offshore loading terminal at Varandey, on the coast of the Pechora Bay. In 2003, 7,600 b/d was exported through this facility.

While providing good engineering experience, this level of exports is not significant. When Lukoil announced its new partnership with ConocoPhillips in the basin, part of their joint venture included raising the capacity of the Varandey facility to 240,000 b/d, which is large enough to change the economics of development in the northern part of the basin for the two joint venture partners.

29 Here Langepasneftegaz includes both the original unit of that name, and the Pokachevneftegaz division carved out in 1999.
30 By 2002, the company had largely abandoned new field exploration in its well picked over part of the Middle Ob.
31 Gregory L. White, 'Russia Assigns Auction Price for Lukoil Stake,' *Wall Street Journal*, August 27, 2004, p. A3.
32 Andrew Jack and Doug Cameron, 'Conoco Plays the Percentage Game with Lukoil Stake Sale,' *Financial Times*, August 31, 2004, p. 19.
33 The agreement between the two companies also contemplates cooperation on the development of the West Qurna field in Iraq, to which Lukoil gained development rights during the Saddam Hussein regime. Lukoil clearly thinks partnering with an American major may secure its dangling interests in Iraq. However, if the Iraqis are ever allowed to decide who their development partners will be, a company from Russia, which supported Saddam Hussein, paired with a firm from America, which invaded their country, may not enjoy the advantage envisioned when this part of the project was conceived.
34 The initial union, between Yuganskneftegaz and the refinery/chemical complex, KuybyshevnefteOrgSintez, provided the 'Yu' and 'kos' of the company name.
35 Hoffman, *The Oligarchs*, op. cit., p. 318.
36 The resources are given as of January 1, 1993, but would not have changed by much between then and the time of the transfer in 1995. Market Intelligence Group, Russian Petroleum Investor, *Russian Petroleum Encyclopedia, Upstream*, 1995, vol. 1, p. 136.
37 Hoffman, op. cit., p. 531. While $100 million is certainly a lot of money, in the context of oil and gas projects, these types of sums are risked regularly on projects by major international oil companies. A total of $100 million would typically cover the costs of drilling two to three big offshore, deep-water prospects.
38 'Unmasking, Yukos Reveals Controlling Shareholders,' *Nefte Compass*, June 27, 2002, p. 7.
39 Having foreigners on the board of a Russian company is neither a necessary nor sufficient condition for success. The presence of directors who are not officers of the company provides a transparency and integrity in company decisions that is usually harder to achieve with all insiders passing on their own decisions. The more 'outside' the board, the better – and one can't get more 'outside' in Russia than being a foreigner.
40 'Output Up, Yukos Claims No. 1 Spot As Production Rises,' *Nefte Compass*, March 27, 2003, p. 4.

41 Yukos, *2002 Annual Report (English)*, p. 20.
42 For financial data for 2000 and 2001: *2001 Yukos Annual Report*, Consolidated Balance and Income Statements. For 2002: *2002 Yukos Annual Report*, Consolidated Balance and Income Statements. Financial data for 2003 apply only to the first three quarters, and was prepared under GAAP standards, but was unaudited: 'Yukos Consolidated Financial Statements as of September 30. 2003.' All other financial statements audited by PriceWaterhouseCoopers under GAAP standards. Reserve data for 2000 through 2003 are SPE/WPC proved, as audited by DeGolyer and MacNaughton. Production data are from *The Almanac of Russian and Caspian Petroleum 2004*, Yukos worksheet.
43 The company's briskly growing investment schedule for producing fields also ensures that depletion, depreciation and amortization will continue to rise. While not part of direct lifting costs, it is a major component of total operating costs. See the financial statement included in the *Yukos 2002 Annual Report*.
44 Gustafson, op. cit., p. 117 provides a short note on the brief esteem enjoyed by Yuganskneftegaz in the mid-eighties (note, Gustafson uses a slightly different transliteration, 'Iuganskneftegaz').
45 Yuganskneftegaz, 'Yukos' (PowerPoint presentation in English, no date – probably early 2003), *www.yukos.com/new_ir/pdf/NYG.pdf*, pp. 39–42.
46 For greater detail, see 'What Charges Face Khodorkovsky?' *Russian Petroleum Investor*, January 2004, p 12.
47 'Putin: No Bankruptcy for YUKOS,' *Russian Journal Daily*, June 18, 2004, *www.russiajournal.com*
48 In Soviet times, all manner of unaccomplished goals were sarcastically expected to be attainable only after the long-awaited graduation from 'socialism' to 'communism.' The development of Priobskoye fell into this category, making it even more amusing that it finally occurred after the transition from what the Soviets called 'socialism' to what the Russians now call 'capitalism.'
49 'Yukos' (PowerPoint presentation), op. cit., p. 49.
50 While Priobskoye is the hero of Yukos, it is also a case study in the overstatement of resources inherent in the Soviet/Russian approach to resource classification. The field's $A+B+C_1$ estimated ultimate recovery (EUR) is cited as 5.8 billion bbls. Using the SPE/WPC definition of remaining reserves, the EUR is 3.9 billion bbls, two-thirds of the Soviet/Russian standard. Using the frugal US SEC definition, the EUR is only 1.5 billion bbls, a quarter of the Soviet/Russian number (see Appendix II). Yet even writing down Priobskoye reserves to a reasonable level, if development continues to be funded at the pace of the period 2001–2003, production will probably top 500,000 b/d in the later part of this decade.
51 Geologists found the first field, Kholmogorskoye, in 1973; it went on line in 1976.
52 This account is basically taken from Freeland, *Sale of the Century*, op. cit., pp. 186–8.

Industry Performance 173

53 Hoffman, *The Oligarchs*, op. cit., p. 320, reports the premium over the minimum price as being $300,000.
54 The estimate of A+B+C$_1$ resources at Noyabrskneftegaz was as of January 1, 1994, but would have been roughly the same two years later when the auction was held. Market Intelligence Group, *Russian Petroleum Encyclopedia*, op. cit., pp. 259–60.
55 Hoffman, *The Oligarchs*, op. cit., pp. 487–9.
56 In 2002, Sibneft announced a horizontal completion drilled at Sugmutskoye that produced at an initial rate of 9,200 b/d, a record for West Siberia. 'Well Being, Sibneft Drills Record-Breaking Well,' *Nefte Compass*, June 6, 2002, p. 4.
57 Financial data for 2002 and 2003 were taken from *Sibneft Annual Report for 2003*, Consolidated Balance and Income Statements for 2003. The data for 2000 and 2001 were taken from *Sibneft Annual Report for 2001*, Consolidated Balance and Income Statements for 2001. Both sets were prepared under GAAP standards, but it is unclear by whom. Oil and gas production data are from *The Almanac of Russian and Caspian Petroleum 2004*, Sibneft workbook. Oil and gas reserves are from Sibneft's web site, www.sibneft.com. They are SPE/WPC proved reserves, as audited by the American petroleum engineering firm Miller and Lents.
58 *The Almanac of Russian and Caspian Petroleum 2004*, Sibneft workbook.
59 For an overview of the drilling and well stimulation plan for 2003, see the Surgutneftegaz, *2002 Annual Report* (English), p. 18.
60 'Putin Ally Surgut Tops List of Possible Buyers for Yukos Unit,' www.bloomberg.com accessed September 9, 2004.
61 Surgutneftegaz's response can be found on its web site, www.surgutneftegas.ru/eng.
62 For financial and production data through 2002, see the 2000, 2001 and 2002 Surgutneftegaz *Annual Reports*, Consolidated Balance Sheets and Income Statements, as audited for 2000 and 2001 by the Russian accounting firm Rosekspertiza and, for 2002, by the Russian firm Aval. The 2003 data on production are from the Surgutneftegaz web site, www.surgutneftegas.ru/eng. Reserves are year-end, SPE/WPC proved as audited by the American petroleum engineering firm, DeGolyer and MacNaughton. Surgutneftegaz, as of October 2004, has not released an annual report, in Russian or English, for 2003 and has not released year-end audited reserve data since the end of 2001. While the company has released financial statements under GAAP rules for 1999, 2000 and 2002, the values above are, to the best that can be discerned, reported under Russian accounting rules. This was done to include the 2002 data. However, it makes comparison to the financial data on other companies in this chapter problematic.
63 Their undeveloped status is why they were 'available' and had not yet been deeded to a producing association.
64 Market Intelligence Group, *Russian Petroleum Encyclopedia*, op. cit, pp. 272, 285–6. The A+B+C$_1$ reserve estimate was as of January 1, 1993. The reserves by the end of the decade, when these transactions took place, would

174   *Russian Oil Supply*

have been less, but it is unknown by how much. However, the estimate of approximately 4 cents a barrel is, nevertheless, probably close.

65 Hoffman, *The Oligarchs*, op. cit., p. 318.
66 Market Intelligence Group, *Russian Petroleum Encyclopedia*, op. cit, p. 155. The A+B+C$_1$ reserve estimate was as of January 1, 1993, but given production rates in 1994 and 1995, it would not have been much different when bought in the Loans for Shares programme at the end of 1995.
67 For the 2002 and 2003 financial data, 'TNK-BP Limited US GAAP Consolidated Financial Statements as of December 31, 2003' (TNK-BP-12M2003-Final.pdf, available at www.tnk-bp.com/investors/financial), as audited under GAAP standards by PriceWaterhouseCoopers. Financial data may not exactly balance because of minority interest charges and rounding. Earnings per share represent the net income divided by the 50,000 ordinary shares reported in the financial statements. Financial data for 2000 and 2001 came from the 2001 financial statements, 'TNK International US GAAP Financial Statements 1999 – H1 2003' (TNK-Int-US-GAAP-Financial-Statements-1999-1H03.xls, available at www.tnk-bp.com/investors/financial), which were also audited by PriceWaterhouseCoopers under GAAP standards. Reserve data for 2000, 2001 and 2002 were all originally reported as January 1 data for the following year, but were moved to the preceding year-end for consistency with other companies' data. The document containing them is available on the TNK-BP web site. The proved reserves were audited under SPE/WPC definitions by the US petroleum engineering firm, Miller and Lents. The 2004 oil reserve data are from the TNK-BP web site *www.tnk-bp.com*, referenced as SPE/WPC definition calculation and presumably audited by the same firm. Although the company had previously reported SPE/WPC proved gas reserves, in 2004, its web site stated that 'Even though TNK-BP has currently no proven gas reserves under SPE/WPC standards on its balance sheet, the company extracts some 4.5 billion cubic meters of associated gas annually.'
68 This was Potanin's first big payday from the Sidanco investment. He sold 10 per cent of Sidanco to BP for $571 million, having paid $130 million for 51 per cent two years earlier – a 22-fold return in two years. Hoffman, op. cit., p. 362.
69 Chernogorneft then began to operate as TNK-Nizhnevartovsk within the TNK structure.
70 This does not appear to have encompassed the northern part of the field operated by Chernogorneft/TNK-Nizhnevartovsk, although its inclusion was probably anticipated at the time it was done.
71 Note also that there are small discrepancies between the total production in this figure and that reported in Table 13. This is because of definitional problems relating to units entering and leaving the company in mid-year.
72 Disposition of the Slavneft assets held jointly with Sibneft awaits resolution as of 2004.
73 Letter (and attachments) to I. Bakaleynik (TNK) from G.B. Knapp (Miller

Industry Performance 175

and Lents, Ltd.), April 3, 2002. Available at www.tnk.com/investor/reports.html.
74 Of this volume, 38 per cent was proved-producing, 36 per cent was proved-nonproducing and the balance was proved-undeveloped.
75 Gregory L. White 'As Westerners Move Into Russia, Its Vast Oil Wealth Keeps Growing,' *Wall Street Journal*, September 30, 2004, p. A1.
76 While $30/bbl oil may seem cheap in October 2004, when Brent crossed the $50/bbl barrier, BP's planning price for project evaluations is probably still in the $18 to $24/bbl range. Projects that do not show at least the required rate of return in discounted cash flow analysis, employing the official planning price and corporate discount rate, are generally not undertaken.
77 It is the economic productivity of investments in a field that matter to profit-maximizing firms in a market economy – not so much whether the field's output is rising or falling. While increasing production *may* lead to greater profitability, TNK-BP can just as easily make profits from a well managed field in decline.
78 Comparing year-on-year production data for the company (by division) since 1998 is problematic because the composition of the corporation has changed so much, so fast. The 14.8 per cent increase estimated by the company probably refers to the increase in existing assets, rather than including the impact of acquisitions (which would make it higher).
79 'High Five, TNK-BP Reveals Five-Year Strategy,' *Nefte Compass*, January 22, 2004, p. 6.
80 In the USA, the most mature producing country, the top 32 companies produce slightly less than half of national production and hold approximately the same share of reserves.
81 Tatneft was an exception.
82 Under the Soviet system, exploration was performed by the Ministry of Geology. When fields were found, delineated and pronounced ready for development, title would be transferred to either the Ministry of Oil or the Ministry of Gas, depending on the type of field. When the USSR collapsed, there were still scores of fields on the books of Ministry of Geology organizations that represented discoveries being prepared for transfer to either oil- or gas-producing organizations. Rather than make those transfers, the Ministry of Geology's exploration organizations kept the fields. With no experience in developing, producing or financing, a number of them invited Western partners to form JVs.
83 Many of these deals included an 'exploration upside,' or the right to explore for new fields within a licence area, as well as develop the field(s) central to the agreement.
84 'BP Makes Find off of East Russia,' *Financial Times*, October 7, 2004, p. 21.
85 It is also why the standard time series that used to separate production from JV and Russian independents now combines those two sources.
86 'Heavy Price, Tatarstan Swims Against Rising Production Tide,' *Nefte*

Compass, September 19, 2002, p. 3.
87 'Lesser Half, Tatneft Profits Hit By Taxes and Transport Costs,' *Nefte Compass*, November 13, 2003, p. 7.
88 Energy Intelligence Group, *The Almanac of Russian and Caspian Petroleum 2004*, Electronic Edition, Tatneft worksheet. This estimate was audited by the American engineering firm, Miller and Lents.
89 The mystery of ownership may be to obscure the position enjoyed by the President of Bashkortostan, M. Rakhimov and members of his family. 'Iron Man, Bashkir President to Maintain Oil Stranglehold,' *Nefte Compass*, January 8, 2004, p. 5.
90 Both Tatneft and Bashneft reserve estimates were reported by Energy Intelligence Group, *The Almanac of Russian and Caspian Petroleum 2004*, Electronic Edition, worksheets for Bashneft and Tatneft. The Tatneft reserve estimates were audited by the American engineering firm, Miller and Lents.
91 In a related action, the government suggested that once it had a majority control of Gazprom again, it would allow the unrestricted sale of the balance of the corporation's stock. Presently, there is a 20 per cent limit on the amount of Gazprom stock that can be held by foreigners. At the same time, there would presumably be a reconciliation of the prices of Gazprom stock, now sold at two different prices, to Russians and foreigners.
92 Subsuming Rosneft into Gazprom also reprises a series of bureaucratic battles in the seventies and eighties when the Soviet ministries of oil and gas were alternatively combined and split, reflecting the rivalry between the two industries.
93 The exceptions were Gazprom, Tatneft and the three producing associations that formed Lukoil, Langepasneftegaz, Urayneftegaz and Kogalymneftegaz.
94 Azerbaijan, the first home of the petroleum industry in what was the USSR, became an independent country.
95 Sidanco (now part of TNK-BP) did or may have had rights to Purneftegaz at some point during the nineties, but repeatedly filed suits, decisions and appeals were too complex to determine how long Purneftegaz may have been out of the Rosneft fold.
96 Financial information, *Rosneft Annual Report 2001* and *Rosneft Annual Report 2002* reports, Consolidated Balance and Income Statements, as audited under GAAP standards (auditor unknown). Data for 2003 represent only January through June and are unaudited (but also prepared under GAAP). Basic earnings per share are net income divided by 19,677 shares of common and preferred stock (only 1 per cent of which is preferred). Net income values may not sum due to rounding. Reserve data for 2000 are Soviet/Russian $A+B+C_1$ definition for both oil and gas and cannot be usefully compared to SPE/WPC definitions. The 2000 resource estimates were reported in the *The Almanac of Russian and Caspian Petroleum 2002*, Rosneft workbook; 2002 production and resource estimates were reported in the

The Almanac of Russian and Caspian Petroleum 2003, Rosneft worksheet.
97 Three of these are Urengoy, Medvezhye and Yamburg. All have produced massive quantities of natural gas for decades and hence have well established infrastructures in place (although admittedly not for liquids handling, except at Urengoy which has always had a small volume of condensate production). The fourth field is Zapolyarnoye, which began production in 2001, and is only a short distance to the east of Urengoy. This does not include the scores of large gas fields immediately in that area that could also make a large collective contribution. Neither does it include the Yamal Peninsula fields, which will probably remain uneconomic as gas producers for some time to come.
98 Linguistically, Russian allows even more latitude in passive voice and conditional statements than even legalize-choked English. The Rosneft statement is a masterpiece of polite, indirect suggestion that it is too valuable to Russia to allow Gazprom to interfere with its existing structure, even if it must merge. *www.rosneft.ru.*
99 The list for 2003 can be found at *www.forbes.com*.
100 The reversal in 1998 was the result of world prices that fell quickly and sharply and the influence of the devaluation of the rouble in and after August.
101 This is shown in greater detail in the Appendix to Chapter 4.
102 Actually, the consumer surplus accounted here was gained only by Russian refineries. For consumers of petroleum products to have benefited, the savings the refineries enjoyed would have to be passed on in low products prices. As the main price control mechanisms were actually applied at the product level, this is generally what happened.
103 The risk of the Putin administration recouping more Yeltsin-era largesse in the Loans for Shares and related programmes is not lost on other oil companies. Russia's majors are in full voice in announcing their tax payments, how they've grown, how no one would use evil tax dodges anymore, the importance to the national budget contributed by each and how much they actually enjoy paying taxes in Russia.
104 The situation outside the oil and gas industry is much more nuanced. There probably is very broad, genuine support for markets in light manufacturing, retailing, services and perhaps increasingly in agriculture. However, the present administration sees strong intervention in energy and other key industrial sectors, guided by the pursuit of broad macroeconomic strategies, as a central part of the state's role.

CHAPTER 6

THE OUTLOOK FOR RUSSIAN OIL SUPPLY

Few analytic endeavours are more feebly rewarded than forecasting oil and gas supplies. Erroneous predictions are inevitably remembered; being right is usually dismissed as predicting the obvious. Nevertheless, the organization of data and thought required to offer a prediction of future supply usually justifies the exercise beyond the narrow value of the numbers. It is in that spirit that this part of the study is offered. Rather than a rigorous mathematical model of Russian oil supply, the information from the preceding chapters is focused here to highlight those factors that will limit and encourage the production of oil in Russia over this and the following decades.

Russia's Resource Base

The immediate supply of oil from any region is from its reserves: the remaining fraction of discovered accumulations that can be recovered using current technology, under prevailing economic conditions and with existing government approvals. Reserves are further divided, based on certainty of technical and economic recoverability in ways that provide more detailed information on the cost, timing and likelihood of production. The size of Russia's oil reserves is a complex topic, but critically important to the future productive capacity of the nation. A detailed comparison of Russian and Western systems of quantifying oil resources is provided in Appendix II.

Proved Reserves. The reserves that constitute a producer's inventory, or ready supply of oil, are its 'proved' reserves, as defined by the US Society of Petroleum Engineers and World Petroleum Congress (SPE/WPC). For these volumes, there is a 90 per cent certainty that they exist, are technically recoverable and economic to produce under existing conditions.

Since about 2000, most large Russian oil producers have reported their oil reserves using SPE/WPC definitions, and, typically, they have been audited by Western petroleum engineering firms specializing in that work. These estimates, therefore, are generally comparable to the reserves reported by Western oil and gas companies and those typically summarized to the national level by government agencies and trade publications.

Table 15 provides the estimates, for this study, of Russian proved reserves by producer. With three exceptions, they are proved reserves reported under the SPE/WPC definitions, drawn from company sources and independently audited. For Bashneft and Gazprom, the most recent company-reported oil volumes were estimated under the Soviet/Russian A+B+C$_1$ system.[1] Because those data are incomparable with the others reported, a simplistic rule of thumb, of annual production equal to 5 per cent of proved reserves, was substituted. The same rule was applied to the collective proved reserves assigned to all of Russia's independents, PSAs, joint ventures and the few miscellaneous producers that do not fall into any other category.

Table 15: Estimate of Russia's Proved Reserves by Producer

Producer	Proved Reserves Billion Bbls	Year End	SPE/WPC 'Proved'	Engineering Audit Company (or method of estimate)
Majors				
Lukoil	16.0	2003	Yes	Miller & Lents
Yukos	14.7	2003	Yes	DeGolyer & MacNaughton
Sibneft	4.6	2002	Yes	Miller & Lents
Surgutneftegaz	6.6	2001	Yes	DeGolyer & MacNaughton
TNK	8.4	2003	Yes	Miller & Lents
Subtotal	*50.3*			
Regional Majors				
Tatneft	5.5	2003	Yes	Miller & Lents
Bashneft	1.8	2003	No	20 times 2003 production
Subtotal	*7.3*			
State Producers				
Rosneft	2.4	2003	Yes	DeGolyer & MacNaughton
Gazprom	1.6	2003	No	20 times 2003 production
Subtotal	*4.0*			
Independent/Other	6.6	2003	No	20 times 2003 production
Total	**68.2**			

The total proved reserves for Russia, as of the end of 2003, estimated here were 68.2 billion bbls.[2] This is very close to the estimate reported by the BP *Statistical Review of World Energy 2004* of 69.1 billion bbls. Proved reserves of 68 billion barrels put Russia seventh in the world;

it possesses the largest proved reserves outside of OPEC (Figure 39). Russian proved reserves are more than double those of the United States.

Russia's reserve-to-production ratio (R/P), reflecting the number of years its proved reserves would last at 2003 production levels, is 22. This is far less than the richest OPEC producers (some of which have R/Ps of greater than 100). However, it is twice that of the USA and from three to four times higher than the top European producers, the United Kingdom and Norway.

As proved reserves are a function of price, the volume credited to Russia at the end of 2004 may be higher than in 2003. There has been a radical increase in world prices; the average for Brent from January through October 2004 was 30 per cent higher than the 2003 average. Due to domestic price controls, the average price of oil on the Russian market has risen far less. Even so, Russia's proved reserves are expected to grow in 2004.[3]

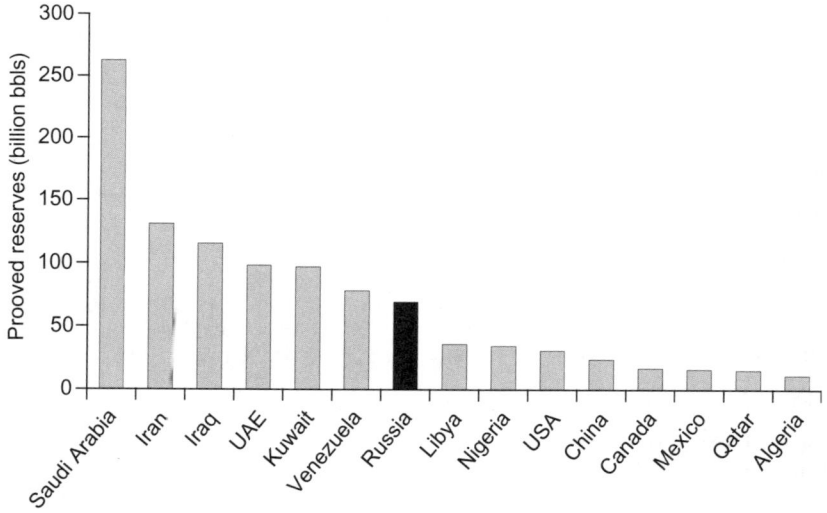

Figure 39: Proved Oil Reserves of the Top 15 Countries

Lesser Categories of Reserves. Within the SPE/WPC schema, there are two lower categories of reserves, 'probable' and 'possible', which reflect less confidence in the technical and economic recoverability of the oil volumes they each include. Probable and possible reserves can be estimated for Russia, based on reporting by the major oil companies.

In addition to proved reserves in Table 15, the five major oil companies reported the lesser reserve categories as well, also evaluated under SPE/WPC definitions and independently audited. All five gave estimates for probable reserves and, four of the five provided possible reserves (Lukoil did not). Therefore, the ratios of probable to proved, and possible to proved, were calculated for each company and averaged. While there were only four to five data points for these averages, the companies involved hold 74 per cent of the nation's proved reserves, so the sample is quite powerful.

On average, probable reserves were 46 per cent of proved and possible were 51 per cent of proved reserves. Applying those averages to the national estimate of proved reserves, at the end of 2003, Russia had an estimated 31.6 billion bbls of probable reserves, and another 34.5 billion bbls of possible reserves. While it is wrong for good mathematical reasons to add proved, probable and possible, as a practical matter it is done all the time and provides sums and ratios commonly used in oil and gas supply analysis (Table 16). The addition of proved plus probable reserves yields a rounded number of 100 billion bbls. Further adding possible produces 135 billion bbls of proved plus probable plus possible (sometimes called the '3Ps').[4]

Table 16: Russia's Conventional Oil Resource Base

Variable Number	Variable	Value	Units
Cumulative Production			
1	Estimated Cumulative Production through 2003	118	Billion bbls
Remaining Discovered			
2	Proved Reserves	68	Billion bbls
3	Probable Reserves	32	Billion bbls
4	Possible Reserves	35	Billion bbls
5	Estimated Ultimate Recovery (1+2)	186	Billion bbls
6	Depletion ((1/5) x 100)	63	Per cent
7	Total Discovered (3+4+5)	253	Billion bbls
8	Total Discovered Produced ((1/7) x 100)	47	Per cent
Estimated Undiscovered			
9	Low Undiscovered Estimate (95% Fractile)	46	Billion bbls
10	Mean Undiscovered Estimate	80	Billion bbls
11	High Undiscovered Estimate (5% Fractile)	132	Billion bbls
Resource Base			
12	Estimated Total Resource Base (7+10)	333	Billion bbls
13	Resource Base Discovered ((7/12) x 100)	76	Per cent
14	Resource Base Produced ((1/12) x 100)	35	Per cent

Russian sources, often obscuring what reserve definitions relied upon, usually claim 'reserves' that are much higher than the 68 billion bbls of proved reserves. Typically, these range from 'over 100 billion bbls' to '100 to 150 billion bbls,' to numbers that are truly fantastic. The controversy is sharpened by recent moves by the Putin administration to resurrect Soviet-era secrecy laws surrounding access to Russian oil resource data.[5]

As explained in detail in Appendix II, relative to SPE/WPC proved reserves, $A+B+C_1$ estimates are systematically inflated by overestimating technical recovery factors and disregarding economic limitations imposed by cost and prices. Nevertheless, the coincidence must be noted that the sums of proved plus probable, and proved plus probable plus possible, define a range that encompasses the more rational of Russian estimates of their 'reserves'.

This lays a foundation for simple comparison of Russia's SPE/WPC reserves with Russians' own estimates, using the Soviet/Russian $A+B+C_1$ system. The difference is what arises between considering technologic and economic limitations (i.e., SPE/WPC proved) and the volume derived when those considerations are progressively, and very substantially, loosened, which is what the categories of probable and possible do on the SPE/WPC side, and the $A+B+C_1$ class does on the Russian side.

Undiscovered Oil. In addition to oil that has been found, an increasing share of future supply will necessarily be drawn from oil that is presently undiscovered, but will be found by exploration. For the period through 2020, the fraction of supply that will come from presently undiscovered fields is very small. After that point, of course, presently undiscovered resources will make a growing contribution.

In its last useful analysis of world oil and gas resources, the US Geologic Survey assessed the undiscovered, conventional, technically recoverable oil resources of Russia with a probabilistic range. They estimated that there was a 95 per cent chance of at least 46 billion bbls of oil remaining to be found in Russia and that there was a 5 per cent chance of at least 132 billion bbls. The mean of the estimated distribution was 80 billion bbls.[6]

According to the USGS 1998 analysis, the undiscovered oil resources of Russia were larger than of any other country in the world. Saudi Arabia and Iraq, the next two, came in at 61 and 45 billion bbls mean estimated undiscovered technically recoverable resources, respectively. Perhaps the USGS analysis, considering the extensive uncertainties surrounding the means, and the subjective methodology employed, should not be leaned on too heavily. However, the most important ordinal result remains robust. It is that Russia's remaining, undiscovered, technically recoverable, conventional oil resources are among the largest on the planet.

What must be applied to that conclusion is an economic filter recognizing that most of the technically recoverable, undiscovered oil in the Arctic Ocean (except in the Pechora Bay) and the Pacific Ocean (except around Sakhalin Island), and some of the volume in East Siberia, is of dubious economic viability, even at long-run world oil prices in the $30/bbl range.

The components of Russia's oil resource base are summarized in Table 16. As closely as possible, these estimates are as of the end of 2003. However, the assessment of Russia's undiscovered resources, carried an 'as of' date eight years earlier.

Future Output from Producing Fields

Through 2010, all but a small volume of oil will be produced from fields that were online in 2003. By 2020, a very large fraction, perhaps over half, still will come from presently productive fields. Therefore, these fields, which contributed almost all of Russia's 68 billion bbls of proved reserves, and all 8.4 million b/d in 2003, are at the centre of the nation's supply.

For the purpose of analysing their future contributions to supply, the stock of producing fields can be divided into two classes. The largest group is composed of those fields in decline; they have already reached their engineering maximums. The second class is fields that are increasing in production because they have not yet hit their engineering capacity peaks.

Fields in Decline. The main producing basins of Russia are moderately to very mature; they have been the objects of exploration and production operations for decades. As would be expected from field size lognormality, and the efficiency of exploration in finding the largest fields early, most of Russian production comes from fields that reached their engineering maximums years ago. The most important post-peak fields are listed in Table 17.

All but a handful of the countries' largest producing fields are in decline. This does not mean that individual fields in this group cannot increase their output over short periods, even years. It does mean, however, that they are not expected ever to exceed their highest historical annual production. Although the field-level data are not yet available for an exact estimate, fields in decline contributed roughly 7 million b/d of the 8.4 million b/d of Russian production in 2003.

In this group, there are many fields, even very large ones, presently enjoying resurgences of output, the result of record high prices and investments, better technology and improvements in engineering management. Nevertheless, with very few exceptions, these fields will not revisit their lifetime peaks. As a class, the fields responsible for over 80 per cent of national output will decline. The question is: how fast?

Table 17: Most Important Post-Peak Fields

Field	Operator
Samotlor	TNK-BP
Romashkino	Tatneft
Mamontovskoye	Yukos
Fedorovskoye	Surgutneftegaz
Lyantorskoye	Surgutneftegaz
Pravdinsko-Salymskoye	Khantymansiyskneftegazgeologiya
Vatyeganskoye	Lukoil
Povkhovskoye	Lukoil
Arlan	Bashneft
S. Yagunskoye	Lukoil

The collective rate of decline for post-peak fields is best conceived as a range, dependent on economic, technical and political conditions. At the low-decline end, using analogues from large, mature regions in the United States and Canada, in the very best case the rate could be as low as 1 per cent annually. This level would obtain if net income to producers from oil sales stays very high. Companies would invest in extra field engineering and extension exploration: buying the best pumps, strategically siting new wells and performing efficient workovers, among other measures.

At the high end, fields in decline could drop at 5 per cent, or even higher, as was seen in Russia a decade ago. A high rate of decline would occur if producers were (again) actually losing money on oil production – that is their net income at the wellhead after taxes was negative. Maintenance would be deferred, causing more wells to fall offline, and few new wells would be drilled in producing fields.

Where the actual rate falls depends, in the first instance, on producers' after-tax net income at the wellhead. In autumn 2004, with Brent over $50/bbl, low wellhead net income does not seem to be a problem.

If world prices of $50/bbl or more persist, and there is no corresponding strong increase in operating costs, tariffs and taxes – all of which would be expected to rise – a decline rate from post-peak fields of 1 per cent annually could be held for several years.

If wellhead net incomes remain at their 2003–2004 levels, it would fund the types of investments in extension exploration and production technologies that give similar US and Canadian basins such low rates of decline. Those types of investments, and their results, have already been seen in Russian fields since 2000. Yukos' re-engineering Mamontovskoye and Surgutneftegaz's frac programme, upgrading pumps at its top fields and generating its own electricity are excellent examples of how investment on the intensive margin of production brings significant new oil to market from old fields. Much of the 2003 14 per cent growth at TNK-BP can also be traced to better engineering of fields past their peaks.

However, in addition to investment, the structure of the North American industry also plays a big role in minimizing its rate of decline. A large and very diverse collection of companies produce oil and gas. The largest fields are typically first developed by the largest companies. Then, as the fields age, the big companies sell off the less productive parts to smaller companies having lower costs and often different ideas on development.[7] These medium to small oil companies also find and develop the majority of fields whose size is below the threshold for the largest companies.

In Russia, however, that hierarchy is very thin. In fact, it is shrinking as small firms are dropping away and being absorbed into the larger ones. There is also a very chilly regulatory, transportation, political and legal environment awaiting those who might desire to form a new independent oil company in Russia.[8]

Of course, the high-price/high-net income scenario is not the only one to be admitted. There is a combination of factors that could drive producers' wellhead net income down in the future. To start with, Russian domestic oil prices, which still set the revenues from nearly two-thirds of national production, are controlled to levels below world price parity. Therefore, while sustained increases in world prices are mirrored in the Russian market, it is at lower and slower levels. That wedge can always be driven further by relatively easy political decisions.

Beyond the problem of revenue from the domestic market, world prices themselves could fall from their present, record levels. If nothing else changed and Brent went to $18/bbl, it would wipe out most of the Russian oil industry's present, prodigious net income (and at some fields – all of it). An expected compensating drop in taxes would offset some of the loss in revenue. However, given the dominant role oil taxes play in the state budget, those reductions will be hard (even perhaps too hard) to make.[9]

In an $18/bbl-world, post-peak fields would probably decline at 3 to 5 per cent annually and the $15–$18/bbl range is the lower edge of world prices which would support decline rates within a 'normal' range. Some in the industry claim that Russian production is robust as low as $8/bbl – but that is sheer bravado.[10] The last time the weighted average sales price of oil in Russia was around $8/bbl was 1993 and 1994 – the industry's worst years since 1942.

Another route to the same destination is a scissors process in which prices retreat, during which there is a large steady increase in the sum of taxes, operating and transportation costs.[11] Operating costs have been in retreat nationally for several years, mainly through the exploitation of one-time gains. They will rise again as field depletion moves producers to ever-higher water cuts, lower well flow rates and smaller recoveries per well. These are the natural signs of aging in basins. Technology and better management may forestall and blunt the ravages of cumulative production, but they cannot be defeated. Transportation costs, as well, may climb to cover the looming need to refurbish ever more miles of the creaking national pipeline network.

Finally, there are taxes. The tax reforms instituted in 2002, if continued and observed, provided two important benefits. One was simplification. At times governments had placed over a dozen levies on oil; now they were consolidated to a few. Secondly, a sliding scale was provided that adjusts the level of excise taxation to the world price of oil. Therefore, as world prices rise, the state is a beneficiary along with producers. If prices fall, the state gets a smaller share.

With record world prices, Moscow has moved to raise its take from oil exports. In 2003, taxes increased dramatically. State policies almost killed the golden goose a decade ago, but now they have seen the limit beyond which higher taxes throttle production and choke tax receipts. Yet given the present level of net income at the wellhead, taxes could be substantially higher without crossing that threshold. The political tenor of the Duma elections in December 2003 exhibited the type of popular backlash against the industry from which higher tax rates spring. After a convincing victory at the polls, the Putin administration made clear that it expects to raise levies on Russian oil producers.[12]

Limits of a 1 per cent annual decline (given continued record world prices and a modest increase in expenses) and as high as 5 per cent (in an $18/bbl-world), suggest a reasonable scenario. It is for an average decline of post-peak fields of 1 per cent for 2004 through 2006 (because of the extremely high prices), 2 per cent from 2007 through 2010, increasing to 3 per cent over the following ten years. In this case, which relies upon high oil prices and high wellhead net income, on average every year over through 2020, Russia will still lose 140,000 b/d due to the decline of fields that are presently beyond their engineering maximums.

This gap of 140,000 b/d (or more, in lower price/lower net income scenarios), must be filled every year, just for Russian production to remain flat at 2003 output. The shortfall must be filled with the output of fields that are growing in production. Therefore, the new fields must increase their collective contribution to supply by at least 140,000 b/d annually for stable Russian production, and more, if there is to be any net increase.

Fields with Increasing Production. With the exception of short spurts by old fields, it is the new fields, the ones that have not yet reached their engineering maximums, which will contribute the most to production growth through 2010. There are scores of these fields in Russia and, collectively, they contributed about 20 per cent or 1.4 million b/d of supply in 2003. They were also responsible for an overwhelming fraction of the growth in national output. This is the premium increment of Russian supply bought by historic world prices and very strong net income to producers. The five most important pre-peak fields are listed in Table 18.

Table 18: Most Important Pre-Peak (Growing) Fields

Field	Operator
Priobskoye	Yukos
Tevlin-Russinskoye	Lukoil
Tyanskoye	Surgutneftegaz
Sugmutskoye	Sibneft
Sporyshevskoye	Sibneft

Of the several scores of fields increasing output (and still below their peaks), these five were dominant. Compared to the 1.6 million b/d net increase in Russian production between 1998 and 2002, the five top fields in Table 18 increased 553,000 b/d – 35 per cent of the total. Between 2004 and the end of the decade, these fields can contribute between 900,000 – 1.5 million b/d annually to Russian supply.

That volume will be critically important to growth. It is enough to fill the annual gap created by the decline of post-peak fields and leave, on average, approximately 1 million b/d for new net national production through 2010, and less thereafter. Of the five top fields, Yukos' Priobskoye is by far the most important. It is the only new oil field online, or under near-term development, capable of making a peak production of > 500,000 b/d. Tevlin-Russinskoye and Tyanskoye follow; both are significantly larger than the final two.

In addition to the five producers in Table 18, there are several scores of fields that have not hit their engineering maximums and will increase for years to come. However, by 2010, most of these fields will peak. The rate at which they decline thereafter will be set by the net income and business environment of the industry in the next decade. But no matter what is the level of their post-peak declines, as each of these fields hits its maximum, subsequent declines all add to the gap formed by those fields declining as of today.

Costs. Production of oil from Russia's discovered fields has increasingly been portrayed as a low-cost proposition, both relative to historical costs and opportunities elsewhere in the world. The former proposition is unquestionably true (Figure 40). The influence of the 1998 devaluation of the rouble is still being felt in operating costs that remain well below their pre-1998 levels. The impact of rouble devaluation was powerfully augmented this decade by better engineering and virgin (low-cost) production from several key new fields.

However, the decline in operating costs is unlikely to continue. At best, it will hold steady for a few years, but is much more likely to rise. High world oil prices and record operator margins always attract

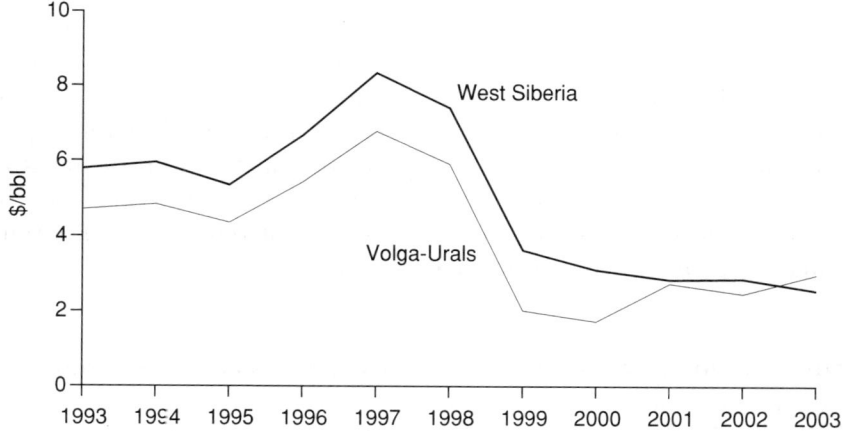

Figure 40: Production Costs in the West Siberian and Volga-Ural Basins

demand-pull premiums on input costs. Capacity utilization is rising in the manufacturing of all inputs to field development. In parallel, the specialized labour market, on which the industry relies, also grows increasingly tight. As evidence, the administrative units covering West Siberia were the only areas in Russia, east of the Urals, to see increased population in the nineties.[13] There is also a very large disparity between oil industry workers in Russia and those in Europe or North America that maintains an undercurrent of upward pressure on wages.

Independent of the macro-industry economic factors, there are the technical dimensions. Higher water cuts and lower flow rates in old fields, lower recoveries per well in smaller fields, and the upward shift in all costs that will attend the early production from remote areas of East Siberia and offshore – all auger for increasing costs. While the influences of technology and better management do offset them, these measures more often soften the rate of increase than actually force costs down.

Operating costs, in isolation, are an important component of the total cost of delivered oil to domestic or export customers. However, for a relevant comparison with competing oil investment alternatives, excise taxes and transportation costs to export points must be added. In several of the largest OPEC producers (like Kuwait and Saudi Arabia), the fields are on or very close to the coast; transportation costs are near zero. West Siberian oil is over 2,000 miles from export points; even Volga-Ural oil must travel 600 miles to leave the country. Geography adds a minimum of several dollars per barrel to the average delivered cost of Russian oil. Moreover, transportation constraints have, this decade, imposed additional delays and costs on exports.

Taxes since Russian independence have consumed one-quarter to one-third of the export price for oil sold at the border. While taxes are set by policy, and policies can change, there is an irreducible minimum fraction that the state, in its sovereign capacity, as well as the mineral owner, will require from operators. Those excise taxes must also be added to derive the total delivered cost of Russian oil at the export ports like Novorossiysk, or as the Druzhba pipeline crosses the Russian border. When viewed from this perspective of oil delivered to the border, reported operating costs of $2–$4/bbl remain an important component of the complete equation, but only a part of it.

Discovered, Undeveloped Oil and Condensate Resources

Virtually all Russian oil through 2010 will come from the hundreds of fields that are now online. However, even before 2010, a critical source of further *growth* will be production from fields that have been discovered, but are not yet producing. There is an inventory of discovered, but non-producing fields in any country. Yet in Russia, there is an abnormally large collection of such fields. Most important to supply is a small number of major projects on the verge of production. The projects with the largest and most immediate impacts are listed in Table 19 and reviewed in greater detail below.

Table 19: Most Important New Field Development Projects

Field	Operator
Lukoil Middle Caspian project	Lukoil
Sakhalin I project	Exxon PSA
W. Salymskoye	Shell JV
Vankorskoye	Rosneft
Lukoil Timan-Pechora project	Lukoil with ConocoPhillips
Komsomolskoye	Rosneft
Prirazlomnoye	Rosneft/Gazprom

Beyond the headline projects about to start production, there are also hundreds of other fields, discovered in the Soviet period, which have received virtually no attention since. Collectively, the discovered undeveloped fields of Russia contain billions of barrels of oil and condensate and trillions of cubic feet of natural gas.

These fields remained undeveloped for a variety of reasons. Some are unlikely ever to be produced. Given their geographic locations and the operations environments at the surface, they fall below a durable minimum economic field size for the regions where they were found. Another subset was beyond the reach of Soviet technology, like the fields off Sakhalin Island. Yet others had size and flow characteristics sufficient to make them work, but lacked transportation. Many of the undeveloped fields, particularly in West Siberia, are large but much smaller than the giant fields that attracted development funding during the Soviet period. A few were about to start production when the USSR came apart and the money disappeared.

Caspian and Timan-Pechora Projects. For the Russian Caspian to produce 250,000 b/d by 2010, as predicted by Lukoil (as opposed to BOE per day – including gas), it will take three to four times the volume of liquids booked by Lukoil through the end of 2003. Kurmangazy, and/or other unidentified targets along the Middle-North Caspian boundary may substantially raise the potential oil capacity for the region, but they will not make it happen earlier. The region can certainly contribute 250,000 b/d, but perhaps not until after 2010.

In addition to the physical volumes of hydrocarbon liquids found, the role of the Middle Caspian oil supply will also depend on how the fields are developed. If they are produced as gas fields (even with good associated liquids output), the contribution to oil supply will be low and slow. If they are seen principally as oil fields, liquids production could rise quite promptly.

In Timan-Pechora, the challenge of increasing production from discovered but undeveloped fields rests purely on money and management.[14] If Lukoil (and the few small operators left) can drill the wells and build pipes from the fields to the Transneft trunk pipelines (or locally export by sea), they can increase output for a decade or more. Of more than 200 oil and gas fields in the basin, less than 10 per cent have produced commercial quantities of oil (although a significant number of remaining fields are gas).

As of 2002–2003, Lukoil's plan called for increasing its production in the basin by about 400,000 b/d by 2010. Given the flow rates possible at the better fields, growth of >50,000 b/d per year would require 20 to 50 new producing wells annually – a do-able task. The test will be in organizing facilities and transportation at the field level for a programme that will necessarily involve developing several new large fields at once. Lukoil's Timan-Pechora subsidiaries sit atop most of the richest undeveloped fields in the basin. The company's announced joint venture with ConocoPhillips, with its own Timan-Pechora experience, increases the likelihood that production growth goals for the basin will be met.

Geologically within the Timan-Pechora basin, but 35 miles offshore, and outside the grasp of Lukoil, is the Prirazlomnoye field. This was discovered in 1989, just as the Soviet curtain dropped. Prirazlomnoye is probably the largest of a small group of discoveries in the Pechora Bay. It has planned peak capacity of 150,000 b/d and an average rate of 70,000 b/d over a 22-year project life.[15] It is favourably situated near existing and planned infrastructure. Being offshore (albeit in shallow water, 60 feet) builds in a natural delay, although a platform is to be set and drilling started in 2004. Being subject to the joint management of Rosneft and Gazprom may slow the project, as neither organization has recently evidenced a strong ability to bring major new fields online.

West Siberian Projects. In West Siberia, three fields stand out among the six or seven dozen fields with $A+B+C_1$ EUR over 50 million bbls, but no production. The Komsomolskoye field is in the hands of Rosneft's

Purneftegaz division and is the most promising of its holdings. This field has a potential to contribute >100,000 b/d, although it has produced at very low levels since 1988. It is geologically complex, but contains large resources and, because of its heterogeneities, could substantially benefit from 3-D seismic, advanced reservoir characterization and horizontal completions.

The Salymskoye project is another of the West Siberian fields that has attracted foreign attention since the early nineties. As of 2003, a project of Shell and the British special-purpose independent oil company, Sibir Energy, appeared to be going forward. Although the project involves several fields, the most important of these is W. Salymskoye. While development is at an early stage, it is projected to produce 116,800 b/d in 2007.[16] That may be optimistic with respect to timing, but not rate.

The Vankorskoye field, although administratively in East Siberia, is geologically in the West Siberian basin.[17] The field is a relatively new find (1990), yet it is in the same group as the Suzunskoye field, discovered in 1972. What makes this play attractive is that these are oil fields in the northern basin, which is otherwise dominated by gas and gas-condensate fields. Vankorskoye appears to be large enough for stand-alone development. It was once the subject of a joint venture with Shell and more recently funded by TOTAL. Nevertheless, as of late 2004, it belongs to Rosneft.[18] The biggest thing Vankorskoye (and neighbouring oil fields) have going for them is the largely arbitrary and fortuitous administrative assignment of their region to divisions of the Krasnoyarsk Kray, in East Siberia – thus avoiding the politics of West Siberia's Tyumen Oblast.[19]

Given Vankorskoye's location, in the extreme north-eastern corner of the basin, hundreds of miles from infrastructure and transport, the timing of its first production is highly uncertain. The transportation plan, naturally the most problematic component, calls for a pipeline straight north to Dikson, a Kara Sea port which is ice-free only some of the time. Operation in such an extreme and distant location will always keep transport and production costs high. If, however, Rosneft's plan is met, the field (with the possible inclusion of neighbouring N. Vankorskoye) will make 120,000 b/d by 2008.[20] As with similar projects, the rate is feasible, but the timing appears wildly optimistic.

East Siberian Projects. There are two areas in East Siberia where large discovered fields might make a contribution to supply before the end of this decade. However, first production is much more likely to be after 2010. The area that will see the quickest commercial operation is north of Lake Baikal. The largest structure in that area is the Nepa-Botubinsk Arch, on which a number of discoveries were made in Soviet times.[21] By age of reservoir, these are among the very oldest hydrocarbon accumulations on the planet, in rocks as old as 1 billion years.

The most attractive field in the area is gas: Kovyktinskoye, with reported $A+B+C_1$ gas resources of 75 trillion cubic feet. Plans call for exporting its gas to China. In the same area are several very large oil accumulations, the most important of which are the Talakanskoye, Chayandinskoye and Upper Chonskoye fields. The hope is that these fields will ride Kovyktinskoye's coat tails to export to China.

The second East Siberian area of highest near-term promise is Baykit. Several giant fields were found there in Soviet times.[22] The most important of these is Yurubchinskoye and there is a handful of fields around it. As of 2003, the dominant player in the area was Yukos, with plans to extract 140,000–150,000 b/d from the field by 2005, expanding output to 260,000 by 2008. The project was the subject of negotiations on joint development with BP.[23] However, these plans have clearly slipped as BP became engrossed in the TNK-BP merger and a separate set of diversions was visited upon Yukos.

The principal problems in East Siberia are the environment of operation and transportation (most likely for export to the Asian market). East Siberia is another example of projects where the forecasted technical production rates are not unreasonable, but timing depends on organization, logistics and economics not yet in place (or in many cases, not even close to being in place).

In December 2003, Rosneft, Gazprom and Surgutneftegaz announced that they would jointly take a leading role in the development of East Siberian oil and gas resources. The combination enjoyed a certain political appeal as the run-up to Duma elections rained heavy rhetoric against private oil companies, seeded by the Yukos Affair. Surgutneftegaz, corporate poster child of the new Slavophiles, has set an enviable standard of technical performance in the last decade. This includes bringing new fields online. Yet Surgutneftegaz has conservatively stayed within its home domain. Joining with Gazprom and Rosneft (now to be combined) may buy political capital, but it hardly builds a team with the innovation and recent engineering accomplishments that East Siberian success will require.

Sakhalin Projects. Off the Pacific coast of the Russian mainland is Sakhalin Island, and the fields located around its northern end. This includes two of Russia's PSAs: the Sakhalin I and Sakhalin II projects. The quickest major liquids production is expected from the former. This

Exxon-operated PSA is based around three fields (Chaivo, Odoptu and Arkhutun-Dagi) located close to shore in relatively shallow water, which is nevertheless heavily influenced by ice. First production from Sakhalin I (Chaivo) is planned for 2005, with the second phase (Odoptu) to begin in 2006. By the end of the decade, if all goes according to plan, the Sakhalin I project could be producing around 250,000 b/d.[24] In September 2004, BP and Rosneft announced a 4 billion BOE discovery in the Sakhalin V licence area.

Undeveloped Condensate Resources. Russia's vast, barely tapped condensate resources are among the more curious parts of the Soviet legacy.[25] As condensate accumulations are associated with natural gas fields, these resources in Soviet times, and today, fall under the purview of Gazprom. Its employees were and are still known as *gazoviki* – men who dealt with gas and nothing else.[26] The fact that any liquids came up the same wells as gas at some fields was to the *gazoviki* more an irritant than an asset.

That there were billions of barrels of condensate (and a much smaller volume of crude oil) in the Neocomian reservoirs of northern West Siberia was interesting to geologists, but not the engineers who ran, and run, Gazprom. A major reason why Gazprom produced the super-giant fields of northern West Siberia almost exclusively from the shallow Cenomanian reservoirs was that gas was dry – no bothersome liquids to process at the surface and transport.[27]

Either because Gazprom finally recognized the commercial value forsaken in ignoring condensate, or perhaps because of impending trouble with licences to the Neocomian reservoirs, in July 2003, the company established a JV with Wintershall, the German gas division of BASF AG.[28] The JV, named Achimgaz (after the Achimov Formation), has set a modest goal of 20,000 b/d of condensate from the super-giant Urengoy gas field. Both sides see this as a pilot project, so presumably higher production will follow.

Although the Wintershall JV is an important first step in the development of Russia's discovered and undeveloped condensate resources, it is a very small one. If the Wintershall project is limited to the Achimov member at the bottom of the productive section, there are substantial condensate resources higher in the Neocomian section. Moreover, this does not begin to address those billions of barrels at Yamburg, Medvezhe, Yubileyskoye and Zapolyarnoye (which finally began gas production in 2001) or the dozens of undeveloped gas fields in the northern part of West Siberia.

With this pace of development, the only increase in Gazprom liquids production through this decade will be tied lock step with its growth in gas production, unless the impending merger with Rosneft gives new motivation to its liquid production programme. By the next decade, it is assumed that market, or political pressures, will force the systematic development of the nation's considerable condensate resources.

Exploration

Through the end of the next decade, production from presently undiscovered fields will play only a small role in Russian oil supply. Beyond that point, however, Russia will be increasingly dependent on the results of future exploration.

The Russians are lucky to have 10 to 15 years to build a portfolio of exploration successes. The reason is that exploration, which fell apart with the USSR, faces two very fundamental problems. The first immediate impediment is the overhang of literally hundreds of discovered fields, which have never been developed. From a macro viewpoint, it is tough for the industry to invest in new exploration, with its associated high risk of failure, when there are billions of barrels of development opportunities, many of them close to infrastructure, which *should* be more profitable to develop.

This has caused tension between the government and the nation's oil companies. The government complains that the companies are proving up too small a volume of new field discoveries each year. At the same time, they say producers are doing too little to develop their inventory of discovered but undeveloped fields, threatening the companies with licence revocation. The companies see licence revocation as a big assault on their reserve bases.[29]

Of course, while pleading capital constraints to the charge of too few wells into the ground, at the same time the companies have shunted big bundles of their discretionary income into mergers and acquisitions. So, while the companies are investing to increase their reserve bases, they have chosen to do it through *buying* reserves, rather than further developing what they have or exploring for more. From the point of view of the Russian government, the companies are simply redistributing existing assets, and doing little to increase the collective discovered resource base of the nation. Market economies do not always align public and private interests.

The second big issue is cost. While the bubble of discovered undeveloped fields will burn off, cost is a much more intransigent problem. Some of the nation's exploration potential in the Volga-Ural basin and the historic producing areas of West Siberia is located where exploration and production costs are in line with those of the past. However, the largest advertised volumes of undiscovered physical hydrocarbon resources reside in the far more exotic locales of East Siberia or under the Arctic or Pacific oceans. The distances and environments surrounding these resources put them in a radically higher cost environment compared with the loci of traditional production.

The physical volumes of oil postulated for these vast domains are repeatedly, widely and loudly trumpeted. But, because of cost, even without the overhang of discovered undeveloped fields, it is not obvious that there will be a rush any time soon to these remote corners to look for new fields.[30]

Nevertheless, there are six principal exploration frontiers in Russia. The two smallest are west of the Ural Mountains: the Russian sector of the Caspian Sea and the Timan-Pechora basin. Next is the now middle-aged West Siberian basin, followed by East Siberia. The final two are Russia's offshore domains beneath the Pacific and Arctic oceans. The North Caucasus, Volga-Ural and the minor European basins hold remaining potential for finding new small to intermediate discoveries. While such finds can mean riches for a small company making the discovery, the only role additional finds in these areas will play is to soften the region's overall rates of decline.

Caspian Sea. The most prospective place west of the Ural Mountains is covered by the North and Middle Caspian basins, particularly their offshore extents. In terms of short-run contributions to supply through new discoveries, the offshore Middle Caspian is the best target. While the five Lukoil discoveries probably picked off some of the best prospects, this is only the beginning of exploration. There are undoubtedly additional discoveries to come in the >100 million barrel of oil equivalent (BOE) range (and perhaps > 1 billion BOE). Lukoil's discoveries proved that the exploration concept worked, although so far their new fields contain a surprisingly high share of natural gas relative to oil.

What is very tantalizing, and within partial reach, is the Kurmangazy structure. It is shallow (above the Permian-age salt that caps Tengiz and Kashagan), sits near the junction of the Middle and North Caspian basins, and also straddles the offshore boundary between Russia and Kazakhstan. It stands a good chance of containing oil and is a large structure.[31] It sits roughly on the regional high separating the two basins. While not perfect analogues, the parallel junction between the Middle and South Caspian basins proved highly oil-prolific.

Immediately to the north, Russia left the division of the Caspian

Sea with Kazakhstan holding only a very small part of the offshore North Caspian basin. The onshore North Caspian yielded Tengiz in Kazakhstan; the large offshore area on the Kazakh side produced the Kashagan discovery in 2000. Onshore in the Russian North Caspian basin is the super-giant Astrakhan gas and condensate field, lending further support to the (disappointing) proposition that the Russian part of the North Caspian offshore will contain much more gas than oil.

Timan-Pechora. Although the Soviets initiated production in the Timan-Pechora basin before the Second World War, it has remained relatively undeveloped. Soviet geologists and geophysicists busied themselves for decades mapping and drilling hundreds of new field wildcat wells. Yet there was never the money or political support to really develop the basin in the Soviet period. Support went first to the Volga-Ural basin, then West Siberia. Thus, there is a very large inventory of discovered fields that has gone undeveloped. There will be little true new field exploration as long as this is the case.

Nevertheless, the Timan-Pechora basin harbours good remaining exploration potential. Along with its Caspian programme, this is a prime exploration focus of Lukoil. Since moving into the basin at the very end of the nineties, the company claims to have discovered several hundred million barrels of new oil. Although such definitions are shaky in Russia, Lukoil also asserts that finding costs were only $0.40/bbl. If this is true, it means that Lukoil is facing very low exploration risk and the fields they are finding are quite large.[32]

West Siberia. New exploration in West Siberia has focused on the basin periphery and on deeper horizons long recognized, but not main exploration targets in Soviet times. The hottest new play on the basin periphery is in the extreme northeast, which has yielded large oil discoveries, the most popular of which is Vankorskoye, with Soviet/Russian C_1+C_2 resources of 912 million bbls (see Appendix II).[33]

Exploration interest extends south along the eastern margin of the basin and turns west to cover the broad southern shelf of the West Siberian basin. There have been discoveries across this entire area and those will continue. However, while the largest are >100 million bbls, no fields of the super-giant class that populate the Middle Ob have been found in the south. The southern margin boasts a much better climate than to the north and northeast. It is also closer to existing pipelines and there is the option of piping oil south and east, rather than the westbound destination of most Middle Ob output.

Going deeper into central and northern West Siberia brings explorationists to the Achimov Formation. As noted at the end of Chapter 3, this is a rather promising play that is likely to produce a good number of discoveries, some of which will be large. It is a more complex geologic and engineering environment than the traditional reservoirs of the Megion and Vartov formations, but enjoys the tremendous advantage of immediate proximity to the world's largest production infrastructure – reducing both operating and transportation costs. As also noted in Chapter 3, the Upper Jurassic Bazhenov shale, which generated most of the basin's oil, is a potential reservoir host as well. It is one, however, that will require extreme technological advances for profitable exploitation on a large scale.

In West Siberia, the problem of overhanging discovered undeveloped fields is most severe. That means, in part, that exploration should attract smaller companies that are fenced out of the opportunity to develop the inventory of fields squirreled away by the majors. This is another facet of the narrow structure of the present Russian oil industry, in which the type of small to medium firms that would be exploring central West Siberia, are vanishing (and there were only a small number, relative to the resource base, to start with).

East Siberia. During the Soviet period, and immediately after it ended, a popular ponder on the future of Russian oil was to look at a map, observe the extraordinary oil and gas resources of West Siberia and wonder if it might not be just as good east of the Yenisey River. Leading Soviet geologists recognized that the Siberian platform would never hold a hydrocarbon density equal to that of West Siberia. But they did preciously little to squelch speculation that it might. In the Soviet structure then, as well as in Western oil companies today, he who convinces management that there's oil in them-thar hills gets funding.

Elementary geology works against the vast region between the Yenisey and the Kolyma rivers. While there are sedimentary basins over much of East Siberia, in many places these rocks are thin or absent. Instead, there is a large volume of igneous and metamorphic rock at or close to the Earth's surface. With almost no exceptions among the tens of thousands of oil and gas fields found worldwide, igneous and metamorphic rocks neither generate nor host hydrocarbons. As a consequence, although East Siberia is vast, a large fraction of it is ram pasture – territory with little or no chance of harbouring oil and gas.

This does not mean that there is no exploration potential in East Siberia – there is. Although they never obtained much of what would now be called commercial production from the region, the Soviets drilled hundreds of exploratory wells. The several dozen fields found include some that are very large in terms of oil in place (as opposed to reserves). These big discoveries do not exist in geologic isolation. If there were dozens, starting at billions of barrels in place, then there are more to be found in the hundreds of millions of barrels range, and exponentially more even smaller than that.

However, as in all remote, extreme Arctic environments, distance and operating costs will conspire to produce very high minimum economic field sizes.[34] Over the next several decades, with the rare exceptions of satellite fields proximate to giants, fields below 100 million bbls EUR may not be profitable to produce. Also, as noted above, until there is basic industry infrastructure in place (most importantly transportation), the requirement of many years lead time will kill all but the very largest projects.

Russian Far East. East of the Kolyma River, along the Russian Pacific margin, but more importantly offshore, there is a series of basins for which analogues exist around the Pacific Rim. These include the prolific basins of southern and central California, the Cook Inlet of Alaska, offshore China, Malaysia and Indonesia. They all share a similar evolution of coastal mountains rising as oceanic crust pushed out from mid-ocean ridges, impinging on the surrounding continental plates.

Erosion of these highlands fed sediments into the Pacific. The rise and fall of sea level over the past 65 million years reworked these sands, cleaning them up to reservoir quality; interbedded are locally rich organic shales, which generated oil and gas. The continual opening of the Pacific Ocean provided tectonic forces not only to raise the mountains above the water line, but to create an extensive system of subsurface uplifts that trap both oil and gas. These are the processes that produced the promising province surrounding the northern end of Sakhalin Island, and, at a larger level, the exploration potential of the Sea of Okhotsk (and, even more remotely, the Anadyr, Khatyrka and other minor basins along the Russian Pacific coast).

The Sakhalin I and II development projects and the exploration potential of Sakhalin rounds III to VI have attracted the greatest investment by the world industry in Russian oil and gas resources.[35] Perhaps, most importantly, the projects are offshore, and the oil can be exported without resort to the pipeline networks of either Transneft, for oil, and Gazprom, for gas.

In other countries, Pacific Rim basins have repeatedly given up multi-billion barrel fields. Therefore, it is likely that further exploration will be rewarded by discoveries of sufficient size to overcome the cost of operation in a sub-arctic environment plagued by icebergs and pack ice. The throttle on exploration in the Pacific offshore is the speed with which the first two major projects (Sakhalin I and II) reach the point of production and then, making money. Once that crucial demonstration is made, and as long as operations are not revisited by bureaucratic delays, exploration around Sakhalin will set the pace and volume marks for the entire nation. Even so, production from structures that are today only undrilled prospects is probably 8 to 12 years away, at the earliest.

Arctic Ocean. In most ways, Russia's most remote exploration frontier lies beyond its northern coast. The Arctic Ocean contains a family of basins, extending from the Barents Sea in the west through the Kara, Laptev and East Siberian seas, to the Chukchi Sea, which borders the United States in the east (Map 1). Very little hard geologic or geophysical data has been collected east of the Kara Sea. There are no offshore wells there and only an extremely small volume of drilling along the coast (a couple of dozen wells, perhaps); there is only a very small volume of seismic data. In considering the next two decades of Russian oil supply, there is no reason to pay attention to any of the Arctic Ocean east of the Kara Sea.

This leaves the Barents and Kara seas, both of which contain discovered hydrocarbons. Both were subjects of a relatively long period of sparsely distributed exploration projects in the Soviet period, with approximately 15 fields discovered and dozens of identified prospects.[36] In the Barents Sea, the prospects fall into two geographic groupings. The first is a set of relatively small fields in the Pechora Bay, which is an offshore extension of the Timan-Pechora basin. The other fields are distributed up to hundreds of miles from the Russian mainland across the Russian sectors of the Barents and Kara seas.

In the Kara Sea, the geology is almost entirely an extension of the northern West Siberian basin. It is likely there is a very large volume of physical hydrocarbons in Mesozoic age rocks under the Kara Sea. While there could well be oil plays in the Kara (particularly along its northern rim), it is more likely that the region is dominated by gas (and condensate) as is the onshore area of the northern West Siberian basin.[37] It is difficult enough to see the point in the distant future when the half dozen discoveries already made will be developed. Why further exploration would take place in the Kara Sea before 2020 is nearly impossible to understand.

The situation in the Barents is different – mainly in the Pechora Bay. The fields discovered there to date are part of the relatively well-understood geology from the Timan-Pechora basin. They are proximate to infrastructure in the northern part of that basin, and this is where a northern oil export terminal may be built in the relatively near future. Many of these fields are oil. After the first fields come online in the Pechora Bay (led by the Prirazlomnoye field) and an offshore infrastructure develops, there will doubtless be additional exploration yielding more discoveries.

The Barents discoveries north and northwest of the Pechora Bay exist in an environment of distance and climate that makes them pretty unattractive economically, despite the fact that there apparently have been relatively large physical volumes of hydrocarbons discovered. The high-profile project of the region is the Shtokmanovskoye gas field. It is a super-giant field that has been the subject of a number of Russian/foreign studies. If and when Shtokmanovskoye is developed, the engineering experience and infrastructure it brings may spark other developments in the northern Barents.

Although there appears to be more oil (as opposed to gas) in the Barents than in the Kara, it is very hard to see the region (outside the Pechora Bay) contributing to supply before 2020. With that framework, it is even harder to reasonably expect new field wildcat exploration in the area, at least any conducted by organizations that are intending to turn an economic profit.

Synthesis

The basic mathematics are clear – the course of Russian oil production through the end of this decade will be almost completely determined by the fields that are presently producing. Among them, the giant old fields, beyond their peaks, are fundamentally important. These same fields will continue to volumetrically dominate output through most of the next decade as well.

For every 1 per cent decline in the production of Russia's post-peak fields, their collective output drops by up to 70,000 b/d. That gap must be filled every year – just to keep output steady. It is the young, growing fields that must fill the shortfall. A field the size of Priobskoye can add oil at a rate of more than 50,000 b/d annually (over its first five to six years), but there are few young fields of that size around.

Were world prices and producers' wellhead net income received in 2003 and 2004 to persist, it is reasonable to expect the gap from declining fields to average as low as 140,000 b/d through 2020 (less before 2010, more after). In the event of a serious erosion of net income, either from increases in taxes and costs or a reduction in world prices, a 4 per cent annual decline enlarges the gap to more than a 250,000 b/d annual loss. To fill *this* hole would take a half-dozen Priobskoyes and once that considerable feat was accomplished, production would only be flat and then just for a few years.

Production through 2010. Obviously, to secure Russian oil supply will take deep and sustained engineering attention to the nation's major, base-load producing fields. That could come from the handful of major oil companies that now control nearly all of them. Yukos, Surgutneftegaz and, more recently, TNK-BP, have made remarkable strides in raising not only the outputs of these fields but their operating efficiencies. Nevertheless, looking forward, Moscow has foreclosed a potentially powerful force in support of these fields by suppressing the development of medium and smaller oil companies. These are the producers that typically farm into late-stage production opportunities, and stretch them further than the big companies that initially found and drilled them.

Given a solid foundation of minimum decline from the giant post-peak fields, the next most important risk point in Russian oil supply is the half-dozen stand-out, growing fields in Table 18. These fields spearheaded the ascent in Russian production from 1998. The largest producer, and the operation in greatest jeopardy, is, of course, Yukos' Priobskoye field. Now, with the dissolution of that company imminent, Priobskoye's rate of growth in the next few years is very problematic. The Putin administration's choice of successor to this asset will immediately indicate the most likely course. If it goes to Surgutneftegaz, the impact on supply will be minimized; if it ends up in the growing pocket of the Gazprom/Rosneft combine, the outlook is much dimmer.

The 2004 level of production, which will be a little over 9 million b/d, can be maintained for several years based entirely on fields presently online. However, while these fields can provide some additional growth, by the end of this decade and beyond, further increases will hinge on the performance of the top new projects in Table 19. In all of these cases, the greatest uncertainty surrounds not the levels of output they can achieve, but when production begins at each.

In one way or another, almost all of the high-profile new projects in Table 19 face very serious technical challenges: offshore Arctic or sub-arctic environments, complex geology or remote locales in very hostile climates. Start dates for Russian projects are notoriously optimistic. Whether these fields commence production on the schedules advertised in 2003 and 2004 or they are pushed back will determine what, if any, growth in Russian supply occurs at the end of this decade.

The new field development projects forming the most immediate source of growth are in the Lukoil Timan-Pechora project. These fields are closest to production and regional infrastructure is in place, hastening the oil to market. A major oil export terminal on Russia's northern coast will also catalyse development. Lukoil, and its new American partner, ConocoPhillips, have a good chance of hitting the goal of >50,000 b/d annual growth. Even if they fall short, tens of thousands of barrels per day of new capacity will come on in the absence of a serious degradation of the industry finances or trouble at Lukoil.

Presumably, the first tranche of significant Sakhalin I supply begins in 2005 or 2006. Around the same time, the Shell-Sibir Energy project at West Salymskoye, in West Siberia, will start. If the Rosneft-Gazprom team actually does install a platform at Prirazlomnoye in 2004, that field could also start making oil in the 2006–2007 time frame. To obtain a collective contribution from all three of 250,000 b/d in 2007, however, would require that *everything* goes right. That is highly improbable. More likely is 100,000 b/d in 2007 or 2008 from these projects, with the possibility of making 250,000 b/d in 2010 or not long thereafter.

As a result of these dynamics, the middle of this decade, while benefiting from the momentum of the last few years, will see a drop in the recent growth rates. The factor that will most powerfully influence whether production flattens just above the 9 million b/d or reaches, or even crosses 10 million b/d will be producer net income. The wildcard is politics. If the Putin administration goes after Sibneft or TNK-BP to further recover assets they deem wrongfully privatized in the nineties, production could drop sharply even in the face of high world oil prices.

While output will continue to rise, because of the path chosen, a growing concern is the increasing fragility of the Russian oil production base.[38] It is again becoming narrow – ever more reliant on a decreasing number of fields. So, even beyond the sources of political risk that could affect one company or another, should a field accident shut down half the production from Tyanskoye, its role is big enough to be reflected in national production. If a rogue iceberg collided with the Orlan platform being installed at Sakhalin I, an important increment of the increase in the output anticipated before 2010 would be deferred, but totally lost to growth this decade

In sum, to produce between 9 and 10 million b/d through 2010 looks relatively easy, if things stay roughly as they were in 2003 and 2004. Production by 2010 over 10 million b/d requires a confluence of positive conditions and most importantly, timing, which is possible. However, as of 2004, such a successful alignment is not obvious nor does it logically flow from the state of the industry today.

Moreover, to push to significantly beyond 10 million b/d by 2010 will require precise execution of brand new projects located in highly challenging technical environments with extreme economic sensitivities.[39] Even if the Russians are successful in breaking the 10 million b/d level, because of the hysteresis of the resource base, pushing 'too hard' over the next few years will undoubtedly reduce the production possibilities thereafter.[40]

Although projects like Tyanskoye, Priobskoye and Tevlin-Russinskoye evidence high engineering and managerial skills, over most of the nineties the industry's ability to bring large new projects online was virtually lost. Producers demonstrated an unexpectedly robust ability to husband their largest producing fields but they were unable to exploit new fields until the last few years.[41] The role of major foreign firms in the Sakhalin projects will provide a good boost to supply from major new fields, but so far, it is only in Sakhalin that outsiders have made a direct and significant contribution to exploiting Russia's oil resources.

Taken together, this analysis paints a band of likely production through 2010 that, in the highest cases, exceeds 10 million b/d but is far less likely to break 11 million b/d. The higher they drive over 10 million b/d, the more technically brittle the production base becomes, and, the more likely that the Russian industry will face the sharply diminishing returns to investment experienced so vividly by the Soviets in the eighties. On the low side of the band, of course, is the possibility of returning to 6 million b/d. However, that path assumes the type of systemic collapse that occurred in the early nineties.

While increases in costs and taxes or a reduction in world prices could drive production down more modestly from its present 9 million b/d level, there will be substantial political pressure opposing declining production.[42] Therefore, the most likely course is in the 9–10 million b/d range.

Production from 2010 to 2020. After 2010, the role of East Siberia will of necessity grow; output from at least the very largest fields in the Nepa-Botubinsk Arch and the Baykit area will become reasonably certain. There will also be greater liquids production from the Sakhalin projects. This includes not only further development of Sakhalin I and II but true new field exploration such as that leading to the 2004 discovery in the Sakhalin V licence area. Sakhalin will be a critical source of Russian export oil for the next two decades. Outside the Sea of Okhotsk (north of Sakhalin Island) and the Pechora Bay (off Timan-Pechora), however, expectations of significant oil before 2020 from the Arctic or Pacific Oceans appear unlikely.

The Russian sector of the Caspian Sea will play a significant role in national production possibilities between 2010 and 2020. If further exploration yields more oil, the region could easily fill in 250,000 b/d to even, optimistically, 500,000 b/d over part of the next decade. If production turns out to be mainly gas, the contribution will be negligible.

Supply in the century's second decade will be a delicate balance. On one side is the decline in old fields, the most important of which will be 30 to 50 years old. The test is not simply to keep them going but to keep their declines in the 1 to 3 per cent range. Also, within the bounds of traditional producing regions, the development of the hundreds of discovered but undeveloped small and medium fields will either heavily cushion declining output in mature basins or their absence will accelerate the fall.

Encouragement of smaller firms will require a deep change in Russian thinking, which almost always equates big with good. Yet, paradoxically, this would be the easiest and cheapest thing the Russian government (mainly by controlling development licenses) could do to extend the present period of growth beyond 2010 and, more importantly, soften the decline that will follow it.

On the other side of the fulcrum of production after 2010 are the new, big projects in remote locations like East Siberia and the Sea of Okhotsk. The challenge to developing these resources is cost. If producers' net income remains very high, cost is not a problem. If world oil prices were to drop to the levels they occupied between 1986 and 1999, little of this oil would be raised.

The band of likely output from 2010 to 2020 has to be widened, relative to that covering the period through 2010. The upper bound must be raised because there is still very substantial exploration potential in Russia and the discovery of several multi-billion barrel fields could significantly change the output profile. The lower bound must be dropped because, although a catastrophic plunge would only attend another national political and economic calamity, after 2010 the Russian oil resource base will be further depleted and only able to sustain a lower equilibrium supply in the face of bad times.

This analysis of production possibilities reviewed what the Russian oil industry *could* do, from the standpoint of economic and technical possibilities – what the rocks and equipment will, and will not, support. Reflection on the country's energy and resource policy options is deferred to the following chapter, this study's conclusions.

Notes

1. Gazprom reported $A+B+C_1$ reserves as of December 31, 2003 at 9.3 billion bbls of condensate and 4.2 billion bbls of oil, for a total of 13.5 billion bbls. *Gazprom Annual Report 2003*, p. 37 (available in English on their website, www.gazprom.ru/eng). Gazprom is particularly egregious at reporting 'reserves' that are economically nonsensical, often, apparently, inventorying any molecule containing a carbon atom. Rosneft reports 'total extractable reserves' of oil equal to 11 billion bbls (available in English on their website, www.rosneft.ru/english).
2. The total, of course, bears the cumulative errors in the individual estimates and, unfortunately, is of necessity the sum of reserve estimates for different years, as 2003 estimates for Sibneft and Surgutneftegaz were unavailable at the time of writing. Reserves change slowly in the absence of acquisitions or divestitures. It was assumed, therefore, that the errors introduced by the differences in vintage were small. Neither company has made large acquisitions. Although acquisitions change company totals, they do not affect the national sum, as they are merely transfers between Russian producers.
3. As reserves constitute a stock variable, they net the difference between the gross addition to reserves and production over the course of the year. Therefore, gross proved reserve additions would have to exceed the 3.3 billion bbls expected to be produced in 2004.
4. The purpose of an estimate of proved reserves is to reflect how much oil is at the immediate disposal of the producer, for which the required investments have virtually all been made. This is not true of the two lesser categories. A roughly applicable analogy, demonstrating why it is wrong to add proved, probable and possible reserves, is as follows. Imagine a vintner, applying for a short-term loan. The vintner has an inventory of wine, which can be used as collateral for the loan. This volume of wine is the result of having harvested the grapes, produced the wine, bottled and stored it. Because of required aging, the wine may need additional time before sale.

   There is some risk on future prices, as all the wine may not be immediately saleable. Nevertheless, all but the costs of storage and transportation to market have been covered and there is little uncertainty surrounding the economic evaluation of the wine collateralizing the loan. The inventory of bottled wine is the vintner's proved reserves.

   In the longer run, the vintner would be expected to add wine that might be produced in future years, including from expansion of the vineyard to new areas of established productivity. These could be considered the vintner's 'probable' reserves. 'Possible' reserves add wine that might be produced in the future, if the vintner is successful in cultivating additional land for which there is only very poor evidence of its productivity and little investment has been made beyond the acquisition of rights to cultivate the land.

A bank, evaluating the vintner's collateral, might consider the future potential that could come through successful expansion of the vineyard. However, for a short-term loan, the vintner's 'bankable' assets are limited to the wine in bottles, his or her proved reserves. To add proved, probable and possible yields a sum that mixes assets that actually exist with those that do not, and are increasingly speculative (see Appendix II for more detail).

5 'Top Secret Oil', *Pravda*, April 29, 2004 (*www.english.pravda.ru* / main/18/89/357/12652_oil.html).

6 C.D. Masters, D.H. Root and R.M. Turner, 'World Conventional Crude Oil and Natural Gas: Identified Reserves, Undiscovered Resources and Futures,' US Geological Survey Open-File Report 98-468 (1998). The data from the study by Masters, et al., were aggregated to the entire former Soviet Union and did not report the Russian Federation separately. The authors did, however, report basin-level assessments.

The basin-level data were used to reform the aggregate for the Russian Federation. This was accomplished using Monte Carlo summation of the basin-level distributions. The data input were the 95 per cent and 5 per cent fractiles reported by Masters, et al. It was assumed that the distributions' functional form was lognormal and that all the basins were statistically independent (both common, but not the only, assumptions used in resource assessment). Further, only very coarse allocation was performed to account for basins that cross national boundaries. Finally, the Masters team analysis was as of the mid-nineties, so there is a vintage problem as well. Therefore, the values reported here for undiscovered resources should be regarded as rough approximations of what the authors would have reported, had they reported a separate analysis for Russia.

Gregory Ulmishek, of the USGS, has provided a series of extremely valuable basin-level updates and expansions of the Masters' world assessment (in which he was the principal assessor for the former Soviet Union). They are in USGS Professional Papers 2201a, c, f and g (all available at the USGS web site, *www.usgs.gov*). However, they do not cover all Russian basins, so cannot be directly used to update the 1998 Masters, et al, aggregate estimates.

7 Lawrence J. Drew and Emil D. Attanasi, 'Firm Size and Performance in the Search for Petroleum,' in S.I. Gass, ed., *Oil and Gas Modeling* (Washington, DC: National Bureau of Standards, 1980), pp. 466–89.

8 It is not that very large firms cannot produce small fields (some state oil companies do it). In general, however, big companies shun such opportunities because they do not fit the big-company cost structures or investment criteria. This is probably the profit-maximizing solution for large firms. However, without an extensive fringe of smaller firms to exploit what are the majority of fields in Russia, it will be increasingly difficult to hold the decline of the key, post-peak field class to a very low level.

9 As of the second half of 2001, it was estimated that the Russian government lost $1 billion (or about 2 per cent of federal revenues) for every one

dollar Brent fell below $18/bbl. 'Mousetrap, Russia Readies for Price War with OPEC,' *Nefte Compass*, September 29, 2001, p. 6. It is likely that the revenue-dependence on the price of oil is higher in 2004 than it was in 2001.
10 'Mousetrap, Russia Readies for Price War with OPEC,' op. cit., p. 6.
11 As early as 2001, Simon Kukes, then CEO of TNK recognized that 'low production costs in Russia are a temporary phenomenon,' citing upward pressure on electricity prices, wages and the funds required for upgrading pipeline transportation. 'Barber of Siberia, Kukes Maps out TNK Restructuring,' *Nefte Compass*, May 31, 2001, p. 6.
12 'Taxman, Putin Pledges to Raise Taxes on Oil Companies,' *Nefte Compass*, December 31, 2003, pp. 5–6.
13 Fiona Hill and Clifford Gaddy, *The Siberian Curse*, op. cit., p. 222.
14 While it would seem that raising Timan-Pechora production is technically trivial, due to the higher cost structure of operations and transport in the basin, its production is much more sensitive to changes in taxes and oil prices than in West Siberia or the Volga-Ural basin, where operating costs are lower.
15 Rosneft, 'Prirazlomnoye Oil Field,' *www.rosneft.ru/english/projects/prirazlomnoye.html*.
16 Sergei Chernyshov, 'Without a PSA,' *Russian Petroleum Investor*, June/July 2003, pp. 15–20.
17 Administratively, the extreme eastern and north-eastern parts of the West Siberian basin fall within the Krasnoyarsk Kray and its subdivisions. Therefore, by the first-order administrative division of the country, they are considered to be in East Siberia.
18 Sergei Chernyshov, 'Rancor over Vankor,' *Russian Petroleum Investor*, August, 2003, pp. 31–7.
19 The Tyumen Oblast is divided into the Khanty Mansiysk Autonomous Okrug (A.O.) in the south and the Yamal-Nenets A.O. in the north.
20 Rosneft, 'Vankorskoye Oil Field,' *www.rosneft.ru/english/projects/vankorsk.html*.
21 For a recent review of the petroleum geology of this area in English, see Gregory F. Ulmishek, *Petroleum Geology and Resources of the Nepa-Botuoba High, Angara-Lena Terrace, and Cis-Paton Foredeep, Southeastern Siberian Craton, Russia* (U.S. Geological Bulletin, 2201-C) (2001).
22 For a recent review of the petroleum geology of this area in English, see Gregory F. Ulmishek, *Petroleum Geology and Resources of the Baykit High Province, East Siberia, Russia* (U.S. Geological Bulletin, 2201-F) (2001).
23 Vladimir Baidashin, 'Seeking a Partner,' *Russian Petroleum Investor*, September 2002, pp. 22–8.
24 The Sakhalin II project has an ongoing liquids component, the development of the Piltun-Astokhskoye field, which went online in 1999 and from 2000 to 2002 produced in the 30,000 b/d range. While liquids production from Sakhalin II is scheduled to increase, the centrepiece of the project is natural gas production to feed 9.6 million tonnes per year liquefied natural gas

(LNG) plant for export to the Asian market. See Vladimir Baidashin, 'New Era for Sakhalin,' *Russian Petroleum Investor*, August, 2003, pp. 38–48.

25 By the Soviet/Russian A+B+C$_1$ standard (which overestimates remaining potential, therefore underestimates depletion), approximately 50 per cent of Russian oil is gone and 25 per cent of its gas, but only 10 per cent of originally recoverable condensate resources has been produced. While the absolute values of these levels of depletion are negatively biased, their relative relationships are probably on the mark.

26 Those of the oil industry were, and are, known as *neftyaniki*, or oil men. There were never any *kondensatniki*, which is why so much of this resource remains today.

27 In their defence, wells to the Cenomanian reservoirs were cheaper (because they were 5,000 feet shallower), they had superior flow rates and higher per well recoveries than the condensate-laden Neocomian reservoirs. The Neocomian reservoirs are also more geologically heterogeneous and often exhibit complex relationships between hydrocarbon phase and reservoir pressure/temperature regimes (making them more expensive and tricky to manage). As a result, tapping the shallow dry gas first was logical. Nevertheless, Gazprom did not just place the condensate reservoirs in second place – they avoided them.

28 Vladimir Baidashin, 'First JV in Yamal,' *Russian Petroleum Investor*, October 2003, pp. 13–19.

29 'Wag the Dog, Companies Question Russian Rules Over Oil Search,' op. cit., pp. 1–2.

30 A part of the problem is high discount rates used in the industry. Given an exploration project initiated immediately in East Siberia or the Kara Sea, even if quickly successful and developed on a fast track, it would not yield first oil for 10–15 years. With the high (explicit or implicit) discount rates used within the companies to evaluate such projects, the net present value of such a programme is doubtlessly too low to attract much investment support. The higher the discount rate used, the exponentially stronger the prejudice against projects with long lead times.

31 Rosneft, responsible for the project from the Russian side, estimated that the recoverable hydrocarbons are in the range of 700 million to almost 3 billion bbls. 'Kurmangazy at a Glance,' *Russian Petroleum Investor*, June/July 2003, p. 41. Note this source reported the oil resources as 'in-place.' They were divided by three to yield the range above.

32 Lukoil, 'Lukoil Plans Activities in North-Western Federal District,' [Press Release], February 2, 2004, *www.lukoil.com/press.asp?div_id=1&id=2200&year=2004*. It is also very uncertain how much of this 'exploration' is drilling out fields that were actually discovered in Soviet times and how much is associated with true new field prospects on which there had been no previous drilling or were not previously identified.

33 Sergei Chernyshov, 'Turn in the Road,' *Russian Petroleum Investor*, June/July 2003, p. 31.

34 In forwarding a proposal to the government in which his company would

take a leading role in developing the fields in the Nepa-Botoubinsk area, Rosneft President Sergei Bogdanchikov, estimated that for development of the area to be profitable, more than 1.8 billion bbls of oil would be required. *Russian Petroleum Investor*, April 2003, p. 27.
35 Not counting the TNK-BP merger.
36 Vladimir Baidashin, 'Arctic Fountain,' *Russian Petroleum Investor*, March, 2003, p. 45.
37 Even the Russian Ministry of Natural Resources, in its estimate of oil and gas resources uses a ratio of 2:1 in favour of gas on a BOE basis in the Kara Sea. Vladimir Baidashin, 'Arctic Virgin Shelf,' *Russian Petroleum Investor*, November/December, 2003, pp. 17–19.
38 This concern applies to a number of the world's major oil exporters, where very high production from a very small number of fields dominates national supply.
39 Estimates that occasionally appear in the Russian and Western press about the possibility of Russia producing 12 million b/d or more by 2010 or 2012 are usually the result of mechanical multiplication and addition of theoretical productive capacities without attention paid to the timing of projects or the probability of their occurrence. See, for example, the estimate of J.J. Traynor of Deutsche Bank in 2003. *Nefte Compass*, November 6, 2003, p. 2.

Another variant on the same theme has been offered by Julian Lee of the Centre for Global Energy Studies. His estimate of future Russian supply, based on a presentation at the Canadian Energy Research Institute Conference (March, 2004), seemed to rely on a rather arbitrarily fit gamma function to Russian historical production data to predict that Russian production will hit a maximum as high as 13.3 million b/d in 2015. Julian Lee, 'Future Russian Oil Production, The CGES View,' Canadian Energy Research Institute 2004 Oil Conference, March 28–30, 2004. See also, Julian Lee, 'Waking the Bear: The Outlook for Russian Oil Production,' *Geopolitics of Energy*, Issue 26, No. 10 (October, 2004), pp. 9–16.
40 The Russian government's long-term energy plan (extending to 2020) also predicts a range of production that, in 2020, gives a base case production of 9 million b/d and optimistic case of 10.4 million b/d. Inessa Barges, 'Long-Term Look,' *Russian Petroleum Investor*, August 2003, pp. 6–14.
41 Eleven years ago, the author and a group of six Russian and American colleagues built a mathematical model to forecast annual oil production from Russia and other former Soviet republics for the period 1993 through 2000. The model was based on engineering analysis of most of the fields mentioned in the present study. Overall, the forecast for Russia was quite accurate. It correctly predicted the end of declines in the mid-nineties; it had only a -3.3 per cent average error in forecasted national production between 1993 and 1999 (-4.4 per cent, including 2000, because of the large increase in production that year) and, throughout the forecast period, actual production was within the 50 per cent confidence intervals for the forecast.

Like this study, fields were divided into groups, including the very largest producers and those projects that were highly promising, but awaiting production. While the national-level forecast had only small errors, the field-group-level forecasts consistently *under*estimated companies' ability to stem the rate of decline at the old major fields. Offsetting this error, however, was a significant *over*estimate of oil coming from the new promising projects that were anticipated over the nineties. It is these projects that, after 1999, finally started to make the contribution that was technically available during the nineties. Therefore, our error in forecasting the supply to be added by new projects was exactly the same one the Russians have consistently made themselves – the predicted productive capacity was correct, but the timing was optimistic. J.D. Grace, A.Z. Zolotov, E.M. Khalimov, N.A. Krylov, D.I. Heather, W.A. Benninger and G.A. Gabrielyants, *CIS Oil 2000* (Dallas, TX: Troika Energy Services, 1993).

42 Political support is assumed but not guaranteed. Even political mismanagement could drive production down. Consider, for instance, the statement by President Putin's key economic advisor, A. Illarionov, that the industry could get along just fine in a $12–$15/bbl-world. At $12/bbl, Russian production would drop sharply. 'Kremlin Adviser's Views,' *Russian Petroleum Investor*, April 2002, p. 12.

CHAPTER 7

CONCLUSIONS

Centuries of Western commentaries have closed with the deduction that Russia is a paradoxical place. Some of their failures to pierce the inconsistencies arose from outsiders' poor understanding – some did not. Like the country itself, Russia's oil industry is what geologists would call a 'type-section,' or exemplar, of ambiguous, and often contradictory, evidence.

Russia holds a massive volume of physical oil, but much of it is uneconomic. Its oil industry enjoys a vast pool of highly educated and experienced labour, but more than could ever be efficiently employed. In the nineties, industry privatization colossally enriched a small clique of insiders; in the present decade, the state may be reclaiming those assets in the name of the people – or maybe just distributing them to a new circle of loyalists.

The context of revolutionary change in Russia over the past 15 years makes understanding its oil industry just that much harder. One strong historical lesson of 135 years of modern oil production in Russia is that it reacts very poorly to an unstable environment. Each major paroxysm, the 1905 Revolution, the First World War-Bolshevik Revolution-Civil War, the Second World War and the collapse of the USSR, terminated a period of record growth in output with a precipitous decline.

So, it is in the midst of a cycle of disruption, when the dynamics of production are least certain, that we seek to answer the question – will Russia recover to set another new, even higher, mark than the 11.4 million b/d made in 1987?

Motivating higher output are prices and producer net incomes unknown in the new industry's 13-year history. Growth is an article of faith for Russia's oil companies. At the field level, they are ready to efficiently apply new investment funds, furthering both short- and long-term projects to increase supply. The present administration in Moscow promotes greater production, particularly exports, not only to feed its oil-and-gas-addicted budget, but as a channel for world political influence it would very much like to enlarge. There are powerful forces supporting escalation.

Yet technical, economic and political constraints bound this pursuit.

Moreover, there are larger questions to be settled on the wisdom of increasing supply, the role of oil in the national economy, the division of the nation's oil wealth, and the political power that comes with it. Oil is central to Russia, so it is critical to get the right answers. High prices and a stable government give the nation and industry the opportunity to make these decisions outside of the crisis exigencies that have filled most of the years since independence from the USSR.

Russia's Oil Resources

Russia has more territory, onshore and offshore, than any other country. It encompasses the world's richest hydrocarbon province, West Siberia, and a prolific convergent margin that stretches 1,200 miles along the western flank of the Ural Mountains. It will doubtlessly benefit from its highly prospective perch on the Pacific Rim, facing a family of basins that has proved very productive elsewhere. Russia's discovered and estimated undiscovered oil resource bases are among the very largest on the planet.

A giant oil resource base is a fairly flexible asset. It will respond to high levels of investment with high levels of production (and to low levels with declines). Because of the magnitude of the resource base and the geology that frames it, Russia has reaped the advantage of having tremendously large fields. As there is perhaps no stronger influence in petroleum economics than scale, these super-giant fields supported levels of output that could not have been achieved had the same volume of oil been distributed over a larger number of smaller fields. If the biggest field in West Siberia had been 1 billion bbls EUR, instead of over 20 billion bbls, the basin might not have been developed at all and Russian supply would have looked much different.

Yet these resources are not limitless. It was the assumption of infinite oil and gas that trapped the Soviet government in a Faustian bargain with the industry: ever more funding for ever more oil and gas. Before depletion intruded, they got away with it. Oil, and then gas, fuelled the largest economic expansion in Soviet history and ultimately made the USSR the world's largest producer of both. But what goes up must come down.

As the finitude of their resources asserted itself in the late seventies and eighties, the limits to supply were swiftly met. It was not that Russia ran out of physical oil. Instead, first they faced the consequences of past short-sighted engineering management: if 'ends justify means' is a bad philosophy in general, it is a disastrous engineering principle. More generally, they hit very sharply and intractably diminishing returns to investment in both exploration and production.

The Soviet economic system caused many of its oil supply problems and exacerbated others. However, the dynamics of the peak in the eighties were much more closely tied to the lognormal distribution of field sizes, efficient discovery of the largest fields first and components of basin maturation that are ideologically neutral. Even if the USSR had somehow struggled on throughout the nineties, oil production would still have crashed (although less dramatically). With further evolution of a market economy for Russian oil in the present decade, these natural constraints may be eased, but they will not be lifted.

While Russia's remaining physical oil resources are gigantic, as inputs to supply they must stand in the context of the capital, labour and environmental costs of their exploitation. Cost and timing divide the nation's discovered oil resources into three cohorts. First, of course, are the proved reserves – 68 billion bbls at the end of 2003. By definition, these volumes are technically recoverable and economic to produce under present conditions; they are immediately available.

Assuming 2004 production will be just over 9 million b/d, Russia's proved reserves can support a plateau at that level for several years, even without the contribution from major, new and imminent projects. Yet production from proved reserves will eventually and inevitably decline. This is because of the natural fall in fields already beyond their engineering maximums and because presently-growing fields, the output of which has boosted Russian production since 1998, will soon hit their own peaks. Moreover, while the 68 billion bbls of proved reserves are presently economic, progressively rising operating costs, tariffs and taxes will erode that volume, unless insulated by sustained extraordinary oil prices (as in 2004).

Economically tougher is the next cohort, composed of oil volumes that fall in probable and possible reserves. Some of this oil is in producing fields. To the extent that it is in good reservoirs the Soviets left behind in their breakneck exploitation of fields' very largest accumulations, these are cherries to be picked. Although they bear capital costs for development, these volumes will share the same transportation costs and (even probably lower) operating costs as proved reserves. To the extent these lesser-quality volumes were left behind by poor Soviet water floods, or in small, thin and tight reservoirs, they are high-cost resources unlikely to be accessed soon.

Finally, there are discovered oil fields, without production, which form the tranche of supply around which the greatest uncertainty exists. At one end of the cost spectrum are excellent development opportunities, proximate to existing infrastructure, which remained unexploited only because of the chaos of the last decade and the capital limitations on Russia's producers. These are, however, generally small- to medium-size fields. While fields this size can be highly profitable, in the West they are typically developed by smaller companies. Collectively, however, their contribution will be to soften the production decline of mature areas, rather than to raise national supply.

In the middle of the last tranche of discovered, non-producing fields are a number of large targets of opportunity for the industry: from the Caspian Sea to onshore Timan-Pechora, continuing offshore into the Pechora Bay, in West Siberia and near the new producers off Sakhalin Island. These fields carry special technical development challenges (e.g., offshore, complex geology, distance from infrastructure), but are large enough that economies of scale will, in the end, secure their contributions to supply. These are the fields with the potential to raise Russian output at the end of this decade and into the next. However, these near-term, high-capacity, moderate cost projects do not exist in large numbers – there are only a dozen or so.

At the distant end of discovered, undeveloped fields, are those very large accumulations in remote and hostile locations: East Siberia and in the Arctic Ocean, under the Kara and northern Barents seas. Capital costs of development and operating expenses will be much higher across the board for these fields. In almost all cases, they must shoulder very large transportation costs, requiring long new pipelines to be built in difficult locations. Moreover, at least initially, the largest projects in each area must underwrite the entire transportation cost. These fields also entail more pressing environmental concerns than attend the less sensitive volumes in proved reserves or fields within established producing areas. These factors not only substantially increase delivered costs, they push the supplies out in time.

The ultimate rate at which Russia exploits its non-producing resources must not only balance volumes against costs at the extensive margin, but a growing share of new production will always be dedicated to filling the gap created every year by the decline in post-peak fields. Here, the performance of Russia's fields since the beginning of this decade has been somewhat deceptive.

Largely by exploiting one-time gains, Russian producers actually got a significant number of their previously neglected post-peak fields to *increase* production. But that trend cannot last long. It has spawned the naïve hope that all Russian fields will continue to increase as long as prices remain high. Yet *all* of the nation's legacy producing fields, which have performed so well over the last few years, will start down again. Technology and better management will defer and cushion their falls, but cannot prevent them.

This describes a resource base, one of the largest in the world, which is already supporting the world's highest or second highest rate of production.[1] It should not be expected to continue the strong growth of the past few years. It *could*, if there were a massive political and economic plan to direct a very large portion of Russia's wealth to that end. Such a programme could come from a renationalized industry bent on world market leadership – irrespective of the cost. It could also come from a private industry buoyed by record oil prices, unfettered by higher taxes, tariffs and costs, transportation bottlenecks or state policies to purposefully limit production. It could also arise from some combination of both.

A more likely path, given Russia's resource base, with its cost and logistic characteristics, is slowing growth, followed by a plateau that can be held for a number of years, then a slow decline.

The Role of Oil in Russia

Since powering the Soviet recovery from the Second World War, oil has remained at the core of the Russian economy. Oil and gas bought the Soviet regime years of longevity, forestalling the consequences of fundamental flaws in its system. The cheap oil began running out at the end of the seventies and the direction of benefit reversed between the Soviet oil industry and the state, the former ultimately consuming far more than it contributed. After that point, rather than oil postponing the inevitable, it hastened it. The financial burden of the bargain between the Soviet government and its oil and gas industries could be borne no longer. It collapsed, with the Soviet structure itself following close behind.

Plummeting oil production in the early nineties mirrored and intensified Russia's macroeconomic disintegration. After the 1998 rouble devaluation and the flourishing of world oil prices, when Russia's oil industry recovered, nearly single-handedly it dragged the nation out of depression.

The surging macroeconomic recovery this decade has restored to the populace some of the massive loss of wealth suffered after the failure of the USSR. Economic strength also bought Russia an essential measure of international independence. The European Union may object to domestic oil and (particularly) gas price controls as free-trade-violating subsidies to Russian manufacturers. But they can be fended off for a

Conclusions   217

few more years simply because the next quarter's federal budget is no longer dependent on international aid.

However, while Russia is now much healthier than it was five years ago, oil has also placed its economy in the ranks of those critically dependent on supplying the rest of the world with highly price-volatile natural resources. Recent worldwide experience indicates that this does *not* consistently lead to sustainable and broad economic development.[2] Moreover, on a psychological level, being chiefly a purveyor of raw materials makes Russia, recently a Superpower, into much more of a Third World Country. That disappointment colours much of Russians' attitudes toward a market economy, oil companies and the role of oil itself.

Despite the liabilities of over-reliance on natural resources, oil and gas continue to propel national policy. President Putin's goal of doubling the nation's gross domestic product by 2015 features income from oil and gas as a primary support. In its image of the nation's energy wealth, Moscow sees a powerful lever to catapult itself into competition and cooperation with its European neighbours as a peer. Russia's natural resources are part of its comparative economic advantage and state management of their performance will ensure that advantage is exploited principally to support national goals.

The present Russian administration does not see markets, particularly in key natural resources, as intrinsically valuable. Instead, they are powerful tools, to be managed by the right hands, directed to the right purposes. Moreover, there are control points that will not be left to markets – like oil and gas transportation, ownership of subsurface minerals and, generally, the right to export natural resources from Russia.[3]

The view of oil and gas as strategic resources under close state control not only sets the limits of Russian companies, it defines the courses available to foreign firms seeking to enter. The current administration's plan for foreign participation in Russian oil is restricted. Outsiders contributing to and leading remote, high-cost, technically complex projects will continue to be allowed – even encouraged. Equity stakes by foreigners in Russian producing companies are also in-bounds. As Russia's financial markets continue to mature, capital of all nationalities will increasingly mix. However, the 50:50 deal between TNK and BP will stand as a high-water mark, unlikely to be revisited.

The Putin government's vision of state-steered economic development explains much of the political marginalia surrounding (and increasingly overprinting) the oil and gas industries. The move against Khodorkovsky and Yukos not only served to renationalize ill-lost assets, but protects administration policy and leaders from the friction of independence and opposition. Renationalization of the gas industry also reverses privatization judged now to have gone too far. The amalgamation of Rosneft and Gazprom forms a single, powerful and ascendant instrument of state policy, the controls of which will be centralized in the small group of men that immediately surrounds the Russian president.

What remains quite uncertain is Putin's goal. Is the pursuit of returning more of Russia's natural resource assets to government control for the benefit of the Russian people, or is it merely a redistribution from individuals who supported Yeltsin to those who serve Putin? A half-dozen of the president's top advisers, in their official capacities, now staking top management positions in oil, gas and electricity, could be inserting ranking state agents directly into energy industry operations. It could also be anointing the next generation of Oligarchs (Bureaugarchs?). That they hail from St. Petersburg, rather than Moscow, and owe their fealty to Putin, rather than Yeltsin, will neither advance the equity of how Russia's wealth is distributed nor contribute to its generation.

Efficiency is also on the line in the revanchism that has and will continue to re-expand direct government management of the oil industry. Gazprom and Rosneft share a mixed technical record. Gazprom is the world's largest producer of natural gas but by dint of inheritance, not recent achievements. Rosneft, while transforming its profile over the last two years, raised output mainly by acquisitions, and those were won with state muscle, not business acumen. It will be increasingly difficult for Moscow to expand the share of productive capacity under its direct management and, at the same time, to expand production.

The New Russian Oil Industry

The development of the post-Soviet Russian industry stands as the most important development in the world oil market since the empowerment of OPEC in the seventies. Its influence derives not just from being the world's largest, or second largest, producer; or for ranking as the biggest, or second biggest, exporter. Those impacts are leveraged because Russian companies, and the environment in which they operate, are still rapidly evolving. This dynamism leads to a much wider band of uncertainty around its future performance than surrounds the oil industries of Saudi Arabia, or the United States. This greater risk enlarges the impact Russian production has on the price of future world supplies.

While still in flux, the one essential change that differentiates today's industry from the Soviet model stands little chance of being undone. Russia's oil producers now raise the revenue required for operations from the sale of oil on markets. They are no longer funded from the state budget. The industry may become more concentrated and the state may play a larger direct role, but probably none of even the most conservative elements of the Putin administration want to see the Soviet Ministry of Oil resurrected.

The economic consequence of the Soviet paradigm was an industry that was morbidly obese and woefully addicted to ever-increasing funding. That a robust collection of producers emerged from such a mire after only a half dozen years of fibrillation is itself remarkable. That the industry is highly concentrated and bears a deep imprint of its Soviet heritage is not surprising, nor is it threatening to future supplies, as long as the present narrow structure does not become ossified.

The asset legacy of the Soviet regime to which Russian producers acceded was not only an exceptional natural endowment, but the (rusting) infrastructure that a decade earlier supported twice the productive capacity. This gave producers, fortified by the income rush after 1998, a very wide spectrum of largely one-time gains to exploit. It also financed development from the Soviet inventory of several very large, untapped fields. Together, these sources raised output from just over 6 million b/d in 1997 to more than 9 million b/d in 2004.

This is not to belittle a 50 per cent increase in production over half a dozen years. Performance since 1998 has been and remains an extraordinary engineering and managerial accomplishment. But much of the gain was ephemeral and not subject to either extension or repetition. Once well repairs at the old fields are complete, Soviet sucker-rod pumps replaced with modern equipment, water floods optimized and well stimulation programmes made routine, the old fields will again begin to decline.

As the five majors and two big regional independents cover 80 per cent of national output, the industry is highly concentrated. Yet, at the same time, among these companies is an unexpected diversity. Surgutneftegaz, Tatneft and Bashneft are archetypes: solidly Russian companies, led by Soviet-era managers and still very much in the moulds of the pre-1992 producing associations from which they sprang. At the other end is TNK-BP – a hybrid unimaginable in Soviet times.

Surgutneftegaz demonstrated that the old model did not have to be replaced, but could be fixed. While it is starting to strain under the resource limits imposed by its Soviet-era geographic domain, Surgutneftegaz has acquired depth and billions of dollars in retained earnings by measured and intelligent investments in engineering. Its technical, managerial and financial strengths, very powerfully augmented by its political orientation, will ultimately allow the company to secure a future that transcends the list of fields it inherited when the USSR dissolved. The company's secrecy and insularity may impede its corporate access to world markets, but $8 billion in the bank and good friends in the Kremlin are probably more valuable right now.

Lukoil occupies the middle ground. As company CEO Alekperov said, Lukoil knows the 'limits.' Staying away from the limits is what puts the company in the middle ground and, at the same time, at the top of the industry. Lukoil genuinely took Western major oil and gas companies as an initial paradigm for corporate structure and strategy. That the blueprint was often poorly translated into Russian is true; 'strategic acquisitions' came out 'shopping binge,' 'international operations' became 'showcase projects,' 'increase capacity' turned out to be 'buy production.'

Nevertheless, the Western integrated major model also gave the company a business attitude that kept its corporate mind in its fields and refineries, rather than courtrooms (like TNK and Sidanco), or distracted by non-oil pursuits (like Yukos). Lukoil has been yeoman-like, but not aggressive, in its management of Western technologies and service-company relationships. It has been number one in the industry by most important measures in all but the last couple of years, when Yukos won several key positions. As Yukos disappears, those remaining first-prize ribbons will be returned to Lukoil.

Lukoil leads the industry because, despite all of its corporate experimentation, it has remained sufficiently focused to turn in a solid technical performance and sober enough to realize where the political boundaries were, and to stay within them. Failure to improve production in its legacy West Siberian fields is a black mark. However at the same time, the company's success in the Caspian demonstrates broad leadership and that region's production may redeem the opportunity cost of poor performance in its home base. The programme for developing Timan-Pechora, which appears to be forming now (several years *after* the acquisitions), is also well founded and potentially advanced by its new partnership with ConocoPhillips.

That the TNK-BP merger occurred, has survived almost two years, and is apparently performing very well is a shocking success. Before the merger, TNK and Sidanco often seemed more like street gangs than oil companies. Time with their British partner appears to have centred the Russians and perhaps enlivened the partner. The company has a profound resource base for both short-term and long-term development.

As a mixed company, it must compete carefully with the unimpeachably full-blooded Russian Surgutneftegaz and Gazprom/Rosneft to retain its East Siberian assets. Because TNK and Sidanco still bear the mark of original sin from the Loans for Shares and kindred programmes of the Yeltsin years, politically wayward moves could be severely answered by Moscow. Yet if it stays within limits, consolidates some within its corporate structure and prices don't fall, prospects are bright.

Sibneft, despite a stand-out performance since the beginning of the decade, is probably in an unstable position, given the configuration of today's industry. It is too small for the league formed by Lukoil, Surgutneftegaz, TNK-BP and Yukos, which is why it was joining Yukos before that company's demise. If there were a hearty band of independent oil companies, Sibneft would head it. But with that sector wobbly and shrinking, it is an unlikely avenue.[4] Sibneft could be acquired by a larger company (including Gazprom/Rosneft – renationalizing more of the assets lost in the Yeltsin years). It could apply for permission in Moscow to take on a foreign partner – giving it the gravitas to be a full-fledged major oil company.

Sibneft stands astride an enviable set of fields; its refinery in Omsk was one of the most modern inherited from the Soviets. The company's management of Western technologies and service company relationships has been effective and a competitive advantage not as fully enjoyed by the larger majors. Yet, Sibneft's distinction as the most contrived of all Loans for Shares schemes could always come back to haunt it. That its largest shareholder, Roman Abramovich, is probably the most ostentatious of the remaining Oligarchs extends its risk. That may be why its principal shareholders are reportedly looking for buyers to convert their holdings into more liquid and fungible assets.

Finally, of course, there is Yukos. Restricting consideration to its performance before and separate from the Yukos Affair, around 1999 or 2000 the company appeared to have changed. Although born into the centre of the Loans for Shares intrigue, in the present decade, it led the industry in financial, reserve and ownership reporting; it became serious about re-engineering legacy fields and, after years of dithering, got the nation's top new field, Priobskoye, rising at a striking rate. Its combination with Sibneft could have been truly win-win – Sibneft getting needed capital, Yukos gaining a fresh slate of undeveloped fields and an accomplished local management team to bring them online.

Yet the transparency at the level of annual reports may have glossed over intricate details that gave rise to the tax charges facing it. That should be determined in an independent judicial framework, but it is unlikely to happen. Irrespective of the finer points of Russian tax law, one thing is certain. Yukos did not understand the limits of operation under the Putin regime, in the way Lukoil did (and that came naturally to Surgutneftegaz). So, all its 'good works' – from drilling to exploit reservoir heterogeneities, to reserve reporting under SEC definitions (as well as using the SPE/WPC and Russian systems), to GAAP financials, to outside (even foreign) directors on its board – came to nothing. Its good works may have even aggravated the crime of being out of bounds, because the company started to look all too Western.

The most telling measure of the jeopardy of private investments in Russia arising out of the Yukos Affair will be the price at which Moscow sells Yuganskneftegaz to settle the Yukos tax claim. If the price is near or above a reasonable range of market values around $15 to $17 billion, President Putin has placed respect for the investments of thousands of (innocent) common stockholders ahead of crushing Khodorkovsky. If the sales price is a fraction of the subsidiary's asset value, uncompensated expropriation of stockholders' interests will have been deemed 'acceptable collateral damage' in the campaign to eliminate the Khodorkovsky threat.

The industry is settling down. Acquisitions that merely traded producing assets, and did not expand national supply, are slowing. Greater attention is being applied to engineering fields in hand, rather than the prowling search for new possessions. Nevertheless, while the acquisitive phase is subsiding, Russian oil companies must more generally confront the question of firm size. Are these business behemoths the most efficient vehicles for either exploitation of existing assets or maximization of shareholder wealth? The same question faces the very largest Western oil companies, with no clear answer.

The other side of the size of firms at the top is the industry's narrowness and concentration. Loss of the small, shrinking second tier of the Russian oil companies looms as a second-order threat to long-run supply. It is not that the large companies cannot produce smaller fields and smaller reservoirs within larger fields, rather that they will not. By allowing those resources to lie fallow, low-cost, more sustainable (and more employment generating) augmentation of supply is forsaken.

A Chance for Choices

Russia's political stability under the Putin administration and the prosperity derived from record oil prices now afford the nation economic and political breathing space that has been absent for decades. It allowed Moscow to rebalance the distribution of power between itself and the oil industry. Within the industry, financial health has sponsored substantial consolidation. It has given engineers in the fields the resources to fix broken equipment, drill new wells and recapture production that was lost, not because it was uneconomic but because of the chaos of the nineties.

The accession of long-desired normalcy provides the opportunity for Russia to examine the larger issues around its oil and is perhaps the best time to take certain actions, the costs of which are dependent on timing. Unfortunately now, when solutions would be best informed by the widest dialogue, the nation's political milieu is ever more unfriendly to diversity of opinion.[5]

Of primary importance is a coherent answer to the question of whether the nation *should* produce more than 10 million b/d by 2010, even knowing that it *could*. This was the question raised in early 2003 by Viktor Kalyuzhnyy, Deputy Minister of Foreign Affairs and oil industry veteran.

Kalyuzhnyy argued that the push to break 10 million b/d will deplete even the nation's moderate-cost oil and raise operating costs to the range of $15 to $18/bbl.[6] The faster the exhaustion of the nation's lower-cost resources, the fewer options either the state or industry has if world prices fall. Critical to longer-run supply, Kalyuzhnyy correctly pointed out that future production is path-dependent. The steps required to exceed 10 million b/d will necessarily damn Russia to a much sharper decline after it peaks, so that by 2020 output could drop as low as 5 million b/d, instead of a shallower path to a higher level of long-run output.

The implications for Russia's choice of output levels will be felt strongly internationally as well as domestically. Therefore, there is much speculation over whether Russia will compete with Saudi Arabia for leadership as the world's premier producer and exporter, or cooperate with it and the rest of OPEC when needed to support the organization's price objectives. Holding the largest proved reserves outside OPEC, Russia's willingness and ability to export is crucial to determining the future of world oil prices. Successful management of exports has two fundamental goals: maximizing revenues and enlarging Russia's international influence.

Russia's relations with other producers, above all OPEC, are central to whatever success is achieved in pursuit of these sometimes conflicting goals. OPEC's ability, and inability, to control supply has been a central determinant of world prices for thirty years. Its future influence depends, more than at any time in the past, on if and how well Russia is willing to support OPEC price targets through controlling its volumes of exported oil. Thus, it is significant that the Crown Prince Abdullah and President Putin have met twice during 2004/2005 and, according to communiqués, discussed cooperation in oil matters.

In the fall of 2004, with world prices vacillating between $40 and $50/bbl, the relationship between Russia and OPEC is of little relevance. Demand largely shapes present prices and the output of nearly all producing nations is at or very near their technical capacities. Production 'discipline' plays no role, as it takes no restraint, in the traditional sense, for a nation to produce as much as it can in the face of record (nominal) prices. OPEC cooperation on volumes is only relevant in a falling market.

In such circumstances, as in 1999 at the beginning of the present period of rising prices, Norway's and Mexico's policies toward OPEC influenced the world market. At that time, OPEC also actively solicited Russia to restrain exports and received weak support. If and when prices swing back down, Russia's attitude toward cooperation with OPEC could either ensure their targets, or make them much easier to break.

While indirectly helpful at times in the early part of this decade, Russia was more often publicly independent of OPEC's strategy. Although it desperately needed export revenues, between 2000 and 2002 Moscow kept one eye focused on export earnings and the other on politics. President Putin aspired to the image of an economic and strategic ally of the West. That political objective required both eschewing 'irresponsibly' high oil prices (for the sake of economic growth in consuming nations) and expressly distancing itself from OPEC.

By 2005, the romance in President Putin's courtship with the West was gone. The government, the industry and the nation have all profited wildly from high prices and the political return to concern over Western economies appears to have all but disappeared. Nevertheless, as long as growing world demand and weak non-OPEC supply outside of Russia keep prices high, Russia's willingness to support or oppose OPEC goals will remain untested.

Cycles in resource prices, however, are the rule. Even so, the recent up-turn in oil prices has prompted a debate about whether this is just another cycle. That is, that demand will eventually slacken at $40+/bbl while both OPEC and non-OPEC producers supply more oil, loosening the market. Or, is the market going through a structural shift, in which prices are lifted onto a new level. In either case, what is Russia to do?

Despite selective use of statistics, Russia cannot deliver oil to consuming nations at a total cost lower than OPEC's main producers.

Therefore, when confronted in the future by lower prices, the margin to Russian producers will be smaller than at least some of the OPEC nations that seek its cooperation. Lower prices, of course, would also hurt Russia. If prices fell precipitously – toward the delivered cost of Russian oil in consuming nations – producers would begin to cut output. In the absence of compensating reductions in tariffs, taxes and operating costs, the first loss would be investments in long-run capacity. With further price erosion, current production would fall. World prices that would throttle investment are less than $20/bbl. Given that $15–$20/bbl oil does not appear likely, this test might also be avoided.

In restraining exports in support of OPEC, Russia would take a bet that the effect will be to increase or hold prices from falling further and that its revenues from less output would be greater than they would have been had it held output and followed prices down. In going for volume, regardless of the price, Russia would be betting that OPEC alone would take the swing. This might work. On the other hand, the experience of 1999 when the rest of OPEC disciplined Venezuela in its drive for market share might hold a lesson for Russia. There is no easy answer. In either case, becoming a member of OPEC is not the question – the question is which bet would best serve Russian self-interest?

A more interesting and likely case would follow from the elevation of OPEC's actual target band from its level in the mid-$20s to $28/bbl into a range between $30 and $40/bbl. Should Russia help defend *those* prices; or would it?

Ultimately, the answer depends on the relationship between the marginal benefit to Russia of higher prices won by cooperation with the cartel and opportunity cost of withheld production (i.e., the sum of revenues from unconstrained exports plus the present value of market share gained by rejecting limits). Whether Russia gains by cooperation or loses cannot be decided on first principles, but must be empirically determined.

Export policy is, however, more than just controlling the physical volumes shipped out of the country. Of looming importance is the choice of currency in which Russian oil is priced and traded – the tie to the US dollar has cost Russia considerably in recent years. The dollar has depreciated significantly against the euro and that currency denominates the largest share of total Russian foreign trade. This has produced a growing consensus in Russia to move oil pricing to a currency basket basis, in which the euro dominates. Economic theory strongly supports a currency basket approach, the reason to maintain a dollar peg is almost completely political, and that advantage is waning.

Finally, while tacit cooperation with OPEC has improved, it has been spotty. Nevertheless, the oil cartel must view the most recent changes in Russia with quiet pleasure. The state's increasing operational control of oil production augers for a faster arrest of the past six years' growth. Escalating resistance to foreign investment in Russian exploration and production will also restrain supply. The Putin administration's overt repatriation of Yukos will doubtless scare even Russian investors, further raising the cost of expanding productive capacity. Rolling delays in improved transportation further interfere with future exports.

Considering these actions as a trend, as impediments to non-OPEC supply work in OPEC's favour at all prices, the cartel might well relax in its contemplation of Russia's future policy toward cooperation. If production generally is restrained by state policies for good resource-conservation reasons (not immediately apparent), or if it is arrested through deteriorating efficiency under poor state management (early signs are there), exports are likely to fall either way. From OPEC's perspective, when and if low prices return, it will make little difference whether Russian oil on world markets is reined in by explicit collaboration or more general moves by Moscow that handicap supply (even if that is not their intent). Russia, we must remind ourselves, is not a 'joiner' of clubs – it pursues its own interests as it sees them.

In addition to the firming influence on world prices of lower Russian production, a lower-and-slower course also plays to the strength of Russia's resource base. With billions of barrels separated from supply by high costs and long lead-times, measured production and consumption create valuable technologic and economic options in the future. It enables what James H. Billington called 'chronopolitics' – the opportunity set that arises when time is on your side.[7]

Setting taxes and policies on export and licensing to guide output between 9 and 10 million b/d could put Russia on a more sustainable course, similar to that blazed by Norway.[8] At the same time, a much more stable technical foundation for production could be constructed. The development of the hundreds of discovered but undeveloped medium and small fields by medium and small companies will add much more productive capacity over a longer period than the handful of high-profile projects in East Siberia and offshore. Moreover, it builds a hierarchy of producers that gives the majors a market for extension and redevelopment opportunities in large fields that fall below the high threshold of major company profitability.

At the other extreme is the path of fastest throughput – extracting, consuming and exporting all the oil in reach. This was precisely the course followed by the Soviets. It produced a voracious industry that by the end did not create economic opportunities for the country, but devoured them. Concomitant extreme price controls put the nation painfully out of sync with the world economy which Russia now aspires to enter. It dogmatically excluded the consequences of inevitable depletion from any consideration.

On the demand side, the present macroeconomic vitality now permits action on domestic oil price decontrol that earlier would have been too expensive to the economy and population. Movement toward a world parity price would focus oil consumption on its highest and best uses, conserving a vital non-renewable resource and reducing the competition that will otherwise unavoidably grow between domestic and export demands.

Domestic price controls generated a large and rather democratic redistribution of a significant part of the nation's hydrocarbon patrimony in the nineties. However, as the depths of the post-independence depression recede, it seems far more efficient and less disruptive for the industry, if the state pursues fiscal goals through tax policy, not price controls.[9] In the end, while oil companies will (now circumspectly) protest higher taxation, when balanced with price decontrol, the combination could, if desired, be producer-revenue neutral.

Increased income to the government from oil could recoup more of the losses suffered in education, health, housing and pensions during the nineties. With the oil industry seen to be paying its 'fair share,' a badly needed process of rehabilitation with the public would begin. Perhaps while bearing a higher obligation to the national treasury, the industry could achieve a concord with the government on environmental remediation. Russia's 2004 ratification of the Kyoto environmental protocols demonstrated the Putin administration's first positive moves in this area. Experience shows that the Russian oil companies that stay in closest step with the Russian president do best.

Almost all the most serious oil-related environmental damage nationally was inherited from the Soviet enterprises. Yet these sites may potentially become the liability of the private companies that succeeded them. Could that liability be traded back to the state, funding required clean-ups out of the higher taxes? If the Russian government seriously pursued it, such public works could also provide substantial employment in many remote areas where thousands are unemployed, or underemployed, and where few alternatives exist.

The Yukos Affair has elicited near-religious professions by Russia's oil industry leaders of their deep devotion to paying taxes and contributing to their workers, communities and the nation. If there was a time to exploit the new corporate *sbornost'*, this appears to be it.[10] The national economic recovery and lush circumstances of Russia's oil industry will, perhaps, continue indefinitely. History, however, suggests cycles. This implies that choices that are feasible today may be much more expensive later. So while the present propitious constellation prevails, latitude exists for securing a rational, sustainable and proportionate role for oil in Russia.

Over the century and a half of the modern world oil industry, Russia has provided the second largest contribution to oil supply and, except during the 1990s, has ranked as the largest or second largest producer. It will remain a dominant force in the world oil market as well as a central support for the Russian domestic economy. While the structure of its industry was radically transformed by the demise of the USSR, what finally emerged in the present decade is a vigorous set of producers. That the industry will take direction from a mix of market signals and government policies may make it more difficult to predict in detail, nevertheless it is unlikely to diminish its leading role.

Notes

1. In the last two years, Russia and Saudi Arabia have traded places twice as the world's leading producer.
2. A survey within a World Bank study of the impact of the extractive industry on a country's economic growth showed an inverse relationship between macroeconomic growth between 1990 and 1999 and the percentage of extractive industry exports of total exports. Alan Beattie, 'World Bank Digs a Hole for Itself,' *Financial Times* (www.ft.com) February 25, 2004.
3. Subsurface minerals, like oil and gas, are owned by the government. They are licensed to both private firms and state entities over fixed periods of time, during which the licensees have specified rights to explore for economic deposits and, if they are found, produce them. The awarding of licences, while officially regulated by federal law, is still diverse. In some areas, licences are auctioned in bid processes, in others they are negotiated. Unless the project is covered by a production sharing agreement (PSA), the licensees are subject to standard Russian law, including tax/royalty rates applied to oil and gas production.
4. While continuing in its present form seems doubtful, after Yukos is broken apart, if Yuganskneftegaz is sold off, it will still leave Tomskneft and Samaraneftegaz and the company's refining assets in the Yukos structure. If this remnant entity is allowed to exist, it would provide company for Sibneft in the ranks of large independent oil companies. This class is now only occupied by Tatneft and Bashneft, which have special positions because of the ethnically based local governments under which they operate (although both are officially joint stock companies).
5. Although the increasingly authoritarian climate of 2004 may not encour-

age critical debate, it is the first real opportunity to connect discussion of systemic changes with the possibility of accomplishing them. Before the Putin administration, the state was not in control of the economy, so the lively discourse on policy of that time was largely moot. Until 2001 or 2002, Russia's immediate economic prospects were so bad that all choices were Hobson's.
6 Viktor Kalyuzhnyy, 'Plany po dobyche perevypolneny. A zachem?' ['Plans for Production Are Overfulfilled – But Why?']. *Neft' Rossii* [*Russian Oil*] (January 2003).
7 James H. Billington, *Russia in Search of Itself* (Baltimore and London: Johns Hopkins University Press, 2004), p. 73.
8 While the oil companies moan in principle about the burden of measured development policies, any of them would be boundlessly happy if every country in which they operated was like Norway.
9 This is not to imply that decontrol will be sudden or unplanned.
10 The old Russian word *sbornost'* 'expresses a desire to find a measure of common purpose for a people and a culture long rent with splits and schisms.' Billington, *Russia In Search of Itself*, op. cit., pp. 145–6.

POSTSCRIPT

In 1991, a non-violent revolution changed Russia's course from the one it had followed for more than 70 years. It liberated the economy from the strictures of the Soviet command system, but failed to build a new structure fast and broad enough to prevent deprivation across the population. The decade that followed was in many ways a freefall, stretching and tearing much of the economic, social and political fabric of the nation. By the new millennium, most Russians, above all, wanted their lives and country to just be 'normal.'

Vladimir Putin's ascendancy to the Russian presidency in 2000 carried a mandate to restore some of the security and order that 'normalcy' requires. He reasserted the primacy of the central government, not only across the vast nation's constituent regions, but over the small clan of 'Oligarchs'. These men, while state power collapsed in the 1990s, pocketed billions of dollars of national assets and came to exercise political power to protect and enlarge their fortunes.

In pursuing a new equilibrium, the Putin government appreciated that a decade of 'market' economics had generated wealth for Russia as only imagined in the Soviet days. But both the government and populace also well knew that the *laissez faire* of Boris Yeltsin's presidency produced a massive distortion in the distribution of much of those riches. Business magnates and government officials, corruptly tied, ensured that very large shares of Russia's natural resource and industrial patrimonies were divided among very few individuals.

Russia is the world's second largest oil exporter. Rising oil prices throughout the Putin administration dramatically leveraged that position, affording the government an opportunity to rebalance the economy in favour of greater state ownership and control. It slowed privatization, tightened enforcement of corporate taxation and regulation (which had become impotent by the end of the 1990s), maintained controls on domestic energy prices and progressively narrowed the prospects for foreign investment in mineral and hydrocarbon resources.

Starting in 2003, the growing state role in the national economy was mirrored politically by increasing intolerance of opposition and application of state action against individuals and institutions perceived as threats to the administration. Some part of the new authoritarianism simply filled the vacuum created by the chaos of the Yeltsin years. However, by momentum or design, centralization of power in the president's hands has reached a level unprecedented in recent Russian history.

In addition to replacement of locally elected leaders with Moscow appointees, President Putin has inserted members of his inner entourage into top management slots in industry, energy in particular. Concentration of authority in the person of the president and empowering personal delegates to fill state and private functions is not the Soviet model. But it *is* Russian: it harks to medieval tsars and their *boyar* retainers, a small class of men who stood both inside and outside court, acting as the eyes, ears and instruments of the tsar, with fealty pledged to him personally.

Of course, neither sixteenth-century tsars nor twentieth-century commissars enjoyed the validation of national elections. Moreover, political opposition is alive, if anaemic, and while 'strategic' industries operate under increasing state control, much of the Russian economy is market-based and likely to stay that way. What the events of the six months since the completion of this book have crystallized is the maturation of a second phase of post-Soviet development. The fact that it roughly mixes medieval instruments and e-commerce perhaps makes it more genuinely Russian – hence a more stable state than the overreaching 'Westernism' of the first post-Soviet decade.

The entwined defence of Kremlin power and recapture of ill-lost national assets from the 1990s was displayed most overtly in the destruction of Russia's largest oil producer, Yukos. As of October 2004, when this study was completed, the outlook for Yukos was grim, with dissolution a near certainty. The largest move in the final act played at the end of year, when the company's central subsidiary, Yuganskneftegaz, was deeded to the state oil company, Rosneft. The rump Yukos, left with a small minority of the original corporate assets, still faces tax judgments doubtlessly exceeding its likely auction value and is therefore insolvent. While some sort of 'Yukos' may survive in name, the corporate entity described here no longer exists; the remaining divisions will likely find new homes in short order.

The dénouement of the 'Yukos Affair' confirmed the worst outcome suggested in Chapter 5, composed of two parts. First was that the government would use its tax case against Yukos to sell Yuganskneftegaz for far less than its market value. Second was that the receiver would be Rosneft, the state oil company only last fall betrothed to the state gas monopoly, Gazprom.

The undervaluation of Yuganskneftegaz demonstrated President Putin's indifference to the loss of equity by common shareholders, those distant from the company's top leadership, who had become the target of Kremlin enmity. That a few individuals ran foul of the Russian president and ended up in jail or exile is not what deterred (particularly foreign) investment in 2004. It was that expropriation became a tool used so bluntly in Russia that it could hit innocent investors whose only offence was loose proximity to enemies of the administration.

In selecting Rosneft to receive perhaps the most promising short-run oil assets in the country, the administration signalled a readiness to trade efficient management for enhancing state ownership and control. Neighbouring Surgutneftegaz, a private company highly loyal to the Kremlin, has the financial and technical resources for effective stewardship of Yuganskneftegaz's fields. It would have probably paid billions more to the state treasury at a real auction. Yet at decision time, state control won over cash and economic efficiency, with Russian oil supply as one of the collateral losers.

Further chilling the environment, in February 2005, with some practical confusion but clear intent, the government announced that henceforth, ownership (and operatorship?) of 'strategic resources,' like some (but not all?) oil and gas fields, would be limited to companies that were at least 51 per cent Russian. While the international oil industry boasts more than a few cases of deep interference in their host nations, Russia is not exactly under the threat of BP hegemony.

Lack of clarity may have been intentional. If 'majority-Russian' and 'strategic assets' are left vague, the policy becomes even more potent in defining narrow spaces in which foreign investment will be allowed. As an independent judiciary is still absent, interpretation can be individualized, giving high-level appointees authority to pass on proposals, based on either national or much narrower interests. The rule also implied that the Putin administration, buoyed by four years of rising oil prices, presumed that the nation's capital requirements can be met internally, and that funding is the only value foreign investment brings.

By March, however, calls of concern arose over recent faltering in economic growth, the threatened prospects for missing long-term national goals and even dropping oil production. Slowing investment and capital flight were seen at the root. Recognizing at least some connection to its destruction of Yukos, the Kremlin again assembled the Oligarchs and scions of ex-Soviet industry. Pardons were proposed for Yeltsin-era crimes; tax authorities would be leashed; Yukos was a 'special case,' they were promised and the protection of future stability was assured – all in return for needed investment (and that the assembled remember the lesson from the last meeting about staying out of politics).

The putative goal of the compact between Putin and the mighty

– raising Russian living standards through greater investment in Russia by Russians – publicly aligned all parties with the national good. Yet in principle, there is not a large difference between the *quid pro quo* of President Putin allowing these men to keep their wealth and the one offered by President Yeltsin giving it to them to start. What the March meeting witnessed on a deeper level was another case of reliance on personal relationships rather than institutional mechanisms to effect change. The individuals gathered in the Kremlin were offered private relief in return for their contribution. The administration did not present broad fiscal or regulatory improvements that would stimulate the market for investment generally – but a set of personal deals tendered to a small group.

These events, played out at much higher scales, have reached down to the oil fields. The rate of growth in Russian oil production, which had averaged 9.6 per cent (year over year) from the beginning of 2003 through the second quarter of 2004, began to fall steadily thereafter. From September 2004 through February 2005 (the latest month available), production actually declined from month to month. Some of the damage traces directly to the demolition of Yukos. Yet output from industry leader Lukoil has been disappointingly flat. Increases at Surgutneftegaz and TNK-BP averted a greater turn down, but even they reportedly declined in January 2005.

The best reading is that the industry is taking a breath after a stunning six-year sprint. Growth surely could be re-fired by several new large fields that are close to production. Moreover, this redoubt shows no signs of the type of collapse that crippled the industry in the early 1990s. It assumes that the 2004 drop at Yukos was ephemeral and Rosneft will restart the engine that raised output by 80 per cent in the previous four years.

A more probable interpretation is that oil production is being hit by the same retreat in investment seen nationally. That Yukos exploded in the oil industry's midst makes it even more likely that investment in the sector is particularly affected. Exacerbating the drop in new money for wells and equipment is that at production levels between 9 and 10 million b/d, Russia is again meeting the steeper, less elastic portion of its supply curve. Some giant old fields, re-invigorated over the last five years, are again slipping into decline; large new projects face delays and higher costs.

Recent drops in production, while informative on the future course of supply, do not now portend fundamental changes. Russia is and will probably indefinitely remain the world's largest or second largest producer and exporter of oil. Oil will remain as a central force in the

Russian economy and in politics. The nation would probably be much better off if oil were not as important. Yet the economic premium to its resources grows in lock step with world prices as well as the dangers of high dependence on a scarce, depletable and volatile resource. The last six months have highlighted, not diminished oil's role.

John D. Grace
6 April 2005
Long Beach, California

APPENDIX I

NOTES FOR MAPS AND FIGURES

Maps

The maps included in this study were generated with ArcMap 8.3 geographic information system (including two of its extensions, Geostatistical Analyst and Spatial Analyst). Almost all of the source data exist in 'shapefiles,' which is a format for map data that is proprietary to Environmental Sciences Research Institute (ESRI), the developer of ArcMap. Shapefiles have the extent .shp. The cartographic information provided for each map gives the coordinate projection systems used in ArcMap.

For maps 2–13, there is a reference map inserted to show the location of each map within Russia (also showing the other republics of the former Soviet Union). The red star in the map is the location of Moscow.

Cartographic Data

The following cartographic standards were used in the generation of the maps appearing in this study. They are reported in the forms used in the coordinate system dialog boxes used in ArcMap.

Table 20: Cartographic Data for Maps

Maps	Projection	Longitude/ Latitude of Centre	Central Meridian	Latitude of Origin	Standard Latitudes	Spheroid
Reference	North Pole Orthographic	100/50				GCS_WGS_1984
1	Asia North Lambert Conformal Conic		100	30	15/65	GCS_WGS_1984
2	Geographic		0			D_North_American_1927
3-6	Asia North Lambert Conformal Conic		60	30	15/65	GCS_WGS_1984
7-13	Asia North Lamber Conformal Conic		72	30	15/65	GCS_WGS_1984

236 *Russian Oil Supply*

Data Sources

Embedded Reference Maps
Country outlines: country92.shp (ESRI).

Map 1
Country outlines: country92.shp (ESRI).
Basin outlines: basin.shp (Earth Science Associates).
All other data (physiography and cities) are from Digital Chart of the World (ESRI)

Map 2
Country outlines: country92.shp (ESRI).
Field outlines: International Exploration and Production Database (fields.shp) (IHS Energy).
All other data (physiography, railroad and cities) are from Digital Chart of the World (ESRI)

Map 3
Country outlines: country92.shp (ESRI).
Field outlines: International Exploration and Production Database (fields.shp) (IHS Energy).
All other data (physiography and cities) are from Digital Chart of the World (ESRI)

Map 4
Country outlines: country92.shp (ESRI).
Field outlines and $A+B+C_1$ Estimated Ultimate Recovery: International Exploration and Production Database (fields.shp) (IHS Energy).
Distribution of sandstone and shale: (Peterson, James A. and James W. Clarke, 'Petroleum Geology and Resources of the Volga-Urals Province, USSR.' US Geological Survey Circular 885 (1983), p. 16) scanned and registered in Equidistant Conic (World), central meridian = 54 and reprojected as described in Table 20.
All other data (physiography and cities) are from Digital Chart of the World (ESRI)

Map 5
Country outlines: country92.shp (ESRI).
Field outlines and $A+B-C_1$ Estimated Ultimate Recovery: International Exploration and Production Database (fields.shp) (IHS Energy).
Top Romashkino structure: (Peterson and Clarke, op. cit., p. 22) scanned

and registered in Equidistant Conic (World), central meridian = 54. Structural contours converted to x,y,z triplets and gridded with ordinary Kriging, second order trend removal, 50 per cent global estimation, default calculation of anisotropy, neighbourhood search with 10 (minimum 5) points and resultant grid reprojected as described in Table 20.

All other data (physiography and cities) are from Digital Chart of the World (ESRI)

Map 6
Country outlines: country92.shp (ESRI).
Field outlines: International Exploration and Production Database (fields.shp) (IHS Energy).
Structural elements: (Peterson and Clarke, op. cit., p. 14) scanned and registered in Equidistant Conic (World), central meridian = 54 and reprojected as described in Table 20.
All other data (physiography and cities) are from Digital Chart of the World (ESRI)

Map 7
Country outlines: country92.shp (ESRI).
Field outlines: International Exploration and Production Database (fields.shp) (IHS Energy).
All other data (physiography and cities) are from Digital Chart of the World (ESRI)

Map 8
Country outlines: country92.shp (ESRI).
Field outlines: International Exploration and Production Database (fields.shp) (IHS Energy).
All other data (physiography and cities) are from Digital Chart of the World (ESRI)

Map 9
Country outlines: country92.shp (ESRI).
Field outlines: International Exploration and Production Database (fields.shp) (IHS Energy).
Samotlor structure: (J.A. Peterson and J.W. Clarke, 'West Siberian Oil-Gas Province' US Geological Survey Open File Report No. 89-192) scanned and registered in Equidistant Conic (World), central meridian = 72. Structural contours converted to x,y,z triplets and gridded with ordinary Kriging, second order trend removal,

238 *Russian Oil Supply*

50 per cent global estimation, default calculation of anisotropy, neighbourhood search with 10 (minimum 5) points and resultant grid reprojected as described in Table 20.

All other data (physiography and cities) are from Digital Chart of the World (ESRI)

Map 10
Country outlines: country92.shp (ESRI).

Field outlines and $A+B+C_1$ Estimated Ultimate Recovery: International Exploration and Production Database (fields.shp) (IHS Energy).

Bazhenov total organic carbon concentration: Gregory F. Ulmishek, *Petroleum Geology and Resources of the West Siberian Basin, Russia*, US Geological Survey Bulletin 2201-G (2003), p. 23 scanned and registered in Equidistant Conic (World), central meridian = 72. Total organic carbon contours converted to x,y,z triplets and gridded with ordinary Kriging, second order trend removal, 50 per cent global estimation, default calculation of anisotropy, neighbourhood search with 10 (minimum 5) points and resultant grid reprojected as described in Table 20.

All other data (physiography and cities) are from Digital Chart of the World (ESRI)

Map 11
Country outlines: country92.shp (ESRI).

Field outlines and $A+B+C_1$ Estimated Ultimate Recovery: International Exploration and Production Database (fields.shp) (IHS Energy).

Hydrocarbon generation from the Bazhenov shale: Calculated based on A.E. Kontorovich, 'Geochemical Methods for Quantitative Evaluation of the Petroleum Potential of Sedimentary Basins' in Gerard Demaison and Roelef J. Murris. *Petroleum Geochemistry and Basin Evaluation* (Tulsa, OK: American Association of Petroleum Geologists), p. 105) scanned and registered in Equidistant Conic (World), central meridian = 72. Total organic carbon contours converted to x,y,z triplets and gridded with ordinary Kriging, second order trend removal, 50 per cent global estimation, default calculation of anisotropy, neighbourhood search with 10 (minimum 5) points and resultant grid reprojected as described in Table 20.

Structural elements: (I.I. Nesterov, 'Tektonicheskaya Karta Mezozoysko-Kaynosoyskogo Platformnogo Chekhla Zapadno-Siberskoy Plity' ['Tectonic Map of the Mesozoic-Cenozoic Platform Section of the West Siberian Plate'''] (1974) in A.E. Kontorovich *Geologiya Nefti I Gaza Zapadnoy Sibiri* [*Geology of Oil and Gas of West Siberia*]

(Moscow: Nedra, 1975) (attached map)) scanned and registered in Equidistant Conic (World), central meridian = 72 and reprojected as described in Table 20.

All other data (physiography and cities) are from Digital Chart of the World (ESRI)

Map 12

Country outlines: country92.shp (ESRI).

Field outlines and $A+B+C_1$ Estimated Ultimate Recovery: International Exploration and Production Database (fields.shp) (IHS Energy).

Neocomian isopach: Derived by subtracting structural contour map of top of Neocomian from structural contour map of top of Bazhenov (J.A. Peterson and J.W. Clarke, 'West Siberian Oil-Gas Province' US Geological Survey Open File Report No. 89-192, pp. 101 and 116.) scanned and registered in Equidistant Conic (World), central meridian = 72. Matrix of differences in depths gridded with ordinary Kriging, second order trend removal, 50 per cent global estimation, default calculation of anisotropy, neighbourhood search with 10 (minimum 5) points and resultant grid reprojected as described in Table 20.

All other data (physiography and cities) are from Digital Chart of the World (ESRI)

Map 13

Country outlines: country92.shp (ESRI).

Field outlines: International Exploration and Production Database (fields.shp) (IHS Energy).

Company assignments and areas: Earth Science Associates.

All other data (physiography and cities) are from Digital Chart of the World (ESRI)

Figures

Figure 1

Note: The Soviet/Russian curve switches in 1992 from the total USSR to only the output of the Russian Federation.

Sources: Russian Soviet Production: For 1860–1915, 1918–20, 1929–40 and 1946–78 Marshall I. Goldman *The Enigma of Soviet Petroleum, Half-Empty or Half-Full?* London: George Allen & Unwin, 1980, pp.14–15 and 22–23; for 1942–1945, Robert E. Ebel, *The Petroleum Industry of the Soviet Union* (Washington, DC: American Petroleum

Institute, 1961), p. 74; for 1941 Robert W. Campbell, *Trends in the Soviet Oil and Gas Industry* (Baltimore, MD: Johns Hopkins University Press, 1976), p. 122; for 1979–91, PlanEcon, *Energy Outlook*, 'Comprehensive Review and Forecasts to the Year 2015 of Energy Developments for the Former Soviet Republics,' Washington, DC: PlanEcon, Inc. (March 1992), p. 5; for 1992–2001, Energy Intelligence Group, *The Almanac of Russian and Caspian Petroleum*, 2002 Edition, New York: Energy Intelligence Group (2002), pp. 7–8; for 2002, US Energy Information Administration, 'Country Analysis Briefs: Russia,' *www.eia.doe.gov/emeu/cabs/russian.html*; for 2003, *Nefte Compass*, January 22, 2004, p. 5. Production data through 1917 are for Imperial Russia, for 1918 through 1991 for the USSR and after 1991 for the Russian Federation.

US Production: For 1860–1970: US Census Bureau, *Historical Statistics of the United States, Colonial Times to 1970* (Bicentennial Edition), Washington, DC: US Government Printing Office (1975), pp. 593–4; for 1971, Pennwell, *1996 Energy Statistics Sourcebook*, 1996 Edition, Tulsa: Pennwell Publishing Company (1986), p. 92; for 1972, Pennwell, *1986 Energy Statistics Sourcebook*, 1986 Edition, Tulsa: Pennwell Publishing Company (1986), p. 82; for 1973–2003, US Department of Energy, Energy Information Administration, June 2004 Monthly Energy Review *tonto.eia.doe.gov/merquery/mer_data.asp?table=T03.01a*.

Saudi Production: For 1938–79: US Department of Energy, Energy Information Administration, Office of Oil and Gas, *Middle East – Crude Oil Potential from Known Deposits* (DOE/EIA - 0298, 1981), pp. 17–18; for 1980–2003, US Department of Energy, Energy Information Administration *tonto.eia.doe.gov/merquery/mer_data.asp?table=T11.01a*; Saudi natural gas liquids data where not included with crude, 1970–2003, US Department of Energy, Energy Information Administration, *www.eia.doe.gov/emeu/ipsr/t43.xls*. For 1938–69 crude oil only, 1970–2003 crude oil plus natural gas liquids.

Figure 2
Source: Basin-wide production: International Exploration and Production Database, IHS Energy.

Figure 3
Note: The logarithmic vertical axis is the estimate of ultimate field recovery (EUR) as made under Soviet $A+B+C_1$ standards (see Appendix II). The three symbol types and three regression lines correspond to the three major structural elements in the core of

the basin (regression statistics for all three lines are given in Table 21).

Sources: A+B+C$_1$ field estimated ultimate recoveries (Oil EUR): International Exploration and Production Database, IHS Energy. The regression was ordinary least square. The regression equations and statistics are:

Table 21: Regressions of Discovery Size versus Discovery Year for Top Volga-Ural Basin Trends (ln (Discovery Size in MM bbls)) = $\alpha + \beta$ (Discovery Year)

Region	α	Standard Error of α	β	Standard Error of β	R^2	Size Halving Time (Yrs)
S. Tatar Arch	170.7	6.04	-0.0852	0.0030	0.25	9.0
Birsk Saddle	163.3	13.66	-0.0812	0.0069	0.23	8.5
Bashkir Arch	260.3	6.85	-0.1304	0.0034	0.62	5.3

Figure 4

Note: Until the end of the sixties, the five largest fields dominated, particularly Romashkino. The second generation consists of 65 fields with A+B+C$_1$ EUR between 100 million bbls and 1.5 billion bbls. The third generation consists of over 700 fields with A+B+C$_1$ EUR less than 100 million bbls.

Source: Annual field production data: International Exploration and Production Database, IHS Energy. Second and third generation fields are classified in this study.

Figure 5

Note: The top of the figure shows the locations of three wells identified in Map 5. The vertical exaggeration is 1:300.

Source: Cross section of Romashkino field modified from James A. Peterson and James W. Clarke, 'Petroleum Geology and Resources of the Volga-Urals Province, USSR,' US Geological Survey Circular 885 (1983), p. 23.

Figure 6

Note: The columns show oil production from the Romashkino field, the line shows percent water of the oil and water mix raised by the field's production wells.

Source: Annual production data and water cut for Romashkino: Earth Science Associates.

242 *Russian Oil Supply*

Figure 7
Source: This study.

Figure 8
Source: Basin-wide production: International Exploration and Production Database, IHS Energy.

Figure 9
Note: The trend is clearly exponentially downward and there has been a smaller, but steady fall in the variance of field sizes discovered each year over the 40-year history of the basin. The line is a linear regression of the log data (regression statistics are given in Table 22)
Source: A+B+C_1 field estimated ultimate recoveries (Oil EUR): International Exploration and Production Database, IHS Energy.
The regression was ordinary least square. The regression equations and statistics are:

Table 22: Regressions of Discovery Size versus Discovery Year for West Siberia (ln (Discovery Size in MM bbls)) = α + β (Discovery Year)

Region	α	Standard Error of α	β	Standard Error of β	R^2	Size Halving Time (Yrs)
West Siberia	160.04	14.33	-0.079	0.007	.18	8

Figure 10
Note: The figure shows the relative contribution to West Siberian production of the three top fields in the basin and the collective contributions of the second, third and fourth generation giant discoveries as well as the output of all 'other' fields in the basin.
Source: Annual field production data: International Exploration and Production Database, IHS Energy. Field generation is classified in this study.

Figure 11
Note: The location of the cross section is shown in Map 9 along line A-B. The numbers in the map correspond to the wells identified by number in this cross section. The field's largest reservoir, the BV_8, is at the top of the Megion Formation. The vertical exaggeration is 1:150.
Source: Modified from A.E. Kontorovich, *Geologiya Nefti i Gaza Zapadnoy*

Sibiri [Geology of Oil and Gas of West Siberia] (Moscow: Nedra, 1975), p. 489.

Figure 12
Note: This figure shows the size range of fields brought on line during the development of the West Siberian basin. The largest and smallest fields are represented by the top and bottom of each bar, the mean EUR is shown by the large dot. Although the mean size declined exponentially, the most abrupt changes were dropping the minimum field size in the eighties and nineties. Note that the y-axis, field size, is logarithmic.
Source: A+B+C_1 field estimated ultimate recoveries (Oil EUR): International Exploration and Production Database, IHS Energy.

Figure 13
Source: This study.

Figure 14
Note: Domestic consumption includes Russian refinery demand for crude oil to produce petroleum products that are exported.
Sources: Soviet and Russian consumption/export data: for 1960–76, Marshall I. Goldman, *The Enigma of Soviet Petroleum,* op. cit., p. 23; for 1977–85, Margaret Chadwick, 'The Growth and Pattern of Soviet Oil Trade,' in Margaret Chadwick, *et al, Soviet Oil Exports,* op. cit., p. 32.; for 1987–2002, Energy Intelligence Group, *The Almanac of Russian and Caspian Petroleum* (2003 Electronic Edition) (New York: Energy Intelligence Group, 2003), Main Indicators workbook; for 1991, PlanEcon, *Soviet Energy* Washington, DC: PlanEcon, Inc. (March 1992), p. 24. Production data through 1991 is for the USSR and after 1991 for the Russian Federation.

Figure 15
Note: Data through 1985 are for the entire USSR, data from 1992 on apply only to the Russian Federation.
Sources: Soviet and Russian production data, see Figure 1.
Number of producing wells: for 1960–72 Robert W. Campbell, *Trends in the Soviet Oil and Gas Industry,* op. cit., pp. 28, 102; for 1973, *World Oil* (August 15, 1974), p. 104; for 1974, *World Oil* (August 15, 1975), p. 124; for 1980, *World Oil* (August 15, 1981), p. 204; for 1984, *World Oil* (August 15, 1985), p. 92; for 1987, *World Oil* (August 15, 1988), p. 74; for 1988, *World Oil* (August 1989), p. 85; for 1989, *World Oil* (August 1990), p. 75; for 1992–2002, Energy

Intelligence Group, *The Almanac of Russian and Caspian Petroleum*, 2003 Electronic Edition, Main Indicators workbook. All other years interpolated.

Figure 16
Note: After 1998 the growth of producing wells came principally from the repair of idle wells rather than drilling new ones.
Sources: Total producing wells, new wells and idle wells: Energy Intelligence Group, *The Almanac of Russian and Caspian Petroleum*, 2004 Electronic Edition, Main Indicators workbook (1987–2004).

Figure 17
Sources: See sources for Figures 1 and 16.

Figure 18
Note: The average sales price of oil is represented by the top of the columns each year. From that value, each of the three cost components is subtracted. From 1993 through 1998, that yielded a loss on each barrel produced (represented by the distance below zero at the bottom of each bar). Starting in 1999, the subtraction of the three cost components from a much higher oil price gave producers net income with which to invest in productive capital.
Source: Estimates of prices, excise taxes, tariffs and operating costs: Earth Science Associates.

Figure 19
Sources: Rouble/dollar exchange rate: Energy Intelligence Group, *The Almanac of Russian and Caspian Petroleum*, 2002 Electronic Edition, Exchange Rate workbook (January 1996–May 2002); Energy Intelligence Group, *The Almanac of Russian and Caspian Petroleum*, 2003 Electronic Edition, Exchange Rate workbook (May 2002–December 2002); www.cbr.ru/eng/currency_base/daily.asp (January 2003–December 2003).

Figure 20
Source: Brent crude price: US Department of Energy, Energy Information Administration, www.eia.doe.gov/emeu/international/Crude1.xls (January 1998–December 2003).

Figure 21
Sources: Monthly Russian crude oil production: *Russian Petroleum Investor* (July 1998–December 2002). Monthly Russian crude oil production:

Nefte Compass (January 2003–December 2003). November 2000 and October 2002 were interpolated.

Figure 22
Note: The area in grey represents total cost, vertical dashes represent total revenue and the cross-hatched area represents consumer surplus captured by Russian consumers through domestic price regulation. The numbers on the production (x) axis in italics in this and Figures 23–26 reflect numbers in the corresponding table. The demand functions in this appendix are not drawn as constant elasticity due to limitations in the drawing software and because it would make little difference, visually, given the low level of estimated elasticity.
Sources: Production: See source for Figure 1
Consumption: See source for Figure 14
World price at Russian border: this study
Domestic price: this study
Elasticity of oil demand: Cooper, 'Price Elasticity of Demand for Crude Oil: Estimates for 23 Countries,' op. cit.
Elasticity of oil supply: this study

Figure 23
Note: In addition to the relationships prevailing in 1987, the world price from 1983 is shown as a grey dashed line. The arrow indicates the large drop in the world oil price between 1983 and 1987. The 1983 supply function is also shown as a grey dashed line (not labelled). The arrow indicates higher costs (and a reduction in supply) in 1987 compared to 1983.
Sources: As for Figure 22

Figure 24
Note: In addition to the relationships prevailing in 1993, total production in 1987 is shown as a grey dashed line. The arrow indicates the large reduction in production between 1988 and 1993. The 1987 supply function is also shown as a grey dashed line. The arrow indicates higher costs (and reduction in supply) in 1993 compared to 1987. The 1987 domestic price is also shown as a grey dashed line, with the arrow indicating its increase to the 1993 level.
Sources: As for Figure 22.

Figure 25
Note: In addition to the relationships prevailing in 1997, total produc-

tion in 1993 is shown as a grey dashed line. The arrow indicates the large reduction in production between 1993 and 1997. The 1993 supply function is also shown as a grey dashed line. The arrow indicates substantially higher costs (and reduced supply) in 1997 compared to 1993. The 1993 domestic price is also shown as a grey dashed line, with the arrow indicating its large increase to the 1997 level.

Sources: As for Figure 22.

Figure 26

Note: In addition to the relationships prevailing in 2002, the supply function from 1997 is shown as a grey dashed line (not labelled). The arrow indicates the large reduction in delivered cost (and increase in supply) between 1997 and 2002, principally due to the devaluation of the rouble in 1997. The 1997 world price is also shown as a grey dashed line, with the arrow indicating its large increase to the 2002 level.

Sources: As for Figure 22.

Figure 27

Note: This figure shows composition of oil production by class of producer. The class of 'independents' includes both Russian independent oil companies and joint ventures with foreign firms. The state sector includes the holding company Rosneft and, between 1992 and 1995, a less organized collection of producers directly under state control, as well as the state natural gas producer – Gazprom.

Source: Production by sector: Energy Intelligence Group, *The Almanac of Russian and Caspian Petroleum*, 2004 Electronic Edition, Main Indicators workbook (1987–2003).

Figure 28

Note: The definition of Langepasneftegaz includes Pokachevneftegaz, which was divided out of the former in 1999. Without acquisitions, post-1999 production would have been flat.

Source: Production by subsidiary: Energy Intelligence Group, *The Almanac of Russian and Caspian Petroleum*, 2004 Electronic Edition, Lukoil workbook (1992–2003).

Figure 29

Source: Production by subsidiary: Energy Intelligence Group, *The Almanac of Russian and Caspian Petroleum*, 2004 Electronic Edition, Yukos workbook (1992–2003).

Figure 30
Source: Well stock and well productivity: Energy Intelligence Group, *The Almanac of Russian and Caspian Petroleum*, 2004 Electronic Edition, Yukos workbook (1993–2003).

Figure 31
Source: Production and well productivity for Noyabrskneftegaz: *The Almanac of Russian and Caspian Petroleum*, 2004 Electronic Edition, Sibneft workbook (1993–2003).

Figure 32
Source: Energy Intelligence Group, *The Almanac of Russian and Caspian Petroleum*, 2004 Electronic Edition, Surgutneftegaz workbook (1992–2003).

Figure 33
Note: The subsidiary Chernogorneft (also known as TNK-Nizhnevartovsk) in certain years was a division of Sidanco. The subsidiary TNK-Nyagan was also formerly a Sidanco subsidiary. The category 'other', added in 2003, mainly includes smaller Sidanco units, brought in through that corporation's merger into TNK-BP.
Source: Production by subsidiary: Energy Intelligence Group, *The Almanac of Russian and Caspian Petroleum*, 2004 Electronic Edition, TNK workbook (1992–2004).

Figure 34
Note: Two large Volga-Ural basin producers dominate the sector, Tatneft and Bashneft. Other independent Russian producers and joint ventures with foreign firms make up the balance. As of 2002, the distinction between Russian independents and joint ventures was dropped because of increased mixing of company capital between foreign and domestic sources.
Source: Production by sector: Energy Intelligence Group, *The Almanac of Russian and Caspian Petroleum*, 2004 Electronic Edition, Bashneft, Tatneft and Main Indicators workbooks (1993–2003).

Figure 35
Note: Originally, independent oil producers did not exist. By 2002, many of both types of firms developed substantial mixes of foreign and domestic capital and personnel. The distinction between the two classes disappeared in the major statistical series on Russian production – with all non-majors and non-state entities classified as independents.

248   *Russian Oil Supply*

Source: Number of independent oil companies and joint ventures, *Russian Petroleum Investor*, various issues reflecting year-end production statistics.

Figure 36
Note: Rosneft and its predecessor agencies held a large number of prolific producing units until 1995. After that point, one producing organization, Purneftegaz has dominated Rosneft's output. The other significant contributor is the state gas monopoly, Gazprom.
Source: Production by state entities: Energy Intelligence Group, *The Almanac of Russian and Caspian Petroleum*, 2004 Electronic Edition, Main Indicators workbook (1993–2003).

Figure 37
Note: The numbers next to each section show the amount in billions of dollars and the percentage of the total of all four categories. The wellhead net income is the amount left from total revenues once the other three expenses have been covered. Excise taxes do not include corporate income tax. All capital expenditures (as well as profits) made by the industry are assumed to have come from wellhead net income.
Source: Division of revenues by operating costs, tariffs, excise taxes and net income: This study.

Figure 38
Note: This shows the relationship between the average domestic price for oil in Russia and the domestic parity price as determined by export price minus the cost of transporting Russian oil from a central domestic sales point (e.g. Ufa in the Volga-Ural basin) to the export sales point. The domestic parity price is the price that would have been paid by domestic consumers of Russian oil (i.e. refineries) in the absence of state price controls.
Source: World parity domestic price and/actual domestic price of oil: This study.

Figure 39
Source: Proved reserves for top 15 nations: BP, 'Statistical Review of World Energy 2004'.

Figure 40
Source: This study.

Appendix One 249

Figure 41
Note: This shows the difference between the Pareto distribution of hydrocarbon accumulations and the lognormal distribution of fields in a hypothetical basin. Economic truncation transforms the Pareto distribution of accumulations into the lognormal distribution of fields contributing to supply. The data are hypothetical.

APPENDIX II

QUANTIFICATION OF OIL RESOURCES

Crustal Abundance vs. Resources

There are many purposes for estimating the quantity of oil in a single reservoir, a field, a basin or collectively for a nation. Therefore, it is not surprising that different standards of measurement apply. From a purely scientific viewpoint, it is interesting and valuable to know the total mass of hydrocarbons in a specified volume of the Earth's crust, like the West Siberian basin or worldwide to a depth of 10 miles from the surface. Geologists and geochemists routinely make such analyses of not only hydrocarbons, but for economic and non-economic minerals generally.[1] These are known as crustal abundance studies, the results of which are usually expressed in grams of the target mineral per tonne of crustal rock.[2]

For instance, on average, there are 0.004 grams of gold in a typical tonne of rock (g/t) at the Earth's surface. These types of studies are performed by collection and geochemical analysis of surface samples and, more importantly, drilling small-diameter cores yielding long, skinny cylinders of rock through the depths penetrated. Some anomalously high concentrations are classified as economic ores. These geochemical anomalies, once located, are assessed by denser core drilling, leading to maps of the extent and grade, or richness, of the ore in three dimensions.

Based on those maps, a mine is designed and the rock cut out of the Earth. As the concentration of the target mineral, even in a rich ore, is usually tiny, a vast volume of total rock must be removed to recover every unit of the mineral.[3] For example, gold is typically mined from rocks with ore grades as low as 0.1 g/t but more commonly from 1 to 20 g/t. The midpoint of that range is 2,500 times the crustal abundance concentration. Nevertheless, it still requires about a three tonnes of rock per troy ounce of gold. A mine continues to produce as long as the combined cost of production and recovering the target mineral from the host rock does not exceed the sales price of the mineral at the mine.[4]

Hydrocarbon Resources. In many ways, oil and gas are like most mineral deposits. The accumulations we care about economically come from anomalously high local concentrations in the Earth's upper crust of special forms of organic carbon. The average concentration of organic carbon in the top six miles of the Earth's crust is approximately 656 grams per tonne of rock or 0.065 per cent.[5]

Only a part of the total volume of organic carbon in the upper crust produces oil and gas.[6] To even generate very widely disseminated volumes, there is a minimum concentration, probably around 0.5 per cent organic carbon, required for successful transformation to hydrocarbons. As this is ten times greater than crustal abundance, these accumulations are relatively rare. Further, even where the required density of organic carbon is achieved, only that fraction, which is exposed to the right level of heat over geologic time, converts to oil and gas. Most of the hydrocarbons generated never escape the fine-grained rocks (generally shales) that typically produce them.

Of the volume that is expelled from the source rock, most does not end up in what we recognize as hydrocarbon accumulations of interest for exploitation. Oil and gas migrate slowly through water-saturated rocks that compose most sedimentary basins. As they are less dense than water, buoyancy makes them move toward the Earth's surface. Because of a variety of forces at play at the molecular level, most individual droplets or rivulets of oil and most tiny bubbles of gas stop in isolation in permeable rocks on a path leading from where they were formed to the Earth's surface.[7]

Finally, there is a significant share of generated hydrocarbons that bubble all the way to the surface. There, they form the types of tar pits found and mined around Baku, or the LaBrea tar pits in Los Angeles. Gas escapes through mud volcanoes as in the South Caspian or Mississippi River delta, or, to form massive, relatively disseminated gas hydrate deposits over parts of the ocean floor and in permafrost.

What is left to fill the world's discovered and undiscovered oil and gas fields is that fraction in between. It is the organic carbon that did get converted to hydrocarbons, which did not remain in the source rocks, get stopped in migration or leak to the surface. This is a tiny part of the original crustal abundance of organic carbon. The accumulation of enough hydrocarbon molecules to form a 'field' requires that mobile hydrocarbons over hundreds, to thousands, of cubic miles of rock be focused, typically by buoyancy and stratigraphy, into traps.

In nature, within each basin, the total range of sizes encompassing all these subsurface accumulations of hydrocarbons appears to follow a mathematical distribution in which the number of accumulations rises exponentially with the exponential decrease in accumulation size.[8]

This means that there are a near-infinite number of accumulations of single molecules of oil and gas, usually surrounded by water molecules, isolated in their own private rock pores. They are alone. Then there are an exponentially smaller number of other water-filled rock pores, with pairs of oil or gas molecules, also isolated. Going down the curve, an even exponentially smaller number of pores host three molecules and so on. As the number of molecules in a single pore goes up, they eventually fill it and spill into neighbouring pores, connecting the pore-level accumulations and displacing the water molecules in the pores downward.

Within petroleum geology, there has been strong and sustained interest in the exact properties of the distribution of hydrocarbon accumulation sizes in nature and the processes that govern them. However, of immediate practical concern is this: given that there are exponentially more accumulations as size declines – at what point is an accumulation of hydrocarbons too small to be of value in oil and gas supply to the economy?[9]

Minimum Economic Field Size. No single subsurface accumulation, no matter how small, can be found and produced with less than a single well. If the economic value of the discovered volume of oil and or gas at the wellhead is less than the cost of drilling, equipping and production, the well is called an 'economic dry hole.' While sometimes there are no measurable hydrocarbons present in the drilling target (called a 'geologic dry hole'), usually there is some small quantity.[10]

Sometimes, accumulations found by a well, which are too small to cover the cost of development and production, are actually produced.[11] However, these are rare exceptions. For an accumulation of hydrocarbons to be produced under market conditions, the volume must be sufficient so that when the discounted present value of its development is calculated, it exceeds a threshold of profitability that reflects the risk and opportunity cost of the investment to develop.

As a consequence, for hydrocarbon accumulations in a region with a common distance to market, reservoir depth and oil quality, an average minimum economic field size arises. That is, there will be a threshold size in the volume of technically recoverable oil and gas, below which, an accumulation will not be produced (but will be counted as a show or an economic dry hole).[12]

Minimum economic field size has exceptions that reflect factors other than size that impact the total cost to bring the oil to market. Because of this, a 500,000-barrel accumulation discovered next to a large producing field may be economic. With infrastructure and transportation close at hand, the total cost before reaching the sales point is small enough to yield a profit. Conversely, the first discovery in a remote, hostile basin, like the Chukchi Sea between Alaska and Russia, may have to be at least 3 billion barrels before it is economic. There is no infrastructure within hundreds of miles of the Chukchi Sea and the physical environment is extremely challenging.

Therefore, the minimum economic field size in a region varies based on a variety of factors. However, one regularity endures: the smaller the size of a discovered oil and gas accumulation, the higher the average cost of development and production. Therefore, the smaller the accumulation found by a well, the more likely it is not called a commercial field and the more likely it is classified as a show or economic dry hole.

Economic Truncation. As a result, although the distribution of hydrocarbon accumulations in nature is probably of the Pareto type, the distribution of discovered hydrocarbon fields is not. The left-hand side of the distribution (representing the smallest accumulations) that exists in nature is truncated economically.[13] The accumulations are physically present, but below the minimum size to be considered a field, so these small accumulations never enter the statistics as fields (or add to supply).

The economic truncation of accumulations, such that the smallest sizes are not counted as fields, transforms the Pareto distribution of accumulations in nature into a lognormal distribution of the fields that supply oil and gas to the economy (Figure 41).[14] Within a single basin, while the distribution of hydrocarbon accumulations in nature is fixed, exploration and economics update the distribution of discovered fields constantly.

On the right-hand side of the distribution, where the largest accumulations and fields reside, the distributions of accumulations and fields are identical because accumulations in the billions of barrels are almost always greater than the minimum economic field size (Figure 41). Going left, the distribution passes through accumulations of hundreds of millions of barrels, the curves usually remain equal. However, at sizes less than 50 to 100 million bbls of technically recoverable oil, the two distributions begin to diverge. While there is an exponentially increasing number of accumulations as size gets smaller, at the same time, more and more accumulations fall below minimum economic field size, and are not considered fields.

At some small size, which depends on the basin and changes over time, fewer and fewer accumulations sport the necessary local advantages to be profitably produced (like proximity to a large field). Eventually, going to the extreme left end of the distribution, there are an exponentially skyrocketing number of accumulations, of which none are classified as fields, because they are all way too small to produce. The best of them are shows.

As a result, the Pareto distribution of accumulations in nature continues to rise toward infinity in Figure 41, and the lognormal distribution falls toward zero. The fall to zero to the left of the mode in the field size distribution (and the parting of the two curves some distance to the right of the mode) is the expression of economic truncation. Within a basin, the truncation point itself moves left over time.[15] As more fields are found, more area is close enough to existing production to make smaller and smaller accumulations profitable to produce.

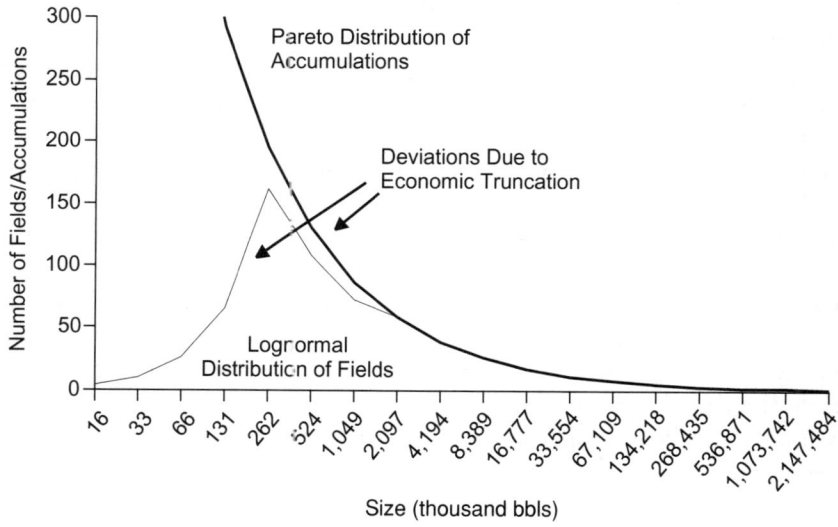

Figure 41: Relationship between Pareto and Lognormal Distribution of Field Sizes

Geology generates the distribution of oil and gas *accumulations* in a basin but economics generate the subset distribution of oil and gas *fields*. This distinction is critical. Only *fields* that contribute to the supply of oil should be counted as oil resources. The distribution of hydrocarbon accumulations in the Earth's upper crust is interesting from a geochemical perspective, but it is an analysis of crustal abundance – not an assessment of the hydrocarbon resources that will enter the human economy as a source of energy.

Recovery Factor. At the reservoir and field levels, the same type of process is at work. Using standard engineering techniques, it is possible to roughly estimate the total volume of oil and gas present within a specific reservoir. This volume is called 'oil in place' in the West and 'geologicheskiye zapasy' [geologic reserves] in Russia. The way in-place volumes of oil and gas are calculated is the same between Russian and Western engineers and geologists and these estimates are pretty uncontroversial.

However, the total volume of hydrocarbon molecules in place within a reservoir never reaches the surface. It does not matter how many wells are drilled, water floods or enhanced oil recovery techniques applied – some oil always remains behind.

Nevertheless, the density of drilling, water flooding, hydraulic fracturing and other well stimulation methods, the use of surfactants in floods, pumping and other measures all influence the fraction of oil in place that is ultimately recovered before a field is abandoned. When a field is finally shut in at the end of its productive life, the cumulative production since inception divided by the estimated total volume of hydrocarbons in place is its ultimate recovery factor.

For oil, recovery factors can, in rare instances, fall below 10 per cent. More typically, around one-third of the oil in place is recovered before a field is abandoned. Less commonly, recovery factors exceed 40 per cent or even 50 per cent.[16]

The recovery factor nets out two sets of influences: one determines the amount of energy required to raise the oil from the rocks to the surface, the other measures the amount of energy applied to the task. The amount of energy required to raise the oil is determined by the geologic characteristics of the field (e.g., reservoir rock permeability, oil viscosity). The second set of factors, reflecting the amount of energy in the reservoir available to move the oil, can be further subdivided. There is natural energy in the reservoir arising from its depth below the Earth's surface. Then there are measures applied by engineers to push the oil toward the surface (e.g., in a water flood), or reduce the amount of energy required to recover the oil (e.g., increase in density of wells drilled, or fracturing and acidizing the rock around well bores). In any field, the more intensive the engineering applications – the greater the recovery factor achieved.

Cost of Recovery. Although more engineering yields more oil, every additional well, every flood programme, frac job or pump costs money. Therefore, a balance is necessarily struck between the cost of investing in these techniques, and the addition to either the rate of production or ultimate volume produced. If the application of a technique (e.g., a surfactant-enhanced water flood) costs more than the value of additional oil it recovers, then it is generally not undertaken. At least in a market system, the producer's prime objective is to maximize economic profit from developing a field – not to maximize the physical volume of oil lifted to the surface.

As all conceivable technologies are not applied to a field because of cost, some (usually most) of the oil in a field is left behind. Even if all economics were suspended and every imaginable technique was applied to a field, oil remains in the rocks. The physics of manipulating forces from the distant surface cannot overcome the electrostatic attraction of oil and gas molecules and rock grains surrounding the pore when only a thin film of hydrocarbon molecules remains.

In sum, the same phenomenon is observed on two scales. There are millions of oil accumulations in the Earth's crust that are too small, or bear other characteristics that make them uneconomic, and prevent their contributing to the supply of oil. They never become fields. In the same way, there are also billions of barrels of oil left behind in commercial reservoirs, when the cost of recovery is greater than economic value of their sale. These volumes never become part of the supply of oil from the fields where they are located.

It is the Russian oil establishment's reluctance to come to grips with these basic facts of oil and gas engineering and economics that most widely separates the Soviet/Russian approach to quantifying oil reserves and resources and the approach generally taken in the West.

The SPE/WPC Reserve Definitions

The Western notion of oil or gas reserves subsets the quantities of hydrocarbons physically present in a reservoir.[17] At their core, the definitions are designed to bridge the distance between the scientific estimation of physical hydrocarbons in place in a field and the economic notion of an inventory. An inventory of oil, for a company producing it, would be a known quantity of oil technically and economically available to the firm.

Reserves are tiered, based on their accessibility to market. The highest level is 'proved,' followed by 'probable' and 'possible.' Proved reserves impose the most stringent requirements, and are the closest to inventories in the sense of on-hand stocks of oil and gas that the producer may bring directly to market, at little additional cost. Probable and possible reserves are encumbered by greater technical and economic uncertainties, and/or, the requirement of additional investments to make those volumes of oil accessible.

Proved Reserves. Proved reserves are defined as:

> Those quantities of petroleum which, by analysis of geological and engineering data, can be estimated with reasonable certainty to be commercially recoverable, from a given date forward, from known reservoirs and under current economic conditions, operating methods and government regulations. Proved reserves may be producing or non-producing.

Proved reserves are limited to those reservoirs that have been drilled and have productivity demonstrated by production or well tests. These may include volumes outside the immediate area of wells, but within reservoir volumes extrapolated only as far as can be reasonably supported by engineering and geologic data. Oil in undrilled reservoirs may not be included.

Only that quantity of the oil that may be extracted under current operating methods qualifies as proved reserves. For instance, take a reservoir where 25 per cent of the oil in place can be recovered in the absence of a water flood and 35 per cent is estimated with a water flood. Until the flood is at least tested with injectors, and a response in production is demonstrated, a recovery factor of 25 per cent must be used for proved reserves.

Likewise, only the recovery factor supported by existing economic conditions may be used. If the price of oil at the time of the reserve audit was $15/bbl and, considering operating costs, only 30 per cent could be extracted from the reservoir at that price, then only 30 per cent of the oil in place qualifies as proved reserves. A higher recovery factor could be achieved by more drilling, better pumps or fracing wells. However, those additional volumes cannot be counted as proved reserves if the prevailing $15/bbl price does not cover the cost of implementing the proposed measures. No oil volumes associated with future investment in wells and facilities can be counted as proved unless they are economic *at existing prices and costs*.

When considering the judgments required in evaluating oil and gas volumes using these criteria, the SPE/WPC guidelines require a 90 per cent level of confidence for proved reserves. This high threshold, limitation to drilled reservoirs, demonstrated recovery methods and availability under prevailing costs and prices are factors designed to strictly limit the volumes. Only oil that is demonstrably there, and immediately recoverable through either existing wells and facilities (or those for which investment is reasonably certain), are included as a high-certainty inventory, much like products stored in a warehouse.

Probable and Possible Reserves. Probable reserves are less certain than proved reserves. Whereas there is a 90 per cent level of confidence in the existence, technical and economic producibility of proved reserves, that standard of certainty drops to 50 per cent for probable reserves. Typically, probable reserves are those volumes in reservoirs requiring more drilling to demonstrate existence and producibility. They also include volumes that could be obtained through additional engineering measures, but those measures have not actually been demonstrated in the reservoir being assessed (or a very close analogue). Probable reserves can, as well, cover oil volumes in the same stratigraphic unit as proved reserves, except that they are separated by faulting or other barriers to hydrodynamic communication with proved volumes.

Possible reserves are those volumes of oil even less certain than probable reserves. They are associated with at least a 10 per cent level of confidence in their existence and technical and economic producibility. These are generally oil volumes in separate and even in some instances undrilled reservoirs not already demonstrated to be commercially productive. Possible reserves cover oil that may be there, but given present operations, could not be produced at a rate high enough to be considered commercially productive. Similarly, this category can include oil that could be obtained with additional investments, but questions exist with respect to the profitability of required investments.

The essence of the proved reserve definition is to admit only those volumes of oil for which there is extreme confidence in their technical and commercial producibility. Generally, the SPE/WPC standard does not demand that all required investments already be made by the 'as of' date of the analysis. The SPE/WPC definitions do require that the volumes of oil would be profitable if produced at that time, so no economic or technical impediment exists that would prevent their production. It is also assumed that the money will be spent and the corresponding oil recovered. The two categories below proved (possible and probable) embrace larger volumes of oil, allowing greater uncertainty on the existence of the oil, its technical recovery and the economic viability of the projects required to produce it.

Since adoption by the World Petroleum Congress, the SPE/WPC definitions have become very widely used in the world industry. They can be calculated by deterministic methods but, increasingly, result from stochastic models that explicitly incorporate and report the uncertainty surrounding estimated reserve volumes and the inputs used to calculate them.

Appendix Two 259

What the SEC Definitions Add

In the United States, an even more conservative standard for reserves is laid on top of the SPE/WPC definitions by the US Securities and Exchange Commission (SEC). The purpose of the SEC regulations is to protect non-specialist investors from being misled and to make reporting by companies under SEC regulations comparable. The SEC goal appears to be identifying that fraction of a company's oil and gas that is most like the inventory of a common firm.

To start, the SEC has only two classes of reserves – proved and unproved.[18] The former are included in the SEC's accounting, the latter are not. The SEC's implicit advice to investors in companies reporting to them is that the only reliable number in assessing the oil and gas assets of a company is its proved reserves.

There are some distinctions between the SPE/WPC and SEC standards that are quite technical (e.g., requiring year-end prices and volumes being within specific distances of completed wells). However, there are two principal differences.

First, some of the criteria of SPE/WPC proved reserves are more simply stringent under the SEC standard. For instance, the SEC is tougher on including volumes that are accessible through enhanced recovery techniques when they have not been demonstrated in the reservoir in question. The SEC also provides explicit guidance on economic producibility demanding that recovery of proved reserves bear a positive net present value rather than the vaguer standard of being 'economic.'

The second difference is more fundamental. The SPE/WPC standard says that there should be no technical or economic impediment to produce proved reserves. SPE/WPC definitions demand producibility characteristics of the reservoir and oil, but place no demands that the producer shows clear intent to develop and sell the proved volumes. The SEC demands that there be a commitment to make the required investments to bring proved volumes to market.

Therefore, if a producer claims non-producing proved reserves, there must be transportation arrangements, financing, sales contracts and other tangible evidence of the decision to spend funds on the volumes claimed. In the same direction, if producing wells are shut-in, even though they may be demonstrably capable of production, the volumes of oil and gas associated must be subtracted from proved reserves as long as they are offline because they are uneconomic.[19]

The joint effect of the differences between the SPE/WPC and SEC standards is that the latter has tried very strictly to limit oil volumes treated as proved reserves to that quantity which is immediately accessible to the producer. In that sense, they have made the meaning of proved reserves as close as possible to the meaning of an inventory.

A company's inventories do not include products that may exist only after major new capital investments; no positive value is assigned to products that cannot be sold at a profit. The common notion of an inventory for a firm is that it consists of products stored at a point in time in a warehouse, ready for retrieval. Because oil and gas also require time for production, in addition to investment, perhaps the closest analogy would be an inventory of wine. When produced, bottled and stored, it needs just the passage of years to be ready for sale. No one would call a few vines on a hillside an inventory of wine. No one should call an undeveloped field without transportation an inventory of oil or gas.

The Soviet/Russian System

The system for quantification of oil resources presently used in Russia is little changed from that developed during the Soviet period.[20] Since then, there have been debates within Russia and refinements proposed. It is, however, fundamentally the old Soviet definitions that operate today. While that system bears some common elements with the SPE/WPC, particularly with respect to the rules for establishing the existence of oil volumes in reservoirs, it was not designed to provide valuable information to an industry operating in a market environment. The USSR was a command economy and thoroughly rejected market mechanisms for all but the last few years of its 75-year history. It should be no surprise, then, that their system for quantifying oil resources should be fundamentally deficient for operations outside a command system.

The Soviet/Russian classification uses a system of letters to differentiate volumes of oil and gas. These classes were based on various criteria, most related to the measure of scientific confidence and engineering evidence for the existence of the volumes of oil covered. The levels go from A, as highest, to D_2, the lowest. All classes require application of a recovery factor to an estimated volume of hydrocarbons in place (called *geologicheskiye zapasy* [geologic reserves]). It is principally in the estimation of this recovery factor that the troubles arise, so discussion of that is deferred to the end of this section and the other aspects of the system are explained first.

Class Definitions. The volume of oil in place, multiplied by a recovery factor, and within the estimated drainage area of a producing well, is classified as an A reserve. If the well is drilled, but not producing, the corresponding volume of oil would be called a B reserve. Except for consideration of how the recovery factor is calculated, Soviet/Russian A reserves would fall within both the SPE/WPC and SEC classifications of proved reserves. With the same caveat, B reserves might or might not qualify as proved reserves – depending on the reason the well was not producing.

If the well was offline because it was new and awaiting facilities for which there was a commitment by the producer to install, then B would be SPE/WPC and SEC proved-nonproducing. If the well was shut in because production costs (including required repairs) exceeded wellhead net income the well would produce, it would not fall under SEC proved and probably not under SPE/WPC proved, either.

There are tens of thousands of idle wells in Russia and sorting them out (at least field by field) would be a large task. This, however, would be required to estimate the number of idle wells that face no economic barriers to production. Those that are economic would be SPE/WPC proved reserves. Of that volume, SEC proved would require a demonstrable commitment by the producers to make the investments required for production.

There are three divisions of the C class reserves. The principal break is between C_3, which is in undrilled exploration prospects, and C_1 and C_2, which cover volumes in drilled reservoirs.

The C_1 class includes the product of multiplying a recovery factor times the oil in place within a reservoir delineated by drilling. It requires that the productivity of the reservoir be demonstrated by production tests. However, the exploitation wells through which oil will be produced remain to be drilled.

Under the Soviet system, after discovery, a set of delineation wells was typically drilled in a field that gained a far denser set of geologic and test data than is typically obtained though Western development practices. Therefore, it was common to have reservoirs drilled on a loose pattern (half the anticipated density of production wells, sometimes less) with no production. In fact, a big share of the hundreds of discovered unproduced fields in Russia are in this state.

The treatment of C_1 volumes under SPE/WPC and SEC is a bit difficult to summarize. The reason is that drilling out a reservoir, at low density with delineation wells not designed to produce oil, is unusual in the Western experience. It is that experience that guides the SPE/WPC definitions. In the West, most commonly, a very small number of delineation wells are drilled. Usually, some, or even all of them are converted to producers. Given this limitation (and ignoring the influence of recovery factor), much of C_1 volumes would be proved-nonproducing under SPE/WPC definitions. Generally, the volume that did not qualify would rest on a finer point of distance from wells. Again, excluding the influence of estimated recovery factor, C_1 volumes that did not qualify as proved would likely make the SPE/WPC probable reserves, or at least SPE/WPC possible categories.

The fraction of C_1 that would qualify under SEC rules is even more problematic (ignoring the influence of recovery factor). The main issue would be the commitment of the field's producer to make the required investment to drill and equip production from the reservoir. If that was highly certain, as evidenced by binding commitments, C_1 volumes could qualify as SEC proved-nonproducing. However, a very large fraction of C_1 volumes in Russia is not in fields facing imminent and certain development. Much of this volume is in fields that were discovered in Soviet times and have languished now for over a decade. They bear highly uncertain prospects for future development. Other C_1 volumes are in reservoirs of producing fields where the commitment to extend development to include them is also questionable. In those cases, C_1 volumes would not qualify for SEC proved.

The class of C_2 covers oil that falls outside specified distances from existing delineation wells. So C_2 volumes tend to be in the undrilled areas of reservoirs that also contain C_1 volumes. This class could also be in reservoirs that were penetrated by exploratory or delineation drilling, but for which production tests have not been run. It is unlikely that any C_2 volumes would qualify as SEC proved and most of the time, the low density of drilling, and/or, absence of production tests would disqualify them under SPE/WPC proved, as well. Some fraction of these volumes could make the SPE/WPC criteria for probable and possible.

The class of C_3 is intended to reflect the estimated volume of oil and gas in place in an undrilled exploration target, times an assumed recovery factor. The target can be within the bounds of a discovered field, in a reservoir not previously drilled. It also includes new field exploration objectives. In all instances, C_3 volumes must be associated with concrete, geologically and geophysically identified exploration targets. They cannot be bulk-volume estimates of resources in a region generally.

Because of the absence of drilling and production tests demonstrating the existence and producibility of hydrocarbons, the C_3 volumes would never qualify as SPE/WPC or SEC proved. It seems they also are too uncertain to be included with SPE/WPC probable. In unusual circumstances within a producing field (i.e., the case of extension exploration), some part of C_3 might qualify as SPE/WPC possible.

The two D categories cover bulk-volume estimates of recoverable resources in a region. They are not associated with identified prospects, but are estimates made on the basis of broad play-level, or basin-level, analysis of geologic and geochemical data and the exploration history of the region. They are by definition, undiscovered oil and gas resources.

The criterion for differentiating the two classes of D appears to have changed since the Soviet period. Generally, the D_1 volumes are in regions where discoveries have shown the regional existence of hydrocarbons (e.g., in the Nepa-Botoubinsk Arch area of East Siberia) and the D_2 are in areas where that demonstration has not yet been made (e.g., the East Siberian Sea). In the West, the term 'reserves' is never properly used to describe undiscovered oil and gas, instead they are referred to as 'resources.' Therefore, the D volumes would never qualify for SEC proved or any of the three SPE/WPC categories.

The Promotion Process. The Soviet/Russian classifications make broad sense within a state-run national industry that was managed through central planning and divorced from the world oil market. Regional geologic and geophysical analysis conducted by the Ministry of Geology assessing a new area would be classified as D resources. When oil volumes included as D had been identified in discrete exploration targets and assessed, corresponding C_3 resources would be credited. After the Ministry of Geology's exploration and delineation teams had drilled successful wells on the prospect, C_1 and C_2 volumes would be declared.

At that point, the Ministry of Geology would engage an independent state organ (called the State Committee on Reserves and known by its Russian initials, GKZ) to certify the reserves and the field would then be titled over to either the Ministry of Oil or Gas for development. As development wells were drilled and facilities prepared on the surface for processing and transportation, volumes in reservoirs intended for production would be further promoted. C_2s would become C_1s with more drilling and tests; C_1s would become Bs when production wells were drilled and Bs would become As when those wells went online. It was a good system for seeing the gross volumes of oil and gas coming down the industry's pipeline. How much of those volumes could and would actually be recovered is another issue, but the system gave an overall view with enough detail on the state of development to facilitate planning.

There are some differences between the SPE/WPC and Soviet/Russian systems based on finer points like how far from a well to include volumes in a specific class. However, the SPE/WPC hierarchy of proved, probable and possible reflects degrees of engineering certainty on existence and technical producibility largely in sync with A, B, C_1 and C_2 volumes. The classes C_3 and below would be regarded as resources in the West and would not enter the *reserve* classification scheme (nor would Russian geologists and engineers claim that they should).

Soviet/Russian Recovery Factors. The fundamental problem differentiating the Soviet/Russian and Western approaches is how the recovery factor is determined, given the demonstrations of existence and technical producibility of specified volumes of oil in place.

In calculating the recovery factor, the Soviet/Russian method seeks to estimate the *maximum* fraction from in-place oil that is technically recoverable. If a stimulation technique would theoretically raise recovery by 10 per cent over production in its absence, the extra 10 per cent would typically be included, even without a demonstration of that result in the field under analysis. From an engineering standpoint, the objective was to include all volumes that *could* be recovered under the most liberal application of existing (and probably promised, but non-existing) technologies. In its most extreme application, oil and gas accumulations under pack ice in the Arctic Ocean are called 'technically recoverable' because someday in the future, an as-yet-undemonstrated technology might be able to somehow operate under or through the ice.

Paralleling the most permissive bounds for what engineering *might* be able to do was a persistent working assumption in Soviet/Russian reserve estimation that economics should not be considered as a constraint. If you were going to assume a technology – you might as well assume the funding to go with it. Generally no comparison was made between prices and costs because, in Soviet times, neither value had meaning as long as oil and gas development was funded from the state budget and products 'sold' back to the state at administrative prices determined by fiat.

Although only a very small fraction of Russian oil production is now funded by the state budget, the mindset persists that reserves are estimated simply assuming the required funding. This can be seen not only in the Arctic Ocean, but with respect to all the gas on the Yamal Peninsula and a very large fraction of the oil resources of East Siberia.

The SPE/WPC requirement of commercial (profitable) production *at existing prices and costs* flies directly in the face of the assumption of limitless money for development. The SEC requirement of positive net present value, with a manifestly evidenced producer's intent to expend the required funds, is light years further than the SPE/WPC standard from the Soviet/Russian assumption that funds will flow as needed.

Russians would argue that their scheme is not based on limitless funding. However, they appear to be unable to show what, if any, role the costs of development and production play and how oil prices influence their calculations.[21] While this difference between Western and Soviet approaches may not have made a difference under the Soviet system, it is incomprehensible why they cling to these concepts today.

As a result, from A volumes all the way to D_2, there is a basic disconnect between what are called reserves in Russia and how they would be described in the West. Even A reserves, which include the areas around producing wells, could include volumes that would not qualify for SEC or SPE/WPC proved – nor even for SPE/WPC probable and possible. The reason is that the inclusion of part of these volumes under the Soviet/Russian system could have been justified on technology that had not been demonstrated. Alternatively, they could be included in A reserves based on additional engineering measures (e.g., fracs or pumps), the cost of which could not be covered given the relationship between existing costs and prices.

Therefore, there is absolutely no simple rule for translating Soviet/Russian reserves into SPE/WPC or SEC based classifications. The notion that generally $A+B+C_1$ equals proved plus probable, or that $A+B+(0.3*C_1)$ equals proved plus probable is just wrong. At a very high level of aggregation (e.g., national statistics), such coarse rules of thumb may have some value. However, to determine the volumes of oil in a field that qualify for the SPE/WPC or SEC classes requires starting with oil in place at the reservoir level and applying the definitions associated with those classifications.

In practice, there is rarely much argument between Russian and Western geologists and engineers on the calculation of oil and gas in place in reservoirs. The divergence begins with what fraction is technically recoverable with the application of existing and demonstrated engineering measures. The divergence then expands very significantly in interpreting what share of that volume can be produced with existing economic conditions (to meet SPE/WPC standards). Going the last step to the SEC level would further require that the economically recoverable volumes enjoy the commitment of producers actually to fund their development.

The use of the Soviet/Russian $A+B+C_1$ volumes in this study as measures of field sizes was accepted for three reasons. First is that with the exception of very few fields, neither SPE/WPC nor SEC reserve analyses exist. Second, while flawed from the viewpoint of understanding their potential contribution to supply, the Soviet/Russian estimates present a highly consistent set of field sizes. In oil supply analysis, consistency is a very good thing. $A+B+C_1$ volumes are not comparable to Western reserves estimates, but internally are a very good basis for comparisons between fields and companies. Finally, the data provided by IHS Energy in its service on Russia (radically improved in the last few years) is an international industry standard.

Comment

If Russia still operated under the command economy strictures and the goals of the USSR, the incompatibility between their reserve classifications, and those used in the West, would be as inconsequential today as it was before the Soviet Union imploded. However, while supply from its oil industry interacts with domestic demand on something of a non-market basis (because of domestic price controls), the production of Russian oil is now overwhelmingly governed by a market system.

That being the case, it is more than confusing why both Russian government agencies, and some of the largest Russian oil companies, so tenaciously embrace a reserve classification system that was designed for a command economy. Not only does it lead to distortions within the Russian oil market and seriously handicap government and company planning – it looks bad internationally.

The issue is not just cosmetics. There is an unfortunate tendency to assume because Russians typically credit fields and regions with unbelievable volumes of 'recoverable' oil and gas that the engineers and scientists responsible for these numbers are incompetent. Whereas, what is inept is the institutional attachment to formulas now wholly irrelevant to the economic conditions under which the modern Russian industry operates.[22]

This is not to say that the SPE/WPC and SEC reserve classification systems are perfect or the only way to quantify oil resources. As repeatedly noted in the West, reserves claimed under these definitions (particularly the latter) grow over time.[23] That is, the reserves booked for a field in its year of discovery are typically only a fraction of the oil recovered when the field is abandoned. There are economic as well as technologic reasons for 'field growth.' Its existence invites serious thought as to how estimates could be made while eliminating the evidenced systemic negative bias.

Perhaps producers worldwide should endeavour to report not only meaningful reserves that include realistic technical and economic constraints, so that they are useful in making investment decisions. They should also give original oil and gas in place as well. That way, consumers of that information would know the current estimate of the total volume of hydrocarbons located in the field. Then, it would be possible to make ancillary assessments of ultimate productive potential, independently of what is claimed at any point in time as proved, probable and possible reserves.

The inherited Soviet system used in Russia does not solve the problem of underestimation in the SPE/WPC or SEC standards. It simply substitutes a system of inherent overestimation. It may be possible that reserves, when strictly defined, so they are as close as possible to the economic notion of inventories, cannot be estimated in a way that does not grow over time. Particularly, as fields in the West (and now in Russia) are not drilled out with a loose set of delineation wells, the learning that necessarily takes place would be expected to add both information and additional volumes of economically recoverable oil.

This is why oil and gas companies in the USA keep two sets of reserve books – although not in the usual nefarious sense of 'two sets of books.' One set reflects the calculations under SEC rules and is used for official reporting to investors. The second set of estimates usually approximate SPE/WPC reserves (or even a looser economic standard, allowing for forecasts of future prices and costs) and is used for internal planning. If that were not done, the company could not conduct any planning longer than its committed investment horizon.

Yet, the Russian insistence on including all the oil that could conceivably be recovered under future technologies and paid for from sources unimagined is not the answer. It sows confusion and probably retards investment (which at some level, exaggeration may be intended to encourage).[24]

For instance, it is not so much that the Russian estimates of Arctic Ocean volumes of hydrocarbons are patently wrong, scientifically. To state that the East Siberian Sea contains 88 billion BOE in hydrocarbon accumulations within its boundaries is not inherently unreasonable (although it seems awfully high).[25] It is, however, a crustal abundance-type number. Considering the environmental conditions prevailing over the East Siberian Sea, most of this volume is in no sense 'technically recoverable,' never mind economic.

As explained in the discussion on crustal abundance at the beginning of this appendix, very small amounts of gold occur in common rock. Gold is also dissolved in sea water (at an even lower concentration, ~

13 parts per trillion). Given the volume of sea water within Russian territorial waters and the average abundance of gold in sea water, it is possible to compute the amount of gold there. The presence of 50 billion grams of gold in four million cubic kilometres of sea water is, perhaps, geochemically interesting. However, multiplying it through by a price per gram of gold to suggest that there are several hundred billion dollars of gold resources demonstrates a basic ability with multiplication, but complete ignorance of economics under which the term 'resources' is constructively used.

The problems caused by happy reserve numbers are not uniquely Russian. On January 10, 2004, Shell, perhaps the most eminent of all Western oil companies, made the humiliating admission that their statement of reserves was exaggerated by 20 per cent.[26] Over the course of spring 2004, the revealed extent of reserve puffery just grew, leading to the resignation of top executives, legal action and a major blow to the company's reputation. Moreover, this type of subterfuge is by no means limited to Shell.

Hopefully, the Russian attachment to big numbers and being Number One by measures that are not informative will dissipate. Juiced numbers, whether used by Russian companies and government agencies, or by Shell, in the end are revealed for what they are. Had the Soviet Union, as claimed in its statistics, actually found 8 billion bbls of new, technically and economically recoverable oil annually between 1985 through 1991 – Russian production would have *never* collapsed – but it did.[27]

Notes

1 Under a strict mineralogic definition, hydrocarbons are not minerals (because they are organic), but that distinction is rarely observed in the geologic literature on mineral resources.
2 For an overview of mineral deposit models, see Dennis P. Cox and Donald A. Singer, *Mineral Deposit Models*, US Geological Survey Bulletin 1693 (1986). In this literature generally, one of the most important contributions is Brian J. Skinner, 'A Second Iron Age Ahead?' *American Scientist*, vol. 64 (May–June, 1976), pp. 258–69. The convention in this study of using English rather than metric units is suspended here as crustal abundances are always stated in metric.
3 There are exceptions to this. When coal is mined, usually a high percent of the rock removed is actually coal. The same is true of certain industrial rocks like limestone and sand.
4 This discussion ignores the 'external' (principally environmental) costs of mineral production and benefaction. Although their internalization is the

putative goal of environmental regulation, as of today, it probably only plays a very small real role in the economics of mineral supply.
5   Ivan I. Nesterov and Vladimir I. Shipil'man estimated 9,000 trillion tonnes of disseminated organic matter in the upper crust. If it is assumed that this estimate included the top ten kilometres from the surface and the average density of rock is 2.7 grams/cubic centimetre, the concentration implied is 0.065 per cent. Ivan I. Nesterov and Vladimir I. Shipil'man, *Teoriya neftegazonakopleniya* [*The Theory of Oil and Gas Accumulation*] (Moscow: Nedra, 1987), pp. 6–8.
6   Organic carbon produces coal too, but the type of organic matter and geochemical transformation are substantially different. What is also ignored here is the fraction of methane that may have formed abiogenically. Abiogenic methane may be significant on a crustal abundance scale, but has not evidenced any role in the supply of natural gas to the human economy.
7   A very large fraction of the generated natural gas goes into solution in the basin's ambient (formation) waters and never concentrates in the types of accumulations of interest for gas supply. An intriguing subset of the volume of gas dissolved in formation waters is that fraction that occurs as gas hydrates. These methane molecules are frozen into 'cages' of water molecules because the temperature and pressure conditions in the rocks or sediments froze the water. So far, hydrates are only of geologic interest, although some accumulations may become natural gas resources in the future.
8   The exact functional form of the size-frequency distribution of hydrocarbon accumulations in nature is beyond the bounds of this study. The most popular are based on the Pareto distribution, including the special case of fractal distributions. For a general discussion of the accumulation size frequency distribution in nature, see Lawrence J. Drew, *Oil and Gas Forecasting* (New York: Oxford University Press, 1990). For discussion of the use of fractal distributions in analysis of hydrocarbon resources see the papers by Christopher C. Barton and Christopher H. Scholz and by Paul R. LaPointe in Christopher C. Barton and Paul R. LaPointe, eds., *Fractals in Petroleum Geology and Earth Processes* (New York: Plenum Press, 1995).
9   While there are more characteristics of an oil or gas accumulation than size that impact its role in economic supply, size will be used here as a proxy for them all. These non-size characteristics include reservoir depth and permeability, oil viscosity, the presence of chemical contaminants in the oil and gas, such as hydrogen sulphide, paraffins and heavy metals. See John D. Grace, 'Assessment of Hydrocarbon Resource Quality,' *Abstracts of the 28th International Geologic Congress*, vol. 1 (Washington, DC, July 1989), p. 572.
10 Above some highly subjective minimum, a noticeable, but sub-commercial accumulation of oil or gas is usually called a 'show.' A show can range, in physical volume, from the tiny film of oil required to make well cuttings exhibit fluorescence under ultra-violet light, to hundreds or thousands of barrels of oil that flow in extended production tests, but at rates that imply

too low a sustained production rate, or ultimate volume per well, to meet investment criteria.
11 If the value of the oil and gas is high enough to cover completing the well, surface production equipment, operating costs and transporting the hydrocarbons to the sales point, 'uneconomic' accumulations are sometimes produced. One reason is that in some instances, those who drilled the well, regarding the well's cost as sunk, make their decision to produce based prospectively, on whether or not subsequent, post-drilling costs, will be covered by the value of what was found. In an economy governed by standard microeconomic theory, a company that consistently made this type of decision would eventually go bankrupt (many do). Even though the strategy covers variable costs, the producer would be losing some of their capital investment in the well each time this decision was made, and in the long run, would not cover fixed (capital) costs.
12 For instance, during the Soviet period in West Siberia, the minimum economic field size (as inferred from the fields that were developed) appeared to be around 50 million bbls of $A+B+C_1$ resources.
13 E.D. Attanasi and L.J. Drew, 'Lognormal Field Size Distributions as a Consequence of Economic Truncation,' *Mathematical Geology*, vol. 17, no. 4 (1985), pp. 335–51.
14 See generally Drew, *Oil and Gas Forecasting* and Gordon M. Kaufman, 'Oil and Gas – Estimation of Undiscovered Resources' in M. Adelman, John C. Houghton, Gordon Kaufman and Martin B. Zimmerman, eds, *Energy Resources in an Uncertain Future, Coal, Gas, Oil and Uranium Supply Forecasts* (Cambridge, MA: Ballinger Publishing Co., 1983).
15 Lawrence J. Drew, Emil D. Attanasi and John H. Schuenemeyer, 'Observed Oil and Gas Field Size Distributions: A Consequence of the Discovery Process and Prices of Oil and Gas,' *Mathematical Geology*, vol. 20, no. 8 (1988), pp. 939–53.
16 For natural gas, the range of recovery factors is higher.
17 Specifically, this discussion is based on the definitions adopted in 1997 by the Society of Petroleum Engineers (SPE) and the World Petroleum Congress (WPC). The definitions are available at the SPE website, *www.spe.org*.
18 See generally US 'SEC Staff Accounting Bulletin: Codification of Staff Accounting Bulletins, Topic 12: Oil and Gas Producing Activities,' *www.sec.gov/interps/account/sabcodet12.htm*. Also very useful in interpreting the guidelines is the SEC document 'Issues in the Extractive Industry,' *www.sec.gov/divisions/corpfin/acctdisc_old.htm*. For a comparison between SPE/WPC and SEC definitions, see D.R. Harrell, L.P and T.L. Gardner, 'Significant Differences in Proved Reserves Volumes Estimated Using SPE/WPC Reserves Compared to United States Securities and Exchange Commission (SEC) Definitions,' Society of Petroleum Engineers Paper #84145 (2003).
19 See SEC, 'Issues in the Extractive Industry,' op. cit. On a very large scale, this can be seen in what happened to booking natural gas at Prudhoe Bay, the largest oil field in the USA. In 1968, after its discovery, the companies originally booked 9.6 billion bbls of oil and 26 trillion cubic feet of natural

gas of proved reserves. After 20 years, when it became clear that there was then no economic way to transport the gas to market (given the existing relationship between prices and costs), the companies were required to subtract all 26 trillion cubic feet of gas from proved reserves.

20 The discussion here is more philosophical than technical. For greater technical detail, see John D. Grace, Robert H. Caldwell, David I. Heather, 'Comparative Reserve Definitions: U.S.A., Europe, and the Former Soviet Union,' *Journal of Petroleum Technology*, (September 1993), pp. 866–72 and John D. Grace, 'Understanding the Soviet Oil and Gas Reserve Classification,' *PlanEcon Energy Outlook for the Former Soviet Republics* (Washington, DC: PlanEcon, 1993), pp. 51–66.

21 The Soviet system also imposed another division of the $A+B+C_1$ volumes. It was the classification of *balansovyye* and *zabalaneovyye zapasy*. The former, 'within balance' volumes, were those estimated recoverable within an enterprise's budget. The latter, 'beyond balance' volumes, were not funded for development. As budgets were unrelated to costs and/or prices of oil and gas, this did not equate to 'economic' or 'non-economic' in the SPE/WPC sense.

22 The problem, at least in the West, is exacerbated by what appears to be an absence at *Russian Petroleum Investor* of writers or editors with technical experience in oil and gas exploration. The terms 'resources' and 'reserves' are continually confused; figures within articles are inconsistent and converted in and out of oil equivalent terms incorrectly and graphs often have axes without labels. The other major English-language source for Russian oil industry news, *Nefte Compass*, is more careful, but rarely treads as far into this type of story as does *Russian Petroleum Investor* (to its credit). The lay, and even business, press outlets (outside of oil and gas industry publications) almost always display a complete lack of understanding of the concepts of resources and reserves.

23 See generally, Emil D. Attanasi and David H. Root, 'The Enigma of Oil and Gas Field Growth,' *Bulletin of the American Association of Petroleum Geologists*, v. 78, no. 3 (1994), p. 321–32.

24 See the claim by Ray Leonard, vice president at Yukos, in 2002 that Russia has 'well over 100 billion barrels' of oil reserves. The road show reported in the same article was to try to convince others that this number is credible in order to 'dramatically increase Russia's international standing as a global energy power....' 'Underground, Russia Challenges Mideast on Reserves,' *Nefte Compass*, March 21, 2002, p. 5.

25 Vladimir Baidashin, 'Arctic Virgin Shelf,' op. cit., p. 17.

26 Carola Hoyos and Tony Tassell, 'Shell Stuns Oil Industry with 20 per cent Reserves Cut,' *Financial Times* (London), January 10, 2004, p. 1.

27 The statistic on Soviet finding rates at the end of the regime was given in Vladimir Baidashin, 'What Price Exploration.' *Russian Petroleum Investor* (October 2002), pp. 7–14.

BIBLIOGRAPHY

Attanasi, Emil D. and Lawrence J. Drew. 'Lognormal Field Size Distributions as a Consequence of Economic Truncation.' *Mathematical Geology* vol. 17, no. 4 (1985): 335–51.

Attanasi, Emil D. and D.H. Root, 'The Enigma of Oil and Gas Field Growth.' *Bulletin of the American Association of Petroleum Geologists* vol. 78, no. 3 (1994): 321–32.

Baidashin, Vladimir. 'Seeking a Partner.' *Russian Petroleum Investor* (September 2002): 22–8.

——, 'What Price Exploration.' *Russian Petroleum Investor* (October 2002): 7–14.

——, 'Arctic Fountain.' *Russian Petroleum Investor* (March 2003): 45–51.

——, 'New Era for Sakhalin.' *Russian Petroleum Investor* (August 2003): 38–48.

——, 'Arctic Virgin Shelf.' *Russian Petroleum Investor* (November/December 2003): 17–19.

——, 'First JV in Yamal.' *Russian Petroleum Investor* (October 2003): 13–19.

Barges, Inessa. 'State Takes the Offensive.' *Russian Petroleum Investor* (February 2004): 6–14.

——, 'Long-Term Look.' *Russian Petroleum Investor* (August 2003): 6–14.

Barton, Christopher C. and Christopher H. Scholz. 'The Fractal Size and Spatial Distribution of Hydrocarbon Accumulations: Implications for Resource Assessment and Strategy.' in Christopher C. Barton and Paul R. LaPointe, eds, *Fractals in Petroleum Geology and Earth Processes,* New York: Plenum Press, 1995.

Beattie, Alan. 'World Bank Digs a Hole for Itself.' *Financial Times* accessed February 25, 2004, www.ft.com.

Berniker, Mark. 'TNK-BP CEO Dudley Banks on Russian Oil, Gas Growth.' *Oil and Gas Journal* accessed January 20, 2004, *ogj.pennnet.com*.

Billington, James H. *Russia in Search of Itself,* Baltimore and London: Johns Hopkins University Press, 2004.

Budkov, A.D. and L.A. Budkov. 'Gody ispytanii (1941–1945 g.g.)' ['Years of Testing (1941–1945)'] in V.A. Dinkov, ed., *Neft' SSSR* [*Oil of the USSR*]. Moscow: Izdatel'stvo Nedra, 1987: 60–75.

Campbell, Robert W. *The Economics of Soviet Oil and Gas,* Baltimore, MD: The Johns Hopkins University Press, 1968.

——, *Trends in the Soviet Oil and Gas Industry, Baltimore, MD: Johns Hopkins University Press, 1976.*

Chadwick, Margaret, David Long and Machiko Nissanke, *Soviet Oil Exports, Trade Adjustments, Refining Constraints and Market Behaviour*, Oxford: Oxford University Press, 1987.

Chernyshov, Sergey. 'Without a PSA.' *Russian Petroleum Investor* (June/July 2003): 15–20.
——, 'Rancor over Vankor.' *Russian Petroleum Investor* (August 2003): 31–7.
——, 'Turn in the Road,' *Russian Petroleum Investor* (June/July 2003): 31.
Cooper, John C.B. 'Price Elasticity of Demand for Crude Oil: Estimates for 23 Countries,' *OPEC Review* (March 2003).
Cox, D.P. and D.A. Singer. *Mineral Deposit Models*, US Geological Survey Bulletin 1693, 1986.

Drew, Lawrence J. *Oil and Gas Forecasting*, New York: Oxford University Press, 1990.
—— and Emil D. Attanasi. 'Firm Size and Performance in the Search for Petroleum.' in S.I. Glass, ed., *Oil and Gas Modeling*. Washington, DC: National Bureau of Standards (1980): 466–89.
——, Emil D. Attanasi and John H. Schuenemeyer. 'Observed Oil and Gas Field Size Distribution: A Consequence of the Discovery Process and the Prices of Oil and Gas.' *Mathematical Geology* vol. 20, no. 8 (1988): 939–53.

Ebel, Robert E. *The Petroleum Industry of the Soviet Union*, Washington, DC: American Petroleum Institute, 1961.
Edwards, Imogene, Margaret Hughes and James Noren. 'US and USSR: Comparisons of GNP,' in Joint Economic Committee, Congress of the United States, *Soviet Economy in a Time of Change*, vol. 1, Washington, DC: US Government Printing Office, 1979: 369–400.
Energy Intelligence Group. *Almanac of Russian and Caspian Oil Petroleum 2002.* (electronic version.)
——, *Almanac of Russian and Caspian Oil Petroleum 2003.* (electronic version.)
——, *Almanac of Russian and Caspian Oil Petroleum 2004.* (electronic version.)

Filina, S.I., M.V. Korzh and M.S. Zonn. *Paleogeografiya i neftegazonosnost' bazhenovskoy svity Zapadnoy Sibiri,* [*Paleogeography and Oil and Gas Potential of the Bazhenov Suite of West Siberia*] Moscow: Nauka, 1984.
Freeland, Chrystia. *Sale of the Century – Russia's Wild Ride from Communism to Capitalism*, New York: Crown Books, 2000.
Forbes website, www.forbes.com.

Gazprom. *Annual Report 2003*.
Goldman, Marshall I. *The Enigma of Soviet Petroleum, Half-Empty or Half-Full?* London: George Allen & Unwin, 1980.
Grace, John D. 'Assessment of Hydrocarbon Resource Quality.' *Abstracts of the 28th International Geologic Congress* vol. 1, (Washington, DC, July 1989): 572.
——, 'Understanding the Soviet Oil and Gas Reserve Classification.' *PlanEcon Energy Outlook for the Former Soviet Republics* Washington, DC: PlanEcon, 1993: 51–66.

———, and George F. Hart. 'Giant Gas Fields of Northern West Siberia.' *Bulletin of the American Association of Petroleum Geologists* vol. 70, no. 7 (July 1986): 830–52.

———, R.H. Caldwell, D.I. Heather. 'Comparative Reserve Definitions: U.S.A., Europe, and the Former Soviet Union.' *Journal of Petroleum Technology* (September 1993): 866–72.

———, David I. Heather and Vladimir I. Shpil'man. *Oil Potential from Idle Wells in Russia*, Dallas, TX: Troika Energy Services, 1993.

———, A.Z. Zolotov, E.M.. Khalimov, N.A. Krylov, D.I. Heather, W.A. Benninger and G.A. Gabrielyants. *CIS Oil 2000*, Dallas, TX: Troika Energy Services, 1993.

Gurevich, Ya.D. 'Vosstanovitel'nyy period i pervyye pyatletki (1917–1922 g.g.)' ['The Period of Reconstruction and the First Five Year Plans (1917–1922)'], in V.A. Dinkov, ed., *Neft' SSSR* [*Oil of the USSR*]. Moscow: Izdatel'stvo Nedra, 1987: 10–30.

Gustafson, Thane. *Crisis Amid Plenty*, Princeton, NJ: Princeton University Press, 1989.

Harrell, D.R., L.P. Gardner and T.L. Gardner. 'Significant Differences in Proved Reserves Volumes Estimated Using SPE/WPC Reserves Compared to United States Securities and Exchange Commission (SEC) Definitions.' Society of Petroleum Engineers Paper #84145 (2003).

Hill, Fiona and Clifford G. Gaddy. *The Siberian Curse – How Communist Planners Left Russia Out in the Cold*, Washington, DC: The Brookings Institution Press, 2003.

Hoffman, David E. *The Oligarchs, Wealth and Power in the New Russia*, New York: Public Affairs, 2002.

Hoyos, Carola and Tony Tassell. 'Shell Stuns Oil Industry with 20% Reserves Cut.' *Financial Times* (January 10, 2004): 1.

IHS Energy. International Energy Exploration and Production Database, Denver, CO: IHS Energy, 2003.

International Monetary Fund. 'Country Report No. 3/145, Statistical Appendix.' Accessed May 2003,

Jack, Andrew and Doug Cameron. 'Conoco Plays the Percentage Game with Lukoil Stake Sale.' *Financial Times* (August 31, 2004): 19.

Kalyuzhnyy, Viktor. 'Plany po dobyche perevypolneny. A zachem?' ['Plans for Production Are Overfulfilled – But Why?'] *Neft' Rossii* [*Russian Oil*] accessed January 2003, press.lukoil.ru.

Kaufman, Gordon M. 'Oil and Gas – Estimation of Undiscovered Resources' in M. Adelman, John C. Houghton, Gordon M. Kaufman and Martin B. Zimmerman, eds, *Energy Resources in an Uncertain Future, Coal, Gas, Oil and Uranium Supply Forecasts*, Cambridge, MA: Ballinger, 1983.

Klemme, H. Douglas. 'Field Size Distribution Related to Basin Characteristics.' in Dudley D. Rice, ed., *Oil and Gas Assessment, Methods and Applications, (AAPG Studies in Geology #21)*. Tulsa, OK: American Association of Petroleum Geologists, 1986: 85–100.
——, and Gregory F. Ulmishek. 'Effective Petroleum Source Rocks of the World: Stratigraphic, Distribution and Controlling Depositions Factors.' *Bulletin of the American Association of Petroleum Geologists* vol. 75, no. 12 (December 1991): 1809–51.
Knapp, G.B. Letter to I. Bakaleyink (with attachments), April 3, 2002. Available at TNK website at www.tnk.com/investor/reports.html.
Kontorovich, A.E. *Geologiya nefti i gaza Zapadnoy Sibiri* [*Geology of Oil and Gas of West Siberia*], Moscow: Nedra, 1975.
——, 'Geochemical Methods for Quantitative Evaluation of the Petroleum Potential of Sedimentary Basins.' in Gerard Demaison and Roelef J. Murris. *Petroleum Geochemistry and Basin Evaluation*, Tulsa, OK: American Association of Petroleum Geologists, 1984: 79–109.

Lagutenko. B. and A. Sakovitch. 'A Step Toward Hyperinflation.' *Russian Petroleum Investor* (April 1992): 38–9.
LaPointe, Paul R. 'Estimation of Undiscovered Hydrocarbon Potential through Fractal Geometry.' in Christopher C. Barton and Paul R. LaPointe, eds, *Fractals in Petroleum Geology and Earth Processes*, New York: Plenum Press, 1995.
Lee, Julian. 'Future Russian Oil Production, The CGES View.' Canadian Energy Research Institute 2004 Oil Conference, March 28–30, 2004.
——, 'Waking the Bear: The Outlook for Russian Oil Production.' *Geopolitics of Energy* Issue 26, no. 10 (October, 2004): 9–16.
Lee, J.R. and J.R. Lecky. 'Soviet Oil Developments.' in Joint Economic Committee, Congress of the United States, *Soviet Economy in a Time of Change*, Washington, DC: US Government Printing Office, 1979: 581–99.
Lukoil. 'History.'
——, 'LUKOIL: Efficient Growth.' PowerPoint investor presentation in English accessed June 2002, *www.lukoil.com*.
——, 'Reserves.' *www.lukoil.com*.
——, *2001 Annual Report* (English).
——, *2002 Annual Report* (English). *www.lukoil.com*.
——, '2002 Financial Results (US GAAP).' PowerPoint investor presentation, *www.lukoil.com*.
——, *2003 Annual Report* (English). *www.lukoil.com*.
——, 'Lukoil Plans Activities in North-Western Federal District.' Press Release accessed February 2, 2004, *www.lukoil.com*.

Maass, Peter. 'The Triumph of the Quiet Tycoon.' *New York Times Magazine* (August 1, 2004): 29.
Maksimov, S.P., ed. *Neftyanyye i gazovyye mestorozhdeniya SSSR* [*Oil and Gas Fields of the USSR*], Moscow: Izdatel'stvo Nedra, 1987.

Market Intelligence Group, Russian Petroleum Investor. *Russian Petroleum Encyclopedia, Upstream,* 1995.

Masters, C.D., D.H. Root and R.M. Turner. 'World Conventional Crude Oil and Natural Gas: Identified Reserves, Undiscovered Resources and Futures.' US Geological Survey Open-File Report 98–468 (1998).

Nesterov, I.I. and V.I. Shipil'man. *Teoriya neftegazonakopleniya* [*The Theory of Oil and Gas Accumulation*], Moscow: Nedra, 1987.

———, N.N. Rostovtsev, M.Ya. Rudkevich, F.K. Salmanov and Yu.G. Erv'ye. 'Otkrytiye Zapadno-Sibirskoy neftegazonosnoy provintsii – pobeda ucheniya I.M. Gubkina.' ['The Discovery of the West Siberian Oil and Gas Province – A Victory for the Scholarship of I.M. Gubkin.'] in *Gubkinskiye Chteniya – K 100 Letiyu so Dnya Rozhdeniya*, [*Gubkin Readings – In Honor of the 100th Anniversary of His Birth,*] Moscow: Nedra, 1972: 42–46.

Nissanke, Machiko. 'Oil Exports and the Soviet Economy.' in Margaret Chadwick, David Long and Machiko Nissanke *Soviet Oil Exports, Trade Adjustments, Refining Constraints and Market Behaviour,* Oxford: Oxford University Press, 1987: 67–97.

Noren, James. 'CIA's Analysis of the Soviet Economy.' *www.odci.gov.*

PennWell Publishing. *Energy Statistics Sourcebook* (11th Edition), Tulsa, OK: Pennwell Publishing, 1996.

Peterson, James A. and James W. Clarke. 'Petroleum Geology and Resources of the Volga-Urals Province. USSR.' *US Geological Survey Circular 885* (1983).

Petroleum Intelligence Weekly. *The Almanac of Russian Petroleum 1993,* New York: Petroleum Intelligence Weekly, 1993.

Riasanovsky, Nicholas V. A *History of Russia,* 5th Edition. New York: Oxford University Press, 1993.

Rosneft. *Rosneft Annual Report for 2001* (English).

———, *Rosneft Annual Report for 2002* (English).

———, website, *www.rosneft.ru/english.*

Sagers, Matthew. 'Oil Production Costs in the USSR.' in *PlanEcon Long Term Energy Outlook,* Washington DC: PlanEcon, 1987: 43–54

——— and John D. Grace. 'Observations on the Russian Oil Sector in 1992 and 1993.' *International Geology Review* vol. 35, no. 9 (September 1993): 855–77.

Sattov, M.M. 'Nadezhda i Sversheniya.' ['Hope and Accomplishments.'] in V.A. Dinkov, ed., *Neft' SSSR* [*Oil of the USSR*]. Moscow: Izdatel'stvo Nedra, 1987: 138–68.

Seligman, Benjamin. 'Long-term Variability of Pipeline-Permafrost Interactions in North-west Siberia.' *Permafrost and Periglacial Processes* vol. 11, no. 1 (January–March 2000): 5–22.

Sibneft. Sibneft website. *www.sibneft.com.*

———, *Sibneft Annual Report 2001* (English).

———, *Sibneft Annual Report 2002* (English).

——, *Sibneft Annual Report 2003* (English).
Skinner, Brian J. 'A Second Iron Age Ahead?' *American Scientist* vol. 64 (May-June 1976): 258–69.
Smith, James L. 'On the Cost of Lost Production from Russian Oil Fields.' *The Energy Journal* vol. 16 no. 2 (1995): 25–57.
Society of Petroleum Engineers. 'Reserve Definitions.' *www.spe.org*.
Stern, Jonathan P. *Soviet Oil and Gas Exports to the West*, Hants, England: Gower Publishing Company Limited, 1987: 123.
Stiglitz, Joseph E. *Globalization and Its Discontents*, New York: W.W. Norton & Co., 2003.
Surgutneftegaz website, *www.surgutneftegaz.ru/eng*.
——, *2000 Annual Report (English)*
——, *2001 Annual Report (English)*.
——, *2002 Annual Report (English)*.
Surtsukov, M. 'The Cost of Doing Nothing.' *Russian Petroleum Investor* (April 1992): 38–41.
Rosneft. 'Vankorskoye Oil Field.' *www.rosneft.ru*.
——, 'Prirazlomnoye Oil Field.' *www.rosneft.ru*.

TNK-BP, 'TNK-BP Limited US GAAP Consolidated Financial Statements as of December 31, 2003' (TNK-BP-12M2003-Final.pdf, available at *www.tnk-bp.com/investors/financial*).
TNK-International, 'TNK International US GAAP Financial Statementes 1999 – H1 2003' (TNK-Int-US-GAAP-Financial-Statements-1999-1H03.xls, available at *www.tnk-bp.com/investors/financial/*.
Tolf, Robert W. *The Russian Rockefellers*, Stanford, CA: Hoover Institution Press, 1976.
Trebin, G.F., N.V. Charygin and T.M. Obkhova. *Nefti mestorozhdenii Sovietsogo Soyuza*, [*Oils of the Fields of the Soviet Union*,] Moscow: Nedra, 1980.
Tretyakova, A. and M. Heinemeier. 'Cost Estimates for the Soviet Oil Industry: 1970–1990.' (CIR Staff Paper No. 20) Washington, DC: US Bureau of the Census, 1986.
Trofimuk, A. A. 'Prognozy I.M. Gubkina v otnosheniye neftegazonosnosti Sibiri.' ['The Predictions of I.M. Gubkin in Relation to the Oil and Gas Potential of Siberia.'] in *Gubkinskiye Chteniya – K 100 Letiyu so Dnya Rozhdeniya*, [*Gubkin Readings – In Honor of the 100th Anniversary of His Birth*,] Moscow: Izdatel'stvo Nedra, 1972: 40–51.

Ulmishek, Gregory F. *Petroleum Geology and Resources of the Middle Caspian Basin, Former Soviet Union*, US Geological Survey Bulletin 2201-A, 2001.
——, *Petroleum Geology and Resources of the Baykit High Province, East Siberia, Russia*, US Geological Survey Bulletin 2201-F (2001).
——, *Petroleum Geology and Resources of the Nepa-Botuoba High, Angara-Lena Terrace, and Cis-Paton Foredeep, Southeastern Siberian Craton, Russia*, U.S. Geological Bulletin, 2201-C, 2001.

———, *Petroleum Geology and Resources of the West Siberian Basin, Russia*, US Geological Survey Bulletin 2201-G, 2003.

US Bureau of Labor Statistics. 'Consumer Price Index.' *ftp.bls.gov*.

US Department of Energy, Energy Information Administration. *www.eia.doe.gov*.

———, *Annual Energy Review 1997*, DOE/EIA-0384(97), Washington, DC, July 1998.

US Federal Reserve. 'Interest Rates.' *www.federalreserve.gov* .

US Securities and Exchange Commission. 'SEC Staff Accounting Bulletin: Codification of Staff Accounting Bulletins, Topic 12: Oil and Gas Producing Activities.' *www.sec.gov*.

———, 'Issues in the Extractive Industry.' *www.sec.gov*.

Valikhanov, A.V. 'I.M. Gubkin i razvitiye neftyanoy promyshlennosti Tatarii.' ['I. M. Gubkin and the Development of the Oil Industry of the Tatar Republic.'] in *Gubkinskiye Chteniya – K 100 Letiyu so Dnya Rozhdeniya*, [*Gubkin Readings – In Honor of the 100th Anniversary of His Birth*,] Moscow: Nedra, 1972: 33–9.

Vyshemirskiy, V.S., ed., *Bazhenovskiy gorizont Zapadnoy Sibiri*, [*The Bazhenov Horizon of West Siberia*], Novosibirsk: Nauka, Siberian Division, 1986.

White, Gregory L. 'Russia Assigns Auction Price for Lukoil Stake.' *Wall Street Journal* (August 27, 2004): A3.

———, 'As Westerners Move Into Russia, Its Vast Oil Wealth Keeps Growing,' *Wall Street Journal* (September 30, 2004): A1.

Yergin, Daniel. *The Prize, The Epic Quest for Oil, Money and Power*, New York: Simon & Schuster, 1991.

Yuganskneftegaz. 'Yukos' (PowerPoint presentation in English, no date – probably early 2003), *www.yukos.com/new_ir/pdf/NYG.pdf*.

———, *Yukos 2001 Annual Report* (English)

———, *Yukos 2002 Annual Report* (English).

———, '*Yukos Consolidated Financial Statements as of September 30, 2003*.'

Newspaper and journal articles

'Barber of Siberia, Kukes Maps Out TNK Restructuring.' *Nefte Compass* (May 31, 2001): 6.

'BP Makes Find off of East Russia.' *Financial Times* (October 7, 2004): 21.

'Chevron Doubles Estimate of Tengiz Oilfield Reserves.' *Alexander's Gas and Oil Connections*. *www.gasandoil.com*.

'Chronicle of the Conflict.' *Russian Petroleum Investor* (January 2004): 8–9.

'Damage Control.' *Russian Petroleum Investor* (August 1998): 5.

'French Kiss: Lukoil Joins Total in Kharyaga.' *Nefte Compass* (October 31, 2002): 3.

'From the Ashes.' *Russian Petroleum Investor* (October 1998): 17.
'Heavy Price, Tatarstan Swims Against Rising Production Tide.' *Nefte Compass* (September 19, 2002): 3.
'Iron Man, Bashkir President to Maintain Oil Stranglehold.' *Nefte Compass* (January 8, 2004): 5.
'Half and Half, Lukoil Halves Timan-Pechora Investments.' *Nefte Compass* (April 11, 2002): 4.
'High Five, TNK-BP Reveals Five-Year Strategy.' *Nefte Compass* (January 22, 2004): 6.
'Kashagan Reserves Estimated to Hold up to 9 bn Barrels.' *Alexander's Gas and Oil Connections*, www.gasandoil.com.
'Kremlin Adviser's Views.' *Russian Petroleum Investor* (April 2002): 12.
'Kurmangazy at a Glance.' *Russian Petroleum Investor* (June/July 2003): 41.
'Lesser Half, Tatneft Profits Hit By Taxes and Transport Costs.' *Nefte Compass* (November 13, 2003): 7.
'Long-Term Look.' *Russian Petroleum Investor* (August 2003): 6–14.
'Lost Innocence.' *Russian Petroleum Investor* (April 1995): 64.
'Lukoil Sells Azeri Assets to Shift Focus to Russia.' *Nefte Compass* (November 21, 2002): 8.
'Lukoil to Sell Some Oil Reserves Amid Industry Shift in Russia.' *Wall Street Journal* (April 19, 2004): A8.
'Mousetrap, Russian Readies for Price War with OPEC.' *Nefte Compass* (September 29, 2001): 6.
'On Borrowed Money.' *Russian Petroleum Investor* (March 1995): 12.
'Open Door.' *Nefte Compass* (November 6, 2003): 1–2.
'Output Up, Yukos Claims No. 1 Spot As Production Rises.' *Nefte Compass* (March 27, 2003): 4.
'Picky, Picky.' *Russian Petroleum Investor* (April 1998): 10.
'Putin: No Bankruptcy for YUKOS.' *Russian Journal Daily* accessed June 18, 2004, www.russiajournal.com.
'Putin Ally Surgut Tops List of Possible Buyers for Yukos Unit,' www.bloomberg.com accessed September 9, 2004.
'Quick Fix.' *Russian Petroleum Investor* (December 1995/January 1996): 13.
'Shopping Spree, Surgut Eyes German Assets.' *Nefte Compass* (November 21, 2002): 5.
'Taking Stock of Russia's Energy Sector.' *Russian Petroleum Investor* (September 1998): 8.
'Tatneft Promotes Differentiated Taxation of Oil Production.' *Radio Free Europe/Radio Liberty Tatar-Bashkir Daily Report* accessed April 12, 2004, www.rferl.org.
'Taxman, Putin Pledges to Raise Taxes on Oil Companies.' *Nefte Compass* (December 31, 2003): 5–6.
'Through, Lukoil Quits Kharyaga Project in Blow to Total.' *Nefte Compass* (September 25, 2003): 1.
'Top Secret Oil.' *Pravda* accessed April 29, 2004, english.pravda.ru.

'Transneft Increases Baltic Pipeline Capacity.' *Alexander's Gas and Oil Connections* vol. 8, no. 23 accessed November 27, 2003, *www.gasandoil.com*

'Underground, Russian Challenges Mideast on Reserves.' *Nefte Compass* (March 21, 2002): 5.

'Unmasking, Yukos Reveals Controling Shareholders.' *Nefte Compass* (June 27, 2002): 7.

'Wag the Dog, Companies Question Russian Rules Over Oil Search.' *Nefte Compass* (June 27, 2001): 1–2.

'Well Being, Sibneft Drills Record-Breaking Well.' *Nefte Compass* (June 6, 2002): 4.

'What Charges Face Khodorkovsky?' *Russian Petroleum Investor* (January 2004): 12.

INDEX

Abdullah, Prince 224
Abramovich, R.A. 131, 133, 157, 221
Access/Renova See TNK-BP, Initial formation
Alaska 133, 199
Alberta 26
Alekperov, V.Yu. 110, 157, 220
Amoco 120
Andropov, Yu.V. 72
Apatit See Yukos, 'Yukos Affair'
Apsheron Peninsula 6–7
ARCO 119
Arctic Ocean 56, 114–15, 183, 200, 204, 264, 267, See also Exploration, Arctic Ocean
Astrakhan 7
Aven, P.O. 139, 157
Azerbaijan 6, 7, 9–10, 12, 16–17, 20–1, 28, 70, 72, 76, 111

Baku 6–8, 10, 12, 76, 251
Baltic Sea 78
Barents Sea 200–1, 215
BASF AG 194
Bashkortostan 15, 107, 148
Bashneft 16, 25, 27, 107, 147–8, 162, 179, 219
Basins
   Anadyr 199
   Cook Inlet (USA) 199
   Gulf Coast (USA) 59, 251
   Khatyrka 199
   Middle Caspian 112, 190, 196, 215
   Niger River delta (Nigeria) 59
   North Caspian 72, 112, 190, 196, 197
   North Caucasus 8–10, 16–17, 20–1, 28–9, 93, 153, 196
   South Caspian 28, 111, 196, 251
   Timan-Pechora See Timan-Pechora basin
   Volga-Ural See Volga-Ural basin
   West Siberian See West Siberian basin
   Western Canadian sedimentary 26
Batumi 7
Baykit 193, 204
Belarus 132
Berezovsky, B.A. 126, 131, 157–8
Billington, J.H. 226
Black Sea 7–8, 78
Bogdanov, V.L. 136–7, 157–8
Brazil 59
British Petroleum 120, 143, 146, 165–6, 179, 193–4

Buroviki [Drillers] 70

California 44–5
Canada 184–5
Carbon, organic 251
Carboniferous Period/System 17, 22, 29
Caspian Sea 2, 6–7, 72, 111–12, 153, 196–7
Caucasus Mountains 7–8
Cenomanian Epoch/Series 60, 194
Central Asia 10, 14, 17, 70
Chechen Republic 8
ChevronTexaco 111
China 122, 199
Chronopolitics 226
Chukchi Sea 200, 253
Chukotka 133
Churchill, Winston 105
Chusovskiye Gorodki 16
Civil War, Russian 8, 12, 212
Coal 3, 36, 67
Columbia 111
Companies, foreign oil 114, 145, 222
   See also: ARCO, British Petroleum, ConocoPhillips, ExxonMobil, Marathon, Shell, Sibir Energy, TOTAL
Companies, Russian independent oil 143–50
   Firm size 147, 149
   Implications of absence in Soviet period 15
   In Volga-Ural basin 15–16, 26–7
   In West Siberian basin 55
   Joint ventures 15, 144, 146
      Production 146–7
      Service joint ventures 144
   Loss of 149–50
      Impact on production 162–3, 185, 202, 222
   Melding of domestic and foreign capital 147
   Production 149
   Role in supply from basins 143
Companies, Russian major oil 4
   Imprint of Soviet past 105, 219
   See also: Lukoil, Sibneft, Surgutneftegaz, TNK-BP, Yukos
Companies, state oil 150–8
   In Loans for Shares 152
   Initial formation 150
   International role 151
   Merger of Gazprom and Rosneft. 150–1, 154, 163
   See also: Gazprom, Rosneft

282   Russian Oil Supply

Condensate 43, 60–1, 111, 154–5, 190, 192, 194–5, 197, 200
  Future supply from 195
ConocoPhillips 109, 115, 118–19, 133, 146, 153, 165, 166, 191, 220
  Timan-Pechora operations 115, 118, 153, 203
Consumer surplus 94–5, 97, 159, 160
  Defined 91
Cost, capital 11, 21, 42, 52, 97, 214
Cost, operating 9, 11, 16, 23, 24, 27, 42, 49, 52, 68, 75, 78–80, 82, 86, 89, 92, 97, 114–16, 123, 135, 148, 151, 158, 167, 185–6, 188, 189, 192, 196, 199, 204, 214, 216, 223, 225, 250, 256–7
  Outlook 189
Cost, production *See* Cost, operating
Cretaceous Period/System 58–9, *See also* Neocomian Epoch/Series
Crustal abundance 250–1, 254, 267

Dagestan Republic 153
Demand, domestic 87
  Defined 90
  Post-war growth 67
Depletion 2, 11, 65, 86, 223
Diminishing returns to investment 70, 86, 214
  In Azerbaijan 7, 9, 11–12
  In North Caucasus basin 9
  In Volga-Ural basin 25
  In West Siberian basin 39
Devonian Period/System 17, 19–20, 22, 28–30
Dikson 192
Drilling technology
  Cable-tool 7, 9
  Directional drilling 51
    Pattern drilling 128
    'Siberian Box' 51
  Rotary 8–9, 20–1
  Turbo 21, 23
    Role in Volga-Ural basin 21
Duma 193

East Siberia 189, 193, 196, 205, 215, 226
  Exploration *See* Exploration, East Siberia
  Plans of Gazprom and Rosneft 193
East Siberian Sea 200, 263, 267
Economic policy, foreign 7, 10
  Role of oil and gas 68
  Role of Volga-Ural oil 26, 35
  Role of West Siberian oil and gas 35
Economic policy, Putin administration
  Balance of power between industry and state 104, 213, 223
  Central role of oil and gas 217
  Decontrol of domestic prices 154, 227
  Increasing state role 109, 151, 163
  Conflict between expanding supply and state role in industry 164
  Impact on supply 218
  Nationalization of gas assets 4, 150, 163, 218
  Nationalization of oil assets 4, 163, 218, 221
  View toward market economics 4, 109, 217
Economic policy, Soviet
  Balance of power between industry and state 11
  Command structure 14–15, 25–6, 54, 87, 105, 260, 263
  Early Soviet period 2, 8–9, 11
  Faustian bargain with oil and gas industries 34–5, 67, 73, 85, 213, 216
  Financing of production from state budget 87
  Late Soviet period 76, 105
  Perestroika 73
  Regulation of domestic prices 94
Economic policy, Yeltsin administration
  Default on sovereign debt 81
  Devaluation of rouble 4, 66, 81, 167, 216
  Impact on costs 82, 88, 98, 188
  Market financing of production 3, 65, 76, 88, 95, 219
  Non-payment of receivables 77–8, 88, 97
  Regulation of domestic prices 65, 77, 83, 88, 96, 160
Economies of scale 10, 20, 34, 53, 55, 65, 162, 213, 215
Economy, national
  Depression in early 1990s 107, 161, 216
  Inflation 77, 89
  Post war expansion 67
  Post-1998 expansion 1, 217, 222
  Role of oil and gas 1, 216
Egypt 111
Electricity 75, 89, 122, 135, 156, 185, 218, *See* Cost, operating
Elektriki [Electrical industry workers] 70
Environmental damage 55, 227
Equatorial Guinea 59
European Bank of Reconstruction and Development 80
European Union 216
Exploration
  Impact of buying reserves 195
  Impact of cost 196, 215
  Impact of discovered fields overhang 195, 198
  In Arctic Ocean 201, 215
  In Caspian Sea 197
  In East Siberia 198–9, 215
  In Imperial period 7

Index 283

In Timan-Pechora basin 115, 197
In West Siberian basin 198
Exports 226
In early Soviet period 9
In Imperial period 7
In Soviet period (1970s and 1980s) 35
Role of hard currency earnings 35, 67, 73, 78, 98
ExxonMobil 111, 146, 164–6
Attempt to invest in Yukos 165
Sakhalin I project *See* Sakhalin Island
Sakhalin III project *See* Sakhalin Island
Standard Oil 7
Faustian bargain *See* Economic policy, Yeltsin administration
Field size
Pareto distribution of accumulation sizes 252–3
Pareto versus lognormal distributions 253
In Volga-Ural basin 18
Lognormal distribution 18, 69, 87, 214
Impact on exploration efficiency in Volga-Ural basin 18
Impact on exploration efficiency in West Siberian basin 39, 53
Impact on industry consolidation 162
Minimum economic 50, 190, 252–4
Economic truncation 253
Role of giant fields 12, 84, 89
In Volga-Ural basin 19–20
In West Siberian basin 34
Role of medium and small fields 162
In Volga-Ural basin 16
In West Siberian basin 43
Fields
Ardalinskoye 115
Arkhutun-Dagi 194
Arlan 16, 25, 29, 69, 147
Astrakhan 197
Azeri-Guneshli-Chirag 111
Balakhany-Sanbunchi-Ramany 6–7
Bibi-Eybat 6–7
Bystrinskoye 135
Chaivo 194
Chayandinskoye 193
Fedorovskoye 40, 46, 116, 134–5
Production 46–7, 69, 71–2
Karachaganak 111
Kharyaginskoye 115, 146
Komsomolskoye 191
Konitlorskoye 136
Kovyktinskoye 193
Krasnoleninskoye 36, 143
Lyantorskoye 134–6
Mamontovskoye 40, 46, 123, 128, 185
Production 47–8, 69, 71, 72
Medvezhe 194
North Pokachevskoye 117

North Vankorskoye 192
Odoptu 194
Pokachevskoye 117
Povkhovskoye 117
Priobskoye 43, 59, 119, 128, 202, 204, 221
Prirazlomnoye 153, 191, 201, 203
Romashkino 14, 16–17, 19, 22, 24–5, 29, 37, 47, 147–8
Discovery 17
Geology 22
In Tatarstan economy 23
Production 24, 69
Production technology 23
Reserves 22
Role of Devonian reservoirs at 17, 22
Water cut 24
Salymskoye 44, 192
Samotlor 40, 46, 116, 129
Application of new technology 73, 142
Geology 47
Oil characteristics 48
Production 35, 46, 48–9
Production collapse in 1980s 48, 71–2
Production collapse in 1990s 49
Reserves 49, 142
Role in Soviet supply 35, 48, 69, 141
Water-cut 49, 71
Well flow rates 48
Shtokmanovskoye 201
South Yagunskoye 117
Sporyshevskoye 85
Sugmutskoye 132
Suzunskoye 192
Talakanskoye 193
Tazovskoye 36
Tengiz 72, 111, 197
Tevlin-Russinskoye 85, 116, 117, 188, 204
Tuymazinskoye 17, 19, 21, 23
Tyanskoye 134–6, 188, 203, 204
Upper Chonskoye 193
Vachimskoye 136
Vankorskoye 153, 192, 197
Vatyeganskoye 117
West Salymskoye 146, 192, 203
Yamburg 114, 194
Yurubchinskoye 193
Zapolyarnoye 194
Fields, discovered undeveloped 55, 162, 195, 215
First World War 8–9, 212
Foreign investment 6
ConocoPhillips *See* Lukoil, Partnership with ConocoPhillips
In Imperial period 6, 10
In Putin administration 164–5, 217, 226

In remote and complex projects 109, 164, 217
Russian attitude toward 166
TNK-BP *See* TNK-BP, British Petroleum, merger with
Friedman, M.M. 139, 157

Gazoviki [Gas industry workers] 155, 194
Gazprom 109, 127, 150–1, 154–6, 164, 168, 179, 191, 193–4, 199, 202, 221
    As receiver of Yuganskneftegaz 151
    Attitude toward condensates 194–5
    'Gas-only' culture 61–4, 155, 194
    Gazneftprom 165
    Liquids strategy 156
    Production 155
    Reserves 151
Generally Accepted Accounting Principles (GAAP) 121, 222
Geologic structures
    Baltica plate 28–9, 56–7
    Birsk Saddle 17, 18, 30
    East African rift zone 57
    Kazakh plate 29, 57
    Nepa-Botubinsk Arch 193, 204, 263
    Nizhnevartovsk Arch 47
    Perm-Bashkir Arch 17, 18, 30
    Siberian plate 29, 56–8
    Tatar Arch 17, 18, 22, 30
Geology
    As a constraint on production 2
    See also Volga-Ural basin, Geology
    West Siberian basin, Geology
Gold 250, 267–8
Gorbachev, M.S. 49, 72–3, 75
Groznyy 8, 10
Gubkin, I.M.
    Role in Volga-Ural basin exploration 16, 36
    Role in West Siberian basin exploration 36
GULAG, Soviet 114, 125
Gusinsky, V.A. 126

Harvard University 137, 138
Hysteresis 2, 54, 204, 223

IHS Energy 266
Indonesia 199
Industry consolidation 222–3
    Acquisition of producing assets 112, 154, 222
    Early 1990s 107, 109, 152
    Post-1998 27, 66, 84, 88, 109, 149–50, 223
International Monetary Fund 81
Iraq 111

Jurassic Period/System 44, 53, 57–8, 60, 198

Kalyuzhnyy, V. 223
Kara Sea 192, 200–1, 215
Kazakhstan 8, 72, 196–7
Kerosene 6, 10–11
Khodorkovsky, M.B. 1, 110, 120, 124–7, 130–1, 157–8, 163, 217, 222
Kolyma River 198–9
Krasnodar Kray 153
Kyoto Protocols 227

LaBrea tar pits (USA) 251
Lake Baikal 193
Laptev Sea 200
Lebedev, P.L. 124–6, 130, 158
Lenin, V.I. 16
Licensing, mineral rights 11
    In Imperial period 6
    Production sharing agreements (PSAs) 115, 146, 179, 193–4
Lithuania 122
Los Angeles 251
Lukoil 76, 105, 107, 109–20, 152, 162, 167, 181, 203, 221
    Acquisition of small companies 111–12, 118
    Industry leadership 109, 111, 121, 220
    International operations 111–12
    Keys to success 110, 220
    Kogalymneftegaz 76, 105, 111, 116–18
    Komineft 107, 115
    Langepasneftegaz 76, 105, 111, 116–17
    Layoffs 113
    Middle Caspian projects 113, 167
    Partnership with ConocoPhillips 109, 118–19, 133–4, 220
        Timan-Pechora joint venture 118, 146
    Permneft 118
    Production
        Role of acquisitions 154, 167
        Tevlin-Russinskoye 116–17
    Production management
        Poor results 110, 116, 220
    Relationship with Putin administration 110
    Reorganization 112
    Timan-Pechora operations 112–13, 115, 167, 191, 197, 203, 220
    Urayneftegaz 76, 105, 111
    Volga-Ural basin operations 16, 27
    Western majors as model 111

Malaysia 199
Marathon Oil 146
Maykop 8, 10
Mesozoic Era/Erathem 36
Mexico 224

Middle Ob region 36–7, 39, 41, 43, 46–8, 54, 58–60, 71–2, 84, 111, 123, 129, 135, 141, 197
Miller and Lents, Ltd. 142
Ministry of Fuels and Energy, Russian 80, 151
Ministry of Gas, Soviet 34, 263
Ministry of Geology, Soviet 34, 41, 51, 149, 263
Ministry of Oil, Soviet 34, 41, 45, 51, 70, 76, 105, 134, 139, 151, 157, 219, 263
Mississippi River 251
Mongol empire 6
Murmansk 122

Nationalization *See* Economic policy, Putin administration
Nefteyugansk 136
Neocomian Epoch/Series 36, 41, 43, 47–8, 59–61, 155, 194
Nigeria 59
Nizhnevartovsk 41, 46–7
Nobel family 6–7, 10–11
Northern Oil 153
Norway 180, 224, 226
Novaya Zemlya 57
Nuclear explosions, peaceful 44

Ob River 26, 37, 40–1, 45–7, 56, 116, 123, 128, 130, 137, 153
Oil in place 255, 260, 265, 267
Oligarchs 1, 107–8, 120, 124–5, 131, 139–40, 157–8, 218, 221
Background of 108
Omsk 221
Organization of Petroleum Exporting Countries (OPEC) 81, 180, 218
Relationship with Russia 1, 224–5

Pacific Ocean 204
Pechora Bay 153, 191, 200–1, 204, 215
Permian Period/System 22, 29–30, 41, 44, 56, 57, 196
Persian empire 6
Polar Lights *See* ConocoPhillips, Timan-Pechora operations
Political instability
Impact on production 11–12
Potanin, V.O. 140, 157
Prices, domestic
Decontrol 77
'Free market' in 1990s 77
Parity with world prices 65, 77, 88, 91–2, 97, 160, 185, 227
Prices, world 224
1986 collapse 35, 73, 87, 94
1998 collapse 81, 166
Brent 5, 77, 81, 83, 89, 120, 131, 139,
140, 180, 184–5
Increases in 1970s 15, 35, 67, 69, 86
Influence on Russian production 55, 66
Post-1998 increase 4, 55, 83, 88, 98, 216
Priobskoye *See* Fields
Privatization 80, 157, 161
Asset value as mechanism of enrichment 157–8
Distribution of government-held stock 106
Gains by Soviet-era managers 106–7, 109, 157
Loans for Shares 108–9, 124, 127, 131, 139–40, 152, 163, 221
Oligarchs' deal with Yeltsin administration 109
See also Sibneft, In Loans for Shares, Yukos, In Loans for Shares
Vouchers for stock 107, 161
Production
Collapse in 1980s and 1990s 66, 74
In Imperial period 7, 12
Post-1998 recovery 82–3, 219
Russian peak 66, 212
Soviet peak 3, 50, 54, 73
Stabilization of output in mid-1990s 80
Production technology
Gas lift 51
Hydraulic fracturing (fracing) 136, 142, 144, 257
In-fill drilling 21
West Siberian basin 52
Pre-modern 6
Pumps 9, 21, 51, 70, 72–3
Electrical submersible pumps (ESPs) 52
Sucker rod pumps 52
Water flood 21, 23–4, 51
Well maintenance 70
Well stimulation 219, 255, *See also* Production technology, Hydraulic fracturing (fracing)
Putin, V.V. 1, 4, 109–10, 125–8, 131, 134, 136–7, 150–1, 153, 155, 158, 163–4, 168, 182, 186, 202–3, 217–19, 222, 224, 227
Centralization of power 1, 4, 126, 151

Railroads 76
Recovery factor 42, 142, 182
Determination 255, 257–60
Influence of cost on 255, 256
Influence of price on 256
Influence of technology on 257
Red Sea 57
Refining 6
In Europe 8
In Volga-Ural basin 16

Reserves 5, 222
  A+B+C$_1$ definitions 260
    Classification criteria 263
    Recovery factor 264
    Role of economics 264, 265
  Comparison of Soviet and Western systems 182, 264
  Possible
    Determination of 181, 258
    Russia 182, 214
  Probable
    Determination of 181, 258
    Russia 182, 214
  Proved
    Determination of 178, 180, 257, 258
    Russia 180, 183, 214
  Reserve to production ratio 180
  SEC definitions 259
    Differences between SPE/WPC and 259–60
  SPE/WPC definitions 121, 178–9, 181, 257, 258–9, 261–2
Reservoir rock units
  Achimov Formation 43–4, 53, 59, 194, 198
  Bazhenov Formation 44–5, 53, 198
  Megion Formation 43–4, 48, 58, 59, 198
  Melekess Formation 22
  Monterey Formation (USA) 44
  Pashiy Formation 22–3, 28
  Vartov Formation 43–4, 48, 58–9, 198
Resources, oil
  Total resource base 183
  Undiscovered 182–3
    In cost context 183
    In relation to other countries 183
Revenues, producer
  Division by cost class 79, 156, 158–9
  From export sales 79
  Losses 79, 80–1, 96
  Wellhead net income 79, 82
    Defined 91
Revolution of 1905 7, 12, 212
Revolution of 1917 2, 8, 10, 12, 14, 212
Risk
  Exploration 42, 115, 197
  Political 203
Romashkino *See* Fields
Rosneft 109, 127, 139, 146, 151–4, 163–4, 166–7, 191, 193–4, 202, 221
  Grozneft 152
  Initial formation 150, 152
  Kurmangazy project 153, 190
  Production 153
    Growth by acquisitions 154
  Purneftegaz 153–4, 156, 192
  Reserves 151
Rothschild family 10, 11

Russian Orthodox Church 134
Russo-Japanese War 7

Sakhalin Island 146
  Sakhalin I project 146, 165–6, 193–4, 199–200, 203–4
  Sakhalin II project 146, 166, 193, 199–200, 204
  Sakhalin III project 165, 199
  Sakhalin IV project 199
  Sakhalin V project 146, 166, 194, 204
Samotlor *See* Fields
Saskatchewan 26
Saudi Arabia 1, 218, 223
Sbornost' [Sense of community] 228
Sea of Okhotsk 199, 204–5
Second World War 3, 9, 10, 14–15, 17, 25, 86, 197, 212, 216
  Impact on production 10, 17
  Oil as German objective 10
Shell 44, 111, 146, 166, 192, 203, 268
Sibir Energy 192, 203
Sibneft 85, 130–4, 158, 162, 166–7, 203, 221
  Acquisition of refining assets 131
  In Loans for Shares 130–1, 221
  Keys to success 132
  Managing Western service contracts and technology 122, 132
  Noyabrskneftegaz 5, 109, 130–1, 153, 247
  Outlook 134, 167, 221
  Production 131, 133
  Purchase of interest in Slavneft 132
  Reserves 131
Slavneft 107, 132, 141
Slavophiles 193
Source rock units
  Bazhenov Formation 36, 43–4, 53, 58–60
    Total organic carbon 58
  Domanik facies 28–9
    Total organic carbon 29
Stalin, J.V. 9, 26
Stalingrad 10
State Committee on Reserves (GKZ) 263
Stavrapol Kray 153
Stocks
  Stockholders
    Minority rights 168
    Value of Russian oil companies. 80–1, 158
Supply and demand
  In 1983 93–4
  In 1987 94–5
  In 1993 95–7
  In 1997 97–8
  In 2002 98–9
Supply, future oil

Costs 189
  Debate on raising 223
  From 2005 through 2010 204, 226
  From 2010 through 2020 205
    Role of Caspian Sea 205
    Role of East Siberia 204
    Role of industry structure 205
  From declining fields 187, 201, 214
    Impact of decline rates 26, 42, 184, 187
    Impact of industry structure 185
    Impact of price 185–6, 202
    Impact of rising costs 186
  From discovered undeveloped fields 54, 190, 215, 226
    Caspian projects 191
    East Siberia 193
    Timan-Pechora projects 191
    West Siberia 192
  From exploration 215
  From fields with increasing production 187–8, 202
    Role of Priobskoye 202
  From producing fields 183, 201
  Impact of industry consolidation 27, 162, 219
Surgut 41, 136–7
Surgutneftegaz 80, 107, 109, 116, 127, 134–8, 147, 162, 167, 185, 193, 202, 219, 221
  As an alternative model 136, 219–20
  As receiver of Yuganskneftegaz 127, 137
  Independence from industry trends 134
  Keys to success 135, 219–20
  Production costs 135
  Production management 135, 136
    Role of drilling 135
  Relations with minority stockholders 138
  Strategic problem 137, 167
Sverdlovsk 36

Tatarstan 15, 23, 107, 148
Tatneft 16, 23–5, 27, 107, 147–8, 162, 167, 219
Taxation
  Excise taxes 78–9, 90–2, 97, 158, 166, 189
  Exploration tax 41–2
  Impact on production 78, 186, 189
  In Imperial period 7, 11
Taymyr Peninsula 57
Taz Gulf 41
Timan-Pechora basin 93, 112, 153, 196, 200, 203, 204, *See also* Lukoil, Timan-Pechora operations
  Attraction to foreign companies in 1990s 114
  Physiography 114

TNK-BP 109, 138–43,162, 166–7, 185, 202–3, 219–21
  British Petroleum, merger with 109, 118, 140, 141, 166, 217, 220
  Chernogorneft 139–41
  East Siberian assets 143, 193, 221
  Financial performance 143
  Glavtyumenneftegaz 139
  Initial formation 139, 165
  KondPetroleum 140
  Krasnoleninskneftegaz 140
  Megionneftegaz 141
  Nizhnevartovskneftegaz 49, 72, 139
  Onako 107, 141, 143, 152
  Production
    Samotlor 49, 141–2
  Reserves 139–40
  Samotlorneftegaz 116, 141
  Sidanco 49, 107, 109, 139–41, 152, 157, 165, 220–21
  Slavneft 132
  TNK-Nyagan 140
  Tyumenneftegaz 139, 143
Tomsk Oblast 129
TOTAL
  Kharyaginskoye project 115, 146
Transportation
  Baltic Transport System 115
  In Imperial period 7, 11
  Pipeline projects 122
  Tariffs
    In Imperial period 7
    In post-Soviet period 65–6, 77–82, 84, 88–9, 97, 109, 115, 123, 158, 167, 185, 189, 214, 216, 225
  Transneft 78, 122, 199
  Varandey export terminal 115
Triassic Period/System 30, 41, 44, 56, 57
Tsars
  Aleksey 134
  Alexander I 6
  Peter the Great 6
  Romanov dynasty 8, 12
Turkey 6–7, 155
Turkmenistan 8
Tyumen Oblast 139, 192

Union of Right Forces 126
Union of Soviet Socialist Republics (USSR)
  Dissolution 87, 212
  Impact on production 75
United Kingdom 180
United States 112, 184–5, 200, 218, 225
  Geological Survey (USGS) 182
  Impact of dependence on oil 69
  Securities and Exchange Commission (SEC) 3, 121, 222, 259, 261–3, 265, 266, 267

Ural Mountains 3, 14, 16, 28, 29, 36–7, 56, 196, 213

Vekselberg, V. 157
Volga River 7, 10, 14, 34
Volga-Ural basin 34, 93, 141, 196–7, 213
   Depletion 3
   Exploration 9
      Cycles 19
      Efficiency 17–18
   Fields
      First generation 19
      Second generation 19, 24
      Third generation 19, 25
   Geology 56
      Juxtaposition of source and reservoir rocks 29, 30
      Tectonics 28
   Industrial development 15
   Oil characteristics 22, 24, 27
   Production
      Decline 24–6, 69, 72
      Decline arrested 16, 25
      Period of increasing 15, 19
      Role in national economy 3, 14, 26, 66
      Role of recognizing Devonian potential 17
   Proximity to transportation and refining 16, 27
   Resources lost to West Siberia 15, 25–6
      Role of medium and small fields 19, 26–7

Wells,
   Flow rates 21, 27, 35, 42–4, 43, 51, 55, 69, 112, 114–15, 117, 128, 144, 186, 189, 191
   Idle 72, 74–5, 79–80, 83, 136, 244, 261
      Cost to repair 75
      Crisis 74
West Siberian basin 3, 15–16, 34–61, 196–7, 200, 213
   Condensate resources 60
   Depletion 86
   Exploration 53
      Cycles 41, 45
      Efficiency 37, 40, 69
      Extension 42
      In post-Soviet period 41–5
      Investment 39, 40
      Strategy in 1960s 37, 43
   Fields
      First generation 37, 40, 46
      Fourth generation 41, 132

      Gas 60
      Other 41, 50, 73
      Second generation 40–1, 46, 69, 73
      Third generation 41, 50, 73
   Geology 52
   Living conditions 55, 70, 71
   Physiography 34
      Arctic swamp 3, 37, 51
   Production
      Outlook 55–6
      Peak 35
   Resource base 36
   Role in national economy 3, 34, 36
   Water-cut 69
Western nations
   Dependence on oil 68
Wintershall 194
World Bank 80, 81

Yabloko 126
Yeltsin, B.N. 3, 4, 80, 81, 88, 106–9, 120, 125, 130–1, 134, 146, 150, 152, 157–9, 161, 167, 218, 221
Yenisey River 58, 198
Yukos 1, 4, 107, 109, 119–30, 152, 158, 162, 165, 166–8, 185, 193, 202, 217, 220–1
   In Loans for Shares 120–1, 124
   Industry leadership 119, 121
   International operations 121
   Merger with Sibneft 122, 130, 133
   Natural gas 122
   Priobskoye 43, 120–1, 123
   Production costs 123
   Reserves 120
   Samaraneftegaz 119, 129
   Sibneft, merger with 221
   Tomskneft 107, 120, 129
   Transportation 122–3
   Yuganskneftegaz 46, 119, 123, 129, 130, 151, 163
      Production management 123, 129
'Yukos Affair' 114–16, 124–8, 193, 222, 227
   Bankruptcy 127
   Charges against Khodorkovsky and Lebedev 124
   Charges against Yukos 125
   Dissolution of company 119, 129, 226
   Elections 125–6
   Menatep Bank (group) 120, 124
   Political lessons 128
   Political manipulation of Duma 126
   Political opposition to Putin 125
   Role of Priobskoye 127
   Sale of Yuganskneftegaz 127, 222